HOW BAKING WORKS

Exploring the Fundamentals of Baking Science

HOW
BAKING
WORKS

Exploring the Fundamentals of Baking Science

SECOND EDITION

Paula Figoni

JOHN WILEY & SONS, INC.

Copyright © 2008 by John Wiley & Sons, Inc. All rights reserved.

Published by John Wiley & Sons, Inc., Hoboken, New Jersey.
Published simultaneously in Canada.

Wiley Bicentennial Logo: Richard J. Pacifico

For general information on our other products and services, or technical support, please contact our Customer Care Department within the United States at 800-762-2974, outside the United States at 317-572-3993 or fax 317-572-4002.

Wiley also publishes its books in a variety of electronic formats. Some content that appears in print may not be available in electronic books.

For more information about Wiley products, visit our Web site at http://*www.wiley.com*.

Library of Congress Cataloging-in-Publication Data:

Figoni, Paula
       How baking works : exploring the fundamentals of baking science /
Paula Figoni.—2nd ed.
           p. cm.
       Includes bibliographical references and index.
       ISBN 978-0-471-74723-9 (pbk. : alk. paper)
     1. Baking.   I. Title.
TX763.F54 2008
641.7—dc22

                                                    2006103521

Printed in the United States of America

10 9 8 7 6 5 4 3 2

CONTENTS

PREFACE

Years ago, there was only one way to become a baker or pastry chef, and that was to apprentice with a master craftsman. The apprentice learned by doing, repeating the necessary skills, year after year, until the skills were mastered. If bakers and pastry chefs understood their ingredients or why they did what they did, it was only after years of experience. Mostly they knew what to do because they did what they had been shown, and it worked.

Today, bakers and pastry chefs have more challenges. They must master more skills. They must adapt to faster-changing trends. They must learn to use a wider array of ingredients from different cultures. They must learn to use still more ingredients devised in the chemist's lab. They must learn all this in a shorter length of time.

Baking and pastry programs in colleges and universities are laying the foundation to meet these new challenges. Part of this foundation includes applying the knowledge of science to the bakeshop. The purpose of *How Baking Works, Second Edition* is to help lay this foundation. Yet, I'm sure some might wonder if this knowledge is necessary, even helpful. After all, isn't it enough to learn the skills of the bakeshop?

After years of working with experienced bakers and pastry chefs and after years of training students, I am convinced that, today, skills are not enough. I have faith that the knowledge of the food scientist can help in facing the challenges in the bakeshop. Finally, I have conviction that this knowledge is useful for the beginner as well as the master.

The food scientist uncovers how different ingredients are processed, views ingredients as made of individual components, and views processes and procedures in the bakeshop in terms of interactions between these components. If ingredients can be viewed in this way, their behavior in the bakeshop begins to make more sense. How they will react under new conditions and new situations can better be predicted, and failures in the bakeshop can be averted. The goal of this book is to share the views of the food scientist with bakers and pastry chefs. Yet, I have tried to keep this book focused on the interests and needs of beginning and practicing bakers and pastry chefs. The only theories presented are those necessary to better understand that which will be immediately useful in the bakeshop.

Beyond the practical usefulness of science, there is a beauty to it, a beauty best appreciated when science is applied to the everyday world. I hope that this book allows those who might not yet see this beauty to at least see the possibility of it.

A NOTE ABOUT TEMPERATURE AND WEIGHT CONVERSIONS

Numbers can sound deceptively precise. For instance, the temperature at which yeast cells die is often cited as 140°F (60°C). But was the heat moist or dry? Was the temperature brought up quickly or slowly? What strain of yeast was used, and how much acid, salt, and sugar were present?

The actual temperature at which yeast cells die depends on these and other factors, and that temperature is not necessarily 140°F (60°C). For this reason, many temperatures provided in this text are converted from Fahrenheit to Celsius in ranges of five degrees. While this may appear inexact, it best reflects the reality of the situation.

Other times, however, temperatures are meant to be precise. For example, it matters when proofing yeast dough whether the temperature is 81°F (27°C) or 85°F (29°C). In this case, temperatures are converted from Fahrenheit to Celsius to the nearest whole degree.

Likewise, weight and volume conversions are not necessarily given to the precise gram or milliliter. In most cases, U.S./imperial units are provided in increments of .25 ounce, while metric units are converted in increments of 5 grams or 5 milliliters. This reflects the reality of the bakeshop, where most equipment reads down to these increments.

CHANGES TO THE SECOND EDITION

While the core format and theme of the text remains the same, several important changes have been made to the *Second Edition* of *How Baking Works.* Material was added to reflect the increasing use of newer ingredients. In particular, stevia, agave syrup, and other sweeteners were added. Along with this, information was added on the source and processing of sweeteners, to increase the depth of understanding of how they differ as well as how they are similar to each other. This is reflected in an expansion of Chapter 8.

At the same time that newer ingredients have been developed, there has been an increased interest in more traditional ingredients, such as stone-ground flours and ancient grains. Chapters 5 and 6 have added information to reflect these interests. The text also reflects new changes to federal law and growing consumer awareness of nutrition and health. This includes information on the labeling of food allergens in the United States, more information on dietary fiber, and additional and updated information on trans fats and trans-free fats in Chapter 10.

An amazing amount of research has been completed in the past few years on gluten structure, in particular, but also on other flour components and their interactions. This comes at a time when scientists are selectively breeding new varieties of wheat with specific properties to meet the changing needs of farmers, processors, and consumers across the globe. Based on this new knowledge, updated information on gluten structure and its interactions is provided in Chapter 7.

Various enzymes and reducing agents have always been important to large-scale commercial bakers, who typically add them as dough conditioners or improvers. However, they are also naturally present in flours and in other common ingredients used in bread baking. Since their special properties are exploited by artisan bakers as they adjust fermentation and mixing conditions, it seemed important to discuss them in more detail. Chapters 5 and 7 include increased coverage of enzymes and reducing agents. Finally, Chapter 9 reflects an improved discussion of starch structure and a more accurate representation of the process of starch gelatinization.

Questions at the end of each chapter have been divided into *Questions for Review* and *Questions for Discussion. Questions for Review* are straightforward; they reflect the material as it is presented in the text. *Questions for Discussion* are questions that in general require a higher level of thinking, that require integration of information from several areas of the chapter, or that apply information in a slightly different manner than is presented in the text.

The main change to the *Second Edition* is the development of exercises and experiments at the end of each chapter. These exercises and experiments are designed to reinforce material from the text in a way that shows rather than tells. Some of the exercises are exclusively paper exercises, with a few involving math. Many more involve the sensory evaluation of ingredients. There are several reasons for including these sensory exercises in the text. First is the narrow objective of learning to identify characterizing traits of ingredients, to better understand the effects that they will have on finished products. Second is the even narrower but very practical objective of learning to identify ingredients that may be unlabeled or accidentally mislabeled. Third is the broad objective of increasing awareness of all the tastes, textures, and sights in the bakeshop, no matter how small or mundane. There is much to be learned in a bakeshop, even when the same items are prepped and baked day after day. The first step to learning is learning to be aware.

An Instructor's Manual (ISBN 978-0470-04512-1) accompanies this book. It can be obtained by contacting your Wiley sales representative. An electronic version of the Instructor's Manual is available to qualified instructors on the companion Web site, at www.wiley.com/college/figoni.

ABOUT THE EXPERIMENTS

While the exercises at the end of each chapter are self-explanatory, the experiments do need some explanation. The experiments allow students to further develop basic bakeshop skills, but that is not the main objective of the experiments. Instead, the emphasis of the experiments is on comparing and evaluating products that vary in some systematic way. The real "products" of these experiments are students' findings, which they summarize in the Results Tables provided at the end of each experiment. There are also specific questions at the end of each experiment, with space provided for students to summarize their conclusions.

The experiments are designed so that one or more can be conducted within a four-hour session by a class divided into five or more groups. Each group in the classroom completes one or more of the products in the experiment. When all products are made and cooled, students evaluate the products, either as a class or individually. Room-temperature water (bottled water, if tap water has a strong taste) should be provided, to cleanse the palate between tastings, and students should constantly return to the control product to make side-by-side comparisons of it with each test product. Whenever possible, two separate groups should prepare the control product for each experiment, in case one turns out unacceptable.

The key to well-conducted experiments is for the products to be prepared and baked under carefully-controlled conditions. This is emphasized by the detail provided in the formulas within each experiment. However, understand that the specific mixing and bake times could change, to adjust to the different equipment and conditions in your classroom bakeshop. What is more important than following the provided methods of preparation exactly as written is that each product made within an experiment by a class be completed exactly as all the others.

Above all else, however, common sense rules when completing experiments. There are times when rigid rules must be forsaken, and chefs and scientists must know when to "work with their ingredients." What this means is that if it is necessary to make adjustments to products because of the nature of the ingredient, those adjustments should be made. An example of when adjustments must be made to products is in the experiment on preparing rolls with different flours, included in different forms in Chapters 5 and 6. If the same amount of water were used for each type of flour, the gluten in the flour would not be properly hydrated. These adjustments are not made lightly, however, and they must be recorded in a Results Table. Notice that a *Comments* column is included in each table, for this very purpose.

While any classroom bakeshop can be used, there are certain modifications that might need to be made to efficiently run the experiments. For instance, the bakeshop should be supplied with multiple versions of smaller-scale equipment and smallwares. As an example, multiple five-quart mixers, one per group, are needed in place of one large mixer. A list of equipment and smallwares for outfitting a bakeshop for these experiments follows.

EQUIPMENT AND SMALLWARES

1. Baker's or electronic scales
2. Measuring cups and measuring spoons, assorted sizes
3. Sieves or strainers
4. Mixers with 5-quart bowls, three-speed Hobart N50, ten-speed Commercial Kitchenaid, or equivalent
5. Flat beaters, dough hooks, and wire whips for mixers
6. Bowl scrapers
7. Bench scrapers
8. Dough cutters, 2" or 2½" or equivalent
9. Oven thermometers
10. Parchment paper
11. Ovens (conventional, reel, deck, etc.)
12. Stovetop burners
13. Half sheet pans
14. Muffin tins and liners (2½ or 3½" size)
15. Half hotel pans
16. Silicone (Silpat) pads, to fit half sheet pans
17. Portion scoops, including #16 (2¾ oz.) and #30
18. Timers
19. Rulers
20. Proof box
21. Stainless steel bowls, especially 2- and 4-quart sizes
22. Mixing spoons, wooden and stainless
23. Spatulas, heat-resistant silicone
24. Stainless steel saucepans, heavy 1½ quart
25. Rolling pins
26. Knives, assorted serrated, paring, etc.
27. Plastic wrap
28. Pastry bags
29. Pastry tubes, plain
30. Vegetable peelers
31. Cake pans, 9-inch round
32. Cutting boards
33. Plastic teaspoons for tasting
34. Cups for water
35. Tape and markers for labeling

ACKNOWLEDGMENTS

I would like to thank the administration of the College of Culinary Arts at Johnson & Wales University (J&W), who first suggested that I write this text. Without their prodding and support, I would not have known that I could really do it.

The faculty in the International Baking and Pastry Institute at J&W deserve a special thanks. They let me into their bakeshops, answered my questions, presented me with practical problems, and made me feel like I was one of them. They demonstrated firsthand to the students through their own knowledge and understanding of science that science does indeed belong in the bakeshop. They have made my years at J&W immensely rewarding, challenging, and fun, and that has made all the difference to me.

In particular, I would like to thank my friend Chef Martha Crawford, whose presence is felt in the classrooms and halls at J&W, even as she has moved on. Chef Crawford taught me many things, including how to begin to think like a pastry chef. She has a knack for getting to the core of any problem and laying out a path to its solution. Whenever I strayed, she firmly and wisely placed me back on track. For this, and for much more, I am grateful. .

I would also like to pay a debt of gratitude to Chef Joseph Amendola, who pioneered the education of bakers and pastry chefs in this country. Chef Amendola had the vision to see where education should head, and he placed us on that path.

I would like to thank the reviewers of the manuscript. Their helpful comments and suggestions strengthened the manuscript. They are Dr. Bill Atwell of Cargill, Inc.; Gloria M. Cabral of Bristol Community College; Kelli Dever of Boise State University; Kathryn Gordon of The Art Institute of New York City; Catherine M. Hallman of Walker State Community College; Monica J. Lanczak of Pennsylvania College of Technology; Simon Stevenson of Connecticut Culinary Institute; and Scott Weiss of Carteret Community College.

Finally, I would like to thank my family. My mother, who taught me how to bake, my father, who taught me to love food, and both my parents, as well as my sisters, who years ago encouraged me to continue even as they ate my first experiments in baking. They helped shape me, and in doing so, they helped to shape this book. Bob deserves a special thanks, because he was on the front line, tolerating my late nights at the computer and steadying my mood as it changed with each day. This book is yours as well as mine.

Paula Figoni
Providence, Rhode Island

CHAPTER 1

INTRODUCTION TO BAKING

CHAPTER **OBJECTIVES**

1. Discuss the importance of accuracy in the bakeshop and how it is achieved.

2. Differentiate between volumetric and weight measurements and specify when each should be used.

3. Differentiate between metric and U.S. common units.

4. Introduce the concept of baker's percentages.

5. Discuss the importance of controlling ingredient temperatures.

 ## INTRODUCTION

Those who enter the fields of baking and pastry arts do so for a variety of reasons. For some, it is the joy of working with their hands, of creating edible works of art from a few basic ingredients. For others, it is the rush they get from the fast pace of the bakeshop, or from its satisfying sights and smells. Still others like the challenge of pleasing and surprising customers. No matter the reason, the decision to work in the field is usually grounded in a love of food, and maybe past experience in a bakeshop or a home kitchen.

Working in a professional bakeshop is different from baking at home, however. Production in a bakeshop is on a larger scale. It takes place day in and day out, sometimes under severe time pressures, in uncomfortably hot and humid conditions, and over long hours. Despite the discomforts and pressures, product quality must remain consistently high, because that is what the customer expects.

It takes specialized knowledge and practiced skills to accomplish these goals successfully. It helps to be attentive to the sights, sounds, and smells of the bakeshop. Experienced bakers and pastry chefs, for example, listen to the sound of cake batter being beaten in a bowl, knowing that changes in sound accompany changes to the batter itself. They push and pummel bread dough to feel how it responds. They use smells from the oven to judge when baking is nearly complete, and they sample their finished products before presenting them to the customer.

Experienced bakers and pastry chefs rely, too, on tools like timers and thermometers, because they know how time and temperature affect product quality. They also rely heavily on accurate scales.

THE IMPORTANCE OF ACCURACY IN THE BAKESHOP

Most bakery items are made of the same ingredients: flour, water, sugar, eggs, leavening agents, and fat. Sometimes the difference between two products is simply the method of preparation used in assembling the ingredients. Other times the difference is the proportion or amount of each ingredient in a formula. Because small differences in method and in proportion of ingredients can have a large effect on the quality of baked goods, it is crucial that bakers and pastry chefs follow methods of preparation carefully and measure ingredients properly. Otherwise, a product may turn out unexpectedly, or worse, it may turn out unacceptable or inedible.

For example, if too much shortening and too few eggs are added to a formula for moist, chewy oatmeal cookies, the cookies will likely turn out crisp and dry. If the same error is made with cake batter, the result will likely be a complete failure, since eggs provide structure and volume. In fact, bakers and pastry chefs require a higher degree of accuracy when measuring ingredients than do culinary chefs in the kitchen.

When the kitchen chef prepares a pot of soup, it doesn't really matter if a little less celery is added or an extra onion is included. The chef still has a pot of soup, and if the flavor is off, adjustments can be made along the way. Bakers and pastry chefs cannot make adjustments along the way. If too little salt is added to bread dough, it will do no good to sprinkle salt onto the bread once it is baked. Instead, ingredients must be weighed and measured accurately at the beginning.

This means that, more so than kitchen chefs, bakers and pastry chefs are chemists in the kitchen. As with chemists, creativity and skill are important for success, but so is accuracy. If a formula calls for two pounds of flour, it doesn't mean around two pounds, more or less. It means two pounds.

BALANCES AND SCALES

Formulas used in the bakeshop are in some ways like recipes in the kitchen. Formulas include a list of ingredients and a method of preparation (MOP). Unlike recipes used by the kitchen chef, however, formulas include exact measurements for each ingredient, and these measurements are usually given in weights. The process of weighing ingredients is called scaling because pastry chefs use scales to weigh ingredients.

The standard scale used in the bakeshop is a baker's balance scale. It measures ingredients by balancing them against known weights. It is an investment that should be selected for its durability and its precision. A good baker's scale can weigh amounts as large as 8 pounds (4 kilograms) or more and as small as 1/4 ounces (0.25 ounce or 5 grams). This provides the precision needed for most quantity food preparation.

Bakers and pastry chefs sometimes use digital electronic scales. While many affordable electronic scales provide the same or better precision than baker's scales, it is not necessarily the case. The precision of a scale—either baker's scale or electronic scale—depends entirely on the scale's design and construction.

HELPFUL HINT

Baker's scales and their accessories (scoops and weights) must be cared for if they are to remain in balance. They should be wiped regularly with a damp cloth and mild detergent, and they should not be banged or dropped. These precautions are necessary to keep the scale reading accurately.

To determine if a scale is in balance, empty both platforms and move the ounce weight indicator to the far left (i.e., to zero). With the scale at eye level, determine whether the platforms are at the same height. If they are not, adjust the weights located beneath the platforms as needed. Repeat this test with a scoop on the left platform and a counterweight on the right. If balancing is needed, do so by adding or removing weight from the counterweight.

MORE ON SCALE READABILITY

The readability of a scale, sometimes represented as *d* for scale division, is literally the increments in weight that are read off the scale's display panel. As weight is added onto a scale with a readability of 5 grams, for example, the reading on the display panel will change from 0 grams, to 5 grams, to 10, 15, 20, and so on. No matter the weight of the ingredient, the scale displays the weight in increments of 5 grams. If a sample in fact weighs 6 grams, the display will read 5 grams. If it weighs 8.75 grams, the display will read 10 grams.

Sometimes a scale fluctuates between readings. Let's say, for example, that the scale in the previous example keeps fluctuating between 5 grams and 10 grams. It is likely that the sample actually weighs about 7.5 grams, which is halfway between 5 grams and 10 grams.

Most digital electronic scales provide information about precision—also called readability—and capacity on their front or back panels. For example, a scale that is marked 4.0 kg × 5 g has a capacity of 4 kilograms, meaning it can measure quantities as large as 4 kilograms (about 8.8 pounds). The *readability* of this scale is 5 grams. Five grams is equivalent to just under 0.2 ounce, which is similar to the 0.25-ounce precision of a good baker's scale.

Consider another electronic scale, one marked *100 oz. × 0.1 oz.* This scale has a capacity of 100 ounces (6.25 pounds or 2.84 kilograms) and a readability of 0.1 ounce (3 grams). The smaller value for readability indicates that this scale provides better precision than a typical baker's scale, making it useful for weighing small quantities of spices or flavorings.

Just as baker's scales need to be checked periodically for accuracy, so too must digital scales. Digital scales typically come with a brass weight calibrated for accuracy. If the scale's reading does not match the mass of the brass weight, follow the manufacturer's instructions to adjust the scale. Because a scale is an important piece of equipment in a bakeshop, it is best to check its calibration at two different points (200 grams and 2000 grams, for example). The scale will need adjustment or repair if either of these two readings is off.

How an ingredient is added to a digital scale can make a difference in the accuracy of the reading. For example, multiple small additions will sometimes read lower than the identical amount added all at once. This can happen because scales are generally designed so that they don't fluctuate excessively with air movement, and the scale cannot necessarily differentiate a small amount of product from air movement. Vibration, heat currents, cordless and cell phones, and static electricity should all be avoided, since they can affect the ability of a scale to read consistently.

HELPFUL HINT

To determine if a scale provides enough precision for the task at hand, consider the readability of the scale. A good rule of thumb is that a scale is acceptable for weighing an ingredient as long as the error in measurement does not exceed 10 percent. To ensure that the error does not exceed 10 percent, be sure that the readability of the scale is 10 percent or less than the amount to be weighed. Stated another way as a workable formula:

Smallest quantity to be weighed = scale readability × 10

Consider a scale where the readability is 0.25 ounce (7 grams). This scale could appropriately weigh quantities as small as 2.5 ounces (70 grams) without more than a 10 percent error in measurement. Likewise, a scale with a readability of 0.1 ounce (3 grams) could adequately weigh quantities as small as 1 ounce (30 grams).

UNITS OF MEASURE

Digital and baker's scales measure in either standard U.S. common units (pounds and ounces; imperial units in Canada) or in metric units (kilograms and grams). Some versatile digital scales switch at the touch of a button from U.S./imperial units to metric units. Most countries throughout the world have adopted the metric

HOW CAN AN OUNCE SCALE PROVIDE THE PRECISION OF A GRAM SCALE?

One gram is a much smaller unit than one ounce (there are 28.35 grams in an ounce), so how is it possible for an ounce scale to provide the precision of a gram scale?

Certainly if the gram scale has a readability of 1 gram and the ounce scale has a readability of 1 ounce, the gram scale will measure more precisely than the ounce scale. But this is rarely the case.

Take, for example, the description of the two electronic scales given earlier. The first scale is a gram scale, with a readability of 5 grams, or 0.2 ounce (5 grams divided by 28.35 grams per ounce). The second scale is an ounce scale with a readability of 0.1 ounce (3 grams). In this particular example, the ounce scale weighs more precisely than the gram scale, because the design and construction of the scale allows it to read smaller amounts.

TABLE 1.1 ■

EQUIVALENCIES BETWEEN U.S. COMMON (IMPERIAL) AND METRIC UNITS

WEIGHT	
1 ounce	= 28.4 grams
1 pound	= 454 grams

VOLUME	
1 teaspoon	= 4.9 milliliters
1 quart	= 0.95 liters

system. This provides a means of sharing formulas more easily across national borders. More importantly, the metric system is simpler to use once you become familiar with it. With the metric system, for example, fewer math calculations are needed when converting a formula to a new batch size. Since 1 kilogram in metric equals 1,000 grams, you simply move decimal points to convert from one size unit to another. For example, 1.48 kilograms is equal to 1,480 grams, and 343 grams is equal to 0.343 kilograms. Try converting as quickly from pounds to ounces, or ounces to pounds! This ease of use is probably the main reason why more bakers and pastry chefs in North America are adopting the metric system for use in the bakeshop.

Using the metric system, for the most part, does not require tedious math conversions from ounces to grams or pounds to kilograms. This makes it much easier to use the metric system than most people believe. Table 1.1 lists the metric equivalents of a few U.S. common (imperial) units, for those times when you do need to convert from one system to another.

It is a common misconception that metric units provide better precision than U.S./imperial units. In fact, metric units are not necessarily more precise, although they are simpler to use. Once again, the precision of measurements depends on the design and construction of the scale, not on the units used.

WEIGHT AND VOLUME MEASUREMENTS

Home cooks in North America use volumetric measurements—measuring containers and measuring spoons—for all ingredients, including dry ingredients. This is a problem when measuring certain ingredients. For example, flour settles over time. When flour settles, there is less air between particles. Density increases, and more flour is needed to fill a container. On the other hand, if flour is sifted before it is measured, there is more air between particles. Density decreases, and less flour is needed to fill a cup.

To avoid these inconsistencies, pastry chefs and bakers do not use volumetric measurements for flour and other dry ingredients. Instead, they weigh dry ingredients—and most liquid ingredients—for accuracy. Density does not affect weight measurements the way it affects volume measurements. A pound of sifted flour weighs the same as a pound of unsifted flour, regardless of the density. They both weigh 1 pound!

TABLE 1.2 ■ A COMPARISON OF THE APPROXIMATE WEIGHTS OF 1 PINT AND 1 HALF LITER (500 MILLILITERS) OF VARIOUS INGREDIENTS

INGREDIENT	APPROXIMATE WEIGHT PER U.S. PINT (IN WEIGHT OUNCES)	APPROXIMATE WEIGHT PER HALF LITER (500 ML) (IN GRAMS)
Splenda	4.0	120
Ginger, ground	6.0	180
Flour, sifted	8.2	245
Flour, unsifted	9.2	275
Sugar, granulated	14.1	420
Oil, vegetable	14.8	445
Cream, heavy	16.4	490
Water	16.7	500
Milk, whole	17.0	510
Eggs, whole	17.2	515
Orange juice	17.4	520
Coffee liqueur	17.5	525
Simple syrup (equal parts sugar and water)	20.6	615
Honey, molasses, and glucose corn syrups	23.0	690

While some pastry chefs and bakers weigh all ingredients using a scale, others measure some liquids volumetrically. They use measuring containers for water and for liquids that have about the same density as water. While practices vary from bakeshop to bakeshop, ingredients that are often measured volumetrically include milk, cream, and eggs. Table 1.2 indicates why. Notice that the weights per pint (or per half liter) of milk, cream, and eggs are around the same as that of water. Measuring 1 pint of each of these ingredients yields about a pound or so (while these ingredients do not weigh exactly 1 pound per pint, they are approximately so; notice, however, that in the metric system, 1 half liter—500 milliliters—of water at room temperature does weigh exactly 500 grams. This is not a coincidence). Many other liquids, including honey, corn syrup, and oil, have densities much different from water. These liquids must be weighed, because 1 pint will not weigh 1 pound.

THE DIFFERENCE BETWEEN DENSITY AND THICKNESS

Density is a measure of the compactness of particles or molecules in a liquid or solid. If the particles or molecules are loosely packed, the liquid or solid is not dense, and the weight per cup or per liter of that ingredient is low. If the particles or molecules are closely packed, the liquid or solid is dense, and the weight per cup or weight per liter of that ingredient is high.

Viscosity or consistency is a measure of how easily a liquid flows. If a liquid's particles or molecules slide past each other easily, the liquid flows easily and is considered thin. If the particles or molecules bump or tangle

HELPFUL HINT

Do not judge the density of a liquid by its thickness. Unless you know for sure that the density of a liquid is close to that of water, assume that it is not; assume that it must be weighed.

TABLE 1.3 ■ VOLUMETRIC CONVERSIONS FOR U.S. COMMON UNITS

1 tablespoon	= 3 teaspoons
	= 0.5 fluid ounce
1 cup	= 48 teaspoons
	= 16 tablespoons
	= 8 fluid ounces
1 pint	= 16 fluid ounces
	= 2 cups
1 quart	= 32 fluid ounces
	= 4 cups
	= 2 pints
1 gallon	= 128 fluid ounces
	= 16 cups
	= 8 pints
	= 4 quarts

with each other, the liquid will not flow easily and is thick. This is the case with fruit purees. Tiny pulp pieces in fruit purees bump and tangle with one another, preventing water and pulp particles from flowing easily past one another. This makes the puree thick.

Some common liquids—honey and molasses, for example—are both dense and thick. The molecules are close together, making these liquids dense, and the molecules do not slide easily past each other, making the liquids thick. But consider vegetable oil. Vegetable oil is thicker than water, yet it is less dense than water (that is why oil floats). Notice how the density of a liquid cannot be judged by looking at its thickness.

THE DIFFERENCE BETWEEN WEIGHT OUNCES AND FLUID OUNCES

Refer to Table 1.3, which lists conversions between U.S. common volumetric measurements. Notice that there are 16 ounces in a pint (2 cups). Recall that there are 16 ounces in a pound. Why, then, did we see from Table 1.1 that a pint does not weigh 1 pound for all ingredients? Likewise, how can there be 16 tablespoons in a cup and 8 ounces in a cup, but 16 tablespoons does not necessarily weigh 8 ounces? These are the problems that result when one word—ounce—is used to represent two different concepts.

The term ounce represents a unit of weight or mass. It can also represent volume or capacity. That is, there are weight ounces that measure weight, and there are fluid ounces that measure volume. Notice that Table 1.3 specifies fluid ounces, not weight ounces, in each conversion. While 1 fluid ounce sometimes does weigh 1 ounce, it is not necessarily so.

Consider feathers and bullets. No one expects 1 cup of feathers to weigh the same as 1 cup of bullets. Likewise, food ingredients vary in how much they weigh per cup. Refer back to Table 1.2, which lists several ingredients—arranged from less dense to more dense—and their weights per pint (2 cups) and per half liter (500 milliliters). Notice the large range in values. This shows that the expression "a pint's a pound the world 'round" is not only false for feathers and bullets, but it is also false for many common bakeshop ingredients. It is approximately true for water and for ingredients with the same density as water. Because 1 fluid ounce of water (and ingredients with the same density as water) weighs about 1 ounce, and 1 milliliter of water weighs 1 gram, for practical purposes it doesn't matter whether water is weighed on a scale or measured volumetrically.

HELPFUL HINT

If a formula includes measurements in ounces, be sure to check carefully to determine for each ingredient whether it is to be measured using fluid or weight ounces. Unless you know the density of an ingredient, do not interchange weight measurements with volumetric measurements, or vice versa.

PHOTO 1.1 A comparison of volumes of equal weights of maple syrup, water, and flour. *Photo by Aaron Seyfarth*

BAKER'S PERCENTAGES

Formulas, especially bread formulas, are sometimes expressed in percentages called *baker's percentages*. With baker's percentages, each ingredient is expressed as a certain ratio or percent of the total amount of flour in the formula. Flour is used as the basis for baker's percentages because it is typically the predominant ingredient in most baked goods. Since the total amount of flour is designated as 100 percent, the percentages of all ingredients add up to more than 100 percent. Table 1.4 provides an example of a bread formula expressed in weight and in baker's percentages. Notice that more than one type of flour is included in this formula, but that together the weight of the flours adds up to 100 percent.

For formulas that do not contain flour, each ingredient is expressed as a percentage of the predominant and characteristic ingredient. In the case of a date filling, for example, each ingredient is expressed as a percentage of the amount of dates (Table 1.5). For baked custard, each ingredient is expressed as a percentage of dairy ingredients—milk and cream.

Baker's percentage—sometimes called *formula percentage* or indicated as "on flour weight basis"—is different than the percentages commonly taught in math classes. In the more common type of percentage, each ingredient is expressed as a certain percentage of the total batch size. In this case, ingredient percentages add up to 100 percent. Table 1.6 shows the bread formula from Table 1.4, this time expressed as a percentage of the total batch.

TABLE 1.4 ■ WHOLE WHEAT BREAD FORMULA EXPRESSED IN WEIGHT AND IN BAKER'S PERCENTAGES

INGREDIENT	POUNDS	OUNCES	GRAMS	BAKER'S PERCENTAGE
Flour, bread	6		3000	60%
Flour, whole wheat	4		2000	40%
Water	5	10.0	2800	56%
Yeast, compressed		6.0	190	4%
Salt		3.0	95	2%
Total	**16**	**3.0**	**8085**	**162%**

Note: Metric measures in this table and throughout the text are not necessarily exact conversions of U.S./imperial measures. This is done to avoid the use of awkward numbers. Because baker's percentages remain approximately the same, products are the same, regardless of the units of measure.

TABLE 1.5 ■ DATE FILLING FORMULA EXPRESSED IN WEIGHT AND IN BAKER'S PERCENTAGES

INGREDIENT	POUNDS	GRAMS	BAKER'S PERCENTAGE
Dates	6	3000	100%
Sugar	1	500	17%
Water	3	1500	50%
Total	**10**	**5000**	**167%**

TABLE 1.6 ■ WHOLE WHEAT BREAD FORMULA EXPRESSED IN WEIGHT AND IN PERCENTAGE OF TOTAL BATCH

INGREDIENT	POUNDS	OUNCES	GRAMS	PERCENTAGE OF TOTAL BATCH
Flour, bread	6		3000	37%
Flour, whole wheat	4		2000	25%
Water	5	10.0	2800	35%
Yeast, compressed		6.0	190	2%
Salt		3.0	95	1%
Total	**16**	**3.0**	**8085**	**100%**

TABLE 1.7A ■ A COMPARISON OF WHOLE WHEAT BREAD FORMULAS EXPRESSED IN WEIGHT AND IN BAKER'S PERCENTAGES (BREAD #1)

INGREDIENT	POUNDS	OUNCES	GRAMS	BAKER'S PERCENTAGE
Flour, bread	6		3000	60%
Flour, whole wheat	4		2000	40%
Water	5	10	2800	56%
Yeast, compressed		6	190	4%
Salt		3	95	2%
Total	**16**	**4**	**8085**	**162%**

TABLE 1.7B ■ A COMPARISON OF WHOLE WHEAT BREAD FORMULAS EXPRESSED IN WEIGHT AND IN BAKER'S PERCENTAGES (BREAD #2)

INGREDIENT	POUNDS	OUNCES	GRAMS	BAKER'S PERCENTAGE
Flour, bread	22		10000	60%
Flour, whole wheat	15		6800	40%
Water	21		9550	57%
Yeast, compressed		18	500	3%
Salt		6	190	1%
Total	**59**	**8**	**26965**	**161%**

Why bother expressing formulas in percentages at all? Percentages allow formulas to be easily compared. Table 1.7 illustrates this point. Compare the two formulas in Table 1.7 by looking at the weights of each ingredient. Can you tell quickly which formula is saltier? Before you conclude that the bottom formula is saltier because it contains 6 ounces (190 grams) of salt compared with 3 ounces (95 grams) in the top formula, notice that the bottom formula also yields a larger quantity of dough. Unless this difference in yield or batch size is accounted for, weights alone won't reveal which bread is saltier.

When baker's percentages for these formulas are used instead of weight for comparison, the difference in batch size is accounted for, and it becomes clear that the formula in Table 1.7A is saltier. The amount of salt in the formula for Bread #1 is about 2 percent of the weight of the flours compared with 1 percent in Bread #2 (Table 1.7B).

Baker's percentages have an advantage over percentages based on total batch size. Baker's percentages require fewer calculations when adding or changing the amount of one ingredient. If percentages used are based on total batch size, then every ingredient percentage will have to be recalculated when any one ingredient is changed, since the total batch size would also change. Needless to say, this is more complicated and time consuming and thus, baker's percentages are preferred by some bakers.

THE IMPORTANCE OF CONTROLLING INGREDIENT TEMPERATURES

The finest ingredients can be selected, they can be accurately weighed and properly mixed, but if temperatures are not carefully controlled, there is still a chance for failure. Why? Many ingredients change properties with temperature. Think of fat, especially fats that melt easily, such as butter. Butter must remain within a narrow temperature range (65–70°F; 18–21°C) as it is spread onto croissant dough. If it is too cold, it will not spread properly; if it is too warm, it melts into the dough and flakiness is compromised.

Often, ingredients that are at widely different temperatures must be carefully combined to avoid damaging one ingredient with the shock of the heat—or cold—of another. In making vanilla custard sauce, for example, cold yolks cannot be added directly to hot milk, or the yolks could curdle. Instead, in a technique called tempering, small amounts of hot milk are stirred into the yolks, diluting them. The diluted yolks can now be safely added to the bulk of the hot liquid.

Tempering is also necessary when stabilizing whipped cream with a gelatin solution. Warmed gelatin hardens into tiny rubbery balls if it is added too quickly to a cold ingredient like whipped cream. The addition of a small amount of whipped cream to the warm gelatin dilutes the gelatin, so it can be added safely to the bulk of the cold whipped cream.

Notice that in the first example of tempering, a small amount of a hot ingredient is added to a cold ingredient, to prevent damage to the cold ingredient. In the second example, a small amount of a cold ingredient is added to a warm ingredient, to prevent damage to the warm ingredient.

Many other examples demonstrate the need for controlling ingredient temperatures and for carefully tempering ingredients. Look for them throughout the text.

HELPFUL HINT

If it is unclear which of two ingredients should be slowly added to the other ingredient, consider the following general rule when tempering ingredients:

Add small amounts of the ingredient that causes problems into the ingredient that is the problem.

In the first example, hot milk could cause egg yolks to curdle. Because the hot milk causes the problem and the yolks, if they curdle, are the problem, hot milk is added to egg yolks, and not the other way around.

Likewise, cold whipped cream could cause gelatin to solidify into tiny rubber balls. This means that the cream (which causes the problem) is added to gelatin (which, solidified into tiny balls, is the problem).

THE IMPORTANCE OF CONTROLLING OVEN TEMPERATURES

Chapter 2 is all about heat transfer and how to control it. Yet, the information in the next chapter is of little use if an oven is not calibrated properly. Nor is it of any use if an oven is not allowed to fully preheat before product is added, or if an oven door is opened too often and for too long. Paying attention to these simple points can go far in assuring that product coming from your bakeshop is of consistently high quality.

HOW IMPORTANT IS OVEN TEMPERATURE WHEN BAKING CAKES?

High ratio cakes are characterized by high percentages, or ratios, of liquid and sugar to the amount of flour. They are formulated to be mixed in a single step that whips large amounts of tiny air bubbles into the batter. While considered by many to be foolproof, things can go wrong when oven temperatures are off.

When the oven temperature is low, for example, a cake's structure sets later than it should. In the meantime, the batter slowly warms and as it does, it thins out. Air bubbles easily rise through the thin batter to the surface of the cake, while starch in the flour sinks to the bottom. If the oven temperature is quite low, the baked cake will have a thick rubbery layer along the bottom and a low volume overall. Or, it could simply have a series of thin tunnels running from bottom to top, tunnels that follow the trail of disappearing bubbles.

QUESTIONS FOR REVIEW

1. Why do bakers and pastry chefs require better accuracy in measuring ingredients than do kitchen chefs?

2. What does it mean for a baker's scale to be out of balance? Describe how to check and adjust a scale for proper balancing.

3. An electronic scale has the following printed on its front display panel: 500 g × 2 g. What does each number refer to?

4. What is the smallest amount that should be weighed on a scale that has 500 g × 2 g on its display panel? Assume that an acceptable amount of error in measurement is 10 percent or less.

5. What is the main advantage of metric weight measurements (grams and kilograms) over U.S. common or imperial measurements (ounces and pounds)?

6. Explain why weighing ingredients in grams is not necessarily more accurate than weighing in ounces.

7. Explain why judging the thickness of a liquid is not a good way to judge how much a cup of it will weigh.

8. When weighing flour that is to be sifted, does it matter whether the flour is sifted before or after it is weighed? Why or why not?

9. What are the two meanings of the word ounce? For which ingredients are they approximately equal?

10. List three ingredients that are sometimes measured using volumetric measures (pints, liters, tablespoons, and milliliters).

11. Why do bakers and pastry chefs prefer weight measurements to volume measurements? Use flour as an example when answering this question.

12. Explain how it is that 1 pint (500 ml) of water weighs approximately 16 ounces (500 grams) while 1 pint of glucose corn syrup weighs much more.

13. What is the main advantage of using formulas that are expressed in percentages?

14. What is an advantage of baker's percentages over percentages based on total yield?

15. What does it mean to temper ingredients?

16. Explain how to temper hot milk and egg yolks.

QUESTIONS FOR DISCUSSION

1. A friend is preparing a 1-2-3 cookie dough (which typically contains 1 pound sugar, 2 pounds butter, 3 pounds flour, and three eggs). Instead of weighing the ingredients, however, your friend uses measuring cups, measuring 1 cup sugar, 2 cups butter, and 3 cups flour. Why is it unlikely that the cookie dough will turn out properly?

2. You are preparing an orange sauce that calls for 32 fluid ounces of orange juice and 1 ounce of starch. You decide to weigh the 32 ounces on a scale. Using the information from Table 1.2, explain whether you will be adding too much or too little orange juice than actually required. Will your orange sauce turn out slightly too thick or too thin?

3. Using the information from Table 1.2, state which of the following measurements will be less accurate if a measuring container is used instead of a scale, when a formula is based on weight units: heavy cream or orange juice? Why?

4. Explain how to combine warmed melted chocolate and chilled whipped cream together, to prevent bits of chocolate from solidifying into small chips in the cold cream.

EXERCISES AND EXPERIMENTS

1. Rye Bread Formulas

Compare the following two formulas for rye bread.

Formula 1

INGREDIENT	POUNDS	OUNCES	GRAMS	BAKER'S PERCENTAGE
Flour, bread	8		3000	80%
Flour, white rye	2		2000	20%
Water	6		2800	56%
Yeast, compressed		6	190	4%
Salt		3	95	2%
Caraway seeds		2.4	75	1.5%
Total	16	4	8085	163.5%

Formula 2

INGREDIENT	POUNDS	OUNCES	GRAMS	BAKER'S PERCENTAGE
Flour, bread	22		10,000	60%
Flour, white rye	15		6,800	40%
Water	21		9,550	57%
Yeast, compressed		15	425	2.5%
Salt		9	260	1.5%
Caraway seeds		4.75	135	0.8%
Total	59	8	27,170	161.5%

1. Based on the amount of caraway seeds added to each, which would you expect to have a stronger caraway flavor? Explain how you got your answer.

2. Based on the amount of yeast added to each, which would you expect to rise faster and possibly have a stronger yeast flavor? Explain how you got your answer.

2. Weight of Ingredients

Complete the formula below by filling in the missing weights for unsifted pastry flour, molasses, and ginger. To do this, use information from Table 1.2 to convert the given volumetric measurements to weight measurements to one decimal place (note that weights are listed in Table 1.2 as "per pint," or 2 cups). Check your work by confirming that the weights in pounds and ounces add up to the total weight given.

INGREDIENT	VOLUME MEASUREMENTS	POUNDS	OUNCES
Flour, pastry, unsifted	9 cups		
Sugar	3 cups	1	5
Butter	2 cups	1	
Molasses	½ cup		
Eggs	3 each		5.2
Ginger	¼ cup		
Baking soda	1 Tbsp.		0.4
Salt	0.5 tsp.		0.1
Total		5	10.7

3. Density and Thickness in Volumetric Measurements

OBJECTIVES

- Show how density affects the weight of a cup of an ingredient.
- Show how thick samples are not necessarily denser than thin samples.
- Show how different methods of adding flour and other dry ingredients affect density.

MATERIALS AND EQUIPMENT

- Flour (any type)
- Small spoon or scoop
- Instant starch, such as National Ultrasperse 2000, or any cook-up starch, such as cornstarch

PROCEDURE

- Prepare a thickened starch solution by adding instant starch to water until noticeably thick, being careful to avoid whisking air into the mixture. *Do not pre-blend starch with sugar* (this will increase the density of the solution and alter the results of the experiment). Or, cook any starch with water (about 25 grams cornstarch into 400 grams water) until noticeably thick; cool to room temperature.
- Weigh 1 level cup (250 ml) of each of the following:
  - Flour lightly spooned into a measuring cup
  - Flour spooned into a measuring cup but shaken after every few spoonfuls to allow flour to settle

- Flour sifted first, then lightly spooned into measuring cup
- Water (room temperature)
- Thickened starch solution (room temperature)

- Record weights in the following Results Table. Be sure to indicate your units of measure—grams or ounces—in the table.
- Record any potential sources of error that might make it difficult to draw the proper conclusions from your experiment.
- Compare your weights and explain.

SOURCES OF ERROR

_____

_____

RESULTS TABLE ■ DENSITY MEASUREMENTS

PRODUCT	WEIGHT PER CUP
Flour, spooned	
Flour, spooned and shaken	
Flour, sifted then spooned	
Water	
Starch-thickened solution	

CONCLUSIONS

1. Rank flour samples—spooned, spooned and shaken, or sifted then spooned—from least dense to densest sample. Based on these results, explain why weight, not volume, is best for measuring flour and other dry ingredients.

_____

_____

2. How did the density (weight per cup) of the starch-thickened solution compare with the density of water? How might you explain these results?

_____

_____

3. Did you have any sources of error that might significantly affect the results of your experiment? If so, what could you do differently next time to minimize error?

_____

_____

CHAPTER 2
HEAT TRANSFER

CHAPTER **OBJECTIVES**

1. Describe the main means of heat transfer in cooking and baking.

2. Describe ways to control heat transfer in cooking and baking.

3. Describe the advantages and disadvantages of various materials used in cookware and bakeware.

 ## INTRODUCTION

We all know that stovetops and ovens generate heat, but how does the heat travel from its source to the food? That is, how is heat transferred? This chapter is all about heat transfer. By understanding heat transfer, bakers and pastry chefs can better control cooking and baking processes and the quality of baked goods.

METHODS OF HEAT TRANSFER

The three main ways that heat is transferred from its source to food are radiation, conduction, and convection. Most methods of cooking and baking—including simmering, sautéing, frying, and oven baking—rely on more than one means of heat transfer (Figure 2.1). A fourth type of heat transfer—induction—takes place on special stovetop surfaces. Each of these means of heat transfer is explained in this section.

Radiation

Radiation is the rapid transfer of heat through space from a warmer object to the surface of a cooler one. Once molecules on the surface of an object absorb heat rays, they vibrate rapidly. The vibration generates frictional heat within the object. At no time does the radiating body come into direct contact with the object, yet heat energy is transferred from one to the other. Because there is no direct contact, radiation is sometimes described as a form of indirect heat. Examples of appliances that heat

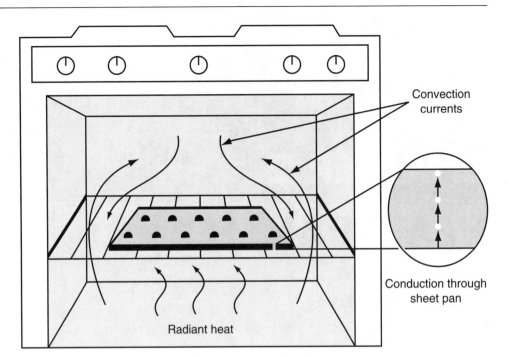

FIGURE 2.1 Radiation, conduction, and convection in an oven

HELPFUL HINT

Radiant heat transfer is important in oven baking, and a large amount of heat is radiated off hot oven walls. This creates "hot spots" in conventional ovens along the oven walls. If product nearest the walls bakes up dark, it is because of this heat radiation. To prevent uneven baking, place pans in the center of the oven, away from the walls. Or, rotate the direction of pans in the oven halfway through baking.

TABLE 2.1 ■ RADIANT HEAT TRANSFER OF VARIOUS MATERIALS

MATERIAL	RELATIVE RADIANT HEAT TRANSFER
Black body (dull)	1.0
Brick	0.93
Aluminum (dull)	0.2
Aluminum (shiny)	0.04

primarily by radiation include toasters, broilers, infrared heat lamps, and conventional ovens.

Hot pans also radiate heat. To prove this, place a hand over—not on—the surface of a hot, empty pan and feel the heat radiating from its surface. Dark surfaces typically radiate more heat than lighter ones because dark surfaces absorb more heat energy to begin with. Likewise, dull surfaces absorb—and radiate—more heat than shiny surfaces. Not surprisingly, dull black sheet pans bake foods faster than bright shiny ones. Table 2.1 lists the relative amount of heat, called *emissivity*, that radiates or is emitted off of several common materials. Notice the high amount of heat that radiates off brick, a material used in traditional hearth ovens.

Radiation is also a means of transferring microwave energy. In a microwave oven, a special tube called a magnetron generates microwave energy. Microwave energy passes through many types of cookware and penetrates the surface of food more easily than radiant heat energy. Still, the principles of heat transfer hold, and the absorbed microwaves generate heat because certain molecules throughout the food flip back and forth from the absorbed energy. The flipping motion generates frictional heat, and the food cooks primarily from heat generated from the movement of molecules.

Microwave cooking tends to heat foods unevenly. This is partly because different substances absorb microwave energy differently, but it is also because some substances require less energy—microwave or otherwise—to heat up. For example, microwave a jelly doughnut and observe that the sugary jelly center will be extremely hot while the outside doughnut will be much less so.

Heating with microwaves is relatively fast because the radiant microwaves penetrate further into the food—typically 1 to 2 inches—than radiant heat energy, which heats surfaces only. But how does heat from microwave energy spread throughout the food, and how does heat from radiant heat energy penetrate beyond the surface of food? Through two different means: conduction and convection.

Conduction

Conduction occurs when heat passes from a hot area of an object to a cooler area. Heat is passed molecule by molecule. That is, as one molecule absorbs heat and vibrates, it passes heat along to a nearby molecule, which vibrates in turn. Conduction of heat energy continues molecule by molecule, until eventually the entire object is hot. Because direct contact is needed for heat transfer by conduction, it is sometimes described as a form of direct heat transfer.

Heat conduction is important in stovetop cooking, where heat is conducted from the heat source—gas flame or electric coils—directly to the outside of a pan bottom. Conduction continues as heat passes through the pan to the food inside the pan. Even when the pan is removed from the heat, conduction continues until the pan and the food reach the same temperature. This is a source of *carryover cooking*—cooking that occurs after food is removed from its source of heat.

Heat conduction is important in baking as well. Once radiation heats the surface of a sheet pan of cookies, for example, conduction transfers heat through the pan and through the cookies. Once the cookies are removed from the oven and from the sheet pan, conduction continues until the cookies are the same temperature throughout (the cookies also begin radiating heat to the bakeshop until they cool to room temperature).

To understand the difference between radiation and conduction, imagine two teams of ten people, each arranged in a row. Each team must pass a ball from the first person to the last. The first team does this quickly by having the first person in the row toss the ball to the last person. The second team passes the ball by handing it from one person to the next, until the ball finally reaches the last person. Think of the first team as radiation and the second team as conduction. Radiation passes the ball (heat) quickly by tossing it through the air. Conduction passes it more slowly by handing it one to the next.

Just as some teams are faster than other teams at passing the ball, some materials pass or conduct heat faster than other materials. Materials that conduct heat fast are described as having high thermal or heat conductivity. In general, solids have higher heat conductivities than liquids and gases because molecules are closer together in solids than they are in liquids and gases. The closeness of molecules makes it easier to pass the heat from one molecule to the next (remember, the "ball" cannot be tossed with conduction).

Heat conduction can be fast or slow through cookware and bakeware, depending on the heat conductivity of the material used in the construction of the vessel. Conduction also varies with the thickness, or gauge, of the material used in a pan's construction. Heavy-gauge material is thicker and conducts heat to food more slowly than light-gauge material. Although they conduct heat more slowly, heavy-gauge pans are often favored over thin-gauge pans because they transfer heat more evenly.

Metals are particularly fast at conducting heat because of their molecular structures. Some metals, however, conduct heat faster than others. See Table 2.2 for the relative heat conductivities of various materials. Additional information about common metals and materials used in the bakeshop follows.

HELPFUL HINT

If old aluminum sheet pans are pocked with bits of blackened baked-on food, they will radiate heat unevenly. For even cooking and browning, keep cookware and bakeware clean of burned-on food.

HELPFUL HINT

Water has low heat conductivity, meaning it is slow to conduct heat. This is why it is useful to bake custard and cheesecake, which are best baked slowly and evenly, in a water bath.

Air's heat conductivity is even lower than water's. Double boilers take advantage of this insulating property of air. With double boilers, the top insert is placed over, not in, boiling water, for very gentle warming of food. Double boilers are useful for warming egg whites, chocolate, or fondant, for example.

TABLE 2.2 ■ HEAT CONDUCTIVITIES OF VARIOUS MATERIALS

MATERIAL	RELATIVE HEAT CONDUCTIVITY
Silver	4.2
Copper	3.9
Aluminum	2.2
Stainless steel	0.2
Marble	0.03
Water	0.006
Teflon	0.002
Wood	0.001
Air	0.0003

WHY DOES MARBLE FEEL COOL TO THE TOUCH, EVEN IN A WARM BAKESHOP?

Touch a marble surface with one hand and a wood surface with the other, and the marble will feel noticeably cooler to the touch. Yet both the marble and the wood, if they have been in the same room for a while, are at room temperature. How can this be?

Marble has a greater heat conductivity than wood, so heat transfers faster from the body to marble than it does to wood. Because the hand touching marble cools more quickly, the marble seems cooler to the touch (when, in actuality the marble is now slightly warmer, because heat was transferred to it from the hand).

Repeat this demonstration by placing one hand on marble and the other on stainless steel or another metal. Because metals have greater heat conductivity than marble, the stainless steel surface will seem cooler than the marble surface.

Again, it seems cooler because heat transfers faster from the hand touching stainless steel than from the one touching marble.

Because of marble's good heat conductivity, marble surfaces are often used in bakeshops to quickly cool hot confectionery products. Why not use a stainless steel surface instead? Generally, the answer has to do with the price: the cost of stainless steel would be prohibitive. Because a thick stainless steel table is very expensive to construct, these tables are typically thin, and thus they heat up too quickly. However, special stainless steel cooling tables are available to confectionery manufacturers. These tables are designed to allow cooling water to circulate within a sandwich of stainless steel. Heat is quickly conducted through the stainless steel surface to the water, where it is carried away through conduction and convection.

COPPER

Copper has very high heat conductivity, which means it conducts heat quickly. For this reason, copper is used in cooking sugar, where it is best to reach high temperatures in a relatively short time. Copper is expensive, however, so it is not used for everyday cookware and bakeware. Copper also reacts with food, and it can be toxic at high levels. To prevent its reacting with food, copper cookware is typically coated with a thin protective layer, usually stainless steel or tin, on surfaces that come into contact with food.

ALUMINUM

Aluminum conducts heat only about half as well as copper. This is still quite fast, however, and unlike copper, aluminum is inexpensive. Like copper, aluminum reacts with food, especially acidic foods. It discolors fruit products and turns milk and egg mixtures an unattractive gray, limiting its use in stovetop cookware. Aluminum mixer attachments also present a problem with reactive foods, discoloring some products. Since aluminum is a soft metal, it is easily scratched and pitted.

Because of its high conductivity and low cost, however, aluminum is commonly used in bakeware, where discoloration is less of an issue. It is easy to burn food cooked or baked on aluminum, however, especially if the pans are of a thin gauge. To minimize this, purchase heavy-gauge pans and use parchment paper. If necessary, for delicate baked items that brown quickly, bake on silicone baking pads placed on aluminum sheet pans, or use a double layer of sheet pans. The layer of silicone, or the cushion of air between the two pans, slows heat conduction to a manageable level.

A newer type of aluminum is called dark hard-anodized aluminum. Anodized aluminum has undergone an electrochemical treatment that changes the surface of the aluminum so that it is hard and durable. Anodized aluminum is nonreactive with foods and easy to clean. Although it does not conduct heat as fast as ordinary aluminum, anodized aluminum is dark in color, so some heat is transferred through radiation. Anodized aluminum typically comes in a heavy gauge so it cooks evenly, but it is more expensive than regular aluminum cookware.

STAINLESS STEEL

Stainless steel is a type of low-carbon steel (iron alloy) that contains a mix of metals including chromium and often nickel. Stainless steel is not a very good conductor of heat. Yet, it is durable, easy to clean, moderately priced, and basically inert—that is, it does not react with food. Stainless also has a light-reflective surface that makes it easy to view food as it cooks.

To improve its heat conductivity, lower-quality stainless steel cookware is manufactured to a thin gauge. However, it is difficult to roll stainless steel, or any metal, to a thin gauge evenly. Because of its unevenness, thin-gauge stainless cookware has hot spots where food is likely to burn. While thin-gauge stainless cookware is inexpensive, it is not a good choice for the bakeshop.

A better alternative for stovetop cooking is stainless steel with an aluminum core. The stainless steel surface provides a nonreactive, light-colored surface that makes it easy to view food and is easy to clean; the aluminum core provides improved heat conduction. The best aluminum-core stainless cookware has aluminum extending up the sides of the pan, for even cooking throughout.

Aluminum-core stainless steel cookware is the best choice for stovetop cooking of fruit mixtures, vanilla custard sauce, and pastry cream.

CAST IRON

Cast iron conducts heat reasonably well and, like aluminum, is best when thick and heavy, to slow down and even out heat exchange. Because it is black, cast iron also transfers heat through radiation. However, iron reacts with food, adding a metallic taste and discoloring the food. Because of this reactivity, cast iron is rarely used in the bakeshop. When it is used, it must be well seasoned before its first use, so it will not stick or rust. To season cast iron, coat with a thin layer of vegetable oil or shortening, then heat in an oven at about 350°F (175°C) for an hour or so.

TIN

Tinware is used in traditional French bakeware. It is lightweight, a good conductor of heat, and inexpensive. Tinware rusts easily and darkens with acid foods, however. If tinware is used in the bakeshop, it must be dried thoroughly as soon as it is washed, to prevent rusting.

GLASS, PORCELAIN ENAMEL, CERAMIC, AND STONEWARE

Glass, porcelain enamel, ceramic, and stoneware all conduct heat poorly. Like most materials that conduct poorly, they retain heat well once they are hot, making them useful for slow cooking. Ceramic ramekins, for example, are ideal for baked custards, which need to bake slowly.

NONSTICK SURFACES

Nonstick surfaces vary in their durability, but some crack and peel, and most scratch after repeated use. The nonstick surface acts as an insulator between the source of heat and any food placed in the pan. This means cooking is slower with nonstick cookware and bakeware, making it more difficult to brown foods. However, nonstick saucepans may be acceptable wherever fast heating is not needed.

SILICONE BAKEWARE, MOLDS, AND SHEETS

Silicone is not a good conductor of heat. For this reason, items bake more slowly and brown more evenly. Professional silicone bakeware, such as Flexipan brand molds,

THE INVISIBLE HELPING HAND

Recall that molecules vibrate when materials and objects are heated. The more they are heated, the faster they vibrate. As they heat up and vibrate faster, they also move farther apart. This movement—this expansion—lowers the density of hot liquids and gases. Less dense hot liquids and gases rise and move away from the source of heat. As the hot air and hot liquids rise, cold liquids and gases—which are denser—fall, moving closer to the source of heat. Convection currents set in, distributing heat more quickly and more uniformly throughout the product. Convection currents occur in the air in ovens, in thin batters baking in the oven, within thin liquids in a saucepan, and within fat in a fryer.

come in many shapes and sizes, and silicone baking mats (Silpat pads) fit inside half and full sheet pans. Silicone products are nonstick and are able to go from oven (up to 580°F/300°C) to freezer. Because they are flexible, product is released with a twist.

CONVECTION

Convection aids heat transfer through liquids and gases, which otherwise conduct heat slowly. Convection involves the constant movement of cold currents of air or liquid toward warmer currents. It occurs because warmer liquids and gases are less dense and therefore rise, while colder liquids and gases are denser and therefore sink. It is like having an invisible hand stirring the pot.

Convection currents work without assistance, but the movement of liquid in a pot, for example, can be increased if it is stirred. This is especially important with thick liquids, where fewer convection currents set in. Likewise, convection currents are at work in any oven, but the movement of air in an oven can be increased if air is forced to circulate. Convection ovens work by doing just that. Some convection ovens have fans that blow hot air, forcing the movement of air throughout the oven. Other ovens—like reel and rotating ovens—work by moving product through the air. In either case, convection ovens work faster than conventional ovens, as hot air moves more rapidly toward the cooler surfaces of the baked good and colder air moves away. This is why convection, reel, and rotating ovens require lower temperatures and shorter bake times. They also work more evenly, with fewer hot spots.

Convection ovens are not appropriate for all products, however. They are best for products made from heavy doughs, such as cookies and pâte à choux (puff pastry). Cakes and muffins, for example, bake up asymmetrically if convection currents are too strong or oven temperatures too high. Sponge cakes and soufflés can lose volume, and custards and cheesecakes overbake.

Convection currents can work against you; as an oven door is opened for viewing its contents, convection currents between the cooler air of the bakeshop and the warmer air of the oven quickly set in, cooling the air in the oven.

HELPFUL HINT

When switching from a conventional to a convection oven, the rule of thumb is to reduce oven temperature by about 25°F (15°C) and to reduce baking time by about 25 percent. When first making this switch, watch products carefully and adjust oven times and temperatures as needed.

HELPFUL HINT

To maximize convection currents in any oven, be sure baking pans are placed so that air movement within the oven is unobstructed. To do this, do not overload an oven, and be sure there is space between baking pans for air to circulate.

HELPFUL HINT

To maintain oven temperatures during baking, minimize the number of times and the amount of time that the oven door is opened. Even when it is opened for a few seconds, convection currents carry a significant amount of the oven's warmth into the bakeshop.

PHOTO 2.1 These cupcakes are misshapen from baking in a convection oven.
Photo by Aaron Seyfarth

Induction

Induction cooking is a new form of heat transfer. It is popular in kitchens and bake-shops in Europe and is becoming more so in North America. Induction cooking takes place on special smooth-top ceramic surfaces, below which are coils that generate a strong magnetic field. The magnetic field causes molecules in a pan to rapidly flip, gen-erating frictional heat within the pan. The pan heats up almost immediately, and the heat is quickly transferred from the pan to the food via conduction.

For a pan to work on an induction burner, it must have a flat bottom (woks will not work) and it must be made of magnetic material. To determine if a pan is made of magnetic material, hold a magnet to its bottom; if it holds, the pan is magnetic. Cast iron and some stainless steel pans work on induction burners, but those made of aluminum or copper do not. Many cookware companies sell pans designed specifically for induction cooking.

Induction cooking is gaining popularity because it is fast and more energy efficient than cooking with gas or electric coils. Since the pan heats directly, less heat is lost to the stovetop or into the air, so the bakeshop stays cooler. Heat is also more easily regulated than with gas or electric, and the stovetop surface stays relatively cool, so it is safer (however, keep in mind that some heat is transferred by conduction from the pan, heating the ceramic surface).

QUESTIONS FOR REVIEW

1. What is the primary means of heat transfer in conventional ovens?

2. Which bake faster and why: shiny new aluminum sheet pans or dark, dull used ones?

3. Explain how heat conduction works.

4. Which should be used when cooking pastry cream: a stainless steel or an aluminum pot? Why?

5. What are the two main features of cookware that affect how quickly heat is conducted through it?

6. Using the example of two teams passing a ball, explain why heat conduction is slower than radiation.

7. Why might cookies be baked on a double layer of sheet pans?

8. What is the main way that heat energy travels to the interior of solid food? In what two ways does it travel to the interior of a liquid?

9. Provide an example of when it is desirable to slow down heat transfer. Explain one way—besides reducing the heat!—that it can be slowed.

10. Explain how induction cooking works. What are its advantages over cooking with gas or electric coils?

QUESTIONS FOR DISCUSSION

1. Aluminum is known to discolor some food products, so why is it the most common material for sheet pans? That is, why might discoloration be less of an issue with baked goods than with sauces cooked in a pot?

2. Some pastry chefs layer sugar on the bottom of a pan when heating milk for vanilla custard sauce. This prevents the milk from burning onto the pan. Does this make the sugar layer a good heat conductor or a poor one? Explain your answer.

3. Explain how cookies baking in an oven are heated by radiation, conduction, and convection.

4. Explain how deep-fat frying—where the frying fat is heated to about 350°F (175°C)—is a good example of heat transfer by conduction and convection.

EXERCISES AND EXPERIMENTS

1. Heat Transfer

Imagine that you are baking cookies in an oven and you need to slow down heat transfer, so that the cookies don't burn on the outside before they are cooked throughout. Explain the reason that each of the following techniques work to decrease heat transfer. As an example, number 1 is completed for you.

1. Use a lower oven temperature.

Reason: This is the most direct way to decrease heat transfer, since it reduces the amount of heat radiated from the heat source.

2. Use shiny metal sheet pans rather than black matte ones.

Reason:

_____

_____

3. Use stainless steel pans instead of aluminum.

Reason:

_____

_____

4. Replace old, stained sheet pans with shiny new ones.

Reason:

_____

_____

5. Use thick-gauge pans rather than thin-gauge ones.

Reason:

_____

_____

6. Use double sheet pans by placing one sheet pan inside another.

Reason:

_____

_____

7. Keep sheet pans away from oven walls.

Reason:

_____

_____

8. Place cookies on a silicone pad (Silpat®) instead of directly on sheet pan.

Reason:

_____

_____

9. Turn off fan in a convection oven.

Reason:

_____

_____

2. The Extent of Hot Spots in a Conventional Oven

It's hard to imagine an oven that heats evenly throughout. The next best thing to having the perfect oven is knowing where the hot spots are in your oven. The fastest and easiest way to "map an oven" is to use an infrared thermometer. Aim the thermometer at various locations throughout the preheated oven, and you will learn very quickly where uneven baking will occur.

Another way to find the hot spots is to bake actual product in different locations in the oven and observe where differences occur.

OBJECTIVES

- Determine if, and where, hot spots exist in an oven.

PRODUCTS PREPARED

- Cookies baked in different locations of a conventional or deck oven (no convection fans)

MATERIALS AND EQUIPMENT

- Plain drop cookie dough that makes 24 cookies or more (for full sheet pans)
- Bowl scraper
- Two sheet pans that are as nearly identical as possible (if necessary, clean sheet pans to remove burned-on food, or use new sheet pans)

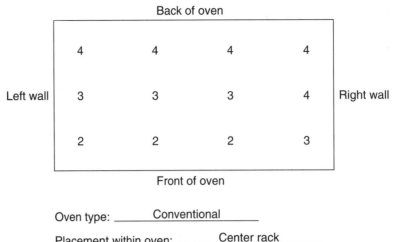

FIGURE 2.2 Sample results for experiment: Full sheet pan placed horizontally on center rack in conventional oven

Oven type: _____Conventional_____

Placement within oven: _____Center rack_____

- Parchment paper
- Small portion scoop, #30 (1 fluid ounce/30 milliliters), or equivalent

PROCEDURE

- Preheat oven according to formula.
- Prepare cookie dough using the formula that follows or any plain drop cookie formula. To minimize experimental error, use shortening instead of butter.
- Select sheet pan size (full or half) based on oven design. Line with parchment paper.
- Label parchment paper, indicating sheet pan placement within the oven (top rack, against left wall of oven, etc.), and which end of pan will be at the front of the oven.
- Using a scoop, portion out cookie dough, spacing it evenly on sheet pans. Place six cookies on half sheet pans and twelve cookies on full sheet pans.
- Use an oven thermometer placed in center of oven to read oven temperature. Record results here _____.
- When oven is properly preheated, place sheet pans in and set timer.
  - Bake cookies according to formula (do not rotate pans during baking), all for same amount of time.
  - Remove pans from oven and cool cookies directly on sheet pan.
  - Record any potential sources of error that might make it difficult to draw the proper conclusions from your experiment. In particular, be aware of any problems with the oven, dents in pan, differences in pan color, etc.
  - Evaluate the amount of browning of each cookie on sheet pans. Use a scale of one to five, one being lightest color.
  - Record evaluations for each cookie by making drawings of sheet pans as shown in Figure 2.1. Label location of walls of oven (left, right, front, back) relative to sheet pan. Also record the type of oven (conventional, reel, etc.) and placement of sheet pan in oven (top, center, or bottom rack; left, middle, right side of deck; etc.). See Figures 2.2 and 2.3 for examples of how to record evaluations.

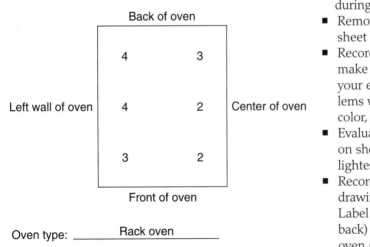

Oven type: _____Rack oven_____

Placement of sheet pan: _____Along left wall of oven_____

FIGURE 2.3 Sample results for experiment: Half sheet pan placed vertically against left wall of deck oven

Drop Sugar Cookie Dough

INGREDIENT	POUNDS	OUNCES	GRAMS	BAKER'S PERCENTAGE
Shortening, all-purpose		13	410	82
Sugar, regular granulated		18	565	113
Salt		0.25	8	1.6
Baking soda		0.25	8	1.6
Eggs		6	185	37
Pastry flour		16	500	100
Total	3	5.5	1676	335.2

Method of Preparation

1. Preheat oven to 375°F (190°C).

2. Allow all ingredients to come to room temperature.

3. Weigh ingredients on digital or baker's scale (*Note:* if readability of scale is higher than 0.1 gram/0.01 ounce, it is better to use teaspoons for measuring baking soda and salt, to minimize error. Use 2 teaspoons (10 milliliters) for 8 grams baking soda; use 1½ teaspoons (7½ milliliters) for 8 grams salt.

4. Blend flour, salt, and baking soda thoroughly by sifting together three times onto parchment paper.

5. Combine shortening and sugar in mixing bowl and mix on low for one minute; stop and scrape bowl, as needed.

6. Cream shortening/sugar mixture on medium for three minutes; stop and scrape bowl.

7. Add eggs slowly while mixing on low for 30 seconds; stop and scrape bowl.

8. Add flour to shortening/sugar/egg mixture and mix on low for one minute; stop and scrape bowl.

9. Cover dough with plastic wrap and set aside until ready to use.

10. Bake cookies for approximately 10–12 minutes.

SOURCES OF ERROR

_____

_____

RESULTS

Type of oven: _____

Location of pan in oven: _____

Type of oven: _____

Location of pan in oven: _____

 **CONCLUSIONS**

1. Which darkened more:

Cookies nearest the oven walls or those furthest from the oven walls? Explain your results.

_____

_____

Cookies near the back of the oven or those near the front of the oven? Explain your results.

_____

_____

2. What do these results tell you about whether there are hot spots in this oven?

_____

_____

3. If there were any, what can you do in the future to compensate for hot spots in this oven, so that they are not a significant source of experimental error?

_____

_____

CHAPTER 3

OVERVIEW OF THE BAKING PROCESS

CHAPTER **OBJECTIVES**

1. Present formulas as a balance of tougheners and tenderizers, moisteners and driers.

2. Discuss the importance of proper mixing technique.

3. Summarize the changes that occur as batters and doughs are mixed, and discuss the importance of water in this process.

4. Provide an overview of the 11 main events that occur as products are baked in the oven.

5. Briefly summarize eight changes that occur as products cool.

INTRODUCTION

Three distinct steps or stages occur in baking once ingredients are weighed. First, ingredients are mixed into batters or doughs. Next, the batter or dough is baked, and finally it is cooled. Many chemical and physical changes occur in products as they pass through each of these three stages. A pastry chef or baker who understands these changes is better able to control them. For example, a pastry chef who understands how mixing, baking, and cooling affect flakiness, tenderness, amount of browning, and crumb structure will be able to control them in baked goods.

This chapter presents an overview of many important and complex processes that occur in baking. Subsequent chapters address each of these processes in more detail.

SETTING THE STAGE FOR SUCCESS

In Chapter 1, the importance of weighing ingredients properly was introduced. Proper weighing of ingredients is important because successful formulas are carefully balanced mixtures of structure builders (tougheners), tenderizers, moisteners, and driers. *Structure builders* are ingredients that hold the volume and shape of baked goods

TABLE 3.1 ■ COMMON MIXING METHODS USED IN THE BAKESHOP

METHOD	DESCRIPTION	EXAMPLE OF USE
Straight dough	All ingredients combined and mixed until dough is smooth and well developed	Yeast-raised breads
Sponge and dough	Liquid, yeast, part of flour, part of sugar mixed into batter or dough (called a sponge or preferment) and allowed to ferment; added to remaining ingredients and mixed until dough is smooth and well developed	Yeast-raised breads made with poolish (liquid sponge), biga (Italian sponge, usually stiff), levain (naturally fermented sponge), or other sponge or preferment
Creaming or conventional	Shortening and sugar creamed; eggs added, then liquids (if any) added alternately with sifted dry ingredients at low speed	Shortened cakes and coffee cakes, cookies, cake-like muffins
Two-stage or blending	Sifted dry ingredients blended on low speed; softened fat cut in with paddle; liquids added slowly to blend in two stages (eggs added in second stage), then beaten to aerate	High-ratio cakes
Liquid shortening	All ingredients blended on low speed, then whipped on high, and finally medium speed, to aerate	High-ratio liquid shortening cakes
Sponge or whipping	Warmed whole eggs (or yolks) and sugar whipped until very light and thick; liquids added, sifted dry ingredients gently folded in, followed by melted butter (if required) or whipped whites (if separated)	Sponge cake (biscuit), genoise, ladyfingers, madeleines
Angel food	Egg whites and sugar whipped until soft peaks form; sifted dry ingredients gently folded in	Angel food cake
Chiffon	Sifted dry ingredients stirred or blended on low speed; oil and other liquid ingredients added and lightly blended until smooth; egg whites and sugar whipped until soft peaks form and folded into flour-oil mixture	Chiffon cake
Muffin or one-stage	Sifted dry ingredients stirred or blended on low speed; liquid fat and other liquid ingredients added in one stage and lightly blended just until moistened	Muffins, quick breads, quick coffee cakes
Biscuit or pastry	Sifted dry ingredients stirred or blended on low speed; solid fat rubbed or cut in by hand or with paddle; liquids stirred in gently	Biscuits, scones, pie pastry, blitz puff pastry

in place. Structure forms when these ingredients interact, building a framework that holds the product together. A certain amount of structure is necessary in all baked goods, but too much causes toughening. In fact, structure builders are often called *tougheners*. Examples of structure builders include flour, eggs, cocoa powder, and starch.

While flour is considered a structure builder, it is specific components in the flour—gluten protein molecules and starch molecules, in particular—that provide the structure. Likewise, it is egg protein molecules that make eggs structure builders. Food, like all matter, is made up of molecules.

Tenderizers are the opposite of structure builders. Tenderizers are ingredients in baked goods that interfere with the formation of structure. A certain amount of tenderizing is necessary in all baked goods so that they are easy to bite into and pleasant to eat, but too much tenderizing causes products to crumble and fall apart. Examples of tenderizers include sugars and syrups, fats and oils, and leavening agents.

Moisteners include water and ingredients that contain water, such as milk, eggs, cream, and syrups. Moisteners also include liquid fat ingredients, such as oil.

Driers are the opposite of moisteners. They are ingredients that absorb moisteners. Examples of driers include flour, cornstarch, dry milk solids, and cocoa powder. Notice that some ingredients fall into more than one category; that is, oil is both a tenderizer and a moistener, while flour is both a structure builder and a drier.

Once the proper amount of ingredients is weighed and measured, they must be combined in a specific manner and often at a specific temperature. Changing the manner of mixing or the temperature at which they are mixed can change the product, sometimes quite dramatically. For example, muffins are often mixed using the muffin method, where the fat is melted and stirred into dry ingredients along with other liquids. An alternative method for mixing muffins is to cream the fat first with sugar, then to add liquid and dry ingredients to this. The muffin method produces dense muffins with a coarse crumb. The creaming method produces a lighter muffin with the finer crumb of a cake. Table 3.1 lists and briefly describes several common mixing methods used in the bakeshop. Many other methods exist that combine certain features from these methods.

STAGE I: MIXING

Mixing distributes ingredients evenly throughout batters and doughs. While this is the obvious reason to mix ingredients, other important events occur during the mixing stage.

For example, during mixing, batters and doughs trap air. In chemically leavened baked goods, acids react with baking soda, producing carbon dioxide gas. Both air and carbon dioxide gas lighten batters and doughs. This makes batters and doughs easier to mix and handle. More importantly, it provides air cells that eventually form the crumb of baked goods.

Air cells are the many bubbles or pockets of air and other gases in batters and doughs. The air cells are surrounded by *cell walls*, which consist of a continuous network of egg and gluten proteins embedded with starch and other particles. These cell walls form the porous crumb structure of finished baked goods.

Because of the ability of batters and doughs to trap air and gas cells, they are sometimes referred to as foams. Once cell walls set into a porous crumb during baking, a baked good is considered a sponge, because air is no longer trapped inside. This term is used whether the product has a springy, spongy texture or not. When bakers and pastry chefs refer to the crumb or grain of baked goods, they are referring to the soft inside of a baked good, viewed when it is sliced.

WHAT IS AIR?

Air is composed of a mixture of gases, mostly nitrogen (close to 80 percent), oxygen, and a small amount of carbon dioxide. Oxygen is the most important gas in air because it is required for life. Oxygen is also required for many chemical reactions important to the baker, including those that strengthen gluten and whiten flour. Certain destructive reactions, such as the rancidity of fats and oils, also require oxygen, which is why some ingredients, such as nuts, are sometimes vacuum-packed to exclude air.

TABLE 3.2 ■ AMOUNT OF WATER IN VARIOUS BAKESHOP INGREDIENTS

INGREDIENT	AMOUNT OF WATER
Strawberries	92%
Lemon juice	91%
Orange juice	88%
Milk, whole	88%
Eggs, whole	75%
Banana	74%
Sour cream	71%
Cream cheese	54%
Jellies and jams	30%
Butter	18%
Honey	17%
Raisins	15%

Source: U.S. Department of Agriculture, Agricultural Research Service.

Most air cells and gas bubbles start fairly large. With continued mixing, large air cells break into many smaller ones. Later, in the oven, these gases and air cells become important, because while more gases are generated during the baking stage, no new air cells form. This means that if baked goods are to have the proper crumb structure, they must be mixed properly.

Throughout the mixing process, the friction of the mixer on the batter or dough breaks up the large particles, allowing them to dissolve or to hydrate faster in water. As particles hydrate, water becomes less able to move freely, and the batter or dough becomes thicker. As you will see, the ability of water (which is the universal solvent) to dissolve or hydrate particles and molecules is a very important part of the mixing process.

The Special Role of Water

All during mixing, water dissolves or at least hydrates many important molecules, both large and small. Even when water is not an ingredient in a formula, it plays a part during the mixing of all batters and doughs, because many ingredients are significant sources of water. Table 3.2 provides information about the amount of water in various bakeshop ingredients. Notice that ingredients do not need to be fluid to contain high amounts of water. Sour cream and bananas, for example, are over 70 percent water, cream cheese over 50 percent, and butter over 15 percent.

Until molecules either dissolve or are hydrated in water, they do not act as expected. For example, undissolved sugar crystals are not able to moisten or tenderize cakes, to stabilize whipped egg white, or to taste sweet. Undissolved salt is unable to slow yeast fermentation or to preserve food. Undissolved baking powder does not produce carbon dioxide for leavening. Each—the sugar, salt, and baking powder—must first dissolve in water before it can act.

Many larger molecules, such as proteins and starches, do not dissolve completely in water, but they do hydrate. *Hydration* occurs when large molecules—proteins and starches, for example—attract and bond to water. Layers of water form liquid shells around hydrated molecules, suspending them. Just as sugar, salt, and baking powder must dissolve before they act, so, too, must large molecules hydrate. Certain flour proteins, for example, must hydrate before mixing transforms them from hard chunks into a large, flexible web called *gluten*. Gluten is important for proper volume and crumb structure in baked goods. Both water hydration and mixing are necessary for gluten development; if either does not occur, gluten will not form.

Besides dissolving and hydrating food molecules, water performs several other important functions that begin during the mixing stage. For example, water activates yeast and allows fermentation to occur. Without sufficient water, yeast cells remain dormant—inactive—or they die.

WHAT IS DOUGH AUTOLYSIS?

Autolysis refers to a rest period that follows a brief, slow mixing of the flour and water that is used in yeast dough. The rest period lasts about 30 minutes, and during that time, water hydrates proteins and starches, improving the extensibility, or stretchiness, of doughs. Autolysis reduces the total mixing time of yeast doughs, which reduces the dough's exposure to oxygen in air. While some exposure to oxygen is desirable for dough development, some bakers believe that too much oxygen causes the flavor of the bread to deteriorate and the color to bleach excessively.

HOW TO MIX PIE PASTRY DOUGH

Pie pastry dough is mixed in a two-step process. Typically, solid fat is first mixed—or rubbed—into flour before water is added. The more the fat is rubbed into the flour, the more thoroughly the fat coats flour particles. Flour particles coated with fat will not easily absorb water. This limits the ability of structure-building gluten to form, and makes for more tender pie pastry. In fact, pie pastries made by rubbing fat thoroughly into flour are considered short or mealy, meaning that they are so tender that they crumble into short or cornmeal-size pieces. Sometimes, mealy pie pastry is desirable, especially for bottom crusts of juicy pies. Mealy pie pastry is less likely to absorb pie juices and toughen.

More often, flaky, rather than mealy, pie pastry is considered desirable. Flakiness requires that solid fat remains in chunks; the larger and more solid the chunks, the flakier the pie pastry. To make dough for flaky pastry, solid fat is rubbed into flour just until it is the size of hazelnuts or lima beans. Then, the dough is rolled to flatten the lumps of fat and distribute them evenly throughout. Notice how flakiness and tenderness are sometimes at odds: For flakiness, fat is kept as large chunks; for tenderness and mealiness, fat is thoroughly rubbed into flour.

Next, water is added and the dough gently mixed. The water must be ice-cold, so that the fat remains in solid chunks. If the fat melts from water that is too warm, the pastry will be mealy, not flaky. Mixing distributes water throughout the dough, but it also increases gluten development and toughening. Flaky pie pastry is particularly at risk for toughening because flour particles in flaky pastry are not well coated with fat. To allow time for water absorption without lengthy mixing, pastry chefs often chill pie pastry dough for several hours or overnight before continuing. This allows for water absorption, and it firms the fat and keeps it from smearing into the dough, for better flakiness. Overall, for a pie pastry that is both tender and flaky, limit the extent of mixing, both before and after water is added, and chill the dough before rolling and baking.

Water is a convenient means for adjusting the temperature of batters and doughs. Using cold water in pastry doughs, for example, keeps fats from melting and ensures a flakier crust. Likewise, carefully controlling water temperature in bread-making ensures that mixed dough is at the proper temperature for fermentation. A small amount of frictional heat is acceptable, even desirable, but too much warms yeast doughs above the ideal temperature for proper fermentation.

The amount of water in batters and doughs affects its viscosity or consistency. In fact, the consistency of a flour mixture defines whether it is a batter or a dough. *Batters* are unbaked flour mixtures that are relatively high in moisture, making them thin and pourable or scoopable. Examples of batters include cake, crêpe, and muffin batters. *Doughs* are unbaked flour mixtures that are relatively low in moisture, making them thick and moldable. Examples of doughs include bread, pie pastry, cookie, and baking-powder biscuit doughs. Batter and dough consistency is important for proper shaping and for proper leavening of baked goods.

Unlike many ingredients used in baking, fats do not dissolve in water, nor are they hydrated by water. Rather, solid fat breaks into small chunks, and liquid fat—oil—breaks into tiny droplets during mixing, forming an emulsion. These small chunks and tiny droplets spread throughout batters and doughs, coating particles by bonding to them. Anything coated with fat or oil cannot absorb water easily. In fact, that is the main reason why fats and oils are effective tenderizers. Fats and oils coat structure builders, such as gluten proteins and starches, and interfere with their ability to hydrate and form structure.

It is easy to see why batters and doughs are considered complex. Yet, compared with what is yet to come, the mixing process is relatively simple and straightforward. The next stage, baking, is where the heat of the oven activates additional chemical and physical changes. These changes are described in the next section as 11 separate events, but they are very much interrelated, and many occur simultaneously.

PHOTO 3.1 On left, pie dough and pastry with fat remaining as large chunks and, on right, pie dough and pastry made from dough with fat thoroughly rubbed into flour
Photo by Aaron Seyfarth

STAGE II: BAKING

Some of the events that occur during baking, such as starch gelatinization, would not happen at room temperature. Others would eventually happen, but the heat from the oven speeds them up. Temperatures are given for some of the events, but they are given only as a guideline because actual temperatures depend on many complex factors. Additionally, there is no upper temperature limit on protein coagulation and on certain other processes, such as starch gelatinization and the evaporation of gases. These processes continue as long as the baked good remains in the oven.

1. Fats Melt

One of the first things that happens when baked goods are placed in the oven is that solid fats melt. The actual temperature at which this occurs varies with the fat and its melting point, with butter melting earlier than all-purpose shortening, for example.

Most fats melt somewhere between 90°–130°F (30°–55°C). As they melt, trapped air and water escape from the fat. Water evaporates to steam vapor, and the air and steam expand, pushing on cell walls so that baked goods increase in volume. In other words, melting fat contributes to leavening. In general, the later a fat melts, the more it leavens, because the gases escape at about the same time that the cell walls are firm enough to hold their shape. While butter, with its low melting point, provides volume and flakiness when used properly, many fats provide more volume and flakiness than butter, because they have higher melting points. Fats with too high a melting point can have an unpleasant waxy mouthfeel, however. An example of fat designed with a very high melting point for maximum volume and flakiness is puff pastry margarine.

Besides melting point, the amount of water and, to a lesser extent, the amount of air in fat affects its ability to leaven. In general, puff pastry margarine, which contains about 16 percent water, provides more leavening than puff pastry shortening, which contains no water. Creamed shortening, which has additional air beaten in, provides more leavening than shortening that has not been creamed. Liquid oil, which contains neither air nor water, does not contribute to leavening at all.

Once melted, fat slithers through batters and doughs, coating gluten strands, egg proteins, and starches. This interferes with these structure builders and prevents them from forming structure. In other words, fats increase tenderness.

The more that fats and oils coat structure builders, the more effectively they tenderize. Usually, fats that melt early in baking tenderize more than those that melt late, because they have more time to coat structure builders. Likewise, liquid oil often tenderizes more than solid fat because the oil begins coating structure builders during the mixing stage.

Finally, as solid fats melt and liquefy, they thin out batters and doughs. Some thinning is desirable, as when cookie dough spreads and cookies bake up thin and crisp. Too much thinning can be undesirable, however, as when cake batter is so thin that it collapses in the oven or forms thin tunnels as it bakes.

2. Gases Form and Expand

The three most important leavening gases in baked goods are air, steam, and carbon dioxide. Steam forms when water is heated. Heat is needed to dissolve slow-acting baking powders, so that they release carbon dioxide. This takes place over a range of temperatures, starting at room temperature and continuing as the temperature reaches 170°F (75°C) and above. Once released, carbon dioxide gas dissolves in the liquid portion of the batter.

As temperatures rise, gases move to the air cells formed during mixing, enlarging them. Heat also causes the gases to expand, which is necessary for leavening and for tenderizing. As gases expand, they push on cell walls, forcing them to stretch. The product increases in size and volume; in other words, it leavens. In fact, this is the main cause of oven spring, the fast expansion of yeast dough during the first few minutes of baking. Because cell walls are stretched during leavening, they are thinner, making the baked good easier to bite through; that is, leavening makes baked goods more tender.

3. Sugar Dissolves

For many batters and doughs, sugar dissolves completely during mixing. However, when batters and doughs are high in sugar or low in moisture—as is the case with most cookie doughs and some cake batters—undissolved sugar crystals are present at the start of baking. These undissolved crystals help thicken and solidify batters and doughs.

When they heat up, however, sugar crystals dissolve in water that is present, forming a sugar syrup. This thins out batters and doughs as they approach 160°F (70°C), much as melted fat thins them out. As with melted fat, dissolved sugar increases cookie spread. Dissolving sugar also thins out cake batter in the oven, making it more susceptible to collapse or tunneling.

4. Microorganisms Die

Microorganisms are small (microscopic) living entities. Examples of microorganisms include yeast, mold, bacteria, and viruses. Most die by about 140°F (60°C), but actual temperature depends on several things, including the type of microorganism and the amount of sugar and salt present.

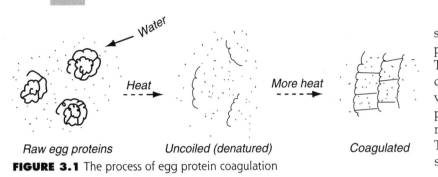

Raw egg proteins   Uncoiled (denatured)   Coagulated

FIGURE 3.1 The process of egg protein coagulation

Once yeast dies, fermentation stops, meaning the yeast no longer produces carbon dioxide from sugars. This is desirable because overfermented dough has an overpowering sour flavor. Besides killing yeast, heat also kills pathogenic microorganisms, like salmonella, that cause illness and even death. Thus, cooking or baking makes food safer to eat.

5. Egg and Gluten Proteins Coagulate

Egg and gluten proteins are two of the most important structure builders in baked goods. When they are heated, egg and gluten proteins coagulate. To visualize what is meant by coagulation, think of the changes that occur as a raw egg cooks. The egg turns from liquid to solid and from clear to opaque. This process typically begins at around 140°–160°F (60°–70°C) and continues as temperatures rise.

While the changes that occur in eggs as they are heated are visible, the protein molecules that cause these changes are not, not even under a microscope. If they were visible, raw egg proteins would appear as relatively large, coiled molecules, surrounded by water. As they are heated and begin to coagulate, the molecules unfold and bond with one another. At the same time, they stretch from the pressure of expanding leavening gases. Eventually, water is released from the proteins, and the bonding proteins become rigid and lose their ability to stretch. It is this rigid structure that helps set the final size and shape of baked goods. Figure 3.1 illustrates the process of egg protein coagulation, which is discussed in more detail in Chapter 11. The changes to gluten proteins are discussed in Chapter 7.

For best volume, protein coagulation must be carefully timed with gas expansion. This occurs only if ingredients are correctly weighed, and if the oven is set and calibrated to the proper temperature. If egg or gluten proteins are stretched too thin, they break, and the baked good could collapse. As you will see in the next section, however, if sufficient starch is present, starch gelatinization contributes to structure in baked goods and prevents collapse.

6. Starches Gelatinize

Starch is often the forgotten structure builder in flour, probably because gluten plays such an important and dominant role in raw bread dough. Yet, once bread is baked, its structure is built as much, or more, on starch than on gluten. This is

MORE ON THE TEMPERATURE OF PROTEIN COAGULATION

Batters and doughs are complex mixtures of ingredients, and the ingredients influence each other. You will see in Chapter 11, for example, that many ingredients, such as sugars, fats, and starches, affect the temperature of egg protein coagulation by increasing it. This makes it difficult to define the temperature at which egg coagulation occurs in baked goods.

WHY DO BAGELS SHINE WHEN THEY ARE BOILED?

The traditional way to make bagels is to briefly boil them in hot water before they are baked. The boiling water gelatinizes starch that is on the surface of the bagel. The gelatinized starch forms a smooth film, a surface so smooth that light reflects off it in an even shine.

because much of the gluten in bread dough stretches so far during baking that it breaks.

Gelatinized starch structure is often softer and more tender than the structure of coagulated egg and gluten proteins. Think of the texture of freshly baked bread. Much of the soft crumb of freshly baked bread is from gelatinized starch. As with protein structure, however, too much starch produces toughness and dryness.

Starch gelatinization occurs when starch granules absorb and trap water as they are heated. Starch granules are small particles or grains that are packed with starch molecules. They are hard and gritty when raw, but they swell to a larger size and soften when cooked. If enough water is present, as it is in lean bread dough, starch molecules can leach out of the granules.

Starch granules grab any water they can get, including water released from protein coagulation. Besides water, starch gelatinization requires heat. Starch granules begin swelling at about 120°–140°F (50°–60°C). By 170°F (75°C), gelatinization is well under way, with granules having absorbed a significant amount of water. This causes the batter or dough to thicken considerably and to take on the final shape of the baked product. Gelatinization is not complete, however, until temperatures approach 200°F (95°C) or so, and only if enough water is available. If it is, granules begin to deform and collapse, as starch molecules move out of granules.

It is rare for all the starch in baked goods to fully gelatinize, because there is usually not enough water or time available for it to occur. For example, very little starch gelatinization occurs in pie or cookie dough, because they contain very little water. Instead, the structure of pie pastry relies mostly on gluten, and that of cookies relies on gluten and egg proteins. In contrast, cake batters are high in water, and the structure of cakes is highly dependent on gelatinized starch (and coagulated egg proteins).

Even when enough water is present, however, other ingredients, such as sugars and fats, increase the temperature of starch gelatinization. This means that starch gelatinizes at a higher temperature in sweet, rich bread dough, dough that is high in sugar and fat, than it does in lean dough.

As with protein coagulation, once starch gelatinization is well under way, the final volume and shape of baked goods—or of pudding and pie fillings—are set. At this stage in the baking process, the baked good is able to hold its shape, but it still has a wet doughy texture, little color, and an off taste.

STARCH IN FLOUR

Did you know that flour contains a very high amount of starch? Even bread flour, which is considered "low" in starch, typically contains a whopping 70 percent starch!

7. Gases Evaporate

While the three main leavening gases are air, steam, and carbon dioxide, baked goods contain other gases, as well. For example, many liquids, including vanilla flavoring and alcohol, evaporate to the gaseous state when heated, and any liquid that evaporates to a gas functions as a leavening gas. Do not underestimate the importance of these other gases to the baking process. Since alcohol is an end product of yeast fermentation, for example, all yeast-raised baked goods contain a measurable amount of alcohol.

Carbon dioxide and other gases are lost in small amounts from batters and doughs as temperatures warm above room temperature. This is because wet cell walls are not completely solid; the network of egg and gluten proteins allows slow but steady movement of gases throughout unbaked products. At a certain point, however, large amounts of gases escape. At about the same time, proteins coagulate and starches gelatinize. That is, as the structure of baked goods becomes more rigid, it also becomes more porous to gases. It is transformed from a foam to a sponge. With bread, this occurs at around 160°F (72°C). It is at this point that bread dough loses its ability to hold carbon dioxide. Eventually, the gases migrate to exposed surfaces and evaporate.

As gases escape from baked goods, several important changes occur. First, a dry, hard crust forms on the surface from a loss in moisture. Depending on the formula and on oven conditions, the crust may become crisp, as it does in properly made French baguettes, or soft, as it does in breads made with milk. In any case, at this stage in baking, the crust is still pale white. Besides developing a dry, hard crust, baked goods lose weight as they lose moisture. On average, 18 ounces (510 grams) of dough must be scaled out to yield a typical 1-pound (450-gram) loaf of bread. The third change that occurs as gases evaporate is a change in flavor. As the bakeshop fills with aromas, like vanilla, it means that these aromas are escaping from the products as they bake. In most cases, however, there is still enough flavor left in the baked good to be enjoyed by the customer. Other flavor changes during this stage of baking are less obvious but still important. For example, alcohol and carbon dioxide are associated with the taste of raw dough. A significant amount of both have evaporated off baked goods by about 170°F (75°C). This causes a subtle yet important change in flavor to products high in these gases, such as yeast doughs.

While tools such as kitchen timers are useful, experienced bakers and pastry chefs rely on all their senses, including the sense of smell, when working in the bakeshop. For example, aromas from the oven are an early indicator that a product must soon be checked for doneness.

WHY IS STEAM INJECTED INTO OVENS DURING BREAD BAKING?

Because of the nature of bread formulas, crusts form fairly quickly on many yeast breads. Once a dry, hard crust forms, bread can no longer expand in volume, even if gases within it continue to expand. At best, the gases may crack the surface of the bread as they escape from the product, but they will not provide more leavening.

If steam is injected into the oven during the early stages of baking, the surface of the bread stays moist and flexible. The bread continues to rise for a longer period of time, and the loaf is higher, lighter, and less dense.

Because the formation of a crust is delayed, steam injection promotes formation of a thinner crust. The crust is crispier and glossier because moist steam facilitates the gelatinization of starch on the surface of the bread.

WHAT DOES MICROWAVED BREAD LOOK AND TASTE LIKE?

Bread that is cooked in a microwave oven does not brown well, and it tastes flat. Unlike oven baking, where the oven is hot and the product heats by conduction from the outside surface to the inside, microwave ovens remain cool and heat a product more evenly throughout. This means that the outside surface of bread does not get very hot in the microwave oven. Without high temperatures, browning reactions do not occur. The crust stays light in color, and the desirable baked flavors from the browning reactions do not form.

8. Caramelization and Maillard Browning Occur on Crust

As long as water continues to evaporate off the crusts of baked goods, evaporative cooling keeps the surface from rising in temperature. Once evaporation slows significantly, however, surface temperatures rise quickly to 300°F (150°C) or so. The high heat breaks down molecules, such as sugars and proteins, on the surface of baked goods. The result is the formation of brown color and a desirable baked flavor. As might be expected, these reactions are important in almost all baked goods because essentially all baked goods contain sugars and proteins.

Bakers and pastry chefs do not always differentiate the type of molecule breaking down. Oftentimes, any formation of brown color and baked flavor is called caramelization. However, strictly speaking, caramelization is the process of sugars breaking down. Place sugar in a pan on the stove and add heat, and the sugar eventually caramelizes to a fragrant, brown mass.

When sugars break down in the presence of proteins, it is called Maillard browning. Because foods contain many different types of sugars and proteins, Maillard browning contributes to the flavor of a wide range of foods, including toasted nuts, roast beef, and baked bread.

While the eight events mentioned previously are the main ones important to bakers and pastry chefs, the following three also occur.

9. Enzymes Are Inactivated

Enzymes are proteins that act as biological catalysts in plants, animals, and microorganisms. They catalyze, or speed up, chemical reactions without actually being used up in the process. This makes enzymes very efficient, so that a small amount goes a long way. Not only can enzymes speed up chemical reactions, they can cause reactions to occur that might not happen otherwise.

All enzymes, being proteins, are denatured by heat. The process of denaturation inactivates enzymes and stops their activity. Most enzymes are inactivated by temperatures of about 160°–180°F (70°–80°C), but they vary in their heat sensitivity. Before they are inactivated, however, rising oven temperatures increase their activity. This increased activity occurs in the early stages of baking only.

Amylase is one example of an enzyme important in yeast-raised baked goods. Amylase is present in a few ingredients used in bread doughs, including malted barley flour, diastatic malt syrup, and certain dough conditioners or improvers. Before it is inactivated, amylase—also known as diastase—breaks down starches into sugars and other molecules. A certain amount of starch breakdown is desirable because this softens bread and keeps it from becoming stale too quickly. If too much starch is destroyed, however, bread turns to mush, because starch is an important structure builder in bread and other baked goods. It is desirable that amylase is rendered inactive by heat, as this controls the amount of starch breakdown.

Other enzymes present in baking ingredients include proteases, which break down proteins, and lipases, which break down lipids (fats, oils, and emulsifiers). Notice that the suffix -ase is part of the name of many enzymes.

10. Changes Occur to Nutrients

Proteins, fats, carbohydrates, vitamins, and minerals are examples of nutrients in food. Heat changes certain nutrients in very important ways. For example, proteins and starches in flour are more digestible once they are heated. This means that baked foods containing flour are often more nutritious than raw foods. Not all the effects of heat on food are positive, however. Heat destroys some nutrients, such as vitamin C (ascorbic acid).

11. Pectin Breaks Down

Pectin is not present in batters or doughs, but many baked goods contain fruit, and pectin is one of the main components holding fruits together. When pectin is heated, it dissolves, and fruits soften and lose their shape. While other changes cause fruits to soften when cooked, pectin breakdown is one of the most important.

STAGE III: COOLING

When removed from the oven, a baked good continues to cook until its temperature cools to room temperature. This is called carryover cooking. Because of carryover cooking, baked goods must be watched carefully during the last few minutes of baking, and they must be removed before—not when—they are baked to perfection.

Even when cooled and properly wrapped, baked goods continue to change during storage. The main changes that occur can be summarized as follows.

1. Gases continue to escape or they contract, and products without sufficient structure, such as soufflés and underbaked items, collapse.

2. Fats resolidify and greasiness decreases. Depending on the fat, however, the product could become hard and waxy, as is the case with puff pastry made with a high-melting fat.

3. Sugars recrystallize on the crusts of low-moisture, high-sugar products, such as cookies and certain cakes and muffins. This gives these products a desirable crunchy crust.

4. Starch molecules bond and solidify, and the structure gets firmer and more rigid. Starch bonding—called retrogradation—continues over the next several days, and it is the main reason for the staling of baked goods. Stale baked goods have a hard, dry, crumbly texture.

HELPFUL HINT

Each product differs in how much heat it retains and how much cooking continues outside the oven. For example, cream-puff shells cool quickly and must be well baked before they are removed from the oven. Baked custards and cheesecakes, however, should still jiggle in the center when they are removed because carryover cooking completes the baking process, firming these products as they cool.

5. Protein molecules also bond and solidify and may contribute to staling. Until delicate baked goods cool and structure solidifies, it is best not to cut into them, so they will not crush.

6. Moisture is redistributed within the crumb of baked goods, and may also contribute to staling.

7. In high-moisture products like bread, moisture moves from moist crumb to dry crust, and the crust loses its crispness over the next day, sometimes becoming tough and rubbery.

8. Flavors evaporate, and over the next day or so, wonderful fresh-baked flavors are lost. Some flavor loss occurs because flavors become trapped by starches as they retrograde. Where this is the case, a brief reheating in the oven recovers some lost flavor—and softens the structure.

QUESTIONS FOR REVIEW

1. Provide examples of tougheners, tenderizers, moisteners, and driers.

2. Provide an example of how a different mixing method can affect the outcome of a baked good.

3. List and briefly describe seven things that happen as ingredients are mixed into batters or doughs.

4. Describe the two main methods used for mixing bread dough.

5. What products are commonly mixed using the creaming method?

6. Why are unbaked batters and doughs sometimes referred to as foams?

7. Why are baked goods sometimes referred to as sponges?

8. What functions does water provide in baking?

9. How, and why, can the same pie pastry dough formula result in a tender, mealy crust in one case and a flaky crust in another?

10. How do fats contribute to leavening in baked goods?

11. Which would be expected to provide more leavening: shortening with a melting point of 130°F (55°C) or margarine with a melting point of 130°F (55°C)? Why?

12. How do fats and oils tenderize baked goods?

13. Which would be expected to provide more leavening: shortening with a melting point of 105°F (40°C) or shortening with a melting point of 130°F (55°C)? Explain why.

14. Which would be expected to give more tenderness: shortening with a melting point of 105°F (40°C) or shortening with a melting point of 130°F (55°C)? Explain why.

15. How do solid fats increase spread in cookies?

16. What is oven spring, and what causes it?

17. What are the three main leavening gases in baked goods?

18. How do leavening agents contribute to the tenderness of baked goods?

19. Provide examples of microorganisms. What happens to them during the baking process? Why is this important? Provide two reasons.

20. Name three structure builders in baked goods.

21. What causes a dry crust to form on baked goods?

22. What three things result from gases evaporating?

23. Provide an example of an enzyme. What happens to it—and other enzymes—during the baking process?

24. Provide examples of nutrients. For one of the nutrients, briefly explain what happens to it during baking.

25. What happens during baking that would cause apples in an apple pie to soften and lose shape?

26. How do sugar crystals affect the thickness of batters and doughs? How does dissolved sugar affect thickness?

27. List and briefly describe eight things that occur as products cool.

28. What is the main reason for the staling of baked goods? What other factors contribute to it?

QUESTIONS FOR DISCUSSION

1. Explain what could happen if protein coagulation occurs too soon—before gas expansion.

2. Explain what could happen if protein coagulation occurs too late—after gas expansion.

3. What do you think would happen if there were few—or no—structure builders in a baked good?

4. As stated in this chapter, for starch gelatinization to occur, there must be enough water and heat. Think about the amount of liquid in each of the following products. For each pair, state which product relies more on starch gelatinization for its structure. That is, in which will more starch gelatinization occur:

- Bread or pie pastry?
- Crisp, dry cookies or muffins?

5. Two of the eight main events that occur in the oven involve gases. Combine the two and describe what happens to gases from the beginning to the end of the baking process and how this affects the product.

EXERCISES AND EXPERIMENTS

1. Microwaved versus Oven-baked Bread

We take it for granted that lean dough, when baked into bread, will have a soft tender crumb, baked-bread flavor, and crispy brown crust. What would happen, however, if one or more of the 11 processes described in this chapter failed to happen? What if they happened but at different stages during baking or in a slightly different manner?

By using a microwave oven to "bake" bread, you will see how the lack of Maillard browning, in particular, changes the flavor of baked goods. You will also see how changes in water evaporation and other baking processes affect the texture of both crumb and crust.

OBJECTIVES

- To demonstrate how a lack of browning affects the flavor of baked goods.
- To demonstrate how the use of a microwave oven to bake bread affects the appearance and texture of bread crust.
- To demonstrate how the use of a microwave oven to bake bread affects the texture of bread crumb.

PRODUCTS PREPARED

- Bread baked in a conventional oven and in a microwave oven

MATERIALS AND EQUIPMENT

- Microwave oven, 1,000 watts, or equivalent
- White bread dough, enough to make 24 rolls

PROCEDURE

- Preheat oven according to formula.
- Prepare bread dough using the following formula or any basic white bread formula, or purchase unbaked bread dough.
- Shape dough into equal-sized rolls, proof, and bake half the rolls in a conventional oven for 15 to 20 minutes.
- Bake remaining rolls in the microwave oven. Record both percent power and bake time here. *Note: Starting at 100 percent power, begin by microwaving rolls for about five minutes. Do not expect the rolls to brown, but they should rise and form a dry crust and crumb. If they do not, adjust time or power as needed.*
- Record any potential sources of error in the space provided. Include things that might make it difficult to draw the proper conclusions from your experiment.
- When rolls are completely cooled, evaluate the sensory characteristics of each and record evaluations in Results Table, which follows the formula for Lean Dough. Compare the rolls that were baked in the microwave to those baked in the oven for the following:
  - Crust color, from very light to very dark, on a scale from one to five
  - Crust texture (thick/thin, soft/hard, crispy, crunchy, soggy, etc.)
  - Crumb appearance (small uniform air cells, large irregular air cells, tunnels, etc.)
  - Crumb texture (tough/tender, moist/dry, spongy, crumbly, chewy, gummy, etc.)
  - Overall flavor (yeasty, floury, sweet, salty, sour, bitter, etc.)
  - Overall acceptability, from highly unacceptable to highly acceptable, on a scale from one to five
  - Any additional comments, as necessary.

Lean Dough

INGREDIENT	POUNDS	OUNCES	GRAMS	BAKER'S PERCENTAGE
Flour	1	2	500	100
Salt		0.25	8	1.5
Yeast, instant		0.25	8	1.5
Water, 86°F (30°C)		10	280	56
Total	1	12.5	796	159

Method of Preparation

1. Preheat oven to 425°F (220°C).
2. Set proof box to 86°F (30°C) and 85 percent relative humidity.
3. Weigh ingredients, including water, on digital or baker's scale. (*Note:* if readability of scale is 1 gram (0.02 oz.) or higher, it is better to use teaspoons for measuring yeast and salt, to minimize error. Use 2-1/2 teaspoons for 8 grams yeast; use 1-1/2 teaspoons for 8 grams salt).
4. Weigh another 5 ounces (140 grams) of water (at 86°F/30°C) and set aside (this will be used for adjusting dough consistency in step 8).

5. Combine flour and salt thoroughly by sifting together three times onto parchment paper.

6. Place flour/salt mixture, yeast, and water into mixing bowl. Attach dough hook.

7. Blend on low for 1 minute; stop and scrape bowl.

8. Add additional water (from step 4 above) slowly and as needed, to adjust consistency.

9. Mix on medium for 5 minutes.

10. Remove dough from mixer.

11. Cover loosely with plastic wrap until ready to use.

12. Continue to follow the Procedure instructions.

SOURCES OF ERROR

_____

_____

RESULTS TABLE ■ SENSORY CHARACTERISTICS OF YEAST ROLLS BAKED IN DIFFERENT TYPES OF OVENS

OVEN TYPE	CRUST COLOR AND TEXTURE	CRUMB APPEARANCE AND TEXTURE	OVERALL FLAVOR	OVERALL ACCEPTABILITY	COMMENTS
Conventional					
Microwave					

CONCLUSIONS

1. How can you tell that the surface of the rolls baked in the conventional oven reached a higher temperature than those baked in the microwave oven?

_____

_____

2. How did this difference in surface temperature affect flavor?

_____

_____

3. What differences did you observe in the crumb texture of your microwaved rolls that might suggest that either different chemical reactions took place in the two ovens, or they took place to different degrees or in a slightly different manner?

_____

_____

4. Overall, how acceptable were the rolls that were baked in the microwave, and why?

_____

_____

5. Were there any sources of error that might significantly affect the results of your experiment? If so, what could you do differently next time to minimize error?

_____

_____

2. The Effect of Method of Preparation on Pound Cake

OBJECTIVES

- To demonstrate how the extent of creaming of fat and sifting dry ingredients in pound cake batter affects:

  - Density of the creamed shortening
  - Thickness of cake batter
  - Volume of pound cake
  - Crumb appearance: coarseness and color of pound cake
  - Overall acceptability of pound cake

PRODUCTS PREPARED

- Pound cake that has undergone:

  - No creaming/no sifting
  - 4 minutes of creaming, three siftings (control product)
  - Other, if desired (4 minutes creaming, no sifting; no creaming, three siftings; 8 minutes creaming, etc.)

MATERIALS AND EQUIPMENT

- Pound cake batter, enough to make one or more 9-inch cakes of each variation
- Two identical clear one-cup measuring cups (or similar size clear containers), for measuring density of creamed shortening
- Cake pans, 9-inch, one per variation
- Ruler

PROCEDURE

- Preheat oven according to formula.
- Prepare pound cake batter using the formula that follows or using any basic pound cake formula. Prepare one batch of batter for each variation. To minimize experimental error, use shortening instead of butter or margarine.
- Cream an excess amount of fat and sugar. For the pound cake that is not creamed, stir sugar into fat just until incorporated. Please note that there are different methods of preparation provided for each batch, and that the Creamed Shortening formula makes double what is needed in cake.

- Measure density (weight per volume) of creamed fat from each batch. To measure density,
    - Carefully spoon sample of creamed fat into tared measuring cup.
    - Visually check cup to confirm that no large air gaps are present.
    - Level the top surface of the cup with a straight-edge.
    - Weigh the amount of creamed fat in each cup and record results in Results Table 1, which follows.
- Measure out the amount of creamed fat into mixing bowls and continue preparing batters for cakes.
- Evaluate consistency of batter, from very thin and runny to very thick, on a scale of one to five. Record results in Results Table 1.
- Weigh batter into cake pans, same weight for each variation (900 grams/9-inch pan).
- Use an oven thermometer placed in center of oven to read oven temperature; record results here_____.
- Place filled cake pans in preheated oven and set timer according to formula.
- Bake until control product (creamed for 4 minutes) is light brown, cake springs back when center top is lightly pressed, and wooden pick inserted into center of cake comes out clean. You may need to bake cakes for different lengths of time because of oven variability. Record bake times in Comments column of Table 1.
- Remove cakes from oven and let stand 1 minute.
- Invert onto wire racks to cool to room temperature.
- Record any potential sources of error that might make it difficult to draw the proper conclusions from the experiment. In particular, be aware of difficulties in measuring densities of shortening; differences in how batter was mixed and handled; and any problems with ovens.
- When cakes are completely cooled, evaluate height and shape as follows:
    - Slice cake from each batch in half, being careful not to compress.
    - Measure height of cake by placing a ruler along the flat edge at the cake's maximum height. Record results in 1/16-inch (10 mm) increments in Results Table 1.
    - Note in Cake Shape column of Results Table 1 whether cake has an even rounded top, or if it peaks or dips in center.
    - Also note whether cake is lopsided, that is, if one side is higher than the other.
- Evaluate the sensory characteristics of completely cooled products and record evaluations in Results Table 2, which follows. Be sure to compare each in turn to the control product and consider the following:
    - Crumb color
    - Crumb appearance (small uniform air cells, large irregular air cells, tunnels, etc.)
    - Overall acceptability, from highly unacceptable to highly acceptable, on a scale of one to five.
    - Add any additional comments, as necessary.

Creamed Shortening Mixture

INGREDIENT	POUNDS	OUNCES	GRAMS
Shortening, all-purpose		10	280
Sugar, regular granulated		20	560
Dried milk solids		1	30
Total	1	15	870

Pound Cake Batter

INGREDIENT	POUND	OUNCE	GRAMS	BAKER'S PERCENTAGE
Creamed shortening (above)		15.5	435	193
Egg		7	190	84
Flour, cake		8	225	100
Baking powder		0.25	7.5	3
Salt		0.1	2.5	1
Water		4.5	125	56
Total	2	3.35	985	437

Method of Preparation (for control product, 4-minute creaming)

1. Preheat oven to 350°F (175°C).
2. Allow ingredients to come to room temperature (temperature of ingredients is important for consistent results).
3. Blend flour, salt, and baking soda thoroughly by sifting together three times onto parchment paper.
4. Place shortening in mixing bowl and stir to soften, low, 15 seconds; stop and scrape bowl.
5. Slowly add sugar while creaming on medium for 1 minute; stop and scrape bowl.
6. Continue creaming on medium for 1 additional minute; stop and scrape bowl.
7. Slowly add dried milk solids (DMS) while creaming on medium, and continue creaming for 2 additional minutes; stop and scrape bowl halfway through.
8. Measure density of creamed shortening/sugar/DMS mixture by following procedure, defined earlier.
9. After density measurements are recorded, place 15.5 ounces (435 grams) of shortening mixture into mixing bowl; discard the rest.
10. Stir on low for 45 seconds, slowly adding slightly beaten eggs; stop and scrape. *Note:* Creamed mixture will likely take on a somewhat curdled look, but it will still be holding a good amount of air. However, do not over mix; if eggs and shortening mixture are well-blended before 45 seconds, begin next step immediately.
11. Add dry ingredients alternately with water in three parts, while stirring on low for 1 minute; stop and scrape bowl.
12. Portion and bake batter as soon as possible.
13. Bake cakes for approximately 30–35 minutes.

Method of Preparation for cake with no creaming or sifting:

Follow the Method of Preparation for the control product (4-minute creaming, sifted three times), except:

- Do not sift ingredients in step 3; instead, stir gently yet thoroughly with a spoon.
- For steps 5 through 7, add sugar and DMS all at once; stir on low until blended but not creamed, about 1 minute.
- Continue with step 8, as shown in the previous method of preparation.

SOURCES OF ERROR

RESULTS TABLE 1 ■ DIFFERENCES IN CAKES MADE WITH DIFFERENT METHODS OF PREPARATION

METHOD OF PREPARATION	DENSITY OF CREAMED MIXTURE	CONSISTENCY OF BATTER	CAKE HEIGHT	CAKE SHAPE	COMMENTS
No sifting, no creaming					
Sifted 3 times, creamed 4 minutes (control product)					

RESULTS TABLE 2 ■ APPEARANCE AND OTHER CHARACTERISTICS OF POUND CAKES MADE WITH DIFFERENT METHODS OF PREPARATION

METHOD OF PREPARATION	CRUMB COLOR AND APPEARANCE	OVERALL ACCEPTABILITY	COMMENTS
No sifting, no creaming			
Sifted 3 times, creamed 4 minutes (control product)			

CONCLUSIONS

1. How did the density of the shortening mixture change with the amount of creaming, that is, did it increase, decrease, or stay the same?

_____

_____

2. How did the amount of sifting and creaming affect batter consistency, that is, did more sifting and creaming result in a thicker, thinner, or no different consistency of the cake batter?

_____

_____

3. How did the amount of sifting and creaming affect crumb appearance? That is, did more sifting and creaming result in much smaller, larger, or no difference in air cells size? How did it affect crumb color? Did it make the cakes lighter or darker?

_____

_____

4. What other changes did you notice as the amount of creaming increased?

_____

_____

5. Which pound cake did you feel was most acceptable overall, and why?

_____

_____

6. Did you have any sources of error that might significantly affect the results of your experiment? If so, what could you do differently next time to minimize error?

_____

_____

7. How do you explain the difference in crumb color between the two cakes, given that both were made from the same amount of the same ingredients?

_____

_____

8. Look through cookbooks and the Internet. List two formulas for baked goods that you would expect to be just as affected by improper sifting and creaming as this cake. Explain why you believe so.

_____

_____

9. Look through cookbooks and the Internet. List two formulas for baked goods that you would expect would be more tolerant of improper sifting and creaming. Explain why you believe so.

_____

_____

CHAPTER 4

SENSORY PROPERTIES OF FOOD

CHAPTER **OBJECTIVES**

1. Introduce the means for objectively evaluating the sensory properties of food.

2. Describe factors that affect the appearance of foods.

3. Discuss the three components of flavor and describe factors that affect the flavor of foods.

4. Provide a brief overview of texture.

INTRODUCTION

The study of sensory perception is the study of how the sensory organs—eyes, ears, nose, mouth, and skin—detect and interpret the world. It is actually receptors on the sensory organs that do the work, with all five active during eating. Examples of sensory receptors include taste buds on the tongue, olfactory cells at the top of the nasal cavity, and nerve endings just beneath the surface of the skin.

The focus of this chapter is the sensory properties of food—appearance, flavor, and texture—and how to objectively evaluate and describe them. As you read through the chapter, notice how the five senses are used individually and together to evaluate these three sensory properties of food. The evaluation of flavor is further developed in Chapter 14.

Evaluating food is not the same as eating for enjoyment. Sensory evaluation takes practice and deliberate concentration, because the perception of food is complex. Yet, professional bakers and pastry chefs must learn to evaluate food if they are to troubleshoot problems. As professionals, they also must prepare foods that they do not necessarily like, and they must evaluate these foods to confirm that they are prepared properly.

Many factors contribute to an individual's ability to objectively evaluate food, including genetics, gender, and health. However, experience is probably the most important factor—experience at paying attention to the smallest of details. This means that, regardless of your current ability to evaluate food, it can be improved, like any skill, through practice.

APPEARANCE

Appearance creates the first impression customers have of food, and first impressions are important. No matter how appealing the taste, an unattractive appearance is hard to overlook. As humans, we do "eat with our eyes" because our sense of sight is more highly developed than the other senses. This is not the case with many animals. Dogs, for example, depend primarily on smell to explore their world.

The sense of sight is so highly developed in humans that messages received from other senses are often ignored if they conflict with what is seen. Yellow candy is expected to be lemon flavored, and if it is grape flavored, many people cannot correctly identify the flavor. Strawberry ice cream tinted with red food coloring seems to have a stronger strawberry flavor than one that has no added food coloring, even when there is no real difference. While, as professionals, you must train your senses so that they are not tricked by your sense of sight, it is also important to understand how appearance influences your customers' perceptions.

Appearance has many different aspects. *Color*, or *hue*—whether food is yellow or red, for example—is an especially important aspect. Other aspects of appearance include opacity, sheen, shape, and size, and a visual evaluation of texture. *Opacity* is the quality of a product that appears opaque or cloudy. The opposite of opacity is clarity or translucency. An example of an opaque product is milk; an example of a clear or translucent one is water. *Sheen* is the state of a product that appears glossy or shiny. The opposite of glossy or shiny is matte or dull. An example of a product with sheen is honey; an example of a product that is dull is a shortbread cookie.

The Perception of Appearance

When light hits an object, it is reflected (bounced off), transmitted (passed through), or absorbed by the object (Figure 4.1). Only light that bounces off or passes through food reaches our eyes and is seen; the light that is absorbed is not.

Factors Affecting the Perception of Appearance

Three main factors affect the perception of appearance. It is these factors that determine whether two products look the same or not. The first two factors—the nature of the light source and the nature of the object itself—affect how light is absorbed, reflected, and transmitted through foods. The third factor—the nature of the surroundings—is more of an optical illusion.

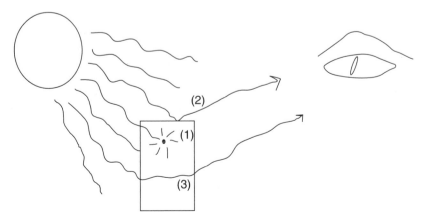

FIGURE 4.1 Light can be (1) absorbed, (2) reflected, or (3) transmitted through an object.

WHAT HAPPENS WHEN LIGHT IS ABSORBED BY FOOD?

When visible light is absorbed by food or by another object, it vanishes from sight. This does not mean that it truly disappears, however. Light, which is a form of energy, is simply converted to another form of energy (such as heat energy or kinetic energy) when it is absorbed by an object.

Objects absorb light selectively, and different objects absorb light differently. For example, a green leaf contains chlorophyll that absorbs most light except green light. Only the green light is reflected off the leaf and reaches the eyes, which is why the leaf appears green in color. Likewise, red raspberries appear red because they absorb most colors except red, and black objects absorb essentially all light, reflecting little to the eyes. Because white light is composed of all colors of the rainbow (hold a prism up to light to see white light separated into its component colors), an object that appears white does so because it absorbs little, if any, light.

NATURE OF THE LIGHT SOURCE

If the light hitting an object changes, the appearance of the object changes. The appearance changes because the light the object absorbs, reflects, and transmits changes. Both the brightness of the light source and the type of lighting—fluorescent, incandescent, or halogen, for example—are important to consider. Bakers and pastry chefs should be aware that what they see in the bakeshop might not be what the customer sees under dining room lights. Bakeshops often have bright, fluorescent lights, while dining rooms tend to have dim, incandescent ones. Dim, incandescent lights have a warm, yellow cast, which tends to mute the appearance of the product.

HELPFUL HINT

If lighting in a work area is different from lighting in the customer service area, be sure to evaluate product appearance in the service area. This way, you can confirm that the product will be acceptable to the customer.

NATURE OF THE OBJECT

Each object has its own characteristic way of absorbing, reflecting, and transmitting light. That is why two objects might look different at different times, even when viewed by the same person under the same light. There are two main reasons that objects might respond differently to light: if they differ in their chemical makeup, and if they differ in their physical structure.

It is logical to expect two products to look different when they differ in their chemical makeup, that is, when they are made from different formulas or when they are made with different raw materials. For example, chocolate icing should look different from vanilla icing because it contains chocolate as an added ingredient. The added chocolate absorbs more light and therefore appears darker than the vanilla icing, which allows more light to reflect off its surface. Likewise, a pastry cream made with pale yellow yolks should be lighter yellow than another made with dark yellow yolks because the darker yolks are chemically different from the lighter ones. The darker yolks contain a higher amount of *carotenoids*, the yellow pigments in eggs that reflect yellow light and absorb the rest.

When products are baked for different lengths of time or at different temperatures, expect additional differences in appearance. A cake baked for 45 minutes instead of 30 minutes will undergo more browning reactions that cause the surface of the product to darken. Likewise, a cake baked at 425°F (220°C) will undergo more browning reactions than one baked at 300°F (150°C). These browning reactions are chemical changes that affect how light is absorbed, reflected, and transmitted.

When egg whites are beaten, tiny air bubbles are trapped within a network of egg white proteins. This changes the physical structure of the egg whites, and it dramatically alters the appearance of egg whites. The egg whites appear white and opaque instead of clear and translucent, because light no longer easily passes through. Instead, the light bounces off the rounded air cells and scatters in many directions. Scattered light appears opaque.

Likewise, if a cake has small air cells—has a fine crumb—it will look lighter or whiter than the same cake with a coarse crumb. That is why an undermixed white cake, with a coarse crumb, looks slightly yellow. Likewise, an undermixed chocolate cake looks darker and richer than one properly mixed, even if both are made from the same formula.

When fondant is properly handled (warmed to body temperature before use), it forms a smooth, white glaze with an attractive sheen. If it is melted above 100°F (38°C), however, it cools to a rougher, grayer, duller surface. The only difference is that the tiny crystals in fondant melt above 100°F (38°C), then recrystallize to form large, jagged crystals as the fondant cools. There is no chemical difference between the fondants; they both contain the same ingredients. The difference is crystal size, and this affects how light is reflected off the surface and viewed by the eye.

NATURE OF THE SURROUNDINGS

Two products can be identical in their chemical and physical makeup, and they can be viewed under the same light, yet if they are placed on different plates, they will likely look different. For example, white cake placed on a black plate will look whiter than the same cake placed on a stark white plate. This is an optical illusion, because it has nothing to do with any real differences in light reaching the eye. Instead, it has to do with how the brain interprets the strong contrast between white and black, making the white seem whiter still. This difference in color perception is no less real to the customer, and it is as important to consider as any other factor.

FLAVOR

Appearance may be the first contact customers have with food, but taste—flavor—of food is what they remember. *Taste* is the everyday word for flavor, but to the scientist, taste is only one small part of what is meant by flavor. Flavor includes the basic tastes, smell, and trigeminal effects, or chemical feeling factors. These three sensations occur when food molecules—chemicals—stimulate receptors throughout the mouth and nose. Because of the chemical nature of these sensations, the three sensory systems that perceive them are called chemical sensory systems. Table 4.1 summarizes information about the three components of flavor and their related sensory systems. Notice that each of these components of flavor—basic tastes, smell, and trigeminal effects—is distinctly different. Each is stimulated by different chemicals. Each is detected by different receptors. Yet, they occur simultaneously, and they also occur at the same time that the brain evaluates appearance and texture. No wonder sensory evaluation is a challenge, one that requires practice and concentration.

TABLE 4.1 ■ THE THREE COMPONENTS OF FLAVOR

SENSORY SYSTEM	EXAMPLES	RECEPTOR	LOCATION OF RECEPTORS	NATURE OF FLAVOR CHEMICAL
Basic tastes	Sweet, salty, sour, bitter (and umami)	Taste cells on taste buds	Throughout mouth, but concentrated on tongue	Must dissolve in water (saliva)
Smell	Vanilla, butter, thousands more	Olfactory cells on the olfactory bulb	Top of nasal cavity	Must dissolve in water (mucous membranes); must be volatile
Trigeminal effects	Pungency, burn, numbing, cooling, and others	Nerve endings underneath the surface of the skin	Throughout mouth and nose	Must absorb through skin; must be volatile to be perceived in nasal cavity

HOW DO CHEMICAL SENSORY SYSTEMS WORK?

For chemical sensory systems—basic tastes, smell, trigeminal effects—to work, flavor chemicals must first reach the receptors. Basic taste chemicals must dissolve in saliva to reach the taste buds, smell chemicals must evaporate to reach the olfactory cells, and trigeminal factors must be absorbed through skin to reach nerve endings.

Once at the site of the receptors, flavor chemicals interact with, or stimulate, receptors in some way, by bonding to them, for example. This generates electrical impulses that travel through nerve cells to the brain, where the information is processed. The organ that actually perceives is the brain—not the eyes, ears, nose, mouth, or skin.

IS THERE A FIFTH BASIC TASTE?

Researchers have reported that there might be a fifth basic taste. The fifth basic taste is called *umami*, which means tastiness or savoriness in Japanese. To get an idea of the taste of umami, dissolve a few crystals of MSG—monosodium glutamate—on the tongue.

Japanese scientists presented the idea of umami as a basic taste in the early 1900s, when monosodium glutamate was first purified from dried seaweed. At that time, many scientists believed that umami was not a basic taste, that it was more likely a blend of other tastes, like sweetness and saltiness. Others classified it as a trigeminal effect (trigeminal effects are discussed in detail in a later section of this chapter). While recent research does provide convincing evidence of umami as a basic taste, it is still a controversy among some scientists.

Basic Tastes

Basic tastes include sweet, salty, sour, and bitter. These sensations are perceived on the tongue and throughout the mouth when taste chemicals—sugars, high-intensity sweeteners, salts, acids, caffeine, etc.—bind to receptor taste cells, or change them in some way.

Taste cells are clustered on taste buds. Taste buds contain around a hundred taste cells apiece, each able to perceive one or more of the basic tastes. While taste buds are scattered throughout the mouth, most are located on the tongue, hidden in crevices beneath papillae, which are small bumps on the tongue. Saliva, which is mostly water, is important to taste perception because it carries taste molecules—sugars, acids, salts, and bitter compounds—into these crevices and to the taste buds. Figure 4.2 illustrates the location of taste buds on the tongue.

It is easier to correctly identify sweetness and saltiness in foods than sourness and bitterness. Sourness and bitterness are often confused, maybe because many foods that are sour are also bitter. Or, maybe it is because each contains an element of unpleasantness. Properly distinguishing sourness from bitterness takes practice, but it is an important skill to learn.

Smell

Smell—also called *aroma*—is often considered the most important of the three components of flavor. It is the most predominant, and it is certainly the most complex. Humans perceive only four—or five—basic tastes, but they can smell hundreds, even thousands, of distinctly different aromas. Most aromas themselves are complex. For instance, there is no one single coffee molecule. Instead, coffee aroma consists of hundreds of separate chemicals.

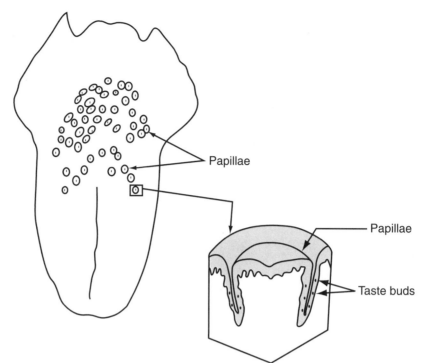

FIGURE 4.2 Taste buds and the perception of basic taste

To produce smell, molecules must be volatile—that is, they must evaporate and escape from food—to reach the top of the nasal cavity where millions of olfactory cells—smell receptors—are located. The olfactory cells are immersed in mucous, which consists mostly of water, so aroma molecules must be at least partly water soluble as well as volatile. To reach the olfactory cells at the top of the nasal cavity, molecules travel either directly from food through the nose (*orthonasal* pathway), or up the back of the throat (*retronasal* pathway), as food is chewed and warmed in the mouth (Figure 4.3).

WHAT IS A SUPERTASTER?

Just as we are born with different eye colors and with different heights and weights, so, too, are we born with different numbers of taste buds. Linda Bartoshuk, a researcher at Yale University, studies taste perception. She and her colleagues have measured the number of taste buds on people's tongues by swabbing the tongue with blue dye and measuring the bumps—the papillae—that stand out in relief on the tongue as pink spots. Because, on average, five or six taste buds are situated below each papilla, the number of taste buds on a person's tongue can be estimated from this swabbing.

Based on these measurements, Bartoshuk has devised three categories of tasters: supertasters, normal tasters, and nontasters. Most—60 percent—of the population fall into the category of normal tasters, while 20 percent are supertasters and another 20 percent are nontasters.

Supertasters have the highest number of taste buds, and it does seem that this affects taste perception. In particular, supertasters seem to be especially sensitive to bitterness. It is not that nontasters cannot perceive any bitterness; it is that bitterness does not seem as strong to them. Being categorized as a supertaster or a nontaster refers only to the number of taste buds on the tongue and does not reflect sensitivities to aroma. Remember, too, that taste perception is influenced by more than the number of taste buds. Experience and training, in particular, are extremely important, because the brain is doing the actual perceiving.

Yet, it is important for bakers and pastry chefs to realize that we live in different taste worlds. If others seem to find flavors much weaker or much stronger than you do, you may need to flavor foods differently from your own liking.

HELPFUL HINTS FOR TASTING SOURNESS, BITTERNESS, AND ASTRINGENCY

To evaluate food for the basic tastes, it often helps to block your nose. This focuses attention on sensations in the mouth. To distinguish between sourness and bitterness, consider the following descriptions.

Sourness is perceived almost instantly, as soon as food is placed in the mouth, while the perception of bitterness is often slightly delayed. Bitterness also tends to linger as an aftertaste. Sourness is perceived more toward the sides of the tongue, while bitterness tends to be perceived toward the back of the throat. If a product is very bitter or very sour, however, it will be perceived throughout the mouth.

A third sensation that is sometimes confused with sourness and bitterness is astringency. While sourness causes the mouth to water, astringency leaves a drying sensation that makes the tongue feel rough. Sometimes astringency is described as having a mouthful of cotton balls. Astringency is not a basic taste; the drying is from tannins in foods binding with proteins in saliva.

Train yourself to identify sourness, bitterness, and astringency in a range of food products. Start with foods that are predominantly sour, bitter, or astringent, such as those from the following lists. Then taste cranberry juice or another food that contains significant amounts of all three, and see if you can identify each sensation. When tasting a new food, it might help to think back to the previous food products and decide if the new food reminds you of any of those.

Foods that are predominantly sour: pickles, yogurt, cultured buttermilk

Foods that are predominantly bitter: strong black coffee, strong dark beer, unsweetened chocolate

Foods that are predominantly astringent: strong black tea, unripe persimmons, grape skins

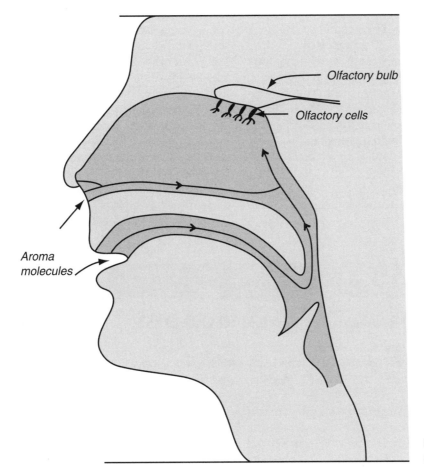

FIGURE 4.3 Olfactory cells and the perception of smell

Smell is considered the most important component of flavor because most of flavor is smell. By some estimates, eighty percent of flavor is from smell. It is also through smell that products are best differentiated and described. Imagine, for example, distinguishing between strawberry and cherry juice without the sense of smell. Appearance, even taste (sweetness and sourness, in this case), would hardly provide enough clues. Most of us would need the sense of smell to tell the two juices apart.

Smell is so important to overall flavor that when people have colds, they often say they cannot taste. Strictly speaking, they can still taste the basic tastes, but they cannot smell. This happens because nasal passages are blocked and odor molecules cannot reach the olfactory cells. Since smell makes up most of flavor, flavor seems lost without it.

Although the receptors for smell are at the top of the nasal cavity, it often seems as if smell takes place in the mouth, not the nose. Recall, however, that perception takes place neither in the mouth nor in the nose, but in the brain. Since the brain senses that food is in the mouth, it perceives smell as coming from there, as well.

HELPFUL HINTS FOR EVALUATING SMELL

Nothing is more frustrating than sitting down with pencil, paper, and product and smelling . . . nothing. Here are some helpful hints for increasing your sensitivity to smell.

Take several small "bunny sniffs." This pulls flavor molecules up to the olfactory cells.

Block your nose while you briefly chew food. Then, release your nose and breathe in deeply. Your olfactory cells will be bombarded with smells as flavor molecules are pulled up the back of your throat.

Move the food around in your mouth as you chew it well. This will help to warm and break up the food, allowing molecules to evaporate more easily to the olfactory cells.

Give your nose frequent breaks. Your olfactory cells—and brain—are easily fatigued. To ease fatigue, move away from what you are smelling and breathe fresh air. By taking breaks, you improve your sensitivity when you return to your evaluations.

Systematically train yourself to identify smells. For example, learn to identify the spices on your spice rack. Start with a few that are very different from each other, like cinnamon, anise, and ginger. Repeat this exercise until you can clearly identify these spices by smell alone. Then, try spices that have similar aromas, such as nutmeg and mace, or allspice and cloves. Once you can identify a small number of spices, increase the number evaluated at one sitting. Next, try variations of one spice. For example, compare cinnamons from different regions of the world. Or, compare aged spices to those freshly purchased.

WHY DO PLEASANT SMELLS BRING TEARS TO OUR EYES?

Have you ever felt emotional after smelling perfume, a flower, or a particular food? If so, then you know firsthand the connection between smell, memory, and emotion.

Aroma is perceived when odor chemicals bind to olfactory cells that are at the top of the nasal cavity. This triggers electrical signals that travel to a part of the brain called the olfactory bulb, where the signals are interpreted as buttery, vanilla, yeasty, and so on. Often, there is a crossing of wires with nearby regions of the brain, especially those related to memory and emotion. The smell triggers memories and feelings. That is what makes perfume so powerful, and why smells from a bakeshop are good marketing tools for selling product.

Trigeminal Effects

Trigeminal effects include the pungency of ginger, the burn of cinnamon, the cooling of mint, the heat from hot peppers, the tingling of carbon dioxide, and the sting of alcohol. The word *trigeminal* refers to the nerve that carries the signal of these sensations from nerve endings in the mouth and nose to the brain. To make matters interesting, this same nerve carries signals of temperature and pressure. Is it any wonder, then, that some trigeminal effects are "hot" or "cooling"?

Trigeminal effects are important to bakers and pastry chefs, even if they never use the term. It is hard to name a spice where the flavor is not dependent on it. Often trigeminal effects go by other names, including chemical feeling factors, *pungency, chemical irritation, chemosensory irritation,* or *chemesthesis.*

Remember that trigeminal effects are part of flavor. As with basic tastes and smell, chemicals in food trigger these sensations. For example, *menthol* triggers the cooling sensation of mint, and *capsaicin* triggers the hot, pungent sensation of chili peppers. These sensations are perceived by nerve endings located just under the skin throughout the mouth and nose (Figure 4.4). To reach these nerve endings, the flavor chemical must first be absorbed through the skin (for the perception of trigeminal effects in the nose, the flavor chemical must also evaporate). Molecules that dissolve at least partially in fat tend to be absorbed more easily.

Factors Affecting the Perception of Flavor

Flavor perception depends on many factors related to the product being evaluated as well as to the person doing the evaluating. These factors determine how flavor is ultimately perceived. A few of the important factors that affect flavor perception are listed in the sections that follow. While it is still unclear exactly how these factors affect flavor perception, it is thought that many work by changing the release of flavor molecules from food. If flavor molecules are released differently, flavor will be perceived differently.

NATURE OF THE INGREDIENT

Different sweeteners provide different qualities of sweetness. Aspartame, also called NutraSweet, may be sweet, but this high-intensity sweetener has a different sweetness than sucrose (table sugar). While sucrose tastes sweet almost immediately, aspartame lags in sweetness. Aspartame also lingers much longer as a sweet aftertaste, and it tastes bitter to many people.

Likewise, malic acid, one of the main acids in apples, has a different sour taste than either citric acid in lemons or acetic acid in vinegar. This is why adding lemon juice or vinegar to mild-tasting apples will not provide the same flavor impact as using apples that are naturally sour.

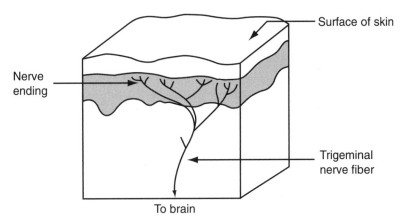

FIGURE 4.4 Nerve endings and the perception of trigeminal effects

PRODUCT TEMPERATURE

Product temperature affects flavor perception in several ways. For example, the perception of saltiness decreases as product temperatures rise. This means that warm baking powder biscuits taste less salty than the same biscuits evaluated at room temperature.

Sweetness increases as product temperatures rise. This means that if sorbet mix tastes properly sweetened at room temperature, it will not taste sweet enough when it is frozen. Aroma also typically increases as product temperatures rise. Since molecules evaporate more readily at higher temperatures, more reach the olfactory cells.

HELPFUL HINT

Because flavor perception changes with product temperature, always evaluate products at their proper serving temperature. If raspberry coulis is to be served cold, evaluate it cold. If it is to be served hot, evaluate it hot.

HELPFUL HINT

Be careful when adding gelatin to Bavarian creams and chiffon pie fillings. Not only does too much gelatin in these products produce a tough, rubbery dessert, but it also reduces the release of flavor.

PRODUCT TEXTURE AND CONSISTENCY

When a product is hard and firm or thick and viscous, it takes a few moments for flavor molecules to dissolve in saliva, to evaporate to the nasal cavity, or to be absorbed through skin. This affects flavor perception, because if flavor molecules cannot reach receptors, they cannot be perceived.

PRESENCE OF OTHER FLAVORS

Add a small amount of acid to a sweet product, and it tastes less sweet. The amount of sugar has not changed, but the presence of acid decreases the perception of sweetness. Likewise, the presence of sugar decreases the perception of sourness in the mix. The same is true of sweetness and bitterness, and sweetness and many trigeminal effects. The job of the pastry chef is often to balance these different flavors and create the most pleasing combination.

Salt and sugar both affect the perception of smell, probably by changing the rate at which molecules evaporate. Sometimes it takes only a small amount of salt or sugar to change and improve the aroma and overall flavor of food products.

AMOUNT OF FAT

Low-fat and fat-free foods are notorious for having an unappealing taste, because fat affects flavor perception, often in unpredictable ways. Many flavor molecules dissolve in fat, so when fat is eliminated, there is a change in the rate of release of flavor molecules to the taste buds, the olfactory cells, and the nerve endings below the skin. With this change comes a change in the perception of flavor. This is why low-fat foods require extra time and effort to flavor properly.

 **TEXTURE**

Texture, like flavor, is complex. Often, texture is ignored unless it is extreme or unpleasant. For example, the texture of breakfast cereal might go unnoticed until it becomes unpleasantly soggy.

The main way texture is evaluated is by touch—how the food feels against the skin, how it feels as it melts from the heat of the mouth, and how it responds to touch as food is squeezed, bitten, and chewed. Although this is the main way texture is evaluated, other senses come into play. The first—although not necessarily the most

WHAT DOES SOUND TELL US ABOUT CRISPNESS?

Sound is just as important as touch (response to pressure) when it comes to evaluating the crispness of foods. Researchers measure the crispness and crunch of food products by setting microphones and recorders to the jaw and measuring the pitch, frequency, and intensity of sound as a person eats crispy foods. The louder the sound, the higher-pitched the sound, and the more frequent the sound, the crispier the food.

accurate—information about texture is based on appearance. A visual evaluation of texture provides the first clues to how soft, firm, gritty, or smooth a product will feel when it is tasted. Sound is important to texture, as well. Tortilla chips are crunchy because of the sound (or vibration) of the crunch.

As with flavor, an experienced baker or pastry chef uses a full vocabulary to completely describe the texture of food. Table 4.2 lists common food texture terms, with examples. Notice that a cookie can be hard or soft, tough or tender, crumbly or chewy, moist or dry, oily or waxy, and more. Sometimes, one textural characteristic predominates, but for professionals, it is important to practice analyzing food as completely as possible.

Texture terms that refer specifically to how food feels against the inside of the mouth are sometimes called *mouthfeel* terms. Mouthfeel terms include smoothness, creaminess, oiliness, and waxiness.

QUESTIONS FOR REVIEW

1. Why is it that humans often "eat with their eyes"?

2. What three things can happen to light as it hits an object?

3. What makes limes green in color?

4. List the three main factors that affect appearance.

5. Explain why the appearance of an object could be different if it is viewed under different lighting.

6. Explain and provide an example of how a difference in the color of a plate or of sauce on a plate could explain why one white cake appears whiter than another.

7. What are the three components of flavor? Which receptor senses each component, and where is each receptor located?

8. Why is saliva necessary for the perception of the basic tastes?

9. Which is generally considered the most important component of flavor, and why?

10. Provide four helpful hints to follow when evaluating aromas.

11. Why does warm food typically have a stronger flavor than cold food?

12. Why is it difficult to taste when you have a cold?

13. Name four products that have trigeminal effects. Name two that do not.

14. What are other names for trigeminal effects?

15. How does the perception of sweetness change when food is served colder than usual?

16. How does the perception of saltiness change when food is served colder than usual?

17. What is meant by mouthfeel?

TABLE 4.2 ■ TEXTURE TERMS FOR DESCRIBING FOOD PRODUCTS

QUESTION	TERM	EXAMPLE
How easily is it pressed or squeezed?	Soft	Fresh Wonder bread
	Firm; hard	Stale Wonder bread
How easily can I bite through it?	Tender	Properly mixed piecrust
	Tough	Overmixed piecrust
Does it hold together?	Chewy (hard; holds together)	Tootsie Roll
	Gummy (soft; holds together)	Chewing gum
	Crumbly, short, mealy (tender; breaks apart)	Corn bread
	Brittle (hard; breaks apart)	Peanut brittle
How quickly does it flow?	Thin	Water
	Thick	Molasses
Does it bounce back?	Plastic (solid; doesn't bounce back)	Shortening
	Springy (bounces back)	Jell-O
	Spongy (tough, springy, airy)	Cake made with extra eggs
How does it feel against the soft tissues of the mouth?	Smooth (no particles)	Creamy peanut butter
	Creamy (thick and smooth)	Vanilla custard sauce
	Gritty (small particles)	Curdled custard sauce; pears with stone cells
	Chalky (gritty and dry)	High-protein bars
	Coarse (large particles)	Coarse sugar
	Pulpy	Orange juice
What shape are the particles?	Flaky (long, flat layers)	Flaky piecrust
Do they run in the same direction?	Fibrous (long, ropelike)	Celery; rhubarb
How much liquid is present?	Dry	Dry cereal
	Moist	Chewy brownies
	Watery	Water
Is the fat liquid or solid?	Oily (thin)	Oil
	Greasy (thick; coats mouth)	Fat-soaked doughnut
	Waxy (firm or solid)	Wax; puff pastry shortening
How much air is present?	Light, airy	Whipped egg white
	Foamy (light, airy, and liquidy)	Steamed milk
	Heavy, dense	Chewy brownies

Adapted from Civille and Szcesniak, Journal of Texture Studies, 4 (1973) 204–223.

QUESTIONS FOR DISCUSSION

1. Explain what is meant by products having differences in their chemical makeup. As part of your explanation, provide two examples of how this could affect the appearance of chocolate cake.

2. Explain what is meant by products having differences in their physical makeup. As part of your explanation, provide an example of how this could affect the appearance of chocolate cake.

3. Why might it be important to know if you are a supertaster or a nontaster?

⟋ EXERCISES AND EXPERIMENTS

1. Taste Buds and Tasters

Using regular (water-soluble) blue food coloring, a cotton swab, and a mirror, apply food coloring to the surface of your tongue. Look in the mirror at the appearance of your tongue. Is it mostly blue with a few pink spots, or is it mostly pink with very little blue? The pink spots are the papillae on your tongue, and the more papillae, the more taste buds. Compare the appearance of your tongue with those of your classmates. Can you predict who might be a supertaster and who might be a nontaster?

2. Ice Cream Storage and Texture

Compare the texture of properly stored (or freshly made) ice cream and ice cream that has been poorly stored (same flavor ice cream, but thawed slightly and refrozen one or more times over the course of several days). Record your evaluations by filling in the Results Table that follows. Use information from Table 4.2 to help you with texture terms.

RESULTS TABLE ■ A COMPARISON OF THE TEXTURE OF PROPERLY STORED AND IMPROPERLY STORED ICE CREAM

ICE CREAM SAMPLE	VISUAL EVALUATION OF SMOOTHNESS (SCALE OF 1–5, 1 BEING NOT VERY SMOOTH; ICY)	SOFTNESS WHEN SCOOPED (SCALE OF 1–5, 1 BEING SOFT, EASY TO SCOOP)	CREAMINESS WHEN EATEN (SCALE OF 1–5, 1 BEING NOT VERY SMOOTH AND CREAMY; ICY)	OTHER
Properly stored				
Improperly stored				

Summarize in one sentence the overall texture differences in the ice cream samples.

_____

_____

3. Texture

Compare the texture of two products of your choice. They can be butter and margarine, fresh and stale bread, two different chocolate couvertures, two different types of cake, two pie fillings, two types of dried fruit, ginger snaps and marshmallows, and so forth. Record the names of the two products in the row headings in the following blank Results Table. Decide on the proper sensory characteristics to evaluate and write these in the column headings of the Results Table. Also write a title for your Results Table. Use information from Table 4.2 to help you with texture terms.

RESULTS TABLE ▪

Product		

Summarize in one sentence the overall texture differences between your two samples.

_____

_____

4. Apple Juice Flavor

Apple juice is a relatively mild-tasting juice, which will be made even milder by diluting with water. Next, ingredients will be added to the diluted juice for you to taste. Some samples might taste very strong to you, others might be difficult for you to perceive. This varies from person to person, since we live in different taste worlds. If necessary, make up a stronger sample of any ingredient that you cannot taste.

Work slowly through this exercise. You will find that your ability to identify and describe differences between samples will progress as you proceed. Taste samples several times, going back and forth from one to the next, as many times as you need.

While diluted apple juice is used to complete this experiment, as you progress through it, think about how the lessons learned using apple juice can be applied to real pastry products, such as pie fillings, coulis, ice cream, even chocolate brownies and cheesecake.

OBJECTIVES

- To identify and describe differences between sourness, astringency, and bitterness
- To demonstrate how sugar affects perception of sourness
- To demonstrate how acid affects perception of sweetness
- To demonstrate the importance of basic tastes and astringency in overall flavor perception
- To create a good-tasting apple beverage that has a pleasing balance of sweetness, sourness, and astringency

PRODUCTS PREPARED

- Diluted apple juice with:
    - No additions (control product)
    - Sugar
    - Acid
    - Tannin powder
    - Caffeine
    - Sugar and acid
    - Other (sugar and tannin powder, sugar and caffeine, different acid or different sugar, etc.)
    - Your choice of additions

MATERIALS AND EQUIPMENT

- Apple juice, 6 quarts (liters) or more
- Water, 2 quarts (liters), bottled or tap

- Sugar, regular granulated
- Caffeine tablets, 200 mg, any brand such as Vivarin or NoDoz Maximum Strength
- Tannin powder (from wine-making store). If unavailable, use alum (sometimes found in supermarkets, with spices or canning supplies).
- Malic or other acid (citric acid, tartaric acid, or cream of tartar)
- Pitchers, to hold one quart (liter) of liquid, one per test product
- Large bowl or pan, to hold 11 quarts (liters)
- Sample tasting cups (1 oz./30 ml soufflé cups, or larger)
- Plain unsalted crackers

PROCEDURE

- Set aside one quart (liter) apple juice.
- Dilute 6 quarts (liters) apple juice by adding 2 quarts (liters) water to it in a large pan or bowl. Add more water if apple juice is very sweet or strong-tasting. Set aside 1 quart (liter) and label sample "diluted apple juice."
- Prepare samples. *Note*: for very small quantities of ingredients, measurements are given in both weight and volumetric measurements. Use measuring spoons with these ingredients if readability of scale is larger than ten times the weight to be measured.
  - Add 1 ounce (30 grams) granulated sugar to one quart (liter) diluted apple juice. Label sample "with sugar."
  - Add 0.15 ounce or 1 teaspoon (4 grams or 5 milliliters) malic acid to one quart (liter) diluted apple juice. Label sample "with acid."
  - Add 0.1 ounce or ½ teaspoon (2.5 grams or 2.5 milliliters) tannin powder to one quart (liter) diluted apple juice. Label sample "with tannin."
  - Add 4 caffeine tablets, crushed finely, to one quart (liter) diluted apple juice. Label sample "with caffeine." *Note:* this is about the same amount of caffeine as in coffee.
  - Add 1 ounce (30 grams) granulated sugar and 0.1 ounce (3 grams) malic acid to one quart (1 liter) diluted apple juice. Label sample "with sugar and acid."
- Set samples aside at room temperature for about one-half hour, to allow powders to dissolve completely. Caffeine, in particular, needs time to dissolve.
- Evaluate the flavor of undiluted apple juice and record results in first row of Results Table 1, which follows. Describe basic tastes and other sensations in the mouth, and flavors other than aroma. If necessary, block your nose so apple aroma is not distracting.
- Evaluate the flavor of diluted apple juice samples with added acid, tannin, and caffeine and also record results in Results Table 1. Be sure to taste each in turn to the control product (diluted apple juice) and to each other. Block your nose, if helpful, and cleanse your palate between samples, using water and unsalted crackers. Go back and re-taste samples as often as needed, and focus on the following.
  - What is perceived (puckering, salivating, drying, general unpleasantness, etc.), other than sweetness and aroma.
  - Where it is perceived (front of tongue, sides of tongue, back of throat, throughout entire mouth, etc.).
  - When—how quickly—sensation is perceived (immediately, slowly, as an aftertaste, etc.).
  - Name foods with this sensation (strong black coffee, unsweetened chocolate, Sour Patch Kids candy, strong black tea, etc.).
- Evaluate diluted apple juice samples with no additions (control product), added sugar, added acid, and added sugar and acid and record evaluations in Results Table 2, which follows. Be sure to compare each in turn to the control product (diluted apple juice) and to each other. Cleanse your palate between samples,

using water and unsalted crackers. Go back and retaste samples as often as needed, and evaluate the following:

- Fullness of flavor
- Sweetness
- Sourness

■ Next, compare each of these products to *undiluted* apple juice, to evaluate for acceptability. Record your results in Results Table 2, as you complete the following.

- Rate each sample as acceptable or unacceptable, and describe what makes it acceptable or unacceptable.
- Add any additional comments, as necessary.

■ Reevaluate the undiluted apple juice, and record results in bottom row of Results Table 2. Be as complete as you can in your evaluation of overall fullness of flavor, sweetness, and sourness. Also evaluate for astringency. If necessary, retaste the diluted apple juice with added tannin powder.

■ Based on your evaluations above, combine samples or add additional ingredients to either match the undiluted apple juice as closely as possible, or to create a good-tasting apple beverage that balances sweetness, sourness, and astringency.

- Keep track of the samples combined and ingredients added; give samples an appropriate name and record in the first column of Results Table 3.
- Describe your apple beverage's flavor and overall acceptability compared to undiluted apple juice. Record in next two columns in Results Table 3.
- Add any additional comments, as necessary.

■ Record any potential sources of error that might make it difficult to draw the proper conclusions from the experiment. Consider, in particular, whether samples were all at same temperature when evaluated; whether powdered ingredients were fully dissolved; whether a large number of samples made evaluations difficult or confusing for you.

SOURCES OF ERROR

_____

_____

RESULTS TABLE 1 ■ A COMPARISON OF SOURNESS, BITTERNESS, AND ASTRINGENCY IN APPLE JUICE

APPLE JUICE	WHAT IS PERCEIVED AND WHERE	WHEN SENSATION IS PERCEIVED	FOODS WITH SIMILAR SENSATION	ADDITIONAL COMMENTS
Undiluted				
Diluted				
Diluted, with acid				
Diluted, with tannin				
Diluted, with caffeine				

RESULTS TABLE 2 ■ HOW A COMBINATION OF INGREDIENTS AFFECTS FLAVOR PERCEPTION IN APPLE JUICE

APPLE JUICE	FULLNESS OF FLAVOR (SCALE OF 1–5, 1 BEING VERY LOW)	SWEETNESS (SCALE OF 1–5, 1 BEING VERY LOW)	SOURNESS (SCALE OF 1–5, 1 BEING VERY LOW)	OVERALL ACCEPTABILITY	COMMENTS
Diluted apple juice (control product)					
With sugar					
With acid					
With sugar and acid					
Undiluted apple juice (final tasting)					

RESULTS TABLE 3 ■ COMPARISON OF FLAVOR AND OVERALL ACCEPTABILITY OF APPLE BEVERAGES TO UNDILUTED APPLE JUICE

APPLE BEVERAGE	DESCRIPTION OF APPLE BEVERAGE FLAVOR	OVERALL ACCEPTABILITY (COMPARED WITH UNDILUTED APPLE JUICE)	COMMENTS

CONCLUSIONS

1. Describe in one sentence the differences between sourness and bitterness.

_____

_____

2. Describe in one sentence the differences between sourness and astringency.

_____

_____

3. How did the addition of sugar affect the perception of sourness in diluted apple juice?

_____

_____

4. How did the addition of acid affect the perception of sweetness in diluted apple juice?

_____

_____

5. Did the addition of sugar increase, decrease, or have no effect on the fullness of flavor in the diluted apple juice? What about the addition of acid?

_____

_____

6. How did your evaluation of undiluted apple juice change, if at all, from the start of the exercise (the results recorded in Results Table 1) to the end (the results recorded in Results Table 2)?

_____

_____

7. Were there any sources of error that might significantly affect the results of your experiment? If so, what could you do differently next time to minimize error?

_____

_____

8. Describe the strategy you used to create a pleasing apple beverage.

_____

_____

9. Provide a specific example of how you could use the information from this experiment to adjust the flavor of a particular pastry product.

_____

_____

CHAPTER 5

WHEAT FLOUR

CHAPTER **OBJECTIVES**

1. Describe the makeup of the wheat kernel and its endosperm.

2. Classify common flours and other wheat products used in bakeshops and describe their characteristics and uses.

3. Describe common flour additives and treatments.

4. List the functions of flour and relate these functions to makeup.

5. Describe how to best store and handle flour.

 INTRODUCTION

Wheat is a cereal grain. Other cereal grains include corn (maize), oats, rice, and rye. Widespread consumption of cereal grains began in the Middle East about 10,000 years ago, when agriculture first began. It was then that wheat was first planted and cultivated.

Today, thousands of different wheat varieties are grown throughout the world. While certain varieties will grow within the Arctic Circle and others will grow near the equator in the Andes mountains, most varieties of wheat require moderate growing conditions. Several locations in North America have ideal conditions for growing high-quality wheat, including the Midwestern United States and the southern prairie region of Canada. Other major wheat-growing countries include China (where more wheat is grown than in any other country in the world), India, France, and Russia.

Wheat is the most popular cereal grain for use in baked goods. Its popularity stems mainly from the gluten that forms when flour is mixed with water. Without gluten, raised bread is hard to imagine. Wheat is also preferred because of its mild, nutty flavor. Both factors, no doubt, contribute to wheat being the most widely grown cereal grain in the world.

WHEAT KERNEL

Wheat kernels are the seeds of the wheat plant, and they are the part of the plant that is milled into flour. Since cereal grains are in the grass family, wheat kernels can be thought of as a type of grass seed. In fact, when a field of wheat starts to grow, it looks like lawn grass.

Wheat kernels have three main parts: the endosperm, the germ, and the bran (Figure 5.1). While whole wheat flour contains all three parts of the kernel, white flour is milled from the endosperm. Whole wheat flour is considered a *whole grain product* because it contains the entire wheat kernel.

The *endosperm* makes up the bulk of the wheat kernel, over 80 percent of it. It is the whitest part, partly because it contains mostly starch—typically 70–75 percent starch. The starch is tightly packed into starch granules, which are embedded in chunks of protein. Two important proteins in the endosperm of wheat kernels are the gluten-forming proteins, *glutenin* and *gliadin*. When flour is mixed with water, glutenin and gliadin form a network of gluten, which is important in the structure of baked goods. In fact, wheat is the only common cereal grain that contains sufficient glutenin and gliadin for the formation of good-quality gluten for bread making. Gluten and its unique properties are described in more detail in Chapter 7.

The *germ* is the embryo of the wheat plant. Given the right conditions, the germ sprouts—germinates—and grows into a new plant (Figure 5.2). Wheat germ makes up only a very small part of the wheat kernel (about 2.5 percent), but it is high in protein (about 25 percent protein), fat, B vitamins, vitamin E, and minerals. These nutrients are important to the germ as it sprouts. While germ protein does not form gluten, from a nutritional standpoint, it is of a high quality.

Wheat germ can be purchased and added to baked goods. When bakers add wheat germ to baked goods, it is usually because of the nutritional value of its protein, vitamins, and minerals. Wheat germ is typically sold toasted. The toasting adds a nutty flavor to the wheat germ. It also destroys enzymes, called lipases, present in wheat germ that break down oils and cause them to oxidize. Because it does not contain gluten-forming proteins, wheat germ will not contribute to structure in baked goods. Because it is high in polyunsaturated oils that oxidize easily, wheat germ is best stored under refrigeration.

The *bran* is the protective outer covering of the wheat kernel. It is usually much darker in color than the endosperm, although white wheat, which has a light bran color, is also available. In either case, bran is high in dietary fiber. In fact, the bran is about 42 percent dietary fiber, most of it classified as insoluble fiber. Bran also contains a good amount of protein (about 15 percent), fat, B vitamins, and minerals. As with wheat germ, bran proteins do not form gluten; in fact, you will see later in this chapter that wheat germ and bran actually interfere with gluten development.

Wheat bran can be purchased as small flakes and added to baked goods. While it may soften slightly, bran remains relatively unchanged during baking because it is neither a moistener nor a drier. Instead, it contributes a dark, rustic appearance, a distinct nutty flavor, and a higher insoluble fiber content to baked goods.

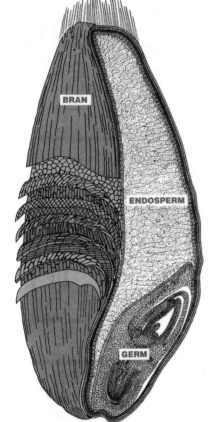

FIGURE 5.1 Longitudinal section of a grain of wheat
Courtesy of the Wheat Foods Council

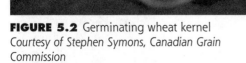

FIGURE 5.2 Germinating wheat kernel
Courtesy of Stephen Symons, Canadian Grain Commission

MORE ON WHOLE GRAIN PRODUCTS

Whole grains consist of the entire grain or kernel. If the kernel is cracked, crushed, or flaked, it still must have the same proportions of bran, germ, and endosperm as the original grain to be called whole grain.

Dark-colored products are not necessarily whole grain. Often, molasses or caramel coloring is added to baked goods to give them a heartier look. Nor do names of products like seven-grain bread or stone-ground flour guarantee that the product is whole grain.

According to the 2005 Dietary Guidelines for Americans, consuming at least 3 or more one-ounce servings (or the equivalent) of whole grains per day can reduce the risk of several chronic diseases and may help with weight maintenance. Based on recent surveys, only about 10 percent of Americans currently meet this guideline.

WHAT IS DIETARY FIBER?

Dietary fiber is plant matter that humans cannot digest. It is classified as either soluble or insoluble. Soluble fiber, when placed in water, will absorb the water, thickening or forming a gel. Insoluble fiber will either sink or float in water, but it remains essentially unchanged because it does not absorb water. Just because it is not digested does not mean that dietary fiber is not important in the diet. Both soluble and insoluble dietary fiber are essential for good health, but they serve different functions in the body. Insoluble fiber, for example, improves intestinal health and is thought to reduce the risks of certain cancers. Soluble fiber lowers blood cholesterol and can reduce the risk of heart disease.

The current recommendation is for healthy North Americans to increase their consumption of dietary fiber to 20–35 grams per day. For many, this means doubling their current intake.

Fiber-rich foods do not necessarily have a fibrous texture. Meats can be fibrous, for example, but those fibers consist of fully digestible proteins and are not dietary fiber. Even fibrous vegetables, like celery, are not necessarily higher in dietary fiber than less fibrous ones. Good sources of fiber-both soluble and insoluble—include most fruits, vegetables, whole grain cereals, nuts and seeds, dried beans, and cocoa powder.

MAKEUP OF FLOUR

White flour—the ground endosperm—contains mostly starch, yet other components naturally present in white flour affect its properties. The main components in white flour are listed in the paragraphs that follow, with approximate percentages provided in parentheses. Of these, the two key components are starch and protein. The circle graph in Figure 5.3 illustrates the major components in flour and the relative amounts of each in typical bread flour.

Starch makes up the bulk of flour (68–76 percent). Even bread flour, considered low in starch, contains more starch than all other components combined. Starch is present in flour as small grains or *granules*. Some starch granules are damaged during the milling process or when flour is stored under damp conditions. When this happens, starch can be broken down by the enzyme amylase into sugars that are readily fermented by yeast. The amount of sugar naturally present in flour (less than 0.5 percent) is rarely high enough for proper yeast

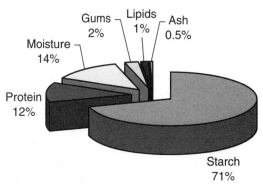

FIGURE 5.3 The makeup of bread flour

fermentation, which is why most yeast dough formulas include at least some sugar or a source of amylase.

Chunks of *protein* (6–18 percent) act as the cement that holds starch granules in place in the endosperm. Together, glutenin and gliadin, the gluten-forming proteins, make up about 80 percent of the proteins in the endosperm. Other proteins in white flour include enzymes, such as amylase, protease, and lipase.

Moisture in flour typically ranges from 11–14 percent. When moisture content rises above 14 percent, flour is susceptible to fungus and mold growth, flavor changes, enzyme activity, and insect infestation. For these reasons, flour must be stored properly, covered and in a cool, dry place.

Other carbohydrates in flour besides starch include gums (2–3 percent), primarily *pentosans*. It is easy to overlook the importance of pentosan gums in white flour because they are present at relatively low levels. But they have at least one important function in flour. Because they typically absorb about 10 times their weight in water, a small amount of pentosan gums makes a large contribution to the water absorption value of flour. Pentosans also increase the viscosity or consistency of batters and doughs. The small amounts present in wheat flour appear to interact with gluten, generally improving its strength and structure. Larger amounts of pentosans have the opposite effect and result in lower volume in baked goods. Pentosan gums are a source of soluble dietary fiber.

Although only a small amount of *lipids* (1–1.5 percent)—oil and emulsifiers—are present in white flour, they are necessary for proper gluten development. Yet, because of its nature, wheat oil oxidizes easily and turns rancid, limiting the shelf life of flour. While not dangerous or unsafe, stale flour has a distinct cardboard flavor that is best avoided by storing flour properly and using it promptly.

Ash is composed of inorganic matter—mineral salts—naturally present in wheat kernels. It includes iron, copper, potassium, sodium, and zinc. Besides providing needed minerals to the diet, ash increases yeast fermentation by contributing minerals to yeast. Ash has a gray color that carries over to the flour. If properly milled, however, white flour is relatively low in ash (less than 0.6 percent), because ash is concentrated in the bran layer, which is separated from the endosperm when white flour is milled. Ash is measured in flour and grain samples by burning the samples at very high temperatures—over 1,000°F (538°C)—and weighing the remains.

Carotenoid pigments are present in white flour in extremely low amounts (1–4 parts per million). They provide the creamy, off-white color to unbleached flour. The carotenoid pigments in white flour are in the same family as beta-carotene, the orange pigment in carrots.

CLASSIFYING WHEAT

Bakers generally classify wheat by the hardness of the kernel, that is, by whether the kernel feels *hard* or *soft* to the touch. Hard wheat kernels are high in protein; soft wheat kernels are low in protein. As the amount of protein in flour increases, the amount of starch decreases. Hard wheat kernels feel harder than soft ones because protein in these kernels forms large, hard chunks that hold tightly to starch granules. Hard wheat kernels typically are higher in carotenoids than soft wheat kernels, and higher in water-grabbing pentosans.

Flours milled from hard wheat kernels are creamy or creamy white in color. They feel slightly gritty and granular, because the hardness of the kernel makes them difficult to mill. This coarseness means that hard wheat flours do not pack easily when squeezed and are good for dusting the bench or workspace. Typically, hard wheat flours form high-quality gluten, meaning gluten that stretches well and forms strong, cohesive films. Because they form strong gluten, hard wheat flours are considered *strong flours*. Strong flours usually have a high water-absorption value and require a longer mixing time to fully develop, but they are tolerant of overmixing. In fact, strong flours require more mixing to fully develop gluten. Strong flours are typically used in yeast-raised products, such as breads, rolls, croissants, and Danish.

Flours milled from soft wheat kernels are whiter in color and finer to the touch than hard wheat flours. Because they are so fine, soft wheat flours tend to pack when squeezed and do not flow or dust the bench easily. Soft wheat flours typically form weak gluten that tears easily, which is why they are sometimes called *weak flours*. Weak flour is not necessarily less desirable than strong flour. It produces more tender products, and this is desirable for many cakes, cookies, and pastries.

PARTICLE SIZE

Wheat and other cereal grains can be milled into many different forms, from very fine flour to cracked or whole kernels. Small, fine particles absorb water quickly. Large particles, such as whole and cracked kernels and coarse meals and flakes, often require soaking or gentle heating in liquid before use, to allow for proper water absorption and softening.

There is evidence that larger particles, such as whole kernels, are absorbed and digested by the body more slowly than fine flours. This is beneficial for diabetics and for others trying to control their blood glucose levels.

Flours

Flours by definition are grains milled to a relatively fine granulation size. Not all flours have the same granulation, however. For example, soft wheat flours are typically ground finer than hard wheat flours because the softness of their kernels allows it.

Granular Products

Granular products are coarser than flour. Like flour, they can be whole grain, if milled from the whole kernel, or not, if milled from the endosperm. Examples of granular wheat products include farina and semolina. *Farina* is coarsely ground from the endosperm of hard red wheat. Cream of Wheat is an example of a brand of farina. Durum semolina is coarsely ground from the endosperm of durum wheat. *Semolina* is from the

PHOTO 5.1 Top row: cracked wheat and whole wheat flour; bottom row: rolled wheat, wheat berries, and whole wheat pastry flour
Photo by Aaron Seyfarth

Italian for farina. Because durum semolina is yellow in color, it can be easily mistaken for cornmeal.

Meals and grits are available in a variety of sizes, from coarse to fine, with each providing a slightly different texture to baked goods. These terms are more commonly applied to grain products other than wheat, such as corn or rice.

Cracked Kernels

Cracked kernels are whole kernels that have been cracked or cut into fragments, not ground like flour. Examples of cracked kernels include cracked wheat or rustic wheat flakes.

Whole Kernels

Grains can be purchased as whole kernels. When whole wheat kernels are purchased, they are generally called *wheat berries*. Whole kernels add a contrasting crunchy texture and visual appeal to bread.

FLOUR AND DOUGH ADDITIVES AND TREATMENTS

Millers often add small amounts of additives to flour. Some of these additives are also available to bakers for mixing directly into dough. The types and amounts of additives that are allowed are strictly regulated by government agencies. By law, millers must label flour with the additives it contains.

There are several different types of flour additives. Some improve the nutrient content of flour and are required by law. Others improve dough handling or baking

WHY IS WHITE FLOUR ENRICHED?

The milling process involves removing bran and germ from the endosperm. When this is done, vitamins and minerals, dietary fiber, and protein and fat from the bran and germ are removed. It is likely that other important unidentified nutrients are also removed. Flour enrichment replaces certain vitamins and minerals that are lost from milling. It does not replace the dietary fiber in the bran, the high-quality protein in the germ, or other potentially important yet unidentified nutrients in the bran and germ.

Flour enrichment began in the United States in the early 1940s after government surveys found that a high incidence of disease was caused by certain vitamin and mineral deficiencies. The enforced enrichment of white flour virtually eliminated two of these diseases, beriberi and pellagra.

Periodically, the U.S. and Canadian governments reevaluate the nutritional needs of North Americans. In the late 1990s, folic acid was added to the list of required vitamins and minerals added to enriched flour. Folic acid prevents certain birth defects, including spina bifida, and can also reduce the risk of coronary heart disease.

properties, or whiten the color of flour. A few of the main flour additives are described in the following sections.

Vitamins and Minerals

Enriched flour is white flour that has iron and B vitamins added in amounts to equal or exceed those in whole wheat flour. Four B vitamins are added to enriched flour: thiamin, riboflavin, niacin, and folic acid. Certain other vitamins and minerals are allowed as optional additives. Essentially all baked goods and pasta products made from white flour in North America are enriched.

Natural Aging

Natural aging occurs when freshly milled green flour is exposed to air for several weeks or more. In naturally aging flour, air is added to it. Air is a powerful additive, causing two main changes. First, it whitens the flour. Second, it strengthens the gluten that forms from flour.

Actually, the active ingredient in air is oxygen, which is considered an oxidizing agent. Oxygen oxidizes the carotenoid pigments in flour, changing their chemical structure and whitening them. Oxygen also oxidizes gluten-forming proteins, allowing them to form stronger gluten. Yeast doughs made from aged flour are easier to handle than those made from green flour, because doughs with stronger gluten are less sticky and less likely to tear when stretched. This, in turn, allows for higher volume and finer crumb on the baked bread.

Natural aging has a few disadvantages. First, it requires time, often several weeks or months. During this time, the flour takes up valuable silo space and is not paying the bills. Besides, the longer flour sits in silos, the more likely it will support mold growth or become infested with insects or rodents. Natural aging also can be inconsistent, and it is not as effective as many chemical bleaching and maturing agents. However, consumers sometimes prefer flours that have been naturally aged over those that contain bleaching and maturing agents. Naturally aged flours are often labeled unbleached.

Bleaching and Maturing Agents

Maturing agents are additives that change the baking properties of flours. Maturing agents are added to flour by the miller or are found in many dough conditioners that are added by the baker.

Some maturing agents strengthen gluten, while others weaken it. Because the same term—*maturing agent*—is used to describe additives that have completely opposite functions, it can be confusing. In this text, maturing agents that strengthen gluten, such as potassium bromate and ascorbic acid, will be called *maturing agents that strengthen*, while those that do not will be called *maturing agents that weaken*. In either case, only very small amounts—parts per million—of maturing agents are necessary to cause the desired changes.

One maturing agent that strengthens is potassium bromate. When it is added to flour, the flour is said to be bromated. Potassium bromate has been in use since the early 1900s, and it is the standard against which all other maturing agents are judged. Despite this, potassium bromate is no longer allowed as a flour additive in Canada or in Europe. Potassium bromate is considered a carcinogen because it has been shown to cause cancer in laboratory animals. While still approved for use in the United States, its use is slowly diminishing, and much lower levels are added to flour today than previously. In California, products containing potassium bromate must carry a warning label.

Many companies are searching for bromate replacers to strengthen their flour. While several bromate replacers are available, *ascorbic acid* is one of the most popular. Another name for ascorbic acid is vitamin C. While ascorbic acid is not as effective as potassium bromate and it works a little differently, its use is increasing because of concerns over the safety of potassium bromate.

Bleaching agents whiten carotenoids. Two common flour bleaching agents are benzoyl peroxide and chlorine gas. *Benzoyl peroxide* is used in all types of flour because it is extremely effective at whitening and because it contributes no maturing effects. It is commonly used in bread, high-gluten, all-purpose, cake, and pastry flours that are bleached.

Chlorine is used in cake flour only. Besides whitening, chlorine improves the baking properties of soft wheat flour by substantially weakening gluten and by allowing starch to absorb water more quickly and easily. You can always tell from the label whether

HOW DO MATURING AGENTS THAT STRENGTHEN WORK?

Maturing agents that strengthen gluten simulate natural aging. That is, they oxidize portions of glutenin and gliadin molecules, altering them so that more bonds form when gluten forms. The more bonds there are, the stronger, drier, and more cohesive the dough becomes. When gases expand during final proof and oven spring, this stronger gluten stretches better without breaking. Loaf volume is higher, and the crumb is less coarse. Many maturing agents are more effective than natural aging at strengthening gluten. For the most part, maturing agents that strengthen do not whiten flour.

While potassium bromate and bromate replacers all work in a similar manner, they work at different times in the bread-making process. That is why commercial dough conditioners often contain a combination of maturing agents to strengthen dough throughout the process. For example, some bromate replacers react rapidly, typically during mixing and makeup. In contrast, potassium bromate works primarily during final proof and oven spring, when strength is needed most. Ascorbic acid works consistently throughout bread production, just not as effectively as potassium bromate.

DOES THE SOURCE OF AMYLASE MATTER?

The source of amylase—more specifically called alpha-amylase—added by the miller makes a surprising difference in the quality of baked bread. This is because not all amylase is alike. Different amylase enzymes are inactivated at different oven temperatures. Since amylase can have its greatest activity on bread dough during baking, its heat stability is extremely important.

Fungal amylase, for example, typically is inactivated before starch granules gelatinize, which is when the granules are most susceptible to its action. If the only reason for the amylase is to improve fermentation, it is acceptable, even

desirable, for amylase to stop working early on. However, the enzyme will not have time to break down enough starch to slow bread staling.

Early versions of bacterial amylase, on the other hand, were inactivated very late in baking, or sometimes not at all. With these enzymes, starch breakdown could be so extensive that bread became gummy. Newer versions of bacterial amylase are inactivated at temperatures that are intermediate to regular fungal amylase and to these early bacterial amylases. They provide an appropriate amount of starch breakdown that delays staling without the gumminess.

flour has been bleached, but you cannot necessarily tell which bleaching agent was used. Ask the manufacturer, if you would like to know.

Notice that chlorine's action on gluten is very different from the action of natural aging or maturing agents like potassium bromate. Chlorine is a maturing agent that weakens, and it is used on soft wheat flour. Potassium bromate and ascorbic acid are maturing agents that strengthen, and they are used on hard wheat flour.

Amylase

Amylase is one of several enzymes important in bread making. Recall from Chapter 3 that amylase breaks down starch in bread dough into sugar and other products. This provides food for yeast fermentation, increases browning, and slows staling. During fermentation, amylase acts on available starch, primarily starch from damaged granules. During baking, amylase activity increases when starch granules gelatinize and become more susceptible to its action. Enzyme activity stops when amylase is inactivated by the heat.

While white flour does contain some amylase, the level is typically too low to be of much benefit. To make up for this deficiency, amylase is sometimes added to flour by the miller. The amylase is from either bacteria or fungi.

If amylase is not added directly to flour, the baker can add any of several ingredients that are rich sources of amylase, including malted flour, diastatic malt syrup, untoasted soy flour, or any number of dough conditioners that contain amylase.

Malted Flours

Malted flours can be thought of as flours with active amylase activity. While any grain can be malted, barley is the most common grain made into malted flour. Malted barley flour is often referred to simply as malted flour, or more simply as malt. Certain brands of flour are sold with added malted barley flour, or the baker can purchase dry malt flour separately and add it to yeast dough at around 0.25–0.5 percent (baker's percentage).

Malted wheat and malted rye flours are also available. They differ from malted barley flour in flavor and in enzyme activity. Malt syrups, also called malt extracts, and dried malt syrups are related products. They are discussed in Chapter 8.

WHAT IS MALTING?

To malt means to sprout or germinate whole grain kernels under controlled conditions, as one might sprout beans or seeds. Malted grains are used in beer-making as well as in baking.

There are three main steps to malting grains for flour: steeping, germination, and drying. To steep grains, whole kernels are gently stirred in a tank of cool water. After they gain close to half their weight in water, the swollen kernels are transferred to a flat bed to germinate. Germinating kernels produce a mix of active enzymes, including proteases, which break down proteins, as well as amylase. After about four to five days germinating in a cool, humid environment, sprouted kernels are transferred to an oven and gently dried to their original moisture (less than 14 percent). This stops germination but leaves the active enzymes intact. The final step is to grind the dried malted kernels into flour.

Dough Conditioners

Dough conditioners are also called *dough improvers*. They are off-white dry, granular products that look similar to flour. Dough conditioners are used in the production of yeast-raised products. Because they contain a mix of ingredients, dough conditioners perform many functions. They are particularly useful when good gluten development is necessary for high volume and a fine crumb, especially when flour quality is poor or when dough undergoes rigorous conditions. For example, large-scale bakery operations will use dough conditioners to strengthen dough that gets rough-handled in automated equipment. Or, they may add dough conditioners to frozen doughs, where ice crystals damage gluten structure. Often, bakeries rely on dough conditioners to reduce mixing and eliminate bulk fermentation.

WHAT ARE IN DOUGH CONDITIONERS?

While many brands of dough conditioners are available, most contain a mixture of the following ingredients:

- Emulsifiers, such as DATEM and calcium stearoyl-2-lactylate, for increasing water absorption and gluten strength. DATEM stands for diacetyl tartaric acid esters of mono- and diglycerides.

- Salts and acids, such as calcium carbonate or monocalcium phosphate, for optimizing gluten development by adjusting water hardness and pH. Calcium carbonate increases both water hardness and pH; monocalcium phosphate increases water hardness while it decreases pH. Monocalcium phosphate, an acid salt, is also present in many baking powders.

- Maturing agents that strengthen, such as potassium bromate, ascorbic acid, potassium iodate, and azodicarbonamide (ADA), for increasing gluten strength.

- Yeast foods, such as ammonium salts, to improve yeast fermentation.

- Enzymes, such as amylase, to improve yeast fermentation and browning, and to delay staling.

- Reducing agents, such as L-cysteine, that break or block bonds in gluten. These agents increase the extensibility and reduce the strength of doughs. They are the opposite of maturing agents that strengthen. Pizza dough, for example, can benefit from the addition of L-cysteine, so that it stretches and handles easily, and doesn't shrink.

Dough conditioners should not be overused. Too much of a good thing yields poor texture and volume—and can be illegal. The United States and Canada both regulate many of the additives present in dough conditioners.

Vital Wheat Gluten

Vital wheat gluten is a dry powder that contains a high amount—about 75 percent—of protein that is vital, that is, protein that forms gluten when mixed with water. It is purchased as a creamy yellow powder. Vital wheat gluten is added to yeast-raised doughs to improve flour quality, to increase mixing and fermentation tolerances, for a finer crumb, and for improving volume. The addition of vital wheat gluten requires an increase in water in a formula, for full hydration. This additional water and the higher volume achieved with added gluten can extend shelf life by keeping the bread softer longer. Care must be taken, however, not to overdo the amount of wheat gluten added to bread formulas. Too much gluten can make a product tough and chewy.

COMMERCIAL GRADES OF WHITE FLOURS

Recall that the endosperm is the whitest part of the kernel and that it is the part of the kernel milled into white flour. Recall, too, that the endosperm contains all the gluten-forming proteins. No wonder that in North America commercial grades of white flour are defined by how much is pure endosperm. Flour that is very high in endosperm must be carefully milled, however, and this makes it higher in price. Of course, high-endosperm flours are whiter in color because they are relatively low in

HOW IS FLOUR MILLED?

Flour milling has two objectives. First, it is a process that separates the endosperm from bran and germ. Second, it involves grinding the grain to fine flour. Ideally, milling separates out as much endosperm as possible without damaging starch granules, but this is difficult to do. In fact, commercial milling operations are able to extract only an average of 72 pounds of flour for every 100 pounds of wheat, for a so-called extraction rate of 72 percent, even though the endosperm makes up 85 percent of the wheat kernel. To accomplish these objectives, the modern milling operation:

1. Cleans the kernels, to remove dirt, weed seeds, stones, and other debris.
2. Tempers the kernels by adjusting moisture content. Tempering toughens the bran and makes the germ more pliable, so the endosperm is easily separated from the bran and germ.

3. Breaks or crushes the kernels between corrugated rollers, loosening chunks of endosperm from the bran and germ.
4. Separates, or purifies the endosperm from the bran and the germ, using sieves and air currents. The resulting farina-size endosperm chunks are called *middlings*.
5. Grinds the endosperm middlings into flour between a series of smooth, reduction rollers.

These last three operations are repeated several times, producing streams of flour in which each progressive stream contains less endosperm and more bran and germ impurities than the last. These streams are selectively combined and sifted to produce commercial grades of flour. The flour is then naturally aged or treated with bleaching and maturing agents. Other approved additives may be blended in before the flour is packaged and sold.

bran and germ impurities. While these so-called high-quality flours are high in baking quality, they are lowest in nutritional quality.

Since wheat bran is naturally high in ash, the traditional way for manufacturers to confirm the grade of flour is to measure its ash content. While ash content is also affected by wheat variety and soil conditions, it does provide some indication of the amount of bran in flour and, therefore, of the flour's commercial grade. The following grades of flour apply to rye flour as well as wheat.

Patent Flour

Patent flour is the highest quality of all commercial grades of white flour. Bakers often use the term *patent flour* to mean patent bread flour, but most flours sold today— whether bread, pastry, or cake—are patent flours. Patent flour is made by combining the first few streams of flour from the milling process. It consists of the innermost part of the endosperm and is essentially free of bran and germ. This makes patent flour lowest in ash and whitest in color. Different grades of patent flours are available, depending on which streams of flour from the milling process are blended. The highest-quality patent flour is called *extra short* or *fancy patent*.

Clear Flour

Clear flour is the lowest quality of all commercial grades of flour. It is milled from the outer part of the endosperm, made from flour streams that remain after patent flour is produced. While different grades are available, all clear flours are relatively high in bran, high in protein and ash, and slightly gray in color. A high grade of clear flour, called *first clear*, remains after the production of hard wheat first patent flour. Most clear flour sold to bakers is first clear from hard wheat flour and typically has a protein content of 13–15 percent.

Clear flour is less expensive than patent flour. While it is higher in total protein than patent flour, the gluten formed from clear flour is typically of lesser quality than that from patent flour. First clear is commonly added to rye and whole grain breads. Its protein provides needed strength to low-gluten grains, while its slight gray cast is hidden by the dark color of the rye or whole grain. Lower, darker grades of clear flour are used in the manufacture of vital wheat gluten.

HOW DID PATENT FLOUR GET ITS NAME?

Traditional gristmills of the mid-1800s had difficulty milling the hard kernels of Midwestern and Canadian spring wheat. A new process using granite millstones was imported from Hungary and greatly improved the ability to process these hard kernels into white flour. But it wasn't until a Frenchman named LaCroix developed a purifier, which improved the yield and quality of white flour, that hard spring wheat was more easily milled into white flour. In 1865, the U.S. patent office granted a patent for the purifier. This was followed by hundreds more patents for refining white flour. These new patented processes— used in the mills of Minnesota—revolutionized the milling industry. Consumer demand for Midwestern patent flour continued to rise in both North America and Europe, and the center of the milling industry in the United States moved from Eastern cities to the upper Midwest, which became an internationally renowned center of milling. Today, the term patent flour still refers to highly purified white flour.

Straight Flour

Straight flour is milled from the entire endosperm. It is made by combining all usable streams of flour from the milling process and contains bran and germ particles that are not easily separated from the endosperm. Straight flour is not commonly used by the baking industry in North America. French bakers, however, use a type of straight flour in breads.

TYPES OF PATENT WHEAT FLOURS

Most flours purchased by the baker and pastry chef today—whether bread, pastry, or cake—are patent flours, milled from the heart of the endosperm. There are many differences among the various patent wheat flours. Some of these differences are due to the type of wheat used in producing the flour. Other differences occur because of differences in milling practices or additives.

Bread

Bread flour is milled from either hard red spring or hard red winter wheat. It is high in protein—typically 11.5–13.5 percent protein—that forms good-quality gluten, essential for high volume and fine crumb in yeast-raised baked goods. Because it is from hard wheat kernels, bread flour is more difficult for the miller to grind into flour. This is why bread flour is coarser in texture than pastry flour, and why it contains a higher percentage of broken and fragmented starch granules. These damaged starch granules absorb more water than intact granules, which is generally considered desirable in bread-making. Damaged granules are also more susceptible than intact ones to breakdown by amylase, making more sugar available to yeast for fermenting into carbon dioxide gas and alcohol.

Bread flour can be purchased unbleached or bleached. Sometimes it contains added malted barley flour to provide for better yeast fermentation, dough handling, and shelf life. Bread flour is typically used for pan breads, rolls, croissants, and sweet yeast doughs.

High-Gluten

High-gluten flour is milled from hard wheat, generally hard red spring wheat. It is naturally high in protein—typically 13.5–14.5 percent protein—and often has potassium bromate or a bromate replacer added to it for even stronger gluten. High-gluten flours require a high amount of water to form an acceptable dough, because of their high protein content and the high degree of damaged starch granules generated during milling. Like bread flour, high-gluten flour sometimes is bleached and can contain added malted flour. It is used almost exclusively for yeast-raised baked goods, particularly those requiring maximum strength and structure. Use high-gluten flour in bagels, hearth breads, thin crust pizzas, and hard rolls.

Do not confuse high-gluten flour with vital wheat gluten, which looks like flour but is best thought of as a flour additive. As with vital wheat gluten, be careful not to overuse high-gluten flour, so that breads are not too tough or chewy.

Artisan Bread

Artisan bread flour, which is milled from hard red winter wheat, resembles French bread flour in its characteristics, that is, it is relatively low in protein (11.5–12.5 percent). The low protein content provides for a crisper crust and a crumb with desirable irregular holes.

Despite having low protein, the quality of protein in artisan bread flour must be high. High-quality protein forms gluten with a good balance between strength and extensibility. If gluten quality is poor, the gluten tears as dough is stretched, and the dough collapses from the rigors of a long fermentation.

Artisan bread flour often has a slightly higher ash content than patent flour. This can create a grayish cast on the flour but is thought to improve yeast fermentation and flavor. Artisan bread flours typically do not contain bleaching or maturing agents and are more likely than other flours to be organic.

Pastry

Pastry flour is milled from soft wheat, generally from soft red winter wheat, but it can be milled from soft white wheat, as well. In either case, it is low in protein—typically 7–9.5 percent—and is easily milled to a fine granulation. Pastry flour is not usually bleached. Because it is typically low in protein, in water-grabbing pentosans, and in damaged starch granules, it has a low capacity to absorb water. Batters and doughs made with pastry flour remain relatively soft and fluid during the early stages of baking. This allows cookie dough to spread further and cakes to rise higher than with a stronger flour.

Cake

Cake flour is milled from soft wheat, generally from soft red winter wheat. It is short or fancy patent flour, meaning that it comes from the absolute heart of the endosperm. This gives cake flour a finer granulation, whiter color, lower protein content—6–8 percent—and a slightly higher starch content than other flours. Cake flour is typically bleached with both chlorine and benzoyl peroxide, yielding a stark white color and a distinctly changed flavor. It is sometimes called chlorinated or high-ratio flour.

Recall that chlorine is a maturing agent that weakens gluten and increases the ability of starch to absorb water. Cookie dough made from cake flour instead of pastry flour is stiff and dry, and the lack of free water prevents much, if any, spread during baking. Cookies made from cake flour are smaller than those made from pastry flour, they brown very little, and they have a cake-like texture.

WHAT IF BREAD IS MADE FROM PASTRY FLOUR?

If bread is made from pastry flour, it will not look or taste the same as bread made from bread flour. First, the dough will be softer, even though less water is required in the mixing. It will readily break and tear and be more easily overmixed.

Once the bread is baked, it will have lower volume. The crust will not brown as readily, and the crumb will be whiter. Air cells in the crumb will tend to be larger and more irregular. Expect a different flavor, and if the bread is stored over several days, it will become stale faster.

Many of these differences are due to the lower amount and quality of protein in pastry flour compared with bread flour.

PHOTO 5.2 The effect of different flours in cookie dough is seen in the differences in height and spread. On the left, cookies made with pastry flour; on the right, cookies made with cake flour.
Photo by Aaron Seyfarth

The importance of chlorine on the properties of cake flour cannot be overstressed. It is as much, if not more, the chlorine treatment as the low protein content that defines cake flour. Researchers are exploring alternatives to chlorination, which is no longer allowed in the European Union. Some promising alternative treatments include the use of heat, enzymes, and additives, such as xanthan gum.

All-Purpose

All-purpose (AP) flour is not always used by professional pastry chefs. However, it is sold in the foodservice industry as H&R flour, which stands for *hotel and restaurant* flour. AP flour typically has between 9.5–11.5 percent protein, but this can vary with the brand. While AP flour is often made from a blend of hard and soft wheat, this is not always the case. Some brands, such as King Arthur flour, are made entirely from hard wheat. Other brands, such as White Lily flour, are made entirely from soft wheat. AP flour comes bleached or unbleached, is typically enriched with vitamins and minerals, and may contain added malted barley flour.

HOW IMPORTANT IS CAKE FLOUR WHEN MAKING CAKES?

Many cakes can be made successfully with pastry or bread flour, but light, sweet, moist, and tender high-ratio cakes cannot. High-ratio cakes are made from formulas that contain a high ratio of liquid and sugar to flour. Without cake flour, these cakes would not rise, or more likely they would rise and then collapse during baking and cooling. Here's why.

Recall that chlorine modifies the starch in flour, so that the flour absorbs more water than it otherwise would. This makes for thicker cake batters, even when large amounts of water and sugar are added. Thick batters are good at holding tiny air bubbles, for a light texture, high volume, and fine crumb. Recall, too, that starch is a structure builder. With so much water and sugar in high-ratio cake batters, and with weakened gluten, chlorine-treated starch becomes essential for keeping the cake from collapsing in the oven, so cake volume stays high and light.

WHAT IF A FORMULA CALLS FOR ALL-PURPOSE FLOUR?

Not all professional bakeshops stock all-purpose flour. What should be used if a formula calls for all-purpose flour and none is available? The standard substitute for AP flour is generally given as a blend of bread and cake flour, usually a 60:40 blend. Yet this is not generally the best substitute.

For yeast-raised products, bread flour is a better choice. Additional water will be needed to form the dough, and longer mixing will be needed to develop the gluten. The dough will handle more easily, the bread will be higher than if it was made from all-purpose flour, and it will have a finer crumb.

For fine-textured, high-ratio cakes, use cake flour instead of AP flour. For most other cakes, such as gingerbread and carrot cake, and for all other products, including pastries and cookies, use pastry flour.

OTHER WHEAT FLOURS

Whole Wheat

Whole wheat flour is sometimes called graham or entire wheat flour in North America and wholemeal flour in Great Britain and other countries. It is a whole grain product because it contains all three parts of the kernel—bran, germ, and endosperm—in the same proportions as they occurred in the original kernel. Whole wheat flour has a shorter shelf life than white flour because the bran and the germ are high in oil, an oil which easily oxidizes to produce rancid, off flavors.

Whole wheat flour comes in different granulations, from coarse to fine. This is true of both stone-ground flour and conventionally (roller) milled flour. Because coarse flours absorb water more slowly than finer flours, they do not form gluten as readily. This is why coarse-grained flours typically result in dense baked goods. Coarse flours are also absorbed and digested more slowly than fine flours, and this helps to control blood glucose levels. Diabetics, in particular, must be careful about controlling their blood glucose.

It is a common misconception that graham flour is either coarser or finer than whole wheat flour. When Reverend Sylvester Graham first created graham crackers in 1829, he used coarsely ground whole wheat flour. However, in both the United States and in Canada today, there are no regulations that differentiate graham flour from whole wheat flour based on particle size.

Whole wheat flour is typically milled from hard red wheat, although whole wheat pastry flour, milled from soft red wheat, is available. In either case, whole wheat flour is higher in protein than white flour milled from the same wheat.

Whole wheat flour is typically high in protein (11–14 percent or more), but it does not form as much gluten as bread flour with the same or even lower protein content. There are several reasons for this:

- Sharp bran particles in whole wheat flour literally cut through gluten strands as they form.
- Bran is high in pentosan gums, which interfere with gluten formation.
- Much of the protein in whole wheat flour is from the bran and the germ, which do not form gluten.
- Wheat germ contains a protein fragment (glutathione) that interferes with gluten development.

WHAT IS STONE-GROUND FLOUR?

Early man made the first stone-ground flour by crushing and pounding whole grains between stones. Over the centuries, the process evolved to the use of stone, or grist, mills. A gristmill consists of two rotating circular granite millstones that rub or crush the grain that is sandwiched between the stones. Grinding can be combined with sifting to separate bran particles from the white flour. Before roller mills revolutionized the milling industry in the late 1800s, there were over 22,000 neighborhood gristmills across the United States, mostly run by windmills or water wheels.

Today, stone grinding is mostly used to mill whole grain flours and meals rather than white flour. While the miller can make some adjustments to the millstones, stone-ground flour is generally characterized by an even distribution of germ oil throughout the flour, and often by small bran particles. When bran particles are small, protein and other nutrients in them are more completely available for digestion. It is for this reason that stone-ground flour manufacturers sometimes advertise the digestibility and higher nutritional value of their products.

Old gristmills grind slowly, generating relatively little heat as the grain is crushed to flour. This can prevent the destruction of active enzymes and prevent the oxidation of oils. The presence of active enzymes in stone-ground flour is a mixed blessing, however. While the low heat of gristmills might not oxidize wheat germ oils, enzymes can. This is probably why stone-ground flours have a short shelf life, and it is probably why they can have a stronger flavor than roller-milled flour.

Roller mills are the primary means for milling flour today. They were invented in Europe as early as the 1500s but did not have widespread use in North America until the late 1800s. Roller mills consist of a sequence of paired iron rollers, either grooved or smooth, that rotate inwards. Because one roller is set to spin at a faster rate than the other, the grains caught in the middle are twisted and chopped. This flattens the bran into large flakes and breaks the endosperm into chunks. This is different than the rubbing and crushing that generally takes place in gristmills.

Whole wheat flour from roller mills is usually made by recombining the endosperm, bran, and germ in the proportions that they were present in the original kernel. Because the germ is flattened in this process and not rubbed throughout the flour, its valuable oils remain in the germ. This is said to minimize oxidation of the oils in the flour. It is also likely that the higher heat of roller milling destroys lipase enzymes, which helps prevent off flavors and helps extend shelf life.

This means that yeast-raised doughs and baked goods made with whole wheat flour will be different from those made from white flour. Specifically, whole wheat bread dough is less cohesive and resilient than that made with bread flour, and 100 percent whole wheat bread is denser and coarser than white bread. This is especially true with coarsely-ground whole wheat flour. Baked goods made from 100 percent whole wheat flour are of course darker in color and stronger in flavor than those made from white flour. To satisfy customers who are unaccustomed to the strong taste of bread made from whole wheat flour, bakers often blend about one-quarter to one-half part whole wheat flour to one part bread or high-gluten flour. As consumers become aware of the positive health benefits of whole grain baked goods, they will likely learn to appreciate the nutty flavor and denser texture of 100 percent whole wheat bread.

Whole White Wheat

Whole white wheat flour is made from either soft or hard white wheat, two new classes of wheat grown in North America. Farmers began growing more white wheat to satisfy the Asian market, where white wheat is preferred to red wheat flour in noodle-making. Although it is less hardy than red wheat, increasing amounts of white wheat are now being grown as North Americans become interested in increasing their consumption

WHAT IS WHEAT FLOUR?

Many bread labels include "wheat flour" as an ingredient. Wheat flour is not the same as whole wheat flour. The names are similar, but the flours are different. Whole wheat flour is a whole grain, milled from the whole wheat kernel. Wheat flour is another name for white flour, milled from the endosperm. It is called wheat flour to distinguish it from rye flour, corn flour, oat flour, or rice flour. This is a helpful distinction for those with allergies to wheat products, but it can mislead consumers into thinking that wheat flour contains all the health benefits of whole wheat flour.

Likewise, wheat bread is not the same as 100 percent whole wheat bread. Wheat bread typically has white flour as its main ingredient. While it contains some whole wheat flour, it often includes caramel coloring or molasses, for the darker look of 100 percent whole wheat bread.

WHAT IS SEMOLINA FLOUR?

Durum wheat is commonly sold either as finely ground flour, called *durum flour*, or as a coarser granular product, called *durum semolina* or simply *semolina*. The particles in durum semolina are about the same size as those in farina. Today, the term *semolina flour* is sometimes used to mean durum flour.

of whole grains. Whole white wheat flour is light in color—golden, not white—and has a sweeter, milder taste than whole wheat flour made from red wheats. This makes it more acceptable to consumers who prefer lighter, milder-tasting breads and pastries. Because it is a whole grain, whole white wheat flour is just as high in dietary fiber as regular whole wheat flour. For this reason, whole white wheat flour is being used in many whole grain breakfast cereals and baked goods.

Durum

Durum flour is made from the endosperm of durum wheat. Durum wheat is not the same as common wheat, which is used in white and whole wheat flours. Durum wheat has a very hard kernel—harder than so-called hard wheat kernels—and it is very high in protein (12–15 percent). Because it is extremely hard, durum wheat is difficult to reduce to a flour, and when it is, the flour is high in damaged starch granules.

Durum flour is high in yellow carotenoid pigments, which provide a desirable golden color to pasta products. Besides being used in pasta, durum products are used in specialty baked goods, such as Italian semolina bread.

 # FUNCTIONS OF FLOURS

Provides Structure

Flour is one of two main bakeshop ingredients that contribute to the toughening or structure building in baked goods, eggs being the other. Structure allows products to hold a new, larger size and shape as gases expand and leaven. It prevents products from collapsing once they are cooled and removed from the pan. Besides its importance in baked goods, flour provides structure—thickening, really—to pastry creams and certain pie fillings.

Gluten and starch are responsible for much of the structure-building properties of flour. Gluten is formed from two proteins in flour, glutenin and gliadin, when flour is mixed with water. While not as important as gluten and starch, pentosan gums also contribute to flour structure. Gums appear either to form their own structure or to interact with gluten.

Which of these structure builders—gluten, starch, or gums—is most important to a particular baked product depends on the type of flour and the formula used. For example, little, if any, gluten forms from cake flour or from nonwheat flours. Instead, starch, or starch and gums, becomes the main structure builder. On the other hand, products low in moisture, like piecrust and crisp cookies, inevitably rely on gluten alone for structure, because starch gelatinization cannot occur in the absence of sufficient water.

Even with flours that contain gluten, gluten is not necessarily the only, or the most important, structure builder. Take yeast-raised baked goods, for example. Gluten and starch share the role of structure building in these products. Gluten certainly is most important for developing structure in unbaked dough, but starch is arguably more important to the structure of the final baked product.

Absorbs Liquids

Ingredients such as flour that absorb liquids are also called *driers*. Starches, proteins, and gums are the three main components in flour that absorb moisture (water) and oil, helping to bind ingredients together. Notice that the same components that form structure are also driers. The difference is that all proteins in flour—not just glutenin and gliadin—absorb moisture, while only glutenin and gliadin form structure.

The absorption value of flour is an important quality factor in bread baking. It is defined as the amount of water absorbed by flour when forming bread dough. High absorption values are desirable in bread baking because the added moisture slows staling. Higher water absorption also means that less flour is needed to make a loaf of bread, so if cost is a factor, this is an important point.

Water absorption values of most bread flours range around 50–65 percent, meaning that 1 pound (450 grams) of flour absorbs over 0.5 pound (225 grams) of water. While several factors affect the absorption value of flour, flours that absorb more water typically have a higher protein content.

Contributes Flavor

Wheat flours have a relatively mild, slightly nutty flavor that is generally considered desirable. Each has a different flavor, however. Expect clear flour, for example, with its higher protein and ash content, to have a stronger flavor than patent flour, like pastry flour. Expect cake flour to have a different flavor because of the treatments it has undergone. Expect whole wheat flour to have the strongest flavor of all.

Contributes Color

Flours vary in color. For example, regular whole wheat has a nut-brown color from pigments in the bran, whole white wheat flour has a golden color, durum has a pale yellow color, unbleached white flour a creamy color, and cake flour a stark white color. These colors carry over to the color of baked goods.

WHY DO FLOURS DIFFER IN ABSORPTION VALUES?

By one estimate, almost half the water in bread dough is held by starch, about one-third by flour proteins, and close to one-quarter by the small amount of gums in white flour. Starch absorbs most of the water in doughs because there is so much starch in flour. Yet, the best way to predict which of two wheat flours will absorb more water is by comparing the amount of protein each contains. Proteins, including gluten-forming proteins, absorb fully one to two times their weight in water, while starch granules absorb only about one-quarter to one-half their weight in water. This means that a small increase in protein has a noticeable increase in the amount of water absorbed in doughs. High-gluten flour absorbs more water than bread flour, and bread flour absorbs more than pastry flour.

Besides the protein in flour absorbing more water, high-protein flours, being from hard wheat, contain more damaged starch granules. Damaged granules take up three to four times as much water as intact granules.

Predicting water absorption from protein values works as long as the wheat flour is not bleached with chlorine. Recall that chlorine changes starch so that it absorbs more water. This is one reason why cake flour absorbs as much water as it does. Another reason is that cake flour is milled finer, and finer particles always absorb water faster.

Flour also contributes protein, small amounts of sugar, and starches for Maillard browning—the breakdown of sugars and proteins—to a dark color on crusts. High-protein flours typically undergo more Maillard browning than low-protein flours. So, for example, expect a browner crust when bread flour is used instead of pastry flour, when making pie crust.

Adds Nutritional Value

Essentially all flours and grain products contribute complex carbohydrates (starch), vitamins, minerals, and protein. However, the protein in wheat is low in lysine, an essential amino acid. This means that wheat protein is not as nutritionally complete as egg or milk protein and is best supplemented with other protein sources for good health.

White flour is a poor source of fiber, but whole wheat flour and whole white wheat flour, being whole grain products, are good sources of dietary fiber from the bran.

STORAGE OF FLOURS

All flours, even white flour, have a limited shelf life. In fact, millers recommend that flours, especially whole grain flours, be stored for no more than six months. The main change that occurs is the oxidation of oils when flour is exposed to air. The result is rancid, cardboard-like, off flavors. While whole wheat flour and wheat germ are most likely to oxidize because of their high amount of oil, even the small amount of oil present in white flour—about 1 percent—eventually causes flavor changes. To avoid problems, rotate stock by following the FIFO rule—first in, first out—and do not add new flour to old. Flour should be stored covered and in a cool, dry area, particularly in the hot, humid days of summer. This prevents the flour from absorbing moisture and odors and from attracting insects and rodents. Wheat germ—and whole wheat flour—is ideally stored under refrigeration, if not used within a few months.

WHAT IS CELIAC DISEASE?

Celiac disease is a disease of the intestinal tract brought about by the consumption of gluten (more specifically, the gliadin in gluten). When people with celiac disease consume gluten—even very small amounts of it—their bodies react by damaging the small intestine, where nutrients are absorbed by the body. Without proper absorption of nutrients, people with celiac disease—also called celiac sprue or gluten intolerance—become malnourished. They may develop a range of symptoms related to intestinal distress or to poor nutrition.

Because people with celiac disease cannot tolerate any amount of gluten, they must adhere to a strict gluten-free diet for their entire lives. This means that they cannot consume any products that contain wheat. They also cannot consume any rye or barley, and oats may be a problem for many.

Celiac disease is genetic, passed down from one generation to the next. Since it is the most common genetic disease in Europe—affecting one out of every 250 Italians, for example—it is likely that many Americans have celiac disease. While celiac disease remains largely undiagnosed in this country, diagnosis is available through a blood test or through biopsy of tissue from the small intestine.

As awareness increases about celiac disease, more gluten-free products are being developed. Preparing gluten-free baked goods can be a challenge, but it is not impossible. Some traditional baked goods are already gluten-free. For example, flourless cakes are made with ground nuts instead of flour as the bulking agent. In place of wheat flour, gluten-free products usually contain some combination of rice, soy, potato, and tapioca flour. Often, xanthan or another gum is added at 1–3 percent, for their ability to trap air. After some experimentation, it is possible to develop acceptable products for sufferers of celiac disease.

QUESTIONS FOR REVIEW

1. Why is wheat so commonly used in the bakeshop? Why not flour from another cereal grain?

2. Identify the three main parts of a wheat kernel. Which is/are milled into white flour? Which is/are milled into whole wheat flour?

3. What components are naturally present in white flour? That is, what is the makeup of the wheat endosperm?

4. Which component in white flour—in the wheat endosperm—is present in larger amounts than all other components combined?

5. What are the main differences between flours milled from hard wheat and those milled from soft wheat?

6. What is the difference between flour and meal?

7. What is added to flour to enrich it? What is lost from milling wheat kernels into white flour that is not replaced with enrichment?

8. What is meant by green flour?

9. What are the two main changes brought about by naturally aging flour?

10. What are the disadvantages of naturally aging flour?

11. Provide an explanation for the advantages of maturing agents that strengthen.

12. What is the standard maturing agent for hard wheat flours, the one that all others are judged against?

13. Which maturing agent has been shown to be a carcinogen?

14. Name a bromate replacer. How does it act differently from potassium bromate?

15. Are potassium bromate and bromate replacers more likely to be added to bread flour or to cake flour? Why?

16. Name the two most common bleaching agents. Which does nothing more than whiten flour? Which also acts as a maturing agent?

17. Name three effects of chlorine on flour.

18. Is chlorine more likely to be added to bread flours or to cake flours? Why?

19. Why might flour contain a small amount of added amylase or malted barley flour?

20. What is meant by patent flour?

21. How does clear flour differ from straight flour? What is the main use for clear flour?

22. How much higher in protein is the typical high-gluten flour compared with the typical bread flour? What else is different between high-gluten flour and bread flour that can explain their different properties?

23. How is artisan bread flour different from regular bread flour? How do these differences affect the qualities of baked bread?

24. How much lower in protein is the typical cake flour compared with the typical pastry flour? What else is different between cake flour and pastry flour that can explain their different properties?

25. What is another name for wheat flour?

26. Which of the following are whole grains: whole wheat flour, wheat berries, wheat flour, durum flour, durum semolina, whole white wheat flour, clear flour?

27. What are the differences in color, flavor, and dietary fiber between regular whole wheat flour and whole white wheat flour?

28. Why does whole wheat flour have a shorter shelf life than white flour?

29. Which of the following are usually milled from hard wheat and which from soft wheat: high-gluten flour, bread flour, artisan bread flour, pastry flour, cake flour, all-purpose flour?

30. Which contains more carotenoids, bread flour or durum flour? How does the amount of carotenoids affect the appearance of flour?

31. One function of flour is that it provides structure or toughening. What structure builder forms from glutenin and gliadin when flour is mixed with water? What else in flour provides structure?

32. One function of flour is that it is a drier. What three components in wheat flour absorb water?

33. What is meant by the absorption value of flour? How can you generally predict which of two flours will absorb more water?

34. You normally use regular bread flour in a formula and switch to high-gluten flour. Will you need more water or less water to fully develop the gluten? Explain your answer.

35. Why does bread flour absorb more water than pastry flour?

36. Why does cake flour absorb more water than pastry flour?

37. Why does flour have a limited shelf life? That is, why should it be stored for no longer than six months?

QUESTIONS FOR DISCUSSION

1. Assume that two samples of wheat flour contain the same amount of protein, yet one forms more gluten than the other. Provide three explanations for why this could be. Assume that the differences are in the flours and their treatments only and not in the formulas or the methods of preparation for making the dough. Be sure to explain your reasons.

2. Assume that a sample of whole wheat flour and one of white flour contain the same amount of protein. Provide three explanations for why less gluten forms from the whole wheat flour than from the white flour. Be sure to explain your reasons.

3. Why do flours vary in the amount of damaged starch granules? How does the extent of this damage affect the flour's water absorption value and its susceptibility to amylase action? Why is this desirable for bread baking? Why is this undesirable for thin, crisp cookies?

4. In what way is flour treated with potassium bromate or ascorbic acid similar to naturally aged flour? In what way is it different?

5. In what way is flour treated with chlorine similar to naturally aged flour? In what ways is it different?

6. How might a high-ratio cake made with chlorinated cake flour differ from one made with pastry flour? Consider appearance, flavor, texture, and height.

EXERCISES AND EXPERIMENTS

1. A Comparison of Different Wheat Flours and Related Ingredients

Use your textbook or other reference to fill out the first three columns of the Results Table that follows. Next, use fresh samples to evaluate the appearance, particle size, and ability to pack of each of the wheat flours or wheat ingredients. To evaluate particle size, rub the grains or particles between your fingers and rate how fine or coarse they feel. To evaluate whether flour packs or holds together, scoop up a small fistful of flour in your hand, and squeeze. Use this opportunity to learn how to identify flours from their sensory characteristics alone. Add any additional comments or observations that you might have to the last column in the following Results Table.

RESULTS TABLE ■ A COMPARISON OF DIFFERENT WHEAT FLOURS AND RELATED INGREDIENTS

TYPE OF FLOUR/FLOUR INGREDIENT	KERNEL HARDNESS	TYPICAL PERCENT PROTEIN	TYPICAL TREATMENTS AND ADDITIVES	APPEARANCE	PARTICLE SIZE	PACKS (YES/NO)	COMMENTS
Bread							
Pastry							
Cake							
First Clear							
High-gluten							
Whole wheat							
Whole wheat pastry							
White whole wheat							
Durum semolina							
Malted barley flour	____	____					
Wheat bran	____						
Wheat germ	____						
Vital wheat gluten	____						

2. The Effect of Flour Type on Qualities of Lean Yeast Dough and Rolls

One way to learn about an ingredient, such as flour, is to make product, like yeast bread, from different types of that ingredient. Because lean dough used in making bread contains little else besides flour and water, it's perfect for learning about the properties of flours, even if some of those flours would never be used in making yeast bread.

OBJECTIVES

To demonstrate how the type of flour affects:

- Amount of water needed to make dough of proper consistency for bread-making
- Strength and extensibility of dough
- Crispness and extent of Maillard browning on the crust of rolls

- Crumb color and structure
- Moistness, tenderness, and height of rolls
- Overall flavor of rolls
- Overall acceptability of rolls

PRODUCTS PREPARED

Lean yeast rolls made with:

- Bread flour (control product)
- High-gluten flour
- Pastry flour
- Cake flour

- Whole wheat flour
- Other, if desired (all-purpose flour, artisan bread flour, white whole wheat flour, etc.)

MATERIALS AND EQUIPMENT

- Proof box
- Lean dough, enough to make 12 or more rolls of each variation
- Muffin tins (2½" or 3½" size)
- Ruler

PROCEDURE

- Preheat oven according to formula.
- Lightly spray or grease muffin tins with pan coating
- Prepare lean dough using the following formula or using any basic lean bread dough formula. Prepare one batch of dough for each flour type.
- Adjust the amount of water included in the dough for each flour, as needed. Record amount of water added to each dough in Results Table 1, which follows.
- Evaluate each dough for its strength and extensibility as follows. Record results in Results Table 1.
  - Take a small amount of dough and stretch it. If it stretches, how much does it resist stretching? This is a measure of dough strength or tenacity.
    - If it is hard to pull, the dough is *strong*.
    - If it is easy to pull, the dough is weak or *soft*.
    - If the dough falls apart and is not cohesive enough to stretch, write *does not stretch* in the appropriate column in the Results Table.

- If it does stretch, continue stretching dough until paper thin, to test extensibility.
  - If the dough stretches to form a thin film without tearing, it is *extensible* and *cohesive*.
  - If it breaks apart or tears easily, it is not extensible or cohesive.
  - If it holds together but won't form a film, it is *pasty*.
- Place dough in proof box for bulk fermentation until doubled in bulk, about 45 minutes.
- Punch down dough to distribute carbon dioxide into smaller air pockets.
- Divide dough into 3-ounce (90-gram) pieces and round into rolls.
- Place in greased muffin tins and label.
- Place rolls in proof box for about 15 minutes, or until nearly doubled in volume and light and airy to touch.
- Use an oven thermometer placed in center of oven to read oven temperature. Record results here _____.
- Place muffin tins in preheated oven and set timer according to formula.
- Bake rolls until control product (made with bread flour) is properly baked. You may need to bake some batches for a different amount of time because of oven variability.
- Transfer to wire racks to cool to room temperature.
- Record any potential sources of error that might make it difficult to draw proper conclusions from the experiment. In particular, be aware of any problems with the ovens and with the amount of water added to each dough.
- When rolls are completely cooled, evaluate height as follows:
  - Slice three rolls from each batch in half, being careful not to compress.
  - Measure height of each roll by placing a ruler along the flat edge at the roll's maximum height. Record results for each of three rolls in 1/16" (10 mm) increments in Results Table 2.
  - Calculate the average roll height by adding the heights of the rolls and dividing this by 3; record results in Results Table 2.
- Enter information from textbook on average protein content of each flour in Comments column of Results Table 2.
- Evaluate the sensory characteristics of completely cooled products and record evaluations in Results Table 3, which follows. Be sure to compare each in turn to the control product and evaluate the following:
  - Crust color, from very light to very dark, on a scale of one to five
  - Crust texture (soft and moist, soft and dry, crisp and dry, etc.)
  - Crumb appearance (small uniform air cells, large irregular air cells, tunnels, etc.)
  - Crumb texture (tough/tender, moist/dry, spongy, crumbly, chewy, gummy, etc.)
  - Overall flavor (yeasty, floury, sweet, salty, sour, bitter, etc.)
  - Overall acceptability, from highly unacceptable to highly acceptable, on a scale of one to five
  - Any additional comments, as necessary.

Lean Dough

INGREDIENT	POUNDS	OUNCES	GRAMS	BAKER'S PERCENTAGE
Flour	1	2	500	100
Salt		0.25	8	1.5
Yeast, instant		0.25	8	1.5
Water, 86°F (30°C)		10	280	56
Total	1	12.5	796	159

Method of Preparation

1. Preheat oven to 425°F (220°C).

2. Set proof box to 86°F (30°C) and 85 percent relative humidity.

3. Weigh ingredients, including water, on digital or baker's scale. (*Note:* if readability of scale is 1 gram (0.02 ounce) or higher, it is better to use teaspoons for measuring yeast and salt, to minimize error. Use 2½ teaspoons for 8 grams yeast; use 1½ teaspoons for 8 grams salt).

4. Weigh another 5 ounces (140 grams) of water (at 86°F/30°C) and set aside (this will be used for adjusting dough consistency in step 8).

5. Combine flour and salt thoroughly by sifting together three times onto parchment paper. *Note:* if all particles (bran particles, for example, in whole wheat flour) do not fit through sieve, stir them back into mixture.

6. Place flour/salt mixture, yeast, and water into mixing bowl.

7. Blend on low for one minute; stop and scrape bowl.

8. Add additional water (from step 4) slowly and as needed, to adjust consistency. Calculate the amount of water added from the amount that remains of the 5 ounces (140 grams); record amount in Results Table 1.

9. Mix using dough hook on medium for 5 minutes, or as needed.

10. Remove dough from mixer.

11. Cover loosely with plastic and label with flour type.

12. Continue to follow the Procedure instructions.

SOURCES OF ERROR

RESULTS TABLE 1 ■ EVALUATION OF WATER ABSORPTION AND DOUGH CONSISTENCY OF LEAN DOUGHS MADE WITH DIFFERENT TYPES OF FLOUR

TYPE OF FLOUR	ADDITIONAL WATER ADDED (OUNCES OR GRAMS)	DOUGH STRENGTH	DOUGH EXTENSIBILITY	COMMENTS
Bread (control product)				
High-gluten				
Pastry				
Cake				
Whole wheat				

RESULTS TABLE 2 ■ HEIGHT EVALUATIONS OF YEAST ROLLS MADE WITH DIFFERENT TYPES OF FLOUR

TYPE OF FLOUR	HEIGHT OF EACH OF THREE ROLLS	AVERAGE HEIGHT OF ONE ROLL	COMMENTS
Bread (control product)			
High-gluten			
Pastry			
Cake			
Whole wheat			

RESULTS TABLE 3 ■ SENSORY CHARACTERISTICS OF YEAST ROLLS MADE WITH DIFFERENT TYPES OF FLOUR

TYPE OF FLOUR	CRUST COLOR AND TEXTURE	CRUMB APPEARANCE AND TEXTURE	OVERALL FLAVOR	OVERALL ACCEPTABILITY	COMMENTS
Bread (control product)					
High-gluten					
Pastry					
Cake					
Whole wheat					

CONCLUSIONS

1. Compare rolls made with high-gluten flour to those made with bread flour (control product). What were the main differences in appearance, flavor, and texture? Explain the main reasons for these differences.

_____

_____

2. Compare rolls made with pastry flour to those made with bread flour (control product). What were the main differences in appearance, flavor, and texture? Explain the main reason for these differences.

_____

_____

3. Compare rolls made with cake flour to those made with bread flour (control product). What were the main differences in appearance, flavor, and texture? Explain the main reason for these differences.

_____

_____

4. Compare rolls made with whole wheat flour with those made with bread flour (control product). What were the main differences in appearance, flavor, and texture? Explain the main reasons for these differences. Explain why whole wheat bread sold in North America is often made with a blend of whole wheat flour and hard wheat flour.

_____

_____

5. Which rolls did you feel were most acceptable overall, and why?

_____

_____

6. Based on the results of this experiment, which flours are not acceptable for use in yeast-raised products? Explain your answer.

_____

_____

7. Did you have any sources of error that might significantly affect the results of your experiment? If so, what could you do differently next time to minimize error?

_____

_____

8. Rank flours in water absorption from the one that required the most amount of water in preparing dough to the least amount. Which of these differences in water absorption can be explained solely by the percent protein in the flour? For those differences in water absorption that cannot be explained by the percent protein in the flour, how can the differences be explained?

_____

_____

9. Rank flours in dough consistency:

   a. From the one that produced the strongest dough to the weakest.

   _____

   _____

   b. From the one that produced the most extensible dough to the least extensible.

   _____

   _____

   c. How can you explain these differences?

   _____

   _____

10. Rank flours in roll height from the one that produced the tallest roll to the shortest. How well did the rankings of dough strength and extensibility match the ranking for roll height?

_____

_____

11. Rank flours in roll toughness from the flour that produced the toughest roll to the most tender. How can you explain these differences in toughness?

_____

_____

3. The Effect of Flour Type on Cookie Quality

There are many types of cookies, and each reacts differently to the type of flour used. This experiment uses a formula similar to one used by millers and manufacturers for evaluating the quality of soft flours. High quality soft flour should be low in protein, in damaged starch granules, and in gums. If it is low in these three driers, cookie dough will thin out when heated, and the cookies will spread to a larger size.

OBJECTIVES

To demonstrate how the type of flour affects:

- Consistency and handling of cookie dough
- Height and spread of cookies
- Appearance of cookies
- Moistness, tenderness, and crispness of cookies
- Flavor of cookies
- Overall acceptability of cookies

PRODUCTS PREPARED

Rolled sugar cookies made with:

- Pastry flour (control product)
- Bread flour
- Cake flour
- Whole white wheat flour (soft)
- Other, if desired (all-purpose flour, whole wheat pastry flour, blend of bread and cake flour [60 percent bread, 40 percent cake], etc.)

MATERIALS AND EQUIPMENT

- Rolled sugar cookie dough, enough to make 12 or more cookies of each variation
- Sheet pans, full or half
- Rolling pin
- Gauge strips, for rolling dough to approximately ¼ inch (7 mm); flat rulers can be used as gauge strips
- Silicone pads or parchment paper
- Cutting board, size of silicone pad or larger
- Circular dough cutter, 2½ inches (65 mm), or similar size
- Ruler

PHOTO 5.3 Measuring the height and spread of cookies
Photo by Aaron Seyfarth

PROCEDURE

- Preheat oven according to formula.
- Prepare cookie dough using the following formula or using any basic rolled sugar cookie formula. Prepare one batch of dough for each flour type.
- Place silicone pad on cutting board and place gauge strips along sides of pad.
- Gently scrape dough from bowl and place six portions of dough at well-spaced points on silicone pad.
- Flatten each dough mound lightly with palm of hand.
- Using gauge strips, roll to thickness of ¼ inch (7 mm) with one forward rolling pin stroke and one return (backward) stroke.
- Cut dough with circular cookie cutter, 2½ inches (65 mm), and remove excess scraps from silicone pad.
- Evaluate each dough for its consistency and ease in handling. Record results in Results Table 1, which follows. In your evaluation, consider the following:
  - Dough softness/firmness, or how much force is required to roll it.
  - Dough cohesion, or how well it holds together
  - Dough adhesion, or how sticky it is
- Slide silicone pad with cookie dough onto sheet pan.
- Use an oven thermometer placed in center of oven to read oven temperature; record results here _____.
- Place sheet pans in preheated oven and set timer according to formula.
- Bake cookies until control product (made with pastry flour) is light brown, approximately 10 minutes. You may need to bake some batches for a different amount of time because of oven variability.
- Remove cookies from oven and let stand one minute.
- Transfer to wire racks to cool to room temperature.
- Record any potential sources of error that might make it difficult to draw the proper conclusions from the experiment. In particular, be aware of differences in the amount of mixing and rolling dough, and any problems with ovens.
- When cookies are completely cooled, measure cookie spread (width) as follows:
  - Slice three cookies from each batch in half, being careful not to compress them.
  - Lay halves from three different cookies edge to edge and measure total width in 1/16" (10 mm) increments; record results in Results Table 2.
  - Calculate the average cookie spread by dividing the total width by 3; record results in Results Table 2.
- Measure cookie height as follows:
  - Stack halves from three different cookies, one atop the other. Place a ruler along their flat edge. Measure the height at the center point of the three cookies in 1/16" (10 mm) increments and record results in Results Table 2.
  - Calculate the average cookie height by dividing the height of the three cookies by 3; record results in Results Table 2.
- Evaluate the sensory characteristics of completely cooled products and record evaluations in Results Table 3. Be sure to compare each in turn to the control product. *Note*: to evaluate crumb, break—rather than cut—cookies in half, so crumb is not compressed by knife edge. Consider the following:
  - Surface color and appearance (smooth, crinkled, etc.)
  - Crumb appearance (small uniform air cells, large open air cells, etc.)
  - Texture (hard/soft, moist/dry, crispy, chewy, gummy, etc.)
  - Overall flavor (sweetness, saltiness, floury flavor, fatty/shortening flavor, etc.)
  - Overall acceptability.
  - Add any additional comments, as necessary.

Rolled Sugar Cookie Dough

INGREDIENT	POUNDS	OUNCES	GRAMS	BAKER'S PERCENTAGE
Shortening, all-purpose		7	200	29
Sugar, regular granulated		14	400	58
Salt		0.25	7	1
Baking soda		0.25	7	1
Milk, whole		5	150	21
Flour	1	8	700	100
Total	3	2.5	1464	210

Method of Preparation

1. Preheat oven to 400°F (200°C).

2. Allow all ingredients to come to room temperature (temperature of ingredients is important for consistent results).

3. Blend flour, salt, and baking soda thoroughly by sifting together three times onto parchment paper.

4. Combine shortening and sugar in mixing bowl and mix on low for 1 minute; stop and scrape bowl, as needed.

5. Cream shortening and sugar on medium for 1 minute; stop and scrape bowl.

6. Slowly add half the milk while mixing on low; mix for a total of 1 minute; stop and scrape bowl.

7. Add flour and mix on low for 1 minute; stop and scrape bowl.

8. Add remaining milk and mix on low for an additional 1 minute.

9. Cover dough with plastic wrap and label with type of flour used.

10. Set aside until ready to use.

11. Bake cookies for approximately 10–12 minutes.

Note: flours vary in their water content and water absorption values. If dough does not hold together well enough to roll, add small amounts of water as needed and record amount added in Comments column of Results Table 1.

SOURCES OF ERROR

_____

_____

RESULTS TABLE 1 ■ DOUGH CONSISTENCY AND HANDLING OF ROLLED SUGAR COOKIE DOUGHS MADE WITH DIFFERENT FLOURS

TYPE OF FLOUR	DOUGH CONSISTENCY	DOUGH HANDLING (COHESION AND ADHESION)	COMMENTS
Pastry (control product)			
Bread			
Cake			
Whole white wheat pastry			

RESULTS TABLE 2 ■ SPREAD AND HEIGHT OF ROLLED SUGAR COOKIES MADE WITH DIFFERENT FLOURS

TYPE OF FLOUR	WIDTH (SPREAD) OF THREE COOKIES	AVERAGE WIDTH (SPREAD) OF ONE COOKIE	HEIGHT OF THREE COOKIES	AVERAGE HEIGHT OF ONE COOKIE	COMMENTS
Pastry (control product)					
Bread					
Cake					
Whole white wheat pastry					

RESULTS TABLE 3 ■ SENSORY CHARACTERISTICS OF ROLLED SUGAR COOKIES MADE WITH DIFFERENT FLOURS.

TYPE OF FLOUR	SURFACE AND CRUMB APPEARANCE	TEXTURE	OVERALL FLAVOR	OVERALL ACCEPTABILITY	COMMENTS
Pastry (control product)					
Bread					
Cake					
Whole white wheat pastry					

CONCLUSIONS

1. Compare cookies made with bread flour to those made with pastry flour (the control product). What were the main differences in appearance, flavor, and texture? Explain the main reasons for these differences.

_____

_____

2. Compare cookies made with cake flour to those made with pastry flour (the control product). What were the main differences in appearance, flavor, and texture? Explain the main reasons for these differences.

_____

_____

3. Compare cookies made with whole white wheat pastry flour to those made with regular pastry flour (the control product). What were the main differences in appearance, flavor, and texture? Explain the main reasons for these differences.

_____

_____

4. Which cookies were acceptable overall and which were not? Explain your answer.

_____

_____

5. Were certain flours more acceptable for certain uses, for example, for decorated gingerbread men, or for traditional shortbread?

_____

_____

6. Did you have any sources of error that might significantly affect the results of your experiment? If so, what could you do differently next time to minimize error?

_____

_____

7. Rank flours from the highest amount of cookie spread to the lowest. How do you explain these differences in spread?

_____

_____

8. Rank flours from the one that produced the tallest cookies to the shortest. Was there a relationship between cookie height and cookie spread? That is, did cookies that tended to spread have more height or less height than those that spread less? How can you explain this relationship?

_____

_____

9. Rank flours from the one that produced the toughest cookies to the most tender.

_____

_____

    a. Which of these differences in toughness can be explained solely by percent protein in flour?

    _____

    _____

    b. For those differences in texture that cannot be explained by the percent protein in the flour, how can the differences be explained?

    _____

    _____

10. Based on the results of this experiment, do you think the type of flour is as important in making cookies as it is in making breads and rolls? Explain your answer.

_____

_____

CHAPTER 6

VARIETY GRAINS AND FLOURS

CHAPTER **OBJECTIVE**

1. Classify common variety grains and flours used in the bakeshop and describe their makeup, characteristics, and uses.

INTRODUCTION

Wheat is the only common cereal grain with a good amount of gluten-forming proteins, making it the most popular grain for baked goods in North America and in many other parts of the world. Yet, other grains and flours are available to the baker. Each has a distinctive flavor and color, which contributes to its value. Bakeshops that limit their products to those made from common wheat miss the opportunity to provide variety to their customers.

Many variety flours contain as much, or more, protein than wheat does. However, because the proteins in these flours do not form gluten (except for rye and triticum grains, to a degree), protein content is not a useful indicator of quality, other than nutritional quality. Figure 6.1 compares the amount of protein in various flours, including

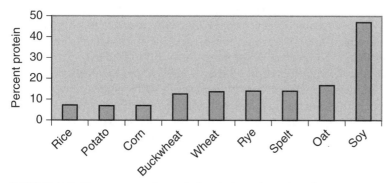

FIGURE 6.1 The amount of protein in whole grain variety flours compared with whole wheat flour
Adapted from the USDA Nutrient Database for Standard Reference, Release 19 (August 2006)

PHOTO 6.1 From left to right, amaranth, quinoa, pearl millet, flaxseed, and spelt
Photo by Aaron Seyfarth

whole wheat flour. As with wheat, most cereal grains are low in the essential amino acid lysine.

This chapter discusses many variety flours available to the baker. Those classified as cereal grains, such as rye and corn, are high in starch.

CEREAL GRAINS

Rye

Rye grass is tolerant of poor soil and cold climates, climates such as those of Russia, Eastern Europe, and Scandinavia, where wheat cultivation is difficult. Not surprisingly, rye bread consumption is high in these regions.

Breads made from rye flour tend to be dense and gummy, and they have a strong flavor. Although rye is as high as wheat in protein, rye flour has, at best, a limited ability to form gluten. While it contains sufficient gliadin, rye flour is low in glutenin. In addition, rye flour is very high in pentosan gums (8 percent or more), which interfere with what little gluten could form. Luckily, the pentosans themselves, along with starch, provide a type of cohesive structure in rye dough.

Because of its high pentosan gum content, rye flour absorbs noticeably larger quantities of water than wheat flour does. For this and other reasons, doughs made from rye flour are gummy and sticky, are easily overmixed and overfermented, and have poor gas-retaining properties during the later stages of proofing and during baking.

Rye bread formulas in North America generally include hard wheat flour—clear, high-gluten, or bread flour—to supply needed gluten and to balance flavor. Standard commercial rye bread formulas generally contain about one-quarter to one-half part rye flour to one part wheat flour. Caraway seed, an ancient spice native to the same regions as rye grass, is a common addition to many rye bread formulas.

Rye flour is not significantly higher in oil than wheat flour. However, rye oil oxidizes more easily, producing rancid, off flavors. To ensure that rye flour is always fresh, purchase it in quantities needed for no more than a three-month period.

As with wheat, a range of commercial rye products is available to the baker. *Light* or *white rye* is patent rye flour, sometimes bleached, from the heart of the rye endosperm. It is the mildest-tasting, most common rye flour used in North America and is used in rye or sour rye breads. Unlike the wheat endosperm, rye endosperm is high in dietary fiber, notably soluble dietary fiber from pentosan gums.

Medium rye is straight flour, from the whole endosperm, and *dark rye* is clear flour, left from the production of light rye. Of light, medium, and dark rye flours, dark rye has the darkest color and strongest flavor, and produces the lowest bread volume. *Whole rye flour*, also called *pumpernickel*, is made from the whole rye kernel. Like whole wheat flour, whole rye flour contains the bran, the germ, and the endosperm. Pumpernickel is sometimes coarsely ground as meal or cut into flakes.

Corn

Corn, or maize, is typically sold as ground cornmeal, but it is also available as a coarser grit or finer flour. The size of the granule affects the quality of the baked good. Coarse-textured cornmeal, for example, makes slightly gritty bread, one that is denser and more crumbly than corn bread made from fine cornmeal.

Corn contains a good amount of protein but none of it is gluten-forming. For this reason, wheat flour is usually added to baked goods that contain cornmeal. Wheat flour provides structure to the baked good, while cornmeal provides an appealing crumbliness, flavor, and color.

Corn products are typically white or yellow, but blue corn products are also available. Yellow cornmeal, because of its high carotenoid content, provides an attractive golden color to baked products such as corn bread and corn muffins.

Most corn products sold today are not whole grain. That is, they are milled from the corn endosperm, since corn germ is extremely high in oil (30–35 percent) and becomes rancid very quickly. Cornmeal milled from the endosperm is sometimes called *degerminated*. Degerminated cornmeal is enriched, to replace vitamins and minerals lost in milling. It has a milder flavor than whole grain cornmeal, but it lasts significantly longer.

Traditional Mexican corn flour used in making corn tortillas is called *masa harina*. Masa harina is made by soaking dried corn in limewater before grinding it into flour. The soaking removes the bran layer, changes the properties and flavor of the corn, and increases its nutritional value.

Oats

Oat products used in baked goods include rolled oats and quick-cooking rolled oats. Steel-cut oats are also available. Oats are most commonly used in cookies, streusel toppings, muffins, and breads. Oats are somewhat higher than most grains in protein, but the protein does not form gluten.

Oat products including oat flour and oatmeal, also called rolled oats, are whole grain because they are made from whole oat kernels, called groats. *Groats* are the kernels of any cereal grain that have had their inedible hulls removed. Regular rolled oats, also called large flake or old-fashioned rolled oats, are whole groats that have been steamed, then flattened between rollers. The steaming makes it easy to flatten the oats. Steaming also inactivates lipase enzymes that could cause the oil in oats to oxidize and produce off flavors. Quick-cooking rolled oats—quick oats—are made by cutting each groat into several thin pieces before steaming and rolling. Quick oats require less cook time because water penetrates thin pieces faster.

Steel-cut or Irish oats are chopped into small chunks rather than rolled. They are chewier and often have a stronger flavor than rolled oats, because they usually are not steamed. The stronger flavor is from active lipase enzymes breaking down oils. Because of their chunky shape and the fact that they have not been previously cooked, steel-cut oats take longer to cook than rolled oats.

Regular rolled oats and quick oats are often used interchangeably in baking formulas. Regular rolled oats, because of their larger size, have a coarser, chewier texture. Cookies made with regular rolled oats may spread excessively if a formula specifies quick oats. The addition of a small amount of white flour may be needed to absorb the free liquid that causes excessive spread.

WHAT'S SO GOOD ABOUT OATS?

If you've ever made oatmeal cereal for breakfast, you likely have experienced the gummy, gluey nature of oats. The gumminess comes from beta-glucan, a gum in oats that functions as dietary fiber in our bodies. While all whole grain cereals, including whole wheat, contain dietary fiber, oatmeal is higher than most in this soluble dietary fiber. Soluble fiber in oat products has been shown to lower cholesterol, which can lower the risk for coronary heart disease. In fact, in the United States, food products made from rolled oats, oat bran, and oat flour that contain enough soluble fiber and are low in fat can make legal claims that they may reduce the risk of heart disease. Barley products that are high in beta-glucan can also make this claim.

Rice

Rice flour, milled from the endosperm of the rice kernel, can be purchased in specialty shops. It is a low-protein flour that contains no gluten, making it a common ingredient in gluten-free baked goods. Rice flour is used in certain cakes and cookies, especially ethnic Middle Eastern and Asian products.

Pearl Millet

Pearl millet (pennisetum glaucum) is the most common of thousands of millet varieties grown throughout the world. These tiny tear-shaped cereal grains originated in Africa thousands of years ago, but once introduced into India, pearl millet became widely grown there, as well. Millet grows despite hot, dry conditions and poor soil, making it a valuable staple in countries where little else will grow. Unless first cooked in water, millet retains a crunchy texture in baked goods. Once ground, pearl millet must be used immediately or it must be refrigerated, to prevent off flavors from developing in the oils. Because it does not contain gluten, pearl millet flour must be combined with wheat for leavened baked goods. In India, pearl millet flour is used in flatbreads (*roti*). Grains of pearl millet pop like popcorn.

Teff

Teff has been grown in Ethiopia for thousands of years, and it is still the most plentiful cereal grain grown in Ethiopia. Teff grains are probably the smallest of any cereal grain. They are traditionally ground into flour, fermented, and made into a mildly sour spongy pancake called *injera*. Teff, in the form of injera and many other baked goods and main meals, is eaten daily in Ethiopia by those who can afford it. As Ethiopian restaurants have become popular in both Europe and North America, the cultivation and use of teff has spread to these areas.

Alternative Wheat Grains

Several variety grains are actually distant ancestors or close cousins to common wheat (triticum aestivum). Each is indeed a type of wheat and does contain gluten. Despite the common misconception that these grains are acceptable for those with celiac disease or with wheat allergies, this is not necessarily the case. In fact, food products sold in the United States that are made with any of the following grains must declare on the label that they contain wheat as an allergen. However, people do vary in their sensitivities to gluten and to allergens, and some who must avoid common wheat can tolerate one or more of these grains.

SPELT

Spelt (triticum spelta) is considered an ancestor to modern wheat. In the United States, spelt has been grown for years, mostly in Ohio as animal feed, but small amounts are now grown for specialty and health food stores. Europe is also showing renewed interest in spelt. Germany and surrounding regions grow significant amounts of spelt, locally called *dinkel*.

Like wheat, spelt can be milled into whole grain or into white flour. Spelt proteins form gluten, but the gluten is weak and easily overworked. Spelt bread dough should be mixed for only a short period of time, to avoid overworking the gluten and reducing its ability to retain leavening gases. Spelt has a lower water absorption value than wheat, so less water is needed when forming batters and doughs. It is best used in place of soft, rather than hard, wheat.

KAMUT

Kamut (triticum turgidum) is considered to be an ancient relative of modern durum wheat. Kamut seeds were first brought to the U.S. from Egypt only about fifty years ago. The seeds were propagated unchanged (not cross-bred with other wheat species) from the ancient seed. Kamut, which is an early Egyptian word for wheat, is a trademarked name that is licensed to those who grow the grain as certified organic. The grain grows well in dry regions of the Great Plains of Montana and in the Canadian provinces of Saskatchewan and Alberta.

Kamut kernels, which are two to three times the size of common wheat kernels, are high in protein, like durum wheat. Like spelt, Kamut has been successfully marketed to consumers as a health and specialty food product. Whole-grain Kamut has a sweeter, milder taste than common wheat, probably because its large size means it has less bran for the amount of endosperm. Kamut products are especially popular in Europe. Because it forms strong gluten similar to durum wheat, it is most commonly used in whole grain pastas, breads, hot cereals, bulgur, and couscous.

TRITICALE

Triticale was developed by plant breeders looking to combine the grain quality of wheat (triticum) with the hardiness of rye (secale). The name triticale comes from a combination of the Latin names of each grain. Because of its superior nutritional quality compared to wheat, there were high expectations in the 1960s and 1970s that triticale would provide the means of feeding growing populations in countries such as India, Pakistan, and Mexico. Today, triticale is used primarily as animal feed in North America and many other places around the world. It is used instead of soft wheat, especially in Mexico, in tortillas, crackers, and cookies.

EINKORN AND EMMER (FARRO)

Ancestors of today's cultivated varieties of einkorn (triticum monococcum) and emmer (triticum dicoccum) originated around the fertile crescent of the Tigris and Euphrates rivers in what is Iraq today. Einkorn is considered the very first wheat grain that was cultivated by man, starting about 10,000 B.C. Before that, einkorn was gathered wild.

WHAT ARE THE EIGHT MAJOR FOOD ALLERGENS?

Food manufacturers selling products in the United States must clearly state on product labels the presence of any of eight food allergens. The eight foods that are sources of these allergens are wheat, soy, milk, eggs, peanuts, tree nuts, fish, and crustaceans. Notice that of these eight allergens, six are commonly used in baked goods. Taken together, these eight trigger 90 percent of food allergy cases in the United States.

Unlike celiac disease or lactose intolerance, allergies occur when certain proteins—allergens— in food trigger a response in the body's immune system. A response to any of the eight allergens described here can lead to death within hours, or even minutes. That is why it is imperative that food preparers know the foods that are on this list.

In Canada, two additional foods are considered top priority food allergens: sesame seeds and sulfites (a food additive in many dried fruits). Although Canadian law does not currently require manufacturers to identify priority allergens by their common names, it will likely do so in the near future.

Emmer has some similarities to spelt, but it is much older, predating spelt by thousands of years. Spelt is often mistakenly identified as emmer. Emmer fell out of favor thousands of years ago when people switched to durum wheat. Like einkorn and spelt, emmer is not free-threshing, meaning that the kernels do not easily fall out of their husks, or hulls. Cereal husks are acceptable as feed for livestock but not as food for humans. However, the very thing that made harvesting these grains difficult in preindustrial times has turned into an advantage. The close-fitting husk protects the kernel from insects and fungus, so these grains are easier to grow organically.

Einkorn and emmer were made into porridge by the earliest civilizations before they were made into bread and beer. Einkorn has a high ratio of gliadin to glutenin, which results in a soft, sticky dough that is not particularly suitable for bread. Emmer, on the other hand, makes satisfactory dough but still heavy-textured bread. Emmer is very likely the wheat that was used by the Egyptians when they first made bread. Today, emmer is grown primarily in the Tuscan region of Italy, where it is known as *farro*.

CEREAL-FREE GRAINS AND FLOURS

The following seeds, legumes, and tubers are often ground into flours and used in baked goods. For this reason, they are included in this chapter. Because they are not cereal grains, none of the following contain gluten.

Buckwheat

Despite its name, buckwheat is not wheat at all. Buckwheat kernels have many similarities to cereal grain kernels. They can be ground into whole grain flour or more coarsely into grits. Or, the endosperm can be separated and milled into a lighter, milder flour. Buckwheat is also sold as whole kernels or groats. Roasted buckwheat groats are called *kasha* and are consumed in parts of Eastern Europe and Russia.

Because of its strong, distinct flavor, dark color, and lack of gluten, buckwheat flour is typically used in combination with wheat flour, usually one-quarter to one-half part

THE NUTRITIONAL BENEFITS OF FLAXSEED

Flaxseed contains a high amount of lignan, an important compound known as a phytoestrogen. In fact, flaxseed contains significantly more lignan than any other plant source. Phytoestrogens are antioxidants that appear to have health benefits. While it is still being researched, lignan is showing promise in preventing certain diseases, such as breast cancer.

Flaxseed is over 40 percent oil, approaching the amount of oil found in peanuts and pistachios. Unlike peanuts and pistachios, however, the oil in flaxseed is particularly high in alpha linolenic acid (ALA), an essential omega-3 fatty acid. Just as flaxseed contains more lignan than any other plant source, so too does it contain more ALA. ALA and other omega-3 fatty acids are important because they appear to reduce the risk of coronary heart disease.

Flaxseed can be ground into flour using a blender or food processor. Unground, flaxseed will keep for a year or more, protected by its hard coating. Once ground, it must be used immediately or refrigerated. ALA, the oil in flaxseed, is a highly polyunsaturated fatty acid, meaning that it oxidizes rapidly. Oxidized ALA has a strong, off flavor, reminiscent of paint or turpentine. This is really not too surprising, since the industrial name for flaxseed is linseed. Boiled linseed oil is one of the main ingredients in oil-based paints.

buckwheat flour to one part wheat flour. Buckwheat is not higher than wheat in protein, but the protein it contains has a more nutritionally balanced profile than wheat. Russian pancakes—*blini*—are traditionally made from buckwheat, as are Breton crêpes, from the north of France, and soba noodles in Japan.

Flaxseed

Flaxseeds are small, oily seeds that are typically dark brown in color. Canada is the world's largest producer of flaxseed, exporting it primarily to the United States, Europe, Japan, and South Korea.

Flaxseeds are oval, like sesame seeds, but they are very hard and should be ground into fine flour before use. Unground flaxseed can pass through the body undigested. If it does, the flaxseed will not provide any nutritional benefits. Yet it is because of its nutritional benefits that flaxseed use has increased dramatically in just a few years.

Flaxseed flour can be added to batters and doughs in small amounts without much change in flavor. Often the amount of fat in the mix can be lowered because of the high amount of oil in flaxseed. Because of the water absorption capacity of its soluble dietary fiber, the amount of water generally needs to be increased when flaxseed flour is added.

Quinoa

Quinoa was a staple crop of the ancient Inca Empire and still grows best in the very high elevations of the Andes Mountains in South America. Quinoa seeds, which are small like sesame seeds, are very high in healthful unsaturated fatty acids. Quinoa is a seed, not a cereal grain. Unlike wheat and most other cereal grains, quinoa is high in lysine, an essential amino acid. When used in multigrain breads, quinoa compensates for their amino acid deficiencies.

Because of its high level of unsaturated fatty acids, quinoa seeds can oxidize fairly quickly, especially once the seeds are ground. It is best to refrigerate quinoa seeds if they are to be kept for a time.

Amaranth

Amaranth is an ancient seed that was a staple crop of the Aztecs and Mayans of South and Central America. Amaranth plants are green herbs, and the seeds are small and light brown. Although not as popular as quinoa, there has been resurgence of interest in amaranth. Like quinoa, amaranth is high in lysine and is used in multigrain breads. Amaranth seeds can be popped like popcorn.

Soy

The soybean is a legume, not a cereal grain. Its composition and characteristics are quite different from wheat and other cereal grains. Compared with wheat, dried soybeans are high in protein (about 35 percent), high in fat (about 20 percent), and low in starch (15 to 20 percent). Soy flour used in baking is typically defatted, which means that some or all of the fat is removed. Soy flour comes toasted or untoasted.

Untoasted soy flour contains powerfully active enzymes useful in yeast breads. One of the enzymes in untoasted soy flour oxidizes carotenoids, whitening flour without the use of chemical bleaching agents. This is the main reason untoasted soy flour is added to bread dough. Only a small amount—0.5 percent—of enzyme-active soy flour is needed; in fact, higher amounts have a detrimental effect on bread flavor and texture.

Amylase is another active enzyme present in untoasted soy flour. Recall that amylase breaks down starch to sugars, improving fermentation, crust color, and bread softness, and delaying bread staling. Other enzymes in untoasted soy flour—proteases—act on proteins, improving dough mixing and gluten development. In a way, untoasted soy flour is a bleaching and maturing agent.

Soy flour has quite different functions when it is toasted. Toasted soy flour no longer contains active enzymes and has a more appealing flavor, so it can be used at higher levels than enzyme-active soy flour.

Soy flour does not contain gluten-forming proteins, but it does provide good nutrition. Soy protein is high in the essential amino acid lysine, so it can be used in breads to improve their protein quality. Soy protein has also been shown to lower the risk of heart disease. In fact, in the United States, food products that contain a certain amount (6.25 grams) of soy protein per serving and are low in fat, saturated fat, cholesterol, and salt can now make legal claims that they may reduce the risk of heart disease.

Like flaxseed, soy contains phytoestrogens. While the phytoestrogens in flaxseed are called lignans, those in soy are isoflavones. Like lignans, isoflavones are antioxidants that are thought to reduce the risk of certain cancers.

Soy flours have other uses in baked goods. They increase water absorption of doughs and reduce fat absorption in doughnuts. Soy flours sometimes function as milk and egg substitutes.

Potato

The potato is a tuber, not a cereal grain, but it can be cooked, dried, and cut into flakes or milled into flour. Potato products are valued in yeast doughs and other baked goods for the starch they contain. The starch in potato flakes, cooked potatoes, and cooked potato water is already gelatinized. Gelatinized potato starch is easily broken down by amylase into sugar and other products. This increases water absorption of doughs and improves fermentation. Breads and other baked goods containing potato products are soft and moist, and they resist staling.

QUESTIONS FOR REVIEW

1. Name four cereal grains besides wheat that are milled into flours or meals.
2. Why does rye flour absorb a large quantity of water as it forms a dough?
3. How does rye bread dough compare to wheat dough in consistency and in its ability to resist overmixing and overfermenting?
4. Which type of rye flour is patent flour, made from the heart of the rye endosperm?
5. Why does white rye flour have a shorter shelf life than white wheat flour?
6. Which of the following are whole grains: degerminated cornmeal, quick-cooking oats, pumpernickel, kasha, white rye flour, rice flour?
7. What is masa harina?
8. How are quick-cooking rolled oats processed differently than regular rolled oats? How does this affect their use in baked goods?
9. What is spelt? What is it used for?
10. What is Kamut? What is it used for?
11. Which two grains were crossed by plant breeders to produce triticale?
12. Why are spelt, emmer, and einkorn easier to grow organically than other grains?
13. List the eight major food sources of allergens.
14. What is ALA and what are its benefits? In which seed is it found?
15. What is a phytoestrogen? Name one found in flaxseed and another in soybean.
16. Why should flaxseed be ground into flour before use? How is this best done?
17. What is the main reason for adding untoasted soy flour to yeast breads?
18. What is the main reason for adding toasted soy flour to baked goods?
19. What effect does potato flour or potatoes have on the quality of baked goods? Why does it have this effect?
20. Which cereal grains contain high amounts of soluble dietary fiber?

QUESTIONS FOR DISCUSSION

1. When rye flour is made into bread, why does the bread come out denser and gummier than when wheat flour is used?
2. Which variety grains are related to wheat (triticum) and therefore have the potential for causing allergic reactions and/or celiac disease?
3. In general, how does the amount and the nutritional quality of protein in wheat flour compare to other flours?

EXERCISES AND EXPERIMENTS

1. Comparison of Grains

Use your textbook or other reference to fill out the first column of the following table. Next, use fresh samples to evaluate the color, smell, and particle size of each of the flours or related ingredients. To evaluate particle size, rub the grains or particles between your fingers and rate how fine or coarse they feel. Use this opportunity to learn how to identify different flours from their sensory characteristics alone. Add any additional comments or observations that you might have to the last column in the table.

TYPE OF FLOUR/INGREDIENT	CONTAINS GLUTEN-FORMING PROTEINS? (Y/N)	APPEARANCE	PARTICLE SIZE	COMMENTS
White rye				
Whole rye (pumpernickel)				
Corn flour				
Corn meal				
Oatmeal, old-fashioned				
Oatmeal, quick				
Rice flour				
Buckwheat flour				
Soy flour				
Quinoa				
Spelt				

2. Flour Type in Lean Yeast Dough

Many of the flours used in this experiment contain no gluten. For this reason, doughs include bread flour as an ingredient. Otherwise, this experiment is identical to one in Chapter 5.

OBJECTIVES

To demonstrate how the type of flour affects:
- Amount of water needed to make lean dough of proper consistency for bread-making
- Strength and extensibility of dough
- Crispness and extent of Maillard browning on the crust of rolls
- Crumb color and structure
- Moistness, tenderness, and height of rolls
- Overall flavor of rolls
- Overall acceptability of rolls

PRODUCTS PREPARED

Lean yeast rolls made with:
- Bread flour, 100 percent (control product)
- White rye, 40 percent and bread flour, 60 percent
- Corn flour, 40 percent and bread flour, 60 percent
- Oat flour, 40 percent and bread flour, 60 percent
- Other, if desired (pumpernickel, cornmeal, oatmeal, buckwheat, soy, spelt, etc.)

MATERIALS AND EQUIPMENT

- Proof box
- Lean dough, enough to make 12 or more rolls of each variation
- Muffin tins (2½" or 3½" size)
- Ruler

PROCEDURE

- Preheat oven according to the Lean Dough formula, which follows.
- Lightly spray or grease muffin tins with pan coating.
- Prepare lean dough using the formula given or using any basic lean bread dough formula. Prepare one batch of dough for each flour type.
- Adjust the amount of water included in the dough for each flour, as needed. Use the control dough as a guide for the consistency of the dough. Record amount of water added to each dough in Results Table 1, which follows.
- Evaluate each dough for its strength and extensibility as follows. Record results in Results Table 1.
  - To evaluate dough strength, take a small amount of dough and stretch it. If it stretches, how much does it resist stretching? This is a measure of dough strength or tenacity.
    - If it is hard to pull, the dough is *strong*.
    - If it is easy to pull, the dough is weak or *soft*.
    - If the dough falls apart and is not cohesive enough to stretch, write *does not stretch* in the appropriate column in the Results Table.
  - If it does stretch, continue stretching dough until paper thin to test extensibility.
    - If the dough stretches to form a thin film without tearing, it is *extensible* and *cohesive*.
    - If it breaks apart into pieces, it is *crumbly*.
    - If it holds together but won't form a film, it is *pasty*.
- Place dough in proof box for bulk fermentation until doubled in bulk, about 45 minutes.
- Punch down dough to distribute carbon dioxide into smaller air pockets.
- Divide dough into 3-ounce (90-gram) pieces and round into rolls.
- Place in greased muffin tins and label.
- Place rolls in proof box for about 15 minutes, or until nearly doubled in volume and light and airy to touch.
- Use an oven thermometer placed in center of oven to read oven temperature. Record the results.
- Place muffin tins in preheated oven and set timer according to formula.
- Bake rolls until control product (made with bread flour) is properly baked. You may need to bake some batches for a different amount of time because of oven variability.
- Transfer to wire racks to cool to room temperature.
- Record any potential sources of error that might make it difficult to draw proper conclusions from the experiment.
- When rolls are completely cooled, evaluate height as follows:
- Slice three rolls from each batch in half, being careful not to compress.
- Measure height of each roll by placing a ruler along the flat edge at the roll's maximum height. Record results for each of three rolls in 1/16" (10 mm) increments in Results Table 2.
- Calculate the average roll height by adding the heights of the rolls and dividing this by 3; record results in Results Table 2.
- Enter information from textbook on average protein content of each flour in Comments column of Results Table 2.

- Evaluate the sensory characteristics of completely cooled products and record evaluations in Results Table 3, which follows. Be sure to compare each in turn to the control product and evaluate the following:

  - Crust browning, from light to dark, on a scale of one to five
  - Crust texture (soft and moist, soft and dry, crisp and dry, etc.)
  - Crumb appearance (small uniform air cells, large irregular air cells, tunnels, etc.)
  - Crumb texture (tough/tender, moist/dry, spongy, crumbly, chewy, gummy, etc.)
  - Flavor (yeasty, floury, sweet, salty, sour, bitter, etc.)
  - Overall acceptability, from highly unacceptable to highly acceptable, on a scale of one to five
  - Any additional comments, as necessary.

Lean Dough

INGREDIENT	POUNDS	OUNCES	GRAMS	BAKER'S PERCENTAGE
Bread flour		11	300	60
Variety flour		7	200	40
Salt		0.25	8	1.5
Yeast, instant		0.25	8	1.5
Water, 86°F (30°C)		10	280	56
Total	1	12.5	796	159

Method of Preparation

1. Preheat oven to 425°F (220°C).
2. Set proof box to 86°F (30°C) and 85 percent relative humidity.
3. Weigh ingredients, including water, on digital or baker's scale. (*Note:* if readability of scale is 1 gram (0.02 ounce) or higher, it is better to use teaspoons for measuring yeast and salt, to minimize error. Use 2½ teaspoons for 8 grams yeast; use 1½ teaspoons for 8 grams salt.)
4. Weigh another 5 ounces (140 grams) of water (at 86°F/30°C) and set aside (this will be used for adjusting dough consistency in step 8).
5. Combine flour and salt thoroughly by sifting together three times onto parchment paper.
6. Place flour/salt mixture, yeast, and water into mixing bowl.
7. Blend on low for 1 minute; stop and scrape bowl.
8. Add additional water (from step 4) slowly and as needed, to adjust consistency. Calculate the amount of water added from the amount that remains of the 5 ounces (140 grams); record amount in Results Table 2.
9. Mix using dough hook on medium for 5 minutes, or as needed.
10. Remove dough from mixer.
11. Cover loosely with plastic and label with flour type.
12. Continue to follow the Procedure instructions.

 **SOURCES OF ERROR**

RESULTS TABLE 1 ■ EVALUATION OF WATER ABSORPTION AND DOUGH CONSISTENCY OF YEAST DOUGHS MADE WITH DIFFERENT TYPES OF FLOUR

TYPE OF FLOUR	ADDITIONAL WATER ADDED (OUNCES OR GRAMS)	DOUGH STRENGTH	DOUGH EXTENSIBILITY	COMMENTS
Bread flour, 100% (control product)				
White rye, 40%; Bread flour 60%				
Corn, 40%; Bread flour 60%				
Oat, 40%; Bread flour 60%				

RESULTS TABLE 2 ■ HEIGHT EVALUATIONS OF YEAST ROLLS MADE WITH DIFFERENT TYPES OF FLOUR

TYPE OF FLOUR	HEIGHT OF THREE ROLLS	AVERAGE HEIGHT OF ONE ROLL	COMMENTS
Bread flour, 100% (control product)			
White rye, 40%; Bread flour 60%			
Corn, 40%; Bread flour 60%			
Oat, 40%; Bread flour 60%			

RESULTS TABLE 3 ■ SENSORY CHARACTERISTICS OF YEAST ROLLS MADE WITH DIFFERENT TYPES OF FLOUR

TYPE OF FLOUR	CRUST COLOR AND TEXTURE	CRUMB APPEARANCE AND TEXTURE	OVERALL FLAVOR	OVERALL ACCEPTABILITY	COMMENTS
Bread flour, 100% (control product)					
White rye, 40%; Bread flour 60%					
Corn, 40%; Bread flour 60%					
Oat, 40%; Bread flour 60%					

CONCLUSIONS

1. Compare rolls made with white rye flour to those made with bread flour (control product): What were the main differences in appearance, flavor, and texture? Explain the main reasons for these differences.

_____

_____

2. Compare rolls made with corn flour to those made with bread flour (control product). What were the main differences in appearance, flavor, and texture? Explain the main reason for these differences.

_____

_____

3. Compare rolls made with oat flour to those made with bread flour (control product). What were the main differences in appearance, flavor, and texture? Explain the main reason for these differences.

_____

_____

4. Which rolls did you feel were most acceptable overall, and why?

_____

_____

5. Based on the results of this experiment:

a. Which flours do you think could be used at a higher level than 40 percent, to improve nutrition without sacrificing quality?

_____

_____

b. Which flours do you think should be used at a lower level than 40 percent, to make them acceptable?

_____

_____

6. Did you have any sources of error that might significantly affect the results of your experiment? If so, what could you do differently next time to minimize error?

_____

_____

7. Rank flours in water absorption from the one that required the most amount of water in preparing dough to the one that required the least amount.

_____

_____

a. Which of these differences in water absorption can be explained solely by the percentage of protein in the flour?

_____

_____

b. For those differences in water absorption that cannot be explained by the percentage of protein in the flour, how can the differences be explained?

_____

_____

8. Rank flours in dough consistency from the one that produced the strongest dough to the one that produced the weakest.

_____

_____

    a. Then rank them from the one that produced the most extensible dough to the one that produced the least extensible.

    _____

    _____

    b. How can you explain these differences?

    _____

    _____

9. Rank flours in roll height from the one that produced the tallest roll to the one that produced the shortest.

_____

_____

    a. How well did the rankings of dough strength and extensibility match the ranking for roll height?

    _____

    _____

10. Rank flours in roll toughness from the flour that produced the toughest roll to the flour that produced the most tender. How can you explain these differences in toughness?

_____

_____

11. Explain why variety breads (those made with rye, oats, corn, etc.) sold in the United States typically contain hard wheat flour in their formulas.

_____

_____

CHAPTER 7

GLUTEN

CHAPTER **OBJECTIVES**

1. Describe what is meant by the unique nature of gluten and of gluten development.

2. List and explain ways to increase or decrease gluten development.

3. Apply this information to various baked goods, including breads, cakes, cookies, and muffins.

4. Differentiate between gluten development and relaxation.

 INTRODUCTION

Gluten is one of three main structure builders in baked goods. The other two are egg proteins and starch. While all three are important, gluten, which forms and develops when flour is mixed with water, is probably the most complex of the three and can be the most difficult to control.

Small changes in a formula or mixing method can have large effects on gluten development. This is especially true with yeast doughs, which rely heavily on gluten for unbaked dough structure. Yet, it is important with any baked good to know when to increase gluten, when to decrease it, and how to make these changes.

 THE IMPORTANCE OF GLUTEN

Gluten is essential for bread-making and important in defining the final shape and volume of many baked goods. Without gluten, yeast-leavened dough is not good at retaining gases produced during fermentation. The dough does not expand well, if at all, and the expansion does not hold throughout the baking process. Cell walls tear, and the final crumb is dense.

THE UNIQUE NATURE OF GLUTEN

Flour consists primarily of a solid matrix of proteins embedded with starch granules. When water is added to flour, the proteins—namely, glutenin and gliadin, unique to the wheat endosperm—absorb water and swell. Mixing promotes the absorption of water, or hydration, by exposing new surfaces of flour particles to water. Mixing also incorporates oxygen from the air into dough, which oxidizes and strengthens gluten. Mixing helps wear down the particles, until they are small and no longer spherical. Finally, mixing distributes the particles evenly throughout the dough, so that ultimately a strong, continuous gluten network forms.

Gluten is a dynamic system, constantly changing, but overall, it becomes stronger as it is mixed. Gluten—and dough—is considered fully developed when it is strong, cohesive, and elastic. Glutenin is thought to provide the strength and cohesiveness of the gluten network, as well as its springiness or elasticity. Gliadin is thought to contribute the stretchiness or extensibility.

HELPFUL HINT

Because gluten strands align in the direction that they are mixed, be sure that dough is evenly mixed in all directions. When using a mixer, this is generally not a problem, since dough moves around the mixing bowl as it is kneaded. If kneading dough by hand, however, dough must be turned 90° with every knead. Likewise, when laminated doughs are folded or sheeted, the dough is rotated with each fold or with each run through the sheeter. Otherwise, gluten strands align in one direction. This becomes especially evident when dough is not allowed to relax before it is shaped and baked. The dough will tend to shrink in the direction that the gluten strands are oriented.

WHAT DOES GLUTEN LOOK LIKE?

Gluten cannot be seen with the naked eye, but scientists are making progress in understanding its structure. The backbone of the gluten network likely consists of the largest glutenin molecules, or subunits, aligned and tightly linked to one another. These tightly linked glutenin subunits associate more loosely, along with gliadin, into larger gluten aggregates. While the complex structure of gluten is not completely understood, portions of glutenin are thought to loop, making gluten stretchy and flexible. Gluten is further made flexible by the presence of compact, coiled gliadin molecules interspersed throughout.

At the next level of gluten structure, gluten aggregates interact to form a tangled network of larger gluten particles that loosely interact with starch granules, fats, sugars, and gums. Altogether, it does seem that gluten structure is held together by some very strong bonds and many more weak ones that break and reform easily. Many bonds break, in particular, during mixing, only to reform around the surfaces of expanding air bubbles during proofing and the early stages of baking. It is this combination of strong and weak forces breaking and reforming that contributes to the unique nature of gluten (Figure 7.1).

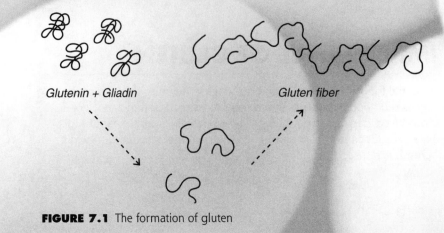

Glutenin + Gliadin   Gluten fiber

FIGURE 7.1 The formation of gluten

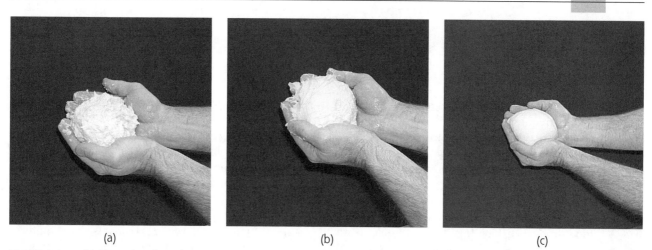

(a)   (b)   (c)

FIGURE 7.2 (a) Flour dough undermixed—out of mixer; (b) Flour dough undermixed—3 minutes mix time; (c) Flour dough optimally mixed—5.5 minutes mix time
Courtesy of USDA Agricultural Research Service and Hard Winter Wheat Quality Laboratory, Manhattan, Kansas

Fully-developed dough has a dry, silky appearance. It stretches into a thin, smooth film without breaking or tearing, yet it still retains some ability to spring back. This process of dough development is sometimes referred to as dough maturation.

Bakers typically evaluate when dough is fully developed, or matured, by performing the windowpane test. To make a windowpane, pull off a piece of dough about one inch or so in diameter. Roll it between your hands to shape into a ball, then gently pull the dough between your hands. Rotate the dough as you do this, so that you are pulling it in all directions, forming a paper-thin sheet of dough. Fully developed dough should form a thin film without tearing.

Although changes to the gluten network during mixing cannot be seen, they are reflected by what is seen in the bakeshop. That is, batters and doughs become smoother, stronger, and less lumpy as they are mixed and kneaded (Figure 7.2), and they are better able to stretch (Figure 7.3) and trap solid particles, liquids, and gases as they expand.

When batters and doughs are baked, most of the moisture evaporates or is absorbed by gelatinizing starch granules. With this loss of moisture and in the presence of heat, gluten coagulates into a firm and rigid yet porous structure that holds its shape. While not unique to gluten (egg proteins, when heated, also coagulate into a firm, rigid structure), this is nonetheless an important feature of gluten.

DETERMINING GLUTEN REQUIREMENTS

It is tempting to generalize and say that, for bread, the more gluten the better, and for pastries, the less gluten the better. But this is oversimplifying the matter. Bread dough can have too much gluten. When it does, it does not stretch easily and bounces back too quickly or too much. Doughs that are tight and bouncy are sometimes described as *bucky*, and they can be difficult to work with. Breads made from these doughs tend to be tough and chewy, have low volume because they cannot stretch, and develop soft and thin crusts. Just as bread can have too much gluten, pastries can have too little. Piecrusts with too little gluten break and crumble easily, cakes collapse, and baking powder biscuits slump.

Still, yeast-raised baked goods require the most gluten of all bakeshop products. Gluten is so important to bread that when bread bakers speak

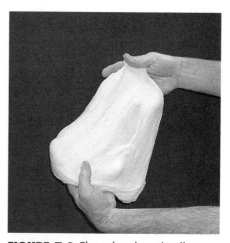

FIGURE 7.3 Flour dough optimally mixed, in stretched windowpane
Courtesy of USDA Agricultural Research Service and Hard Winter Wheat Quality Laboratory, Manhattan, Kansas

HOW UNIQUE IS GLUTEN?

Gluten's makeup and structure are responsible for its unique nature, which scientists describe as viscoelastic. Viscoelasticity is the ability of a material to stretch and easily change shape—like a thick or viscous liquid—without breaking or tearing, and to partly bounce back to its original shape—like an elastic or rubber band. Viscoelastic products can be thought of as part liquid, part solid. Few food products exhibit this dual nature as clearly as gluten. Consider the following products that are not viscoelastic.

Corn syrup is not viscoelastic because it does not have elasticity or rubberiness. That is, corn syrup cannot bounce back to its original shape once it flows. Corn syrup is also not strong and solid enough to capture and hold expanding gases.

Shortening is not viscoelastic because it cannot stretch or flow like a liquid. While it is soft enough to change shape yet solid enough to hold its shape, shortening cannot stretch and hold expanding gases.

Peanut brittle is not viscoelastic because it is too firm and rigid. While it holds its shape quite nicely, peanut brittle will not stretch or change shape easily. If gases were able to expand at all in peanut brittle, the brittle would not expand. Instead, it would crack and shatter from the buildup of pressure.

of flour quality, they are generally referring to the amount and quality of gluten that forms from the flour. Bread dough made from high-quality flour is best at holding gases produced during fermentation and oven spring. The baked bread typically has large loaf volume and a fine crumb.

Of common breads, hearth breads—those that are baked directly on sheet pans or baking stones—usually require the most gluten, if high volume is desired. Without sufficient gluten—and without pans—to hold them in shape, hearth breads flatten under their own weight. Bagels, with their fine crumb and chewy texture, also have high gluten requirements. In contrast, rustic artisan breads, those with a large, open grain and crisp crusts, require much less gluten. With less gluten, the dough breaks and tears more readily, forming the desired large air pockets characteristic of this type of product.

IS HIGH-QUALITY FLOUR ALWAYS BEST?

Flour quality should be judged by its intended use. Often, however, certain flours, typically those high in gluten-forming proteins, are described as high quality. While bread bakers rightfully describe flour as high quality when it forms strong, cohesive gluten, this does not mean that so-called high-quality flour is best for all baked goods, or even for all breads. Pastry chefs would argue that a high-quality flour allows cookies to spread and cakes to rise high and have a fine, tender crumb. Pastry flour that is of high quality typically is low in gluten, has a very fine granulation, is relatively low in pentosans and other gums, and has few damaged starch granules.

Bread bakers also are not necessarily looking for the highest protein content in their flour. To achieve a soft, open crumb in their products, artisan bread bakers typically use flour with a lower amount of gluten than what is in traditional bread or high-gluten flours.

Nor is high-quality flour particularly high in nutritional quality, even when enriched. Because it is white flour, it contains no bran or germ particles. This means that it is not a good source of dietary fiber. It also means that it will be low in lysine, an essential amino acid, and, therefore, its protein will not be nutritionally complete. In contrast, wheat germ in whole wheat flour contains protein that is more nutritious, but of course, wheat germ proteins do not form gluten.

While it is easy to say that pastries require less gluten than breads do, it is often difficult to compare the gluten requirements of various pastries, since they are complex mixtures of tougheners and tenderizers, moisteners and driers. It is probably safe to say, however, that products containing significant amounts of other structure builders require the least amount of gluten for their structure. Liquid shortening cakes, which rely on the soft structure of gelatinized starch, and sponge cakes, with their high egg content, both require very little gluten.

CONTROLLING GLUTEN DEVELOPMENT

There are three main ways that gluten is developed during bread-making. One way is by mixing and kneading, sometimes called mechanical dough development. A second way is by chemical dough development, through the use of ascorbic acid and other maturing agents that strengthen. Finally, gluten is developed over time during bulk fermentation and final proof.

While these are the main ways that gluten is developed, there are many more ways to control gluten development, whether to increase it so that dough is stronger and more cohesive, or alternatively, to decrease it so that dough is softer and more extensible. The following list includes the most common ingredients or processes that affect gluten development. Many were introduced in Chapters 5 and 6. They are included again here to present a comprehensive list that can be helpful with problem solving in the bakeshop.

- Type of flour
- Amount of water
- Water hardness
- Water pH
- Mixing and kneading
- Batter and dough temperature
- Fermentation
- Maturing agents and dough conditioners
- Reducing agents
- Enzymes
- Tenderizers and softeners
- Salt
- Other structure builders
- Milk
- Fiber, bran, fruit pieces, spices, and the like

Some of these items, such as dough conditioners and heat-treated milk, apply exclusively to yeast-raised doughs. Others apply to all baked goods. Even so, most items on the list tend to have their greatest effect on baked goods that rely heavily on gluten, and not on eggs and starch, for structure.

Besides yeast doughs, pie pastry relies heavily on gluten for structure. Expect pie pastry quality to suffer noticeably when too much or too little gluten develops, and expect it to be affected by many items on the list.

In contrast, high-ratio liquid shortening cakes and other baked goods made from cake flour contain very little gluten to begin with. Only those items on the list—such as fats, sugars, and water pH—that also affect other structure builders like eggs and starch will have a large effect on the structure of liquid shortening cakes.

Type of Flour

One way to control gluten development is through proper flour selection. For example, the *type of grain* is an extremely important consideration because wheat flour is the only common grain with the potential for forming a good amount of high-quality gluten. Rye flour has about the same amount of protein as wheat, but recall that very little rye protein forms gluten. Any gluten that forms from rye flour is of such poor quality that, except for certain specialty rustic loaves, most formulas for rye bread in North America contain added wheat flour. Other flours, such as oat, corn, buckwheat, and soy, do not form gluten at all. Baked goods made from these flours do not have good gas-retaining or structure-building properties and are dense and compact if no wheat flour is added.

Different *varieties of wheat* vary in the amount and quality of gluten that form from them. Recall from Chapter 5 that currently thousands of different varieties of wheat are grown throughout the world, but that they are generally classified as either soft wheats or hard wheats. Soft wheats are low in protein, and the protein quality is typically poor (from the standpoint of gluten development), meaning that there is a lower amount of glutenin for the amount of gliadin, and the glutenin subunits tend to be smaller in size. Soft wheat flours form gluten that is weak and tears easily.

Hard wheats are high in protein, contain a higher percentage of glutenin for the amount of gliadin, and the glutenin subunits tend to be large in size. Strong wheat flours form gluten that is strong, cohesive, and elastic. While the quality of protein in flour depends mostly on which variety of wheat is grown, the amount of protein is highly dependent on environmental conditions, such as climate, soil quality, and the amount of fertilizer applied.

Whole wheat flour is typically the same or higher in protein than white flour. Yet, this does not translate into more gluten development. Recall that the bran and germ interfere with gluten development, and that the proteins from these components do not form gluten. Glutenin and gliadin are found exclusively in the endosperm.

WHAT IS AN ALVEOGRAPH?

There are several tests used by cereal chemists, grain millers, and bakeries to evaluate the quality of wheat flour. One test, which is especially popular in Europe, is run on an instrument called the Chopin alveograph. The alveograph blows air into dough made from flour, water, and salt, forming an expanding bubble. This mimics the fermentation process, where gas cells expand in a similar manner.

Three values from this test are particularly useful. First is a measure of dough strength. This is designated as W, and is especially important in understanding dough behavior during proofing and baking. Dough with a W value that is too high will be difficult to shape because it will be bucky and bounce back easily. Dough with a too-low W will stretch easily, but it won't hold its shape during proofing and baking.

A second value measured on the alveograph is often designated as P, and it is called dough tenacity. *Dough tenacity* is a measure of the pressure reached as the bubble is inflated. Dough with a high tenacity will have a higher water absorption capacity than dough with a low tenacity. Not surprisingly, bread flour typically has a higher P value than pastry flour.

A third value, L, represents dough extensibility. Dough extensibility is a measure of the extent that a dough bubble stretches before it breaks. The greater the L value, the better the dough's ability to rise during fermentation.

Often, the P and L value are expressed as a ratio, which provides a combined index of gluten behavior. Notice how the alveograph measures similar characteristics that bakers evaluate when they produce a windowpane from developed dough.

Amount of Water

Recall that gluten is not actually present in flour itself. Glutenin and gliadin, which are present in flour, form a gluten network as they hydrate and swell with up to two times their weight in water.

Water hydration is absolutely essential for gluten development. In fact, one way to control gluten development is by adjusting the amount of water in a formula. For example, gluten in pie and biscuit doughs is starved for water, so it develops poorly, and the product remains tender. If a small amount of water is added to gluten that is not fully hydrated, more gluten develops and the dough toughens. This will not happen with most cake batters. Cake batter usually contains excess water. Since there is enough water to fully hydrate gluten, adding more water to most cake batters does not increase gluten development. Instead, adding more water dilutes out proteins, weakening gluten.

Water is sometimes added as an ingredient in its own right. More often, however, water is added as a part of other liquids or other ingredients, such as milk or eggs. Liquid oil, however, contains no water at all, and it does not contribute to gluten development. In fact, oil, being a tenderizer, interferes with gluten development.

Water Hardness

Water hardness is a measure of the amount of minerals, like calcium and magnesium, in water. Hard water is high in minerals, while soft water is low in minerals. If you ever see hard white mineral deposits, called scale, on equipment surfaces, you know the water is hard.

Because minerals strengthen gluten, yeast doughs prepared from hard water are often too strong and elastic. They do not stretch when gases expand, or they stretch only to quickly bounce back. Doughs prepared from soft water are often too soft, slack, and sticky. Ideally, water for bread baking is neither too hard nor too soft.

WHEN SHOULD "TOO MUCH" WATER BE ADDED TO BREAD DOUGH?

If you've ever wondered how coarse-grained rustic breads get their appealing large, irregular holes, it helps to understand that they form when gluten is weak and tears relatively easily. Artisan bakers use several approaches to achieve this. First, they use flour with a relatively low protein content. Second, they may add excess water, so that the amount of water is sometimes over 70 percent (baker's percentage), compared with 50–60 percent for regular lean dough. This produces a well-hydrated dough, one that is a cross between batter and dough. Although messy to work with, superhydrated doughs can produce fine artisan breads. Not only is the grain coarsened by the additional water, but a longer bake time is needed to dry out the bread, resulting in a thicker, crispy crust. (See Photo 7.1.)

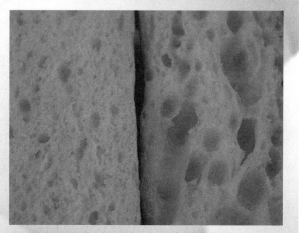

PHOTO 7.1 The baguette on left is made from regular lean dough, and the baguette on the right from a well-hydrated lean dough.
Photo by Aaron Seyfarth

WHY ARE SOME WATERS HARD AND SOME SOFT?

Water becomes hard as it picks up minerals from contact with the earth. Ground water, which percolates through soil on its way to water wells, is usually harder than surface water from lakes and reservoirs. Since the earth varies in composition from one location to another, water hardness also varies. For example, parts of Florida, Texas, and the Southwest have hard water, while most of New England's water is soft. (See Figure 7.4.)

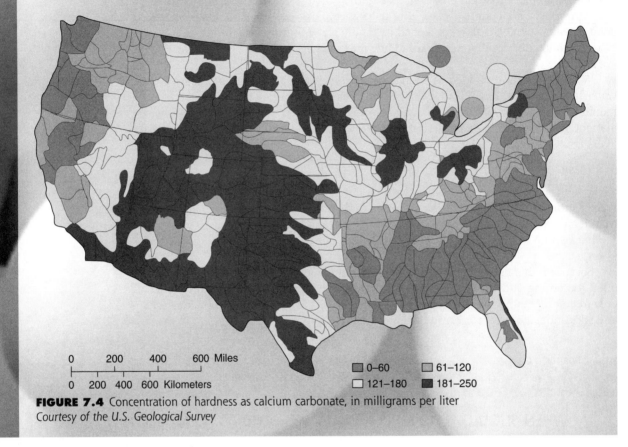

| 0 | 200 | 400 | 600 Miles |
| 0 | 200 | 400 | 600 Kilometers |

■ 0–60   ☐ 61–120
☐ 121–180   ■ 181–250

FIGURE 7.4 Concentration of hardness as calcium carbonate, in milligrams per liter
Courtesy of the U.S. Geological Survey

If water is either too hard or too soft, there are several ways to compensate. First, there are dough conditioners designed specifically for soft water and others designed for hard water. Dough conditioners for soft water contain calcium salts, such as calcium sulfate, to increase the mineral content. Dough conditioners for hard water contain acids that prevent minerals from interacting with gluten.

Probably a more common solution with hard water is to treat all incoming water with a water softener system. Water softeners remove calcium and magnesium from the water. Not only does this prevent the effects of minerals on gluten, it also eliminates damage to equipment from scale buildup. Water that is treated with a water softener, however, is high in sodium, which in some people can contribute to high blood pressure.

Water pH

Just as water hardness is a measure of the amount of minerals, pH is a measure of the acidity or alkalinity of water. The pH scale (see Figure 7.5) runs from 0 to 14. At pH 7, water is neutral—neither acidic nor alkaline (basic). If acid is present, pH falls below 7. If base or alkali is present, it rises above 7. Water supplies rarely have a neutral pH. Areas of North America plagued by acid rain—Canada and the United States along the Atlantic coast, for example—typically have water with a low pH.

The ideal pH for maximum gluten development is slightly acidic, at a pH of about 5–6. This means that adding acid so that the pH falls below 5, or adding alkali so it rises above 6, will reduce gluten strength. It is easy to adjust pH by adding acids or alkalis, and bakers and pastry chefs do this all the time. Examples of acids commonly added to baked goods include cream of tartar, fruits and fruit juice, cultured dairy products, and vinegar. For example, vinegar or another acid is added to strudel dough to dissolve gluten and reduce its strength, so that the dough is more extensible and easier to stretch without tearing. An example of an alkali is baking soda. Adding a small amount of baking soda to cookie dough provides for a porous, open and more tender crumb.

Although water hardness and water pH are completely different concepts, they can influence each other. For example, certain minerals that increase water hardness also increase pH. Some acids that decrease pH also decrease the effects of water hardness. Just the same, it is helpful to keep these two concepts—water hardness and water pH—separate in your mind.

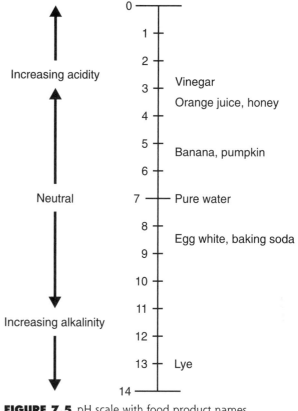

FIGURE 7.5 pH scale with food product names

Mixing and Kneading

Besides water, gluten requires mixing and kneading for development. However, too much mixing can develop too much gluten. For all products except yeast-raised doughs, over-mixing refers to toughening from too much gluten. Products vary in their

CONTROLLING SPREAD IN COOKIES—pH

Cookie dough spreads across a cookie sheet if the dough is liquid enough to spread. When most cookie doughs heat up in the oven, their consistency becomes more liquid and the dough will spread. At a certain temperature, heat sets the gluten and egg proteins so that the dough thickens and stops spreading.

Whether this is desirable or not depends on what kind of cookie you wish to bake, but often some spread is desirable. There are many ways to increase cookie spread. One way is to add a small amount of baking soda—as little as 0.25 to 0.5 ounce (5 to 15 grams) for 10 pounds (4.5 kilograms) of cookie dough. This increases pH of the dough, and it raises the set temperature of the gluten and egg proteins. With more free water and less structure for a longer time, cookies that contain baking soda spread more and have a coarser, more porous crumb. Since moisture evaporates from a porous crumb more easily, baking soda often provides for a crisper crumb, as well.

Measure baking soda carefully. Baking soda increases browning significantly, and if used at too high a level, it leaves a distinct salty-chemical off flavor. Too much baking soda also causes eggs in baked goods to turn grayish green.

When working at high altitudes, omit baking soda from cookie dough. The lower air pressure at high altitudes already encourages spread.

WHY DO TUNNELS FORM IN OVERMIXED MUFFINS?

Traditional muffin batter is relatively low in tenderizing fats and sugars. To keep them from toughening, traditional muffins are mixed just long enough to dampen flour. Even the slightest amount of overmixing produces tough muffins pocked with tunnels. Tunnels are a defect that occurs when overmixing develops too much gluten in muffins. When overmixed batter is baked, evaporating gases have difficulty escaping from the product. Thick, gluten-reinforced cell walls prevent muffins from slowly letting off steam. Instead, gases build up, until finally enough pressure forces them to escape upward, much as volcanoes erupt. On their way out, the gases bore tunnels through the batter, marking their escape route.

One way to prevent this toughening and tunneling, of course, is to not overmix. Another way is to use soft flour and to add tenderizers to the formula, making it difficult to overmix. Today, many muffin batters are made with cake or pastry flour and contain high amounts of tenderizing fats and sugar. While this solves the tunnel problem, today's muffins often resemble tender cupcakes more than they do the coarse-grained, rustic muffins of yesterday.

susceptibility to overmixing. Baking powder biscuits, for example, require a certain amount of light mixing or kneading to develop some gluten. Too little mixing, and biscuits slump during baking from a lack of structure. Too much and they hold their shape but are tough. The right amount of mixing allows biscuits to remain tender yet still hold their shape.

It is hard to imagine certain batters developing much, if any, gluten from mixing. Consider high-ratio liquid shortening cakes made with cake flour. Despite several minutes of mixing, the use of cake flour and of a high amount of water and tenderizers practically eliminates any concern over gluten development. High-ratio liquid shortening cakes should still be mixed no longer than recommended, however. They rely on proper mixing for adequate air incorporation and leavening.

With yeast-raised doughs, adequate mixing is required to disperse glutenin particles well enough so that a strong continuous network of gluten forms, one that can trap and hold gases. Undermixed doughs are sticky and lack smoothness, and when baked, the bread has low volume and a coarse crumb from tearing.

The longer or more vigorously bread doughs are mixed, the more mechanical dough development takes place, at least up to a point. If dough is mixed beyond that point, the gluten network breaks down. This is sometimes called the letdown stage of mixing, and it is what is meant by overmixed yeast dough. The dough becomes soft and sticky, it tears into stringy pieces when stretched and it no longer retains water or gas. Bread made from overmixed dough suffers from poor loaf volume and a coarse crumb. Doughs most susceptible to overmixing are those that do not develop strong gluten to begin with. Doughs made from rye flour, low-quality wheat flours, or those high in sugar and fat are least resistant to overmixing.

Knowing when yeast dough is adequately mixed is an art as well as a science, since many factors affect the amount of mixing needed for proper dough development. First, different flours require different mixing times, with hard flours that are high in glutenin tolerating, even requiring, longer mix times than flours that are soft. Rye flour, which contains little glutenin, is very easily overmixed. Different formulas have different mixing requirements. Rich yeast doughs require less mixing to fully develop and are highly susceptible to over-mixing. A mixer's design and speed must be considered, as well. Finally, dough that will undergo a long bulk fermentation should be mixed for less time, since fermentation also contributes to dough development. The knowledge that is required to properly mix yeast dough comes from both proper training and practical experience.

Batter and Dough Temperature

Batter and dough temperature is also a factor in controlling gluten development. Dough temperature is often controlled through the temperature of ingredients, especially water and other liquids. The warmer the temperature, the faster flour particles hydrate and proteins oxidize. Faster hydration and oxidation means faster gluten development and dough maturation.

Controlling temperature has other benefits besides controlling gluten development. In yeast-raised doughs, proper dough temperature is important for controlling yeast fermentation, as well as for controlling gluten development. The ideal dough temperature for fermentation is typically somewhere between 70°–80°F (21°–27°C), although this varies from one formula to the next. If dough temperatures are too high, fermentation occurs too rapidly and flavor suffers.

In products such as pie pastry dough, the use of cold water not only minimizes gluten development, it also prevents solid fat in the dough from melting. Fat must remain solid in pie pastry dough if the pie is to be flaky.

Fermentation

Fermentation involves allowing yeast in dough to convert sugars into carbon dioxide. It typically occurs in two separate stages—bulk fermentation and final proofing—and can take several hours to complete. Besides the need for the production of leavening gases and for the development of flavor, fermentation strengthens gluten, improving its cohesiveness and elasticity. In other words, fermentation contributes to dough maturation.

It is the action of expanding air bubbles pushing on gluten that helps strengthen it. At the same time, bonds that were broken during mixing slowly reform around these expanding bubbles, so that bread ultimately develops higher volume and a finer crumb.

Just as too much mixing tears gluten strands and weakens gluten strength and elasticity, so does too much fermentation. The end result of overfermented dough is similar to overmixed dough—softness, stickiness, and a loss of gas-retaining ability.

Maturing Agents and Dough Conditioners

Recall that maturing agents are sometimes added to flour to affect baking qualities. Maturing agents do this partly or exclusively through their effects on gluten. Some maturing agents, primarily chlorine gas, weaken gluten (don't forget that chlorine also whitens carotenoids and changes starch so that it absorbs more water). Others, such as ascorbic acid and potassium bromate, strengthen gluten.

The main role of dough conditioners is to increase gluten strength, contributing to *chemical dough development.* This is especially important when dough undergoes extreme conditions, as when it is run through high-speed commercial equipment. Recall from Chapter 5 that dough conditioners contain a mix of ingredients. The main ingredients in dough conditioners are maturing agents that strengthen, but other ingredients important for strengthening gluten include emulsifiers and enzymes, as well as salts and acids that adjust water hardness and pH. The amount of dough conditioner to use varies with the brand, but it is typically 0.2–0.5 percent of the weight of the flour.

Reducing Agents

Reducing agents have the opposite effect of maturing agents that strengthen. While maturing agents like ascorbic acid oxidize gluten-forming proteins, allowing them to form more bonds that hold gluten together more strongly, reducing agents alter

WHAT IS NO-TIME DOUGH?

No-time dough is yeast-raised dough that does not undergo bulk fermentation. Instead, the dough undergoes a simple 10- or 15-minute bench rest before being divided. This saves an hour or sometimes several hours of time, depending on the type of bread produced. But, how can an important step like bulk fermentation be eliminated?

Gluten develops and matures through mixing, through fermentation, and through the use of maturing agents such as ascorbic acid. If dough undergoes mechanical dough development by intensive high-speed mixing, or if it undergoes chemical dough development through the use of chemical maturing agents and dough conditioners, less fermentation time is needed for the dough to properly mature.

While intensive high-speed mixing requires special equipment, any bakeshop can use chemical maturing agents and dough conditioners to shorten or eliminate bulk fermentation. Because no-time doughs undergo a final proof, carbon dioxide needed for proper leavening is not sacrificed, despite the elimination of the bulk fermentation step.

Before trying no-time doughs, however, the baker should consider the pros and cons. Certainly, no-time doughs take less time to prepare, and time is money. And, while there is the added cost of the chemicals, this is somewhat offset by a higher amount of water absorbed by the doughs. However, breads develop a good amount of flavor during bulk fermentation. When this step is eliminated, bread may lack the subtle flavors that are the pride of the baker.

gluten-forming proteins so that they form fewer bonds and hold together more weakly. The most common reducing agent used by large-scale commercial bakeries is L-cysteine. L-cysteine is an amino acid naturally found in proteins throughout our bodies. It is a common ingredient in dough conditioners. L-cysteine and other reducing agents are sometimes added to dough so that the dough mixes faster and more easily and generates less frictional heat. The softening and slackening effect of the reducing agent is later counteracted with maturing agents like potassium bromate, which help rebuild gluten structure during proofing and baking, when structure is needed most.

Probably the most potent reducing agent is not necessarily added intentionally. This reducing agent is called glutathione. Glutathione is a fragment of a protein that is found in fluid milk and many milk products; in active dry yeast and other yeast products that contain dead yeast cells; and in wheat germ.

When active dry yeast is used improperly, that is, when water or dough temperature is low, glutathione is released into dough and can weaken it. For this reason, professional bakers seldom use active dry yeast. Most prefer compressed or instant yeast, which do not release glutathione.

Interestingly, so-called no leavening yeast is sold that intentionally contains a high amount of glutathione. This is sometimes used in large-scale bakeries for pizza and tortilla production, so that doughs will stretch more easily and not shrink when baked.

Glutathione is also found in wheat germ. Recall that weaker gluten develops from whole wheat flour than from white flour. One reason for this is the glutathione in wheat germ. Wheat germ can be purchased raw or toasted, however. Toasted wheat germ will not have the same high glutathione activity as raw wheat germ.

Enzyme Activity

Recall that amylase is an enzyme that breaks down starches. Likewise, proteases are enzymes that break down proteins, such as gelatin and gluten. When gluten is broken down into smaller pieces by a protease, it becomes softer and more extensible. Like reducing agents, proteases are sometimes added to dough by large-scale commercial bakeries so that the dough mixes faster and more easily.

More often, however, protease enzymes are not added by the baker, but they are naturally present in flours. Flours that have been malted, for example, contain many enzymes, including protease. Rye flour contains more protease activity than wheat flour, and whole grains contain more than white flour, because whole grains include protease-rich bran. Because clear flour contains the inner bran layer, clear flour is higher in protease activity than patent flour.

Autolysed dough—that is, yeast dough that undergoes a rest period after a brief, slow mixing—experiences a certain amount of protease activity. This is especially true if salt is withheld at this stage, since salt slows enzyme activity.

Protease activity can be especially high in a sourdough. Sourdoughs, as the name suggests, are acidic and have a low pH, and proteases are particularly active at low pH. Protease activity is also high in a poolish or sponge, which is a so-called preferment made by adding a small amount of yeast to flour and water well before bread dough is mixed. While enzyme activity can take place in any preferment, a poolish is made of equal parts flour and water, so it is watery, and that allows for a high amount of enzyme activity. When salt is added to a preferment, enzyme activity is slowed, but most preferments do not contain salt.

Protease activity weakens gluten but also makes it more extensible. That is, bread dough made with a poolish or one that has been autolysed will stretch easily but will also be sticky and tear more easily. This provides volume and a large, open crumb. The breakdown of protein from protease activity also releases amino acids that are valuable for the flavor of bread.

Tenderizers and Softeners

Some tenderizers, such as *fats, oils,* and certain *emulsifiers*, work by coating gluten strands (and other structure builders). This reduces gluten development in at least one way. Proteins coated with fat cannot absorb water and properly hydrate. Unless they hydrate, glutenin and gliadin proteins cannot adequately bond and form a large gluten network. Short gluten strands form instead, and the product is tenderized. The use of the term *shortening* to mean *fat* is derived from this ability of fats to shorten gluten strands.

Besides fat, another important tenderizer in baked goods is sugar. Sugars tenderize by interacting with both water and gluten proteins, keeping the gluten proteins from properly hydrating and interacting. Rich sweet doughs, such as brioche, contain large amounts of both fat and sugar. If flour containing too little gluten is used in these doughs, they could collapse and lose volume during proofing or the early stages of baking.

Leavening gases also tenderize baked goods through their action on gluten strands. As leavening gases expand during baking, they stretch gluten strands—and egg proteins. Stretched gluten strands form thin, weaker cell walls that are easily broken. With the right amount of leavening gases, baked goods are weak enough to be pleasantly tender, yet strong enough to keep from collapsing.

Salt

Salt is added to bread dough at approximately 1.5–2 percent or so of the weight of flour. Salt has several functions in baked goods. It modifies flavor, increases crust color, and controls the rate of yeast fermentation and of enzyme activity. This is especially important with dough containing rye flour, since rye flour is relatively high in enzyme activity and in the rate that it ferments. Salt also strengthens gluten, improving its cohesiveness and making it less sticky. This means that salt prevents

CAN OVERWORKING PIE PASTRY DOUGH PRODUCE A TENDER CRUST?

The first stage in making pie pastry dough is to cut fat into the dry ingredients. For the flakiest pie crust, fat chunks should be kept fairly large, about the size of a hazelnut. If fat is worked into the flour until it is the size of cornmeal, will too much gluten develop?

Before answering this question, recall that two things—water and mixing—are needed for gluten to develop. As long as water is not present, gluten cannot form and there is no risk that dough will toughen, no matter how much mixing occurs. Instead, overmixing fat into flour distributes the fat more completely, thoroughly coating flour particles. The result is less water absorption, less gluten development, and more tenderness. In fact, working the fat into flour is one way to produce a tender, mealy pie crust. It is only after water is added to pie crust dough that mixing develops gluten and toughening.

DOES SALT BLEACH FLOUR?

When bread is made without salt, the crumb takes on an off-white cast. At first glance, it appears that salt bleaches flour, much as chlorine and benzoyl peroxide do. However, this is not the case. Instead, salt acts by strengthening gluten, preventing it from tearing when it stretches from the pressure of expanding gases. The result is a fine, even crumb. Light bounces off a fine crumb more evenly than it does off a coarser crumb. This makes the bread appear whiter, even when the flour has the same amount of carotenoids—the pigments that color flour—as the coarser, off-white bread.

excessive tearing when gluten stretches, so bread is easier to handle and has better volume and a finer crumb.

Because salt noticeably strengthens gluten, bread bakers sometimes delay the addition of salt to dough made from strong flour, adding it late in the mixing process. The dough mixes faster and cooler, because there is less resistance and frictional heat generated during mixing. Once salt is added, the dough tightens and is more difficult to stretch, but it will stretch further without tearing.

Other Structure Builders

Starches, including corn, rice, and potato starches, sometimes partially replace flour in cakes, cookies, and pastries. For example, genoise sponge cake is often made with up to half the flour replaced with cornstarch, for tenderness. This works best in products with a limited amount of water. With limited water, only a limited amount of starch gelatinizes. Unlike gelatinized starch, which contributes structure to baked goods, ungelatinized starch granules act as inert fillers that interfere with gluten forming its network. With today's soft cake flour, however, it is probably unnecessary to use starch to tenderize baked goods, except in special circumstances.

Eggs are also structure builders. Even with the fat in egg yolks, adding eggs to baked goods provides more structure once the eggs coagulate. But raw eggs in bread dough interfere with gluten development during mixing and fermentation. The final baked bread might be tougher than if eggs were not added, but the added toughening is due to coagulated eggs, not gluten.

Milk

Fluid milk, above all else, is a source of water. In fact, it is primarily water—about 85–89 percent water. This means that anytime milk is added to baked goods, water, which is necessary for gluten development, is also being added.

Fluid milk also contains glutathione, the reducing agent that softens dough. This becomes important in the production of yeast-raised baked goods, where the effects become noticeable during fermentation. If glutathione is not first destroyed, bread dough softens and becomes slack, and oven spring decreases. The result is lower loaf volume and coarser texture.

Heat destroys glutathione. Pasteurization, a heat process applied to essentially all milk sold in North America, is not enough heat to inactivate it. This is why bakers typically scald fluid milk before using it in yeast doughs. To scald milk, heat it in a saucepan until it reaches a simmer (180°F; 82°C), then cool.

Likewise, not all dry milk solids (DMS) have been exposed to sufficient heat to destroy the protein. Only DMS labeled as high-heat have been heated sufficiently. The milk used in high-heat DMS has been held at 190°F (88°C) for 30 minutes prior to drying. High-heat DMS are the only DMS used in yeast doughs. They are also perfectly acceptable for use in other baked goods.

Fiber, Bran, Fruit Pieces, Spices, and the Like

Any particle that physically gets in the way of the forming gluten strands will decrease gluten development. Surprisingly, even spice particles interfere with gluten formation.

DOUGH RELAXATION

To rest or relax dough means to allow it to sit awhile. For example, bread dough requires a short bench rest before it is shaped. Laminated doughs, including croissants, Danish, and puff pastry doughs, usually rest in the refrigerator between folds. This rest period is important. It makes it easier to shape, roll, and fold the dough properly.

Bread, croissant, and Danish doughs need to rest because the gluten is well developed, meaning that it is strong and elastic. Elasticity—the tendency of dough to shorten up or bounce back—can be a problem when dough is rolled and shaped. The further dough is stretched and the more it is worked, the more stressed it is. By relaxing dough once it has been worked, gluten strands have a chance to adjust to the new length or shape. Bread dough will continue to relax for up to 45 minutes or longer after mixing, depending on the dough. Pastry doughs relax in less time. Once dough has relaxed, it is easier to continue shaping, and it will shrink less upon baking.

Do not confuse dough relaxation with yeast dough bulk fermentation or proofing. During fermentation and proofing, yeast continues to produce carbon dioxide gas, slowly stretching gluten strands. The stretching helps to further develop the gluten and mature the dough. During dough relaxation, gluten strands are not necessarily stretched. The dough rests, and gluten strands adjust to a new length or shape.

Pie pastry dough benefits from a rest period after mixing, to make it easier to roll and shape. Some pastry chefs also relax rolled and shaped pie dough before baking, so it will not shrink during baking. As with laminated doughs, pie pastry dough is usually chilled during the rest period. Chilling solidifies fat, allowing for flakier pastry.

There is yet a third reason to allow pie pastry dough to rest for at least several hours before use. Recall that pie dough contains very little water, to keep gluten development at a minimum. If water is not mixed in properly, the dough may become crumbly in some spots and soggy in others. On the other hand, if dough is mixed thoroughly to

MORE ON DOUGH RELAXATION

To understand why worked dough needs a relaxation period, it helps to view gluten at the molecular level. Recall from earlier in this chapter that gluten consists of a three-dimensional tangled network held together with a mix of both strong and weak bonds. As dough is rolled and shaped, weak bonds are apt to break, allowing particles to slide past one another. Once rolling and shaping stops, new bonds form and the dough takes on a new shape.

When dough is stretched and pulled quickly, it doesn't stretch as far as when it is stretched and pulled more slowly. Instead, the dough resists stretching and is apt to tear. If the dough is pulled slowly, it has time to make small adjustments along the way. It is as if the gluten strands in the dough are acting like a bowl of noodles. If you try to pull on one noodle in the bowl quickly, it will likely break. If instead you pull on it slowly and evenly, it will wiggle its way out without breaking.

assure even distribution of water, gluten overdevelops. If instead dough rests for several hours, water distributes itself evenly throughout the dough. This is important in pie pastry doughs, which are barely mixed and contain little water. It is also important when working with grains having large particles, such as durum semolina.

In summary, the main thing that happens as doughs relax is that gluten strands have time to adjust to their new length or shape. This makes them easier to roll and shape and less likely to shrink during baking. Some doughs rest to allow time for gluten and starch to properly absorb water. Finally, when refrigerated during resting, the fats in dough harden, for better lamination and flakiness.

QUESTIONS FOR REVIEW

1. Describe the three main characteristics of good-quality gluten.

2. What is the difference between extensibility and elasticity? Which protein, glutenin or gliadin, is primarily responsible for each?

3. What does the bread baker mean by high-quality flour?

4. Will a small increase in the amount of water added to pie pastry dough be likely to increase or decrease gluten development? Explain your answer.

5. Will a small increase in the amount of water added to superhydrated bread dough be likely to increase or decrease gluten development? Explain your answer.

6. How would you describe the difference between water hardness and water pH? How does each affect gluten development?

7. Will a small amount of baking soda added to cookie dough increase or decrease cookie spread? Why might baking soda have this effect?

8. What is meant by overmixed baking powder biscuit dough? What is meant by overmixed bread dough?

9. What is one cause of tunnels in muffins? How can using a formula high in sugar and fat reduce the likelihood that tunnels will form?

10. What is meant by dough maturation?

11. How does dough temperature affect gluten development? What else does dough temperature affect in pie pastry doughs? In bread doughs?

12. What three processes occur during dough fermentation? Which of these three can also be accomplished by intensive high-speed mixing or by chemical maturing agents?

13. What is meant by no-time dough? What is the main advantage of no-time dough? What is the main disadvantage?

14. What is meant by a reducing agent?

15. What is glutathione and where is it found?

16. What are proteases and how do they affect gluten?

17. Which of the following in each pair is likely to have more protease activity: rye flour or wheat flour; white flour or whole wheat flour; thin preferment with a high amount of water, or a heavier preferment with a lower amount of water?

18. Why will pie pastry dough bake up more tender when the fat is well worked into the flour (before water is added) than when it is left in larger chunks?

19. How does salt affect gluten in yeast-raised doughs?

20. Why is it that bread made with salt has a whiter crumb than bread made without salt?

21. Why is fluid milk usually scalded before it is used in yeast-raised doughs?

22. What is meant by high-heat DMS? What is it used for?

23. You are shaping pizza dough, but it shrinks before you have a chance to add toppings and bake. What should you do?

24. What is the difference between gluten development and gluten relaxation?

25. What are the three reasons why pie pastry dough might be chilled and allowed to rest several hours or overnight?

QUESTIONS FOR DISCUSSION

1. Since high-ratio liquid shortening cakes are made with cake flour that contains very little gluten, how is it that the amount of fat and sugar in liquid shortening cakes can have a large effect on the tenderness of these cakes?

2. Explain why developing the maximum amount of gluten is not necessarily desirable in bread baking.

3. Explain why developing the minimum amount of gluten is not necessarily desirable with pastries.

4. Why is the careful selection of flour more important with breads than with cookies?

5. Explain why the use of cake flour and of a high amount of water and tenderizers in high-ratio liquid shortening cakes practically eliminates any concern over gluten development.

6. A brioche dough rose beautifully only to collapse during the early stages of baking. What changes might be needed in the method of preparation? Consider changes that might be needed in mixing, fermentation, pretreating milk, and so forth. *Note:* brioche is made from a sweet, rich dough that generally contains eggs, butter, sugar, and fluid milk (as well as bread flour, yeast, and salt).

EXERCISES AND EXPERIMENTS

1. Increasing Gluten Development in Batters and Doughs

In the spaces that follow, list all the ways you know that will increase gluten development in batters and doughs. Be sure to start each line with an action word, such as the following: add, increase, decrease, change, omit, include, use. While each item might not apply to all types of products, each should work in at least one. Follow the format used in the first two, which are done for you, and see if you can add at least ten more ways.

1. Use bread flour instead of pastry flour.
2. Increase the amount of water in dough where gluten is not fully hydrated.
3. _____
4. _____
5. _____
6. _____
7. _____
8. _____
9. _____
10. _____
11. _____
12. _____
13. _____
14. _____
15. _____

2. Functions of Ingredients in Bread

On a sheet of paper, copy the name of each ingredient listed on the label of any brand of bread from the supermarket. State what the ingredient is (flour, variety grain, sweetener, fat or oil, emulsifier, maturing agent, etc.), then briefly explain its function in the bread. Use your entire textbook—not just this chapter—as a reference. For the flour, state whether it is bleached or unbleached; if it is bleached, state which bleaching agent you believe was likely used. Also state whether the flour is enriched, why it is enriched, and which vitamins and minerals were added for enrichment. Attach the original label to the assignment.

3. Amount and Quality of Gluten in Various Flours

OBJECTIVES

To gain an increased understanding of different flours and the gluten they contain by:
- Kneading doughs by hand
- Separating out the gluten contained in each flour
- Measuring the amount of gluten from each flour
- Evaluating the qualities of gluten from each flour

PRODUCTS PREPARED

Gluten balls made from:
- Vital wheat gluten
- High-gluten flour
- Bread flour

- Pastry flour
- Cake flour
- Whole wheat flour
- White rye
- Other, if desired (all-purpose flour, artisan bread flour, white whole wheat flour, corn flour, durum flour, etc.)

MATERIALS AND EQUIPMENT

- Bowls, one per gluten ball, four-quart (four-liter) or larger
- Sieves or strainers, one per gluten ball

PROCEDURE

- Prepare dough from each flour by combining 8 ounces (250 grams) flour with 4 ounces (125 grams) water. Set aside a small amount of the 8 ounces (250 grams) of flour to use to dust the table surface.
- Add more water to each flour, as necessary, until dough is able to be kneaded. You do not need to keep track of the amount of water added to the dough.
- Knead by hand for 5–7 minutes, or until gluten is fully developed. Use flour set aside to prevent dough from sticking; do not add any additional flour, unless necessary. If additional flour is necessary, weigh the amount of flour. Record the total weight of flour (8 ounces or 250 grams plus any additional flour) in Results Table 1, which follows.
- Place dough in bowl and fill bowl with cool water. Time permitting, let gluten ball soak in water for twenty minutes. (See Photo 7.2.)
- Knead and gently tear dough by hand while it is submerged, until water is very cloudy (cloudiness is primarily from the starch, bran particles, and gums coming from the flour). For flours that have little or no cohesive gluten (corn flour, cake flour, rye flour), dough will fall apart easily when placed in water; for these flours, swish the bits of dough through water to remove starch.
- Gather bits of dough into a ball and drain off cloudy water, replacing it with fresh cool water. If necessary, use a sieve or strainer to prevent loss of dough from flours that have little or no cohesive gluten. Also use sieve or strainer to retrieve bran particles from whole wheat flour and add back.
- Continue this process until water squeezed from gluten ball is clear; this will take 20 minutes or more of continuous kneading for most doughs.
- When water is completely clear, drain off and squeeze the gluten ball to remove as much excess water as possible.
- Pat gluten ball dry (for low-gluten flours, retrieve bits of dough as efficiently as possible).
- Weigh gluten ball on scale and record results in Results Table 1.
- Estimate the percent of gluten in flour as follows, and record results in Results Table 1:

$$\text{Percent Gluten in Flour} = \frac{100 \times \text{Weight of Gluten Ball}}{3 \times \text{Weight of Flour}}$$

This calculation is based on the estimate that gluten absorbs two times its weight in water, meaning that

PHOTO 7.2 In back, rinsing and kneading a gluten ball. In front, gluten balls made from bread, pastry, and cake flours. *Photo by Aaron Seyfarth*

every ounce (or gram) of the gluten ball is ⅓ ounce (or gram) gluten. This calculation also assumes that the gluten ball is only gluten. In fact, lipids, ash, and some starch and gums are in gluten balls. Where the total amount of flour is 8 ounces, the formula can be simplified to 4.2 × Weight of Dough. For 250 grams flour, the simplified formula is 0.13 × Weight of Dough.

- Find information on the typical percent protein content for each flour from textbook or another reference and record information in Results Table 1.
- Allow gluten ball to relax for a minimum of fifteen minutes, to allow time for gluten network to recover from the washing process.
- Evaluate each relaxed gluten ball for its consistency (elasticity, strength, cohesiveness) as follows. Record results in Results Table 2, which follows.
  - Elasticity/springiness: press finger on gluten ball and release. How well does the gluten ball spring back? The more fully the ball springs back, the more elastic.
  - Strength/tenacity: Take a small amount of dough and stretch it. If it stretches, how much does it resist stretching? The harder it is to stretch, the stronger the gluten. If the gluten ball falls apart and is not cohesive enough to stretch, write *does not stretch* in the appropriate column in Results Table 2 and include an appropriate description of its consistency in the Comments column. For example, some gluten balls are pasty and others are crumbly.
  - Cohesiveness: Continue stretching the gluten ball, if possible, while rotating it until it is paper thin, like a windowpane. The better it forms a good film without tearing, the more cohesive and extensible the dough.
- Record any potential sources of error that might make it difficult to draw the proper conclusions from the experiment. Consider, in particular, whether gluten ball was thoroughly rinsed; whether it was kneaded completely; and whether bits of gluten were lost during the rinse.

SOURCES OF ERROR

RESULTS TABLE 1 ■ EVALUATION OF AMOUNT OF GLUTEN IN DIFFERENT FLOURS

TYPE OF FLOUR	WEIGHT OF FLOUR (OUNCES OR GRAMS)	WEIGHT OF GLUTEN BALL (OUNCES OR GRAMS)	ESTIMATED PERCENT GLUTEN IN FLOUR (FROM CALCULATION)	TYPICAL PERCENT PROTEIN IN FLOUR (FROM TEXT OR OTHER SOURCE)	COMMENTS
Vital wheat gluten					
High-gluten					
Bread					
Pastry					
Cake					
Whole wheat					
White rye					

RESULTS TABLE 2 ■ EVALUATION OF QUALITIES OF GLUTEN EXTRACTED FROM DIFFERENT TYPES OF FLOUR

TYPE OF FLOUR	ELASTICITY	STRENGTH/TENACITY	COHESIVENESS	COMMENTS
Vital wheat gluten				
High-gluten				
Bread				
Pastry				
Cake				
Whole wheat				
White rye				

CONCLUSIONS

1. In general, how did the size of the gluten balls change with the amount of protein present in each flour?

_____

_____

2. How did the cake flour gluten ball differ in size and quality from the pastry gluten ball? That is, which was much smaller? Which was much weaker and much less cohesive? How do you explain these differences?

_____

_____

3. How did bran particles affect the cohesiveness of the whole wheat flour gluten ball? How might this explain why whole wheat bread typically has a denser volume than white bread?

_____

_____

4. For which flours did the calculated percentage of gluten match the typical percentage of protein listed in the text?

_____

_____

5. For which flours did the calculated percentage of gluten not match the typical percentage of protein listed in the text? Can you explain these discrepancies?

_____

_____

6. How do you think forming a gluten ball from flour can help predict the suitability of the flour for use in bread baking?

_____

_____

7. Did you have any sources of error that might significantly affect the results of your experiment? If so, what could you do differently next time to minimize error?

_____

_____

CHAPTER 8

SUGAR AND OTHER SWEETENERS

CHAPTER **OBJECTIVES**

1. Present the basic chemistry and describe the production and makeup of various sweeteners.

2. Classify common sweeteners and describe their characteristics and uses.

3. List the functions of sweeteners and relate these functions to their makeup.

4. Describe how to best store and handle sweeteners.

 ## INTRODUCTION

While granulated sugar is the most common sweetener in the bakeshop, many other sweeteners are available to the baker and pastry chef. Successful bakers and pastry chefs have a clear understanding of the advantages and disadvantages of each sweetener. They know when they can substitute one for another, and they know how to do it. The first challenge in understanding sweeteners is sorting through the terminology.

 ## SWEETENERS

Sweeteners can be divided into two main categories: dry crystalline sugars and syrups. A third category—specialty sweeteners—covers sweeteners that do not fit neatly into either of the first two categories. Although less commonly used and often expensive, specialty sweeteners fulfill needs that cannot easily be met by the common sweeteners. Before discussing each category of sweeteners, it will help to cover some general points.

Sugar generally means sucrose, the most common sugar in the bakeshop. Other sugars include fructose, glucose, maltose, and lactose. Any of these can be purchased as dry white crystals, although, except for sucrose, it is more common to purchase them in syrup form.

WHAT IS GLUCOSE?

The most abundant sugar in nature, glucose, has an abundance of names. For example, glucose is typically called dextrose when purchased as dry crystalline sugar. Dextrose is added to processed food products, including cake mixes, chocolate chips, sausages, and hot dogs. It provides many of the properties of sugar with less of the sweetness. Commercially, the main source of crystalline dextrose is corn, so dextrose is sometimes called corn sugar.

Glucose is present in nearly all ripened fruit, but its presence in grapes is essential to the fermentation of grapes to wine. This is why winemakers call glucose grape sugar.

Another name for glucose is blood sugar, because it is the sugar that flows through the bloodstream. People with diabetes tend to have high blood sugar levels unless they control it through diet and/or medication.

Glucose is also shorthand for glucose syrup, commonly called corn syrup in the United States (because it is usually derived from cornstarch). To minimize confusion, this text refers to the syrup as glucose corn syrup. While glucose corn syrup does contain a certain amount of the monosaccharide glucose, it generally contains significant amounts of other components as well, so the name is somewhat misleading. Historically, however, glucose corn syrups were manufactured for the glucose they contained, so while misleading, the name is logical. Many other syrups contain the monosaccharide glucose, including honey, molasses, invert syrup, and malt syrup.

All sugars are classified as simple carbohydrates, molecules that consist of carbon, hydrogen, and oxygen atoms arranged in a specific way. Sugars are further classified as monosaccharides or disaccharides. *Monosaccharides* consist of one (*mono*) sugar unit (*saccharide*) and are considered simple sugars. The two main monosaccharides are glucose and fructose, although there are others. These two sugars are naturally present in many ripened fruits and are important in the makeup of certain syrups.

The skeletal molecular structure of the monosaccharide glucose is sometimes shown as a hexagon, while fructose is sometimes shown as a pentagon (Figure 8.1). Understand that these skeletal figures overlook the true complexity of sugar molecules. For one, they do not show the carbon, hydrogen, and oxygen atoms that form the structure of the molecules.

Disaccharides consist of two sugar units bonded together (Figure 8.2). Maltose, or malt sugar, is one example of a disaccharide. It consists of two glucose molecules. Maltose is commonly found in glucose corn syrup and malt syrup. Lactose, or milk sugar, is a disaccharide found only in dairy products. Sucrose, the most common sugar in the bakeshop, is also a disaccharide. It consists of one molecule of glucose bonded to fructose.

In addition to monosaccharides and disaccharides, two other main classifications of carbohydrates are oligosaccharides and polysaccharides. *Oligosaccharides* are made up of a few (*oligo*) sugar units, usually three to ten, bonded into a chain. Oligosaccharides, which are called *higher saccharides* or dextrins by the sweetener industry, are present in many syrups used in the bakeshop. Figure 8.3 shows the skeletal structure of two higher saccharides.

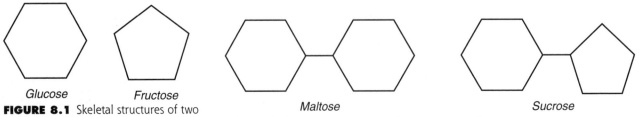

Glucose *Fructose*

FIGURE 8.1 Skeletal structures of two common monosaccharides

Maltose

Sucrose

FIGURE 8.2 Skeletal structures of two common disaccharides

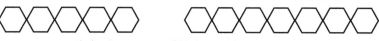

Polysaccharides are very large molecules made up of many (*poly*), often thousands, of sugar units. Two polysaccharides discussed in this chapter are *starch* and *inulin* (not to be confused with insulin, the hormone that controls blood glucose levels in our bodies). The sugar units in starch are glucose; those in inulin are primarily fructose.

FIGURE 8.3 Skeletal structures of higher saccharides

Sugar crystals are highly ordered arrangements of sugar molecules bonded together. They form because sugar molecules of the same type are attracted to one another. Crystal growth can be desirable, as when making rock candy; or it can be unwanted, as when making nut brittle, pulled sugar, or smooth and creamy fondants and icings.

For the most part, sugar crystals are pure. This means, for example, that crystals of sucrose consist entirely of sucrose, even when they form from syrups that contain a mix of sugars. The mix just makes it more difficult for crystals to form, because it makes it difficult for molecules of the same type to come together. Because they are pure, sugar crystals are naturally white in color and do not need to be bleached. When crystals are off-color, it is because impurities are trapped between the crystals.

The Hygroscopic Nature of Sugar

All sugars are *hygroscopic*, at least to some degree, meaning that they attract and bond to water. Because sugar is typically more attracted to water than are proteins, starches, and gums, sugar will pull water away from these structure builders and driers. When this occurs in batters and doughs, they will soften and thin out. The proteins, starches, and gums are no longer able to hydrate, trapping and holding water. Instead, the water is released to sugar, forming a thin syrup as part of the batter or dough.

Highly hygroscopic sugars, such as fructose, readily pick up water from moist air. The hygroscopic nature of sugars is considered desirable when soft, moist cookies must stay soft and moist, or when icings must not dry, crack, or dull. When used in this manner, hygroscopic sugars are sometimes called *humectants*.

The hygroscopic nature of sugars is sometimes undesirable, as when a dusting of powdered sugar on a doughnut liquefies; when the surface of cookies, cakes, and muffins becomes gummy or soggy; or when spun or pulled sugar becomes sticky and collapses.

DRY CRYSTALLINE SUGARS

Sucrose is naturally present in maple tree sap, palm tree sap, dates, ripe bananas, and many other ripened fruits. Commercial production of sucrose involves removing and purifying natural sucrose from sugarcane or from sugar beets. Various forms of dry crystalline sugar are available, each differing primarily in granulation or particle size. Some contain additional ingredients such as cornstarch or molasses. Most have more than one name. Sometimes the name refers to particle size of the crystals (extrafine, superfine); other times it refers to use (sanding sugar) or to user (confectioners' sugar, baker's special sugar). Going from largest to smallest in particle size:

coarse > regular > superfine > 6X powdered > 10X powdered > fondant sugar

Regular Granulated Sugar

Regular granulated sugar is also called fine or extrafine sugar. In Canada, granulated sugar is mostly purified from sugarcane; in Europe, it is mostly purified from sugar beet; in the United States, about half is from sugarcane, the other half from sugar beets.

A BRIEF HISTORY OF SUGAR

Sugarcane is a tall reedy grass that was first cultivated in the South Pacific at least eight thousand years ago. It migrated west to India, then China and Persia (Iran), countries that have extracted and purified sugar from the cane—either as syrup or as crystals—for the past two or three thousand years.

Europeans were relatively late in using cane sugar, relying on more available sweeteners, such as honey and ripened fruit. When cane sugar was eventually introduced to Europe during the Crusades in the eleventh and twelfth centuries, it was considered so precious that it was used mostly in medicines.

Sugarcane is a tropical crop that does not grow well in much of Europe, so for years sugar was under the control of Arab traders. However, once the Spanish and Portuguese brought the cultivation of sugarcane into Africa and the New World, sugar became readily available throughout Europe. Although still a luxury, by the 1600s sugar was used in confectionery and in coffee, tea, and hot chocolate. As demand grew, slaves were brought from Africa to the New World to work the sugar plantations. Still, it wasn't until the 1800s, when sugar refining methods were improved, that prices came down and sugar became readily available to the middle class.

The use of beets for sugar manufacture was a more recent development, first commercialized by a Prussian (German) chemist in the 1700s. The process was adopted and refined by the French in the early 1800s, when the Napoleonic Wars created a need for a domestic source of this important ingredient. The antislavery movement in Europe and the Americas further drove interest in sugar beet cultivation, because sugar beets grow in temperate climates without extensive labor. Over the years, sugar beets have been selectively bred to contain high amounts of sucrose. Today, they contain about 17 percent sucrose, over twice the amount in beets from the 1700s, and slightly more than that in sugarcane. Sugar beets remain the predominant source of sugar in Europe today.

Regular granulated sugar from either cane or beets is more than 99.9 percent pure sucrose, meaning that both are extremely pure and highly refined. For most practical applications, sugar refined in North America from either source can be used interchangeably. However, even very small amounts of impurities can cause undesirable crystallization and browning in sugar confectionery. When this occurs, it is often necessary to add or to increase the amount of cream of tartar added to a formula. Cream of tartar and other acids prevent both crystallization and browning by lowering pH.

Today, there is a trend towards using sugars that have not gone through the complete refining process. They go by many different names, but mostly they are called evaporated cane juice or natural cane juice crystals. These sugars have been refined through one—rather than three—washings and centrifuge cycles. They also have not been filtered to decolorize. Sometimes called first crystallization sugar, these sugars retain a small amount of lightly-colored refiners' syrup—generally less than two percent. They have a pale gold color and a very mild flavor, much closer to regular granulated sugar than to brown sugar. They will function in baked goods as regular granulated sugar, except for a slight off-white cast they give to light-colored products.

These semi-refined sugars are marketed as a substitute for granulated sugar to the natural foods industry and can be made to various granulation sizes, just like regular granulated sugar. Organic cane sugars, that is, sugars made from sugarcane grown organically, are often sold semi-refined.

When deciding on the best sweetener for your particular needs, make an informed decision. Do not consider these sugars—including the organic versions—to have improved health or nutritional benefits, and keep in mind that they are typically two to three times the price of regular granulated sugar.

HOW SUGAR IS PROCESSED

The manufacturing of white sugar involves two basic steps, which often take place at separate locations: the production, or milling, of raw sugar from sugarcane or sugar beets, and the refining of this inedible, raw sugar into pure white sugar. The specifics are somewhat different for cane sugar than for beet sugar. In both cases, however, the sucrose is not changed chemically during the process. Instead, through a series of steps—filtration, crystallization, washing, and centrifugation—sucrose is physically separated from impurities naturally present in the sugarcane or sugar beet. The following is a general description of cane sugar milling and refining.

The first step in milling cane sugar is crushing freshly harvested sugarcane and extracting the juice with water. Next, lime (calcium oxide, an alkali) and carbon dioxide are added to this cloudy juice, to trap impurities. The impurities settle to the bottom and the liquid is strained to remove these impurities from the clear juice. Water is evaporated from the clear juice until it is a thick yellow syrup. The syrup is filtered then concentrated by gently heating it in vacuum pans. As water evaporates and the syrup becomes supersaturated, sugar crystals form. The crystallized mixture is centrifuged—spun, as in a salad spinner—to separate crystals from the dark, thick syrup (molasses), and the crystals are washed and recentrifuged. The light-brown crude raw sugar is ready to be refined into pure white sugar.

In the meantime, the molasses from the centrifuging of sugar cane syrup is recycled, often two or three times, by heating and recentrifuging until no more sucrose crystals can be easily extracted. With each extraction the amount of sugar in the molasses decreases while the color, flavor, and ash increase. Final-extraction molasses has little easily extracted sucrose. While so-called first, second, and third extractions of cane molasses are sometimes blended and sold for food use, final-extraction molasses is generally not. It is considered too dark in color and too harsh in flavor for use by humans.

The crude raw sugar—considered unclean and inedible in North America—is sent to a sugar refinery, where it undergoes a series of processes involving more washing, centrifuging, clarifying, and filtering. The sugar syrup is also decolorized, meaning that it is passed through an ion exchange or activated carbon filter, much as you would pass water through a water filter. A few cane (but not beet) sugar manufacturers still use bone char from cattle for decolorizing, which strict vegetarians find unacceptable.

Finally, the pure sugar is crystallized for the last time, then dried, screened through wire meshes, packed, and sold. The remaining syrup, commonly called molasses, is referred to as *refiners' syrup* by the sugar industry. This differentiates it from molasses syrup left from the milling operation of sugar manufacture.

Coarse Sugars

Coarse sugars have larger crystals than regular granulated sugar. They are useful as a garnish on muffins and other baked goods. Their large, clear crystals do not readily dissolve, and they have an attractive sparkle. One example of a coarse crystalline sugar is sometimes called sanding sugar, although that term also refers to a different product called pearl sugar.

Coarse white sugars are often best for the whitest fondants and confections and the clearest syrups, because they have the fewest impurities of all granulated sugars. Being pure, coarse sugars are significantly more expensive than regular granulated sugar. The high purity-often—exceeding 99.98 percent—is necessary, however, if large, sparkling crystals are to form. One coarse sugar, designed for the whitest confections, is called AA confectioners. Do not confuse this pure, coarse sugar with finely pulverized powdered sugar.

PHOTO 8.1 Sugars for garnish, clockwise from left: coarse, pearl, and demerara/turbinado
Photo by Aaron Seyfarth

Powdered Sugar

Powdered sugar is often called *confectioners' sugar* in the United States and *icing* or *fondant sugar* in Canada. It consists of sucrose crystals finely pulverized into powder and is available in various degrees of fineness. The fineness of grind is sometimes indicated by a number before an X—the higher the number, the greater the fineness. Two common powdered sugars are 6X and 10X. Of the two, 10X is best for the smoothest uncooked icings and confections, where anything coarser would be too gritty. For decorative dustings on desserts, 6X powdered sugar is the better choice, since its coarser grind means it is less likely to cake or liquefy.

Powdered sugars typically contain about 3 percent cornstarch, which absorbs moisture and prevents caking. This can help to stiffen and stabilize meringues and whipped cream. However, you might notice a raw starch taste when using powdered sugar in certain applications.

Superfine Granulated

Superfine sugar has crystals that are intermediate in size between powdered sugar and regular granulated sugar. Superfine sugar—also called ultrafine—dissolves more quickly in liquids than does regular granulated sugar. It also allows the incorporation of smaller air cells into batters and creamed shortenings, and it is good for sugaring baked goods.

WHAT IS PEARL SUGAR?

Pearl sugar consists of opaque white irregular granules that do not dissolve readily. Pearl sugar is used much like coarse crystalline sugar, to provide a crunchy decorative topping on sweet baked goods, but it has a very different look than the clear, glistening crystals of coarse crystalline sugar. Pearl sugar is sometimes called sanding sugar, decorative sugar, or nibs.

WHAT'S IN A NAME?

Each of the following sugars is similar in particle size to superfine granulated. It is interesting to see that each name says something about the sugar and how it is used. For practical purposes, these sugars can be used interchangeably, although they vary slightly in particle size.

Fruit sugar—dissolves quickly when sprinkled on fresh fruit (do not confuse this with fructose, also called fruit sugar because it is found in fruit).

Baker's sugar—used by bakers to produce the finest crumb in certain cakes; it also produces greater spread in cookies and is good for sugaring doughnuts.

Bar sugar—dissolves quickly in cold beverages.

Caster or castor sugar—named for the small container used for serving sugar in British homes.

While not all bakeshops stock superfine sugar, those that do find that it produces a finer, more uniform crumb in certain cakes; it reduces beading in common meringues; and it increases spread in cookies.

Regular Brown Sugar

Brown sugar generally refers to fine granulated sugar with a small amount—usually less than 10 percent—of molasses or refiners' syrup. Because some, or all, of the molasses is on the surface of tiny sugar crystals, brown sugar is soft, sticky, and tends to clump. Depending on the color and flavor of the molasses that is used in its production, brown sugar is considered light brown (golden) or dark brown. Sometimes, but not always, dark brown sugar has caramel coloring added, for an even darker color. In North America, there is very little—if any—difference in the amount of molasses added to regular light and dark brown sugars.

Brown sugar is commercially made one of two ways. The first way is to partially refine sugar crystals, that is, to leave some molasses syrup and other impurities with the crystallizing sugar. Another way is to blend cane sugar molasses with granulated white sugar, coating the crystals with molasses. Both methods are common. The first method is typically used when brown sugar is made from sugar cane. The second is always used when brown sugar is made from sugar beets.

Brown sugar is used primarily for its color and distinct molasses flavor; the small amount of molasses in brown sugar has little, if any, effect on the moistness of baked goods or on its nutritional value. Use light or dark brown sugar in cookies, cakes, confections, and breads, replacing regular granulated sugar, pound for pound. Brown sugar is soft and tends to clump because it is higher in moisture (3–4 percent) than regular granulated sugar, so it must be stored in an airtight container.

If brown sugar is unavailable, substitute about 1 pound (or 1 kilogram) molasses and 9 pounds (or 9 kilograms) sugar for every 10 pounds (or 10 kilograms) brown sugar in a formula. The color, flavor, and overall quality of the final product will depend on the color, flavor, and quality of the added molasses.

Specialty Brown Sugars

There are several brown sugars available to the baker in addition to regular light and dark brown sugars. While the processes used in making these products vary with the manufacturer, they are described in this section in general terms. All brown sugars

PHOTO 8.2 Brown sugars, left to right: regular light brown, dark muscovado, Sucanat, and demerara/turbinado
Photo by Aaron Seyfarth

retain small amounts of vitamins and minerals from the molasses they contain, but none are a significant source of either.

Muscovado sugar is the darkest, richest-tasting brown sugar. It is soft and moist, consisting of powdery-fine crystals enrobed in molasses. Muscovado sugar is sometimes called Barbados sugar, after the island in the Caribbean where it was produced in the 1700s. It was originally made by draining excess molasses from crystallized raw, unrefined sugar before shipping the sugar to England for refining. The word *muscovado* is derived from the Spanish word for unrefined.

Today, two main types of muscovado sugar are sold: dark and light. Dark muscovado retains the full amount of molasses (13 percent) from the sugar cane syrup. Light muscovado contains less molasses (6 percent) and has a correspondingly lighter color and flavor.

Sucanat is the trademarked name for free-flowing brown sugar that is made from cane sugar with the full amount of molasses (13 percent) added back. Despite having about the same amount of molasses as muscovado, Sucanat typically has a golden color and a less intense flavor. Sucanat (SUgar CAne NATural) is slowly stirred as it dries and cools, forming granules rather than crystals. It is sometimes labeled dehydrated cane juice. *Rapadura* is the brand name of an organic dehydrated cane juice which is similar in appearance and texture to Sucanat. Rapadura is also the generic name in Brazil for so-called noncentrifugal sugars.

Turbinado sugar is similar in taste and color to light brown sugar, but it is dry and free-flowing, rather than soft and moist. Turbinado sugar is sometimes called raw, washed raw, or unrefined sugar, but these terms are somewhat misleading. A better description might be to call it partially refined. To make turbinado sugar, crude, raw sugar is first cleaned by steaming it. It is then washed and centrifuged to remove surface molasses before it is crystallized and dried. These refining steps turn crude raw sugar into an edible light golden brown sugar that typically retains about 2 percent molasses. The name turbinado comes from the use of the centrifuge, also called a turbine, in the refining process of this and all sugars except artisanal noncentrifugal ones. Sugar In The Raw and Florida Crystals are two brands of turbinado brown sugar.

Demerara sugar is a type of turbinado sugar. It is a light brown sugar with large, golden crystals. It is popular in Great Britain as a sweetener in coffee or on cereal. Because its crystals are large, crunchy, and glistening, demerara is also used as a decorative sanding sugar on muffins and other baked goods. Demerara sugar is named after a region in Guyana, the country in South America where quantities of it were first made.

NONCENTRIFUGAL SUGARS—ARTISAN SUGARS FROM AROUND THE WORLD

In some areas of the world, sugarcane juice is still evaporated in open pans until it is dry, to produce a crude, unrefined brown sugar, much as it was made thousands of years ago. These unrefined raw sugars are sometimes called noncentrifugal sugars, since they have not been centrifuged, or spun, to remove molasses at any stage in the process.

All unrefined sugars retain the rich, hearty flavor of molasses; in fact, they can be thought of as crystallized molasses or evaporated whole cane juices, with nothing removed at any stage. Each is unique because of differences in regional practices. Most come in varying degrees of color, from golden to dark brown, depending on how they are boiled and what clarifying agents and additives are used. The sugar is generally consumed where it is produced, but quantities are available through specialty distributors, as interest in the unique flavor of each region's sugar has grown.

Jaggery, made in the villages of India, where it is often called *gur*, is the most common example of an unrefined sugar. Jaggery is made by boiling and stirring sugarcane juice until it evaporates to a thickened crystallized syrup. The hot, fudgelike mixture is cast in cylindrical molds or formed into cakes and cooled to harden. Sometimes jaggery is grated from hardened blocks and sold as powdery crystals, called *shakkar* (Hindi for sugar). When it is washed with water, centrifuged, and crumbled into grains, the resulting semi-refined product is called *khandsari*. About one-third to one-half of the sugar consumed in India is still in the form of jaggery, shakkar, and khandsari. Jaggery is also used throughout Southeast Asia.

Other examples of unrefined sugar include *panela*, made in Colombia and sold as rectangular or round flat loaves throughout South America; *rapadura*, from Brazil; cone-shaped *piloncillo* from Mexico; and *panocha* from the Philippines.

A refined artisan sugar made in Japan is called *wasanbon toh*. Wasanbon toh, made from a special variety of sugarcane, is refined by repeatedly mixing sugar crystals with water, kneading the mix by hand, and pressing it with stones to remove molasses syrup. When the process is completed, the sugar takes the form of a fine, ivory-white powder. Wasanbon toh is said to have a delicate flavor that is important in traditional Japanese sweets.

Today, much of the demerara—and muscovado—sugar sold is produced on the island of Mauritius, off the coast of Africa, and exported to Europe.

SYRUPS

Syrups are mixtures of one or more sugars dissolved in water, usually with small amounts of other components, including acids, colorants, flavorants, and thickeners. Although these other components are present in small amounts, they are extremely important because they provide the unique character of each syrup.

Most syrups contain about 20 percent water, but there are exceptions. For example, invert syrup typically contains about 27 percent water, maple syrup has about 33 percent water, and simple syrup often contains 50 percent water.

Sometimes, the thicker the syrup, the less water it contains. Usually, however, syrups are thick because they contain higher saccharides in addition to sugar. The larger size of higher saccharides makes them slower to move and apt to bump and tangle, which is why they thicken. Higher saccharides are present in glucose corn syrups and other thick syrups, such as honey and molasses.

Sometimes syrups can be used interchangeably, but often one syrup, because of its makeup, excels over others at a particular function. For example, most syrups tend to sweeten, moisten, and brown when used in baked goods. But syrups high in fructose, such as invert syrup, high fructose corn syrup, agave syrup, and honey,

TABLE 8.1 ■ COMPOSITION OF COMMON SWEETENERS (%)

SWEETENER	TOTAL SOLIDS	SUCROSE	FRUCTOSE	GLUCOSE	MALTOSE	HIGHER SACCHARIDES
Invert, medium	73	50	25	25	0	0
Honey	83	2	47	37	8	5
Molasses, premium	80	54	23	23	0	0
Corn syrup, low conversion	80	0	0	7	45	48
Corn syrup, high conversion	82	0	0	37	32	31
High fructose corn syrup	71	0	42	50	2	6
Agave syrup	71	0	80	10	0	0
Malt syrup	78	0	0	3	77	20
Maple syrup	67	90	5	5	0	0
Brown sugar, light	96	95	2	3	0	0
Brown sugar, dark	96	95	2	3	0	0

excel at these functions. As the makeup and functions of syrups are described in the following sections, notice how these syrups are similar in other ways. Table 8.1 summarizes and compares the average compositions of various syrups and other sweeteners.

WHAT IS BRIX? WHAT IS BAUMÉ?

Syrups are sometimes described by their solids content. For example, a typical glucose corn syrup contains about 80 percent solids and 20 percent water. Such a syrup is described as having 80° Brix. Brix—named after Adolf Brix, the German scientist who created the scale—is a measure of the percentage of soluble solids (sugar, primarily) in syrups and other products, including fruit juices.

Just as temperature is measured in Fahrenheit or Celsius, the solids content of syrups can be measured in Brix or Baumé units. Baumé (Bé) units—named after Antoine Baumé, the French scientist who created the scale—are familiar to many pastry chefs. Brix and Baumé units can both be measured using a hydrometer, sometimes called a saccharometer, meaning sugar meter. A hydrometer actually measures specific gravity, which is related to density. Syrups having a high Brix or Baumé reading have a higher specific gravity, are denser, and therefore contain more soluble solids and less water than those having a lower reading.

A typical glucose corn syrup with a Brix of 80 will have a Baumé reading of about 43. A typical simple syrup, one used in sorbets, has a Brix just over 50 and a Baumé of 28, while most sorbet mixes have a Brix of 27 and a Baumé of 15. Brix units can be converted to Baumé units using a formula or a special conversion chart. For the range of syrups typically used by pastry chefs, the following formula provides a good estimate of the relationship between the two:

$$\text{Baumé} = 0.55 \times \text{Brix}$$
$$\text{Brix} = \text{Baumé}/0.55$$

While pastry chefs have traditionally used hydrometers and Baumé units, many have switched to Brix units. They are also using different devices, called refractometers, to measure Brix. Refractometers are more expensive than hydrometers, but they are faster and easier to use, and they require a much smaller sample.

Simple Syrup

The simplest syrup is called simple syrup. Bakers and pastry chefs typically make simple syrup by heating equal parts by weight of granulated sugar and water, although other ratios of sugar to water can be used. The ratio of sugar to water in simple syrup should not go above 2:1, or the sugar is likely to crystallize. Often, a small amount of lemon juice or sliced lemon is added to simple syrup. The acid in lemon could help prevent darkening and possibly crystallization, especially in syrups high in sugar.

Simple syrup has many uses. For example, it is used for moistening cake layers, glazing fresh fruit, thinning fondant, poaching fruit, and preparing sorbets. Simple syrup is the only syrup made by bakers and pastry chefs. All others, including invert syrup, molasses, glucose corn syrup, maple syrup, honey, and malt syrup, are purchased.

Invert Syrup

The term *invert syrup* is sometimes used by bakers and pastry chefs to describe any liquid syrup, including glucose corn syrup, maple syrup, honey, and molasses. The term has a more specific meaning, however. It refers to a type of syrup that contains approximately equal amounts of fructose and glucose.

To produce invert syrup, the manufacturer treats a sugar (sucrose) solution with an enzyme or heats it with acid (Figure 8.4). Recall that sucrose is a disaccharide consisting of fructose and glucose bonded together. The enzyme, or a combination of heat and acid, breaks the bond between the two monosaccharides, releasing

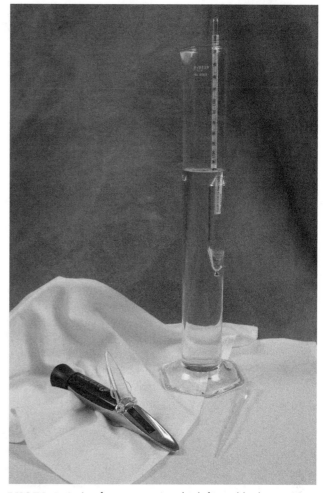

PHOTO 8.3 A refractometer (on the left) and hydrometer (on the right) in use
Photo by Aaron Seyfarth

them. The process is sometimes called inversion, and what remains is invert syrup—equal parts fructose and glucose dissolved in water, with a small amount of residual acid. There are two main types of invert syrup commonly used in bakeshops. The first is called total or full invert syrup, and it contains little, if any, remaining sucrose. The second, called medium invert syrup, is invert syrup blended with an equal amount of sugar. Medium invert syrup is easier to use since it is less apt to crystallize.

Invert syrup is also sometimes called invert sugar, or simply invert. It comes as a clear light-colored liquid or a thicker opaque cream, which contains tiny crystals of sugar suspended in syrup. Several brands are available to bakers and pastry chefs, including Nulomoline, Trimoline, and FreshVert.

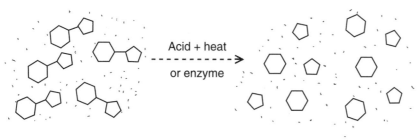

Sucrose in water   Acid + heat or enzyme   *Glucose + fructose in water*

FIGURE 8.4 The commercial production of invert syrup

WHAT IS GOLDEN SYRUP?

Golden syrup, also known as light treacle, is popular in Great Britain. It is a refiner's syrup, a by-product of the sugar refining process, with a golden color and a mild, caramelized sugar flavor. Golden syrup contains a moderate amount of invert sugar, so it has the properties of medium invert syrup. Golden syrup is used in cooking and baking, as pancake syrup, and as ice cream topping.

Invert syrup is only slightly more expensive than sucrose, but it, like all syrups, is messier to use and has a shorter shelf life. This means that syrups like invert should be used only if they have properties that sugar cannot provide.

Several properties of invert syrup make it valuable in bakeshops and pastry shops. One is that it keeps baked goods soft and moist longer. Another is that it keeps icings, fondants, and confections smooth, shiny, and free from cracking and drying. A third is that it prevents the formation of ice crystals in frozen desserts, keeping them softer while frozen. Soft frozen desserts are easier to scoop, slice, and eat straight from the freezer.

Invert syrup is sweeter than sugar and browns much faster. When it is used in baked goods, oven temperatures should be lowered by about 25°F (15°C), to prevent excessive browning. Even with a lower oven temperature, no more than 25 percent of the sugar in a formula should be replaced with invert syrup. Too much invert tends to make baked goods dark, dense, gummy, and too sweet. Use even less invert syrup—if any—in white cake, so the cake stays white. If necessary, a small amount of cream of tartar can be added, to lower pH and slow browning.

Although bakers and pastry chefs do not produce invert syrup in bulk in the pastry shop, small amounts are produced in the normal course of creating many confections. For example, when acid, such as cream of tartar or tartaric acid, is added during the boiling of sugar to reduce browning, a certain amount of sugar is inverted to fructose and glucose. This mix of sugars helps reduce sugar crystallization, so the confection is smoother, shinier, and less apt to crack and dry.

A small amount of lemon juice is sometimes added to simple syrup. Depending on the amount added and the length of time the syrup is heated, the acid allows a certain amount of sucrose to invert to fructose and glucose. Again, the mix of sugars helps prevent concentrated syrups from crystallizing.

WHAT GIVES INVERT SYRUP ITS SPECIAL PROPERTIES?

At first glance, it appears that the water in invert syrup is what gives it its special properties. After all, one of the main properties of invert syrup is keeping baked goods and confections soft and moist. But adjust formulas for water, or compare invert syrup with most other syrups, and invert would still be superior at moistening and at certain other functions.

In fact, the reason invert syrup has different properties than sucrose is because it contains the monosaccharides fructose and glucose. While sucrose is made up of fructose and glucose, in sucrose they are bound to each other as a disaccharide. In full invert syrup, they are not.

Recall, for example, that fructose is particularly hygroscopic, meaning it is better than most sugars, including sucrose, at moistening. Recall, too, that a mixture of sugars crystallizes more slowly than pure sugar. Adding a small amount of invert syrup to icings, fondants, and confections means less sugar crystallization and more softness, creaminess, and shine. Additionally, monosaccharides such as fructose and glucose, being smaller in size, are better at lowering the freezing point of water than sucrose is. Fructose and glucose are also more reactive, meaning that they break down and brown faster than sucrose.

WHAT IS TREACLE?

Treacles are dark cane syrups sold in Great Britain. Just as molasses varies in color and flavor, so do treacles. Black treacle is equivalent to a low-grade edible blackstrap, very dark in color and bitter in taste. Medium treacles are made by blending molasses with higher-grade refiner's syrups.

Molasses

Molasses is the concentrated juice of sugarcane. It is used primarily for color and flavor, although a moderate amount of invert sugar in molasses provides moistness and softness to baked goods. Many grades of molasses are available to the baker and pastry chef. The highest grades are sweet, light in color, and mild in flavor. They are more expensive than lower-grade molasses but are not necessarily best for baking. Strong flavors from spices and whole grains can easily overwhelm the mild, sweet flavor of premium, imported molasses. A darker, lower-grade molasses might be more suitable.

Several factors affect molasses grading. Molasses made by directly boiling and concentrating sugarcane juice, with no sugar crystals removed, is considered premium grade; in Canada, it is called fancy molasses. The best premium-grade molasses is imported from the Caribbean. An example of premium imported molasses is Home Maid.

Lower grades of molasses are by-products of cane sugar milling, often blended from first-, second-, and third-extraction molasses. Because some of the sugar has been removed and the molasses has undergone more processing, lower-grade molasses is darker in color, less sweet, and more bitter than premium molasses. In Canada, two lower grades of molasses are table and cooking molasses. Lower-grade molasses can be an excellent choice when a hearty, robust flavor and dark color are desired.

In the United States, blackstrap molasses usually refers to inedible final extraction molasses, extremely bitter and not very sweet. In Canada, blackstrap is another name for low-grade but edible cooking molasses.

Glucose Corn Syrups

Glucose corn syrups—glucose, for short—are clear syrups produced from the hydrolysis, or breakdown, of starch. By far the most common starch used in the production of glucose corn syrup is cornstarch, but any starch, including potato or wheat, can be used. Throughout this text, the term glucose corn syrup refers to these syrups, although the small amount of syrup made from noncorn starches, such as potato starch, are not properly called corn syrups.

Starch is a carbohydrate that consists of hundreds, even thousands, of glucose molecules bonded together. To produce glucose corn syrup, the manufacturer heats starch in the presence of water and acid and treats it with enzymes (Figure 8.5), breaking the large starch molecules into smaller units. The syrup is filtered and refined, to remove color and flavor. The manufacturer controls the acid, heat, enzymes, and refining processes, producing a range of glucose corn syrups, each best for a particular use.

Whatever the process, all glucose corn syrups contain a certain amount of sugar (primarily glucose and maltose), which sweetens, browns, moistens, and tenderizes. The rest remains as larger fragments, called higher saccharides. Higher saccharides do not have the properties of sugar; that is, they do not sweeten, brown, moisten, or tenderize. However, because of their larger size, they thicken and add body and pliability to products. They are superior at interfering with the movement of molecules, so sugars are less likely to crystallize and water molecules are less likely to form ice in the presence of higher saccharides.

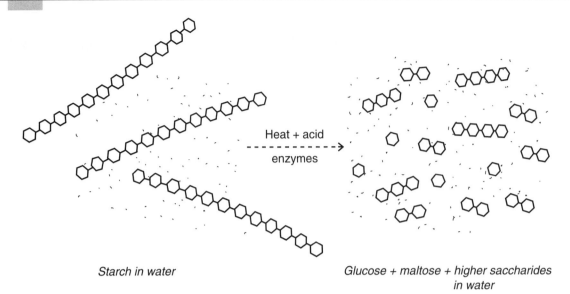

Starch in water

Glucose + maltose + higher saccharides
in water

FIGURE 8.5 Glucose corn syrup production

Glucose corn syrups are often classified by the amount of conversion to sugar that the starch has undergone. High-conversion syrups undergo a high amount of hydrolysis are high in sugars (and low in higher saccharides); low-conversion syrups undergo a low amount of hydrolysis and are low in sugars (and high in higher saccharides). Medium-conversion syrups fall between the two extremes. There are other differences among glucose corn syrups, but the degree of conversion is one that is important to bakers and pastry chefs.

While many different glucose corn syrups are available to bakers and pastry chefs, most bakeshops stock two or three, at most. Regular glucose corn syrup, a medium-conversion syrup (DE of 42), is a good all-purpose glucose corn syrup. The sugar in regular glucose corn syrup provides some tenderness and sweetness to baked goods (although not as much as sucrose), and it moistens and browns (although not as well as invert syrup). While it is never used alone in baked goods, regular glucose corn syrup is sometimes added along with granulated sugar. Karo light corn syrup is similar to regular glucose corn syrup, although it also contains fructose, salt, and vanilla.

HISTORY OF GLUCOSE CORN SYRUP

The history of glucose corn syrup is tied to the political history of Europe. In the early 1800s, when the Napoleonic Wars were being fought in Europe, England set up blockades around France. These blockades prevented imported items—including food—from entering France. Needing to feed his army and his country, Napoléon offered cash rewards for new ways to produce and preserve food domestically.

One cash reward was given for the production of sugar from native plants. Starch sugar was originally produced by treating potato starch with acid. The resulting starch sugar was not as sweet as cane sugar, so when the blockade was lifted, France stopped producing it. Production began again in the mid-1800s, this time in the United States. Shortly thereafter, Americans began producing starch sugar from cornstarch instead of potato starch, and the corn syrup industry was born. Today, more than half of the 150 pounds (68 kilograms) of sweeteners consumed annually by each American comes from corn, exceeding the consumption of cane and beet sugars combined.

WHAT IS DE?

DE stands for dextrose equivalent. It is a measure of the degree of conversion of starch to sugar in glucose corn syrups. Pure cornstarch has a DE of 0, while pure dextrose has a DE of 100. Low-conversion syrups have DEs between 20 and 37; medium-conversion syrups are between 38 and 58; high-conversion have DEs between 58 and 73; and very high conversion syrups have DEs greater than 73.

Regular glucose corn syrup can be used in candies and confections, but low-conversion glucose corn syrups are much more suitable. Low-conversion glucose corn syrups (DE of 27 to 36) are very thick, barely sweet, and unlikely to brown or crystallize. They are best for the whitest, smoothest, shiniest icings, confections, and fondants. They are also useful for increasing the pliability and strength of pulled and spun sugar, and at preventing ice crystallization in frozen desserts. Glucose Crystal is one example of a low-conversion glucose corn syrup. Glucose Crystal is imported from France and is also highly refined, giving it a crystal-clear appearance and a premium price.

Dark corn syrup is regular light glucose corn syrup with added molasses or refiner's syrup, caramel coloring, and flavoring. An example of dark glucose corn syrup is Karo dark corn syrup, which also contains salt and an antimicrobial agent. Dark glucose corn syrup can be used as an inexpensive substitute for molasses in baked goods and confections, although it is much milder tasting than most molasses syrups.

MAKING FUDGE SMOOTH AND CREAMY

Perfect fudge is smooth and creamy. Like fondant and other crystalline confections, fudge consists of many microscopic crystals suspended in a thin layer of syrup. The crystals provide body and bulk while the syrup provides a smooth creaminess and shine. If too few crystals form, fudge is soft and sticky. If they grow too large, the fudge feels gritty.

There are several tricks to preparing the smoothest, creamiest fudge. One is to use a thermometer to best determine when fudge is properly cooked (238–240°F; 114–116°C). Another is to properly use key ingredients. A key ingredient in many fudge formulas is cream of tartar. Cream of tartar is an acid, and the combination of heat and acid breaks down a certain amount of sucrose into invert sugar—equal parts fructose and glucose. Fructose and glucose are considered interfering agents because their very presence interferes with the growth of large, gritty crystals of sucrose. The result is smoother, shinier fudge.

The disadvantage of relying on acid to invert sugar is that the process is difficult for pastry chefs to control. Too little inversion and the fudge is dull, hard, and gritty; too much and the fudge may not crystallize and set up. This guesswork is eliminated, however, by simply adding a measured amount of invert syrup or glucose corn syrup.

Low-conversion glucose corn syrup—one that is low in sugar and high in the higher saccharides—is best to use as an interfering agent in fudge and other confections. Higher saccharides thicken the sugar mixture, greatly slowing crystallization. Low-conversion glucose corn syrup is particularly ideal for fondant and other confections that are prized for their white appearance, because it does not contain large amounts of sugars that brown. Avoid adding too much glucose corn syrup, however. Especially when they are low-conversion syrups, too much glucose corn syrup prevents so much crystallization that fudge takes on the consistency of chewy icing.

High fructose corn syrup is one of the newer corn syrups. Called glucose-fructose in Canada, it was first popularized in the 1970s and 1980s, when high sugar prices and improved syrup quality made it the standard sweetener in the United States for carbonated beverages. The name glucose-fructose is particularly appropriate, since the most common high fructose corn syrup (HFCS) contains approximately equal parts fructose and glucose, making it essentially the same as invert syrup in composition and in properties. Other versions of HFCS contain up to 90 percent fructose. While bakers and pastry chefs do not commonly use high fructose corn syrup, it is useful to know that it is a high-quality, low-price substitute for invert syrup.

Honey

Honey, flower nectar collected and processed by honeybees, was probably the first sweetener. An early cave painting shows Neolithic man collecting wild honey from a hive. Honey remained the primary sweetener in Europe for thousands of years, until the use of sugar became widespread in the 1700s.

Today, honey is an expensive ingredient, used primarily for its unique flavor. After it is collected from beehives, it is separated from the waxy honeycomb, heated to dissolve crystals and destroy spoilage yeast, and filtered to remove impurities. Honey is sold mostly as syrup, but honey cream is also available, consisting of tiny crystals suspended in concentrated syrup.

Honey is sometimes called a natural invert syrup because enzymes in the honeybee invert sucrose in the nectar to fructose and glucose. Like invert syrup, honey is very sweet, browns easily, and has the ability to keep baked goods and icings soft and moist.

Honeys are named for the flower that the nectar is collected from. The most common honey throughout the world is sweet clover honey, but others—orange blossom and tupelo, to name two—are also popular. Many expensive specialty honeys are available, but they should be considered flavoring agents and not be used in general baking. Either clover honey or baker's honey is appropriate for baking. Baker's honey is a relatively inexpensive blend that has a darker color and stronger flavor than straight clover honey.

Maple Syrup

Maple syrup is made by boiling and evaporating the sap of the sugar maple tree, which begins to flow in early spring. It is produced throughout northeastern United States and southeastern Canada, where over 80 percent of the world's supply of maple syrup is produced. Like jaggery and other unrefined noncentrifugal sugars, maple syrup is boiled in open pans, often over a wood fire. Because sap is only 2 or 3 percent sugar, about 40 gallons (151 liters) of sap are needed to produce 1 gallon (4 liters) of maple

SUBSTITUTING HONEY FOR GRANULATED SUGAR

The National Honey Board recommends the following substitution for using honey in place of granulated sugar. This substitution accounts for both the amount of water in honey and for its intense sweetness: use 1 pound honey in place of 1 pound granulated sugar; reduce water (or other liquid) in the formula by 2.5–3 ounces. Or, use 500 grams honey in place of 500 grams granulated sugar; reduce water (or other liquid) in the formula by 80–95 grams.

syrup. This makes maple syrup an extremely expensive sweetener. It is prized for its unique and very sweet aroma, which develops from the Maillard reactions that occur as sap is boiled over high heat.

Do not confuse maple-flavored pancake syrup with real maple syrup. Pancake syrup is made from inexpensive glucose corn syrup, with added caramel coloring and maple flavoring.

While flavor is important, real maple syrup is graded primarily by color. Usually, lighter-colored syrups are produced early in the season and darker ones later. Darker-colored syrups have a stronger flavor, lower grade, and lower price. An all-purpose maple syrup is Grade A Medium Amber in the United States (Canada No. 1 Light). A lighter, more delicate-flavored maple syrup, U.S. Grade A Light Amber (Canada No. 1 Extra Light), may be more appropriate for use in candies and confections, while stronger-flavored, darker ones, such as U.S. Grade A Dark Amber (Canada No. 1 Medium) or Grade B (Canada No 2. Amber) may be best for baking.

The sugar solids in maple syrup are almost entirely sucrose, with a small amount—usually less than 10 percent—invert sugar. Because it is low in invert sugar, do not expect much more added moistness and softness from maple syrup than you would get from sugar and water. Instead, enjoy maple syrup for its flavor.

Malt Syrup or Extract

Malt syrup is produced by malting, or sprouting, cereal grain, dissolving it in water, then concentrating it to a syrup. Malt syrup, like malted flour, can be made from any cereal, but barley and wheat are most commonly used. The malting process initiates many biological processes in the cereal, including the breakdown of large starch molecules to sugars.

Malt syrup, which is also called malt extract, has a distinct flavor and color that is somewhat similar to molasses. Unlike molasses, malt syrup is very high in maltose. Maltose and, to a lesser degree, trace amounts of protein and ash, improve yeast fermentation, one reason why malt syrup is often used in bread, bagels, biscuit, and cracker production. Malt syrup is also often added to the water used for boiling bagels, for added sheen.

The two main types of malt syrup are diastatic and nondiastatic. Diastatic malt syrup contains a small amount of enzymes from the malting process. Nondiastatic malt syrup has been heated to eliminate all active enzymes, but it still contains the distinct flavor and the maltose that is characteristic of all malt syrups.

HOW DOES MALTOSE AID FERMENTATION?

During fermentation, yeast breaks down sugars and, in the process, generates carbon dioxide gas. If there is an adequate supply of carbon dioxide throughout fermentation and proofing, bread leavens properly. For this to occur, it is best to have sugars available throughout the entire fermentation process.

Sucrose, fructose, and glucose are all quickly broken down and fermented by yeast in the early stages of bulk fermentation. Lactose is generally not fermented at all, while maltose is fermented slowly. By including maltose in yeast-raised formulas, yeast food is available through final proof, and this ensures adequate gassing during this critical stage. The result is properly leavened bread. Besides malt syrups, good sources of maltose include malted barley flour and certain glucose corn syrups.

SPECIALTY SWEETENERS

Dextrose

Dextrose is another name for glucose, the monosaccharide. It is the name used when the monosaccharide is purchased as dry sugar. Dextrose is sold as crystals or as pulverized powder. It is less sweet than sucrose and is useful when the properties of sugar are desired, but the sweetness is not. For example, dextrose provides bulk without much sweetness in chocolates and chocolate products. Dextrose also improves the shelf life of confections, because it is more effective than sucrose at inhibiting microbial growth.

Powdered dextrose, also called dusting or doughnut sugar, is superior to powdered sugar at dusting and coating doughnuts and plated desserts. Dextrose, even when finely pulverized, does not easily dissolve, so it is less likely to liquefy when exposed to heat and humidity.

Expect a different flavor from dextrose, especially when it is undissolved. Dextrose is less sweet than sucrose, and dextrose crystals provide a cooling sensation when they melt in the mouth. Dusting sugar may contain other ingredients besides dextrose, such as vegetable oil. Vegetable oil helps the sugar to adhere to doughnuts and baked goods, but it changes the mouthfeel and produces an off flavor as it ages and oxidizes.

Dried Glucose Syrup

Dried glucose syrup, also called corn syrup solids or glucose solids, is glucose corn syrup with most of its water removed (only 7 percent or less water remaining). Just as there are many different types of glucose corn syrups, so are there many types of dried glucose syrups. Dried glucose syrup is used wherever the functionality of glucose corn syrup is desired without the added water. For example, dried glucose syrup can provide added body to the mouthfeel of ice cream and other frozen desserts.

Fondant Sugar

Fondant sugar is an extremely fine powdered or icing sugar, as much as one hundred times finer than 10X sugar. It is ideal for quickly preparing the smoothest fondant, glaze, or cream praline centers without cooking. It provides a higher sheen than regular powdered sugar, and because it generally does not contain cornstarch, it exhibits no raw starch taste. Fondant sugar may contain ingredients (maltodextrin, for example) to reduce stickiness and improve icing's ability to adhere to baked goods. An example of fondant sugar is Easy Fond.

WHY DOES DEXTROSE COOL THE TONGUE?

Dextrose crystals require a relatively large amount of energy to dissolve, because they are held together with strong bonds. When dextrose crystals are placed in the mouth, the energy needed to break the bonds and dissolve the crystals comes from the heat of the mouth. So much heat is needed that the temperature inside the mouth drops briefly, creating a cooling sensation.

Prepared Fondant

Prepared fondant is sold as soft cream or as firm sheets or rolls (massa Ticino). Although it can be made from scratch, fondant requires time and skill to prepare. Cream fondant, warmed and thinned, is used for glazing doughnuts, petit fours, and other baked goods. It also serves as a base for cream praline centers and for uncooked icings. Rolled fondant is used primarily on wedding cakes.

To use prepared cream fondant as a simple icing or glaze, warm it gently to 98°–100°F (37°–38°C). Add simple syrup, pasteurized egg white, flavored liqueur, or any other liquid to thin it before use. To maintain a soft, smooth consistency and an attractive sheen, do not heat fondant above the recommended temperature. Otherwise, small sugar crystals melt, only to reform as large, coarse crystals on cooling.

HELPFUL HINT

When warming prepared fondant, always do so in a double boiler, and stir while warming. This way, the fondant will soften without exceeding the critical 98°–100°F (37°–38°C), which is necessary to maintain its consistency and sheen.

Isomalt

Isomalt is a relatively new sweetener made by chemically modifying sucrose. Isomalt is not found in nature. It has been approved for use in the United States only since 1990. Isomalt is purchased as a white powder or small beads, and while it is expensive, it has some advantages over sucrose in certain decorative sugar pieces, such as spun, poured, and pulled sugar. Isomalt does not easily brown, pick up moisture, or crystallize and grain, so sugar work remains relatively dry and white. However, isomalt does not have the same melt-in-the-mouth sensation as does sucrose. Isomalt also serves as a bulking agent in low-calorie and "sugar-free" hard candies and confections.

Isomalt is about half as sweet as sucrose. Although it sweetens and is derived from sugar, chemically isomalt is not a sugar. It is classified as a polyol, a type of sugar replacer.

WHAT ARE POLYOLS?

Polyols are also known as sugar alcohols, although they are neither sugars nor alcohols. Like sugar, polyols are carbohydrates. Just as there are many different types of sugars, so too are there many different types of polyols. Some are purchased as dry crystals, others as liquid syrups. Examples of polyols include sorbitol, glycerine (glycerol), maltitol, mannitol, and xylitol.

In general, polyols provide sweetness and bulk and certain other functions of sugar, except browning. They are lower in calories than sugar and do not promote tooth decay. Products sweetened exclusively with polyols can be labeled sugar-free. Because they are not readily absorbed by the body, polyols can be useful in products for diabetics and for those on reduced-calorie diets. However, most polyols have a laxative effect, which can cause diarrhea when consumed in large quantities.

Maltitol is the closest to sugar in taste and other properties and can be used as a one-to-one replacement for sugar in confections and baked goods. Glycerine and sorbitol, which are both hygroscopic, have been used by confectioners and pastry chefs for years, to provide softness and moistness to confections. Xylitol, like dextrose, provides a cooling sensation when used in crystalline form. Its most common application is in sugar-free gum.

Some polyols, such as isomalt, are not found in nature, while others are. Dried plums (prunes), for example, contain about 15 percent sorbitol, according to the California Dried Plum Board. This high amount of sorbitol, in addition to even higher amounts of glucose and fructose, make dried plums—and the baked goods that they are added to—soft and moist.

Fructose

Fructose is sometimes called levulose or fruit sugar. While it is present in many syrups, including honey, molasses, invert syrup, and high fructose corn syrup, fructose can be purchased as dry, white crystals. Crystalline fructose is expensive, but it has a clean, distinct sweetness that complements fruit flavors. It is most commonly used in fruit-based desserts, sorbets, and confections. Commercially, fructose is produced from high fructose corn syrup. It is considered sweeter than sugar, so generally less is needed than sucrose.

Agave Syrup

Agave syrup is made from the sap of the agave, a succulent plant farmed in Mexico. To make agave syrup, the core of the agave is heated and sap pressed from the plant. The sap contains the polysaccharide inulin, along with smaller amounts of glucose and fructose. Heat and/or enzymes break down inulin to fructose, much as starch is broken down to glucose in the making of glucose corn syrup. Enzymes can also convert glucose to fructose in the same way that high fructose corn syrup is made from glucose corn syrup. The sap can be clarified, filtered, and concentrated.

There are several brands of agave syrup, also called agave nectar, on the market. Some are dark in color and strong in flavor, while others are highly refined and pale in color. Some are made from organically grown agave and marketed as a raw food, which means it has not been heated above 120°F (50°C) or so. Raw foods retain their heat-sensitive nutrients and natural enzyme activity.

Like high fructose corn syrups, agave syrups vary in the amount of fructose that they contain. This variability can occur because of differences in how the sap is processed or because of differences in the amount of fructose-containing inulin naturally present in the agave. For example, the blue agave, which is also the only agave plant allowed in the making of tequila, is naturally high in inulin. Because of this, blue agave syrup is typically higher in price than agave syrup from other sources.

There are few, if any, higher saccharides present in the various brands of agave syrups, making them easy to use because they are very thin and pourable. Besides containing 50–90 percent fructose, agave syrups contain varying amounts of the monosaccharide glucose. The more fructose and less glucose in agave syrup, the less likely it will crystallize and the sweeter it will be. Agave syrups, especially those highest in fructose, are said to have a low glycemic response.

Rice Syrup

Rice syrup is made from rice starch, much as glucose corn syrup is made from cornstarch. Rice syrup usually undergoes less refining than glucose corn syrup, so it has a brownish tan color and a distinct flavor. Because it is less refined than many other sweeteners, rice syrup is marketed as a sweetener to the health food industry.

High-Intensity Sweeteners

High-intensity sweeteners, sometimes called nonnutritive or artificial sweeteners, are typically two hundred or more times sweeter than sugar. They provide one function in baked goods—sweetness. High-intensity sweeteners are largely unsuitable for pastry and bakery products, which rely on sugar for many functions besides sweetness.

WHAT IS THE GLYCEMIC RESPONSE?

Glycemic response is a term that refers to how fast sugars—and foods that contain sugars and other carbohydrates—break down during digestion and provide energy to the body. The faster carbohydrates in a food product are digested, the faster they raise blood sugar levels and the higher the glycemic response. Proteins and fats, not being carbohydrates, do not raise blood sugar levels. Dietary fiber, although made of carbohydrates, pass through the body undigested, so they also do not raise blood sugar levels.

The most common numerical measure of the glycemic response of foods is the glycemic index. If glucose itself is arbitrarily given a glycemic index (GI) of 100, then sucrose has a GI of 60, fructose is 20, whole milk is 35, and white flour is 70.

The usefulness of this information is currently in dispute by nutritionists and health professionals, although some weight loss diets have touted low GI foods as a means of reducing hunger, aiding in weight loss, and assisting diabetics in controlling their insulin levels. Although high-glycemic foods might be great for quick energy needed to run a sprint, low-glycemic foods are generally considered better for health. Fructose and high-fructose sweeteners like agave syrup are sometimes touted as healthful because of their low GI. Low GI foods are thought by some to reduce hunger, aid in weight loss, and help diabetics control their blood insulin levels. Yet, there are also indications that sweeteners high in fructose could increase blood insulin levels and promote obesity because of the way that they are metabolized.

The U.S. 2005 Dietary Guidelines Advisory Committee, Health Canada, and other groups responsible for public health recommendations in North America have not yet made diet recommendations based on the glycemic response of food products.

This is a complex topic that may take years to resolve. Realize that it is normal for scientists to have widely different views and for scientific studies to sometimes produce conflicting results. Science at its best is a process, with a lively exchange of ideas supported by solid research. Each research study provides another piece of the puzzle until finally, the big picture is clear. Until that time, it is best to keep an open mind, to be aware of your customers' changing needs, and to be prepared to alter your practices as needed.

The four most common high-intensity sweeteners in the United States are saccharin, the sweetener in Sweet 'n' Low; aspartame, also known as NutraSweet and Equal; acesulfame potassium, more commonly known by its brand names Sunett and Sweet One; and sucralose, also known as Splenda. A fifth sweetener, neotame, was approved for use in the United States in 2002, but it is not yet in general use.

Of these five high-intensity sweeteners, Splenda is the best choice for baking and other applications. Unlike aspartame, for example, sucralose does not lose its sweetness from the heat of the oven. It's safety is also less in question by consumers and consumer advocacy groups.

Besides containing sucralose, Splenda contains maltodextrin as a bulking agent. The maltodextrin-sucralose blend in Splenda can substitute one for one for sucrose (by volume, not weight). Maltodextrins have some of the properties of sugar, so Splenda provides some of the volume, tenderness, and browning of sugar. Start with the one-for-one replacement of Splenda for sugar, but expect some differences in appearance, taste, and texture in the finished product. By adjusting levels of Splenda and other ingredients, an acceptable, if not identical, product can usually be made.

Stevia is a sweet herb that grows wild in South and Central America. It has been used for centuries by native Americans in Paraguay and Brazil to sweeten beverages. Stevia is sold in several forms, from a dry herb to a concentrated liquid extract. It has a long-lingering sweetness, and at high levels, is bitter. Stevia remains sweet when heated.

MORE ABOUT STEVIA

Stevia is available for sale in the United States as a dietary supplement but is not allowed to be added to food products sold in this country. So-called dietary supplements do not have to undergo the stringent safety testing that food additives must undergo. This means that consumers can purchase stevia from health food stores and add it to foods themselves, but food manufacturers cannot sell products sweetened with stevia. While this might seem like a contradiction, it does mean that stevia, which has not yet been proven safe, is limited to low levels of use. Besides the United States, Canada, Australia, and the European Union do not allow stevia to be added to foods. However, China, Japan, much of Southeast Asia, and countries in South America allow its use.

FUNCTIONS OF SWEETENERS

As with other important ingredients in baked goods, sweeteners provide many functions. Some of the functions of sweeteners are related to their hygroscopic properties—their ability to attract and hold water.

Main Functions

SWEETENS

All sugars and syrups sweeten, but not to the same degree. Fructose is generally considered sweeter than sucrose. The other common sugars are less sweet. While the following rankings for sugars and syrups are only approximate (relative sweetening

PHOTO 8.4 Pound cakes made with different amounts of sugar. Left to right: low amount of sugar, regular amount of sugar, and high amount of sugar
Photo by Aaron Seyfarth

power depends on concentration, pH, and other factors), they indicate how substituting one sweetener for another can change a product's sweetness.

Sugars: fructose > sucrose > glucose > maltose > lactose
Syrups: clover honey > invert > medium-conversion glucose corn syrup

TENDERIZES

Sugars, once dissolved, interfere with gluten formation, protein coagulation, and starch gelatinization. In other words, sugars delay the formation of structure, and in doing so, they tenderize. At least some of the tenderizing effect of sugars is related to their hygroscopic nature. Since gluten, egg, and starch structure all require the presence of water, sugar's strong ability to attract water keeps the water from the structure builders. It is also likely that sugar interacts with the structure builders themselves.

The more sugar added, the more tender the baked good. If too much sugar is added to a product, too little structure forms, and it will never rise, or it will rise and collapse as it cools.

While most tender products are also soft and moist, some are not. Shortbread cookies, for example, are tender yet dry and crumbly. Sugar contributes to this form of tenderness, as well.

RETAINS MOISTNESS AND IMPROVES SHELF LIFE

The hygroscopic nature of sugars increases the softness and moistness in freshly baked products. It also extends shelf life by keeping baked goods from drying and staling.

In general, fructose, being the most hygroscopic of common sugars, provides more moistness and a longer shelf life than other sugars. Syrups containing a significant amount of fructose, such as invert syrup, honey, high fructose corn syrup, and agave syrup provide more moistness than other syrups or granulated sugar. Differences are particularly noticeable after several days of storage.

CONTRIBUTES BROWN COLOR AND A CARAMELIZED OR BAKED FLAVOR

While some sweeteners, such as brown sugar, molasses, malt syrup, and honey, have a brown color, most sweeteners contribute brown color—and a pleasant caramelized or fresh-baked flavor—through the processes of caramelization and Maillard browning.

Because caramelization and Maillard browning have similar end results, the distinction between the two is often overlooked. Strictly speaking, caramelization is the process that sugars undergo when heated to a high temperature. Maillard browning is a similar process but proteins, in addition to sugars, are required. Only a small amount of protein is required to greatly speed up the process, so less heat is needed. In fact, if enough time is allowed, Maillard browning occurs at room temperature. For example, sucrose must be heated to around 320°–340°F (160°–170°C) before it caramelizes, but dry milk solids undergo Maillard browning and develop off flavors after a year or so of storage at room temperature. Table 8.2 compares the processes of caramelization and Maillard browning.

Another distinction between caramelization and Maillard browning is the flavor that each provides. While caramelized flavor is best described as that of cooked sugar,

TABLE 8.2 ■ COMPARISON OF CARAMELIZATION AND MAILLARD BROWNING

BROWNING REACTION	REACTING MOLECULES	TEMPERATURES REQUIRED	EXAMPLES
Caramelization	Sugars (and certain other carbohydrates)	Very high	Caramelized or burnt sugar
Maillard browning	Sugars (and certain other carbohydrates) and proteins	Lower temperatures; can occur at room temperature	Roasted cocoa, coffee, nuts; crust on baked goods; discoloration of white chocolate during storage

WHERE DO CARAMELIZED BURNT SUGAR COLORS AND FLAVORS COME FROM?

When sugars are heated, a series of complex chemical reactions occur that break down sugars into smaller fragments. These smaller molecules evaporate easily and trigger our sense of smell, providing the wonderful aromas associated with caramelized sugar. With continued heating, the fragments react with one another and form large molecules called polymers. Large polymers do not evaporate, but they do absorb light, imparting a brown color. With continued heating, bitter-tasting polymers form. That is why it is important not to overheat sugars.

Similar reactions occur with Maillard browning, that is, when sugars and proteins react together.

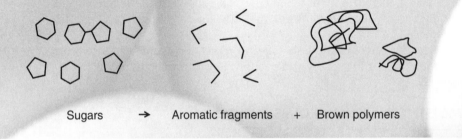

Sugars → Aromatic fragments + Brown polymers

the flavors of Maillard browning are as diverse as roasted cocoa, roasted coffee, roasted nuts, toffee, maple syrup, and molasses (maple tree sap and sugarcane provide small amounts of protein for Maillard browning). Much of the flavor and color in the crust of baked goods also comes from Maillard browning.

Maillard browning is generally considered desirable, but it sometimes causes brown discoloration and the development of off flavors during storage. For example, dry milk solids undergoing Maillard browning at room temperature is undesirable. Another is white chocolate stored for a year or more. Notice that dry milk solids and white chocolate both contain dairy ingredients. Products that contain dairy ingredients are particularly susceptible to Maillard browning because they contain milk proteins and lactose, a sugar that browns relatively quickly.

Monosaccharides brown faster than most disaccharides. This is true with both caramelization and Maillard browning, and it is why invert syrup, which contains the monosaccharides fructose and glucose, browns faster than granulated sugar. Isomalt, the polyol used in pulled, poured, and spun sugar, hardly browns at all. Roughly, the rate of browning of the various sugars and isomalt is as follows:

fructose > glucose > lactose > sucrose > maltose > isomalt

HELPFUL HINT

For the whitest possible sugar showpieces, use all the tricks to prevent browning. Start with sugar relatively free of impurities, such as coarse AA confectioners. Use water that is pure. If necessary, use distilled water, which should have a neutral pH and be free of minerals. If a formula calls for glucose corn syrup, use a low-conversion syrup, which is low in sugars that brown. Add a small amount of acid, such as tartaric acid, during the last stage of cooking or after sugar is removed from heat. Or, use isomalt in place of sugar.

The browning of sugar increases in the presence of salt and certain minerals, including copper, iron, and lead. All that is needed is a very tiny amount—parts per million—of minerals for browning to be significantly increased. Minerals are present in some water supplies, in unrefined syrups (malt, molasses, maple, honey, rice), and in salt.

Acids and alkalis also affect browning by their affect on pH. A small amount of baking soda, which increases pH, is often added to baked goods to increase browning. Buttermilk, which is acidic and lowers pH, slows browning, as does cream of tartar. Since water often contains minerals, acids, and alkalis, it can be a factor in the extent of browning, especially with confections.

ASSISTS IN LEAVENING

There is air between sugar crystals, which are irregular in shape, while there is little or no air in syrups. Whenever dry sugar is added to batters and doughs, air—one of the three main leavening gases in baked goods—is added. This is also true when fats are creamed with sugar. Only dry sugars, not syrups, assist in leavening in this manner.

PROVIDES BULK AND SUBSTANCE TO FONDANT AND SUGAR-BASED CONFECTIONS

Sugar crystals provide bulk and substance to fondant, confections, and certain other products. To understand what this means, consider that fondant contains 90 percent or more crystallized sugar. Without these solid sugar crystals, fondant would consist of liquid syrup.

While sugar is not considered a structure builder in baked goods (remember, the more sugar, the more tender the baked good), in fondant and other products that contain sugar crystals, the solid crystals do provide substance. This substance defines the size and shape of these products. In this sense, solid sugar crystals do provide a type of structure.

STABILIZES WHIPPED EGG FOAMS

Sugar, if added properly, stabilizes whipped egg whites, meaning that sweetened whipped whites—meringue—will be less likely to collapse and weep. Sugar also stabilizes whipped whole egg and whipped yolk in foam-type cakes, such as genoise and chiffon. More on sugar's ability to stabilize whipped egg white will be discussed in Chapter 11.

PROVIDES FOOD FOR YEAST FERMENTATION

All common sugars, except lactose, are fermented by yeast. Through yeast fermentation, these sugars provide carbon dioxide gas for leavening doughs. Sucrose, fructose, and glucose are fermented quickly, maltose more slowly.

Additional Functions

ADDS FLAVOR

All sweeteners provide sweetness, of course, but certain sweeteners are also valued for the distinctive flavor they provide. This is true for brown sugar, honey, maple syrup, malt syrup, rice syrup, dark agave syrup, molasses, and dark glucose corn syrup. Other sweeteners are more neutral in flavor, providing mostly sweetness. Examples of sweeteners that are neutral in flavor include granulated sugar, powdered sugar, light glucose corn syrup, and invert syrup.

REDUCES ICINESS AND HARDNESS IN FROZEN DESSERTS

Sugars lower the freezing point of frozen desserts by holding on to water and interfering with the formation of ice crystals. Increasing the amount of sugar in frozen desserts makes them softer and less icy. The monosaccharides—fructose and glucose—are more effective at lowering freezing point than disaccharides.

Thick syrups, such as low-conversion glucose corn syrups, are also extremely effective at preventing iciness. The large higher saccharides in low-conversion glucose corn syrups interfere with ice crystal formation by preventing water molecules from easily moving around. This limits water's growth into large, sharp ice crystals.

PROVIDES A SOURCE OF ACID FOR LEAVENING

Most syrups contain some acid, while most dry sugars do not. The acid in syrups, when combined with baking soda in baked goods, produces carbon dioxide for leavening. For example, the pH of honey is typically 3.5–4.5, meaning that it is quite acidic. The National

Honey Board recommends the use of ½ teaspoon (1.2 milliliters) baking soda to neutralize the acid in one cup—approximately 12 weight ounces (340 grams)—of honey. This provides about the same amount of carbon dioxide as 1 teaspoon (5 milliliters) baking powder.

PREVENTS MICROBIAL GROWTH

When used at low levels, sugars are a source of food for microorganisms, encouraging their growth. At very high levels, however, sugars have the opposite effect and act as preservatives, preventing the growth of microorganisms. That is why rich, sweet doughs ferment and proof more slowly than those with less sugar. The high sugar content of jams, jellies, sweetened condensed milk, candied fruit, and many candies and confections explains, in part, their ability to resist microbial growth.

ADDS SHEEN TO ICINGS

Syrups, in particular, add a glossy sheen to icings and many confections. They do this by forming a smooth, mirrorlike surface over the jagged irregularity of sugar crystals.

PROMOTES A CRISP CRUST ON CERTAIN BAKED GOODS

Often, baked goods form an attractive surface cracking as they bake and a desirable crisp crust as they cool. The cracked, crisp crust forms when moisture evaporates and sugars crystallize. This is particularly noticeable with cookie, brownie, and pound cake formulas that are high in sugar and low in moisture. Hygroscopic sweeteners, such as fructose, sorbitol, invert syrup, and honey, which keep baked goods soft and moist and interfere with sugar crystallization, prevent the formation of crisp crusts.

PROMOTES SPREAD IN COOKIES

Sugar, once dissolved, promotes spread in cookies. To understand this, recall that sugar is hygroscopic and that it a tenderizer. It keeps proteins, starches, and gums from hydrating and absorbing liquids, and it interferes with their ability to form structure. This means that the cookie dough will thin out as it warms from the heat of the oven, at least until proteins coagulate. Sugars with a finer granulation promote more spread because they dissolve sooner, and only dissolved sugars tenderize and thin out doughs. Powdered sugar, when it contains cornstarch, prevents spread in cookies, despite its finer grind.

PROVIDES ENERGY FOR THE BODY

Sugars, and most carbohydrates, provide energy for the body. This is another way of saying that they provide calories. Since most sweeteners are pure and consist almost entirely of carbohydrates, few nutrients besides calories are provided. Molasses is an exception; although it is low in most nutrients, it can be a good source of calcium, potassium, and iron.

STORAGE AND HANDLING

All sweeteners should be stored covered to prevent them from picking up odors. It also prevents them from absorbing or losing moisture. This is particularly important for powdered and brown sugars, which cake when they pick up and lose moisture. If powdered sugar does cake or clump, pass it through a sieve before use. If this occurs to brown sugar, warm it gently in the oven or microwave before passing it through a sieve.

When dry sugars are stored covered, they have an unlimited shelf life. That is not the case with syrups. Certain syrups—invert syrup and some glucose corn syrups, for example—darken when stored for too long, particularly when temperatures are warm.

If light syrups darken, do not discard them. Instead, use them in dark products, such as brownies or whole wheat bread.

Syrups high in moisture, such as maple syrup and simple syrup, must be refrigerated to prevent mold growth. It is best not to refrigerate other syrups. Refrigeration causes syrups high in glucose to crystallize. This occurs with honey, invert syrup, and high fructose corn syrup. If syrup does crystallize, stir well to distribute the crystals evenly throughout. While it is generally unnecessary to heat the syrup to dissolve crystals, you may do so. Be sure to heat gently, especially with delicate syrups, like honey. Honey's flavor may be damaged when the syrup is heated above 160°F (70°C).

Substituting Syrup for Sugar

Recall that syrups contain one or more sugars and water. Most syrups contain about 80 percent sugar and 20 percent water. This means that 1 pound (or 1 kilogram) of syrup typically contains 0.8 pound (or 0.8 kilogram) sugar and 0.2 pound (or 0.2 kilogram) water. Because a 1:1 substitution of granulated sugar with syrup changes the amount of sugar solids in a product by about 20 percent, it is sometimes desirable to calculate and adjust the amount of syrup and liquid when making a substitution. Starting guidelines for changing between granulated sugar and many syrups (those that are 80 percent sugar and 20 percent water) are as follows. *Note:* The following calculations do not adjust for differences in sweetness or other properties of sweeteners. Recall, for example, that the Honey Board recommends substituting honey 1:1 for sugar while reducing the amount of water.

- *To substitute syrup for granulated sugar:* Divide the weight of sugar by 0.80 to determine the weight of syrup to use. Reduce the amount of water or other liquid by the difference between the two. For example, for 1 pound (16 ounces) of sugar, use 20 ounces of syrup and reduce the amount of liquid by 4 ounces. For 500 grams of sugar, use 625 grams of syrup and reduce the amount of liquid by 125 grams.

- *To substitute granulated sugar for syrup:* Multiply the weight of syrup by 0.80 to determine the weight of granulated sugar to use. Increase the amount of liquid by the difference between the two. For example, for 1 pound (16 ounces) of syrup, use 12.8 ounces of sugar and increase the amount of liquid by 3.2 ounces. For 500 grams of syrup, use 400 grams of sugar and increase the amount of liquid by 100 grams.

QUESTIONS FOR REVIEW

1. Draw out and label two monosaccharides and two disaccharides. Which of these represents the structure of regular granulated sugar?

2. What are other names for glucose, the monosaccharide?

3. How would you describe sugar crystals?

4. Which is more likely to crystallize sooner—syrup containing only one type of sugar molecule, or syrup that is identical in every way except that it contains two or more types? Explain your answer.

5. What does it mean to say that sugars are hygroscopic? Which of the common sugars is most hygroscopic?

6. Provide an example of when using a highly hygroscopic sweetener is desirable; provide an example of when using a highly hygroscopic sweetener is undesirable.

7. What is the main difference between extrafine, coarse, and superfine sugars? What is another name for each?

8. How does evaporated cane juice compare to regular granulated sugar in color, flavor, and crystalline size?

9. Coarse sugar is more expensive than regular granulated sugar. In fact, it can be three times the price of regular granulated sugar. Why use it?

10. What is another name for powdered sugar? Why might powdered sugar have a different flavor and sweetness than regular granulated sugar?

11. What is the difference between 6X and 10X powdered sugar? What is each best used for?

12. About how much molasses is in light brown sugar? About how much is in dark brown sugar? What are the main reasons for using brown sugar in baked goods?

13. Since light and dark brown sugar typically contain about the same amount of molasses, what is the difference between the two?

14. Which is the brown sugar equivalent of coarse sugar?

15. Provide an example of an unrefined noncentrifugal sugar. How are noncentrifugal sugars made?

16. How would you define syrup?

17. How can two syrups contain the same amount of water, but one be much thicker than the other?

18. What is the makeup of full invert syrup?

19. Draw out the process for the commercial production of invert syrup.

20. What are the advantages of invert syrup over sucrose in baked goods? In icings, confections, and fondants?

21. What are the characteristics of premium-grade molasses? Why is it not necessarily the best molasses for baking?

22. Draw out the process for the commercial production of glucose corn syrups.

23. What are the differences in makeup between a high-conversion glucose corn syrup and a low-conversion one?

24. What is meant by the DE of glucose corn syrup?

25. What are the properties of high-conversion glucose corn syrups? What are the properties of low-conversion glucose corn syrups?

26. Which type of corn-derived syrup is most similar in composition to invert syrup?

27. What is dextrose? What is it used for?

28. What is the difference between glucose corn syrup with a DE of 42 and dried glucose syrup with the same DE?

29. What is isomalt? Why is it sometimes used instead of sugar?

30. Which polyol is closest to granulated sugar in taste and in other properties? How does it—and other polyols—compare to sugar in caloric content?

31. What are the most common uses for crystalline fructose?

32. What ingredient, besides sucralose, is added to Splenda? What is its function?

33. What are the eight main functions of sweeteners? Which one of these is the only function that high-intensity sweeteners typically provide?

34. Why might granulated sugars assist in leavening while syrups do not?

35. What are the two components in milk that allow it to undergo Maillard browning?

36. Why might white chocolate darken and develop off flavors as it ages?

37. Explain the proper procedures for handling and storing honey.

QUESTIONS FOR DISCUSSION

1. Rank the following sugars from highest amount of molasses to lowest: demerara, regular granulated sugar, evaporated cane juice, dark brown sugar, muscovado.

2. What might happen to the quality of white cake if too much invert syrup is added? When answering this question, assume that you've adjusted your formula for the amount of water in syrup.

3. You prepare simple syrup from two parts sugar to one part water. After several days of refrigeration, the syrup becomes cloudy as the sugar crystallizes. What could have been added to the syrup to prevent sugar crystallization?

4. You want to make soft, moist cookies. Which syrup will be best to add to your formula: regular glucose corn syrup or invert syrup? Why?

5. You're substituting 8 pounds (or 8 kilograms) of sucrose in a formula with glucose corn syrup. How much glucose corn syrup should you add and how should you adjust the water so that you end up with the same amount of sweetener and water as in the original formula? Show your work.

6. You're substituting 8 pounds (or 8 kilograms) of sucrose in a formula with maple syrup, which is 67 percent—not 80 percent—sugar solids. What adjustments should be made to this formula?

EXERCISES AND EXPERIMENTS

1. Evaluate the Sensory Characteristics of Each of the Following Sugars and Sweeteners

Using the Results Table that follows, first fill in the Description column with the brand name of each sweetener. Include additional information that further describes and differentiates the sweetener from others of the same kind (granulated sugar, for example, could be identified as cane or beet sugar, and whether it is fine or extrafine). Next, compare and describe the sweeteners in appearance, smell, and taste. Use this opportunity to identify different sugars from their sensory characteristics alone. Add any additional comments or observations that you might have to the last column in the table.

RESULTS TABLE ■ A COMPARISON OF DIFFERENT SUGARS AND SYRUPS

TYPE OF SWEETENER	DESCRIPTION	APPEARANCE	SWEETNESS/FLAVOR	COMMENTS
Regular granulated				
Evaporated cane juice				
Powdered				
Coarse				
Light brown				
Dark brown				
Crystalline fructose				
Isomalt				
Splenda				
Invert syrup				
Glucose corn syrup, medium DE				
Glucose corn syrup, low DE				
Molasses				
Honey				

2. How the Amount of Sugar Affects the Overall Quality of Pound Cake

OBJECTIVES

To demonstrate how the amount of sugar affects:
- The shape of baked cake
- The crispness and the extent of Maillard browning on the crust of pound cake
- The moistness, tenderness, crumb structure, and volume of pound cake
- The sweetness and overall flavor of pound cake
- The overall acceptability of pound cake

PRODUCTS PREPARED

Pound cake made with:
- Full amount of sugar (control product)
- No sugar
- Half the amount of sugar
- One and a half times the amount of sugar
- Double the amount of sugar
- Other, if desired (three-quarters the amount of sugar, one and one-quarter the amount of sugar, etc.)

MATERIALS AND EQUIPMENT

- Pound cake batter, enough to make 24 or more cupcakes of each variation
- Muffin tins (2½" or 3½" size) and liners or pan spray
- Size #16 (2¾ ounce) portion-control scoop or equivalent
- Ruler

PROCEDURE

- Preheat oven according to formula.
- Lightly spray or grease muffin tins with pan coating; label with amount of sweetener to be added to cake batter.
- Prepare cake batter using the high-ratio pound cake formula, or using any basic high-ratio pound cake formula. Prepare one batch of batter for each variation.
- Scoop batter into prepared muffin tins using #16 scoop (or equivalent); save excess batter.
- If desired, place muffin tins onto half sheet pans.
- Use an oven thermometer placed in center of oven to read oven temperature; record results here _____.
- Place filled muffin tins into preheated oven and set timer according to formula.
- Bake until control product pulls away slightly from sides of pan, cake springs back when center top is lightly pressed, and wooden pick inserted into center of cake comes out clean. Control product should be lightly browned. Remove *all* cupcakes from oven after same length of time, even though some will be paler in color or have not risen properly. If necessary, however, adjust bake times for oven variances. Record bake times in Comments column of Results Table 1, which follows.
- Transfer to wire racks to cool to room temperature.
- Record any potential sources of error that might make it difficult to draw proper conclusions from the experiment. In particular, be aware of difficulties in how batter was mixed and handled, and any problems with ovens.

- When cupcakes are completely cooled, evaluate average height as follows:
  - Slice three cupcakes from each batch in half, being careful not to compress.
  - Measure height of each cupcake by placing a ruler along the flat edge at the cupcake's maximum height. Record results for each of three cupcakes in 1/16" (10 mm) increments in Results Table 1.
  - Calculate the average cupcake height by adding the heights of the cupcakes and dividing this by 3; record results in Results Table 1.
  - Evaluate the shape of cupcakes (even rounded top, peaked top, dips in center, etc.) and record results in Results Table 1.
- Evaluate the sensory characteristics of completely cooled products and record evaluations in Results Table 2. Be sure to compare each in turn to the control product and consider the following:
  - Crust color, from very light to very dark, on a scale of one to five
  - Crust texture (soft and moist, soft and dry, crisp and dry, etc.)
  - Crumb appearance (small uniform air cells, large irregular air cells, tunnels, etc.; also, evaluate color)
  - Crumb texture (tough/tender, moist/dry, gummy, spongy, crumbly, etc.)
  - Sweetness, from not sweet at all to extremely sweet, on a scale of one to five
  - Overall flavor (egg flavor, floury taste, saltiness, etc.)
  - Overall acceptability, from highly unacceptable to highly acceptable, on a scale of one to five
  - Add any additional comments, as necessary.

High-Ratio Pound Cake

INGREDIENT	POUND	OUNCE	GRAMS	BAKER'S PERCENTAGE
Flour, cake		12	350	100
Shortening, high-ratio		8	230	66
Sugar, granulated		14	400	115
Dried milk solids		1.4	40	11
Salt		0.2	7	2
Baking powder		0.4	10	3
Water		6	175	50
Eggs, whole		8	230	66
Total	3	4	1442	413

Method of Preparation (for control product, full amount of sugar)

1. Preheat oven to 375°F (190°C).
2. Allow ingredients to come to room temperature.
3. Blend flour, dried milk solids, salt, and baking powder thoroughly by sifting together three times onto parchment paper.
4. Place sifted dry ingredients and granulated sugar in bowl; add shortening and half the water (3 ounces or 87 grams).
5. Mix on low for 30 seconds; stop and scrape bowl and beater.
6. Continue mixing on low for an additional 4 minutes, stopping once a minute to scrape the bowl and beater. Batter should be smooth.
7. Combine the remaining water (3 ounces or 88 grams) and lightly beaten eggs with a whisk.
8. Add half water/egg mixture to batter and mix on low for 4 minutes; stop and scrape bowl.
9. Add the remaining water/egg mixture and mix on low for 4 minutes. Batter should be thin.
10. Scrape bowl and set aside batter until ready to use.
11. Bake cupcakes for approximately 20–22 minutes.

Method of Preparation for cakes with varying amounts of sugar:

Follow the Method of Preparation for the control product (full amount of sugar), except add the following amounts of sugar in step 4:

1. For half the amount, add 7 ounces (200 grams) sugar.

2. For one and a half times the amount, add 1 pound, 5 ounces (600 grams) sugar.

3. For double the amount, add 1 pound, 12 ounces (800 grams) sugar.

SOURCES OF ERROR

_____

_____

RESULTS TABLE 1 ■ EVALUATION OF THICKNESS OF BATTER AND SIZE AND SHAPE OF HIGH-RATIO POUND CAKES MADE WITH DIFFERENT AMOUNTS OF SUGAR

AMOUNT OF SUGAR	HEIGHT OF THREE CUPCAKES	AVERAGE HEIGHT OF ONE CUPCAKE	CUPCAKE SHAPE	COMMENTS
Full amount (control product)				
None				
Half the amount				
One and a half times the amount				
Double the amount				

RESULTS TABLE 2 ■ SENSORY CHARACTERISTICS OF POUND CAKES MADE WITH DIFFERENT AMOUNTS OF SUGAR

AMOUNT OF SUGAR	CRUST COLOR AND TEXTURE	CRUMB APPEARANCE AND TEXTURE	SWEETNESS	OVERALL FLAVOR	OVERALL ACCEPTABILITY	COMMENTS
Full amount (control product)						
None						
Half the amount						
One and a half times the amount						
Double the amount						

CONCLUSIONS

1. Did the amount of sugar affect the *shape* of the baked cupcakes? That is, did a change in amount make the cake flatten, peak, or fall?

_____

_____

2. How did the amount of sugar affect the *color* of the baked cupcakes? That is, did more sugar make the cakes lighter or darker or have no effect?

_____

_____

3. How did the amount of sugar affect the overall flavor of the cupcakes, that is, did more sugar make the cakes more or less eggy, salty, etc.?

_____

_____

4. How did the amount of sugar affect the *tenderness* of the cupcakes, that is, did more sugar make the cakes tougher or more tender or have no effect?

_____

_____

5. As the amount of sugar *decreased* from the amount in the control product, how did cake volume change? How did the cake volume change as the amount of sugar increased?

_____

_____

6. How did the amount of sugar affect the sweetness and overall flavor of the pound cakes?

_____

_____

7. Did you have any sources of error that might significantly affect the results of your experiment? If so, what could you do differently next time to minimize error?

_____

_____

8. Why might a change in the amount of sugar affect the shape of cupcakes?

_____

_____

9. Why might a change in the amount of sugar affect the color of the pound cakes? That is, what reaction increases as the amount of sugar increases?

_____

_____

10. Why might a change in the amount of sugar affect the tenderness of the pound cakes?

_____

_____

11. Which pound cake had the lowest volume, and how does your knowledge about the effects of sugar on the formation of structure help explain why volume was low for this cake?

_____

_____

12. Which pound cake had the highest volume, and how does your knowledge about the effects of sugar on the formation of structure help explain why volume was high for this cake?

_____

_____

3. How the Type of Sweetener Affects the Overall Quality of Pound Cake

OBJECTIVES

To demonstrate how different sweeteners affect:

- The density of cake batter
- The crispness and the extent of Maillard browning on the crust of pound cake
- The moistness, tenderness, crumb structure, and volume of pound cake

- The sweetness and overall flavor of pound cake
- The overall acceptability of pound cake

PRODUCTS PREPARED

Pound cake made with

- Regular granulated sugar (control product)
- Dark (or light) brown sugar
- Honey (formula adjusted for amount of water in honey)
- Invert syrup (formula adjusted for amount of water in syrup)

- Splenda (formula adjusted so that sugar is substituted with Splenda 1:1 *by volume*)
- Other, if desired (glucose corn syrup, malt syrup, molasses, maltitol, agave, etc.)

MATERIALS AND EQUIPMENT

- Pound cake batter, enough to make 24 or more cupcakes of each variation
- Muffin tins (2½" or 3½" size) and liners or pan spray
- Size #16 (2¾ ounce) portion-control scoop or equivalent
- Ruler

PROCEDURE

- Preheat oven according to formula.
- Lightly spray or grease muffin tins with pan coating; label with type of sweetener to be added to cake batter.
- Prepare cake batter using the high-ratio pound cake formula given previously, or using any basic high-ratio pound cake formula. Prepare one batch of batter for each variation.
- Scoop batter into prepared muffin tins using #16 scoop (or equivalent); save excess batter.
- If desired, place muffin tins onto half sheet pans.

- Use an oven thermometer placed in center of oven to read oven temperature; record results here _____.
- Place filled muffin tins into preheated oven and set timer according to formula.
- Bake until control product (made with regular granulated sugar) pulls away slightly from sides of pan, cake springs back when center top is lightly pressed, and wooden pick inserted into center of cake comes out clean. Control product should be lightly browned. Remove *all* cupcakes from oven after same length of time, even though some will be paler or darker in color or have not risen as high. If necessary, however, adjust bake times for oven variances. Record bake times in Comments column of Results Table 1, which follows.
- Transfer to wire racks to cool to room temperature.
- Record any potential sources of error that might make it difficult to draw proper conclusions from the experiment. In particular, be aware of difficulties in how batter was mixed and handled, and any problems with ovens.
- Measure density (weight per volume) of cake batter. To measure density,
  - Carefully spoon sample of cake batter into tared measuring cup.
  - Visually check cup to confirm that no large air gaps are present.
  - Level the top surface of the cup with a straight-edge.
  - Weigh the amount of cake batter in each cup and record results in Results Table 1.
- When cupcakes are completely cooled, evaluate average height as follows:
  - Slice three cupcakes from each batch in half, being careful not to compress.
  - Measure height of each cupcake by placing a ruler along the flat edge at the cupcake's maximum height. Record results for each of three cupcakes in 1/16" (10 mm) increments in Results Table 1.
  - Calculate the average cupcake height by adding the heights of the cupcakes and dividing this by 3; record results in Results Table 1.
  - Evaluate the shape of cupcakes (even rounded top, peaked top, dips in center, etc.) and record results in Results Table 1.
- Evaluate the sensory characteristics of completely cooled products and record evaluations in Results Table 2. Be sure to compare each in turn to the control product and consider the following:
  - Crust color, from very light to very dark, on a scale of one to five
  - Crust texture (soft and moist, soft and dry, crisp and dry, etc.)
  - Crumb appearance (small uniform air cells, large irregular air cells, tunnels, etc.; also, evaluate color)
  - Crumb texture (tough/tender, moist/dry, gummy, spongy, crumbly, etc.)
  - Sweetness, from not sweet at all to extremely sweet, on a scale of one to five
  - Overall flavor (egg flavor, floury taste, saltiness, molasses, caramelized, etc.)
  - Overall acceptability, from highly unacceptable to highly acceptable, on a scale of one to five
  - Add any additional comments, as necessary.

Method of Preparation for cakes made with different sweeteners:

Follow the Method of Preparation for the control product (regular granulated sugar) except make the following adjustments when using these sweeteners:

1. For cake made with brown sugar, substitute brown sugar for granulated sugar in step 4.

2. For cake made with honey (80°Brix), measure 17.5 ounces (500 grams) honey and add it in step 4 along with the dry ingredients and shortening; omit sugar and water in this step and reduce water in step 7 to 2.5 ounces (70 grams).

3. For cake made with invert syrup (73°Brix), measure 18.5 ounces (535 grams) invert syrup and add it in step 4 along with the dry ingredients and shortening; omit sugar and water in this step and reduce water in step 7 to 1.5 ounces (40 grams).

4. For cake made with Splenda, measure 1.75 ounces (50 grams) Splenda and add it in step 5 along with the other dry ingredients, shortening, and water; omit sugar in this step.

 **SOURCES OF ERROR**

_____

_____

RESULTS TABLE 1 ■ EVALUATION OF DENSITY OF BATTER AND SIZE AND SHAPE OF HIGH-RATIO POUND CAKES MADE WITH DIFFERENT AMOUNTS OF SUGAR

TYPE OF SWEETENER	DENSITY OF BATTER	HEIGHT OF THREE CUPCAKES	AVERAGE HEIGHT OF ONE CUPCAKE	CUPCAKE SHAPE	COMMENTS
Granulated sugar (control product)					
Brown sugar					
Honey					
Invert syrup					
Splenda					

RESULTS TABLE 2 ■ SENSORY CHARACTERISTICS OF POUND CAKES MADE WITH DIFFERENT SWEETENERS

TYPE OF SWEETENER	CRUST COLOR AND TEXTURE	CRUMB APPEARANCE AND TEXTURE	SWEETNESS	OVERALL FLAVOR	OVERALL ACCEPTABILITY	COMMENTS
Granulated sugar (control product)						
Brown sugar						
Honey						
Invert syrup						
Splenda						

CONCLUSIONS

1. Compare density of batters made with syrups to those made with regular granulated sugar (control product) and brown sugar. Overall, did batters made with syrups have higher or lower *densities* than those made with crystalline sugars?

_____

_____

    a. Did this carry over to differences in *cupcake height*? Explain why this might be so.

    _____

    _____

2. Compare cupcakes made with brown sugar to those made with regular granulated sugar (control product). What were the main *differences* in appearance, flavor, and texture? Why might there be these differences?

_____

_____

    a. What were the main *similarities* in appearance, flavor, and texture? Why might there be these similarities?

    _____

    _____

3. Compare cupcakes made with *invert syrup* to those made with regular granulated sugar (control product): What were the main differences in appearance, flavor, and texture?

_____

_____

4. Review your text for the composition of invert syrup and record here:

_____

_____

    a. How does its composition explain why cupcakes made with invert syrup might be different in *color* from those made with regular granulated sugar (control product)?

    _____

    _____

    b. How does its composition explain why cupcakes made with invert syrup might be different in *crust texture* from those made with regular granulated sugar (control product)?

    _____

    _____

5. Review the adjustments to the formula for cupcakes made with invert syrup; record information here:

_____

_____

    a. Use this information to explain why the fact that invert syrup contains water *does not* explain any differences in pound cakes made with invert syrup and with granulated sugar.

    _____

    _____

6. Compare cupcakes made with *honey* to those made with *invert syrup:* What were the main differences in appearance, flavor, and texture?

_____

_____

    a. Based on the results of this experiment, is the fact that honey is an invert syrup reflected in the appearance, flavor, and texture of cupcakes made with honey? That is, were cupcakes made with honey similar to those made with invert syrup? Explain.

    _____

    _____

7. Compare cupcakes made with Splenda to those made with regular granulated sugar (control product). What were the main differences in appearance, flavor, and texture?

_____

_____

    a. According to the manufacturer, the recommended starting level for Splenda is the 1:1 replacement for sugar (by volume) that was used to make the Splenda cupcake in this experiment. Based on sweetness alone, would you increase, decrease, or keep the same usage of Splenda in this formula, if you were to make it again?

    _____

    _____

8. Which pound cakes did you feel were acceptable overall, and why?

_____

_____

9. Did you have any sources of error that might significantly affect the results of your experiment? If so, what could you do differently next time to minimize error?

_____

_____

10. Go to www.splendafoodservice.com, a website by the manufacturer of Splenda, and read tips for using Splenda in cooking and baking. Which of their suggestions might be worthwhile trying, to improve the quality of the pound cake made with Splenda? Explain your answer.

_____

_____

11. Select one sweetener from those tested (besides Splenda) that did not produce the "perfect" cupcake. If you could change anything in the formula or the method of preparation, what would you change to make the product more acceptable?

_____

_____

CHAPTER 9

THICKENING AND GELLING AGENTS

CHAPTER **OBJECTIVES**

1. Define various thickening and gelling agents used in bakeshops and describe their characteristics and uses.

2. Describe the process of starch gelatinization and factors that affect it.

3. Describe the functions of thickening and gelling agents.

4. Provide guidelines for selecting a thickening or gelling agent.

 INTRODUCTION

The simplest way to thicken food is to add an ingredient that is itself thickened or gelled. Heavy cream, sour cream, many cheeses, jams and jellies, fruit purees, thick syrups, yogurt, and buttermilk are useful thickeners in the bakeshop. These ingredients do more than thicken, of course. They add flavor, they alter appearance, and they contribute to the nutritional value of the final product.

Other ingredients are added exclusively—or almost so—to thicken and gel. These so-called thickening and gelling agents—gelatin, vegetable gums, and starches—are added to fillings, glazes, sauces, and creams. They function by absorbing or by trapping large amounts of water. The most common thickening and gelling agent in the bakeshop is not often thought of as one, however, because it is used in so many products for so many reasons. This common thickening and gelling agent is the egg. Eggs will be discussed separately in Chapter 11.

There are other ways to thicken and gel food products besides adding an ingredient. For example, the formation of an emulsion or foam provides thickening and sometimes gelling. This is why heavy cream, which is an emulsion of butterfat droplets in milk, is thicker than milk. When it is whipped, the heavy cream foams, and in the process it thickens further. The more the cream is whipped, the more it foams and the stiffer it becomes—all without the use of a thickening agent.

THE PROCESS OF THICKENING AND GELLING

Thickening and gelling agents—gelatin, vegetable gums, and starches—have one thing in common: They are all composed of very large molecules. Some, such as starches and gums, are polysaccharides. Others, such as gelatin, are proteins.

Polysaccharides are very large molecules made of many (*poly*) sugar molecules (*saccharides*) linked one to the next. Often, thousands of sugar molecules are linked together in a single polysaccharide molecule. Sometimes, all sugar molecules in a polysaccharide are the same, but often there is a mix of two or more different sugars. What distinguishes one polysaccharide from another is the type of sugar that makes it up, how many are linked together, and how they are linked. Recall from Chapter 8, for example, that starch molecules are made up of glucose sugars and inulin consists primarily of fructose. Besides being different in the type of sugar, starch and inulin differ in the number of sugars. Starch, with thousands of sugar units, is a much more effective thickener and gelling agent than inulin, which has, at most, sixty sugars. Both, however, are classified as polysaccharides.

Proteins are very large molecules made of many amino acids linked one to the next. Often, thousands of amino acids are linked together in a single protein molecule. More than twenty common amino acids make up proteins. What distinguishes one protein from another is the number and arrangement of these amino acids within the protein molecule.

Thickening occurs when water and other molecules or particles in a product move around rather slowly. For example, this will happen when large molecules, such as polysaccharides and proteins, bump and entangle. It also happens when water is absorbed and trapped by starch granules, or when air bubbles (in foams) or fat droplets (in emulsions) slow water movement.

Gelling occurs when water and other molecules in a product are prevented from moving around at all. For example, this will happen when large molecules, such as polysaccharides and proteins, bond with one another, forming a large web or network that traps water and other molecules. It also happens when an extremely large number of air bubbles or fat droplets are incorporated into food.

Some thickening and gelling agents do both; that is, some thicken when used at low levels and gel when used at higher levels (Figure 9.1). Examples of thickening and gelling agents that both thicken and gel include gelatin, cornstarch, and pectin. Other ingredients only thicken. They will not gel, no matter how much is used. Instead, they get thicker and gummier. Examples of ingredients that only thicken include guar gum, gum arabic, and waxy maize starch.

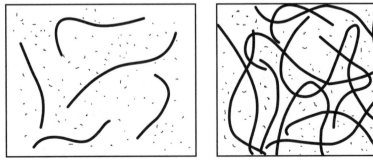

FIGURE 9.1 The difference between thickening and gelling

Thickening   *Gelling*

🥤 GELATIN

Gelatin—whether in powder form or sheets—is a staple in the bakeshop. When properly prepared, it forms an appealing crystal-clear gel with bounce and spring. Best of all, gelatin melts quickly and cleanly in the mouth.

Gelatin has many uses. It is a necessary ingredient in Bavarian creams, fruit mousses, and cold soufflés. It is a good stabilizer for whipped cream and many cake fillings, and it provides the characteristic texture of marshmallows and gummy confections. Gelatin mixtures, when cooled to thicken, can be whipped, much as egg whites can be whipped.

Gelatin is an animal protein. Most food-grade gelatin is extracted from pigskin, although small amounts are from cattle bones and hides. A specialty form of gelatin is purified from fish; fish gelatin is called isinglass. Gelatin is not found in any vegetable sources.

How Gelatin is Produced

Food-grade gelatin is sometimes called Type A gelatin, A for the acid treatment it receives. To produce Type A gelatin, clean, chopped pigskins are soaked for several hours or days in cold acid. This breaks down the pigskin's connective tissue, transforming its rigid, ropelike protein fibers (called collagen) into smaller, invisible strands of gelatin. Hot water is then used for dissolving gelatin and extracting it from the pigskins. This process is repeated up to six times, with each extraction occurring at a progressively higher temperature. By the last extraction, water is at the boiling point and the last bits of usable gelatin are removed.

The best-quality gelatin comes from the first extraction. It has the strongest gel, the clearest, lightest color, and the mildest flavor. Later extractions produce weaker gelatin that is darker in color and slightly meaty in flavor. To standardize gelatin from batch to batch, manufacturers blend solutions from several extractions. Once blended, the gelatin is filtered, concentrated, formed into sheets or "noodles," dried, and ground. The ground gelatin is either sold as is or made into sheet gelatin. To make sheet gelatin, powdered gelatin is redissolved, reheated, then cast, cooled, and dried as a gel film.

Gelatin is rated by its gel strength, also called Bloom rating. Gelatin with a high Bloom rating forms firm gels. Because Bloom rating is related to gelatin quality, gelatin with a high Bloom rating also has a light color and clean flavor. It sets fast and produces a short, less stringy gel than gelatin with a lower Bloom rating.

A BRIEF HISTORY OF GELATIN

Early recipes calling for gelatin describe how to first boil calves' hoofs. Not until the early 1800s was purified gelatin available for purchase, although a British patent for its manufacture was issued as early as the mid-1700s. Throughout the 1800s, gelatin was sold shredded or in sheets.

Powdered gelatin was a later invention. It came about in America in the late 1800s at the request of housewives. In response, Knox Gelatine dried gelatin sheets until brittle, then pulverized them into granules, which were easy to measure with measuring spoons. Granular gelatin also had the advantage of dissolving faster than shredded gelatin. The powdered gelatin industry was born, with Jell-O gelatin just a few years away.

THE BLOOM GELOMETER AND BLOOM RATINGS

The Bloom scale is a rating system that was invented in the 1800s. It was named for the French chemist who devised a standard test and an instrument—the Bloom gelometer—for measuring gel strength. The gelometer measures the force it takes for a small plunger to sink a certain distance into a gelatin gel prepared under standardized conditions. The more force required, the higher the bloom rating and the stronger the gel. Although more reliable instruments have replaced the gelometer, gel strength is still reported as Bloom rating, also called Bloom value or Bloom strength.

Most food-grade gelatins range from about 50 to 300 on the Bloom scale. Gelatin sold to pastry chefs is rarely, if ever, labeled with its Bloom rating, but manufacturers can provide that information. Most powdered gelatin in bakeshops in North America is rated about 230 Bloom.

Sheet gelatin is often designated by the name of a precious metal. At about 250 Bloom, platinum-labeled gelatin sheets are closest in Bloom rating to powdered gelatin. Platinum sheets weigh 0.06 ounces (1.7 grams). Gold-labeled sheets are rated about 200 Bloom and weigh 0.07 ounces (2 grams) per sheet; silver-labeled are about 160 Bloom and weigh 0.09 ounces (2.5 grams) per sheet; and bronze-labeled are about 140 Bloom and weigh 0.12 ounces (3.3 grams) per sheet. Notice that the weight of the sheet increases as the Bloom rating decreases. This makes it easy to switch from one quality of sheet gelatin to another, as long as sheets are counted, not weighed. If a formula calls for ten sheets, use ten sheets of gelatin, no matter the Bloom rating. The actual amount being added is automatically adjusted by the change in weight per sheet.

North America and the European Union follow strict quality control guidelines for gelatin manufacture. These guidelines have been reviewed and updated since mad cow disease spread through cattle herds in Great Britain in the late 1980s. Mad cow disease (bovine spongiform encephalopathy) is a disease that infects the brain and spinal cord of cattle. To date, it has not been found in gelatin products, but precautions are taken to ensure that all raw materials used in gelatin manufacture are from healthy animals that have been approved for human consumption.

How to Use Gelatin

The term *bloom* has another meaning besides gelatin gel strength. It also refers to the method used for hydrating gelatin—for adding it to cold liquid and allowing it to swell. Gelatin is first hydrated so that it is less likely to clump later in use.

To bloom gelatin, add powder to five or ten times its weight in cold liquid. Sheets are typically added to excess cold water, then removed and gently squeezed. Use almost any liquid to bloom gelatin, as long as the liquid is cold. However, certain fruit juices, such as pineapple, kiwi, and papaya, must be heated and cooled before use. Heat inactivates the protease enzymes in these fruits. Protease enzymes break down gelatin and other proteins, preventing them from gelling. Liquids that are high in acid, such as lemon juice, may weaken gelatin slightly, but they will not liquefy it. If gelatin is used with highly acidic ingredients, a slightly higher level of gelatin may be needed.

HELPFUL HINT

Inexperienced pastry cooks sometimes have difficulty adding gelatin solutions to cold preparations. If they are not careful, the gelatin lumps, and the mixture must be discarded. This can happen when stabilizing whipped cream with gelatin, for example.

To avoid lumps, be sure the gelatin solution is hot—at least 140°F (60°C)—and not just warm. Temper the mixture by stirring a small amount of whipped cream into the hot solution, then add this mixture slowly to the whipped cream. Tempering serves to dilute the gelatin while it is still warm, so that as it cools, it gels more slowly and uniformly.

FROM HOT LIQUID TO SOFT SOLID

Gelatin dissolved in hot liquid can be thought of as invisible strands moving around rapidly. As the solution cools, the invisible strands begin to slow. Sections of strands coil up like telephone cords, and the coiled sections double over onto themselves. Often, a section from one strand wraps itself around another strand's coil. Over time, these tangled sections stack up, forming junctions. Water, trapped in this three-dimensional web, is unable to move around. The mixture is now a soft solid.

These junctions are very fragile and easily broken with the smallest amount of heat. In fact, gelatin generally melts completely to a liquid at about 80°–90°F (27°–32°C), which is lower than body temperature. This provides for a pleasant mouthfeel. The actual melting temperature, however, depends on the gelatin's Bloom rating and on the level of gelatin used.

Most of the gelled junctions in a gelatin web form within the first hour or two of chilling, but the process continues over the next 18 hours or so. Mousses and creams prepared with gelatin are always firmer the second day, even when they are well covered and have not dried out.

Gelatin powder and gelatin sheets typically take from 5 to 10 minutes to hydrate properly. Once bloomed, gelatin is heated gently in a saucepan to melt before adding it to cold preparations.

If a formula calls for hot liquid, there is no need to heat gelatin separately to melt. It is faster and easier to add the bloomed gelatin directly to the hot liquid. Do not allow gelatin to boil, and remove it from heat as soon as the gelatin dissolves. Extended heat damages gelatin and lowers its Bloom rating.

Switching between Sheets and Powders

Which is better, gelatin sheets or gelatin powder? This question has no one right answer. Some bakers and pastry chefs favor sheet gelatin, others favor powder. Sheet gelatin is more popular in Europe than in the rest of the world.

Whichever they favor, versatile chefs know how to use either sheet or powdered gelatin, and they know how to substitute one for the other. Before discussing how to do this, it is helpful to first understand the advantages and disadvantages of each form of gelatin.

Sheet gelatin cannot spill, so it is less messy than powder. Sheets can be counted, and many find this easier than weighing, at least for small-scale production. For large-scale production, however, this is no longer an advantage; it is easier to weigh large quantities of sheets than to count them. When the sheets are added to excess water, the user must be careful that they do not dissolve and disappear completely in too-warm water.

Powdered gelatin is produced worldwide and in much larger quantities than sheet gelatin. This high volume provides for economies of scale that keep prices low. And, because powder is produced in the United States, there are no added import costs to drive up prices.

HELPFUL HINT

When blooming gelatin sheets in excess water, the water should be about room temperature (70°F; 21°C) or cooler. Don't forget that water from the tap is warmer in the summer than it is in the winter, and that it is warmer in Tucson, Arizona, than it is in Toronto, Ontario. Some chefs bloom sheet gelatin the same way as powdered gelatin, by adding it to five or ten times its weight in water.

Convenience is as important as—sometimes more important than—cost. Convenience means different things to different people. While some find counting sheets more convenient than weighing powder, others find the opposite to be true. Probably the greatest inconvenience, however, is running out of an ingredient altogether. If this happens with sheet gelatin, it could be difficult to receive a new shipment

WHAT IS INSTANT GELATIN?

Instant gelatin is a new gelatin product that does not need to be bloomed and heated before use. Instant gelatin has undergone a special drying process. It is a fine-grained powdered gelatin that dissolves instantly in cold water. To prevent lumping, instant gelatin must be mixed with other ingredients—sugar, for example—before it is added to water. Unlike regular gelatin, which requires about 18 hours to firm up, instant gelatin firms up in less than 30 minutes.

quickly. Sheet gelatin is a specialty item imported from Europe, and it is not available from all purveyors. Powdered gelatin, however, is readily available from most purveyors and, in a pinch, can be purchased at a supermarket.

In theory, sheet and powdered gelatin can be used interchangeably. In practice, the conversion between sheets and powder depends on Bloom rating. For powdered gelatin with a rating of 230 Bloom, the following conversion holds:

17 gelatin sheets = 1 ounce (28 grams) gelatin powder

This does not necessarily mean that 17 gelatin sheets weigh 1 ounce (28 grams), although that is essentially true for platinum sheets. Instead, it means that 17 sheets of any grade provide about the same gelling strength as 1 ounce (28 grams) of powder. When converting from powder to sheets, or vice versa, or when converting from one brand or type of gelatin to another, it is always a good idea to prepare a test batch first, to confirm that the conversion works.

Also remember when converting between sheets and powder that gelatin absorbs about five times its weight in water. That is, 1 ounce (30 grams) of gelatin absorbs about 5 ounces (150 grams) of liquid. While this water is always listed in formulas using powdered gelatin, it is not listed in formulas where sheets are placed in excess water. This difference in water should be considered when converting between sheets and powder.

VEGETABLE GUMS

Vegetable gums are polysaccharides that absorb large quantities of water, swelling to produce thick liquids and gels. While some gums have a gummy texture, most do not when used correctly. All are vegetable in origin, meaning that they are extracted and purified from trees, bushes, shrubs, seeds, seaweed, or microorganisms. Many are all natural. Others, such as cellulose gum, are from natural sources but are chemically modified to improve their properties.

All vegetable gums are an excellent source of soluble dietary fiber. Dietary fiber consists of polysaccharides that are not digested by the human body. Health experts recommend that consumers eat more fiber, since it offers certain health benefits.

Pectin

Pectin is present in all fruits, but fruits vary in the amount of pectin they contain. Fruits high in pectin include apples, plums, cranberries, raspberries, and citrus peel. These and other fruits high in pectin can be made into jams and jellies without any added pectin.

Pectin thickens and, in the presence of acid and high amounts of sugar, it gels. Pectin gels are clear, not cloudy, and they have an attractive sheen and clean flavor. This makes pectin a great choice with fruit products. Pectin is commonly used in mirrors, glazes, jams and jellies, bakery fillings, and fruit confections. It can be purchased as a dry powder, which is typically extracted and purified from citrus peel or apple skins.

Agar

Agar—also called *agar-agar*, or *kanten* in Japan—is derived from any of several species of red seaweed (*Gracilaria* or *Gelidium*, for example). Asian cultures have used agar for centuries. Today, it is harvested worldwide and commonly sold in the United States as dry powder or as strands. While strands require soaking and several minutes of boiling in water to dissolve, agar powder dissolves in hot water in about a minute. Both strands and powder gel quickly as they cool, much more quickly than gelatin.

Agar is a polysaccharide and not a protein like gelatin, but it is sometimes nicknamed the vegetable gelatin because gels made from agar are similar to those made from gelatin. While they are similar, agar and gelatin gels are not identical. For one thing, much less agar is needed than gelatin, and agar gels stay firm without refrigeration. This makes agar useful for firming piping gels and in certain jellied confections. Agar is also a good warm-weather stabilizer for icings and fillings, and it can be used to replace pork-based gelatin whenever dietary or religious restrictions warrant its use. However, because agar does not melt as readily as gelatin, it does not have as pleasant a mouthfeel, especially if used improperly.

Agar cannot be whipped, as gelatin can. This means it cannot substitute for gelatin in aerated products, such as Bavarian cream, fruit mousses, and marshmallow.

The often-cited conversion between gelatin and agar is eight to one, meaning that agar is eight times stronger than gelatin. However, agar and gelatin are both natural products and, like all natural products, they vary in gel strength from one manufacturer to another. The only way to know how much agar to use in a product is to evaluate a series of products prepared with different levels of agar.

PHOTO 9.1 Red seaweed and two forms of agar, which are derived from it
Photo by Aaron Seyfarth

A BRIEF HISTORY OF CARRAGEENAN

It is interesting to see how chefs make creative use of local ingredients. For example, red seaweed was once a popular gelling agent in Europe. Cooks would make a flan-type pudding by boiling seaweed with milk, then cooling. One source of the seaweed was off the coast of Ireland near a town called Carragheen. Today, the gum purified from this seaweed is called carrageenan.

Carrageenan

Carrageenan, like agar, is extracted from a red seaweed (*Chondrus*). Pastry chefs are generally less familiar with carrageenan than with agar, but it is used in many commercial food products for thickening and gelling. It is particularly effective when used in milk products, which is why it is added to eggnog, chocolate milk, ice cream, and instant flan mixes. In another form, carrageenan is called Irish moss. Irish moss is popular in the Caribbean for thickening beverages and as an aphrodisiac.

Guar and Locust Bean Gum

Guar gum and locust bean gum are from the endosperm of beans growing in pods that look much like string beans or pea pods. Guar gum is from the beans of a plant (*Cyamopsis tetragonoloba*) that grows in India and Pakistan. Locust bean gum, also called carob gum, is from the beans of an evergreen tree (*Ceratonia siliqua*) that is originally from the Mediterranean. While locust bean gum is from the bean, another food ingredient, carob flour, is from the locust bean pod. To make carob flour, locust bean pods are roasted, then ground, and used as a cocoa powder substitute.

Both guar gum and locust bean gum are used as thickeners in a broad range of products, including cream cheese and sour cream. They also are commonly used in frozen foods, such as ice cream and frozen pasteurized egg whites, to prevent ice crystal growth and freezer damage.

Gum Arabic

Gum arabic is purified and dried from the *exudate*—gummy sap—of a tree (*Acacia*) that grows in northern Africa. The sap forms when a tree trunk or branch has been damaged, either through extreme climatic conditions or deliberate knife cuts. Gum arabic is good at stabilizing emulsions while maintaining a pleasing, nongummy mouthfeel. That is why it continues to be used in icings, fillings, and certain flavorings, even when its supply is scarce.

Gum Tragacanth

Gum tragacanth is obtained in a way similar to gum arabic, but it is from a shrub (*Astragalus*) that grows in the Middle East. Much thicker than gum arabic, gum tragacanth is probably best known to pastry chefs as an ingredient in gum paste, used by cake decorators for creating flowers and other designs. Gum tragacanth is extremely expensive because its main supply is in a politically unstable part of the world. For this reason, gum tragacanth is being replaced by other gums in most foods.

Xanthan Gum

Xanthan gum is a fairly new gum, in use since the 1960s. It is produced when a certain microorganism (*Xanthomonas campestris*) undergoes fermentation. Xanthan gum thickens without feeling thick and heavy, so it is commonly used in salad dressings to keep ingredients suspended.

Xanthan gum is often used along with starch, often rice starch, to replace wheat flour in gluten-free baked goods, including breads and cakes. Xanthan gum, used at about 2–3 percent, helps batters and doughs hold in gases, leaven, and provide an acceptable crumb to these baked goods.

Methylcellulose

Methylcellulose—also called *modified vegetable gum*—is one of several gums derived from cellulose. Cellulose makes up the cell walls of all plants and is the most plentiful polysaccharide on earth. Modified vegetable gum is made commercially by chemically modifying wood or cotton cellulose fibers. It is not considered a natural gum because of these chemical modifications.

Modified vegetable gum has a unique property, however, that makes it useful in bakery fillings. While most gels thin out at oven temperatures and thicken as they cool, modified vegetable gum gels at oven temperatures and thins out as it cools. Instead of bleeding and running as it is baked in Danish pastries, a bakery filling made with modified vegetable gum holds its shape.

 STARCHES

Like gums, starch molecules are polysaccharides. This means that they are large, complex carbohydrate molecules made of many sugar units bonded one to the next. In the case of starch, the sugar units are glucose molecules.

Not all starch molecules are alike, however. Glucose units in starch can be arranged in one of two ways: either as long straight chains or as short but highly branched ones. Straight-chain starch molecules are called *amylose,* while the larger, branched starch molecules are called *amylopectin* (Figure 9.2). Although amylose is a straight chain, the chain typically twists into a helical shape, while amylopectin, with its many branches,

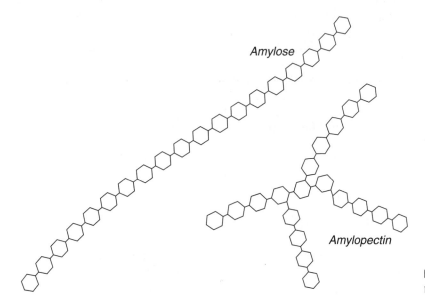

FIGURE 9.2 Parts of starch molecules

TABLE 9.1 ■ COMPARISON OF HIGH-AMYLOSE AND HIGH-AMYLOPECTIN STARCHES

HIGH IN AMYLOSE	HIGH IN AMYLOPECTIN
Cloudy when cooled	Relatively high clarity
Forms a firm, heavy-bodied gel when cooled	Thickens, does not gel
Gel tightens and weeps over time	Much less likely to weep over time
Not freezer-stable; tends to tighten and weep	Much less likely to weep when thawed
Much thicker cold than hot	Essentially the same thickness hot or cold
Tends to mask flavors	Less likely to mask flavors

looks like a flat coral fan. Whether amylose, amylopectin, or a mix of both, starch molecules are tightly packed in an orderly fashion inside starch granules.

Starch granules are small, gritty particles that are found in the endosperm of cereal grains, such as wheat and corn grains. Starch granules are also found in the tubers and roots of certain plants, including potatoes, yuca (also called cassava or manioc), and arrowroot. Starch granules vary in size and shape, depending on the starch. For example, potato starch granules are relatively large and oval in shape, while cornstarch granules are much smaller and more angular. Starch granules also grow larger over time, forming rings of starch molecules, much as growth rings form on a tree as it matures.

Different types of starches—corn, potato, arrowroot, or tapioca—have properties uniquely their own. Some of the differences have to do with the distinctive size and shape of each starch's granules. Other differences occur because of the amount of amylose and amylopectin in each. Table 9.1 summarizes the major differences between high-amylose starches, such as cornstarch, and high-amylopectin starches, such as waxy maize. Root starches, which could be considered medium-amylose, have properties somewhere between the two.

This section covers four main types of starches—cereal starches, root starches, instant starches, and modified food starches. Actually, all starches begin as either cereal or root starch. Instant starches and modified food starches are manufactured from these.

Cereal Starches

Cereal starches are extracted from the endosperm of cereal grains. Cornstarch, for example, is from the endosperm of corn kernels. Other cereal starches include rice starch, wheat starch, and waxy maize.

Cornstarch is the most common starch used in the bakeshop. In North America, cornstarch has the advantage of being inexpensive and readily available. Cornstarch should be your first choice for starch in the bakeshop, unless for some reason it does not meet your particular needs.

Waxy maize is a type of cornstarch, one that is extracted from a very different corn kernel and has different properties than regular cornstarch (see Table 9.1). While most cereal starches are high-amylose starches, waxy maize is a high-amylopectin starch. Waxy maize starch, sometimes called waxy cornstarch, will be discussed in the section on modified food starch, because it is almost always used in its modified form.

Root Starches

Root starches are extracted from various root or tuber plants. Root starches differ from cereal starches in many ways, mostly because they are lower in amylose and higher in amylopectin. While they are generally more expensive than cornstarch, they do not

WHEN IS WHEAT STARCH USED IN THE BAKESHOP?

Recall that regular white flour is about 68–75 percent starch. Any time flour is used in the bakeshop wheat starch is being used. Flour also contains gluten-forming proteins, which, along with wheat starch, contribute to thickening and gelling.

Besides its use in batters and doughs, flour is sometimes used instead of cornstarch to thicken pastry cream and home-style apple pie. It adds a subtle taste of its own and a creamy, off-white color.

have a cereal taste and they have better clarity and produce a softer gel. Potato starch, arrowroot (*Maranta arundinacea*), and tapioca are examples of root starches. All are sold as fine powders, also called flours. Tapioca is extracted from yuca root, also called manioc or cassava. Yuca—not to be confused with the cactus yucca—is a versatile root used in South America and in the Caribbean in the same way potatoes are commonly used. It is the most common starch, besides cornstarch, used in North America. Since it is imported, primarily from Thailand or Brazil, tapioca is much more expensive than cornstarch.

Besides being sold as finely-ground flour, tapioca is available as quick-cooking granules or as various-sized pearls. Granules and pearls are made from tapioca starch that has been agglomerated, or clumped, and gently heated. The heating gelatinizes the outer layer of starch. Granules and pearls tend to cook into a short, less stringy texture than unmodified tapioca flour. Quick-cooking granules, such as Minute brand tapioca, dissolve quickly, while pearls must be soaked for several hours before use. Tapioca pearls become translucent when cooked, but they retain their size and shape in the finished product.

Notice from Table 9.1 that high-amylose starches, such as cornstarch, are cloudy when cooled, and they tend to have a heavy body and a cereal flavor. While these are not always disadvantages, they can be. When they are, root starches are a better choice.

Modified Food Starches

Modified food starches are starches that have been treated by the manufacturer with one or more chemicals approved for use by government agencies. Modified food starches are designer starches; that is, they are designed by the manufacturer to have certain desirable features. While any native starch—corn, potato, arrowroot, tapioca, or waxy maize—can be modified, most modified food starches are made from waxy maize starch. Waxy maize starches start with many desirable properties. Compared with regular cornstarch, for example, waxy maize starches are relatively clear and clean tasting. They are modified in one or more ways to increase their stability against excessive heat, acid, and freezing. They can be modified for other reasons, as well. For example, starches can be modified to change their texture or to speed up or slow down how quickly they gelatinize. Probably the main reason to use a modified food starch in the bakeshop is for its added stability. Some modified food starches—for example, Colflo 67—are called cook-up starches, because they must be cooked just like any regular starch. Other modified food starches are instant starches.

Instant Starches

Instant starches thicken and gel without heat. They are different from modified starches, although most instant starches are also modified. Instant starches are sometimes called *pregelatinized* or *cold-water swelling*. To make a starch instant, the manufacturer either

HELPFUL HINT

Be careful when whisking instant starch into cold liquids. The starch thickens so quickly that it is easy to whisk and trap air bubbles. If necessary, the mixture can be gently warmed after whisking to allow air bubbles to dissipate.

HELPFUL HINT

To prevent an instant starch from clumping when adding it to liquids, first blend it with sugar or another dry ingredient. The rule of thumb is to blend four parts sugar with one part instant starch. However, some instant starches are designed to blend easily with water, so not every instant starch requires this high amount of sugar.

precooks (pregelatinizes) and then dries the starch, or makes some other change to the starch so that the granules absorb water without heat. While instant starches do not require heat to thicken, most are not damaged if they are heated.

Because instant starches do not require heat to thicken, they are ideal for thickening products that are heat-sensitive. For example, the bright green color and delicate flavor of a kiwi coulis is not damaged when the coulis is thickened with an instant starch.

Instant starches are also fairly quick to use. This makes them ideal for last-minute thickening of sauces for plated desserts, for example. Remember, though, that instant starches are specialty starches and, as such, cost more than regular cornstarch, often two or three times more. Instant starches also do not necessarily have the same texture as regular cook-up starches and cannot totally replace cornstarch in the bakeshop.

Instant Clearjel and Ultrasperse 2000 are the names of two common instant starches. Both are waxy maize starches that have been modified as well as precooked. This makes them both instant and stable.

Process of Starch Gelatinization

Recall from earlier in the chapter that starch molecules are tightly packed in an orderly fashion inside starch granules. When starch granules are place in cold water, the molecules inside the granules attract water and the granule swells slightly. If the water is heated, the starch granules undergo an irreversible process called gelatinization. Gelatinization is disruption of the orderliness of starch granules and the swelling of these granules, caused by large amounts of water being attracted to the molecules within the granules. Large granules typically gelatinize first, with smaller granules taking a longer time to fully absorb water and swell.

Since water is trapped by gelatinized starch molecules, it cannot move freely, so the product thickens. This thickening is the beginning of a process sometimes called pasting. As heating continues, the granules continue to swell and starch molecules, especially amylose molecules, leach into the hot liquid from the granules. At this point, with most of the granules fully swollen and only some starch leached from the granules, the starch mixture is properly cooked. It should be removed from the heat and cooled.

If the mixture is instead heated more, and if enough water is present, the granules continue to release their contents, becoming smaller and more deformed in shape, until

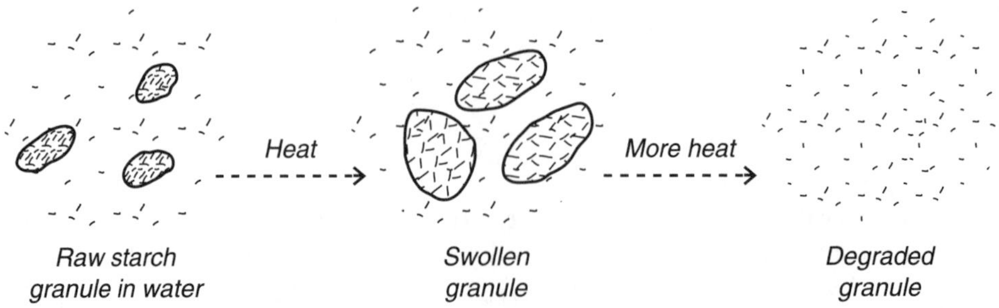

FIGURE 9.3 The process of starch gelatinization

Raw starch granule in water   Heat →   *Swollen granule*   More heat →   *Degraded granule*

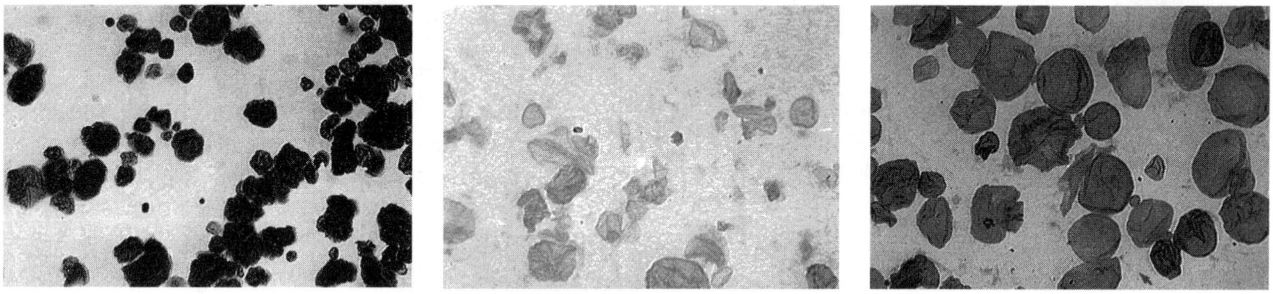

FIGURE 9.4 (a) Starch granules undercooked; (b) Starch granules overcooked; (c) Starch granules properly cooked
Courtesy of National Starch and Chemical Co.

finally they rupture completely. At this point, all that is left are small granule fragments and freed starch molecules. Mixing and stirring speeds up the rupturing of starch granules, since large, swollen granules are easily broken apart. Figure 9.3 shows the process of starch gelatinization.

As the starch solution cools, starch molecules slow down and entangle, trapping additional water and thickening. If there is a high enough concentration of entangled amylose molecules, the solution gels as it cools.

Notice that there is an optimum amount of heat for maximizing thickening and gelling. Too little heat and too few granules swell, let alone release starch molecules. Too much heat and too many granules degrade. Either way—undercooking or overcooking starch mixtures—causes too little thickening and gelling. Figure 9.4 compares the appearance of starch granules under the microscope, when cooked to varying degrees.

Undergelatinizing starch—undercooking it—creates other problems, as well. Because raw granules are hard and dense, undercooked starch feels gritty in the mouth. Undercooked starch is more opaque and typically has a raw starch taste. If stored for a day or more, undercooked starch mixtures tend to weep, meaning unattractive droplets or even pools of water form around the gel. Because undercooked starch has different characteristics than overcooked starch, it is easy to tell if a too-thin starch mixture has been undercooked or overcooked. Table 9.2 summarizes the characteristics of undercooked and overcooked starches.

Many factors affect the gelatinization temperature of starches and the amount of cooking required to fully gelatinize them. The higher the gelatinization temperature, the longer it takes for starch to gelatinize and the greater the tendency for the starch to be easily undercooked. Likewise, the lower the gelatinization temperature, the less time it takes for the starch to gelatinize and the greater the tendency for the starch to be easily overcooked. The most important factors that affect the gelatinization temperature of starch are itemized in the bulleted list that follows.

- *Type of starch.* Each type of starch has an optimum amount of heat required for proper gelatinization. Check with the manufacturer for guidelines on the use of a modified food starch, since some gelatinize at a higher temperature than cornstarch and others gelatinize at a lower temperature. The amount of time required to fully gelatinize root starches varies with the formula, but it is always less than the amount of time required to fully gelatinize cornstarch. Most times, unmodified root starches should not be brought to a boil. When cooked for too long, unmodified root starches become excessively stringy in texture. If this occurs, the sauce or filling should be remade and cooked for a reduced length of time, or the root starch should be replaced with a modified one.

TABLE 9.2 ■ COMPARISON OF UNDERCOOKED AND OVERCOOKED STARCH SOLUTIONS

UNDERCOOKED	OVERCOOKED
Too thin	Too thin; may be stringy
Gritty	Smooth
Opaque	Extremely clear
Raw starch taste	No raw starch taste
Tends to weep	Does not weep

HELPFUL HINT

If a formula for a starch-thickened sauce or pie filling is high in sugar, withhold half the sugar until after the starch has gelatinized. This way, the starch has a chance to absorb water before the hygroscopic sugar grabs the water and prevents the starch from gelatinizing.

HELPFUL HINT

The tendency for starch to be overcooked when acid is present can be somewhat compensated for by reducing the cook time, by increasing the amount of starch, or by adding acid after the starch mixture has fully gelatinized and cooled. However, by far the best solution to dealing with starch and acid is to switch to a starch that is more acid-resistant. The most acid-resistant starches are modified food starches, but root starches and waxy rice starch are somewhat more resistant than cornstarch.

- *Amount of tenderizers: sweeteners and fats.* Sweeteners and fats slow the rate at which starch granules absorb water. The more slowly they absorb water, the longer it takes starch granules to gelatinize. In fact, if enough sugar is present, it completely prevents starch from gelatinizing. This is one way that sugars and fats tenderize baked goods: They reduce the amount of structure-building starch gelatinization that occurs. Sugar also increases the translucency of starch-thickened mixtures.

- *Amount of acid.* Acid hydrolyzes large starch molecules into smaller ones, reducing their thickening power. Acid also disrupts starch granules so that they gelatinize more quickly and easily. In fact, if enough acid is present, gelatinization occurs so quickly that the starch mixture appears to not thicken at all.

Selecting a Starch

The number and variety of starches available to the pastry chef can seem bewildering at first. There are many native starches—cornstarch, rice, tapioca, arrowroot, and potato starch—plus modified and instant starches. When confronted with as many choices as this, it is helpful to systematically think through your needs, then systematically consider the options available.

The list of questions in Table 9.3 was designed to help narrow the choices when selecting a starch or a gum. Understand, however, that cornstarch should be the first choice in the bakeshop because it is a good all-purpose starch, low in cost and readily available.

For more details on the advantages and disadvantages of different starches and gums, refer to Table 9.4.

PHOTO 9.2 Tapioca and cornstarch cooked for the same amount of time; the overcooked tapioca on the left has a stringy texture. *Photo by Aaron Seyfarth*

TABLE 9.3 ▪ QUESTIONS TO CONSIDER WHEN SELECTING A THICKENING AND GELLING AGENT

Is clarity important? If yes, use a root starch or a modified food starch; better yet, don't use a starch. Use gelatin or a vegetable gum such as agar or pectin.

Are you thickening or gelling a heat-sensitive product, such as kiwi or strawberry? If yes, use an instant starch, or use gelatin.

Is a sharp, clean flavor important, such as in a fruit pie filling or glaze? If yes, use a root starch; better yet, use gelatin or pectin.

Are you thickening a product that contains a high amount of acid, such as lemons or cranberries? If yes, use a root starch; better yet, use a modified food starch.

Are you planning to freeze the product? If yes, use a root starch; better yet, use a modified food starch.

What is the desired consistency? For example, would you prefer a soft gel to a firm, heavy-bodied one? If yes, use a root starch, or use cornstarch and stir mixture as it cools.

Are there any price constraints? If yes, your best choice is cornstarch, but all starches are relatively inexpensive when compared to most other thickening and gelling agents.

TABLE 9.4 ▪ A COMPARISON OF THE PROPERTIES AND USES OF STARCHES AND GUMS

STARCH	PROPERTIES	IDEAL USES
Cornstarch	Cloudy when cooled; good sheen	Puddings, cream pies
	Heavy body; gels if concentration is high	
	Not stable to excessive heat, acid, freezing, mixing	
	Gel tightens and weeps over time	
	Masks many flavors	
	High gelatinization temperature	
Arrowroot	Moderate to high clarity; high sheen	Fruit pies and sauces
	Soft gel; can be stringy	
	Relatively stable against acid, heat, mixing, freezing	
	Relatively low gelatinization temperature	
	Relatively clean flavor	
Tapioca	Moderate to high clarity; high sheen	Fruit pies and sauces
	Soft gel; can be stringy	Tapioca pudding
	Relatively stable against acid, heat, mixing, freezing	
	Relatively low gelatinization temperature	
	Relatively clean flavor	
	Available as pearls, granules, powder	
Waxy maize	Moderate to high clarity	Base for many modified starches; not typically available unmodified
	Thickens, does not gel	
	Relatively stable against acid, heat, mixing, freezing	
	Relatively clean flavor	
Modified food starch	Highly stable against acid, heat, mixing, freezing	Frozen foods
	Variable gelatinization temperature	Steam table applications
	Other properties vary with brand	High-acid products

(Continued)

TABLE 9.4 ■ (Continued)

STARCH	PROPERTIES	IDEAL USES
Instant starch	No heat required	Last-minute plating
	Properties vary with brand	Heat-sensitive products
Flour	Cloudy; yellow-tinged color	Pastry cream
	Heavy body	Home-style pie fillings
	Imparts a flavor; masks or mellows flavors	
Gelatin	High clarity, high sheen	Gelatin desserts
	Forms firm, bouncy gel	Stabilized whipped cream
	At typical usage levels, melts in the mouth and at room temperature	Confections (gummy bears)
	Clean flavor	
	Available as sheets, powder	
Agar	Moderate to high clarity	As a gelatin substitute for:
	Forms very firm gel, bouncy gel	a. Vegetarians and people with religious dietary restrictions
	Stable (does not melt) at room temperature or in mouth	b. Use with raw pineapple, etc.
	Usage level varies with purity	
	Available as sheets, strands, and powder	
Pectin	High clarity, high sheen	Fruit jams, jellies, fillings
	Thickens or gels	Glazes
	Clean flavor	High-quality jelly confections
	Generally requires high acid and high sugar concentrations	

FUNCTIONS OF THICKENING AND GELLING AGENTS

Main Functions

PROVIDES A THICKENED OR GELLED TEXTURE

To say that an ingredient provides a thickened or gelled texture to sauces, fillings, glazes, and creams is to say that the ingredient provides structure. While thickening and gelling is the formation of a very soft structure, recall that starch, in particular, also contributes to structure in baked goods.

INCREASES STABILITY

Thickening and gelling agents are sometimes called stabilizers, meaning that they prevent undesirable changes from occurring in foods. Actually, thickening and gelling agents typically provide this stability by thickening and gelling. The goal is added stability, and the stability comes from thickening and gelling. For example, gelatin

STARCH RETROGRADATION—THE FORMATION OF TOO MUCH STRUCTURE

Starch retrogradation is a process in which starch molecules in a cooked or baked and cooled product bond more and more closely over time, increasing structure. It is as if the starch molecules wish to return—retro—to the tightly bonded state of ungelatinized starch granules. When this happens to starch-based creams and pie fillings, products shrink and firm up, becoming tough and rubbery. The shrinking network of tightly bonded starch molecules squeezes out water, causing weeping, also known as syneresis. It is this process that makes high-amylose starches, such as cornstarch, inappropriate for creams and fillings that are to be frozen or refrigerated for any length of time.

When starches retrograde in baked goods, the soft crumb becomes dry, hard, and crumbly.

In other words, starch retrogradation is a primary cause of staling in baked goods. Water may be squeezed out of the starch, but it is not evident in baked goods because other ingredients are likely to absorb the water.

Starch retrogradation—staling—of baked goods can be delayed by covering products to prevent moisture loss; by storing products at room temperature or in the freezer—not in the refrigerator, where retrogradation is fastest; and by adding ingredients that slow down the process. Sugars, proteins, fats, and emulsifiers are all effective at delaying starch retrogradation. Because pastries contain large amounts of these ingredients, they are slower to stale than breads and rolls.

---

stabilizes whipped cream primarily by gelling. This solidifies the walls surrounding air bubbles in whipped cream and prevents them from breaking. Guar gum stabilizes frozen egg whites primarily by thickening them. This prevents the formation of large, damaging ice crystals and allows the egg whites to whip fully.

PROVIDES GLOSS OR SHEEN TO SAUCES, FILLINGS, AND GLAZES

Many thickening and gelling agents form a smooth layer that clings to the surfaces of ingredients. This smooth layer reflects light in a way that provides gloss or sheen to many sauces, fillings, and glazes.

Additional Functions

SOFTENS AND TENDERIZES BAKED GOODS

Starch added to baked goods interferes with the formation of gluten and egg structure. This is especially true when there is not enough water for starch to gelatinize, as is the case for cookies and pie dough. It is only through gelatinization that starch forms structure; otherwise it consists of hard, gritty particles that interfere with protein webs that gluten or eggs form.

ABSORBS MOISTURE

Recall that flour is a drier because it contains starch, gums, and proteins. All starches and gums, in fact, are driers because they absorb moisture and, often, fats and oils.

Cornstarch, in particular, is added to dry powdered products to absorb moisture. This prevents caking and keeps the dry powder free-flowing. For example, cornstarch is added to finely pulverized confectioners' or icing sugar. Cornstarch is also commonly added to baking powder. Besides keeping baking powder free-flowing, cornstarch serves as a bulking agent to standardize baking powders. It also prevents losses in activity. As cornstarch absorbs moisture, it prevents the reaction of acid and baking soda and the release of carbon dioxide, an important leavening gas.

STORAGE AND HANDLING

All thickening and gelling agents should be stored covered. This prevents them from absorbing moisture.

The following guidelines should be followed when working with starches, to ensure maximum thickening and gelling.

Separating Granules

Before heating starches—and many other thickening and gelling agents—be sure dry particles are well separated from each other. If granules are not separated before heating, they will clump. If this happens, they must be sieved out, and this lessens the thickening ability.

Following are the three main ways of separating dry granules from one another. The first two are commonly used in bakeshops.

- Blend granules with other dry ingredients, such as granulated sugar. The rule of thumb is to add at least four or five parts sugar to one part dry starch (or gelatin, or gum).

- Add granules first to *cold* water, making a paste or slurry. This technique is used with gelatin when it is bloomed, and it can be used with most starches except instant starch. Many instant starches—and other ingredients like guar gum that absorb cold water quickly—clump when added directly to cold water. These ingredients must be blended with dry ingredients first, or blended with fat.

- Blend granules with fat, such as butter or oil. Culinary chefs use this technique whenever they prepare roux, which is flour blended and cooked in melted butter.

Cooking and Cooling Starch

HELPFUL HINT

Creams that contain egg yolks in addition to starch, in particular, must not be undercooked. Besides the possibility of bacteria growth, egg yolks contain amylase, which breaks down starch molecules and destroys thickening and gelling power. Heat destroys amylase and other enzymes, eliminating this concern.

Likewise, chefs must be careful not to double-dip into starch-based products. The amylase in saliva is particularly strong, and it can thin out starch-based products in minutes.

Be sure to cook starch long enough without overcooking it. Cornstarch mixtures start to thicken before they come to a boil, but continue heating them to ensure that all starch granules are fully hydrated and swollen. A good rule of thumb for cornstarch is to bring it to a boil and boil gently for 2 or 3 minutes. This is a guideline that works well with most cornstarch mixtures, but it is too much heating for root starches, which should not be brought to a boil.

Be sure to stir a starch mixture evenly and constantly while cooking, to prevent scorching or burning. Cool immediately upon cooking, to avoid overcooking. For a creamy-smooth texture, stir while cooling; for maximum thickening and gelling, cool without stirring.

QUESTIONS FOR REVIEW

1. What units make up all polysaccharides? Describe the difference between starch and inulin in the type and number of units each contains.

2. What units make up all proteins? Which common thickening and gelling agent is a protein?

3. Describe the difference between thickening and gelling.

4. Describe the process used for producing most food-grade gelatin.

5. What is meant by Bloom rating? How is it measured?

6. Why must fresh pineapple juice be heated before it can be added to gelatin?

7. How do acidic ingredients, such as lemon juice, affect gel strength?

8. Name a gum extracted from each of the following vegetable products: seaweed, apple peel, sap from a tree, endosperm of a seed.

9. Which gum is particularly useful for thickening and gelling fruit products?

10. Which gum is sometimes used as a gelatin substitute and is sometimes called vegetable gelatin?

11. What thickening and gelling agent is extracted from the endosperm of cereal grains?

12. Give examples of cereal starches and root starches.

13. What two reasons could explain why starches differ from each other in properties (gel strength, clarity, flavor, stability, etc.)?

14. Describe the main differences in properties between a typical cereal starch and a root starch.

15. Why should cornstarch not be used to thicken pastry cream that will be frozen? What starch is the best choice to use instead?

16. What is the main reason for using a modified food starch?

17. What are the two main reasons for using an instant starch?

18. How should an instant starch be used so it is less likely to clump?

19. Draw out the process of starch gelatinization. Label your drawings, and be sure to show the major differences in raw, swollen, and degraded granules.

20. What two things happen to starch granules as they are heated in the presence of water? Describe how each contributes to thickening and gelling.

21. Which is more likely to require more heat to gelatinize: cornstarch or a root starch?

22. You switch from cornstarch to tapioca as a thickener in a fruit sauce. The sauce becomes unacceptably stringy when it cools. What should you do differently next time, to prevent this from happening?

23. Does sugar speed up or slow down the process of starch gelatinization?

24. Does acid speed up or slow down the process of starch gelatinization?

ⓦ QUESTIONS FOR DISCUSSION

1. About how much water will 5 sheets of gelatin absorb when they are properly bloomed? Show your work, and assume that the sheets weigh 0.1 ounce (3 grams) each.

2. A formula calls for 5 sheets of gelatin but only powdered gelatin is available (assume Bloom rating of 230 for powdered gelatin). How much powdered gelatin should be weighed out? What adjustments should be made with water, if any? Show your work.

3. A formula calls for 5 sheets of gelatin but only powdered gelatin is available. The proper calculations to convert from sheets to powder were made, but a Bavarian cream comes out too firm. Assume ingredients were weighed properly. What went wrong?

4. Why might a butterscotch cream pie—which is high in sugar—have half the sugar added after the cornstarch-milk-egg mixture is already cooked? If all the sugar were added to the butterscotch cream pie before the mixture is cooked, what might happen to the texture, appearance, and mouthfeel of the pie?

5. A starch-thickened cherry pie filling doesn't taste tart enough, so more lemon juice is added. Why is it best to add the lemon juice after the cherry pie filling is cooked and cooled? Even better than adding the lemon juice at the end of the cook time is to use a starch that is stable to acid. What starch is the best choice for acid stability?

6. Your assistant shows you a starch-thickened sauce that is too thin. Explain how you can tell by looking at and tasting the sauce whether the starch was undercooked or overcooked.

EXERCISES AND EXPERIMENTS

1. Sheet versus Powdered Gelatin

Fill in the following table, summarizing the relative advantages and disadvantages of sheet and powdered gelatin.

GELATIN FROM	HOW MEASURED—SMALL AMOUNTS (WEIGHED OR COUNTED)	HOW MEASURED—LARGE AMOUNTS WEIGHED OR COUNTED)	EASE IN CLEANUP	PRICE	AVAILABILITY
Sheet					
Powdered					

2. Thickening Agents in Bakeshop Products

Look up formulas for the common bakeshop products listed in the left column of the following table and place a checkmark in the box indicating which of the thickening agents listed in the top row contribute to the thickening and gelling of each.

PASTRY PRODUCT	EGGS (SPECIFY WHOLE, WHITES, OR YOLKS)	GELATIN	STARCH	FRUIT PULP/FRUIT PECTIN	CHEESE
Pastry cream					
Crème brûlée					
Banana cream pie					
Fruit pie filling					
Chiffon pie					
Bavarian cream					
Cheesecake					
Pumpkin pie					

3. How Different Brands and Forms of Gelatin Compare in Gel Firmness in Stabilized Whipped Cream

This experiment uses stabilized whipped cream as a means of understanding different forms of gelatin and how they differ in use and usage levels. Gelatin solutions will be prepared using 10 sheets of gelatin or using one ounce (28 grams) of powdered gelatin.

This is the standard conversion used by some pastry chefs, and you will see for yourself whether this conversion holds true.

OBJECTIVES

- To compare stabilized whipped cream made with sheet gelatin and powdered gelatin
- To determine a conversion factor between sheet gelatin and powdered gelatin
- To compare stabilized whipped cream made with sheet gelatin of different quality levels
- To demonstrate the affect of overstabilizing products on flavor, texture and mouthfeel, and overall quality
- To practice tempering hot mixtures into cold

PRODUCTS PREPARED

Whipped cream stabilized with:

- No added gelatin (control product)
- Powdered gelatin, Knox brand or equivalent (230 Bloom), one-half the full amount of gelatin solution
- Powdered gelatin, Knox brand or equivalent, full amount of gelatin solution
- Powdered gelatin, Knox brand or equivalent, 1½ times the full amount of gelatin solution
- Sheet gelatin, bronze, 130 Bloom, full amount of gelatin solution, using 10 sheets for 1 ounce (30 grams) gelatin powder.
- Sheet gelatin, platinum, 250 Bloom, full amount of gelatin solution, using 10 sheets for 1 ounce (30 grams) gelatin powder.
- Other, if desired (different brands of powdered gelatin, silver or gold sheet gelatin, commercial stabilizer, agar in place of gelatin [at 8 to 1 conversion, or 12 percent the amount of gelatin]).

MATERIALS AND EQUIPMENT

- Plates, 6 in. (18 cm), or equivalent
- Plastic wrap

PROCEDURE

- Prepare stabilized whipped cream samples (whipped to very soft peak, only), using the following formula or using any basic formula for whipped cream stabilized with gelatin.
- Place samples from each batch of cream onto small plates; cover with plastic wrap to prevent drying. Label each sample with type and amount of gelatin added and time it is placed under refrigeration.
- In the meantime, record from each box of sheet gelatin the net weight of gelatin in the whole box; record in Results Table 1, which follows.
- Weigh 10 sheets of each grade of sheet gelatin and record weights in Results Table 1.
- Calculate the average weight per gelatin sheet by dividing the weight of 10 sheets by ten. Record calculated weight per sheet in Results Table 1.
- Calculate the number of sheets per box by dividing the weight per box by the weight per sheet and record in Results Table 1.
- Record in the Comments column of Results Table 1 how the different grades of sheet gelatin compare in feel (which feels thicker, heavier)?

- Refrigerate cream samples until all are cooled to 35°–40°F (2°–4°C). Record length of time that each sample is cooled in Comments column of Results Table 2, which follows.
- Record any potential sources of error that might make it difficult to draw the proper conclusions from this experiment. In particular, be aware of differences in the extent that the creams were whipped, how long each was cooled, whether all were cooled to the same temperature, and any difficulties tempering warm gelatin with cold heavy cream.
- Evaluate the sensory characteristics of cooled samples and record evaluations in Results Table 2. Be sure to compare each in turn to the control product and consider the following:
  - Appearance
  - Flavor intensity, from very low in flavor to very high, on a scale of one to five
  - Firmness, from very soft to very firm, on a scale of one to five
  - Mouthfeel (lightness/heaviness on tongue, mouthcoating, how quickly it melts)
  - Overall acceptability, from highly unacceptable to highly acceptable, on a scale of one to five
  - Add any additional comments, as necessary

Stabilized Whipped Cream

INGREDIENT	POUND	OUNCE	GRAMS	BAKER'S PERCENTAGE
Heavy cream		8	250	100
Sugar, granulated		1	30	12
Gelatin solution		variable	variable	variable
Vanilla (1 tsp)		0.2	5	2
Total		9.7	275	120

Method of Preparation

1. Chill heavy cream, bowl, and whip attachment thoroughly.
2. Prepare gelatin solution as follows:
   - Add 1 ounce (30 grams) gelatin powder or ten sheets gelatin (weight is variable) into 5 ounces (150 grams) cold water. (Note: If desired, sheets can be used the traditional way, adding sheets into excess water and squeezing gently; however, the amount of water absorbed by the gelatin tends to vary with water temperature, soak time, and amount of squeezing.)
   - Allow to bloom for 5–10 minutes.
   - Warm bloomed gelatin gently, just until gelatin dissolves. Keep warm.
   - Smell warmed gelatin solutions; record strength of meaty aroma of sheet gelatin solutions in Comments column of Results Table 1, comparing each to the aroma of the powdered gelatin solution.
3. In the meantime, whip heavy cream and sugar on medium to a very soft peak only.
4. Weigh gelatin solution into a warm bowl, using the following amounts:
   - For one-half the amount of solution, use 0.25 ounce (7.5 grams).
   - For full amount of solution, use 0.5 ounce (15 grams).
   - For 1½ times the amount of solution, use 0.75 ounce (22.5 grams).
5. Add a small amount of whipped cream to warm gelatin solution, to temper.
6. Quickly add tempered solution into whipped cream, whipping rapidly without overwhipping.
7. Taste a small amount of stabilized whipped cream to confirm that it is smooth and that gelatin did not bead or ball up. If whipped cream is not smooth, discard and begin again.

SOURCES OF ERROR

_____

_____

RESULTS TABLE 1 ■ COMPARISON OF DIFFERENT QUALITY GRADES OF SHEET GELATIN

GELATIN GRADE	WEIGHT PER BOX	WEIGHT PER TEN SHEETS (FROM WEIGHING)	WEIGHT PER SHEET (FROM CALCULATION)	NUMBER OF SHEETS PER BOX (FROM CALCULATION)	COMMENTS
Silver					
Bronze					

RESULTS TABLE 2 ■ SENSORY CHARACTERISTICS OF WHIPPED CREAM STABILIZED WITH DIFFERENT TYPES AND AMOUNTS OF GELATIN

TYPE AND AMOUNT OF GELATIN	APPEARANCE	FLAVOR INTENSITY	FIRMNESS AND MOUTHFEEL	OVERALL ACCEPTABILITY	COMMENTS
No added gelatin					
Powdered, Knox, 0.5X					
Powdered, Knox, 0.75X					
Powdered, Knox, full amount					
Sheet, bronze, full amount					
Sheet, silver, full amount					

CONCLUSIONS

1. How did flavor strength, firmness, and mouthfeel change as the amount of gelatin solution increased from none to 1½ times the full amount of powdered gelatin?

_____

_____

2. How did creams stabilized with the two grades (bronze and silver) of sheet gelatin compare to each other in flavor intensity, firmness, mouthfeel, and overall acceptability?

_____

_____

3. Based on your evaluations, are bronze and silver sheets interchangeable, sheet for sheet, when stabilizing whipped cream (with both solutions made with the same number of sheets)? Why or why not?

_____

_____

4. Based on your weight measurements of the different grades of sheet gelatin, would you expect bronze and silver sheets to be interchangeable, weight for weight, when stabilizing whipped cream (with both solutions made with same weight of sheets)? Why or why not?

_____

_____

5. Based on your evaluations of stabilized creams made with different levels of powdered gelatin and with bronze sheets, what might be an approximate conversion between Knox gelatin powder and bronze gelatin sheets? That is, are 10 bronze sheets approximately equal in gel strength to 1 ounce (30 grams) of powdered gelatin, or is it closer to 5, 15, or 20 sheets? In your estimate, what is the weight of the number of bronze sheets that are equal in gel strength to 1 ounce (30 grams) of powdered gelatin?

_____

_____

6. Were there any sources of error that might significantly affect the results of your experiment? If so, what could you do differently next time to minimize error?

_____

_____

4. Comparing Different Starches and Cook Times for Thickening a Fruit Juice Filling

🔔 OBJECTIVES

To compare the appearance, flavor, and texture of fruit juice fillings:
- Made with different starches
- Cooked for different lengths of time

🔔 PRODUCTS PREPARED

Fruit juice fillings prepared with:
- No added starch
- Cornstarch, boiled gently 2 minutes (control product)
- Cornstarch, not boiled
- Cornstarch, boiled gently 8 minutes
- Tapioca starch/flour (or arrowroot or potato), boiled gently 2 minutes
- Tapioca or potato, quick-cooking granules
- Instant starch (such as National Ultrasperse 2000 or Instant Clearjel), not cooked
- Other, if desired (tapioca pearls, rice starch, bread flour, National Frigex HV, ColFlo 67, or other modified food starch)

MATERIALS AND EQUIPMENT

- Plates, 6″ (18 cm) and clear cups, 4 ounces (125 ml), or equivalent
- Plastic wrap

PROCEDURE

- Label plates or cups with type of starch to be used to thicken fruit juice filling.
- Soak tapioca granules in cold water to soften.
- Prepare fruit juice fillings using the formula that follows, or using any basic fruit juice filling made from clear juice. Prepare at least 16 ounces (450 grams) of each.
- Transfer hot filling to a tared stainless steel bowl and cool in ice water bath to 110°–120°F (40°–50°C), stirring occasionally.
- Weigh bowl and filling; add back water to replace any lost to evaporation.
- Record amount of water added back in Comments column of Results Table 1, which follows.
- Transfer filling to labeled plates and clear cups, filling all plates and all cups to the same level.
- Evaluate consistency (thickness/thinness) of fruit fillings at 110°–120°F (40°–50°C) and record evaluations in Results Table 1. Evaluate fillings on a scale of 1–5, 1 being very thin.
- Cover samples with plastic wrap and refrigerate to cool to 35°–40°F (2°–4°C).
- Record any potential sources of error that might make it difficult to draw the proper conclusions from the experiment. In particular, be aware of difficulties in controlling the rate of cook and total cook time, the amount of stirring as samples cooled, and final sample temperature.
- Evaluate the sensory characteristics of completely cooled fruit fillings and record evaluations in Results Table 1. Be sure to compare each in turn to the control product and consider the following:
    - Appearance (shiny/dull, translucent/opaque, thick/thin/gelled, short body/long body, stringy/smooth, etc.)
    - Flavor (raw starch taste, sweetness, sourness, fruit flavor, etc.)
    - Mouthfeel and texture (smooth/gritty, thick/thin/gelled, heavy-bodied, mouthcoating, etc.)
    - Overall acceptability, from highly unacceptable to highly acceptable, on a scale of one to five
    - Any additional comments, as necessary

Fruit Juice Filling

INGREDIENT	POUND	OUNCE	GRAMS	BAKER'S PERCENTAGE
Fruit juice, clear, any flavor		16	450	100
Starch		0.8	22	5
Sugar, granulated (optional)		1	30	6
Total	1	1.8	502	111

Method of Preparation

1. Select any clear fruit juice, such as apple or cranberry.
2. Place starch and sugar (if added) in bowl; stir to blend.
3. Add 5 ounces (150 grams) fruit juice to starch/sugar and whisk until dispersed.
4. Place remaining fruit juice in saucepan and bring to a boil.

5. Add starch/juice mixture to boiling liquid, stirring constantly with a heat-resistant silicone spatula.

6. For unboiled fillings, remove from heat immediately and begin to cool, following Procedure.

7. For boiled fillings, return mixture to a boil and boil for the stated amount of time (2 or 8 minutes), stirring constantly. For fillings boiled for 8 minutes, add a measured amount of water, if necessary, to prevent burning from excessive water evaporation.

8. Remove from heat and cool slightly; use a separate tasting spoon to taste a small amount of thickened fruit filling, confirming that it is smooth and that starch did not bead or ball up (do not confuse grittiness of undercooked starch with beading/balling of improperly dispersed starch). If filling is not smooth, do not strain; discard and begin again. Do not reuse tasting spoon without first washing it thoroughly.

For fruit filling thickened with instant starch:

1. In step 3, sprinkle starch/sugar onto full amount of cold fruit juice.

2. If starch begins to clump (this may occur with instant starches that are very fine powders), start by first blending starch with additional sugar, up to five parts by weight.

3. Evaluate consistency of fruit filling immediately after water is added; record evaluation in Results Table 1.

4. Transfer filling to cups and plates, cover, and refrigerate with rest of samples.

SOURCES OF ERROR

_____

_____

RESULTS TABLE 1 ■ SENSORY CHARACTERISTICS OF THICKENED FRUIT FILLINGS MADE WITH DIFFERENT STARCHES HEATED FOR DIFFERENT LENGTHS OF TIME

TYPE OF STARCH	CONSISTENCY WHILE HOT[1]	APPEARANCE	FLAVOR	MOUTHFEEL/TEXTURE	OVERALL ACCEPTABILITY	COMMENTS
No added starch						
Cornstarch, 2 minute boil (control product)						
Cornstarch, not boiled						
Cornstarch, 8 minute boil						
Tapioca starch						
Tapioca granules						
Instant starch						

[1]For instant starch, consistency is when first mixed

CONCLUSIONS

1. Which starch resulted in the filling with best clarity? Which had the most cloudiness or opacity?

_____

_____

2. Which starch resulted in the filling with the firmest gel or most thickening? Which had the softest gel or least amount of thickening?

_____

_____

3. Which starch had the cleanest flavor, that is, which allowed the flavor of the fruit to come through best? Which had the strongest taste of its own, or masked the flavor of the fruit?

_____

_____

4. How can you tell when cornstarch is undercooked? (Compare fruit filling not boiled to filling boiled 2 minutes.)

_____

_____

5. How can you tell when cornstarch is overcooked? (Compare fruit filling boiled 8 minutes to filling boiled 2 minutes.)

_____

_____

6. How did the filling made with tapioca granules compare to fine tapioca starch/ flour in texture? (Compare.)

_____

_____

7. In general, how do root starches compare overall to cornstarch (2-minute boil) in clarity, flavor, and mouthfeel/texture?

_____

_____

8. Were there any sources of error that might significantly affect the results of your experiment? If so, what could you do differently next time to minimize error?

_____

_____

CHAPTER 10

FATS, OILS, AND EMULSIFIERS

CHAPTER **OBJECTIVES**

1. Present the basic terminology and chemistry of fats, oils, and emulsifiers.

2. Describe the process and the importance of hydrogenation.

3. Classify fats, oils, and emulsifiers and describe their makeup, characteristics, and uses.

4. List the functions of fats, oils, and emulsifiers and relate these functions to their makeup.

5. Discuss the use of fat replacers in baked goods.

6. Describe how to best store and handle fats, oils, and emulsifiers.

INTRODUCTION

High-quality baked goods require a balance between tougheners and tenderizers, moisteners and driers. Any good formula will already contain the proper balance of ingredients, but it is still helpful to understand the ingredients that most contribute to this balance.

Fats, oils, and emulsifiers are indispensable moisteners and tenderizers. Yet, recommendations for a healthful diet include reducing intake of certain fats, namely-saturated fats and trans fats. North Americans are aware of these recommendations and have health and diet concerns about fat. While most baked goods cannot be made without fats, it is important to use them properly and to understand the concerns of your customers.

CHEMISTRY OF FATS, OILS, AND EMULSIFIERS

Lipids are loosely defined as substances that do not dissolve in water. Fats, oils, emulsifiers, and flavor oils (peppermint oil and orange oil, for example) are all classified as lipids.

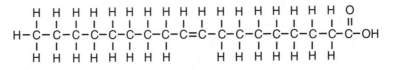

An unsaturated fatty acid

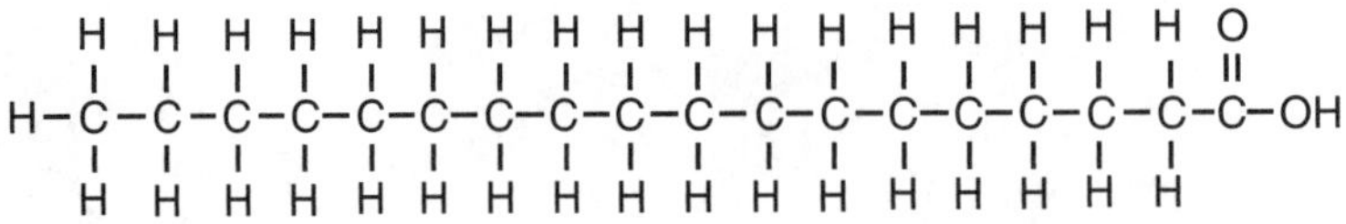

A saturated fatty acid

FIGURE 10.2 Unsaturated and saturated fatty acids

C – FA
|
C – FA
|
C – FA

C = carbon

FA = fatty acid

FIGURE 10.1
A triglyceride

Fats are, strictly speaking, lipids that are solid at room temperature. The term fat is also commonly used to refer to any lipid, whether fat, oil, or emulsifier. For example, the amount of fat listed on food labels includes the amount of solid fat, liquid oil, and emulsifier present in the food product.

Oils are lipids that are liquid at room temperature. Oils are typically from vegetable sources, such as soybean, cottonseed, canola, and corn. *Tropical oils*, such as coconut, palm, and palm kernel oil, are solid at room temperature (70°F; 21°C), but they melt quickly in a warm room.

Chemically speaking, fats and oils are *triglycerides*. Triglycerides consist of three (*tri-*) fatty acids attached to a three-carbon glycerol (glycerin) molecule (Figure 10.1). *Fatty acids* are composed of carbon chains that typically contain anywhere from four to twenty-two carbon atoms. Because they are important to the makeup of fats and oils, it is worthwhile to take the time to understand the chemistry of fatty acids in more detail. As you go through the next few paragraphs, notice how terms commonly used by consumers (saturated, monounsaturated, polyunsaturated, trans fats) are based on the chemical structures of fatty acids.

Fatty acids can be saturated or unsaturated (Figure 10.2). Carbon atoms on *saturated fatty acids* are saturated with hydrogen atoms. That is, they cannot hold more hydrogen, and all bonds between carbon atoms are single. *Unsaturated fatty acids* contain two or more carbon atoms that are not fully saturated with hydrogen atoms. Carbon atoms that are not saturated form double bonds. The unsaturated fatty acid in Figure 10.2 is

WHY FATS DON'T MELT LIKE ICE

Solid fats contain many tiny fat crystals. Fat crystals consist of fat molecules arranged in an orderly fashion, bonded one to the next. For solid fat to melt, these bonds must break, just as ice crystals must break apart for ice to melt.

Unlike pure water, which consists of identical molecules of H_2O, fats contain a mix of different fatty acids. While identical water molecules melt at the same temperature (32°F; 0°C), each fatty acid melts at its own distinct temperature.

When fats soften, it is because some fat crystals have melted while others have not. For example, butter noticeably softens at around 80°F (27°C) because many of the bonds between shorter fatty acids have broken. It is not until 90°F (32°C) and above that bonds break between the longer fatty acids in butter, and the butter liquefies completely.

Fats, such as butter, that melt quickly and completely from body heat, have a pleasant mouthfeel. Fats that melt slowly or incompletely, such as all-purpose shortening, tend to have a less pleasant, often waxy mouthfeel.

called a *monounsaturated fatty acid* because it has only one (*mono*) double bond between carbon atoms. Unsaturated fatty acids are either monounsaturated or polyunsaturated (having more than one double bond between carbon atoms).

All common food fats contain a distinct mix of saturated, monounsaturated, and polyunsaturated fatty acids. Typically, the higher a fat is in saturated fatty acids, the more solid the fat. That is why animal fats, tropical oils, and cocoa butter, which are all naturally high in saturated fatty acids, are solid at room temperature. Most vegetable oils are liquid at room temperature because they are low in saturated fatty acids. Dietary guidelines for North Americans recommend that intake of saturated fatty acids be limited because saturated fatty acids have been shown to raise blood cholesterol and increase the risk of coronary heart disease.

Trans fatty acids are unsaturated fatty acids where the two hydrogen atoms of a double bond are on opposite sides of each other. Most naturally occurring unsaturated fatty acids—"cis" fatty acids—have the two hydrogen atoms on the same side of the double bond. (Figure 10.2) This seemingly small difference in structure has a big affect on health. This affect will be discussed in the next section of this chapter.

HYDROGENATION

Check the ingredient labels of fats and oils used in the bakeshop and you will notice that many of them—including all-purpose shortenings, high-ratio shortenings, margarine, lard, even liquid oils—have been hydrogenated.

Fats and oils are hydrogenated by exposing them to hydrogen gas in the presence of high heat, pressure, and a catalyst, such as nickel. Catalysts speed up chemical reactions without actually being used up in the reaction. Recall from Chapter 3 that enzymes are biological catalysts. Nickel is a metal catalyst. The nickel is removed before the hydrogenated fat is packaged and sold.

Hydrogenation of fats is a process where hydrogen is added to unsaturated fatty acids at their double bonds. Hydrogenation saturates carbon atoms with hydrogen, converting an unsaturated fatty acid to a saturated one (Figure 10.3). Fully saturated fats are so solid that they are hard to work with, so fats have traditionally been partially hydrogenated. Partial hydrogenation leaves some fatty acids unsaturated, so that the fat is soft and plastic. The manufacturer controls the process to achieve the desired degree of hydrogenation for the desired consistency.

Notice that hydrogenation is not the same as adding air to fats. Hydrogenation is a chemical process that changes the fatty acid molecule by forcing hydrogen onto it.

Aeration occurs when air is whipped into solid fat, as when fat is creamed. For fats to be properly aerated, however, they must have a soft, plastic, consistency. The process of hydrogenation is one way to create this consistency in liquid oils.

Why Hydrogenate?

There are two main reasons to hydrogenate fats and oils. The first is to increase the solidity of a fat or oil. Solid fat is desirable, for example, for flakiness and volume in pastry or to decrease the greasiness in doughnuts and cookies.

The second reason to hydrogenate fats and oils is to increase stability against oxidative rancidity. Oxidative rancidity is the breakdown of fatty acids that leads to rancid off flavors. The more unsaturated the fatty acid, the faster it undergoes oxidative rancidity. This means that monounsaturated fats oxidize faster than saturated ones, and polyunsaturated fats oxidize fastest

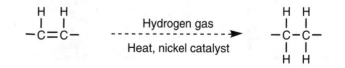

Unsaturated liquid oil   *Saturated solid fat*

FIGURE 10.3 Hydrogenation of liquid oil into a solid fat

ARE PLASTIC FATS EDIBLE?

Plastic fats are not made from plastic. Rather, they are edible fats that have a plastic consistency, meaning that they are soft, moldable solids, such as Play-Doh. Plastic fats are part liquid and part solid. That is, they consist of liquid oil trapped in a network of solid fat crystals. Examples of fats that are plastic at room temperature (70°F; 21°C) include all-purpose shortening, lard, and butter. Fats that are not plastic at room temperature include vegetable oils, which are liquid at room temperature, and cocoa butter, which is a hard solid.

Plasticity depends on temperature. Butter is plastic at room temperature, but it is rock solid in the freezer and completely liquid in a hot bakeshop. All-purpose shortening is plastic when refrigerated and is still plastic when the bakeshop warms. That is one of the advantages of shortening—it keeps its soft, work-able consistency over a wide range of temperatures.

of all. In fact, highly polyunsaturated fats can oxidize one hundred times faster than highly saturated ones.

Hydrogenation reduces oxidative rancidity by converting unsaturated fatty acids into saturated ones, and polyunsaturated fatty acids into less unsaturated ones. Even a small amount of hydrogenation helps delay rancidity. That is why vegetable oils, which remain liquid and therefore don't appear hydrogenated, sometimes are.

Regular soybean oil, in particular, is highly polyunsaturated when extracted from the soybean. By hydrogenating the polyunsaturated fatty acids, soybean oil is much less likely to oxidize to an unpleasant beany, fishy, or painty smell. Today, because of its use in shortenings, margarines, and vegetable oil, soybean oil is the most common vegetable fat in the bakeshop. In fact, soybeans are the second largest crop in the United States, second only to corn. Figure 10.4 shows mature soybeans in a pod. Standard mature, dried soybeans contain about 20 percent oil, over half of it polyunsaturated.

An unfortunate downside of hydrogenation is that it generates saturated fatty acids. A diet high in saturated fat is thought to increase blood cholesterol and the risk of coronary heart disease. A greater downside is that the process of partial hydrogenation typically generates trans fatty acids. While small amounts of trans fatty acids—sometimes called trans fats—occur naturally in butter, by far the greatest source of trans fats in the North American diet is from partial—but not total—hydrogenation of fats and oils. Since January 2006, food manufacturers are required by law to disclose on the nutrition label the amount of trans fat present in their products, directly below the amount of saturated fat.

Trans fatty acids are of concern because they tend to increase bad (LDL) cholesterol while also decreasing good (HDL) cholesterol levels in the blood. In doing so, trans fats increase the risk of coronary heart disease even more than naturally saturated fatty acids. Trans fats have also been implicated in certain cancers, particularly breast cancer.

In response to these concerns, people are reminded to minimize their intake of fats, especially saturated and hydrogenated fats.

FIGURE 10.4 Mature soybeans in pod
Courtesy of the U.S. Department of Agriculture, Agricultural Research Service

TRANS-FREE FATS AND OILS

New versions of vegetable fats and oils have been developed that are trans-free yet have the stability and functions approaching that of regular fats and oils. For example, soybeans and other oil sources can be specially bred to be naturally low in polyunsaturated fatty acids without having to undergo hydrogenation. These new liquid oils, often called low-lin oils (because they are low in alpha linolenic acid (ALA), a polyunsaturated fatty acid that is highly susceptible to rancidity), have the advantage of better stability against rancidity. Certain sunflower, canola, and soybean oils currently on the market are made from these new oil sources.

It is also possible to produce trans-free plastic fats. For example, trans-free shortenings and margarines can be made from fats that are naturally saturated, such as palm oil and coconut oil. Because they are naturally saturated, these tropical oils do not need partial hydrogenation to achieve a soft plastic consistency and are therefore trans-free.

Another common way trans-free plastic shortenings and margarines are manufactured is by blending fully hydrogenated fats with liquid oils. Since full hydrogenation, unlike partial hydrogenation, does not generate trans fats, a fully hydrogenated solid fat can be blended with liquid oil to achieve the desired plastic consistency, trans free.

Bakers and pastry chefs cannot replace all saturated fats with unsaturated ones in the bakeshop, despite the concerns of their customers. Yet, it is still important to understand that baked goods and fried foods have been implicated as the two major sources of saturated and trans fats in our diet.

FATS AND OILS

Fats (and oils) differ from each other in cost, flavor, consistency, amount of fat, amount of air, amount of water, and melting point. Some contain additives, such as emulsifiers, antioxidants, salt, colors, flavors, antimicrobial agents, milk solids, and more (Table 10.1). These differences affect how each fat functions in the bakeshop.

Butter

Butter is made from heavy cream, an emulsion of butterfat suspended in milk. While some of the fat in chilled cream is in the form of liquid globules, a large amount consists of tiny solid fat crystals, so tiny that cream, while thickened by these solid crystals, seems totally liquid in the mouth. Butter manufacturing is the separation of this fat, both solid fat crystals and liquid globules, from much of the remaining liquid, or buttermilk.

As with other fats, butter provides many important functions, including moistness, tenderness, flakiness, and volume. But this does not explain the widespread use of butter in quality bakeshops, because butter does not excel at any of these functions. Instead, butter's two main advantages are its flavor and mouthfeel. No other fat can match butter in these two attributes. Margarine may contain natural butter flavor and have a low final melting point, but it still does not have the superior flavor and texture of butter.

Final melting point is defined as the temperature at which no solid fat crystals are visible, that is, when the fat appears as a completely clear liquid. Butter's final melting

HELPFUL HINT

Butter is too hard to work at 50°F (10°C) and too soft at 80°F (27°C). In fact, the best temperature for working with butter is within the narrow range of about 65°–70°F (18°–21°C). With laminated doughs, however, where flakiness and volume are important, butter should be as solid as possible. Puff pastry and other laminated doughs are chilled between folds, to keep butter solid and assure maximum flakiness and volume.

TABLE 10.1 ■ COMMON ADDITIVES TO FATS AND OILS

ADDITIVE	DESCRIPTION	COMMON USE IN FATS AND OILS
Annatto	Natural coloring from the seed of the annatto (anchiote) shrub	Color for butter
Beta carotene	A form of vitamin A	Color for margarine
BHA	Synthetic antioxidant; butylated hydroxyanisole	Minimizes oxidative rancidity
BHT	Synthetic antioxidant; butylated hydroxytoluene	Minimizes oxidative rancidity
Citric acid	Organic acid, especially high in citrus fruits	Minimizes oxidative rancidity, especially in lard
Cottonseed oil, partially hydrogenated	From seed of cotton plant	Added to plastic shortening to encourage formation of proper crystal structure for creaming
Dimethylpolysiloxane	Silicone derivative	Added to frying fats to reduce foaming
Lecithin	Emulsifier	Added to margarine to minimize spattering during pan sautéing
Mono- and diglycerides	Emulsifier	Added to high-ratio shortenings to increase moistness, tenderness, prevent staling of baked goods
Palm oil, partially hydrogenated	From flesh of palm fruit	Added to plastic shortening to encourage formation of proper crystal formation for creaming
Polyglycerol esters	Emulsifier	Prevents clouding in salad oil
Potassium sorbate	Potassium salt of sorbic acid, a natural organic acid	Added to margarine to prevent microbial growth
Propyl gallate	Synthetic antioxidant	Minimizes oxidative rancidity, especially in lard
Propylene glycol monostearate	Emulsifier	Highly effective emulsifier in high-ratio liquid shortenings
Salt	Sodium chloride	Flavoring and preservative in butter and margarine
Sodium benzoate	Sodium salt of benzoic acid, a natural organic acid	Added to margarine to prevent microbial growth
Stearic acid	Natural saturated fatty acid	Added to high-ratio liquid shortening as an emulsifier
TBHQ	Synthetic antioxidant; tert-butylhydroquinone	Minimizes oxidative rancidity, especially in lard
Tocopherols	Mixture of vitamin E and related molecules; Antioxidant	Minimizes oxidative rancidity
Vitamin A palmitate		Added to margarine as a vitamin
Vitamin D		Added to margarine as a vitamin

point is often stated as around 94°F (34°C), because that is when essentially all the fat crystals have melted to liquid. However, the butter has been melting all along.

Butter has many disadvantages. For example, it is expensive. Butter can be several times more expensive than margarine, and its price fluctuates with the seasons and with supply. Butterfat is an undesirable fat from a health standpoint. It is the highest of common bakeshop fats in saturated fat—even higher than lard—and it contains cholesterol.

Butter is also one of the most difficult fats to work with because it has a narrow plastic range. It is too hard when used directly out of the refrigerator, and it melts quickly

HOW BUTTER IS MANUFACTURED

At one time, cream was agitated in wooden butter churns. Today, butter is manufactured in large batches or even larger continuous commercial operations. Either way, the first step in butter manufacture is to pasteurize cream, then cool it to 60°F (16°C). If desired, small amounts of natural yellow annatto color may be added before the cream is vigorously agitated, or churned. At first, the churning action produces whipped cream, as air is whipped in. Solid fat crystals surround and stabilize the air cells, but soon, warm temperatures soften the fat crystals. Continued violent agitation causes fat crystals and fat globules to clump. Eventually, large pools of liquid buttermilk seep out and chunks of butter form, as the whipped cream collapses.

After churning, the butter chunks are washed with cold water, salted if desired, then worked or kneaded, to shape and to remove excess water. Because kneading also softens butter, it is sometimes called work softening. What remains is a smooth mixture of solid fat crystals, with droplets of water, air bubbles, milk solids, and liquid butterfat trapped throughout.

from the heat of hands or a warm bakeshop. Its low melting point also means that oven temperatures must be set properly and the butter must be well-chilled to achieve the best volume for puff pastries and other baked goods that rely on butter for leavening.

Butter spoils faster than other fats, especially if it is unsalted. It is susceptible to bacterial spoilage if it is not refrigerated for the short term or frozen for the long term. Butter that has undergone bacterial spoilage has either a sour milk or rancid off flavor.

CLASSIFYING BUTTER

Butter can be classified by the type of cream used in its production. The two types of butters are cultured butter and sweet cream butter. *Cultured butter* is made from sour cream, where bacteria have converted lactose to lactic acid. Cultured butter, also called ripened butter, has a distinct sour flavor, similar to sour cream. It is rarely, if ever, salted. *Sweet cream butter* has a milder flavor than cultured butter. It is called *sweet cream* because the cream has not been soured, not because it contains a sweetener.

While both types are available worldwide, there are regional preferences. Sweet cream butter is traditional throughout North America and Great Britain. Cultured butter is traditional in certain countries in Europe, particularly France, Germany, and Switzerland. *European-style butter* made and sold in North America is either cultured butter or sweet cream butter with an added cultured cream flavor. Plugrá is an example of a European-style butter made with an added cultured cream flavor.

MAKEUP OF BUTTER

The minimum amount of butterfat required in butter in the United States and in Canada is 80 percent, slightly lower than the 82 percent minimum required in most European countries. European-style butters, like European butters, typically contain a minimum of 82 percent butterfat. While 82 percent is the minimum allowed in Europe, it is not uncommon for European butters to have as much as 86 percent butterfat, or more. Butter containing a higher percentage of butterfat typically has a smoother, creamier mouthfeel.

Butterfat consists mostly of triglycerides with a small amount of natural emulsifiers. The emulsifiers, which make up about 2–3 percent of butterfat, include mono- and diglycerides and lecithin. Butterfat also contains cholesterol and vitamin A, a fat-soluble vitamin.

The remaining 20 percent of butter's makeup includes water (typically 16 percent), milk solids, and salt, if added. Milk solids consist of proteins, lactose, and minerals.

THE GRADING OF BUTTER

In the United States, there are three grades for butter: Grades AA, A, and B. U.S. Grade AA and Grade A are the quality ratings most often seen, but some U.S. Grade B butter is available. The grading of butter is a voluntary system administered by the U.S. Department of Agriculture (USDA).

Flavor is considered the most important attribute of butter, and a preference in the United States for mild-tasting butter is reflected in the USDA scoring system. Of the three grades, USDA Grade AA butter is made from the freshest cream. It has a mild butter flavor with minimal flavor defects. USDA Grade A butter has a stronger, slightly sour but still pleasant flavor. Grade B butter has a flavor that is more like cultured butter, a flavor that some prefer.

A lesser part of butter's score is related to its body or consistency and its color. U.S. Grade AA butter must have a smooth, creamy consistency and uniform color. The cow's diet strongly influences butter consistency, as does the season of the year that the cow is milked. The manufacturer, however, has control over other factors that influence butter consistency. These factors include the percentage of fat and milk solids in butter, the heating and cooling of cream, and how the butter is churned and worked.

Canada has one grade for butter, Canada 1. Canada 1 butter can be mild-flavored or sour, depending on whether it is made from sweet cream or cultured cream. Other characteristics of Canada 1 butter are similar to USDA Grade AA or A.

HELPFUL HINT

The proteins and lactose in butter may be browned deliberately to make browned butter, or *beurre noisette*. *Noisette* is French for hazelnut, and browned butter has an appealing nutty flavor and the rich color of hazelnuts. To brown butter, cook it in a sauté pan until the water evaporates and the butter has a golden brown color. Remove from heat and strain the clear liquid beurre noisette from the solids. Discard the solids.

If butter is heated just until the water evaporates and is skimmed and strained before milk solids brown, it is called clarified butter. Clarified butter is a staple on the line in restaurant kitchens. Because milk solids have been removed, clarified butter is less likely to scorch, smoke, or burn when foods are sautéed under high heat.

Proteins and lactose in milk solids contribute to Maillard browning in baked goods. Water and a small amount of air in butter provide for leavening.

A few optional ingredients are allowed in butter in the United States and Canada. For example, natural butter flavor and annatto, a natural coloring, can be added. Salt can be added for flavor, and bacterial cultures can be added if the butter is cultured.

Bakers and pastry chefs generally use unsalted butter in the bakeshop for good reason. First, the amount of salt added to butter can be unpredictable, as it varies from one brand to the next. Second, the amount of salt in butter may be too high for certain products, such as buttercream. Finally, it is easier to detect off flavors in unsalted butter than in salted butter. While butter in North America will be free of off flavors when initially graded, it can pick up odors if stored improperly. If salted butter is used in the bakeshop, formulas must be adjusted accordingly (assume the amount of salt added to butter is about 2.0–2.5 percent).

Unsalted butter is sometimes confusingly called sweet butter. It is best to stay away from this term because it is easily mistaken for sweet cream butter, which is butter made from sweet cream. Sweet cream butter can be either salted or unsalted.

Lard

Lard, rendered from hog fat, is a by-product of the meat industry. It was once a common ingredient in cooking and baking in North America, Great Britain, Spain, and many other countries around the world. The highest grade lard, called leaf lard, surrounds the kidneys and abdomen of the animal. Other grades of lard include hard fat

HOW A LACK OF REFRIGERATION GAVE US DIFFERENT STYLES OF BUTTER

The very act of making butter—of churning cream and removing buttermilk—is a form of food preservation, because buttermilk supports bacterial growth. Yet, butter still contains some buttermilk, which is rich in nutrients, so it can still spoil. This was a problem in the days before refrigeration.

Where salt was available, it was used as a preservative in butter. Salt is a very powerful antimicrobial agent, and salted butter could contain a fairly high amount of buttermilk and not spoil.

In countries where salt was not readily available, other means were needed for preservation. As milk sat out for cream to slowly rise to the surface, the milk and cream would sour before the cream was churned. The "friendly" bacteria in sour or ripened cream slow the growth of undesirable spoilage bacteria. Since this is not as effective as salt in preventing bacterial growth, a higher amount of buttermilk often was removed in the production of cultured butter. This may explain why some European butters are very high in butterfat.

Some countries, notably India, simmer butter to destroy bacteria and to remove water. The resulting liquid butterfat, called ghee, has a distinctive nutty flavor, from the Maillard reaction that occurs when milk proteins and milk sugar (lactose) are heated. Since it contains essentially no water, ghee lasts longer than butter.

Today, refrigeration is more readily available, yet many cultures still prefer butter made in the style of their culture. In North America, more than 95 percent of butter sold is salted sweet cream butter.

---

from the back; soft fat from around muscle tissue; and caul fat from around the stomach and intestines.

Lard's unique crystalline structure makes it valuable for providing flakiness to pastries and piecrusts. It is also prized for its mild meaty flavor, characteristic of certain traditional ethnic pastries. Except for these uses, lard has largely been replaced by shortening in North America. However, there has recently been a small resurgence in interest in the use of lard in pastries.

Today's lard is highly refined for a mild flavor, white color, and better uniformity. It is 100 percent fat, usually with small amounts of antioxidants added to protect it from developing rancidity. Like all plastic fats, lard traps air, useful for leavening. To improve upon this feature, lard is sometimes hydrogenated and otherwise processed to give it a less greasy feel and to improve its creaming ability. While this allows lard to produce fine-textured cakes, it is at the expense of providing flakiness to pastries and piecrusts.

WHAT'S SO UNIQUE ABOUT LARD?

All solid fats contain solid fat crystals. Depending on the source of fat, how the fat is processed, and how it is cooled, liquid fats can solidify into one of several different crystalline structures. The three main crystalline structures are called alpha, beta prime, and beta. Each has its own distinct features. For example, beta prime crystals are relatively small. They solidify to a smooth, creamy white solid and hold in lots of small air bubbles when creamed. Beta prime crystals are ideal for producing light, airy cakes with a fine crumb. While today's all-purpose shortenings are designed to solidify into beta prime crystals, lard naturally will not. Instead, lard tends to form larger beta crystals. That is why it is not the best choice for producing fine-textured cakes. Beta crystals are what gives lard its translucent appearance and coarse, grainy texture. Beta crystals are what make lard uniquely suited to providing flakiness in pastries.

WHAT IS OLEO?

On occasion, consumer recipes call for oleo. Oleo is just another name for margarine. The French chemist who invented margarine in the 1860s made it from beef fat and gave it the full name oleomargarine. Beef fat consists primarily of oleic acid and two saturated acids (palmitic and stearic acids), which, in the 1800s, was called margaric acid.

The U.S. FDA (Food and Drug Administration) shortened the name of oleomargarine to margarine in 1951, but some people—mostly those who remember the days before 1951—still refer to margarine as oleo.

Margarine

Margarine is imitation butter. While great improvements have been made over the years in margarine quality, it is still not the real thing, and it does not have the superior flavor and mouthfeel of butter. Yet, margarine has several advantages over butter, and this probably explains why sales volume of margarine in North America has exceeded that of butter since the late 1950s.

One advantage of margarine is its lower price. Another advantage is that margarine contains no cholesterol, and soft margarines are lower in saturated fats than butter is (although they may contain trans fats). A third advantage of some margarines is their stronger flavor. While this might sound like a contradiction since butter is prized for its flavor, margarine flavor can be more assertive, if less refined.

HELPFUL HINT

Margarine, or a blend of margarine and butter, can in theory be used instead of butter in just about any product, but it is best to use butter wherever mouthfeel or butter flavor is especially important. For example, while margarine, or a blend of margarine and butter, might be acceptable in chocolate brownies, butter alone is best in buttercream, where butter flavor and mouthfeel stand out.

Don't forget to adjust a formula for salt if salted margarine is used in place of unsalted butter.

MAKEUP OF MARGARINE

Most margarines are made from soybean oil, but they can be made from any vegetable or animal fat. True margarine has a similar composition to butter; that is, it contains a minimum of 80 percent fat and about 16 percent water, and a similar amount of air is trapped in margarine as in butter. This means that margarine has the same number of calories as butter. While low-fat and fat-free "margarines"—called *spreads*—do exist, these products do not generally work well in baking. Low-fat and fat-free spreads consist of a high amount of water. They rely on gums and starches to provide a butterlike consistency.

Margarine made without coloring and flavoring would be white and bland-tasting, like shortening. That is why margarine contains coloring—usually beta-carotene—and butter flavoring, either natural or artificial. Margarine, like butter, can be purchased salted or unsalted.

Besides salt, several other optional ingredients can be added to margarine, including milk solids, lecithin, and antimicrobial agents. When margarine contains salt and antimicrobial agents and does not contain milk solids, like shortening, it does not need refrigeration.

CLASSIFYING MARGARINE

Margarine is a designer fat, meaning that the manufacturer can blend or hydrogenate it to any degree of firmness and plasticity. One way to classify margarine is by its firmness and its final melting point. The following three types of margarine are listed with approximate final melting points.

WHY RESOLIDIFIED SHORTENING IS DIFFERENT

Once shortening is melted and rehardened, it looks different. Instead of being smooth, creamy and white, it appears hard, translucent, and somewhat gritty. This is the first clue that things have changed.

In fact, beta prime crystals have not reformed. Instead, larger, more stable beta crystals have formed, and the shortening will no longer cream as well.

Baker's margarine (typical final melting point: about 90°–100°F, or 32°–38°C), also called cake margarine, has the softest consistency and the lowest melting point of the three types of margarine. Baker's margarine is good for creaming; it is the margarine of choice for cookies and cakes made by the creaming method, and for icings (if using margarine for icing, remember to select an unsalted brand). While baker's margarine has a final melting point similar to butter's, it does not have the same pleasant mouthfeel as butter. Instead, it can be somewhat greasy or oily. Mouthfeel is complex and is related to the total melting behavior of fat, not just final melting point.

Puff pastry margarine has an extremely high final melting point (typically 115°–135°F, or 47°–57°C) and a firm, waxy consistency. Puff pastry margarine is excellent for picture-perfect light and flaky pastries, but the pastries tend to have an unpleasant waxy mouthfeel.

Roll-in margarine has a medium final melting point (typically 100°–115°F, or 38°–46°C) and medium consistency. Roll-in margarine is acceptable for providing a moderate amount of flakiness and volume in puff pastries, croissants, and Danish pastries, without contributing excessive waxiness.

Shortenings

The main differences between shortening and margarine are that shortening is 100 percent fat, contains no water, and is white and bland. As with margarines, most shortenings are made from soybean oil, but they can be made from any vegetable or animal fat. Smaller amounts of either palm and/or cottonseed oil are typically added to shortening, to encourage the formation of beta prime crystals, which are so important when shortening is creamed.

Shortening was originally developed as a replacement for lard. Like margarine, shortenings are designer fats, so many types are available to the baker and pastry chef. The three main types of shortenings used in the bakeshop are all-purpose shortening, high-ratio plastic shortening, and high-ratio liquid shortening. Other shortenings are available, however, including ones designed specifically for frying and others designed to make the softest, lightest icings.

CLASSIFYING SHORTENING

All-purpose (AP) shortening contains no added emulsifiers. Its final melting point varies with the brand, but it is typically anywhere from 110°–125°F (43°–52°C). AP shortening contains about 10 percent air trapped in the fat, important for leavening. Shortening (and butter) manufacturers often aerate shortening with nitrogen instead of air. Air contains oxygen, which causes fats to undergo oxidative rancidity. Recall that air itself is almost 80 percent nitrogen, so nitrogen is perfectly safe in foods.

All-purpose shortening is used in products where shortening is creamed or where it is rubbed into flour, as with pie dough and biscuits. It is plastic and workable over a wide temperature range, making it easier than butter to work with.

LIQUID OIL IN SHORTENING

Did you know that a typical all-purpose shortening at room temperature contains about 80 percent liquid oil? The remaining 20 percent consists of a network of solid fat crystals that gives AP shortening its solidity.

AP shortening is also acceptable for frying. Many AP shortenings contain small amounts of antifoaming agent, to prevent fat from foaming excessively in a fryer. An example of an antifoaming agent is dimethylpolysiloxane, a silicone additive.

High-ratio plastic shortening looks like all-purpose shortening, but it has emulsifiers added. The most common emulsifiers added to high-ratio shortenings are mono- and diglycerides. High-ratio shortenings—sometimes called emulsified shortenings—are best used in icings and cakes, or in any product that includes a relatively high amount of liquid or air. They are also useful in bread doughs, where the emulsifiers help delay starch retrogradation that leads to staling. They should never be used in frying, because the emulsifiers easily break down and smoke under high heat, and while high-ratio plastic shortening can be used in pie dough, there is no advantage to this. Pie dough contains very little liquid or air and it has no tendency to stale, so emulsifiers are unnecessary.

The emulsifiers in high-ratio shortenings provide plain icings with a lighter, fluffier texture that holds more liquid ingredients without breaking (the same is true of buttercreams made with whipped egg white). Cakes and other baked goods made with high-ratio shortenings are generally moister, more tender, and have a finer crumb. High-ratio shortenings also extend shelf life in baked goods, because the emulsifiers prevent starch retrogradation and staling.

High-ratio liquid shortening, like high-ratio plastic shortening, has added emulsifiers. However, it usually contains a much higher level of extremely effective emulsifiers. High-ratio liquid shortening is much less hydrogenated than high-ratio plastic shortenings. While it is fluid and can be poured, it does contain some fat crystals, giving it an opaque, creamy look at room temperature.

High-ratio liquid shortening is primarily used in liquid shortening cakes, where it provides, by far, the highest volume, most moistness, finest and most tender crumb, and the longest shelf life of any fat or oil. High-ratio liquid shortenings are so effective at

WHAT DOES HIGH-RATIO MEAN?

Procter & Gamble first added emulsifiers to shortenings in the 1930s. Cakes made with these new shortenings were moister, more tender, and had a finer crumb and longer shelf life because of the emulsifiers.

Cake batters made with emulsified shortenings also held a higher ratio of water to flour because emulsifiers are effective at holding oil and water together. Since the batters held more water, they also held more sugar, which dissolves in water. A higher ratio of water and sugar meant that the ability of emulsified shortenings to increase moistness, tenderness, and shelf life went well beyond the abilities of the emulsifiers themselves. It also meant that the cost of making cakes was lowered, since water and sugar are both inexpensive ingredients. No wonder the importance of the higher ratio of water and sugar in cake was reflected in the name of the shortening itself.

moistening and tenderizing that manufacturers often recommend that the amount of shortening be reduced by about 20 percent when switching from a plastic shortening to a liquid one.

High-ratio liquid shortenings are extremely effective at incorporating air into cake batters. This, of course, makes for a lighter, more tender product, but it does more. It lowers costs, and it has changed the way cakes are made in this country. Instead of creaming shortening as a first step in cake making, liquid shortening cake batters are mixed in a simple one-step process.

Substitutions of Shortening and Butter

Recall that shortening and lard are 100 percent fat, while butter and margarine are only 80 percent or so fat. In many formulas, one fat can be substituted directly for another, one for one. Products made with the 80 percent fat will be slightly different in texture—generally less moist and tender—and they will have the characteristic flavor of the fat. While it is generally acceptable to substitute one plastic fat for another, oils should be used only in recipes developed for their use.

Because a one-for-one substitution of shortening and butter, for example, changes the amount of fat in a product by about 20 percent, it is sometimes desirable to calculate and adjust the amount of fat and liquid when making these changes. Starting guidelines for changing between butter (or margarine) and shortening (or lard) are as follows.

- *To substitute butter for shortening:* Divide the weight of shortening by 0.80 to determine the weight of butter to use. Reduce the amount of liquid (milk or water) by the difference between the two. For example, for 1 pound (16 ounces) of shortening, use 20 ounces of butter and reduce the amount of liquid by 4 ounces. For 500 grams of shortening, use 625 grams of butter and reduce the amount of liquid by 125 grams.

- *To substitute shortening for butter:* Multiply the weight of butter by 0.80 to determine the weight of shortening to use. Increase the amount of liquid by the difference between the two. For example, for 1 pound of butter, use 12.75 ounces of shortening and increase the amount of liquid by 3.25 ounces. For 500 grams of butter, use 400 grams of shortening and increase the amount of liquid by 100 grams.

Oil

Even though it is liquid, oil contains no water; it is 100 percent fat. Oil used in the bakeshop is sometimes called vegetable oil because it is extracted from a vegetable source, such as soybeans or cottonseed. Vegetable oils are sometimes labeled salad oils because of their use in salad dressings. The most common vegetable oil worldwide is soybean oil, but others are available, including cottonseed, corn, canola, and peanut. While these oils vary slightly in flavor and color, they can be used interchangeably in baking.

Oil is the only common lipid that does not contribute to leavening in baked goods. Unlike plastic fats, oil does not contain trapped air or water. Unlike high-ratio liquid shortenings, it does not contain emulsifiers that allow batters to trap and hold large volumes of air. In fact, oils generally destabilize the foaming of cake batters, especially when they contain anti-foaming agents, which is generally the case with oils designed to be frying oils.

Oil is used in quick breads, muffins, and chiffon cake for a distinctively moist and tender, yet dense, coarse crumb. Oil is also sometimes used in piecrusts, especially the bottom crusts of juicy pies. Oil crusts are not flaky. While they are not flaky, crusts made with oil do not absorb as much water when they are mixed, so they bake up tender. Once baked, they are resistant to soaking up wet, juicy fillings. They do not become soggy or toughen, as flaky bottom crusts tend to do. Mealy pie crusts also do not splinter like flaky crusts, so they cut more cleanly.

WHAT IS WINTERIZED OIL?

When salad oil is refrigerated, it remains crystal clear and liquid, even when fully chilled. Do the same with olive oil and it will harden and cloud. That is because salad oils have been winterized and most olive oils have not.

Winterizing is a process in which oil is stored at cold temperatures to allow higher-melting triglycerides to crystallize. The oil is filtered to physically remove these solid fat crystals. What is left is salad oil, which consists only of triglycerides that are liquid at cold temperatures.

OLIVE OIL

Olive oil is the most expensive of all oils used in the bakeshop. It can be refined like other oils to be mild-flavored and light in color, but then it would lack its attractive green-gold color and fruity flavor. Refined olive oil is sometimes labeled *light* in the United States. Light olive oil is light in color and flavor only; olive oil, refined or not, has the same amount of fat (100 percent) and the same number of calories as any oil. Because olive oil is high in desirable monounsaturated fatty acids, it is often considered the fat of choice for a healthful diet.

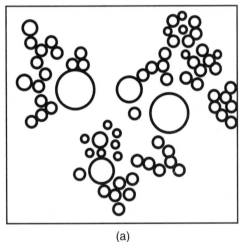

Olive oil is most often sold unrefined, or virgin. Most countries follow the grades set by the International Olive Oil Council (IOOC) in defining olive oil products. Virgin olive oil is squeezed and separated from crushed olives without the use of heat and without altering the natural oil in any way. While virgin olive oil is commonly described as cold-pressed, today virgin olive oil is not so much pressed as it is centrifuged, or spun, to separate it out.

The quality of virgin olive oil is defined by the quality of its flavor and by the amount of free fatty acids present in the oil. Free fatty acids are fatty acids that are not part of a triglyceride molecule. The amount of free fatty acids is an indication of the level of care taken in handling and processing the olives. Extra-virgin olive oil is the highest-quality virgin olive oil, with a fine, fruity aroma and the lowest level of free fatty acids.

Within the world of extra-virgin olive oils, there is a wide range of flavor characteristics and prices. In all cases, however, extra-virgin olive oils become bitter and lose their fine flavor when they are exposed to high heat. Extra-virgin olive oils are best used where there is minimal heat exposure. For applications that involve high heat, less expensive virgin or refined olive oil may be more appropriate. Olive oil is most commonly used in savory flatbreads, focaccia, pizza, and yeast-raised doughs, but it also shows up in regional Mediterranean specialty desserts.

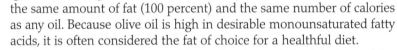

(a)

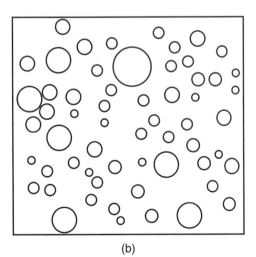

(b)

FIGURE 10.5 Effect of added emulsifier on the dispersion of fats and oils in cake batter (a) Butter without added emulsifier (b) Butter with added emulsifier

Emulsifiers

Emulsifiers have been mentioned throughout this chapter, but they are so important in baking that they deserve more consideration. Many different emulsifiers provide a wide range of functions in baked goods. In all cases, emulsifiers function by interacting with other ingredients. For example, emulsifiers interact with fats and oil droplets, helping to disperse them more evenly throughout batters and doughs (Figure 10.5). Better distribution of fats means more tender, better-textured baked goods. Emulsifiers interact with proteins, improving their

WHAT DO EMULSIFIERS LOOK LIKE?

Emulsifiers can be either liquid or solid, just like fats and oils. While some have pretty complicated molecular structures, mono- and diglycerides, the emulsifiers added to high-ratio shortenings, have relatively simple structures. Mono- and diglycerides consist of a mixture of molecules of monoglycerides and molecules of diglycerides. *Mono* means one and *di* means two. Instead of having three fatty acids, like triglycerides (fats and oils), monoglycerides have one fatty acid (FA) attached to glycerol, and diglycerides have two. The fatty acid part of the molecule is attracted to fats and oils, while the rest of the molecule is attracted to water.

$$
\begin{array}{lll}
C - FA & C - FA & C - FA \\
\mid & \mid & \mid \\
C & C - FA & C - FA \\
\mid & \mid & \mid \\
C & C & C - FA \\
\end{array}
$$

Monoglyceride   Diglyceride   Triglyceride

strength and flexibility so they stretch without breaking. Stronger, more flexible proteins in cake batters hold air exceptionally well, which means better-textured baked goods. Emulsifiers interact with starch molecules, preventing them from retrograding or bonding with one another, which is the primary cause of staling. This, too, translates to better-textured baked goods.

Emulsifiers can be purchased separately and added with fats to batters and doughs; however, it is not common for bakers and pastry chefs to do so. Instead, the main sources of emulsifiers in the bakeshop include:

- Dough conditioners used in yeast-raised doughs
- High-ratio shortenings
- Dairy ingredients and egg yolks, which naturally contain complex mixtures of emulsifiers, lecithin being the best known

FUNCTIONS OF FATS, OILS, AND EMULSIFIERS

Main Functions

PROVIDES TENDERNESS

Fats, oils, and emulsifiers tenderize by coating structure builders—gluten proteins, egg proteins, and starch granules—and preventing them from hydrating and forming structure. Tenderness is the opposite of toughness. A tender product is easy to break, chew, squeeze, or crumble because it lacks a strong structure.

Tenderness is usually considered a good thing. After all, baked goods that are tender are pleasantly easy to bite. Tenderizers, however, must be balanced with structure builders—tougheners. Too much tenderness is undesirable because overly tender products collapse or break apart, or are excessively crumbly or mealy.

Another name for tenderness is shortness because lipids literally shorten gluten strands by coating them. While all-purpose shortening is named for this ability to provide shortness, all fats, oils, and emulsifiers serve this function. All lipids do not provide shortness—tenderness—to the same degree, however.

Butter and margarine, having only 80 percent fat (and containing water besides), tenderize less effectively than shortening and lard, which contain 100 percent fat. This is true unless formulas are adjusted when converting between fats, as described earlier.

The softer or more fluid the fat, the more easily it mixes into batters and doughs, coating flour particles and egg proteins. In other words, all else being equal, the softer or more fluid the fat, the more it tenderizes. This explains why piecrust made with oil is short and mealy. It also explains why plastic fats that are softened by creaming tenderize better than ones not creamed. Finally, it explains why highly saturated, very hard cocoa butter in chocolate does little to tenderize baked goods.

In the case of pie pastry dough and certain other products, tenderness increases the more fat is worked into flour before water is added. The more it is incorporated, the smaller the piece size of the fat, and the more it coats structure-building flour particles. This is why French piecrust—pâte brisée—is short and mealy. French chefs achieve this texture through fraisage, a process where fat and flour are kneaded with the heel of the hand until they are thoroughly blended.

Emulsifiers, like those added to high-ratio shortenings, are extremely effective at providing tenderness. They accomplish this in at least two ways. First, emulsifiers help fats and oils disperse throughout baked goods, so the fats and oils coat structure builders more completely. Second, emulsifiers themselves are extremely effective at coating structure builders. In fact, the amount of fat in baked goods can be reduced when emulsifiers are added. Check the labels of low-fat baked goods and you will see that many are high in emulsifiers, such as mono- and diglycerides.

Finally, the more leavening provided by the fat or oil, the more it tenderizes, because leavening stretches and thins cell walls, weakening them. This is why oil might excel at tenderizing pie pastry, but it actually might toughen a cake.

In summary, the shortening or tenderizing abilities of lipids depend on the following:

- The amount present; the more fat, oil, or emulsifier, the more tenderizing
- How soft and fluid it is; the more soft and fluid the fat, the more tenderizing
- Piece size; the smaller the piece size of the fat (from more mixing), the more tenderizing
- The presence of emulsifiers, such as mono- and diglycerides
- The ability of the fat, oil, or emulsifier to leaven

PROVIDES FLAKINESS IN LAMINATED DOUGHS

Flakiness refers to the number of layers in a baked laminated product. A flaky product has many distinct layers. Flakiness requires that flattened chunks of plastic fat separate bits of dough. When heated in the oven, the fat melts, while structure in the layers solidifies. This leaves distinct layers of baked dough. The more layers, and the more distinct the layers, the flakier the pastry. To keep layers distinct, chunks of fat should be kept large. To ensure this, some chefs prefer using their fingertips instead of mixers to work fat into flour because mixers can quickly overblend fat with flour. Notice how flakiness can be at odds with tenderness, which is greatest with small pieces of fat.

If solid fat melts too early in the baking process, layers will not form. Instead, the melted fat seeps into the dough, tenderizing it. That is why pie or any laminated dough made with butter is best chilled before baking, and why the higher the melting point of the fat, often the flakier the pastry.

In summary, the ability of lipids to provide flakiness depends on the following:

- How solid it is; the more solid the fat and the higher its melting point, the more flakiness
- Piece size; the larger the piece size of the fat, the more flakiness

THE PERFECT PIECRUST

The perfect piecrust is both tender and flaky. It is tender enough to bite easily, and it is also flaky, so that distinct layers of dough are clearly visible. To create piecrust that is both tender and flaky, keep the chunks of fat large for flakiness, and use other means besides piece size to achieve tenderness. For example, be sure the protein content in the flour is low, and keep the amount of flour dusted on the work surface to a minimum. Increase the amount of fat in the formula, if necessary, and be sure only a minimum amount of water is added. Finally, do not overwork the dough once water is added. If necessary, chill dough for several hours or overnight, to allow time for water to passively migrate throughout dough.

ASSISTS IN LEAVENING

As with eggs, fats help incorporate air into baked goods, but they do it in a very different way. They are not leaveners themselves—air, steam, and carbon dioxide are the leaveners—but they play an important role in the leavening process.

Fats assist in leavening in three main ways. The traditional way is in the creaming of plastic fats, where tiny air cells are incorporated into the fat. Cookies and cakes made by the creaming method rely on plastic fats for the bulk of their volume and fine crumb. This is true even when baking powder is used.

All plastic fats contain entrapped air even when not creamed, and some—butter and margarine—contain water for leavening. Puff pastries, in particular, rely on entrapped air and water in fats for leavening. For maximum height, use fat with a high melting point, and use margarine—which contains water—instead of shortening. Recall, however, that high-melting-point fats tend to leave a waxy mouthfeel. If butter or another low melting fat is used, be sure the fat is thoroughly chilled before use, and chill the prepared dough until ready to bake.

The third way for fats to assist in leavening is related to the ability of emulsifiers in high-ratio shortenings to assist proteins in batters in trapping and holding air as they are mixed. High-ratio liquid shortening cakes rely on this means of leavening for their light, airy texture.

In summary, the three main ways that fats contribute to leavening in baked goods are as follows:

- Through the incorporation of air during the creaming of plastic fats
- By the air and water already present in certain plastic fats
- Through the assistance of emulsifiers in high-ratio shortenings

CONTRIBUTES MOISTNESS

Moistness is a characteristic of all fluid ingredients because moistness is the sensation of something being liquid. Both moisture (water) and liquid oil provide moistness. Notice the distinction made between moistness and moisture. Liquid oil provides moistness but not moisture. Butter, which contains moisture, usually contributes less moistness than oil does.

Moistness is not the same as tenderness, but the two can be related. Often, anything that is moist is also tender. However, chewy foods are moist but not tender, and crisp crumbly cookies are tender without being moist.

Not all fats contribute significantly to moistness; only those, like oil, that are fluid at body temperature do. Emulsifiers also contribute to moistness. Interestingly, fats often contribute more moistness to baked goods than does water. This is probably because much of the water in baked goods is either driven off or becomes tightly bound to proteins and starches.

In summary, the moistening ability of lipids depends on the following:

- How fluid it is; the more fluid the fat at body temperature, the more moistening
- The presence of emulsifiers, such as mono- and diglycerides

PREVENTS STALING

Lipids—especially emulsifiers such as mono- and diglycerides in high-ratio shortenings—interfere with the process of retrogradation of gelatinized starch. One way that they do this is by preventing starch granules from gelatinizing in the first place. Since starch retrogradation is the major cause of staling in baked goods, lipids prevent the hard, dry, crumbly texture and loss of flavor associated with staling.

CONTRIBUTES FLAVOR

A major reason for using butter is for its unsurpassed flavor. Other fats that contribute a distinct flavor include lard, olive oil, and margarine. While margarine does not have the fine flavor of butter, it can be an acceptable substitute in certain situations.

Even neutral fats contribute to flavor because all fats add a certain richness. And, in the case of fried foods, desirable fried flavor comes from the breakdown of fats and oils exposed to high heat.

Additional Functions

CONTRIBUTES COLOR

Some fats—butter and margarine, in particular—provide a distinct golden-yellow color to baked goods. Fats that contain milk solids—butter and certain margarines—undergo Maillard browning on the surfaces of baked goods, contributing further to color. All fats increase the rate of heating of baked goods, and in doing so allow for faster browning. This is especially noticeable when comparing low-fat baked goods to regular baked goods. The low-fat baked goods inevitably are paler in color.

PROVIDES A FINE CRUMB TO BAKED GOODS

Plastic fats and emulsifiers provide a finer, less coarse crumb to baked goods. There are probably several reasons for this, including the ability of plastic fats and emulsifiers to allow the incorporation of many tiny air cells into batters and doughs.

ADDS CREAMINESS TO SAUCES, CUSTARDS, CONFECTIONS, AND FROZEN DESSERTS

Many sauces, confections, and frozen desserts are emulsions of liquid fat droplets in milk or another liquid. For example, vanilla custard sauce, ganache, and ice cream are all emulsions. The droplets of liquid fat are like very tiny balls that roll over the tongue, which is perceived as a rich, creamy texture.

CONDUCTS HEAT

Fats and oils conduct heat from the oven, pan, or fryer directly to food. Fats and oils can be heated to a much higher temperature than water—350°F (177°C) compared with 212°F (100°C)—before they evaporate or break down. This high heat allows for the formation of a dry, crisp, brown crust in deep-fried foods and often in baking.

PROVIDES BULK AND SUBSTANCE TO ICINGS AND FILLINGS

Solid fat crystals provide bulk and substance to icings, fillings, and certain other products. To understand what this means, consider that icings contain anywhere from 30 to 50 percent solid fat. Without this solid fat, icings would consist of loose sugar crystals, or crystals dissolved or suspended in egg white or another liquid.

While fats are not considered structure builders in baked goods (remember, the more fat, the more tender the baked good), in icings and other products that contain solid fat, the solid crystals do provide substance. This substance defines the size and shape of these products. In this sense, solid fat does provide a type of structure.

PROMOTES SMOOTHNESS IN CONFECTIONS

Fats, oils, and emulsifiers interfere with sugar crystallization, providing a desirable smoothness to confections.

BLENDS FLAVORS AND MASKS OFF FLAVORS

When fats are removed from baked goods, flavors become disjointed and the baked good doesn't taste as rich and full-flavored. Fat affects taste perception probably because many flavors dissolve in them.

ACTS AS A RELEASE AGENT

Lipids, either applied to grease the pan or added to a formula, help ensure that baked foods are easily removed from their pans.

INCREASES THE SOFTNESS AND EXTENSIBILITY OF DOUGHS

Lipids lubricate gluten strands, making them softer, stretchier, and less likely to break. This is advantageous during yeast fermentation since it allows for a higher volume. Certain emulsifiers, in particular, are used for this purpose, including sodium stearoyl-2-lactylate and DATEM. You will often see one or both of these emulsifiers in dough conditioners for use in yeast doughs.

Water and other moisteners also provide a certain amount of softness to doughs. When the amount of lipids added to batter or dough is increased, often the amount of water and other moisteners must be reduced, to maintain the proper consistency of the batter or dough. Likewise, when the amount of lipids is reduced, the amount of other moisteners must be increased accordingly.

THINS OUT CHOCOLATE COUVERTURES AND COATINGS

Fats, oils, and emulsifiers—especially lecithin—coat and lubricate solid particles in melted chocolate couvertures and coatings, allowing the particles to slide past each other more easily. This thins the consistency of the coating, allowing it to be applied in a thin, even layer over pralines and confections. Pastry chefs typically use cocoa butter to thin out chocolate couvertures because of its pleasing mouthfeel. Butter and other fats can be used, but the chocolate will not harden as well and, when cooled, will have less snap.

INCREASES SPREAD IN COOKIES

Fats, oils, and emulsifiers coat and lubricate solid particles in doughs—for example, cookie doughs—reducing mixing time and thinning the doughs. This allows for more spread when the cookie bakes. The more fat, usually the more spread.

HELPFUL HINT

To reduce excessive spreading and thinning of cookies during baking, be sure dough is well-chilled and sheet pans are not warm before baking.

TABLE 10.2 ■ FAT REPLACERS IN BAKED GOODS

TYPE	EXAMPLE
Butter flavor	Natural and artificial butter flavorings
Emulsifiers	Mono- and diglycerides
Certain fruits	Prune paste, applesauce
Gums	Pectin, cellulose gum
Nondigestible lipids	Olestra
Oat-based ingredients	Oatmeal, oat flour
Starches and starch by-products	Potato starch, maltodextrins
Sugars and sweeteners	Dextrose, granulated sugar

Fats that liquefy early in the baking process, like butter, often increase cookie spread to a greater degree than later-melting fats, like all-purpose shortening. This effect is magnified when the dough is warm as it is placed in the oven.

Fat Replacers

Fats perform many functions in baked goods, making it difficult for any single fat replacer to complete the job. For example, one fat replacer might provide a buttery flavor but not increase tenderness. Another might increase tenderness and moistness but not flavor. Few, if any, provide flakiness, and only one, olestra, can be used in frying. Even when a combination of fat replacers is used, it is difficult to replace fat completely, especially without trial and error. Usually, it makes sense to reduce the amount of fat in a baked good instead of eliminating it completely. Remember, too, that it is not necessarily the total amount of fat that makes a product unhealthful. Rather, it is the amount of specific types of fats—saturated and trans fats—that are important to reduce.

To decide which of the many fat replacers to use, first decide which functions the fat provides in your high-fat product. Next, select one or more fat replacers that perform those same functions. See Table 10.2 for examples of fat replacers used in baked goods. Notice that sugars and sweeteners are listed as fat replacers. Sugars and sweeteners provide two important functions of fats, moistening and tenderizing. Dried plum (prune) paste and applesauce have been used over the years as fat replacers in baked goods. These fruit products provide sugars, sorbitol, and fruit pulp that moisten and tenderize. They provide varying degrees of success in replacing fat in baked goods.

STORAGE AND HANDLING

Two properties of fats that must be protected during storage are flavor and texture (plasticity). Fats and oils develop off flavors primarily from three sources: oxidative rancidity, which occurs with exposure to heat, light, air, and metal catalysts; bacterial spoilage, which occurs only in butter and those margarines that contain milk solids; and absorption of odors from the bakeshop.

The more unsaturated a fatty acid, the faster it will oxidize and have a stale, rancid flavor. Expect oils that are relatively high in polyunsaturated fatty acids, such as safflower oil, to oxidize many times faster than oils that are higher in monounsaturated fatty acids, such as olive oil. Likewise, expect most plastic fats, which are typically low in unsaturated fatty acids, to oxidize slowest of all. However, because oilseeds today are bred and processed in ways that affect the oil's stability, it is no longer possible to generalize and say, for example, that all soybean oils are highly susceptible to oxidation (although years ago that was the case). No matter the fat or oil, however, all should be stored properly to minimize oxidative rancidity. This means covering them when not in use and storing them in a cool, dark place.

Fats and oils sometimes contain antioxidants to slow oxidative rancidity. Examples of antioxidants include BHA, BHT, TBHQ, and vitamin E (tocopherols). Bacterial spoilage is slowed by the addition of salt or friendly bacteria, as when cream is cultured before use in butter.

To prevent changes in flavor and texture, cover the fat or oil tightly. This will keep out moisture, air, light, and strong odors. It is acceptable to store fats and oils in a cool, dry place, but butter must be stored at 40°F (4°C) or below. Do not expose fats to light, and do not allow plastic fats to melt. Melting changes the crystalline structure of fats, altering their texture and ability to cream. It also reduces the amount of air in fat, lowering its ability to assist in leavening. As with all ingredients, follow the FIFO (first in, first out) system to rotate stock.

QUESTIONS FOR REVIEW

1. What is a triglyceride? What is a fatty acid?

2. What is the difference between the chemical structure of a saturated fatty acid and an unsaturated fatty acid? Which is more likely to increase risk of coronary heart disease? Which are liquid oils high in?

3. Which oils are solid at room temperature?

4. Which common fats are solid because they are naturally high in saturated fatty acids? Which are solid because they have been hydrogenated or otherwise treated to increase their level of saturated fatty acids?

5. Draw out the process of hydrogenation, starting with an unsaturated fatty acid. Provide two reasons why fats and oils are hydrogenated.

6. Why might liquid oils oxidize faster than solid fats?

7. Why might vegetable or salad oil be partially hydrogenated?

8. How would you define a plastic fat? Which of the following fats are plastic at room temperature (70°F; 21°C): vegetable oil, high-ratio liquid shortening, all-purpose shortening, butter, lard, cocoa butter?

9. How does hydrogenation affect the healthfulness of fat?

10. Where are trans fatty acids typically found in our food supply? Why are trans fats considered undesirable?

11. What is meant by low-lin vegetable oil?

12. Name two ways that shortening and margarine processors are able to manufacture trans-free plastic shortenings.

13. Which of the following fats and oils are considered 100 percent fat: vegetable oil, high-ratio liquid shortening, all-purpose shortening, butter, margarine, high-ratio plastic shortening, lard? Which are only around 80 percent fat? Which contain air? Which contain water?

14. What are the two main advantages of using butter in baked goods? That is, what does butter excel at compared with other fats? What are four disadvantages?

15. How do European butters differ from North American butters in butterfat content?

16. Classify the two main types of butters by the type of cream used in their production. Which is the most common in North America? Which is common in Europe?

17. What are the advantages of margarine over butter?

18. List the three main types of margarines. In what way are they different? What are the main uses for each, and why?

19. When does margarine not require refrigeration?

20. Will margarine with the same final melting point as butter have as desirable a mouthfeel? Why or why not?

21. What are the main differences between margarines and shortenings? List two.

22. What is in high-ratio shortening that is not in all-purpose shortening? What are two differences between a high-ratio plastic shortening and a liquid one?

23. Which would you expect to be more fully hydrogenated, and why: baker's margarine, roll-in margarine, or puff pastry margarine?

24. Which baked goods are traditionally made with liquid oil?

25. Why is oil sometimes used instead of shortening or butter for the bottom crusts of juicy pies?

26. Why will muffins made with oil be denser than those made with all-purpose shortening?

27. What are mono- and diglycerides and where are they found?

28. Which is more hydrogenated, high-ratio liquid shortening or high-ratio plastic shortening?

29. Why is too much tenderness in baked goods undesirable?

30. What are the two main ways that emulsifiers contribute to tenderness in baked goods?

31. Why does oil result in a more tender but less flaky piecrust than plastic shortening? Why might oil result in a less tender cake than shortening?

32. What is the difference between moistness and tenderness?

33. Why might low-fat baked goods bake up paler than regular baked goods?

34. Why are sugars and some sweeteners listed as fat replacers? That is, which functions of fat do sugars and some sweeteners also provide?

35. What is oxidative rancidity? How can it be delayed?

36. What do antioxidants prevent in fats and oils? Name an antioxidant.

QUESTIONS FOR DISCUSSION

1. Besides being more tender, what else is different about a cake made from high-ratio liquid shortening than one made from other fats, such as an AP shortening?

2. Describe three reasons why butter might give you a less tender cake than high-ratio liquid shortening. In answering this question, assume formulas for each cake are identical except for the type of fat.

3. Name three ways that plastic fats contribute to leavening in baked goods.

4. You have two sunflower oils with very different fatty acid profiles. One has 69 percent polyunsaturated fatty acids; the other has 9 percent. Which will oxidize and taste rancid sooner, and why?

5. A biscuit formula calls for 7 pounds 8 ounces (3,750 grams) of shortening, but you wish to use butter instead. It also contains 12 pounds (6,000 grams) water. Show your calculations for determining how much butter should be used in place of the shortening, so that the amount of fat stays the same. Also show how the amount of water added will change.

EXERCISES AND EXPERIMENTS

1. How to Increase Flakiness in Pastry

Recall that flakiness results from dough being layered with bits of fat, which melt in the oven, leaving gaps that expand from the heat. Imagine that you have a formula, but the pastry is not as flaky as you wish. Explain why each of the changes listed as follows could work to increase flakiness. The first is completed for you.

1. Increase the amount of fat.

Reason: The more fat, the more layers can be formed between layers of dough.

2. Switch to a higher melting fat.

Reason:

_____

_____

3. Refrigerate fat before use and chill dough before rolling and shaping.

Reason:

_____

_____

4. Minimize the extent that the fat is worked into the dry flour.

Reason:

_____

_____

5. Increase oven temperature.

Reason:

_____

_____

6. Switch to a fat that contains water.

Reason:

_____

_____

2. How to Decrease Tenderness in Pastry

Recall that tenderness in pastry is achieved primarily by minimizing the development of a strong gluten structure. Imagine that you have a formula for making pastry that is too tender, that is, that falls apart too easily. Explain why each of the changes listed as follows could work to decrease tenderness. The first is completed for you.

1. Decrease the amount of fat or increase the amount of flour.

Reason: The less fat for the amount of gluten in flour, the more gluten structure can form.

2. Switch to a higher-melting fat.

Reason:

_____

_____

3. Refrigerate fat before use and chill dough before rolling and shaping.

Reason:

_____

_____

4. Minimize the extent that the fat is worked into the dry flour.

Reason:

_____

_____

5. Increase the amount of water.

Reason:

_____

_____

6. Increase the amount of kneading and rolling.

Reason:

_____

_____

7. Switch to stronger flour, for example, switch some or all pastry flour to bread flour.

Reason:

_____

_____

3. Comparison of Different Fats and Oils

In the Results Table that follows, use your textbook to fill in the percent fat and recommended uses for each fat and oil. Next, record from its package the brand name and list of ingredients for each fat and oil. Finally, use fresh samples brought to room temperature to evaluate the appearance and consistency as well as the aroma of each fat and oil. Use this opportunity to identify different fats and oils from their sensory characteristics alone.

RESULTS TABLE ■ A COMPARISON OF DIFFERENT FATS AND OILS

TYPE OF FAT	PERCENT FAT	BRAND NAME	RECOMMENDED USES	APPEARANCE	CONSISTENCY	AROMA	INGREDIENT STATEMENT
All-purpose shortening							
High-ratio plastic shortening							
High-ratio liquid shortening							
Vegetable oil							
Butter							
Margarine, regular bakers'							
Margarine, rollin or puff pastry							
Lard							

4. How the Type of Fat Affects Batter Consistency and the Overall Quality of Liquid Shortening Sponge Cake

High-ratio liquid shortening can be used to make a light and airy sponge cake using a one-step mixing method. While it is usually not recommended that the method of preparation specifically designed for one fat be used for very different fats, we will do just that in this experiment. In doing so, you will experience how differences in consistency, fat content, and the presence of emulsifiers affects the function of various fats in baked goods.

OBJECTIVES

To demonstrate how the type of fat affects:
- The lightness and volume of cake batter
- The crispness and the extent of Maillard browning on the crust of cake
- The moistness, tenderness, crumb structure, and volume of cake
- The overall flavor of cake
- The overall acceptability of cake

PRODUCTS PREPARED

Sponge cake, liquid shortening type, made with:
- High-ratio liquid shortening (control product)
- High-ratio plastic shortening
- Vegetable oil (without dimethyl-polysiloxane or other anti-foaming agent)
- Butter, unsalted
- Butter, unsalted, melted
- Other, if desired (olive oil, margarine, puff pastry shortening, all-purpose shortening, all-purpose vegetable oil [with dimethylpolysiloxane], lower amount of liquid shortening [one-half or three-quarters the full amount], mixture of butter and high-ratio liquid shortening, etc.)

MATERIALS AND EQUIPMENT

- Cake batter, enough to make 24 or more cupcakes of each variation
- Muffin tins and liners (2½" or 3½" size) or pan spray
- Size #16 (2¾ ounce) portion-control scoop or equivalent
- Ruler

PROCEDURE

- Preheat oven according to formula.
- Line muffin tins with cupcake liners or spray with pan spray; label with the type of fat to be used in cake.
- Prepare cake batters using the formula for sponge cake, which follows, or using any basic sponge cake formula designed for liquid shortening. Prepare one batch of batter for each variation.
- Scoop batter into prepared muffin tins using level #16 scoop (or any scoop that fills cup one-half to three-quarters full); save excess batter.
- Use an oven thermometer placed in center of oven to read oven temperature; record results.
- Place filled muffin tins in preheated oven; place on sheet pan, if desired. Set timer according to formula.
- Measure the volume of excess batter for each product in fluid ounces (milliliters) using measuring cups; record results in Results Table 1, which follows.

- Bake cakes until control product (made with high-ratio liquid shortening) is light brown, springs back when center top is lightly pressed, and wooden pick inserted into center of cake comes out clean. Remove all cupcakes from oven after same length of time, even though some will be paler or darker and will not have risen as high. If necessary, however, adjust bake time for oven variances and record bake time in Comments column of Results Table 1.
- Cool to room temperature on cooling racks.
- Record any potential sources of error that might make it difficult to draw the proper conclusions from the experiment. In particular, be aware of differences in how batter was mixed and handled, any difficulty in dispensing equal volumes of batter into muffin tins, and any problems with ovens.
- When cupcakes are completely cooled, evaluate weight as follows:
  - Weigh three cupcakes on scale and record total weight in Results Table 1.
  - Calculate average cupcake weight by dividing total weight by three. Record in Results Table 1.
- Note in Cake Shape column of Results Table 1 whether cupcakes have evenly rounded tops, or if they peak or dip in center. Also note whether cakes are lopsided, that is, if one side is higher than the other.
- Evaluate the sensory characteristics of completely cooled products and record evaluations in Results Table 2, which follows. Be sure to compare each in turn to the control product and consider the following:
  - Crust color, from very light to very dark, on a scale of one to five
  - Crust texture (soft and moist, soft and dry, crisp and dry, etc.)
  - Crumb appearance (color and size/shape of air cells, etc.)
  - Crumb texture (tough/tender, moist/dry, spongy, crumbly, etc.)
  - Overall flavor (butter, egg, sweetness, saltiness, flour taste, etc.)
  - Overall acceptability, from highly unacceptable to highly acceptable, on a scale of one to five
  - Add any additional comments, as necessary.

Sponge Cake Using Liquid Shortening

INGREDIENT	POUND	OUNCE	GRAMS	BAKER'S PERCENTAGE
Flour, cake		10	300	100
Baking powder (4 tsps, 20 ml)		0.8	24	8
Salt (1 tsp, 5 ml)		0.2	6	2
Sugar		13.3	400	133
Fat or oil		6	180	60
Milk		5.3	160	53
Eggs, whole		15	450	150
Total	3	2.6	1520	506

Method of Preparation

1. Preheat oven to 350°F (220°C).
2. Have ingredients at room temperature (except melted butter; cool slightly before use).
3. Sift dry ingredients together three times.
4. Place milk, eggs, and fat or oil in mixing bowl; add sifted dry ingredients on top.
5. Using whip attachment on mixer, blend on low for 30 seconds; stop and scrape whip and bowl.
6. Whip for 3 minutes on high; stop and scrape.
7. Whip for 2 minutes on medium.
8. Use batter immediately.
9. Bake cupcakes for approximately 20–22 minutes.

SOURCES OF ERROR

RESULTS TABLE 1 ■ EVALUATION OF AMOUNT OF BATTER AND CUPCAKE HEIGHT AND SHAPE OF SPONGE CAKE MADE WITH DIFFERENT TYPES OF FAT

TYPE OF FAT	EXCESS BATTER, IN FLUID OUNCES (MILLILITERS)	WEIGHT OF THREE CUPCAKES	AVERAGE WEIGHT OF ONE CUPCAKE	CUPCAKE SHAPE	COMMENTS
High ratio liquid shortening (control product)					
High-ratio plastic shortening					
Vegetable oil					
Butter, unmelted					
Butter, melted					

RESULTS TABLE 2 ■ SENSORY CHARACTERISTICS OF SPONGE CAKES MADE WITH DIFFERENT TYPES OF FAT

TYPE OF FAT	CRUST COLOR AND TEXTURE	CRUMB APPEARANCE AND TEXTURE	OVERALL FLAVOR	OVERALL ACCEPTABILITY	COMMENTS
High ratio liquid shortening (control product)					
High-ratio plastic shortening					
Vegetable oil					
Butter, unmelted					
Butter, melted					

CONCLUSIONS

1. Which fat or oil produced the greatest volume of cake batter? Which produced the least? How do you explain these differences in air incorporation?

_____

_____

2. Which fat or oil produced the heaviest cupcake? Which produced the lightest? Did these differences, for the most part, relate to differences in volume of batter produced from fat or oil? Explain.

_____

_____

3. What were the main differences in appearance, flavor, and texture between the cake made with butter and the one made with high ratio liquid shortening (the control product)?

_____

_____

    a. State and explain three reasons why these cakes differed in tenderness.

    _____

    _____

4. What were the main differences in appearance, flavor, and texture between the cake made with oil and the one made with high ratio liquid shortening (the control product)?

_____

_____

    a. Explain why the cake made with oil had a different crumb color than the control product.

    _____

    _____

5. What were the main differences in appearance, flavor, and texture between the cake made with unmelted butter and the cake made with melted butter?

_____

_____

    a. Which made the more acceptable cake, and why?

    _____

    _____

6. Which fats and oils produced cupcakes that were totally unacceptable using this method of preparation, and why?

_____

_____

7. Were there any sources of error that might significantly affect the results of your experiment? If so, what could you do differently next time to minimize error?

_____

_____

5. How the Type of Fat Affects the Overall Quality of a Simple Icing

OBJECTIVES

To demonstrate how the type of fat affects:

- The lightness and volume of icing
- The appearance, flavor, and mouth-feel of icing
- How easy icing is to spread
- The overall acceptability of icing for various uses

PRODUCTS PREPARED

Simple icing made with:

- Butter, unsalted, sweet cream (control product)
- Butter, cultured cream, higher fat (European or European-style)
- All-purpose plastic shortening
- High-ratio plastic shortening
- Half butter, half high-ratio plastic shortening
- Other, if desired (salted butter, unsalted margarine, icing shortening, three-quarters butter/one-quarter shortening, one-quarter butter/three-quarters shortening, etc.)

MATERIALS AND EQUIPMENT

- Simple icing, enough to make about 1 pound (500 grams) or more of each variation
- Cakes, cupcakes, or plates, for spreading icing onto
- Measuring cups (eight ounces or 250 ml)

PROCEDURE

- Prepare icings using the formula for the simple icing, which follows, or using any simple buttercream icing. Prepare one batch of icing for each variation.
- Be sure icings are all at room temperature.
- Measure density (weight per volume) of icings to evaluate the relative amount of air incorporated into each variation. To measure density,
  - Carefully spoon creamed icing into tared measuring cup (eight ounces or 250 milliliters).
  - Visually check cup to confirm that no large air gaps are present.
  - Level the top surface of the cup with a straight-edge.
  - Weigh the amount of icing in each cup and record results in Results Table 1, which follows.
- Evaluate how well icing can be spread on a cake. To do this, spread icing on cooled cupcakes, cake, or the back of a plastic or paper plate. Rate the softness, smoothness, and overall ease of spreading the icing.
- Record any potential sources of error that might make it difficult to draw the proper conclusions from the experiment. In particular, be aware of differences in temperature of fats and how icings were mixed.

- Evaluate the sensory characteristics of icings and record evaluations in Results Table 1. Be sure to compare each in turn to the control product and consider the following:
  - Appearance (smoothness and color)
  - Mouthfeel (light/heavy, oily/waxy, etc.)
  - Flavor (butter, egg, sweetness, saltiness, etc.)
  - Add any additional comments, as necessary.

Simple Icing

INGREDIENT	POUND	OUNCE	GRAMS	BAKER'S PERCENTAGE
Fat		6	180	60
Sugar, powdered		10	300	100
Egg whites, pasteurized		1	30	10
Total	1	1	510	170

Method of Preparation

1. Bring all ingredients to room temperature.
2. If two fats are used, soften the firmer of the two first by mixing it using the flat beater attachment on low speed.
3. Cream the fat(s) on low for 3 minutes, or until smooth and light.
4. Add powdered sugar and blend on low for 1 minute; stop and scrape bowl and beater.
5. Whip on high for 6 minutes; stop and scrape bowl and beater after every 2 minutes.
6. Add egg whites and whip on high for 5 additional minutes or until smooth and light.
7. Cover, label, and hold at room temperature until ready to evaluate.

RESULTS TABLE 1 ■ EVALUATION OF LIGHTNESS (DENSITY), EASE IN SPREADING, AND SENSORY CHARACTERISTICS OF ICING MADE WITH DIFFERENT TYPES OF FAT

TYPE OF FAT	DENSITY (WEIGHT/VOLUME)	EASE IN SPREADING	APPEARANCE	MOUTHFEEL	FLAVOR	COMMENTS
Butter, sweet cream, unsalted						
Butter, European						
All-purpose plastic shortening						
High-ratio plastic shortening						
Half butter, half high-ratio plastic shortening						

CONCLUSIONS

1. Which fat whipped to the lightest (least dense) consistency? Which was the most dense? Did this affect mouthfeel?

_____

_____

2. What were the main differences in appearance, flavor, and texture between the icing made with the cultured cream butter (European) and the cake made with sweet cream butter (the control product)?

_____

_____

    a. Which of these two icings did you prefer in a buttercream, and why?

    _____

    _____

3. What were the main differences in appearance, flavor, and texture between the icing made with high-ratio plastic shortening and the icing made with butter (the control product)? What accounts for the differences in mouthfeel between the two icings?

_____

_____

4. What were the main differences, if any, in appearance, flavor, and texture between the icing made with high-ratio plastic shortening and the icing made with all-purpose plastic shortening?

_____

_____

    a. Is there any advantage to using one of these shortenings over the other in this particular icing? If so, what is it?

    _____

    _____

5. Which icing(s) do you believe would be acceptable for use on a white wedding cake, and why?

_____

_____

6. Which icing(s) do you believe would be acceptable as a flavorful buttercream, and why?

_____

_____

7. Which icing(s) do you believe would be acceptable as a butter-flavored icing during hot summer months, and why?

_____

_____

8. Were there any sources of error that might significantly affect the results of your experiment? If so, what could you do differently next time to minimize error?

_____

_____

CHAPTER 11

EGGS AND EGG PRODUCTS

CHAPTER **OBJECTIVES**

1. Describe the makeup of eggs.

2. Classify eggs and egg products and describe their characteristics and uses.

3. List the functions of eggs and egg products and relate these functions to their makeup.

4. Describe the process of egg coagulation in custards and the main factors that affect it.

5. Describe the process of whipping egg whites and the main factors that affect it.

6. Describe how to best store and handle eggs and egg products.

INTRODUCTION

Because of eggs' versatility, nearly all baked goods contain them. This, in turn, partly explains why the production of eggs in North America has evolved to become a large commercial operation. Today in the United States, most eggs come from companies having flocks of 75,000 hens or more, with some companies having 5 million hens or more. The average hen lays from 250 to 300 eggs per year, over twice as many as 50 years ago. This increase is the result of improvements in breeding, nutrition, housing, and management practices. In turn, the price of eggs has remained steady over the years.

THE MAKEUP OF AN EGG

Eggs have six distinct parts: thin white, thick white, yolk, shell, air cell, and chalazae (Figure 11.1). About two-thirds of the weight of the edible part of an egg is egg white; about one-third is the yolk. Overall, most of the whole egg is moisture, with smaller amounts of protein, fat, and emulsifiers (Figure 11.2).

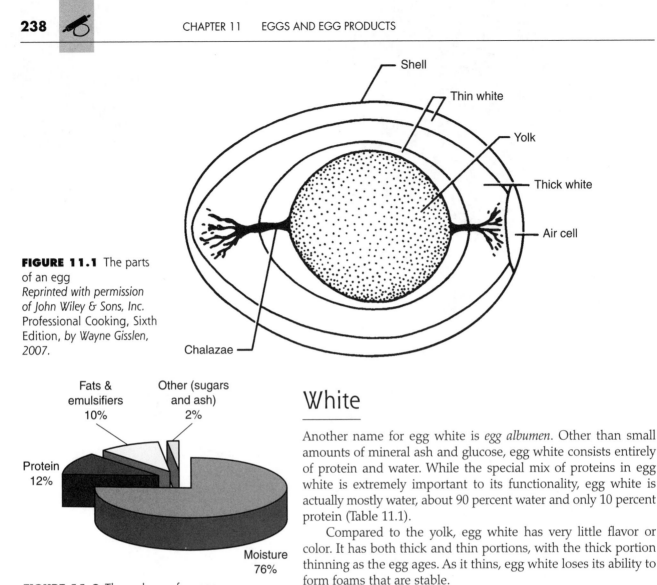

FIGURE 11.1 The parts of an egg
Reprinted with permission of John Wiley & Sons, Inc. Professional Cooking, Sixth Edition, *by Wayne Gisslen, 2007.*

FIGURE 11.2 The makeup of an egg

White

Another name for egg white is *egg albumen.* Other than small amounts of mineral ash and glucose, egg white consists entirely of protein and water. While the special mix of proteins in egg white is extremely important to its functionality, egg white is actually mostly water, about 90 percent water and only 10 percent protein (Table 11.1).

Compared to the yolk, egg white has very little flavor or color. It has both thick and thin portions, with the thick portion thinning as the egg ages. As it thins, egg white loses its ability to form foams that are stable.

Yolk

Egg yolks are about half moisture and half yolk solids. As eggs age, yolks pick up additional moisture from the white. When this happens, the yolk thins out and flattens when the egg is cracked onto a smooth surface. It has a protective membrane that weakens as it ages, making it more difficult to separate the yolk from the white. The weakening of this membrane also increases the possibility that bacteria will pass into the nutrient-rich yolk where they can multiply if the egg is not kept cold.

The solids in egg yolks consist of proteins, fats, and emulsifiers (Table 11.1), with small amounts of mineral ash and yellow-orange carotenoids. Egg yolk proteins are not the same as egg white proteins. Many egg yolk proteins are lipoproteins, proteins bound to fats and emulsifiers, which are both lipids.

TABLE 11.1 ■ A COMPARISON OF THE MAKEUP OF WHOLE EGGS, EGG WHITES, AND EGG YOLKS

COMPONENT	WHOLE	WHITE	YOLK
Moisture	76%	88%	50%
Protein	12%	10%	17%
Fat and emulsifiers	10%	0%	30%
Other (sugars and ash)	2%	2%	3%

ALKALINITY OF EGG WHITES

Did you know that egg white is one of the few foods that is naturally alkaline? Fresh egg whites have a pH approaching 8, and this increases to 9 or 10 as eggs age and lose carbon dioxide. While the natural alkalinity of egg whites helps reduce bacterial growth, egg whites should still be cooked or pasteurized before consumption.

Besides egg whites, the only other common alkaline food ingredients are baking soda and hard water. Dutched cocoa is also alkaline, but only because it is treated with an alkali.

WHAT IS LECITHIN?

Lecithin is not a single substance. It is a complex mixture of emulsifying lipids widely found in nature. Besides egg yolks, lecithin is found in dairy ingredients, cereal grains, and soybeans. Lecithin is sold as a dark, oily liquid, or sometimes as powder or granules.

The emulsifying lipids in lecithin are classified as phospholipids. Phospholipid molecules look something like triglyceride molecules. Recall from Chapter 10 that triglycerides consist of three fatty acids attached to glycerol. Phospholipids consist of two fatty acids attached to glycerol. Instead of the third fatty acid, phospholipids contain a so-called phosphate group. The fatty acids are attracted to fats and oils (lipids) in food, while the phosphate group is attracted to water. It is this ability to attract both lipids and water that allow phospholipids such as lecithin to act as emulsifiers.

The most well-known emulsifier in egg yolk is lecithin. Egg yolk contains an incredibly high amount of lecithin, about 10 percent. Like most of the lipids in egg yolk, lecithin is bound as lipoproteins. The emulsifying lipoproteins perform many functions in foods, most notably bonding to both water and oil. By bonding to both, emulsifiers and emulsifying lipoproteins hold together, or bind, complex mixtures of ingredients, such as cake batters.

An important factor in the color of egg yolk is the hen's feed. The more carotenoids in the feed, the more yellow-orange the yolk. Alfalfa and yellow corn, which are both high in carotenoids, produce deeply colored yolks. Wheat, oat, and white corn produce lighter yolks. When feed is naturally low in carotenoids, marigold petals, which are a rich source of carotenoids, can be added for color.

The hen's feed also affects the flavor of the yolks. This explains why some brands of eggs taste different from others. Sometimes, for example, organic eggs taste different from regular eggs. It isn't that being organic necessarily gives them a different flavor; more likely, the growers are using a particular feed that—organic or not—has a distinct flavor that passes into the egg.

Omega-3-fatty acids are sometimes added to feed for hens so that the eggs are high in this healthful oil. Eggs that contain omega-3-fatty acids will have a different flavor from regular eggs.

Shell

Eggshell represents about 11 percent of the weight of eggs. Although it serves as a hard protective covering, the eggshell is porous. This means that odors penetrate eggshells, and moisture and gases (primarily carbon dioxide) can escape. In commercial practice, shell

WHAT IS MEANT BY CERTIFIED ORGANIC?

The use of organic eggs in the United States more than doubled during the 1990s and continues to grow at an annual rate of about 15 percent a year. In response to the growing popularity of organic products, the United States initiated the National Organic Program in 2002 to unify the use of the term organic across the country. Organic growers must now be certified, or they cannot use the term organic to describe their products.

Organic food is produced by farmers who use renewable resources and conservation to enhance environmental quality. Organic eggs come from animals that are given no antibiotics or growth hormones. The hens are fed organic feed, which is produced without using most pesticides, synthetic fertilizers, irradiation, or genetic engineering. Before a product can be labeled organic, a government-approved certifier inspects the farm where the food is grown to make sure the farmer is following all the rules necessary to meet USDA organic standards. The safety and nutritional quality of organic eggs is not necessarily different from that of standard eggs.

eggs are washed and sanitized to remove dirt and to reduce the likelihood of salmonella contamination. They are also lightly coated with mineral oil to delay moisture loss.

Eggshell color can be either brown or white, depending on the breed of hen. Hens with white feathers and white earlobes lay white eggs; hens with red feathers and red lobes lay brown eggs. While most (95 percent) commercial breeds produce white eggs, hens bred in parts of New England produce brown eggs. Shell color has no effect on flavor, nutrition, or functionality of eggs.

Air Pocket

Eggs contain two protective membranes between the shell and the white. Soon after an egg is laid, an air cell forms between the membranes at the egg's larger end. As the egg ages, loses moisture, and shrinks, the air pocket increases in size. This is why older eggs float in water while fresh ones sink.

Chalazae

The chalazae are twisted white cords that hold the yolk to the center of the egg. They disintegrate as the egg ages. Chalazae are an extension of the egg white and are completely edible, although pastry chefs typically use a chinois or sieve to strain them from certain products, such as custards.

COMMERCIAL CLASSIFICATION OF SHELL EGGS

Shell eggs are eggs purchased in their shells, either by the dozen or in *flats*. One flat holds 2½ dozen or 30 eggs. There are 12 flats in a case, which means that one case contains 30 dozen or 360 eggs.

Shell eggs are sometimes called fresh eggs, but this is misleading. Shell eggs might be several weeks or months old, so they are not necessarily fresh. Shell eggs are sorted and classified according to grade (quality) and size. The U.S. Department of Agriculture (USDA) and Agriculture and Agri-Food Canada (AAFC) offer programs to classify and label eggs with both a grade and a size classification. In Canada, the program is mandatory; in the United States, it is voluntary, with about 30 percent of all eggs sold in the United States graded by the USDA.

Grade

The three USDA grades for acceptable shell eggs are U.S. Grades AA, A, and B. Canada has two acceptable grades: A and B. Quality grades do not reflect product safety or nutritional quality, and Grade B eggs—stored properly—are safe to eat and will have the same nutritional quality as higher-grade eggs.

Usually, USDA-graded eggs are washed, packed, and graded within a day to a week of being laid, but they can be legally graded for up to 30 days. They must be labeled with the date that they were packed and graded; often they will also have a sell-by or expiration date. The sell-by date is defined as no more than 30 days from the time the eggs were packed and graded. This means that USDA-graded eggs can theoretically be sold for up to two months after they are laid, although most will be sold within 30 days or less.

Prior to 1998, eggs that were nearing their expiration date could be returned to the packer to be washed, packed, and graded a second time, extending their usable life. This is no longer allowed in the United States, for safety reasons.

Grades A and AA are the most common eggs purchased for the bakeshop. The main difference between USDA Grade AA and Grade A eggs is in the firmness of the white and the size of the air cell. Only eggs with the firmest whites and the smallest air cells can be labeled USDA Grade AA. Firm whites—and yolks—are particularly important when frying or poaching eggs because they hold their shape best (Figure 11.3). They are less important for baking.

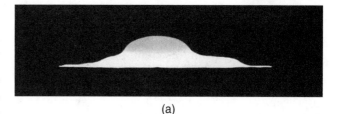

(a)

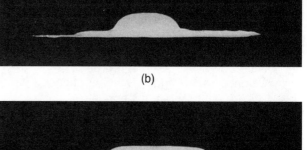

(b)

(c)

FIGURE 11.3 Egg grades: (a) Grade AA (b) Grade A (c) Grade B
Courtesy of U.S. Department of Agriculture

Grade B eggs may have one or more of the following defects: stained shells, large air cells, watery whites, small blood spots in the white, or an enlarged, flattened yolk. Grade B eggs are acceptable for general baking, but whites from Grade B eggs may not whip properly, if they are watery.

While the quality grade of eggs does not necessarily reflect age, quality does decline over time. Even properly refrigerated eggs stored in their carton will decline from Grade AA to Grade A in about one week. In about another five weeks, they will drop from Grade A to Grade B, as the whites thin and the air pockets enlarge. However, a properly handled and refrigerated egg will retain its nutritional value and wholesomeness for a considerably longer time.

Size

Size classifications for eggs are different from quality classifications. The six size classifications for shell eggs in North America are based on minimum weights per dozen; it does not refer to the dimensions of an egg or how large it is. The most common size

HOW ARE EGGS GRADED FOR QUALITY?

Candling is the primary method used for measuring the quality of eggs. In candling, a bright light passes through the egg still in its shell and exposes the size of its air pocket, thickness and clarity of the white, the position and stability of the yolk, the presence of blood spots or a developing embryo, and more.

When a formula calls for a certain number of eggs, assume the formula is based on large-size eggs, with the edible portion of the egg weighing approximately 1.75 ounces (50 grams). Recall that two-thirds (1.2 ounces or 33 grams) of this is egg white; about one-third (0.55 ounce or 17 grams) is yolk.

For consistency, it is always best to weigh the amount of egg in a formula instead of counting the number of eggs. To calculate the amount of egg to weigh, use the following formulas:

Weight of whole eggs = number of eggs × weight of 1 egg

Weight of egg yolks = number of yolks × weight of 1 yolk

Weight of egg whites = number of whites × weight of 1 white

For example, if a formula calls for three large eggs, it is best to weigh out 3 × 1.75 ounces (3 × 50 grams), or 5.25 ounces (150 grams). If it calls for three egg yolks, weigh out 3 × 0.55 ounce (3 × 17 grams), or 1.65 ounces (50 grams). If it calls for three egg whites, weigh out 3 × 1.2 ounces (3 × 33 grams), or 3.6 ounces (100 grams).

classifications for eggs used in the bakeshop are large, extra large, and jumbo (the three other classifications are medium, small, and peewee). Because the size classifications are based on minimum weights for an entire dozen, individual eggs themselves will vary in weight.

EGG PRODUCTS

Egg products include various forms of eggs that are sold removed from their shells. The range of products includes egg whites, egg yolks, and whole egg products sold refrigerated, frozen, or dried. Liquid and dried egg products have been available since the late 1800s, but quality was generally poor. Today, however, about one-third of the eggs used in the United States are egg products.

Changes in processing have improved over the years so that frozen and refrigerated liquid egg products can be used in place of shell eggs in most bakeshop applications. While the viscosity of frozen products changes somewhat over time, for the most part, this does not affect their properties. Dried egg products are less popular in the bakeshop than liquid egg products, although they, too, can be used successfully in many applications.

Advantages of Egg Products

Egg products are steadily replacing shell eggs in the bakeshop, and there are several reasons for this. The main one is safety. By law, egg products must be pasteurized so that they are free from salmonella bacteria. This means that it is safe to use egg products in uncooked items, such as buttercream and sorbet.

There are other advantages to egg products besides food safety (Table 11.2). Cost, however, is not usually one of them, because egg products can be expensive. However, egg products save time, so if labor is expensive, they can save money in the long run.

Types of Egg Products

FROZEN WHITES

Frozen egg whites often contain an added thickener, such as guar gum. A small amount of guar gum protects egg whites from ice crystal damage. Guar gum also increases viscosity, improving the ability of frozen whites to foam. Whipping agents—such as triethyl citrate

TABLE 11.2 ■ MAIN ADVANTAGES OF EGG PRODUCTS

Safety—because they are pasteurized, by law
Save time in cracking and separating eggs; can reduce labor costs
Take up less space
No loss due to breakage
Longer shelf life—as long as products remain dry or frozen
No leftover whites or yolks from separating shell eggs
Uniformity in quality

AUTOMATED EGG BREAKING

Did you know that as many as 162,000 eggs per hour or 45 eggs per second can be broken on modern automated egg-breaking machines? This, according to the American Egg Board, is because technology for these machines has improved dramatically in recent years.

HOW ARE EGGS PASTEURIZED?

Pasteurization is a process that eliminates pathogenic (disease-causing) microorganisms, such as salmonella, in food products. The most common means of pasteurizing food is to apply heat for a specific period of time. The higher the heat, the less time is needed to ensure food safety. With most food products, high pasteurization temperatures are desired because the shorter heating time inflicts less quality damage to the food. Eggs, however, cannot be pasteurized at high temperatures or the egg proteins coagulate. A typical commercial pasteurization process for liquid whole eggs is to heat the eggs for 3.5 minutes at 140°F (60°C). Other pasteurization processes exist. For example, dried egg whites can be pasteurized by holding them at 130°F (54°C) for seven days. For the most part, pasteurization does not affect the properties of the eggs.

or sodium lauryl sulfate—are sometimes added to frozen whites, so that frozen (thawed) egg whites often whip up faster and higher than whites from the shell.

Frozen egg whites can be used in most applications requiring egg whites, including meringue and angel food cake. In some cases, however, frozen egg whites do not form as firm or as stable a foam as whites from fresh shell eggs. This seems to be the case with the making of Swiss meringue, where egg whites and sugar are warmed together in a double boiler before whipping. When this is a problem, fresh or dried whites can be blended with frozen whites to assure better whipping.

Like all egg products, frozen whites are pasteurized and are preferred to shell whites in uncooked products. In fact, in many areas, laws mandate that raw egg not be used in uncooked or undercooked products.

Separation of thick and thin whites may occur upon thawing, so be sure to shake or stir thawed whites before use.

FROZEN SUGARED YOLKS

Frozen yolks contain added sugar or glucose corn syrup, generally 10 percent. The added sweetener lowers the freezing point, preventing excessive ice crystal damage that causes yolk proteins to gel irreversibly to a thick gummy solid. Even then, frozen sugared yolks thaw to a thicker consistency than yolks that have not been frozen. However, this should not negatively affect functionality. In fact, thicker yolks might assist in the formation of stable emulsions.

For general use, replace regular yolks directly with sugared yolks. For products that contain a high amount of yolk, such as vanilla custard sauce, you may wish to adjust the amount of sugar and yolks in the formula.

To make this adjustment for sugar, replace each pound of yolks with 1.1 pounds (about 1 pound, 1.5 ounces) of sugared yolks. Reduce the amount of sugar in the formula by 0.1 pounds (about 1.5 ounces). Using metric units, replace each kilogram of yolks

WHAT CAUSES A GRAY-GREEN COLOR TO FORM IN EGGS?

You may recall seeing a gray-green ring surrounding the yolk in hard-boiled eggs. While harmless, this discoloration is unattractive. It is caused by a chemical reaction that occurs when eggs, especially old ones, are heated for extended periods. This is how.

Proteins in egg whites are high in sulfur. You cannot see or smell sulfur in fresh eggs, but as eggs are heated, some of the sulfur is released. When sulfur from egg white combines with iron from egg yolk, an iron sulfide forms. This iron sulfide has a gray-green color.

Iron sulfide is especially likely to form when eggs are heated for too long, or when they are heated in water that is high in iron. High pH also favors this reaction. Recall that the pH of an egg increases as it ages. Not surprisingly, old eggs are more likely to discolor than fresh ones.

The formation of iron sulfide in the presence of high pH explains why baked goods with too much added baking soda—which raises pH—can have a slight greenish tinge.

with 1.1 kilograms of sugared yolks. Reduce the amount of sugar in the formula by 0.1 kilograms (100 grams).

REFRIGERATED LIQUID YOLKS

Unlike yolks sold frozen, refrigerated liquid yolks do not contain additives to lower the freezing point and protect the yolks from gelling. Since excessive gelling reduces the ability of egg yolks to aerate and mix well with other ingredients, it's best not to freeze liquid yolks sold for refrigerated storage. This is especially important if the yolks are to be used in biscuit (sponge cake), French buttercream, or bombe mixtures, which rely on whipped egg yolks for volume.

Refrigerated liquid yolks are most apt to be used in the kitchen, not the bakeshop. They are useful in hollandaise sauce, Caesar salad dressing, and other products where the sugar added to frozen yolks is undesirable.

FROZEN WHOLE EGGS

Frozen whole eggs contain whites and yolks in their natural proportion. While whole eggs will thicken when frozen, the thickening is typically minimal. Often, frozen whole eggs contain a small amount of added citric acid. The citric acid prevents a gray-green discoloration from occurring when whole eggs are heated.

LIQUID WHOLE-EGG SUBSTITUTE

Whole-egg substitutes, such as Egg Beaters, are made from egg whites. They generally contain over 99 percent egg white, making them fat-free and cholesterol-free. Whole-egg substitutes are available for those interested in lowering the amount of fat and cholesterol in their diet.

Whole-egg substitutes often contain added beta-carotene, for a yellow color. Other optional ingredients include dry milk solids, vitamins and minerals, gums, and seasonings. Be sure to read ingredient labels before using whole-egg substitutes. Some contain garlic and other seasonings that are inappropriate for use in sweet baked goods.

Instead of using whole-egg substitutes in low-fat baked goods, consider using egg whites. Egg whites

HELPFUL HINT

Be sure to watch bake times closely when substituting egg whites for whole eggs, since egg white proteins coagulate fast. If you are not careful, baked goods made with egg whites will be tough, spongy, and dry.

WHAT IS MERINGUE POWDER?

Meringue powder, as the name suggests, is used for making meringue, royal icing, and other products made from whipped egg whites. In addition to pasteurized dried egg whites, meringue powder typically contains sugar, stabilizers (starch and gums), free-flowing agents (silicon dioxide), whipping aids (cream of tartar, sodium lauryl sulfate), and flavor.

work quite well, often at a substantially lower price and with better flavor. If necessary, add a small amount of yellow-orange food coloring to your batter or dough for the look of whole egg.

DRIED EGGS

Pasteurized dried whole eggs, egg yolks, and egg whites are also available for use in the bakeshop. They are dried until less than 5 percent moisture remains and can conveniently be stored in a cool dry place until reconstituted. Drying can reduce the acceptability of eggs in certain applications because of changes to color, and flavor.

While not commonly used in the bakeshop, dried egg products are perfectly acceptable for use in baked goods, such as muffins, breads, cookies, and some cakes. Follow the manufacturer's instructions for reconstituting dried egg products, or sift the egg powder with other dry ingredients and add a measured amount of water with the liquids.

Because of their heat sensitivity, dried egg whites are processed differently than dried whole eggs and egg yolks. First, the liquid whites are treated with an enzyme to remove the small amount of glucose that is naturally present in egg whites. If this glucose is not removed, dried egg whites darken through Maillard browning to an unattractive tan color during drying, storage, and baking. Once dried, the egg white powder is typically held for a week to ten days in a hot room at 130°F (54°C). The heat pasteurizes the egg whites, but it does more. It improves the egg white's gel strength and its whipping ability.

Pastry chefs sometimes add dried egg whites to liquid egg whites, to increase body and improve the stability of meringue. Because they are glucose-free, dried egg whites are sometimes used in baked meringue shells, to minimize browning. Finally, dried egg whites are often used instead of liquid egg whites when making royal icing, an uncooked icing that dries to a glossy hard finish.

FUNCTIONS OF EGGS

Eggs provide many complex functions in baked goods, some of which overlap. For example, the ability of eggs to bind ingredients is related to their ability to emulsify and to form structure.

Main Functions

PROVIDES STRUCTURE

Coagulated egg proteins in both egg whites and egg yolks are important structure builders in baked goods (see Photo 11.1). For example, eggs are as important as flour—sometimes more so—in building structure in cakes. In fact, without eggs, most

PHOTO 11.1 From left to right, cupcakes made with egg yolks and whole eggs retain their structure, while those made without eggs do not. *Photo by Aaron Seyfarth*

cakes collapse. Eggs also contribute to structure in quick breads, cookies, muffins, and certain yeast breads.

Coagulated egg proteins also provide thickening and gelling—a form of structure—in pastry cream, crème anglaise, cream pie, and custards. Because egg coagulation is so important to the structure of custards and related products, it will be discussed in more detail later.

Eggs are considered tougheners because of their ability to provide structure. Eggs are probably the only common bakery ingredient containing significant amounts of both tougheners (proteins) and tenderizers (fats and emulsifiers). The tenderizers in eggs are concentrated in the yolk.

Because of the tenderizing fats and emulsifiers in the yolk, egg yolks contribute less toughening—less structure—than an equal weight of egg whites. The proteins in yolk, bound as lipoproteins, do not coagulate as quickly as egg white proteins and produce a shorter, more tender structure.

A ranking of the structure-building abilities of eggs is as follows:

whites > whole > yolks

Be sure that you are clear that egg yolks, despite containing tenderizers, are classified as tougheners or structure builders. Egg yolks are not tenderizers.

WHAT WOULD HAPPEN IF EGGS WERE LEFT OUT OF MUFFINS?

Traditional muffins and quick breads rely as much, or more, on eggs than on flour for their coarse, crumbly structure. They are typically made with pastry flour, or a combination of pastry and bread flour. If eggs were left out of muffin batter and replaced with milk or water, the muffins would be more tender and have a lower volume. While they might be acceptable to some, the muffins would be white in color and bland in flavor. In fact, eggless muffins taste more like sweet baking powder biscuits than flavorful muffins.

IF EGG YOLKS CONTAIN TENDERIZERS, WHY ARE THEY NOT CALLED TENDERIZERS?

Actually, sometimes egg yolks are referred to as tenderizers. When they are, it is usually when the yolks are compared to whole eggs. And it is true that baked goods made with egg yolks have a more tender crumb than those made with the same weight of whole eggs. However, this is not the same as saying that egg yolks are true tenderizers. They are still tougheners; they simply produce a more tender structure than whole eggs.

Here's another way of looking at it. Add more of a tenderizer, such as sugar or fat, to batters and doughs, and baked goods will be more tender. Add more yolks, and baked goods toughen (just less so than if the same amount of whole eggs were added). Think of it as a tug of war between tougheners and tenderizers in yolks, and the tougheners win.

AERATES

Eggs are unique because they are especially good at aerating, producing a relatively stable foam. Foams consist of tiny bubbles of air or another gas surrounded by a liquid or solid film. By aerating, eggs assist in the leavening process. The actual leavener is air. Eggs simply form the foam that allows air to be incorporated into baked goods. Examples of baked goods that rely heavily on the foaming ability of eggs for leavening include sponge, genoise, chiffon, and angel food cakes.

The foaming power of eggs refers to how high they can be whipped. Egg whites, which have a very high foaming power, can whip up to eight times their volume. However, whites whipped this high have extremely thin cell walls consisting of overstretched proteins. When placed in a hot oven, these proteins stretch even more and are likely to break and collapse. There are ways to prevent the overwhipping of eggs and egg whites so that baked goods don't collapse in the oven. These are discussed later in this chapter.

Whole eggs and egg yolks also foam, just not as well as egg whites. The foaming of whole eggs is important, however, in the leavening of genoise, while egg yolks contribute to the lightness of many sponge cakes. A ranking of the foaming power of eggs is as follows:

whites > whole > yolks

The foaming of egg whites will be discussed in more detail later in this chapter, when meringues are discussed.

EMULSIFIES

Egg yolks are effective emulsifiers, meaning that they can keep fat and water from separating. Egg yolks are particularly effective at emulsifying because of their lipoproteins and emulsifiers, including lecithin. Without this ability, eggs would not be effective at binding ingredients in batters and doughs.

Eggs are also often added to creamed butter or shortening to emulsify and stabilize the mixture. Care must be taken when adding eggs to creamed shortening. If eggs are added too quickly or while still cold, the emulsion breaks. While the subsequent addition of flour and other ingredients appears to bind the emulsion back together, a poorly emulsified batter bakes into a cake that may not rise properly and that has a coarse crumb.

CONTRIBUTES FLAVOR

The rich flavor of eggs comes mostly from egg yolk, partly because that is where the fat is concentrated.

WHAT WOULD HAPPEN IF EGG YOLKS REPLACED WHOLE EGGS IN CAKES?

If egg yolks replaced whole eggs in liquid shortening cake, the cake baked with egg yolks would be richer in flavor, more yellow in color, and often more crumbly and dry.

Baked goods become crumbly when they are so tender and dry that they break into tiny pieces when cut or chewed. Cakes made with egg yolks can be crumbly because the yolks are both lower in moisture, making the cake drier, and higher in tenderizers than are whole eggs.

In some cake formulas, however, direct substitution of whole eggs with egg yolks produces a denser, tougher product. This happens if water is so limited that there is much less steam produced to leaven and therefore tenderize the cake.

HELPFUL HINT

Do not use aluminum bowls, beaters, or saucepans when working with egg mixtures. Use stainless steel instead. The eggs discolor aluminum, and worse, aluminum discolors egg mixtures to a dull gray.

CONTRIBUTES COLOR

Yellow-orange carotenoids in yolk provide a rich, yellow color to baked goods, creams, and sauces. Once highly variable from season to season, egg producers control yolk color through feed supplements, such as marigold petals.

Eggs also contain protein (and a small amount of glucose) that contributes to the brown color from Maillard reactions.

ADDS NUTRITIONAL VALUE

Egg proteins in both the yolk and the white are of the highest nutritional quality. Eggs also contribute vitamins and minerals. The yellow-orange carotenoids in egg yolks, like all carotenoids, are antioxidants important to health. In particular, these carotenoids—specifically, one called lutein—are thought to reduce the risk of macular degeneration, the leading cause of severe vision loss in people over the age of 50.

While hens today are bred and fed to produce yolks that are lower in fat and cholesterol, egg yolks are still a significant source of both. Fat, in particular, is considered a contributing factor to many diseases. Both fat and dietary cholesterol are thought to increase the risk of high blood cholesterol and coronary heart disease. While health guidelines for the consumption of eggs have been relaxed in recent years, health authorities still recommend limiting egg consumption.

Additional Functions

PREVENTS STALING

Fats, emulsifiers, and proteins in eggs interfere with the process of starch retrogradation, which is the cause of staling in baked goods.

ADDS SHINE TO THE SURFACE OF BAKED GOODS

Egg proteins dry to a glossy brown film when egg wash is applied to the surface of doughs. Egg wash can be made with eggs diluted with water or, for additional browning, eggs diluted with milk.

SERVES AS AN EDIBLE GLUE

Eggs help nuts, seeds, spices, and sugar crystals adhere to baked goods. Eggs also allow batters to adhere to foods that are fried.

SHOULD EGG WHITES BE ADDED TO SORBET?

Sorbets are smooth frozen ices made without milk or other dairy products. The mark of a fine sorbet is a soft texture, free of large ice crystals. While any good ice cream freezer can make a smooth sorbet, the addition of egg white helps sorbets stay smoother during storage. Egg whites affect other qualities of sorbets, too, and whether these differences are desirable comes down to personal preference.

For example, sorbets made with added egg white have a milder, less intense flavor than ones made without. Because the whites are aerated in the ice cream freezer, sorbets containing egg white are also lighter and airier. Because of their airiness, they also have a paler color.

If you choose to add egg white to sorbet, be sure the whites are pasteurized. If you do not have access to pasteurized egg whites, it is best to leave egg whites out of sorbet.

WHY DOES ADDING EXTRA EGGS MAKE BROWNIES CAKE-LIKE?

Some people like their brownies dense and fudgy, others like them light and cakey. Everybody has their favorite brownie formula, which can vary widely in the proportion of chocolate to sugar, fat and other tenderizers, and to flour, eggs and other structure builders. Brownie formulas also vary in mixing methods.

Sometimes, however, the difference is as simple as the number of eggs added. Eggs can provide aeration, and cake-like brownies are lighter than fudgy ones. But the added lightness from cakey brownies is as likely from the moisture in the eggs. Moisture converts to steam when heated, and steam is very powerful leavening gas, important in lightening the texture of baked goods. The moisture in eggs also allows starch to more fully gelatinize, and gelatinized starch is essential for a cake-like crumb.

PROMOTES SMOOTHNESS IN CONFECTIONS AND FROZEN DESSERTS

Fats, emulsifiers, and proteins in eggs interfere with sugar and ice crystallization, promoting a velvety smooth texture in icings, confections, and frozen desserts. French-style ice cream is ice cream that contains added egg yolks for creamy smoothness and richness.

ADDS MOISTURE

Whole eggs contain approximately 75 percent moisture. Any time eggs are added to batter or dough, a good amount of moisture is also added. Remember that baking involves balancing moisteners with driers. If eggs are increased in a formula, other liquids—milk or water, for example—must be decreased.

Do not confuse adding moisture with adding moistness. Because eggs also contain structure-building proteins, the use of eggs often makes a product taste tougher and drier.

INCREASES SOFTNESS IN RAW DOUGH

Eggs interfere with gluten development in raw dough, even as they provide structure of their own once baked. Gluten proteins bond with other gluten proteins, and egg fats, emulsifiers, and proteins interfere with this bonding.

HELPFUL HINT

Brioche is a rich yeast dough, high in egg, sugar, and butter. It can be helpful to withhold some of the eggs in brioche dough until after the dough has been well mixed. This way, gluten can develop properly before eggs have a chance to interfere with the process.

MORE ON COAGULATION—BASIC EGG CUSTARD

A basic egg custard consists of eggs, milk or cream, sugar, and flavoring. The mixture is thickened or gelled through the heat coagulation of egg proteins. Examples of egg custards include crème caramel, crème brûlée, and crème anglaise—vanilla custard sauce. Many other products have a custard base. For example, pumpkin pie filling, cream pie filling, bread pudding, rice pudding, pastry cream, quiches, even cheesecakes are variations on the basic egg custard.

A properly cooked custard-based product is a moist, tender gel or a smooth, creamy sauce. The thickening and gelling occurs over time as the temperature of the mixture increases and the eggs coagulate.

A Description of the Process of Egg Coagulation

As eggs are heated, proteins in both the whites and the yolks gradually denature or unfold (Figure 11.4). The unfolded proteins move through the liquid and bond, or aggregate, with one another. In fact, protein coagulation is sometimes called *protein aggregation*. Properly aggregated egg proteins form a strong, yet often flexible network that traps water and other liquids.

The more eggs are heated, the more egg proteins aggregate, and the tighter, firmer, and more rigid the protein network becomes. Eventually, the proteins overcoagulate, shrinking and squeezing out liquids, much as a sponge shrinks and releases water when it is wrung. Overcoagulation is sometimes called *curdling*, and it results in *weeping* or *syneresis*, where bits of tough gel float in pools of squeezed-out liquid.

Often, however, water that is released from overcoagulated proteins evaporates, or it is absorbed by other ingredients. This happens in cakes and other baked goods, where gelatinizing starches absorb water that is squeezed out of overcoagulated egg proteins. The protein network and the cake, however, still shrink to a dry, rubbery toughness.

In general, it is beneficial to slow down coagulation. This reduces the risk of overcoagulation and provides the highest-quality custard or baked product—one that is soft, moist, and tender.

While heat is the most common means of coagulating proteins, proteins are also coagulated by acid, salt, freezing, whipping, and drying.

Factors Affecting Egg Coagulation

There are several ways to slow down coagulation and reduce the risk of overcoagulation. When coagulation is slowed, it takes a higher temperature to bring it about. Following is a discussion of the main factors that affect the rate of egg protein coagulation, the temperature at which it occurs, and the risk of overcoagulation. Temperatures given are approximate.

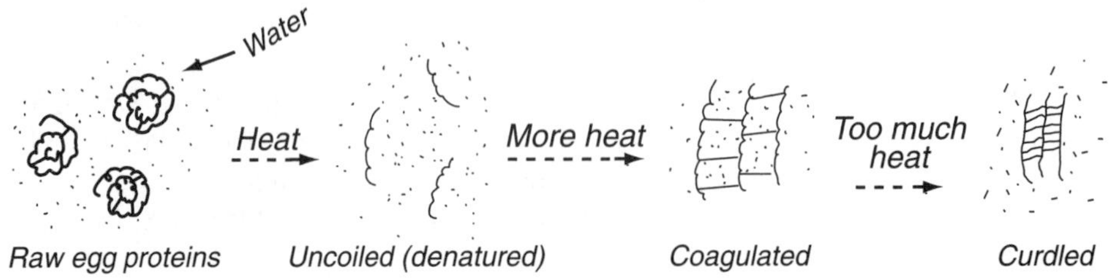

FIGURE 11.4 The process of egg coagulation

Raw egg proteins — Uncoiled (denatured) — Coagulated — Curdled

HOW DOES SUGAR "COOK" EGG YOLKS?

When sugar is placed on egg yolks and not stirred in, the yolks gel and appear to cook. Sugar, being hygroscopic, pulls water from the egg yolks (recall that yolks are about 50 percent water) and dries them. Without water, proteins in the yolk are closer together and quickly aggregate, as if heat was applied.

To avoid this, never add sugar to yolks without stirring the two together. The yolks will thicken, but they will not solidify.

AMOUNT OR PROPORTION OF EGG

Proteins in an undiluted egg properly coagulate by about 160°F (70°C). Dilute the egg with milk, water, or other ingredients, and the coagulation temperature increases. For example, the coagulation temperature for most vanilla custard sauce formulas is between 180°–185°F (82°–85°C). The dilution of egg proteins with milk, sugar, and cream makes it more difficult for the proteins to bump into one another and bond. This reduces the risk of overcoagulation. When bonding does eventually occur, expect a softer, more tender product when the additional liquid is trapped in the coagulated protein network.

RATE OF COOKING

Egg coagulation does not happen instantaneously. It requires time, and the faster the rate of cooking, the less time it takes. However, when eggs coagulate too quickly, the egg proteins do not unfold properly and are less likely to thicken or gel as well. For example, crème anglaise—vanilla custard sauce—cooked over high heat is not only more likely to curdle and burn, it is also less likely to fully thicken. To maximize thickening, use a low heat setting while stirring constantly.

PART OF EGG USED

Egg yolks coagulate at a higher temperature (150°–160°F; 65°–70°C) than egg whites (140°–150°F; 60°–65°C), making them less likely to weep and curdle. Recall that egg yolk proteins are lipoproteins, bonded to fats and emulsifiers. The fats and emulsifiers make it more difficult for proteins to aggregate. Ranking the parts of the egg from highest to lowest in the rate of coagulation and the tendency to overcoagulate:

egg whites > whole eggs > egg yolks

SUGAR

Besides diluting protein molecules, sugar slows egg protein coagulation in custards and baked goods by preventing the proteins from unfolding. If the proteins are slow to

HELPFUL HINT

An important technique in the bakeshop is the tempering of ingredients—the careful addition of one ingredient to another when two ingredients start at different temperatures. The goal of tempering is to avoid damaging either ingredient.

Tempering is important when adding eggs to hot mixtures. If eggs are added directly to hot milk, for example, heat from the milk prematurely cooks the eggs, and bits of coagulated egg form in the mixture.

This is avoided by slowly adding a small amount of hot milk to the eggs before they are added to the bulk of the milk. This dilutes the eggs without significantly raising their temperature. Once they are diluted, the eggs are much less likely to be heat damaged as they are added to the rest of the milk.

Some formulas call for other ingredients, such as sugar, to be added to eggs before they are tempered with hot milk. Adding sugar or another room-temperature ingredient is yet another way to dilute and protect eggs from the effects of heat.

HELPFUL HINT

Water baths are good for baking egg custard, bread pudding, and cheesecake. Water baths rarely exceed simmering (180°–190°F; 82°–88°C), even when the oven is set at 325°F (165°C) or more. This slows the process and evens out baking so that the outside of the custard does not become tough, rubbery, and curdled before the inside bakes.

To use a water bath, place filled containers to be baked in a pan. Place the pan in the oven and fill with hot water at least halfway up the sides of the containers. Do not fill so high that water sloshes into your product.

unfold, they will be slow to coagulate, unless temperatures are raised. This means that sugar helps prevent curdling. It is why quiches, which are essentially egg custard made without sugar, are more apt to curdle and weep than egg custard itself.

It is no surprise that sugars are considered tenderizers in baked goods; by slowing coagulation, sugars slow the formation of egg structure (sugars also slow the formation of gluten structure and starch structure). If enough sugar is present, coagulation is stopped completely, and the baked good will remain raw, even after extended baking.

LIPIDS

Like sugars, lipids—fats, oils, and emulsifiers—interfere with coagulation of egg proteins and so tenderize custards much as they tenderize baked goods. Lipids slow coagulation by coating egg proteins, just as they tenderize gluten structure by coating gluten proteins.

Actually, custards made with a high amount of lipids—from either cream or egg yolk—are more than just soft and tender. Cream and egg yolks provide an added dimension, a smoothness and creaminess not seen in custards made without these ingredients. This creamy texture is the hallmark of well-made crème brûlée, which is custard prepared from heavy cream and egg yolks, topped with a crisp burnt sugar crust.

ACID

Acid speeds up egg coagulation, lowering the temperature of coagulation. The acid comes from added lemon or other fruit juice, raisins or other fruits, or cultured dairy products. When using acidic ingredients in custard products, be sure to carefully monitor baking times.

STARCH

Starch increases the temperature of egg coagulation by interfering with the process. To understand how effective starch is at slowing the process and increasing the temperature of egg coagulation, compare the cooking of pastry cream to that of vanilla custard sauce. Pastry cream is essentially custard sauce with added cornstarch or flour. Pastry cream is—must be—brought to a boil and boiled for 2 or more minutes. Vanilla custard sauce could not survive 2 minutes of boiling. In fact, custard sauce generally curdles before it reaches 185°F (85°C). While other differences between the two formulas exist, the main reason pastry cream can be boiled without curdling is because it contains added starch.

OTHER FACTORS

Calcium in hard water and in dairy ingredients strengthens the coagulation of egg proteins. Imagine egg custard made with water instead of milk. The custard would be very soft and barely set. Using hard water to replace the milk restores much of the lost gel strength—but none of the rich dairy flavor.

Protease enzymes break down egg proteins much as they break down gelatin protein. Try to make a baked custard with added uncooked pineapple, which contains active protease, and the custard will not set. Cook the pineapple first, inactivating the enzyme, and the intact egg proteins in the custard will coagulate.

Stirring eggs as they are heated also affects coagulation. Compare baked egg custard, for example, with stirred vanilla custard sauce. Custard sauce is typically made with egg yolks and part heavy cream, while baked custard is made with whole eggs and whole milk. From

---

HELPFUL HINT

Vanilla custard sauce is easily curdled. As long as the curdling is not too excessive, the sauce can be saved by blending it until smooth in a blender or food processor. There will be differences, however, between a saved sauce and one properly made. For example, the extra heat will noticeably increase egg flavor and deepen the yellow color. The extent of blending will increase the airiness of the sauce, making it slightly foamy, at least initially. Finally, and surprisingly, a saved sauce is typically thicker than one not overcooked. This is partly because of the air incorporated into the sauce, but it is also because the egg proteins are fully cooked and coagulated.

this alone, you would expect a softer set from the custard sauce than from the baked custard. Yet, there is also a striking difference in procedure. Custard sauce is stirred in a saucepan as the eggs are heated, while baked custard is not. Constant stirring keeps egg proteins from aggregating into a solid mass, so the sauce thickens instead of forming a firm solid (and, if not stirred, custard sauce would burn the bottom of the pan).

MORE ON AERATION—MERINGUE

Meringue is egg white whipped with sugar. It is used for lightness and volume in mousses, soufflés, angel food and sponge cakes, and icings. It can also be baked in a low-temperature oven for macaroons, cake layers, and tartlet shells.

Meringue could not form without the unique combination of proteins that are present in egg white. Four egg white proteins—*ovalbumin, conalbumin, globulin,* and *lysozyme*—work together for maximum foaming power and foam stability.

A Description of the Process of Egg Foam Formation

As eggs are whipped, two things happen simultaneously. Air bubbles are beaten into the liquid, and certain egg proteins denature, or unfold (Figure 11.5). The unfolded proteins quickly move through the liquid to the surface of the bubbles. Once there, neighboring proteins bond or aggregate around the bubbles, forming a filmy network. Surrounded by these strong, flexible films, air bubbles are less likely to collapse, so more bubbles can be beaten in, even as the walls of the film thin out.

Notice that what happens to egg proteins during whipping is similar—but not identical—to what happens to egg proteins when they are heated. In both cases, protein molecules unfold and bond, forming a type of structure.

Factors Affecting Meringue Stability

Stability in a meringue is important. Stable meringue is firm yet flexible and resilient, so it can hold up to folding, piping, and baking. Often, the very things that increase stability decrease volume and tenderness. As always, the goal of the pastry chef is to balance opposite features. In this case, the goal is to balance stability with volume and tenderness.

Following is a discussion of the main factors that affect meringue stability.

> **HELPFUL** HINT
>
> Because sugar reduces volume and slows whipping, it is best to withhold sugar in a common meringue until the egg whites have already begun to foam.

SUGAR

Sugar greatly stabilizes meringues even as it slows whipping and decreases volume slightly. For a common meringue—one in which room-temperature egg whites are whipped with granulated sugar—sugar stabilizes best if it is added slowly, and only if

Raw egg proteins → *Whipping* → Egg proteins denatured: air bubbles beaten in → Egg proteins coagulated, forming film around air bubble

FIGURE 11.5 The process of egg foam formation

ONE WAY TO CLASSIFY MERINGUES

A useful way to classify meringue is by the ratio of sugar to egg whites. Using this means of classification, the two main types of meringue are hard meringue and soft meringue. Hard meringue uses about two parts sugar for every part egg white, by weight. This means that about 2.4 ounces (66 grams) of sugar is needed for every large egg white (about 1.2 ounces or 33 grams). Soft meringue uses equal weights of sugar and egg white.

Hard meringue is denser and less tender than soft meringue, but it is more stable and it can be easily piped. Use a hard meringue for baked torte layers or for baked meringue shells or cookies. Use a soft meringue for a light-textured topping on a lemon meringue pie, for example, but only if it is to be served fairly soon after production.

Hard meringue is more common in the bakeshop because of its stability.

the proper amount is added. Sugar should be added slowly to provide time for crystals to dissolve and not weigh down the foam. In addition, if sugar is added too quickly, protein molecules may not unfold properly. The result is a softer meringue or, in extreme cases, whites that will not whip.

Sugar stabilizes meringue by slowing the unfolding and aggregation of protein molecules. This aids stability because it protects against overwhipping. There is another way that sugar stabilizes meringue. As it dissolves in meringue's liquid film, sugar forms a thick, viscous syrup that is slow to drain. This protects the bubbles from collapse. The sugary syrup also adds a satiny sheen to the appearance of meringue.

> **HELPFUL HINT**
>
> Undissolved sugar crystals weigh down meringue, weakening it. Once baked, these crystals attract moisture and sometimes form unattractive beads of syrup. To minimize beading and volume loss, sift sugar first and add it slowly, allowing it to dissolve between additions. Otherwise use superfine or another finer grind of sugar, so the sugar dissolves faster.

LIPIDS

Lipids—fats, oils, and emulsifiers—interfere with aeration. Depending on the type and the amount, lipids either slow down aeration or prevent it from happening at all. This is especially true of egg yolk lipids, more so than of shortening or vegetable oil. Even a small amount of yolk can prevent whites from whipping.

Lipids interfere with aeration by coating proteins, preventing them from unfolding and aggregating. But they do more. Lipids compete with proteins for a spot at the foam's bubble surface. Since lipids themselves cannot form a strong, cohesive network like egg proteins, lipid-coated bubbles expand rapidly, only to collapse.

> **HELPFUL HINT**
>
> To avoid problems with fats, oils, and emulsifiers when whipping meringue, be sure to use a clean bowl, carefully remove any stray bits of yolk from your whites, and stay away from plastic bowls and utensils, which absorb fats and oils and cannot easily be cleaned.

ACID

Acid stabilizes meringue by lowering pH. Cream of tartar is the most common acid used, but lemon juice and vinegar also stabilize. Too much acid leaves a sour, off taste and should be avoided.

Add acid early on. Whipping might take longer, but the protein network that forms will be flexible and stable against overwhipping, folding, piping, and baking. The meringue will also be whiter.

TEMPERATURE OF WHITES

Egg whites right out of the refrigerator will not whip well. The ideal temperature to whip a common meringue is room temperature—about 70°F (20°C).

Besides making common meringues, bakeshops also prepare Swiss and Italian meringues. Any of these three can be made soft or hard, that is, made with equal parts sugar to whites, or with two parts sugar to whites. Swiss meringue is made by warming sugar with egg whites in a double boiler prior to whipping. This process dissolves sugar crystals, and the higher temperature—to 110°–120°F (40°–50°C)—undoubtedly has an effect on the unfolding of egg proteins. Swiss meringue is used more often in the bakeshop, and when properly prepared, is more stable than common meringue.

Probably because frozen egg whites have already been heated to pasteurize, care must be taken when using them in Swiss meringues. Warm the whites just until sugar crystals dissolve, then immediately remove from heat.

An Italian meringue is essentially a cooked meringue. Hot sugar syrup, heated to 248°–250°F (120°–121°C), is slowly added to whipped egg whites. The hot syrup coagulates the whipped egg proteins. An Italian meringue is the most stable of the three types of meringue. However, an Italian meringue has the lowest volume and the most dense, least tender mouthfeel.

> **HELPFUL** HINT
>
> If egg whites need to be warmed to reach room temperature, take extreme care. It is best to warm them gently over a hot—not boiling—water bath and to stir constantly while warming. If overheated, egg whites coagulate and will not whip.

THICKNESS OF WHITES

Thin, older whites whip more easily to a higher volume than thick, fresh ones. Yet, once whipped, the foam from thin whites is less stable, because the liquid film drains more easily from the bubbles. If volume is more important than stability, then older eggs are better.

For the most part, however, eggs purchased through normal channels have already aged, often by several weeks. For better stability, a good rule of thumb is to use fresher eggs for meringues, saving older ones for general baking.

WHIPPING TIME

Both underwhipped and overwhipped egg whites are unstable. If underwhipped, proteins are not fully aggregated to form a strong film. In time, underwhipped whites weep.

When whipped too quickly or for too long, proteins denature and aggregate extensively, and the protective film that surrounds each air bubble becomes overstretched and rigid. The whites eventually collapse, forming tightly bonded, inflexible clumps of protein floating in squeezed-out liquid. In other words, too much whipping has a curdling effect on egg protein structure similar to the effect of too much heat. Overwhipped whites should be discarded.

> **HELPFUL** HINT
>
> Whip egg whites no faster than medium-high speed and carefully follow each formula's guidelines for when to stop whipping. Time your work carefully so that the whipped whites are used immediately.

OTHER FACTORS

Other factors that affect the stability of meringue include the presence of copper or salt, and the type of whisk used. Whipping in a copper bowl increases meringue stability in much the same way that cream of tartar works; that is, it improves the flexibility of a protein network so that it is stable against overwhipping, folding, piping, and baking. With copper bowls, tiny particles of copper are whipped into the whites each time the whisk hits the bowl. Egg whites whipped in copper have a slight golden color.

Salt appears to decrease meringue stability, so it is best left out of whites when they are whipped. Large wires or blades on a whisk produce larger, less stable air cells than thinner ones. When choosing a whisk, it is best to use a finer piano whisk for whipping whites.

STORAGE AND HANDLING

The U.S. Food and Drug Administration (FDA) classifies shell eggs as a potentially hazardous food—even if the eggs are clean, whole, and uncracked. Dry eggs that have been reconstituted and frozen egg products that have been thawed are also potentially hazardous.

The following guidelines should be followed when working with eggs, to ensure microbiological safety.

Receiving and Storing Eggs and Egg Products

- Check the temperature of a shipment of whole shell eggs by breaking one or two into a small cup and immediately measuring the temperature with an accurate thermometer. The temperature of an incoming shipment of eggs should be 45°F (7°C) or below, by law.

- Evaluate one or two eggs from a shipment for freshness. Check for cleanliness of shell, thickness of white and yolk, and odor.

- Refrigerate or freeze eggs and egg products immediately upon delivery. Store dry egg products at room temperature in a cool dry area. Store shell eggs in their original containers. The ideal storage conditions for shell eggs is 38°–40°F (3°–4°C) with 75–85 percent relative humidity. This helps maintain the overall quality of eggs. At the very least, be sure to refrigerate shell eggs, reconstituted dry eggs, and thawed frozen egg products at temperatures at or below 45°F (7°C).

- Unopened refrigerated liquid egg products can be held for up to 12 weeks, if kept at or below 40°F (4°C). Once opened, use within a few days. To keep track of product age, label cartons with thaw dates. Always rotate stock: first in, first out (FIFO).

- Treat opened thawed frozen liquid egg products as you would refrigerated products. Refrain from refreezing unused product, since it is freezing and thawing that causes the most damage to frozen foods, including egg products.

WHAT IS SALMONELLOSIS?

Salmonella is a type of bacteria that causes one of the most common foodborne infections, salmonellosis. An estimated 118,000 illnesses per year in the United States are caused by the consumption of eggs contaminated with salmonella. Symptoms of salmonellosis include diarrhea, fever, intense abdominal pain, and vomiting. Mild cases often last two to three days. Severe cases last longer and can be fatal, especially for young children, the elderly, or those with weak immune systems.

Since salmonella cannot be completely eliminated from raw foods of animal origin, it must be carefully controlled by the food preparer. Eggs and dairy products are two common bakeshop ingredients that are potential sources of salmonella and must be handled properly.

Usage

- Discard eggs that have even the smallest of cracks or that have a strong off odor.

- Do not wash eggs before use; eggs have been washed and sanitized by the packer.

- Do not crack and pool large amounts of eggs for later use, since eggs out of the shell are particularly susceptible to growth of bacteria.

- Do not crack an egg directly into a bowl containing other ingredients or other eggs; crack into a small cup or bowl, inspect for shell pieces, then add to batch.

- When breaking eggs, do not allow shell to come in contact with egg contents. Although sanitized by the egg processor, eggshells could subsequently pick up dirt or microorganisms. *Hint:* Use a metal spoon and not a piece of shell to remove yolk inadvertently dropped into whites.

- Do not thaw frozen eggs at room temperature; follow the guidelines given in the following section.

- To avoid cross contamination be sure to sanitize equipment, utensils, and counter-tops that have come in contact with eggs.

- Also to avoid cross contamination, wash hands thoroughly after handling raw eggs and before handling other foods.

- Minimum cook time for shell eggs: hold at or above 140°F (60°C) for at least 3.5 minutes.

- Use pasteurized egg products whenever eggs are needed for products that are not heated and held at 140°F (60°C) for at least 3.5 minutes.

- If a cooked product, such as a vanilla custard sauce, is to be cooled before service, cool quickly in an ice water bath and hold at or below 40°F (4°C), to minimize time in temperature danger zone; use within one day.

How to Thaw Frozen Egg Products

There are two acceptable ways to thaw frozen egg products. The first is to thaw frozen eggs under refrigeration. This method is preferred, but it requires planning ahead.

The second acceptable way to thaw frozen egg products is to place unopened containers under cold running water. Do not thaw containers under hot water. This could cook the eggs, destroying their functionality. Do not thaw containers at room temperature; the time it takes for the inner core to thaw exposes the outer area to potentially dangerous temperatures for too long.

How to Use Dried Eggs

There are two ways to use dried eggs in baked goods. The easiest way is to blend dried eggs with other dry ingredients, being sure to increase the amount of water in your formula accordingly.

The second way to use dried eggs is to reconstitute with cool water before use. Allow time for reconstituted egg to stand (refrigerated) before use. Wait at least 1 hour for reconstituted yolks, 3 hours for whites. This allows time for eggs to hydrate properly.

QUESTIONS FOR REVIEW

1. How much (in fractions or a percentage) of the edible part of an egg is egg white? How much is egg yolk?

2. How many dozen eggs are in a flat?

3. How do egg whites and egg yolks compare in moisture, lipids (fat and emulsifiers), and protein content?

4. Name an emulsifier present in egg yolks.

5. Which component in egg yolk provides yellow color? Why might the color of yolk vary from one egg producer to another and throughout the season?

6. Which component in whole eggs (fats, emulsifiers, proteins, water, minerals, etc.) provides structure or toughening? Which two components are considered tenderizers? Where is each of these components located (white, yolk, or both)?

7. Overall, is a whole egg considered a toughener or a tenderizer? What about egg white? Egg yolk?

8. Which—whole egg, egg white, or egg yolk—provides the most toughening? Which provides the least?

9. Why do the FDA and the American Egg Board call eggs purchased in the shell shell eggs and not fresh eggs?

10. What is meant by an egg product? What are the advantages of egg products over shell eggs?

11. Why should egg products be used instead of shell eggs in uncooked buttercream or sorbet?

12. Why is citric acid often added to frozen pasteurized whole eggs? Why is guar gum often added to frozen pasteurized egg whites? Why is sugar often added to frozen pasteurized egg yolks?

13. Rank egg whites, egg yolks, and whole eggs from highest to lowest in each of the following functions: structure-building and toughening, leavening, color, flavor, and emulsification.

14. Why will the addition of extra egg whites (which are about 90 percent water) to cake batter likely produce a drier, rather than a moister, cake?

15. How do sugars and fats affect the process of egg coagulation? That is, do they speed it up and increase the likelihood of curdling and toughening due to overcooking, or do they slow it down and decrease the likelihood of curdling and toughening?

16. Which is better for producing the highest-quality baked custard: using an oven temperature that is slightly too high, or using one that is slightly too low? Explain.

17. Besides producing softer and more tender custards, how else do fats—from cream and egg yolks, for example—affect the texture of custards?

18. How is the volume of freshly whipped foam affected when steps are taken to increase stability? That is, as you increase the stability of whipped egg whites, will volume most likely increase, decrease, or stay the same?

19. What is the difference between a hard meringue and a soft meringue? When is one used instead of the other?

20. Briefly describe differences in the preparation of common, Swiss, and Italian meringues. Which is the most stable? Which is the least stable?

21. What happens to the thickness of an egg white (and yolk) as it ages? How does this affect its ability to whip?

22. How does sugar affect the stability of whipped egg whites? What happens when sugar is added too fast or too soon to whipping eggs?

23. How do fats and egg yolks affect the ability of a meringue to form?

24. How does acid affect the stability of whipped egg whites?

QUESTIONS FOR DISCUSSION

1. A formula calls for 35 whole eggs. How much whole egg should you weigh out?

2. A formula calls for 10 egg yolks. How much egg yolk should you weigh out?

3. A formula calls for 6 egg whites. How much egg white should you weigh out?

4. Why might a slightly greenish cast develop in baking powder biscuits? How can it be prevented?

5. Draw out the process of the heat coagulation of egg proteins. Include in your drawing what happens when eggs receive too much heat. Explain in words what is happening at each step, and be sure to properly label all your squiggles and dots.

6. You need to temper room-temperature eggs with hot milk to avoid coagulating the eggs. Explain how you will do this, and explain how it prevents coagulation of eggs.

7. You have extra egg yolks and decide to use them instead of whole eggs in a cake. You use 1 pound (or kilogram) egg yolk for each pound (or kilogram) of whole eggs called for in the formula. What differences might you expect in the cake baked with egg yolks compared with the cake baked with whole eggs?

8. Describe the process of egg foam formation.

9. List steps to follow when receiving and storing eggs and egg products, and explain why each is important.

10. Provide six safety guidelines to follow when using eggs and egg products, and explain why each is important.

EXERCISES AND EXPERIMENTS

1. Comparison of Baked Custards

Use information from the following three baked custard formulas to answer the questions that follow. Be sure to examine both the type and amount of each ingredient before answering these questions, and explain your answers. *Note:* percentages are baker's percentages, based on dairy liquid (milk, cream) at 100 percent.

INGREDIENT	BAKED CUSTARD 1 BAKER'S %	BAKED CUSTARD 2 BAKER'S %	BAKED CUSTARD 3 BAKER'S %
Eggs, whole	40.0%	40.0%	0.0%
Eggs, yolks	0.0%	0.0%	40.0%
Extract, vanilla	1.2%	1.2%	1.2%
Salt	0.2%	0.2%	0.2%
Cream, heavy	0.0%	50.0%	0.0%
Milk, whole	100.0%	50.0%	100.0%
Sugar, granulated	20.0%	20.0%	20.0%
Total Baker's Percentage	161.4%	161.4%	161.4%

1. Which custard would have the deepest yellow color, and why?

2. Which custard would have the firmest gel, and why?

3. Which custard would have the smoothest, creamiest texture, and why?

2. How to Minimize Weeping and Curdling in Baked Custard

Imagine that you have a baked custard formula that tends to weep and curdle during baking. You can make any change to the formula or to the method of preparation. You list the following changes that could decrease weeping and curdling because each decreases the rate of egg coagulation. While some of these changes will not work in every situation, and some work better than others, each is a possibility. Explain the reasons that each could work. The first is completed for you.

1. Use lower oven temperature.

   Reason: This is the most direct way to slow the rate of coagulation, since it reduces the rate of heat that reaches the outside of the custard, reducing the likelihood that the outside does not weep and curdle before the inside bakes.

2. Replace whole egg with yolk.

   Reason:

   _____

   _____

3. Use cream instead of milk.

   Reason:

   _____

   _____

4. Increase amount of sugar.

   Reason:

   _____

   _____

5. Place custards in water bath.

   Reason:

   _____

   _____

6. Decrease amount of egg.

   Reason:

   _____

   _____

3. An Experiment on How the Type of Egg Affects the Overall Quality of Muffins

OBJECTIVES

To demonstrate how the type of egg affects:
- Consistency and appearance of muffin batter
- Crispness and the extent of Maillard browning on the crust of muffins
- Crumb color and structure
- Moistness, tenderness, and height of the muffins
- Overall flavor of the muffin
- Overall acceptability of the muffin

PRODUCTS PREPARED

Muffins made with:

- Whole egg (control product)
- No egg (with additional water and oil to replace the bulk of the egg)
- Egg white
- Egg yolk
- Liquid whole egg substitute (e.g., Egg Beaters)

- Other, if desired (one-half egg yolk and one-half water [to replace water from egg white], dried whole egg, dried egg substitute, frozen pasteurized whole egg, etc.)

MATERIALS AND EQUIPMENT

- Muffin batter, enough to make 24 or more muffins of each variation
- Muffin tins (2½" or 3½" size) and liners or pan spray
- Size #16 (2¾ ounce) portion-control scoop or equivalent
- Ruler

PROCEDURE

- Preheat oven according to formula.
- Line or lightly spray muffin tins with pan coating; label with type of egg to be added to muffin batter.
- Prepare muffin batter using the following formula or using any basic muffin formula. Prepare one batch of batter for each variation.
- If desired, place muffin tins onto half sheet pans.
- Use an oven thermometer placed in center of oven to read oven temperature; record results.
- Place filled muffin tins into preheated oven and set timer according to formula.
- Bake until control product (made with whole eggs) springs back when center top is lightly pressed, and wooden pick inserted into center of cake comes out clean. Control product should be lightly browned. Remove all muffins from oven after same length of time, even though some will be paler in color or have not risen properly. If necessary, however, adjust bake times for oven variances. Record bake times in Comments column of Results Table 2, which follows.
- Transfer to wire racks to cool to room temperature.
- Record any potential sources of error that might make it difficult to draw the proper conclusions from the experiment.
- Evaluate the consistency and appearance of the batter, from very thin and runny to very thick, on a scale of one to five; record results in Results Table 1, which follows.
- When muffins are completely cooled, evaluate height as follows:
  - Slice three muffins from each batch in half, being careful not to compress.
  - Measure height of each cupcake by placing ruler along the flat edge at the cupcake's maximum height. Record results for each of three muffins in 1/16 inch (10 mm) increments and record results in Results Table 1.
  - Calculate the average muffin height for each batch by adding the heights of the muffins and dividing by 3; record results in Results Table 1.
  - Evaluate the shape of muffins (even rounded top, peaked top, dips in center, etc.) and record results in Results Table 1.
- Evaluate the sensory characteristics of completely cooled products and record evaluations in Results Table 2. Be sure to compare each in turn to the control product and consider the following:
  - Crust color, from very light to very dark on a scale of one to five
  - Crust texture (soft and moist, soft and dry, crisp and dry, etc.)
  - Crumb appearance (small uniform air cells, large irregular air cells, tunnels, etc); also, evaluate color

- Toughness/tenderness, from extremely tender to extremely tough, on a scale of one to five
- Crumb texture (moist/dry, gummy, spongy, crumbly, etc.)
- Overall flavor (egg flavor, floury taste, saltiness, sweetness, etc.)
- Overall acceptability, from highly unacceptable to highly acceptable, on a scale of one to five.
- Any additional comments, as necessary

Basic Muffin Batter

INGREDIENT	POUND	OUNCE	GRAMS	BAKER'S PERCENTAGE
Butter		7	200	35
Eggs, whole		6	170	30
Milk	1		455	80
Flour, pastry	1	4	570	100
Sugar, granulated		8	225	40
Salt (1 tsp)		0.2	6	1
Baking powder (2½ tsp)		1.2	35	6
Total	3	10.4	1661	292

Method of Preparation

1. Preheat oven to 400°F (200°C).
2. Sift dry ingredients together into bowl.
3. Melt butter; cool slightly.
4. Whisk egg lightly; blend in milk and melted butter.
5. Pour liquids onto dry ingredients and mix just until flour is moistened. Batter will look lumpy. *Do not overmix!*
6. Use batter immediately, baking muffins for approximately 20–22 minutes.

 **SOURCES OF ERROR**

_____

_____

RESULTS TABLE 1 ■ EVALUATION OF BATTER CONSISTENCY AND SIZE AND SHAPE OF MUFFINS MADE WITH DIFFERENT TYPES OF EGG

TYPE OF EGG	CONSISTENCY AND APPEARANCE OF BATTER	HEIGHT OF THREE MUFFINS	AVERAGE HEIGHT OF ONE MUFFIN	MUFFIN SHAPE	COMMENTS
Whole egg (control product)					
No egg (water and oil as replacement)					
Egg white					
Egg yolk					
Liquid whole egg substitute					

RESULTS TABLE 2 ▨ SENSORY CHARACTERISTICS OF MUFFINS MADE WITH DIFFERENT TYPES OF EGG

TYPE OF EGG	CRUST COLOR AND TEXTURE	CRUMB APPEARANCE AND TEXTURE	OVERALL FLAVOR	OVERALL ACCEPTABILITY	COMMENTS
Whole egg (control product)					
No egg (water and oil as replacement)					
Egg white					
Egg yolk					
Liquid whole egg substitute					

CONCLUSIONS

1. Did the type of egg affect the appearance and consistency of the batters? If so, how?

_____

_____

2. Rank the muffin tops from lightest to darkest. Explain any differences in appearance.

_____

_____

3. Rank the muffins from least tender to most tender. Explain any differences in tenderness.

_____

_____

4. What were the main differences in appearance, flavor, and texture between the muffins made without egg and the muffins made with whole egg (the control product)?

_____

_____

    a. Why might the muffins made without egg not collapse? What also provides structure?

    _____

    _____

5. What were the main differences in appearance, flavor, and texture among the muffins made with egg white, whole egg substitute, and whole egg (the control product)?

_____

_____

a. Whole egg substitute consists primarily of egg whites, but they do contain other ingredients. Use the whole egg substitute's packaging label to explain what ingredients contribute to specific differences between the muffins made with the substitute and those made with egg whites.

_____

_____

6. You wish to use egg whites instead of whole egg to make a muffin with less fat and no cholesterol. What adjustments would you recommend making to the formula and to the method of preparation so that the muffins made with egg white will more closely match those made with whole egg?

_____

_____

7. What were the main differences in appearance, flavor, and texture between the muffins made with egg yolk and the muffins made with whole egg (the control product)?

_____

_____

8. Besides the muffins made with whole eggs (control product), which muffins did you feel were acceptable overall, and why?

_____

_____

9. Did you have any sources of error that might significantly affect the results of your experiment? If so, what could you do differently next time to minimize error?

_____

_____

4. How Various Ingredients and Treatments of Egg White Affect the Overall Quality and Stability of Meringue

OBJECTIVES

To demonstrate how various ingredients and treatments affects:
- The time it takes to fully whip meringue
- Meringue volume
- Meringue stability
- The appearance, flavor, and mouth-feel of meringue
- The overall acceptability of meringue

PRODUCTS PREPARED

Meringue prepared the following ways:
- Common soft meringue, sugar added slowly (control product)
- With cream of tartar
- With sugar added all at once, in beginning
- More sugar (hard meringue, two parts sugar to one part white)
- No sugar
- Swiss meringue method
- Italian meringue method
- Other (with small amount of egg yolk or with shortening on bowl; made with frozen pasteurized egg whites; made with dried egg whites, whites not warmed before whipping, whipped on high speed, added salt, etc.)

MATERIALS AND EQUIPMENT

- Clear volumetric measuring cups (one pint/one liter, or equivalent, one per test product; one quart/two liter, or equivalent)

PROCEDURE

- Prepare meringue using the formula that follows, or using any basic common soft meringue formula. Prepare one batch of meringue for each variation.
- Measure the time it takes for soft peaks to form; record results in Results Table 1, which follows.
- Record any potential sources of error that might make it difficult to draw the proper conclusions from the experiment.
- Measure density of meringue as follows:
  - Carefully spoon sample of meringue into tared measuring cup.
  - Visually check cup to confirm that no large air gaps are present.
  - Level the top surface of the cup with a straight-edge.
  - Weigh the amount of meringue in each cup and record results in Results Table 1.
- Measure stability of meringue as follows:
  - Hold samples at room temperature for thirty minutes (longer, if time permits).
  - Evaluate loss in volume and increase in liquid at bottom of container. Record results in Results Table 1.
- Evaluate the sensory characteristics of freshly-whipped meringue and record evaluations in Results Table 2, which follows. Be sure to compare each in turn to the control product and consider the following:
  - Appearance (air cell size, gloss, whiteness)
  - Flavor (sweetness, sourness, fresh egg flavor, off-flavors)
  - Mouthfeel (density and body, softness/firmness)
  - Overall acceptability for use on a lemon meringue pie
  - Add any additional comments, as necessary.

Note: There is a small but real risk of the presence of salmonella bacteria in egg white. Where consumption of unpasteurized egg white is outlawed or undesired, evaluate flavor by smell only, omit evaluation of sweetness, and use fingertips or a spoon to evaluate texture in place of mouthfeel. Or, conduct this experiment using pasteurized egg whites.

Common Soft Meringue

INGREDIENT	POUND	OUNCE	GRAMS	BAKER'S PERCENTAGE
Egg whites		6	230	100
Sugar, granulated		6	230	100
Total		12	460	200

Method of Preparation

1. Warm egg whites to room temperature.
2. Pass sugar through sieve, if necessary, to remove lumps.
3. Using wire whip, beat egg whites at medium speed. If adding cream of tartar, add ¼ teaspoon (1.25 ml) when whites just begin to foam.
4. After whites begin to foam, begin adding sugar gradually and whip until soft peaks form.

Method of Preparation for Swiss Meringue

1. Combine egg whites and sugar in a double boiler that contains hot (not boiling) water.
2. Whip mixture continuously until it reaches 115°F (45°C).

Method of Preparation for Italian Meringue

1. Begin heating sugar with 1½ ounces (45 grams) water; stir to dissolve.
2. Boil sugar syrup, without stirring, until temperature reaches 245°F (118°C).
3. In the meantime, whip egg whites at medium speed.
4. Continue whipping egg whites while gradually adding hot sugar syrup in a slow, steady stream.
5. Continue to whip until meringue is cool.

RESULTS TABLE 1 ■ EVALUATION OF WHIP TIME, MERINGUE VOLUME, AND MERINGUE STABILITY FOR DIFFERENT TREATMENTS OF MERINGUE

TREATMENT	TIME TO REACH SOFT PEAK (MINUTES)	DENSITY OF MERINGUE	MERINGUE STABILITY	COMMENTS
Common soft meringue (control product)				
With cream of tartar				
Sugar added all at once, in beginning				
More sugar (hard meringue)				
No sugar				
Swiss meringue				
Italian meringue				

RESULTS TABLE 2 ■ SENSORY CHARACTERISTICS OF DIFFERENT TREATMENTS OF MERINGUE

TREATMENT	OVERALL APPEARANCE	SWEETNESS	OVERALL FLAVOR	MOUTHFEEL	OVERALL ACCEPTABILITY	COMMENTS
Common soft meringue (control product)						
With cream of tartar						
Sugar added all at once, in beginning						
More sugar (hard meringue)						
No sugar						
Swiss meringue						
Italian meringue						

CONCLUSIONS

1. Rank meringues from lowest density to highest, when freshly made. Explain these differences in density.

_____

_____

2. Rank meringues from lowest stability to highest. Explain these differences in stability.

_____

_____

3. Which meringue whipped up fastest? Which whipped up slowest?

_____

_____

4. What were the main differences in appearance, flavor, and mouthfeel among the hard meringue (made with two parts sugar to one part egg white), the soft meringue (control product), and the meringue made with no added sugar?

_____

_____

5. What were the main differences in appearance, flavor, and mouthfeel between the meringue with added cream of tartar compared to the one without (the control product)?

_____

_____

6. What were the advantages and disadvantages, if any, of adding sugar all at once and adding it slowly (control product)?

_____

_____

7. What were the main differences in stability, appearance, flavor, and texture among the Swiss, Italian, and common (control product) meringues?

_____

_____

8. Did you have any sources of error that might significantly affect the results of your experiment? If so, what could you do differently next time to minimize error?

_____

_____

9. Identify which meringue might be best for each of the following applications; justify your answers.

    a. Angel food cake

    _____

    _____

    b. Lemon meringue pie, to be served immediately

    _____

    _____

    c. Lemon meringue pie, to be held for three days before serving

    _____

    _____

    d. Smooth, rich, and full-bodied buttercream

    _____

    _____

    e. Light and airy buttercream

    _____

    _____

    f. Baked meringue shells

    _____

    _____

CHAPTER 12

MILK AND MILK PRODUCTS

CHAPTER **OBJECTIVES**

1. Define milk and milk products used in bakeshops and describe their makeup, characteristics, and uses.

2. List the functions of milk and milk products and relate these functions to their makeup.

3. Describe how to best store and handle milk and milk products.

 ## INTRODUCTION

Milk and milk products—dairy ingredients—sold in North America are produced mostly from domesticated cows. They are complex ingredients that contain a mix of proteins, sugar (lactose), vitamins, minerals, emulsifiers, and milk fat. While dairy ingredients are not absolutely essential to many baked goods, they do provide some valuable functions, making them important ingredients in the bakeshop.

Both the U.S. and Canadian federal governments regulate minimum milk fat amounts in milk and milk products. They also regulate processing conditions for pasteurization, maximum allowable bacterial counts, acidity levels, and additives allowed. Certain states and provinces have more stringent regulations that are enforced within their borders. Milk fat requirements and pasteurization times and temperatures provided below represent U.S. and Canadian federal standards.

For information on butter, see Chapter 10.

COMMON COMMERCIAL PROCESSES TO MILK AND MILK PRODUCTS

Pasteurization

Essentially all dairy products sold in North America are pasteurized (certain aged cheeses are the exception). *Pasteurization* is a process that eliminates pathogenic—disease-causing—microorganisms and reduces the number of many other microorganisms in

WHY DRINK BOXES OF MILK DO NOT REQUIRE REFRIGERATION

Milk is usually purchased in the dairy case and stored in the refrigerator. How is it, then, that milk, such as Parmalat milk, can be sold in drink boxes that are not refrigerated?

Think of drink boxes of milk as the modern equivalent of canned milk. The milk in these boxes has been ultrapasteurized, then cooled and specially packaged under sterile conditions so that the product inside is essentially bacteria-free. The process is called aseptic processing, and no preservatives or food irradiation are involved. A similar process is used for processing and packaging coffee cream in single-use plastic containers.

Because the product is essentially bacteria-free and is in containers that do not allow entry of microorganisms, milk in sealed drink boxes is as safe as canned milk. Once opened, however, milk that has been aseptically packed in drink boxes or that has been canned, must be refrigerated.

food, without adversely affecting the overall quality of the food. Louis Pasteur invented the process of pasteurization in the mid-1800s.

The most common commercial means of pasteurizing milk is high-temperature, short-time (HTST) pasteurization, in which milk is heated to a high temperature, at least 161°F (72°C) for a minimum of 15 seconds. Ultra high temperature (UHT) pasteurization—*ultrapasteurization*—involves heating the product to an even higher temperature, often 280°F (138°C), for 2 seconds. UHT milk has a slightly different flavor than HTST milk because milk flavor is very heat sensitive. UHT milk also has a longer shelf life because the higher temperature is much more lethal to bacteria, destroying essentially all bacteria in milk. However, unless UHT products are specially packaged to prevent the entry of microorganisms, they must be treated like HTST products and refrigerated at all times.

Homogenization

If fresh milk is taken straight from the cow and allowed to sit, cream eventually rises to the top. To prevent this separation, most dairy products sold in North America are homogenized. *Homogenization* is a process in which milk is forced under high pressure through small openings in a metal plate, forcing the milk fat into tiny droplets (Figure 12.1). As soon as the droplets form, milk proteins and emulsifiers surround each one, forming a protective film that prevents them from reuniting. The tiny droplets stay suspended indefinitely, and milk fat no longer separates and rises to the top as a cream layer. In other words, homogenized dairy products are stable emulsions of fat droplets suspended in milk.

Separation

Cream is easily separated from milk in a milk separator. A separator is a type of centrifuge that spins very quickly, causing cream in milk to separate off because of its lighter density. The process is much faster than relying on gravity for the cream to rise.

 MAKEUP OF MILK

Milk directly from the cow contains proteins, lactose, vitamins, minerals, and milk fat. From Figure 12.2, however, it is clear that milk is composed mostly of water. Not counting milk fat, the solids in milk are appropriately called *milk solids not fat*, or

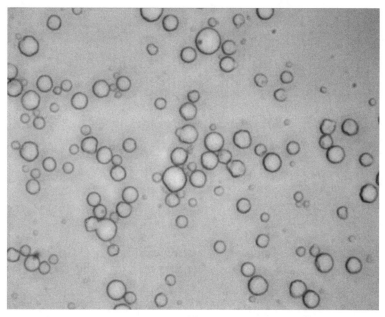

(a)

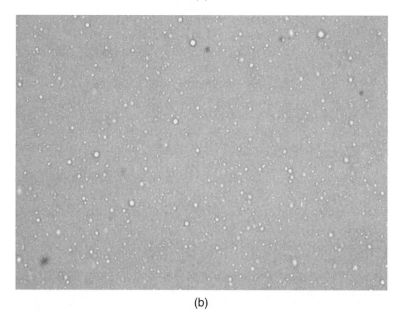

(b)

FIGURE 12.1 Effect of homogenization on milkfat in whole milk
(a) unhomogenized, (b) homogenized
*Courtesy of Dr. Alexandra Smith, Department of Food Science, University of
Guelph, Guelph, Ontario*

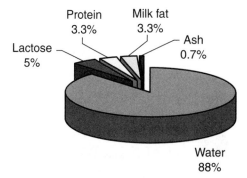

FIGURE 12.2 The makeup of whole milk

MSNF. There are legal minimum requirements for the amount of milk fat and MSNF in most dairy products.

Other than a slight sweetness, the flavor of fresh milk is relatively mild. As the amount of milk fat in milk products increases, however, the rich dairy flavor increases, because most dairy flavors are in the fat.

Small amounts of the emulsifiers lecithin and mono- and diglycerides are also in milk fat, as are carotenoid pigments. Carotenoids provide dairy products with a slight yellowish color. Mostly, however, milk fat contains triglycerides, or fat molecules, especially saturated ones.

Although milk contains only about 3.5 percent protein, the proteins in milk are very important. These proteins fall into two main categories: casein proteins and whey

WHY IS MILK WHITE?

Casein proteins in milk associate with calcium and phosphorus to form small spherical structures called micelles. Like the tiny droplets of fat in milk, micelles are too small to see or feel. Yet, light cannot pass through the casein micelles. Instead, it bounces off them in many directions. When light scatters like this, it appears white. Most of the whiteness of milk is from the scattering of light off casein micelles. Some of the light, however, is scattered off fat droplets, making whole milk appear whiter and more opaque than fat-free milk. As the amount of milk fat increases much higher, as it does in heavy cream and certain cheeses, the product takes on a buttery-yellow appearance from the carotenoids in the milk fat.

proteins. *Casein proteins* are easily coagulated with acids or enzymes. Coagulated, or clabbered, casein proteins aggregate with one other in a manner somewhat similar to coagulated egg proteins. Like egg proteins, casein proteins thicken and gel as they coagulate. This is the basis for the manufacture of cheeses, yogurt, sour cream, and other cultured dairy products.

When cheese is made, a clear greenish liquid drains from the cheese curd. While coagulated casein proteins form the cheese curd, the clear liquid, known as whey, contains whey proteins. *Whey proteins* form a film along the bottom of pans and on the surface of milk when milk is heated. Milk must not be left unattended on the heat because a film of whey quickly burns onto the pan bottom, ruining flavor and color.

If sugar is in a formula where milk or cream is heated, add some or all the sugar to the milk before heating, to prevent whey proteins from coating and sticking to the bottom of the pan.

Whey proteins are just one of the nutrients in whey. Whey is also rich in lactose, calcium salts, and riboflavin. The slight greenish tinge in whey is from riboflavin, one of the B vitamins in milk.

Lactose, also called milk sugar, makes up about 50 percent of the MSNF of milk. Its sweetness, which is about one-fifth that of sucrose, contributes to the characteristic flavor of milk. Lactose is a disaccharide consisting of a glucose molecule bonded to galactose. Unlike most sugars, lactose is not fermented by yeast.

WHAT IS LACTOSE INTOLERANCE?

Many people experience intestinal discomfort after consuming large quantities of milk. This lactose intolerance occurs because their bodies do not contain high enough levels of an enzyme—lactase—that breaks down lactose to glucose and galactose. The undigested lactose passes into the lower intestine, where bacteria break it down and produce acid and gas.

Lactose intolerance causes intestinal discomfort, but it is not a life-threatening allergy. Those experiencing the discomforts of lactose intolerance should consume only those dairy ingredients low in lactose, such as cultured dairy products and cheese. Another strategy is to add a product called Lactaid to milk before it is consumed. Lactaid contains lactase, which breaks down the lactose to glucose and galactose. Because glucose and galactose are sweeter than lactose, milk treated with Lactaid is sweeter than regular milk.

A third successful strategy for those with lactose intolerance is to slowly consume larger and larger quantities of dairy ingredients. By taking it slowly, lactose-intolerant individuals gradually increase the level of enzyme in their bodies, so they can enjoy more dairy products in their diet.

MILK PRODUCTS

Fluid Milk

Fluid milk is classified by its fat content, which is standardized by the processor. Fat content in milk ranges from 3.25 percent or higher for whole milk to essentially 0 percent for fat-free (skim) milk. The minimum MSNF for milk is 8.25 percent in the United States and 8.0 percent in Canada; the rest is water.

For freshest dairy flavor, fluid milk is the product of choice. Fluid, not dry, milk is best in baked custards, cream pies, vanilla custard sauce, frozen desserts, and pastry cream. When using fluid milk in yeast doughs, scald it first by heating to about 180°F (82°C). This denatures the whey protein (glutathione) that interferes with gluten development.

Dry Milk

Dry milk solids (DMS) are made by removing most—all but about 3–5 percent—of the water from fat-free or whole milk. Most DMS is made by the spray-dry process, in which partly evaporated milk is sprayed as a fine mist into a heated chamber. The milk dries almost instantly and falls to the bottom of the chamber as a powder.

Dry milk takes up less space in the bakeshop than fluid milk, and it requires no refrigeration. When DMS is made from whole milk, it is sometimes called dry whole milk or powdered whole milk. Because dry whole milk contains milk fat, it oxidizes easily, producing a rancid, off flavor. When DMS is made from fat-free milk, it is sometimes called nonfat dry milk, powdered skim milk, NDM, or NFDM. Nonfat dry milk has a much longer shelf life than dry whole milk and is much more common in bakeshops.

DMS does not have the same fresh dairy flavor as fluid milk, so it should not be used in custards and creams. Instead, use DMS in baked goods like breads, cakes, and cookies. Although many cake, bread, and muffin formulas call for fluid milk, dry milk solids are acceptable, even desirable, in these products.

DMS can be purchased with varying amounts of heat treatment. High-heat DMS is held at 190°F (88°C) for a minimum of 30 minutes, then dried. It is the best choice for use in yeast-raised baked goods because the heat treatment denatures the whey protein that reduces gluten development and bread quality. The heat treatment also increases the ability of milk proteins to absorb water.

Low-heat DMS is not often used in the bakeshop, although it would be acceptable for all baked goods except yeast-raised doughs. Instant nonfat dry milk purchased in the supermarket is an example of low-heat DMS. While it has a fresher taste than

HOW TO USE DRY MILK SOLIDS

It is very easy to convert formulas that call for fluid milk to ones using dry milk solids. For every pound of fluid whole milk, use 2 ounces (0.12 pounds) DMS and 14 ounces (0.88 pounds) water. If your formula is in metric units, use 120 grams DMS and 880 grams water for every liter of milk. Blend the DMS with dry ingredients, such as flour and sugar, or cream it with shortening. DMS does not easily mix with water, so it is best not to reconstitute it before use.

TABLE 12.1 ■ MINIMUM MILK FAT STANDARDS FOR CREAM PRODUCTS SOLD IN THE UNITED STATES AND CANADA

NAME	U.S. MINIMUM STANDARD	CANADIAN MINIMUM STANDARD
Heavy cream	36%	—
Whipping cream	30%	32%
Cream	—	10%
Light cream	18%	—
Half-and-half	10.5%	—

high-heat DMS, low-heat DMS does not provide the added benefits to baked goods that high-heat DMS provides. Where dry milk solids are added to increase the solids of ice cream mixes, low-heat DMS would be the best choice.

Cream

Cream sold in North America is pasteurized, often under UHT conditions. The main advantage of UHT—ultrapasteurized—cream is that it has an extended shelf life. While cartons of cream used in the bakeshop are often UHT pasteurized, they are not aseptically packed and therefore must be refrigerated.

Besides being pasteurized, cream is usually homogenized. Homogenization makes whipping more difficult, but many heavy creams and whipping creams contain added emulsifiers and stabilizing gums to aid in whipping. At very high levels of fat—around 40 percent—even homogenized cream whips easily.

Cream is classified by the amount of milk fat it contains. Milk fat contributes much of the creamy rich flavor of cream. It forms tiny oil droplets and small solid fat particles that stay suspended when the cream is homogenized. It is the presence of these droplets and fat particles that gives cream its thick, smooth consistency. Because cream is high in fat, it is also high in carotenoid pigments that dissolve in fat, giving it a yellowish creamy tinge.

In the United States, heavy cream contains between 36 and 40 percent milk fat. It is often the only cream stocked in the bakeshop. Other cream products include whipping cream, light cream, and half-and-half. Light cream from the United States can be made by mixing equal parts heavy cream and whole milk; half-and-half can be made by mixing equal parts light cream and whole milk.

Nationally, Canada has two types of cream: cream and whipping cream. Canadian provincial governments often regulate the milk fat content of other cream products, such as table cream, half-and-half, cereal cream, and light cream sold regionally. Table 12.1 lists the minimum milk fat standards for cream products in both the United States and Canada.

WHAT IS DOUBLE CREAM?

England is known for the quality of its dairy products, including its cream. Two common types of cream sold in Great Britain are single cream and double cream. Single cream is equivalent to American light cream. Double cream, at over 48 percent milk fat, is thicker and richer than any cream commonly sold in North America. Double Devon cream, from Devonshire, England, is considered by many to be the finest in Great Britain.

Evaporated Milk and Sweetened Condensed Milk

Evaporated milk and sweetened condensed milk are specialty ingredients that have occasional uses in the bakeshop. They are generally purchased in cans, which can be stored at room temperature until opened. Both are made by removing water from milk. Evaporated milk is concentrated until it contains twice the milk fat and twice the MSNF of regular fluid milk. Sweetened condensed milk has had more water removed and has sugar added. Low-fat and fat-free versions of both evaporated and sweetened condensed milk are available.

Evaporated milk and sweetened condensed milk cannot be used interchangeably. The main difference between the two products is the sugar that is added to sweetened condensed milk. Because of this sugar, sweetened condensed milk is thicker, sweeter, and denser, and has a more caramelized color and flavor, than evaporated milk. The color and flavor are the result of Maillard browning that occurs from heating the products.

The added sugar in sweetened condensed milk means that it can be—but usually is not—left open at room temperature for days and it will not spoil.

Evaporated and sweetened condensed milks cost more than liquid whole milk, but there are advantages to each. They are easier to store because they take up less space, and they last indefinitely at room temperature until opened. This is particularly important in tropical regions where refrigeration is not readily available. More importantly, the low water content and caramelized flavor in these products can be used to an advantage. For example, a common use of sweetened condensed milk is in making Mexican flan, which is custard with a caramelized milk flavor. Mexican flan is traditionally made with milk that has been boiled and evaporated with sugar, which is essentially sweetened condensed milk. Other common uses for sweetened condensed milk and evaporated milk are pumpkin pie, fudge, and caramel, where it provides a creamy smooth texture. Evaporated milk substitutes for cream in certain low-fat products.

Cultured Dairy Products

Cultured dairy products are fermented by the addition of live bacteria, usually lactic acid bacteria. *Lactic acid bacteria* ferment lactose to lactic acid and other flavorful products. The lactic acid lowers the pH of cultured dairy products and provides a pleasant sour

HOW DOES SUGAR PREVENT SPOILAGE IN SWEETENED CONDENSED MILK?

How is it that the addition of sugar allows an opened can of sweetened condensed milk to sit at room temperature and not spoil? After all, sugar is a source of food for most microorganisms.

Microorganisms require more than food to survive. They require moisture and warmth, for example, and most require air (oxygen). Moisture is extremely important to microorganisms, as it is to all living things. If moisture is unavailable, microorganisms dehydrate and their cells shrivel and malfunction.

Recall that sugar is hygroscopic, that is, it attracts water and bonds to it. When water is bound to sugar, it is unavailable to microorganisms. Just as sailors at sea cannot quench their thirst with seawater, microorganisms cannot easily quench their thirst with sugar syrup. Their cells shrivel and cannot function, as if water were not present at all. The water activity is said to be lowered and the osmotic pressure raised by the high concentration of sugar or salt. Below a certain water activity and above a certain osmotic pressure, microorganisms cannot survive.

This is what happens in sweetened condensed milk. Even though it is liquid, it has a low water activity, so it will not easily spoil. Other foods preserved with high amounts of sugar include honey, molasses, jams, and jellies.

WHAT IS A PROBIOTIC?

Fermented—cultured—dairy products have a long history of use for their health benefits. It is thought that when the friendly bacteria from these products make it to the intestinal tract, they help maintain the health of the intestinal tract by reducing the growth of undesirable bacteria. When consumed for health benefits, these live bacteria are often called probiotics. Recall from Chapter 3, however, that bacteria and other microorganisms die during the baking process. Whatever health benefits provided by the probiotics in cultured dairy products are lost during baking.

flavor. It also thickens and gels cultured dairy products because the acid causes casein proteins to coagulate. Lactic acid bacteria are considered friendly bacteria because they have positive effects on the flavor and texture of dairy products and because they help prevent the growth of undesirable spoilage bacteria in these foods. It is because of friendly bacteria that cultured dairy products have a longer shelf life than milk products that are not cultured.

Often, formulas for baked goods that contain cultured dairy products also contain baking soda. When acid from the dairy product reacts with baking soda, carbon dioxide gas is produced. This can be a significant source of leavening for some baked goods. If there is more acid in the dairy product than is needed to react with the baking soda, the excess acid will lower the pH of the mix, tenderizing and whitening the baked product.

CULTURED BUTTERMILK

Originally, buttermilk was the fluid remaining after cream was churned into butter. Today, cultured buttermilk is made by adding lactic acid bacteria to milk, usually low-fat or fat-free milk. It is thicker than regular milk because of the effect of acid on the casein proteins.

Cultured buttermilk is used in buttermilk biscuits and certain other baked goods for flavor, whitening, tenderizing, and leavening. Cultured buttermilk can also be purchased as a dry powder.

A reasonable substitute for cultured buttermilk is *sour milk*, prepared by adding 1 tablespoon (15 milliliters) vinegar to 8 ounces (225 grams) fluid milk. Sour milk does not have the thick consistency of cultured buttermilk and it has a sharper sourness, but it does provide the same tenderness, whiteness, and leavening. Notice that sour milk is not the same as soured milk, which is milk that has spoiled. Soured, spoiled milk has an unpleasant flavor and should never be used in baked goods.

Other cultured milk products include kefir cultured milk and acidophilus cultured milk. These products are similar to buttermilk but are cultured with different bacteria, giving them distinctive flavors.

SOUR CREAM

In the United States, sour cream is made by adding lactic acid bacteria to light cream (18–20 percent milk fat). In Canada, sour cream can be slightly lower in milk fat (14 percent minimum). The lactic acid causes the proteins in sour cream to coagulate to a gelled consistency; gums and starches may be added to further thicken the product. Use sour cream in cheesecakes, coffee cakes, and certain pastry doughs. Low-fat and fat-free sour cream products are available. These products are higher in moisture and less rich in flavor than regular sour cream. Low-fat sour cream, which is essentially cultured half-and-half (minimum 10.5 percent milk fat), is often satisfactory as a substitute for regular sour cream in baking.

CRÈME FRAÎCHE

Crème fraîche is a cultured cream product used throughout France. The traditional way of making crème fraîche is to set unpasteurized milk in a pan at room temperature, allowing cream to rise to the top. After about 12 hours, the cream is skimmed off. During that time, natural bacteria in the unpasteurized milk ripen the cream, turning it into a mildly sour, thickened product. Because crème fraîche is high in fat (minimum 30 percent in France), it is much smoother, richer, and more velvety than sour cream. In Mexico, a similar product is called *crema fresca*.

Pastry chefs sometimes make a substitute crème fraîche by adding a small amount of cultured buttermilk or sour cream to heavy cream and allowing it to stand in a warm spot for 8 hours or more before refrigerating. As the cream ripens from the growth of the lactic acid bacteria, it thickens and develops a sour flavor. This product is similar to sour cream, except it has a higher milk fat content.

CLOTTED CREAM

Clotted cream is a thick, spreadable dairy product with a minimum fat content of 55 percent. The most prized clotted cream is from Devonshire, the region in England where it has been made for centuries. The traditional way of making Devonshire clotted cream starts like crème fraîche, with ripened cream rising from milk set out in shallow pans. Once separated, however, the cream is slowly heated to about 180°F (82°C) and held for about an hour until it starts to form a golden-colored crust. The scalded cream is removed from the heat and slowly cooled, and the thick crust of buttery clotted cream is skimmed off the top. Clotted cream is traditionally paired with jam and served on scones at teatime in England.

Small quantities of clotted cream are still made the traditional way at dairy farms in western England, but clotted cream today is more likely to be made from unripened (not cultured) pasteurized cream.

Cheeses

Cheese is made when coagulated casein milk proteins—curds—are separated from whey. Most, but not all, cheeses are classified as cultured dairy products, meaning that live bacteria produce acid that forms cheese curd.

Cheese can be unripened or ripened (aged). Soft, unripened cheeses, like cream cheese, Neufchâtel, baker's cheese, ricotta, and mascarpone, are the most common cheeses used in the bakeshop. Ripened cheeses typically have stronger, more distinct flavors. Examples of ripened cheeses include Parmesan cheese, blue cheese, cheddar cheese, and Brie.

MAKE A SIMPLE CHEESE

The simplest cheese to make is yogurt cheese. Yogurt cheese—*labneh*—is traditional in the Middle East. It is made by draining liquid whey from yogurt. Any yogurt—including low-fat or fat-free yogurt—can be used, but avoid brands that contain added starches or gums. Starches and gums prevent whey from draining freely.

To drain, simply place yogurt on several layers of cheesecloth and hang over a bowl to catch the whey. Keep it loosely covered and refrigerate. The process takes as little as several hours, but continue to drain for a day or more, if drier cheese is preferred.

The resulting yogurt cheese is similar to cream cheese in texture, but it has a stronger acid bite. Try yogurt cheese as a substitute for cream cheese in cheesecake.

CREAM CHEESE, NEUFCHÂTEL, AND BAKER'S CHEESE

Cream cheese, Neufchâtel, and baker's cheese are similar. Their curds form from the addition of lactic acid bacteria and often enzymes to milk or cream. Once liquid whey is drained off, the curds are processed until they have the right consistency. All three cheeses have a mild, slightly acidic flavor and a soft, smooth texture. All are used in pastry fillings and cheesecakes. Often, gums are added to increase creaminess and firmness, especially in the lower fat cheeses. Usually, a combination of xanthan gum and locust bean gum are added.

Of the three, cream cheese is the highest in fat. It must contain a minimum of 33 percent milk fat (30 percent in Canada), the same as whipping cream. Neufchâtel is lower in fat (20 percent minimum) than cream cheese; in fact, Neufchâtel is often labeled low-fat cream cheese. Baker's cheese is essentially fat-free and is sometimes labeled fat-free cream cheese. Baker's cheese is less expensive than cream cheese but it is also noticeably less rich.

Because low-fat and fat-free versions of cream cheese often contain high levels of gums, these products can be successfully used in products like low-fat cheesecake without sacrificing texture. The flavor of low-fat cheesecake, however, is usually not as rich, full, and satisfying unless some adjustments are made. Many flavors dissolve in fat, and when fat is removed, flavors are released differently, often more quickly. With a little bit of experimenting, however, full-flavored lower-fat versions of cheesecake and many other dairy-based desserts can be created. Chapter 14 provides suggestions for improving the flavor of food products, including low-fat foods.

> **HELPFUL HINT**
>
> Soft, unripened cheeses blend well into other ingredients as long as they are added properly. When making cheesecake, soften the cream cheese by beating it with a paddle before blending it with softer, more liquid ingredients. If the cream cheese is not first softened in this manner, it forms lumps in the batter that remain once the cheesecake is baked. In fact, a good rule of thumb is to never blend two ingredients together that have different consistencies before first softening the firmer ingredient to the consistency of the softer.

RICOTTA CHEESE

Ricotta cheese has a slightly grainy consistency and a mildly sweet dairy flavor. Originally, thrifty Italian housewives made ricotta cheese by adding acid to liquid whey that was left over from cheese making. Today, ricotta is often made by adding acid or bacteria and enzymes to whole milk or part skim milk. This soft, moist cheese is used in cannoli, ricotta cheesecake, and other Italian specialties.

MASCARPONE

Mascarpone is an Italian cheese best known as an ingredient in tiramisu. At 70–75 percent milk fat, mascarpone is almost as high in fat as butter is. Its flavor and texture are a cross between cream cheese and butter, or similar to a very rich clotted cream. Mascarpone is commonly made by adding acid to heated heavy cream. The combination of acid and heat coagulates the casein, forming a fine, smooth curd that drains slowly from liquid whey. Since mascarpone is a relatively easy cheese to make, some specialty pastry shops prepare their own.

> **HELPFUL HINT**
>
> Be careful when mixing or creaming mascarpone cheese. Unappealing butter lumps form when it is overmixed, much as cream turns to butter when it is overwhipped. To avoid overmixing, mix on low speed no more than necessary.

QUARK

Quark originates from Germany. Different versions of this mild, unripened soft-curd cheese are available with different amounts of fat. Quark has a texture that is slightly smoother than ricotta. If quark is unavailable, ricotta cheese can be substituted by

CREATING DAIRY-FREE PRODUCTS FOR THOSE WITH LACTOSE-INTOLERANCE

Because dairy ingredients are complex mixtures, they provide many functions in pastries and baked goods. However, the effects are usually not large, except for products like custard-based products. This means that, unlike eggs, fat, or flour, milk is relatively easy to leave out of baked goods. Often simply substituting milk with water is all that is needed. Other times, any number of products can be used in place of milk or cheese, including rice milk, almond milk, soy milk, or soybean curd (tofu). As with using low-fat dairy ingredients, the problem often becomes one of balancing flavor, not one of improving texture.

blending it in a food processor; for higher-fat quark, mix ricotta cheese with cream cheese. Quark is used in German cheesecake and in other pastries.

WHEY PRODUCTS

Recall that liquid whey, the greenish by-product of cheese manufacturing, is high in proteins—whey proteins—and lactose. It is also high in many vitamins and minerals, such as riboflavin, calcium, and phosphorus.

Liquid whey was once discarded or used as animal feed. Today it is converted into many valuable products. One such product is dry whey powder, made by pasteurizing and drying liquid whey. Dry whey is similar in many ways to DMS and can be used in baked goods at a lower cost.

FUNCTIONS OF MILK AND MILK PRODUCTS

The following functions apply primarily to fluid milk and to dry milk solids (DMS). Where a function applies specifically to one dairy product and not to others, it is specified.

Main Functions

INCREASES CRUST COLOR

The combination of proteins and lactose, a fast-browning sugar, in dairy products provides the right mix for Maillard browning. Recall that Maillard browning is the breakdown of sugars and protein, and that it contributes color and fresh-baked flavor to baked goods. When baked goods are prepared with milk instead of water, baking times and temperatures may need to be lowered to reduce excessive browning.

DELAYS STALING

Several components in dairy products, including proteins, lactose, and milk fat, prevent starch retrogradation—staling—in the crumb of baked goods. This is particularly noticeable in lean yeast breads, which are typically low in stale-retarding ingredients, like sugar and fat. By preventing staling, dairy products extend shelf life in baked goods.

INCREASES CRUST SOFTNESS

Products like bread and cream puffs that are made with milk instead of water have softer crusts than those made with water. For example, crusty French baguettes contain water. Soft-crusted pullman or pan bread contains milk. Softening occurs because milk proteins and sugar absorb water, delaying its evaporation from the crust.

BLENDS FLAVORS AND PROVIDES RICHNESS IN FLAVOR

Milk modifies the flavor of baked goods. In cakes and breads, for example, milk blends flavors and reduces saltiness. In baked custards, vanilla custard sauces, and pastry cream, milk products provide a rich, full flavor, especially when they are high in milk fat.

PROVIDES A FINE, EVEN CRUMB TO BAKED GOODS

Some baked goods—yeast breads, in particular—have a finer, more even crumb when prepared with milk or dry milk solids. It is likely a combination of milk proteins, emulsifiers, and calcium salts in milk that help stabilize small air bubbles. The smaller the air bubbles, the finer the crumb.

FORMS A STABLE FOAM

Cream whips into foam if it has a minimum milk fat content of about 28 percent. Both whipping cream and heavy cream can be whipped satisfactorily, but heavy cream, because of its higher fat content, produces a more stable foam.

Besides using cream with a higher fat content, you can stabilize whipped cream by first chilling the cream to solidify the milk fat; by slowly adding sugar while whipping; or by folding in a gelatin solution or another stabilizer. Many brands of heavy cream contain added emulsifiers, such as mono- and diglycerides, to aid whipping.

Milk proteins also form stable foams. For example, the froth on cappuccino is from milk proteins trapping air. Evaporated milk, which is high in milk proteins, can be whipped to a stable foam when chilled, producing a whipped cream substitute.

Other Functions

AIDS IN THE CREAMING OF SHORTENING

The addition of dry milk solids to creamed shortenings aids air incorporation and stabilization. The emulsifiers and proteins in dry milk seem to provide these benefits.

HOW IS WHIPPED CREAM LIKE WHIPPED EGG WHITE?

Both whipped cream and whipped egg white are relatively stable foams, meaning that they contain air bubbles trapped in liquid. Both are more stable with the addition of sugar. Beyond that, whipped cream and whipped egg white are quite different. While it is the proteins in eggs that stabilize whipped egg white, it is milk fat that stabilizes whipped cream. Here is how it works.

Whipping disrupts the protective film that surrounds fat globules suspended in cream. The unprotected fat globules form tiny clumps with bits of solidified milk fat. These clumps of milk fat surround each air bubble, stabilizing them.

Fat clumps are not as effective as egg proteins in stabilizing foams, so while egg white increases up to eight times in volume, cream barely doubles.

ABSORBS MOISTURE

Proteins in milk act as driers, absorbing moisture and increasing the water absorption rate of yeast doughs. The amount of extra water needed in yeast doughs is ounce for ounce about the same as the amount of DMS added. This means yeast doughs made with milk require more liquid than doughs made with water. This ability to absorb water contributes to the ability of milk proteins to delay bread staling.

AIDS IN THE COAGULATION OF EGG PROTEINS

Custards made with water instead of milk do not firm up properly, because milk aids egg coagulation. Milk also has been shown to firm up the crumb in cakes, making them spongier and more resilient. It appears that both milk proteins and the calcium salts in milk strengthen egg structure, much as the calcium salts in hard water strengthen gluten structure.

PROVIDES MOISTURE

Because fluid milk is about 88 percent water, anytime it is used in baked goods, it contributes moisture for dissolving sugars and salts and for developing gluten. Even heavy cream is over 50 percent water.

ADDS NUTRITIONAL VALUE

Milk contains high-quality protein, vitamins—riboflavin, vitamin A, and vitamin D—and minerals, especially calcium. This reflects the fact that milk is the sole source of food for the newborn calf. However, dairy products, such as heavy cream, that contain milk fat are high in saturated fat, which increases blood cholesterol and contributes to coronary heart disease.

Milk is a significant source of calcium in North America. Calcium is needed for bone growth, and a lack of calcium in the diet has been associated with osteoporosis, which is a serious loss of bone structure. Milk is fortified with vitamin D because vitamin D aids in the absorption of calcium in the body.

STORAGE AND HANDLING

Fluid milk and reconstituted dry milk products spoil easily. Bacteria multiply and produce acids and off flavors, souring the milk. While it is usually not harmful, soured milk has an unpleasant flavor and should be discarded.

Beyond bacterial spoilage, the flavor of milk is highly susceptible to other changes, either from absorbing aromas or from chemical reactions that occur from exposure to excessive heat or light.

Pasteurized whole milk has a shelf life of about two weeks. It and all other dairy products are marked with a shelf life or use-by code. These codes are meant as a guide. Actual shelf life depends on many factors, the main one being how well the product has been stored. Always smell and taste dairy products before use, and use your judgment in deciding whether an ingredient is appropriate or not. Do not mistake the formation of a layer of fat in heavy cream for a sure sign of spoilage. If a layer of fat forms, shake the container before use.

The following guidelines should be followed when handling fluid milk, to ensure microbiological safety and freedom from the development of off flavors.

- Check the temperature when it is delivered; it should be 45°F (7°C) or less. If it is warmer, reject the shipment.

- Always refrigerate milk when not in use, ideally at 34°–38°F (1°–3°C).

- Close containers immediately after use. Stray microorganisms from the air can land in open cartons and shorten shelf life.

- Maintain a clean refrigerator. Odors from other foods or from unclean conditions can pass through containers and be absorbed. If necessary, use separate refrigerators for foods that have strong odors.

- Protect from light. Fluid milk is susceptible to ultraviolet (UV) light damage.

While cultured dairy products like yogurt, buttermilk, and sour cream have an extended shelf life, their acid content continues to increase over time. Their flavor gradually becomes stronger, sharper, and more pronounced. Mold can grow on cultured products that have been improperly stored or stored too long. Any cultured dairy product containing mold should be discarded.

Soft, unripened cheeses used in the bakeshop are highly perishable. Those high in moisture, such as ricotta cheese, are especially perishable. Once opened, ricotta cheese should be used within two to five days. Cream cheese, Neufchâtel, and baker's cheese last a little longer. Once opened, they should be tightly wrapped or covered to prevent drying, and they should be stored in the refrigerator for no more than two weeks.

Nonfat dry milk is easy to store. It needs no refrigeration unless reconstituted, but it should be covered and kept in a cool, dry place. This keeps dry milk from absorbing strong odors or from clumping and caking with changes in moisture. If nonfat dry milk absorbs water and hardens or clumps, pulverize and sift it before use. While it has a long shelf life—at least a year and possibly up to three, if properly stored—nonfat dry milk eventually develops off flavors and darkens and browns. Whole dry milk contains milk fat that oxidizes to a rancid, off flavor. Whole dry milk has a maximum shelf life of only six months, even when stored under ideal conditions.

Canned evaporated and sweetened condensed milk do not spoil even after several years, if unopened. Over time, however, they darken, develop stronger flavors, and change in consistency. Once opened, evaporated milk requires refrigeration, and it is best to do so with sweetened condensed milk as well.

WHAT IS LIGHT-INDUCED FLAVOR?

Ultraviolet light from the sun or from fluorescent lighting is high in energy and causes chemical changes to occur in foods. Some of these changes produce off flavors in milk stored in transparent containers. These changes can occur quickly, within an hour of exposure. They significantly reduce the acceptability of milk with consumers, and they can reduce the nutritional quality of milk.

One light-induced chemical change involves the breakdown of an amino acid in milk protein. This reaction takes place in the presence of the vitamin riboflavin. The result is the production of an off flavor in milk and a loss of riboflavin. The light-induced, off flavor is sometimes described as

the smell of burnt feathers or burnt potatoes, and it can happen within minutes of exposure to bright sunlight, longer under fluorescent lighting.

Another light-induced flavor change in milk is the breakdown of vitamin A, which is most likely to occur in low-fat and fat-free milk products. When vitamin A breaks down, it produces an oxidized, off flavor that is sometimes described as the smell of wet cardboard or old oil. Again, the nutritional quality of the milk is reduced from exposure to light, this time with the destruction of vitamin A. Ironically, this cardboard flavor is more likely to occur in milk stored in clear plastic containers, not those stored in cardboard cartons.

QUESTIONS FOR REVIEW

1. Why is milk pasteurized? Why is it homogenized?

2. What is UHT milk? How does it differ from regular pasteurized milk?

3. What are MSNF?

4. What is in milk fat?

5. Name the two main categories of proteins in milk.

6. What does whey consist of?

7. What is DMS? Why is DMS not recommended for use in custard cream pie?

8. What is the difference between low-heat and high-heat DMS? Which is more commonly used in the bakeshop? In what products is it commonly used?

9. Why might it be better to add DMS with sugar when creaming fat than to add it later with flour and other dry ingredients?

10. A formula calls for light cream but all that is available is whole milk and heavy cream. What should you do?

11. A formula calls for evaporated milk, but all that is available is sweetened condensed milk. Can sweetened condensed milk be used instead of evaporated milk? Why or why not?

12. What is meant by a cultured dairy product? Provide examples of cultured dairy products.

13. What is a probiotic? How does heat from the oven affect probiotics?

14. How do cultured dairy products contribute to leavening in baked goods?

15. How do cultured dairy products contribute to a whiter crumb in baked goods?

16. What is the difference between cream cheese, Neufchâtel, and baker's cheese?

17. Which types of dairy products can be successfully whipped into a stable foam?

18. List four factors important in producing stable whipped cream.

19. How do dairy products, such as milk, extend the shelf life of baked goods?

20. Why should dry milk solids be stored covered in a cool dry place?

QUESTIONS FOR DISCUSSION

1. A formula calls for 32 ounces (1 liter) of milk, but you would like to use dry milk instead. How much dry milk and water should be substituted for liquid milk?

2. You want to produce a baked custard dessert for people with lactose intolerance. You try using soy milk instead of whole milk, but find that the baked custard doesn't set up properly. Why might this be?

EXERCISES AND EXPERIMENTS

1. Comparing the Quality of Éclair Shells Prepared with Different Liquids

Pâte à choux is the name of the dough used in making cream puffs, profiteroles, and éclairs. It is just as often made with milk as it is made with water. While either liquid can be used, the results are somewhat different. In this experiment, you will prepare pâte à choux—also called choux paste or éclair paste—and bake up éclair shells using both liquids and evaluate the results for yourself.

OBJECTIVES

To demonstrate how the type of liquid used in pâte à choux affects:

- The crispness and the extent of Maillard browning on the crust of éclair shells
- The moistness, tenderness, and height of the éclair shells
- The overall flavor of the éclair shells
- The overall acceptability of the éclair shells

PRODUCTS PREPARED

Éclair shells made with:

- Water (control product)
- Milk
- Other, if desired (50:50 blend of water and milk, soy milk, milk with butter instead of shortening, etc.)

MATERIALS AND EQUIPMENT

- Heavy-bottom saucepan
- Pâte à choux dough, enough to make 12 or more éclairs of each variation
- Large pastry bags and plain tube
- Ruler

PROCEDURE

- Preheat oven according to formula.
- Line sheet pans with parchment paper; label with the type of liquid to be used in pâte à choux.
- Prepare pâte à choux doughs using formula below or using any basic pâte à choux formula (use all-purpose shortening instead of butter to eliminate milk solids coming from fat). Prepare one batch of dough for each variation.
- Place a plain tube in pastry bag and fill bag with pâte à choux.
- Pipe dough onto lined sheet pans into strips about ¾ inch (2 cm) wide and 3 inches (8 cm) long.
- Use an oven thermometer placed in center of oven to read oven temperature; record results here _____.
- Place filled sheet pans in preheated oven and set timer according to formula (note that most pâte à choux formulas have oven temperature lowered after first 10–15 minutes).
- Bake éclairs until brown and firm to touch. To confirm doneness, remove one éclair from oven and allow to cool; if éclair holds its shape and does not collapse, remove remaining éclairs from oven. Record bake times in Results Table 1, which follows.
- Allow éclairs to cool slowly to room temperature on sheet pans in a warm place.
- Record any potential sources of error that might make it difficult to draw the proper conclusions from the experiment. In particular, be aware of difficulties in how dough was mixed and handled, how long dough was heated, and any problems with ovens or with bake times.
- When éclairs are completely cooled, evaluate average height as follows:
  - Slice three éclair shells from each batch lengthwise, being careful not to compress.

- Measure height of each éclair shell by placing a ruler along the flat edge at its center. Record results for each of three éclair shells from each batch in 1/16" (10 mm) increments in Results Table 1.
- Calculate the average éclair shell height by adding the heights of the éclairs and dividing this by 3; record results in Results Table 1.

- Evaluate the sensory characteristics of completely cooled products and record evaluations in Results Table 2, which follows. Be sure to compare each in turn to the control product and consider the following:

  - Crust color, from very light to very dark, on a scale of one to five
  - Crust texture (soft and moist, soft and dry, crisp and dry, etc.)
  - Inside appearance (color, amount of webbing, etc.)
  - Inside texture (tough/tender, moist/dry, etc.)
  - Overall flavor (egg flavor, floury taste, saltiness, etc.)
  - Overall acceptability, from highly unacceptable to highly acceptable, on a scale of one to five
  - Add any additional comments, as necessary.

Pâte à Choux

INGREDIENT	POUND	OUNCE	GRAMS	BAKER'S PERCENTAGE
Water		8	225	181
Shortening, all-purpose		3	85	68
Salt		0.1	3	2.4
Bread flour		4.4	125	100
Eggs, whole		8	225	181
Total	1	7.5	663	532.4

Method of Preparation

1. Preheat oven to 425°F (220°C); bake at 425°F (220°C) for the first 10 minutes, then reduce heat to 375°F (190°C) and finish baking at that temperature, for about another 10–15 minutes.

2. Have eggs at room temperature.

3. Combine liquid, shortening, and salt in a heavy saucepan. Bring to a full boil, melting shortening completely.

4. Remove pan from heat and add flour all at once; stir quickly and vigorously with a wooden spoon.

5. Return to heat and continue stirring vigorously until dough forms a smooth, dry ball that does not cling to the spoon or to the sides of the pan. Do not overcook or dough will not puff properly.

6. Transfer dough to bowl of mixer and add eggs slowly (about 2 ounces/60 grams at a time), beating on medium speed after each addition. Eggs should be completely mixed in before the next portion is added. If desired, eggs can be beaten in by hand.

7. Continue beating mixture until all egg is absorbed. Dough should hold its shape when lifted on the end of a spoon, but it should still be smooth, moist, and workable.

8. Use dough immediately.

SOURCES OF ERROR

RESULTS TABLE 1 ■ EVALUATION OF BAKE TIMES AND HEIGHT OF ÉCLAIR SHELLS MADE WITH DIFFERENT LIQUIDS

TYPE OF LIQUID	BAKE TIME (IN MINUTES)	HEIGHT OF EACH OF THREE ÉCLAIR SHELLS	AVERAGE HEIGHT OF ONE ÉCLAIR SHELL	COMMENTS
Water (control product)				
Milk				

RESULTS TABLE 2 ■ SENSORY CHARACTERISTICS OF ÉCLAIR SHELLS MADE WITH DIFFERENT LIQUIDS

TYPE OF LIQUID	CRUST COLOR AND TEXTURE	INSIDE APPEARANCE AND TEXTURE	OVERALL FLAVOR	OVERALL ACCEPTABILITY	COMMENTS
Water (control product)					
Milk					

 **CONCLUSIONS**

1. Compare éclair shells made with milk to those made with water (control product). What were the main differences in appearance, flavor, and texture? Explain the main reasons for these differences.

_____

_____

    a. Which of the two did you prefer, and why?

    _____

    _____

2. Were there any significant differences in bake times for the different éclair shells? If so, why might this be?

_____

_____

3. Did you have any sources of error that might significantly affect the results of your experiment? If so, what could you do differently next time to minimize error?

_____

_____

CHAPTER 13
LEAVENING AGENTS

CHAPTER OBJECTIVES

1. Review the process of leavening.
2. Discuss the three main leavening gases in baked goods.
3. Discuss different types of yeast.
4. Discuss different types of chemical leavening agents.
5. List and discuss the functions of leavening agents.

 ## INTRODUCTION

Baking powders are all alike, right? Not exactly. In fact, baking powders have some interesting and important differences that are often overlooked. This chapter discusses these differences. It also discusses each of the three main leavening gases in baked goods—air, steam, and carbon dioxide—as well as others.

Sometimes, bakers and pastry chefs categorize leavening by the method used for forming or adding the leavening gases into batters and doughs. The three categories are physical, biological, and chemical leavening. Information about each of these categories runs throughout the chapter, particularly in the section on leavening gases. As you read this information, notice how each leavening gas is added to baked goods in its own characteristic way. Also notice that leavening often starts before baked goods are placed in the oven.

THE PROCESS OF LEAVENING

Leavened baked goods are light and porous. They are higher in volume and more tender than if unleavened. Leavened baked goods are also easier to digest.

Before discussing the leavening process, understand that there are three forms of matter: *solid, liquid,* and *gas.* When temperature changes, matter can change from one form to another. For example, as temperatures rise, solid ice melts to liquid water, and liquid water evaporates to gaseous steam. Heat causes these changes, and in the

A BRIEF HISTORY OF LEAVENING

The very first breads were unleavened. They were more like flat tortillas made by moistening and baking ground nuts, cereal grains, or seeds. The Egyptians were probably the first to leaven bread. As early as 2,300 B.C., they used breadmash, which contained wild yeast from the air, to lighten doughs.

For many centuries after that, yeast was the only leavening agent added to baked goods. Chemical leavening agents were not introduced until the late 1700s. The first popular chemical leavening agent was pearl ash, a crude form of potassium carbonate, an alkali. Pearl ash was removed from the ashes of wood. Next came baking soda, also called sodium bicarbonate, which was used with sour milk or a cultured dairy product.

Almost a hundred years went by before cream of tartar, the acid by-product of winemaking, was commercially available. It was used in the first commercial baking powder, made by mixing cream of tartar and baking soda with cornstarch. This first baking powder was produced in San Francisco, near the winemaking region of California.

Baking powders were refined throughout the 1800s and 1900s, with newer, more versatile acids replacing cream of tartar. Today, several types of baking powders are available. They are discussed later in this chapter.

While these advancements were happening with chemical leavening agents, improvements were also made with yeast. Baker's yeast was first purified and sold in the 1800s. No longer was the baker at the mercy of the flavor and gassing properties of wild yeast starters. Few changes were made until the 1940s, when active dry yeast was developed. While active dry yeast is much less perishable than fresh yeast, it did not perform as well as fresh yeast and was not widely used by professional bakers. Not until the late 1970s, when instant yeast was developed, was there a product that combined the convenience of dry yeast with the performance of fresh.

process, molecules move faster and spread further apart. This expansion is the basis for leavening.

As gases expand from the heat of the oven, the force from these expanding gases pushes on wet, flexible cell walls, causing them to stretch. As long as structure builders stretch without excessive breaking, volume increases. When baked goods are removed from the oven, gases evaporate or contract back to their original volume. Products with strong structure retain their shape. Those with weak structure—such as soufflés and underbaked cakes—shrink in size or collapse as the gases evaporate or contract.

Timing is important. For best volume, gas expansion must occur while the baked good's structure is still stretchy and flexible, yet intact. In the case of yeast-raised baked goods, these ideal conditions occur during bulk fermentation, proofing, and the early stages of baking. Bread dough made with rye and other flours that do not contain sufficient gluten does not rise properly because, without gluten, the dough is not stretchy or intact. The gases from fermentation escape from the dough soon after they are formed.

LEAVENING GASES

Recall from Chapter 3 that the three main leavening gases in baked goods are steam, air, and carbon dioxide. Actually, all liquids and gases expand when heated, so all liquids and gases leaven, at least to some degree. It is just that steam, air, and carbon dioxide are common and plentiful in baked goods. Other liquids and gases that can be important in certain baked goods include alcohol and ammonia.

Steam

Steam, or water vapor, is the gaseous form of water. It forms when water, milk, eggs, syrups, or any other moisture-containing ingredient is heated. Steam is a very effective leavening agent because it expands to occupy over 1,600 times more space than water. Imagine the power of this huge increase in volume.

All baked goods rely on steam for at least some of their leavening because all baked goods contain water or another liquid. In fact, many baked goods rely on steam for leavening more than one might imagine. Sponge cakes, for example, rely on steam as much as air. That is because sponge cake batters are high in eggs, which are high in water.

Certain baked goods, such as popovers and choux pastry, are leavened almost exclusively by steam. These steam-leavened baked goods contain large amounts of liquid and are baked in very hot ovens.

Steam has other uses in baked goods. For example, steam is injected into ovens during the early stages of bread baking. This keeps crusts from forming too early, allowing bread to rise to its fullest potential without the constraints of a hardened crust.

Steam also affects the quality of bread crust once it does form. Because crust formation is delayed, the crust remains thin, and there is enough time and moisture from the steam to fully gelatinize starches. Gelatinized starches are needed to form a crisp, glossy crust.

HELPFUL HINT

If volume is low in baked goods, it could be that leavening was not properly timed with structure formation. Ask yourself the following questions, and make the appropriate changes.

- Is the oven working properly, and is it set to the correct temperature? For example, a low oven temperature slows the formation and expansion of gases. This is a problem especially with steam-leavened baked goods, such as choux pastry, puff pastry, and certain sponge cakes. On the other hand, if oven temperature is set too high, the outside crust could form and harden on the baked good before leavening gases have a chance to expand.

- Is the product properly formulated, and were ingredients measured accurately? High amounts of sugar and fats slow the coagulation of proteins and the gelatinization of starches, causing gases to be released before structure sets.

- Is the baking powder too fast- or slow-acting? You will learn shortly that baking powders vary in how quickly carbon dioxide is released, with slow-acting baking powders releasing most of their gases late in the baking process.

- Was unbaked batter left out too long before it was baked? Small bubbles tend to migrate to large bubbles in thin batters, and large bubbles tend to rise to the surface and escape.

THE MAGIC PUFF OF CHOUX PASTRY

Choux paste leavens by steam and bakes into hollow shells that can be filled with pastry cream, whipped cream, or savory fillings. Although thick and pasty, choux paste contains a large amount of liquid from water or milk, and eggs. It is baked in a very hot 425°F (220°C) oven, which allows the liquid to quickly evaporate to steam during the first 10 minutes of baking. This powerful leavening potential is captured by the high amount of eggs in choux paste.

Recall that raw egg proteins are twisted and coiled. As steam expands, egg proteins uncoil and stretch, and the paste puffs. Steam continues to expand, putting pressure on the stretched egg proteins. Eventually, most of the egg protein structure breaks from the pressure, creating a characteristic cavity in the baked choux paste. However, the outside shell wall—dry from the high heat—resists breakage. Gelatinized starch and coagulated egg proteins in these walls harden and set, defining the shell's final volume and shape.

Choux pastry shells must be thoroughly baked. If side walls are even slightly moist, they will be weak. When the shells are removed from the oven and steam evaporates and condenses back to water, egg proteins in still-wet walls recoil. When this happens, shells shrink and collapse.

To keep shrinking and collapsing from happening, do not rely on color alone to determine if choux pastry shells are properly baked. Instead, remove a test shell from the oven, break it open, and check that it is dry. If it is dry and does not collapse, then it is safe to remove the entire batch from the oven.

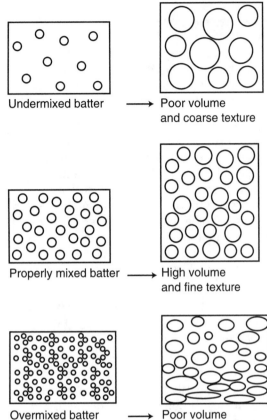

Undermixed batter → Poor volume and coarse texture

Properly mixed batter → High volume and fine texture

Overmixed batter → Poor volume and dense texture

FIGURE 13.1 The effect of mixing on the volume and crumb structure in baked goods

Air

It is easy to understand the importance of air to angel food cake and to sponge cake. After all, both contain egg whites that are whipped, and this adds volumes of air to the batter. It is a little harder to understand the importance of air to other baked goods, such as cookies and biscuits, because these batters and doughs do not noticeably change in volume after mixing.

Yet, without air, baked goods would not leaven.

Before discussing the importance of air to leavening, it is important to understand how air gets into batters and doughs. Air is added to batters and doughs by physical means—by creaming, whipping, sifting, folding, kneading, and even stirring. In fact, it is nearly impossible to mix ingredients without adding some air. These physical processes also serve to break large air cells into smaller ones, for a finer, more uniform crumb. For example, bread dough that has undergone bulk fermentation is punched down, to subdivide enlarged gas bubbles into many smaller ones.

AIR'S IMPORTANT ROLE IN LEAVENING

Like water, air is present in all baked products. Unlike water, air is already a gas. Recall from Chapter 3 that air is composed of a mixture of gases, primarily nitrogen. While it expands a little when heated, air is already a gas and does not expand nearly as much as water.

Air's role is subtler but no less important. Here's why. When air is added to batters and doughs, it is added as small air bubbles or air cells during the mixing stage. These air or gas cells present in the raw batter or dough can be thought of as seed cells. During baking, steam and carbon dioxide gas move to these seed cells, enlarging them. No matter how much water vaporizes into steam, no matter how much carbon dioxide is produced, no new air cells form during baking. Instead, steam and carbon dioxide fill and enlarge the seed cells that are already present in the batter or dough. Without these seed cells, there would be no place for the gases to go except out. Without these seed cells, there would be no leavening.

Understand this: Steam and other leavening gases may be formed during the baking process, but no new air cells form. The existing ones simply increase in size.

This leads to an explanation of air's important role in baking. The number of air cells in batters and doughs helps define the baked good's crumb structure. Figure 13.1 shows the relationships among the amount of mixing, the number of seed cells, and the final texture and volume of baked goods.

For example, if cake batter is undermixed and too few air cells are whipped into it, the cake's crumb will likely be coarse and the baked cake will be low in volume. Gases that expand during baking move to the few air cells formed during mixing, making them very large. The fewer the air cells, the larger those few will grow. Large air cells in baked goods mean a coarse crumb.

Likewise, overmixed batters and doughs will contain many seed cells. Egg and gluten proteins in the cell walls become overstretched, and cell walls are thin and weak. During baking, these thin cell walls stretch further and collapse. Again, the baked good will have poor volume.

PHOTO 13.1 Cakes made from properly creamed batter (top) and from undercreamed batter
Photo by Aaron Seyfarth

Carbon Dioxide

Carbon dioxide is the only one of the three main leavening gases that is not present in all batters and doughs (while carbon dioxide is present in air, it is present in trace amounts only). Carbon dioxide forms from yeast fermentation or from the use of chemical leavening agents. Yeast fermentation is a *biological source* of carbon dioxide. Chemical leavening agents, such as baking soda and baking powder, are considered *chemical sources* of carbon dioxide. Each is discussed in the sections that follow.

Sometimes the role of carbon dioxide in the leavening process is overestimated. Certainly, carbon dioxide is extremely important in yeast-raised baked goods and is very important in certain other products, such as baking powder biscuits. Many cakes, however, are leavened more by steam and air than by carbon dioxide. Liquid shortening cakes, for example, with their high-ratio liquid shortenings, are mixed until the batter is extremely light and filled with many tiny air cells. Being high in water, these cakes produce volumes of steam. Baking powder plays only a minor role in leavening liquid shortening cakes.

 # YEAST FERMENTATION

The biological or organic production of carbon dioxide results primarily from yeast fermentation. Yeast cells are very small single-celled microorganisms, so small that approximately 15 trillion of them are in one pound of compressed yeast. Fermentation is a process in which yeast cells break down sugars for energy. Yeast uses the energy for survival and for reproduction. Figure 13.2 shows a yeast cell reproducing by budding. Over time, the bud enlarges and eventually pinches off from the mother cell. Visible on the yeast cell in Figure 13.2 are scars from previous buddings. Although yeast breads had been produced for thousands of years, it wasn't until the mid-1800s that Louis Pasteur proved that living yeast was necessary for fermentation.

Yeast can be thought of as tiny enzyme machines, breaking sugars into smaller and simpler molecules with every step. Yeast lacks amylase and cannot break down starch into sugar, however. That is why amylase is an important additive in bread baking,

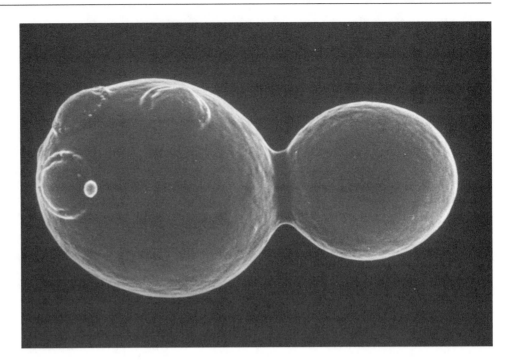

FIGURE 13.2 Budding yeast cell
Courtesy SPL/Photo Researchers

especially in lean doughs—those consisting of little more than flour, water, salt, and yeast. Malted barley flour—dry malt—is the most common means of adding amylase into lean doughs.

Before it was understood that there are many steps in the breakdown of sugars to carbon dioxide, it was thought that an enzyme called zymase was responsible. We now know that there are many steps to this process, called glycolysis, and separate enzymes control each step. The term *zymase* is still sometimes used to refer to the many enzymes in yeast that take part in the breakdown of sugars. The overall process is as follows.

$$\text{sugar} \xrightarrow{\text{yeast}} CO_2 + \text{alcohol} + \text{energy} + \text{flavor molecules}$$

When asked, many bakers would say that the most important end product of fermentation is carbon dioxide. However, fermentation produces as much alcohol as it does carbon dioxide. Alcohol evaporates to a gas and expands during the early stages of baking. This adds significantly to oven spring, the fast rising of bread during the first few minutes of baking, making alcohol an important leavening gas in yeast-raised baked goods.

Besides carbon dioxide and alcohol, small amounts of flavor molecules, including many acids, are produced during fermentation. These molecules are sometimes overlooked because there are too many to name, and each is generated in such small amounts. Yet, they are the source of the distinctive aroma of freshly baked yeast bread. Often long, slow fermentation is best for developing the most desirable flavor molecules.

Factors Affecting Yeast Fermentation

The rate of yeast fermentation is affected by several important factors. Fast fermentation is desirable when time is a constraint. Slower fermentation is desirable for developing both flavor and gluten strength. Bakers often adjust one or more of the following factors to optimize the rate of fermentation.

■ *Temperature of dough.* Yeast is dormant at 32°–34°F (0°–1°C) and begins to be quite active starting at about 50°F (10°C). As dough temperature rises above this, the

HOW BAKERS CONTROL THE FLAVOR OF BREAD

Bread flavor comes from three main sources: flavor of the ingredients themselves, especially from the flour; Maillard browning that occurs during baking; and flavor generated during yeast fermentation. All three of these can be controlled by the baker.

Artisan bread bakers, in particular, actively work to improve bread flavor through controlling the process of yeast fermentation. Preferments, for example, are commonly used to add flavor to breads, especially those that have a short fermentation time. A preferment—either a liquid batter (poolish) or stiff dough (sponge)—contains yeast along with a portion of flour and water from a bread formula. The preferment is allowed to ferment for several hours or overnight, allowing for the development of a distinctive but not overpowering flavor.

Another method used by bakers is to add a portion of dough from a prior batch into a new batch. This so-called old dough, or pâte fermentée, usually adds a slightly stronger, more acidic flavor than a poolish or sponge, because it has already been through a full fermentation.

Bagels are typically retarded overnight, or for up to 18 hours. To retard, divided and formed dough is held refrigerated at 35–42°F (2–5°C). At this temperature, lactic acid bacteria (present in flour and yeast) are still active, even as yeast are greatly slowed. As they ferment, these bacteria produce flavors that are different in character from those from yeast fermentation.

For stronger flavor still, bakers can prepare a natural starter that relies on the action of wild yeast and bacteria. Natural starters are described below.

rate of yeast fermentation increases. By about 120°F (50°C), fermentation slows, because yeast cells begin to die. Fermentation essentially stops at 140°F (60°C), when most yeast cells are dead (these temperatures are estimates only; actual temperatures depend on the dough formula and on the strain of yeast in question). Optimum fermentation is often given as about 78°–82°F (25°–28°C).

- *Amount of salt.* Salt retards, or inhibits, yeast fermentation. While the typical amount of salt in yeast doughs is 1.8–2.5 percent (baker's percentage), bakers can vary the amount of salt in a preferment, making up the difference in the final mix. A preferment contains yeast and a portion of other ingredients from the formula. It is fermented before the makeup of the final dough. For a short fermentation, the preferment is made with a low amount of salt or none at all; for a longer one, it contains more.

- *Amount of sugar.* Small quantities—up to 5 percent (baker's percentage)—of sugar increase yeast activity. Large amounts—especially those above 10 percent—slow fermentation. For this reason, a common method for preparing rich, sweet doughs is to use a sponge or other preferment. Because large amounts of sugar are not added to the sponge, yeast can ferment without inhibition.

- *Type of sugar.* Sucrose, glucose, and fructose are all fermented rapidly; maltose is fermented slowly; lactose is not fermented at all. A mix of both fast- and slow-fermenting sugars is important with lean yeast doughs—those with low levels of added sugar. This provides for continued gassing through final proof.

- *pH of dough.* The optimum pH for yeast fermentation is an acidic 4 to 6. Above and below that pH, yeast fermentation slows. As yeast ferments, it produces acids that lower pH to this ideal range.

- *Presence of antimicrobial agents.* Certain antimicrobial agents slow or stop yeast fermentation. For example, when calcium proprionate is added to commercial doughs to prevent mold growth in breads, it must be added properly so that it does not prevent yeast fermentation. Most spices, including cinnamon, have strong antimicrobial activity and can slow yeast fermentation. Instead of mixing cinnamon directly into dough, make cinnamon breads and rolls by sprinkling cinnamon and sugar onto the dough. Then roll and shape the dough as a jelly roll before baking.

- *Amount of yeast.* For the most part, the more yeast, the faster the fermentation. However, a large amount of yeast can add an undesirable yeasty flavor. A large amount of yeast can also exhaust dough, especially a lean dough, of sugars needed for fermentation during final proof and oven spring. That is why it is best to use a small amount of yeast when using a long fermentation time.

- *Type of yeast.* Some yeast products sold to bakers contain fast fermenting yeast, good for no-time doughs. This is particularly true of instant yeast, discussed in the following section. Quick-fermenting yeasts are not as desirable, however, when a long fermentation time is used, since there might not be enough yeast activity to survive through final proof.

Some yeast strains grow well in rich doughs, doughs that are high in sugar. Yeast that grow well in high-sugar environments are sometimes called *osmophilic yeast*. The name osmophilic comes from the fact that sugar increases the osmotic pressure in dough by tying up water.

When regular (nonosmophilic) yeast is used in sweet, rich doughs, it can take an hour or more for the yeast to adapt to the high-sugar environment. Until it adapts, the yeast will not produce much carbon dioxide or alcohol. Even then, it can take two to three times the amount of yeast to get the same gas production as in a lean dough.

Types and Sources of Yeast

Bread can be made from a traditional, naturally fermented sourdough starter, called *levain* in French. Starters are prepared by mixing flour and water and allowing wild yeast—and lactobacilli bacteria—from the flour and air to ferment the mix. Sometimes rye flour, onion, potato or another source of food for microorganisms is added to the flour and water.

After a few days to a week of caring and feeding, the starter is ready to use. A portion of it is made into a sponge and allowed to ferment, then used to leaven a batch of bread. Because different microorganisms and different ways of handling a starter affect flavor, not all sourdough breads taste alike. While San Francisco sourdough bread is noticeably sour, French sourdough bread (*pain au levain*) is usually milder.

Fresh starter does not need to be made for each new day's production. Instead, a small amount of starter is mixed with fresh flour and water and saved for the next day's bread. Or, as described earlier, a piece of raw dough from one day's production is added to the next day's sponge. In fact, some bakeshops pride themselves on the number of years they have continued to bake from their original starter.

A more consistent source of yeast is to use pure yeast cultures. While all yeast purchased for bread baking consist of baker's yeast or *Saccharomyces cerevisiae*, many different strains and several different forms of baker's yeast are available. The three main forms of yeast available to the baker today are compressed, active dry, and instant. As you read the descriptions that follow, notice that each type of yeast works best within a specific temperature range. These temperature ranges are important for achieving optimum results with each product.

COMPRESSED YEAST

Fresh compressed yeast comes as moist cakes or blocks that are about 30 percent yeast, the rest moisture. Compressed yeast lasts up to two weeks when stored wrapped in plastic and refrigerated, and three to four months when frozen.

Fresh compressed yeast can vary in color, but it generally has a light grayish tan color, crumbles easily, and has a pleasant yeasty aroma. Do not use compressed yeast if it has darkened extensively and turned gummy, or has an off aroma. This could indicate bacterial contamination. The most common way to use compressed yeast is to first dissolve it in twice its weight of warm (100°F; 38°C) water. While compressed yeast can be crumbled directly into dough, this is not recommended, since it risks uneven distribution of yeast throughout the dough.

ACTIVE DRY YEAST

Active dry yeast comes as dry granules sold in vacuum-packed jars or pouches. It is widely available to consumers. The low moisture and vacuum packaging extend shelf life. Once open, active dry yeast lasts several months at room temperature, longer if frozen or refrigerated.

Active dry yeast is dried in a spray drier to less than 10 percent moisture. Spray-drying is a fairly harsh treatment, and the outside layer of each granule consists of dead yeast cells. In fact, every pound of active dry yeast contains about one-quarter pound of dead yeast. Since dead and damaged yeast release a substance—glutathione—that is detrimental to the quality of gluten in dough, active dry yeast is not popular with professional bakers. It tends to produce slack, sticky doughs and dense loaves. However, this tendency to slacken dough can be used to an advantage when active dry yeast is used in pizza or tortilla production, where extensible dough is desirable. If active dry yeast is used, dissolve it in four times its weight in very warm (105°–115°F; 41°–46°C) water, and use about half as much active dry as you would fresh compressed.

INSTANT YEAST

Instant yeast was developed in the 1970s. It is instant because it can—and should—be added directly to dough without first hydrating in water. As with active dry yeast, instant yeast is sold dried and vacuum-packed. However, the drying process—a fluidized bed—that produces instant yeast is much gentler than the one used for active dry yeast, so while there are still some dead and damaged yeast present, there is not the same high level. Instant dry yeast is more vigorous than either compressed or active dry, so it is easy to overproof doughs leavened with it. For this reason, instant yeast is best used when fermentation time is short, as it is in conventional or no-time doughs. Use only one-quarter to one-half instant yeast for the amount of fresh compressed yeast called for in a formula, and be sure when using instant yeast that initial dough temperatures are between 70°F (21°C) and 95°F (35°C). Instant yeast, if unopened, will last up to one year at room temperature without loss in activity. If it is opened, refrigerate for several months or more, or freeze.

CHEMICAL LEAVENERS

The chemical production of gases occurs when chemical leaveners break down in the presence of moisture or heat, giving off gases. Before discussing chemical leaveners, bench tolerance should be defined. *Bench tolerance* is a measure of how well batters and doughs withstand—or tolerate—a delay before baking without risking a large loss in leavening gases. Bench tolerance is an important consideration for commercial bakeshops, which need to produce consistent product, time after time, even if a batch is large and sits on the bench for a while before it is baked. While heavy doughs typically have better bench tolerance than thin batters, bench tolerance is also affected by the leavening agent used.

The most common chemical leavener is baking soda combined with one or more acids. The acids are either added separate from the baking soda, or both are added together in the form of baking powder. Baking ammonia is another chemical leavener, more common in Europe than in North America.

BAKING AMMONIA

Baking ammonia is another name for ammonium bicarbonate, used for leavening. When ammonium bicarbonate is exposed to heat in the presence of moisture, it quickly decomposes into ammonia, carbon dioxide, and water. All three are sources of leavening in baked goods.

Many European packaged cookies and crackers are leavened with baking ammonia. In fact, the best application of baking ammonia is in small dry cookies and crackers or choux paste. When properly used in these products, baking ammonia leaves no chemical residue. Be careful with baking ammonia, however; do not breathe in the powder, which has a very strong ammonia smell.

Baking ammonia has certain unique features that make it particularly suited for use in small, dry baked goods and unsuitable for use in large or moist products. Baking ammonia:

- Reacts rapidly in the presence of water and heat
- Increases uniformity and spread in cookies
- Increases browning
- Produces a crisp, porous crumb
- Adds an ammonia-like, off flavor to still-moist baked goods

Unlike baking soda and certain baking powders, baking ammonia is not very reactive at room temperature, which means that batters and doughs containing baking ammonia have good bench tolerance. However, baking ammonia quickly breaks down in the presence of heat (104°F; 38°C), so it is considered relatively fast-acting.

Baking ammonia should be used only in small products that bake to a low moisture content (less than 3 percent moisture), so that the ammonia gas can fully bake out. Otherwise, baked goods will have an ammonia off flavor. This means that one should never use baking ammonia in muffins, biscuits, cakes, or soft and moist cookies.

Baking Soda + Acid

Baking soda is another name for sodium bicarbonate or bicarbonate of soda. Like baking ammonia, baking soda decomposes to carbon dioxide and other gases in the presence of moisture and heat. However, baking soda by itself is not a practical leavening agent because very high amounts are needed to produce sufficient leavening gas. High amounts of baking soda produce yellow or green discoloration and a strong chemical off flavor in baked goods.

When baking soda is used for leavening, it is used with one or more acids. Acids react with baking soda in the presence of moisture, so the baking soda breaks down more quickly and easily to carbon dioxide and water. With acid, less baking soda is needed to produce carbon dioxide for leavening, so there is less discoloration and fewer chemically off flavors.

Any acid can be used with baking soda. Table 13.1 lists common acid ingredients used in baking. Each reacts differently and each produces a different salt residue, but the overall reaction is as follows:

$$\text{baking soda} + \text{acid} \xrightarrow{\text{moisture}} \text{carbon dioxide} + \text{water} + \text{salt residue}$$

Both unreacted baking soda and the remaining salt residue contribute to off flavors when high levels of baking soda are added to baked goods.

There are a few disadvantages to using the ingredients from Table 13.1 as acids in baked goods. One disadvantage is that they can vary in acid content. For example, buttermilk, sour cream, and yogurt increase in acidity as they age. Another disadvantage is that these ingredients tend to react with baking soda almost immediately, especially in thin batters. Where this is true, the batter has poor bench tolerance and must be baked immediately upon mixing.

TABLE 13.1 ■ COMMON ACID INGREDIENTS USED IN BAKING

Buttermilk
Yogurt
Sour cream
Fruits and fruit juices
Vinegar
Most syrups, including molasses and honey
Brown sugar
Unsweetened chocolate and natural cocoa

Baking Powders

There are several different types of baking powders. All contain baking soda, one or more acids—in the form of acid salts—and dried starch or another filler. Acid salts release acid once they dissolve in water. For example, cream of tartar is an acid salt, also called potassium acid tartrate. When cream of tartar dissolves in batter or dough, tartaric acid is released. The tartaric acid reacts with baking soda to produce carbon dioxide gas for leavening. Often, for simplicity, acid salts are simply called acids.

All baking powders release the same minimum amount of carbon dioxide, by federal law, 12 percent, by weight of baking powder. This means that most baking powders are more or less interchangeable—as long as they are still fresh. While they are interchangeable, they are not necessarily identical. To discuss baking powders and their differences, it is helpful to categorize them.

It was once useful to categorize baking powders as either single- or double-acting. This is no longer useful, since essentially all baking powders sold today are double-acting. Instead, a good way to categorize baking powders is by their reaction rates. Another is by the type of acid each contains. You will see shortly that these two categories are related.

HOW IS DRR MEASURED?

The DRR—dough reaction rate—test is used to measure the amount of carbon dioxide released from baking powder when it is used under controlled conditions. When DRR is tested, biscuit mix is placed in an airtight mixing bowl. The bowl is attached to a device that measures the amount of gas released as water is added and as the mixture is stirred at a specified temperature for a specified length of time. Often, the DRR—the percentage of carbon dioxide that is given off—is defined after 2–3 minutes of mixing and again after 8 or 16 minutes of bench time.

DOUGH REACTION RATES

As mentioned earlier, all baking powders release about the same amount of carbon dioxide and essentially all are double-acting, releasing some gas at room temperature and the rest when heated. Baking powders differ, however, in how much carbon dioxide is released at room temperature, how much is released with heat, and how quickly all this happens. In other words, baking powders differ in their dough reaction rates (DRR).

Bakers often speak of baking powders as being fast-acting or slow-acting. A fast-acting baking powder has a fast DRR and releases more of its carbon dioxide during the first few minutes of mixing and less of it in the oven. For example, a common fast-acting baking powder releases about 60–70 percent of its total carbon dioxide during mixing and another 30–40 percent during baking. A slow-acting baking powder releases a smaller amount of carbon dioxide during mixing and a larger amount in the oven. For example, a common slow-acting baking powder releases about 30–40 percent of its total carbon dioxide during mixing and another 60–70 percent during baking.

TABLE 13.2 ■ A COMPARISON OF COMMON ACID SALTS IN BAKING POWDERS

ACID SALT	MAJOR FEATURES
Cream of tartar	Fast-acting—releases over 70 percent of carbon dioxide during mixing, which is too quick for general use; very clean flavor, little aftertaste; fast action lowers pH, to give a whiter crumb than most; expensive.
MCP (monocalcium phosphate)	Fast-acting—releases almost 60 percent of carbon dioxide during mixing; often coated so it dissolves and reacts more slowly; relatively clean taste; a very common acid salt in household and commercial baking powders, when combined with slower-acting SAS or SAPP.
SAS (sodium aluminum sulfate)	Slow-acting—requires heat to release acid, but releases it all during early stages of baking, by about 120°F (50°C); bitter aftertaste when used alone; combined with fast-acting MCP for the most common household baking powder.
SAPP (sodium acid pyrophosphate)	Many kinds available, all slow-acting—releasing only 25–45 percent of their carbon dioxide within 16 minutes of bench time; most have noticeable unpleasant chemical aftertaste; combined with fast-acting MCP for the most common commercial baking powder.

WHY MIGHT CAKE DOUGHNUTS REQUIRE A DIFFERENT BAKING POWDER THAN CAKES?

Cake doughnuts and cakes both do best with slow-acting baking powders, where more carbon dioxide is released after heat is applied than before. However, cake doughnuts require faster release of carbon dioxide than cakes do. With doughnuts, which fry up in minutes, if carbon dioxide releases too slowly, the crust sets before leavening occurs. Once leavening takes place, the force of expanding gases cracks the doughnut's surface or produces pinholes on it. If this happens, the doughnut absorbs fat in its cracks and pinholes, and it becomes soggy and greasy.

For best volume and symmetry in cakes, generation of carbon dioxide must be timed with protein coagulation and starch gelatinization. Cakes, especially liquid shortening cakes, contain high amounts of fat and sugar that delay the coagulation of egg proteins and the gelatinization of starches. If the generation of carbon dioxide is to be timed with these processes, then the baking powder must be slower-acting than most.

Because most commercial baking powders are designed more for cakes than for doughnuts, bakers and pastry chefs often use mixes when frying doughnuts. Doughnut mixes already contain the proper type and amount of baking powder—and other ingredients—for optimum doughnut quality.

TYPE OF ACID

A listing of acids used in baking powders reads like alphabet soup—MCP, SAS, SAPP, SALP, and more. The important point here is not to memorize names and features but to understand that differences in acids exist. A comparison of the four major acids used in baking powders is given in Table 13.2. Notice in the table that acids differ in reaction rates, flavor, and price.

Baking powders for professional bakeshops are designed to provide some carbon dioxide quickly, to lighten batters and doughs during mixing, but to generate most of it when baking is well under way, for best bench tolerance and product expansion. Baking powders for professionals are most apt to contain a mixture of SAPP and MCP, but they can also contain SAS and MCP. Eagle double-acting is a SAPP/MCP baking powder; Clabber Girl is an SAS/MCP baking powder.

Functions of Chemical Leaveners

Chemical leaveners, such as baking ammonia, baking soda, and baking powders, contribute a number of functions to baked goods, including the following.

LEAVEN

With chemical leaveners, leavening occurs when gases form from the breakdown of the leavening agents and when these gases expand during the baking process.

TENDERIZE

As with all leavening, as gases form and expand, cell walls in baked goods stretch and thin out. This makes them easier to bite through; that is, this makes them more tender.

ADJUST pH

Many batters and doughs have a neutral pH if no baking powder, baking soda, or other chemical leavener is added. Cream of tartar—an acid—tends to decrease pH, while baking ammonia and baking soda—both alkalis—tend to increase pH. Fast-acting

PHOTO 13.2 The effect of adding an alkali to chocolate biscotti is seen in the differences in spread, crumb structure, and color. From left to right, chocolate biscotti made with baking soda and without.
Photo by Aaron Seyfarth

baking powders, which release acidic carbon dioxide quickly, decrease pH of batters and doughs, while slow-acting baking powders do not, and can even increase pH.

Changes in pH affect many things in baked goods, including color, flavor, crumb texture, and gluten strength. For example,

- A small amount of baking soda in chocolate brownies or gingerbread provides a darker, richer-looking product. The higher pH also smoothes out the flavor in gingerbread and chocolate, so that it is mellower and less sharp (unless a very high amount of baking soda is added; high levels of baking soda give baked goods a sharp, chemical taste).

- A small amount of baking soda or baking ammonia in cookies increases pH, weakening gluten. The result is more spread, more tenderness, and a coarser, more open crumb that dries and crisps more quickly (see Photo 13.2). The higher pH from baking soda also increases the rate of browning.

- A small amount of cream of tartar in baking powder biscuits decreases pH and weakens gluten. The result is more tenderness. Unlike with baking soda, the lower pH from cream of tartar also provides a whiter crumb, often one that is fine and tight.

PROVIDE FOR A FINER CRUMB

Recall that creaming, whipping, sifting, folding, kneading, and stirring are physical processes that add small air cells—seed cells—to batters and doughs. Chemical leaveners—those that release carbon dioxide during mixing—contribute to the size of these seed cells, which through continued mixing, increase the number of seed cells in batters and doughs. Seed cells are important for defining the crumb of baked goods. The more small seed cells in batters and doughs, the finer the crumb of the baked good.

The addition of carbon dioxide also makes batters and doughs thicker, less dense, and easier to mix.

HELPFUL HINT

Be careful when weighing baking soda and other chemical leavening agents. While a small amount can be beneficial to flavor, texture, and color, too much often leaves a bitter chemical aftertaste and discolors baked goods.

WHY IS CORNSTARCH ADDED TO BAKING POWDER?

Cornstarch serves two main functions in baking powder. First, cornstarch absorbs moisture, so that baking soda and acid do not react in the box. Don't tempt fate, however; even with cornstarch, baking powders should be covered after each use.

Cornstarch also serves to standardize baking powders, so that an ounce of one brand provides the same leavening potential as an ounce of another.

ADD FLAVOR

Small amounts of baking powder and baking soda have a distinct salty-sour flavor that is characteristic of certain baked goods, such as baking powder biscuits, scones, and Irish soda bread.

STORAGE AND HANDLING

All chemical leavening agents should be stored in tightly covered containers at room temperature. Even then, baking powder has a shelf life of only six months to one year. Leaving baking powder containers uncovered can significantly reduce shelf life, since uncovered chemical leaveners easily absorb moisture, and moisture absorption leads to a loss in potency and to caking. Chemical leaveners also pick up off odors if left uncovered.

QUESTIONS FOR REVIEW

1. What are the three main leavening gases in baked goods? Which two contribute significantly to leavening in *all* baked goods?

2. What are three ways of categorizing how leavening gases are added or formed in baked goods?

3. How are air cells added to batters and doughs?

4. Why is it important not to undermix batter? Why is it important not to overmix?

5. From what is steam generated? From what is carbon dioxide generated?

6. Name a baked good leavened primarily by steam. Name two leavened by steam and air. Name two in which carbon dioxide contributes significantly to leavening.

7. How is a sourdough starter made and what is it used for?

8. List and describe factors that affect the rate of yeast fermentation.

9. List the three main forms of baker's yeast available. Describe an advantage and a disadvantage of each.

10. At what temperature range should each of the three main forms of baker's yeast be used?

11. Would you use baking ammonia in a cake? Why or why not?

12. What two things are needed for baking soda to generate carbon dioxide? Why is acid usually added along with baking soda, when baking soda is added for leavening?

13. What is the difference between baking soda and baking powder?

14. What are two ways of categorizing baking powders?

15. Which requires heat for the release of all of its carbon dioxide: a single- or a double-acting baking powder?

16. What is meant by bench tolerance? Which provides better bench tolerance to batters: a fast-acting or a slow-acting baking powder?

17. If the amount of baking powder in a batter or dough is doubled, will the volume double? Why or why not?

18. Besides leavening, what are the other functions of chemical leaveners in baked goods?

19. Which of the following would be better leavened with baking ammonia: crisp, dry cookies or soft, moist cookies? Explain your answer.

20. What would happen to the volume of a cake made with a single-acting baking powder if the batter were left sitting out awhile before being baked?

QUESTIONS FOR DISCUSSION

1. Describe the process of leavening. That is, what occurs as products rise during baking?

2. You are short on time. Why will an increase in chemical leaveners not make up for a decrease in mixing time?

3. Describe the process of yeast fermentation. Be sure to include a description of the starting material and the end products.

4. What do you think will happen if the proteins in a baked good coagulate and the starches gelatinize before much carbon dioxide is generated? Explain.

5. Why do you think a formula for gingerbread might contain both baking powder and baking soda?

6. Why do cake doughnuts require a slightly faster-reacting baking powder than most cakes?

7. If a little bit of baking powder is good, will more be better? Why or why not?

8. Why do you think some choux paste formulas include a small amount of baking ammonia rather than baking powder?

9. Why do you think a formula for chocolate biscotti might contain both baking soda and baking powder?

EXERCISES AND EXPERIMENTS

1. A Comparison of Chemical Leavening Agents

Complete the results table, which follows. In the second column, record brand names and any descriptive information (bench-tolerant, fast-acting, double-acting, etc.) from the package labels of each of the chemical leavening agents to be evaluated. In the third column, copy the ingredient list from the package. You will prepare the tartrate baking powder yourself, from the formula that follows. Use fresh samples to evaluate the appearance and taste of each product. Because they all are white powders, it is particularly important that you taste them and describe what you taste. Use this opportunity to identify different chemical leavening agents from their sensory characteristics alone. Add any additional comments or observations that you might have to the last column in the Results Table.

Baking Powder—Tartrate Type

INGREDIENT	OUNCE	GRAMS
Baking soda	1	30
Cream of tartar	2	60
Cornstarch	0.5	15
Total	3.5	105

Method of Preparation:

Sift ingredients together three times onto parchment paper.

RESULTS TABLE ■ A COMPARISON OF CHEMICAL LEAVENING AGENTS

CHEMICAL LEAVENER	BRAND OR DESCRIPTION	INGREDIENT LIST	APPEARANCE	TASTE	COMMENTS
Cream of Tartar					
Baking soda					
Baking powder, SAPP type					
Baking powder, SAS type					
Baking powder, tartrate type					

2. How the Type and Amount of Leavening Agent Affects the Overall Quality of Baking Powder Biscuits

OBJECTIVES

To demonstrate how the type and amount of leavening agent affects:

- Crispness and the extent of browning on the crust of baking powder biscuits
- Crumb color and structure
- Moistness, tenderness, and height
- Overall flavor
- Overall acceptability

PRODUCTS PREPARED

Baking powder biscuits made with:

- Full am ount of commercial SAPP baking powder (control product)
- No baking powder
- Twice the amount of SAPP baking powder
- Full amount of tartrate baking powder
- Commercial SAPP baking powder with added cream of tartar

- Baking soda instead of baking powder
- Other, if desired (half the amount of baking powder, SAS baking powder, etc.)

MATERIALS AND EQUIPMENT

- Biscuit dough, enough to make 12 or more biscuits of each variation
- Rolling pin and height guide
- Ruler

PROCEDURE

- Preheat oven according to formula.
- Line sheet pans with parchment paper; label with type and amount of leavening agent to be added.
- Prepare biscuit dough using the formula below or using any basic baking powder biscuit formula. Prepare one batch of dough per variation.
- Roll out dough to a thickness of ½ inch (1.2 centimeters), using a height guide to keep consistency throughout.
- Cut with a floured biscuit cutter and place on lined sheet pan. Space biscuits evenly, placing six on half sheet pan or twelve on full sheet pan.
- Use an oven thermometer placed in center of oven to read oven temperature; record results.
- Place sheet pans in preheated oven and set timer according to formula.
- Bake biscuits until control product (with full amount of SAPP baking powder) is light brown. Remove *all* biscuits from oven after same length of time. If necessary, however, adjust bake times for oven variances. Record bake times in Comments column of Results Table 1, which follows.
- Remove biscuits from oven and transfer to wire racks to cool to room temperature.
- Record any potential sources of error that might make it difficult to draw the proper conclusions from your experiment. In particular, be aware of differences in mixing, kneading, and rolling, and any problems with the oven.
- When rolls are completely cooled, evaluate height as follows:
  - Slice three biscuits from each batch in half, being careful not to compress.
  - Measure height of each roll by placing a ruler along the flat edge at the biscuit's maximum height. Record results for each of three biscuits in 1/16" (10 mm) increments in Results Table 1.
  - Calculate the average biscuit height by adding the heights of the three biscuits and dividing by 3; record results in Results Table 1.
- Note in Biscuit Shape column of Results Table 1 whether biscuits have slumped or held their shape. Also note whether biscuits are lopsided, that is, if one side is higher than the other.
- Evaluate the sensory characteristics of completely cooled products and record evaluations in Results Table 2, which follows. Be sure to compare each in turn to the control product and consider the following:
  - Crust color, from very light to very dark, on a scale of one to five
  - Crust texture (soft and moist, soft and dry, crisp and dry, etc.)
  - Crumb appearance (flaky, dense, airy, etc.)
  - Crumb texture (tough/tender, moist/dry, flaky, etc.)
  - Overall flavor (buttery, sweet, salty, metallic/chemical, sour, etc.)
  - Overall acceptability, from highly unacceptable to highly acceptable, on a scale of one to five
  - Add any additional comments, as necessary.

Baking Powder Biscuits

INGREDIENT	POUND	OUNCE	GRAMS	BAKER'S PERCENTAGE
Flour, pastry	1		500	100
Salt		.3	10 .	2
Sugar, granulated		1	30	6
Baking powder		1	25	6
Shortening, all purpose		6	190	38
Milk		9.5	300	60
Total	2	1.8	1055	212

Method of Preparation

1. Preheat oven 425°F (220°C).
2. Allow ingredients (except milk) to come to room temperature.
3. Blend dry ingredients thoroughly by sifting together three times onto parchment paper.
4. Place dry ingredients into bowl and cut in shortening on low speed for 1 minute; stop and scrape bowl.
5. Add milk slowly and stir on low speed for 20 seconds; dough should just barely hold together.
6. Transfer dough to a lightly floured surface and knead lightly about five or six times.
7. Cover dough with plastic wrap and set aside until ready to use.
8. Bake 2-inch biscuits for about 20 minutes.

 **SOURCES OF ERROR**

_____

_____

RESULTS TABLE 1 ■ EVALUATION OF HEIGHT AND SHAPE OF BISCUITS MADE WITH DIFFERENT AMOUNTS AND TYPES OF CHEMICAL LEAVENERS

TYPE AND AMOUNT OF LEAVENER	HEIGHT OF EACH OF THREE BISCUITS	AVERAGE HEIGHT OF ONE BISCUIT	BISCUIT SHAPE	COMMENTS
Commercial SAPP baking powder (control product)				
No baking powder				
Twice the amount of baking powder				
Tartrate baking powder				
Commercial SAPP baking powder with added cream of tartar				
Baking soda instead of baking powder				

RESULTS TABLE 2 ■ SENSORY CHARACTERISTICS OF BISCUITS MADE WITH DIFFERENT TYPES AND AMOUNTS OF CHEMICAL LEAVENERS

TYPE AND AMOUNT OF LEAVENER	CRUST COLOR AND TEXTURE	CRUMB APPEARANCE AND TEXTURE	OVERALL FLAVOR	OVERALL ACCEPTABILITY	COMMENTS
Commercial SAPP baking powder (control product)					
No baking powder					
Twice the amount of baking powder					
Tartrate baking powder					
Commercial SAPP baking powder with added cream of tartar					
Baking soda instead of baking powder					

CONCLUSIONS

1. How did changing the amount of baking powder affect height, shape, color, flavor, and texture?

_____

_____

2. Why did the height of the biscuits not double when double the amount of baking powder was added?

_____

_____

3. How do you account for differences in tenderness when different amounts of baking powder were added?

_____

_____

4. What were the main differences in height, shape, color, flavor, and texture between the biscuits made with tartrate baking powder and those made with a regular commercial baking powder (the control product)?

_____

_____

  a. Which of these two biscuits did you prefer, and why?

_____

_____

5. What were the main differences in height, appearance, flavor, and texture between the muffins made with baking soda and those made with baking powder (the control product)?

_____

_____

6. How can you tell when baking soda instead of baking powder is used by mistake? How can you prevent baking soda from mistakenly being used instead of baking powder, and vice versa?

_____

_____

7. How do you account for differences in browning of the biscuits made with baking soda instead of baking powder, the ones made with added cream of tartar, and the control product?

_____

_____

8. Did you have any sources of error that might significantly affect the results of your experiment? If so, what could you do differently next time to minimize error?

_____

_____

CHAPTER 14

NATURAL AND ARTIFICIAL FLAVORINGS

CHAPTER **OBJECTIVES**

1. Define the different natural and artificial flavorings used in bakeshops and describe their characteristics and uses.

2. Describe how to best store and handle flavorings.

3. Provide helpful hints for improving the flavor of food products.

 INTRODUCTION

When asked why a particular food is liked, most people comment on its flavor, or taste. It is not that appearance and texture are unimportant. It is just that flavor is most important of all. Flavor should likewise be uppermost on the chef's mind when preparing food. A chef should taste every batch of product made each and every day. This is one way to develop a sense of taste. More important, it is a good way to catch mistakes before they reach the customer.

Developing a sense of taste is a skill that is as important as piping chocolate or folding gelatin into whipped cream. As with any skill, it is developed through practice and experience. This idea was first introduced in Chapter 4. Because of the importance of flavor to food, it is worthwhile exploring this in more detail.

To best develop a sense of taste, practice describing flavors in a broad range of ingredients and products. Retreat to a quiet spot, smell and taste the ingredients and products, and record your comments. Compare one ingredient directly with another, one product directly with another. For example, compare the taste of molasses with dark corn syrup; compare toasted to untoasted hazelnuts; compare vanilla custard sauce made with vanilla extract to one made with vanilla bean. You will learn much more by these close comparisons than by tasting any number of items individually. If possible, discuss your evaluations with others. Try to describe the flavor of each product as completely as possible. Recall from Chapter 4 that smell and memory are connected. Take advantage of this connection to help in identifying and remembering smells.

That is, if you cannot identify a smell in words, record what it reminds you of or where else you remember experiencing it.

For example, maybe you are not sure of the name of a spice, but its smell reminds you of your grandmother. Record that information, then think of why you make that memory connection. Maybe your grandmother used that particular spice in cookies she baked for you when you were young. Or, maybe she had potpourri that contained that spice. Once you connect that memory with the smell and with the name of the spice, it will be easier to identify and name it in the future.

To develop a sense of taste, it helps to understand flavor profiles and food flavorings.

A BRIEF REVIEW OF FLAVOR

Recall from Chapter 4 that flavor consists of three main parts: basic tastes, trigeminal effects, and smell. Basic tastes include sweet, salty, sour, and bitter sensations perceived throughout the mouth. *Trigeminal effects*, or *chemical feeling factors*, include the pungency of ginger, the burn of cinnamon, the cooling of mint, and the sting of alcohol. Smell—also called aroma—is often considered the most important of the three components of flavor. It is certainly the most complex. Butter aroma, for instance, is actually composed of hundreds of different chemical compounds.

FLAVOR PROFILES

A *flavor profile* is a description of a product's flavor from when it is first smelled until after it is swallowed. For example, the flavor profile of a particular milk chocolate might start with the aromas of vanilla and roasted cocoa, continue with a sweet taste and a milky caramelized flavor, and end with lingering bitterness. The term flavor profile is also used to describe the distinctive flavor combinations that characterize the food of a particular culture. For example, the flavor profile of American apple pie generally includes cinnamon and lard, or the blander shortening, but not butter. In contrast, many European apple tarts and desserts, such as apple charlotte, feature butter as a predominant flavor, often supplemented with lemon, apricot, or vanilla.

Whatever the culture, a flavor is most satisfying when it contains a full flavor profile. A full flavor profile has top notes, middle notes, background or base notes, and an aftertaste or finish. Top notes are the smells that provide instant impact, the ones that first fill the bakeshop when pastries bake. Because they provide the first impression of a product's flavor, when a product is described as low in flavor, it is often low in top notes. Volatile flavors are the main sources of top notes in foods. *Volatile flavors* are flavors that evaporate easily, usually because they consist of molecules that are small and light. The smells of freshly-cut lemons and ripe strawberries and peaches are classified as top notes. Because these are highly volatile, they are perceived almost immediately, but they are also easily lost once the fruit is cut and when it is cooked.

Middle notes follow top notes in a flavor profile. They come from flavor molecules that evaporate more slowly, usually because they are larger and heavier than top notes. Middle notes provide a satisfying staying power to flavor. Many caramelized, cooked fruit, egg, cream, and coconut flavors are classified as middle notes. Roasted nuts, cocoa and chocolate, and coffee also are rich in middle notes, because of Maillard browning, which occurs during the roasting process.

Background or *base notes* consist mostly of the largest, heaviest molecules that are nonvolatile. Nonvolatile flavors evaporate slowly or not at all. Basic tastes and trigeminal effects are part of a flavor's background notes. If a product seems thin or weak and seems to need "something," it probably lacks middle and background notes.

Aftertaste—or *finish*—is the final flavor that remains in the mouth after food is swallowed. It is a final chance for food to leave a lasting positive impression. Again, basic tastes—especially bitterness—and trigeminal effects, often from cloves, ginger, and other spices, are important to aftertaste.

TYPES OF FLAVORINGS

Most, if not all, ingredients added to foods provide flavor. By *flavorings*, however, we are referring to ingredients added to foods primarily for their flavor, especially their aroma. This eliminates honey, almonds, and cocoa from being classified as flavorings, because they are equally important for the appearance, texture, and nutrition that they contribute to foods. Sugar and salt also do not fall into this category, because they provide basic tastes rather than aroma (and alter foods in many other ways).

While food flavorings contribute to a total flavor profile, they are especially good at providing aroma top notes and often trigeminal effects. Flavorings used by bakers and pastry chefs can be categorized as *herbs and spices* and as *processed flavorings*.

Herbs and Spices

Most, but not all, spices come from hot, tropical climates. The American Spice Trade Association defines a spice as any dried plant product used primarily for seasoning. Spices come from the bark of a tree (cinnamon), dried fruit (allspice and star anise), seeds (cardamom, nutmeg, anise, and sesame), flower buds (clove, lavender, and rose), roots (ginger), and leafy herbs (mint, oregano, parsley). Notice that this definition includes herbs as a type of spice. While not commonly thought of as spices, citrus peel, coffee beans, and vanilla pods also fall into this definition.

All spices contain high amounts of volatile oils. *Volatile oils*—also called *essential oils*—are oils that evaporate easily and provide strong, pleasing top notes. This makes them different from cooking oils.

The quality of a spice is related to the amount of volatile oil it contains. For example, Vietnamese (Saigon) cinnamon is considered the highest quality cinnamon because it is very high in cinnamon oil. Often it contains twice the amount of volatile oil as Indonesian cinnamon. Its price is often twice as high, too.

Besides top notes from volatile oils, spices provide trigeminal effects. Cinnamon, allspice, cloves, ginger, anise, and many other spices provide valuable pungency to foods.

Spices are desirable because they are the real thing, but they do have certain disadvantages. Because they are agricultural products, they can vary greatly in quality, strength, and price, and insect infestation can occur. A few of the many factors that affect quality include plant variety, country of origin, method of harvesting and

WHEN MIGHT A LOW QUALITY SPICE BE THE RIGHT CHOICE?

High quality cinnamon is high in cinnamon oil, but this might not be what you need. For example, when cinnamon is sprinkled generously on pastries as a garnish, a so-called high quality cinnamon, such as Vietnamese cinnamon, might be too intense. Instead, the mildest, least expensive cinnamon is likely the ideal choice.

THE MAKING OF VANILLA BEANS

Vanilla beans are the seed pods of a particular orchid. They are classified primarily by region of origin. For example, vanilla beans can be Mexican, Tahitian, Indonesian (Java), or from Madagascar. Madagascar vanilla is often called bourbon vanilla because Madagascar was once a Bourbon Island.

Cultivation of vanilla beans takes about a year of intense labor. Plants are hand-pollinated to produce flowers, which bloom for just a few hours before forming pods. The pods remain on the vine for up to nine months to ripen. At this point, they are mostly green in color and still flavorless. Once harvested, vanilla beans are cured to develop their characteristic aroma and chocolate-brown color.

The curing process varies with region. In all cases, though, it starts with heating the pods to stop the ripening process. Some producers dip the beans in boiling water; others lay them in the sun to bake or on mats over an open fire. The beans are next alternately exposed to heat by day, then covered by night, to sweat. This process is repeated for several weeks before the beans are slowly dried, then covered and aged. If properly cultivated and cured, vanilla beans can develop up to 2 percent natural vanillin. Vanillin is the main flavor molecule in vanilla.

Each type of vanilla has its own characteristic flavor because the climate and local curing practices are different. The most popular vanilla in the United States is bourbon (Madagascar) vanilla. It has a deep, rich flavor, reminiscent of wood and rum. Tahitian vanilla is distinctly different in flavor because it is from a different orchid plant. It has a sweeter, more floral aroma with hints of cherry. Very little (less than 1 percent) of all vanilla imported into the United States is Tahitian. The bulk of Tahitian vanilla is imported into Europe.

handling, annual climatic conditions, manufacturer's processing, and the age and storage conditions of the flavoring.

To minimize problems, purchase spices from a reputable dealer and treat them as the raw agricultural products that they are. Or instead, consider using a processed flavoring.

Processed Flavorings

Processed flavorings include extracts, liqueurs, compounds, oils, emulsions, and powders. Other processed flavorings are available but are not common in bakeshops. Processed flavorings can be natural or artificial.

Processed flavorings have several advantages over spices. They are generally more consistent in flavor quality and strength. There is little or no concern over insect infestation, and they can be faster and easier to use than spices. For example, it is easier to measure an ounce of lemon extract or dried lemon peel than it is to zest a lemon.

The one main disadvantage of processed flavorings sometimes cancels out these advantages. That is, the flavor of certain processed flavorings—even natural ones—can be less true, rich, or full than the original spice. For example, lemon extract, even if natural, rarely has the same true flavor as lemon zest, and almond extract does not taste much like almonds.

EXTRACTS

The most common processed flavorings in the bakeshop are extracts. All extracts contain alcohol. Alcohol dilutes and dissolves the flavor ingredients and preserves them by preventing microbial growth. Common flavors sold as extracts include vanilla, peppermint, orange, lemon, ginger, anise, and almond. Extracts can be natural or artificial, depending on whether the added flavor is natural or artificial. Because vanilla is, by far, the most popular flavor used in baked goods in North America, this section focuses on vanilla bean and vanilla extract, which is also the most complex of extracts.

MAKE YOUR OWN VANILLA EXTRACT

If you like the flavor of certain vanilla beans but want the convenience of an extract, consider making your own vanilla extract. Slice vanilla pods lengthwise, scrape them with a knife, and chop them into small pieces. Place the finely chopped beans in a tightly closed jar with one fluid ounce (30 milliliters) of 80-proof vodka for each pod (about 0.1 ounce or 3 grams). Shake occasionally. After two or more weeks, you will have the equivalent of one-fold vanilla extract. The quality of your vanilla extract will depend on the quality of the beans.

Most extracts are made by dissolving flavoring agents in alcohol. For example, lemon extract consists of a certain amount of lemon oil added to an alcohol solution. With other extracts, however, alcohol solutions are used for extracting, or removing, flavor from the plant product. Alcohol is used because it is better than water at dissolving and extracting many flavor molecules.

Pure vanilla extract, for example, is made commercially by infusing an alcohol solution with vanilla bean. The dilute alcohol gently percolates through mashed vanilla beans, often for several weeks, before aging. In the United States, a minimum of 13.35 ounces of vanilla bean is required to make one gallon (128 ounces) of extract (in Canada, the minimum is 10 grams of vanilla bean for 100 milliliters of vanilla extract). This is equivalent to about one vanilla bean for each fluid ounce (two tablespoons or 30 milliliters) of extract. Vanilla extract must also contain a minimum amount of alcohol (35 percent) and vanillin extracted from the bean. Vanillin is an important flavor chemical naturally present in pure vanilla. While it is only one of many flavor chemicals present, it is a convenient gauge of overall quality.

Vanilla bean provides a somewhat different flavor than vanilla extract. To use, vanilla bean is first split and scraped, then allowed to infuse in hot liquid, often milk. After a time, the liquid becomes infused with vanilla flavor and the bean is removed. Because the infusion time is often minutes instead of hours, and because the infusing liquid often does not contain alcohol and is not aged, vanilla beans provide a different flavor than the equivalent amount of vanilla extract. Besides flavor quality, there are other points to consider when deciding between vanilla bean and vanilla extract. Table 14.1 lists some of the advantages of each.

HELPFUL HINT

To make top-quality product consistently time after time, do not reuse vanilla beans. Spent vanilla beans have lost much of their flavor, especially their top notes.

Instead of discarding spent vanilla beans, add them to dry sugar. Vanilla flavor will infuse into the sugar, which can be used in baked goods. Or, add the used vanilla beans to vanilla extract, to reinforce its flavor. Beans can also be dried, ground in a spice grinder, sieved, and used for their visual appeal.

TABLE 14.1 ■ ADVANTAGES OF VANILLA BEAN AND OF VANILLA EXTRACT

	ADVANTAGES
Vanilla bean	Can select a specific type of bean for a signature flavor
	No alcohol taste
	Can include natural flecks for visual appeal
	Less likely to darken or discolor background color of light sauces
Vanilla extract	Consistent flavor from one use to the next
	Faster and easier to use
	Longer shelf life (often several years)

Concentrated vanilla extracts that contain a higher amount of vanilla "extractives" for the amount of alcohol are available. The usual ratio of vanilla bean to alcohol produces a so-called 1× or *one-fold vanilla extract*. Higher folds are available. For example, a 2× vanilla extract is made by doubling the amount of vanilla bean for every gallon or liter of extract. While the price per ounce or gram is higher for a two-fold extract, the price per use is lower, and the quality is just as good. If you use a two-fold extract, remember to use half as much as you would when using a one-fold. Good-quality vanilla extract can be purchased up to a four-fold concentration.

LIQUEURS

In terms of using them in the bakeshop, think of liqueurs as extracts with sugar added. As with extracts, liqueurs can contain natural or artificial ingredients. Liqueurs are very useful for flavoring pastries, but they can be expensive because of the tax on alcohol. The more popular ones can be purchased as concentrated flavorings for a lower cost. Concentrated flavorings are ideal for use in creams, where large amounts of alcohol could curdle the dairy ingredients. They can also be useful for frozen desserts, where alcohol lowers the freezing point and at high levels can prevent freezing from happening at all. Finally, concentrated liqueur flavorings can be used in products for customers who, for religious or personal reasons, choose not to consume alcohol. While concentrated flavorings have advantages over liqueurs, remember that alcohol has a taste, too. Without the burn from a liqueur's alcohol, a product might lack flavor, even when the flavor concentrate is of high quality.

Liqueurs come in all flavors and all prices. With some, such as Frangelico (hazelnut), amaretto (almond), or peppermint schnapps, a single flavor predominates. With others, such as Benedictine or Drambuie, the flavor is more complex and less easily defined. As with all flavorings, expect different brands of the same liqueur to taste different. For example, Kahlúa and Tia Maria are both coffee-flavored liqueurs, but they differ in flavor quality and sweetness. Do not assume that price is an indication of quality. The only way to know which best meets your needs is to taste and compare.

FLAVOR COMPOUNDS AND BASES

Compounds and bases contain flavorings and sugar added to ingredients such as puréed fruit, chocolate, ground nuts, or ground vanilla beans. Think of compounds as highly flavored food ingredients. They are easy to use, and their ingredients contribute to a full flavor profile. Still, the quality of a compound depends on the quality of its ingredients, and brands vary widely. Compounds come in a variety of flavors, including strawberry, raspberry, lemon, and vanilla. Marzipan, which is made from ground almonds, sugar, and almond oil, is essentially an almond compound.

FLAVOR OILS

Recall that the volatile or essential oils in spices are major sources of aroma. These oils can be purified—distilled or pressed—from the plant and sold separately. Examples of available oils include peppermint, lemon, orange, bitter almond, cinnamon, and clove.

Flavor oils are highly concentrated and must be used with care. They are most commonly used in products where high levels of moisture are undesirable, such as chocolate products and pralines. While flavor oils have their advantages, they are not for everyday use. Instead, extracts are better than oils for everyday use because they are less concentrated and easier to measure. Read labels and you will see that many flavor extracts are oils diluted with alcohol. For example, peppermint extract contains peppermint oil, lemon extract contains lemon oil, and almond extract contains almond oil, each diluted with alcohol.

A disadvantage of flavor oils is that they provide little more than top notes. They lack a full flavor profile and are best used as a flavor supplement. For example, lemon oil or lemon extract used alone provides the flat flavor of a lemon lollipop. Combined with lemon juice and zest, the flavor becomes rich and full.

FLAVOR EMULSIONS

Flavor emulsions are flavor oils dissolved in water with the aid of a starch or gum. The starch or gum—often gum arabic or xanthan gum—acts as an emulsifier, allowing the oil to blend more easily with other ingredients. This makes flavor emulsions easier to add to batters and doughs, for example.

DRIED AND ENCAPSULATED FLAVORINGS

Dried flavorings, such as vanilla powder, are used in dry mixes, like cake or muffin mixes. They can be natural or artificial. Encapsulated flavorings are dry spices or flavorings that are specially coated to protect the flavor from moisture, light, heat, and air. Encapsulated flavorings have a longer shelf life than spices and generally survive the heat of the oven better than other flavorings.

FLAVOR TIPS AND TRICKS

Sometimes, reaching for the bottle of extract or the jar of compound is not the best way to improve the flavor of a product. Here are some suggestions for other ways to improve flavor in problem products.

If flavor is weak in a mousse or cream, back off on the amount of thickener, whether it's gelatin, starch, or flour. Thick and heavy products prevent flavor molecules from escaping for taste.

Often, a combination of two basic tastes provides an interesting flavor contrast in foods. For example, sour fruit sauce is an interesting contrast to sweet cream.

To provide richness and a full-bodied flavor to pastries, add ingredients that supply middle notes. Eggs, milk, and cream are probably the most common ingredients pastry chefs use for richness. But consider, too, coconut milk, banana puree, caramelized sugar, and maple syrup for this purpose. Small amounts of aged rum, brandy, wine, and vanilla provide depth to fruit flavors, as does the slightly "jammy" character from cooked berries, such as raspberries.

If flavor in a product disappears too quickly, remember that a full flavor profile includes an appropriate finish, or aftertaste. The pungency and burn of ginger, cinnamon, and other spices might provide just the lingering flavor note that the product is lacking.

While a strongly bitter aftertaste is unpleasant, a small amount from coffee, cranberries, citrus peel, or unsweetened chocolate adds interest to the aftertaste, as long as it is properly balanced with sweetness.

If a fruit sauce isn't fruity enough, consider adjusting the amount of sugar and acid. Each fruit has a characteristic sweet-sour balance that is important to its overall flavor, and sometimes the best way to increase fruitiness is to add a small amount of sugar or acid—or both.

If ginger molasses cookies lack a snappy flavor, back off on the baking soda. The color will lighten and the cookies will spread less, but the flavor will be improved.

For chocolate cheesecake, try layering chocolate with cheese instead of mixing them together. Cheesecake has a low pH, but chocolate tastes best when its pH is neutral. When chocolate is separated from the cheese, the chocolate is at its proper pH. And, there is the added bonus of a flavor contrast between bittersweet chocolate and salty-sour cheesecake.

To balance cost and quality, consider layering two or more flavorings. For example, use an inexpensive liqueur flavor concentrate to boost the flavor provided by a liqueur, or use fresh lemon peel and lemon extract to boost the flavor of bottled lemon juice.

For the look of real vanilla beans without splitting and scraping vanilla pods, consider purchasing vanilla bean paste, a compound of vanilla extract mixed with vanilla bean seeds and sugar.

If a formula calls for a pinch of salt, do not omit it. Salt is a flavor enhancer, which means it blends and improves flavors even when the salt itself cannot be tasted. A pinch of salt is less than 1/16 teaspoon (just over ¼ milliliter).

Artificial Flavorings

Artificial flavorings are created from sources that sometimes have no relation to the natural flavor. Maybe this is why they are sometimes looked on with suspicion. By law, artificial flavorings must be labeled as either *artificial* or *imitation*. Likewise, natural flavorings must be labeled as either *natural* or *pure*. (Liqueurs are the exception to this rule. In the United States, liqueurs are regulated by the Bureau of Alcohol, Tobacco, and Firearms [BATF]. The BATF does not require the labeling of flavorings in liqueurs.) All processed flavorings, including extracts, liqueurs, compounds, oils, emulsions, and powders, can be natural or artificial, or a combination of both.

All artificial flavorings are not created equal. Many have improved over the years, and some are quite good. The comments that follow are general comments that apply to some and not others. Before deciding which to use, determine your needs and those of your customer, then purchase accordingly.

The most common reason for using artificial flavorings is to reduce cost. While cost is not an issue for some operations, for many it is. If using artificial vanilla in chocolate mousse allows you to splurge on real vanilla bean in ice cream, it is worth considering. And, because of advances in flavor chemistry, low cost no longer necessarily means low quality.

Imitation almond extract, for example, is an excellent substitute for natural almond extract. Natural almond oil is a very simple flavor, consisting of little more than a single flavor chemical, and it is easily imitated with an artificial flavoring.

Pure vanilla, however, is more difficult to reproduce because it consists of hundreds of flavor chemicals that provide deep, rich middle notes in addition to top notes. Some artificial vanilla flavorings consist of only one or two flavor top notes—primarily vanillin. Often, these simple mixtures are best at supplementing pure vanilla rather than replacing it. This is especially true where vanilla is the predominant flavor, as in vanilla ice cream, vanilla sauce, or Chantilly cream.

What many artificial flavorings lack in complexity, however, they often make up in strength. If they appear weak, it is because they lack a full flavor profile. Whenever a flavoring lacks a full flavor, it is unlikely that doubling or tripling it will make up for this lack. Instead, the result will likely be flavor burn. Flavor burn is a sharp flavor or an unpleasant sting on the tongue that occurs when flavorings—either natural or artificial—are used at too high a level. It is a common problem with certain artificial flavorings, since they can be abruptly sharp. While this can be a problem in some situations, it is an advantage in others. For example, the strong taste of artificial vanillin is often needed to balance the equally strong flavors of chocolate. In fact, a large number of chocolate products contain vanillin in place of pure vanilla.

Their robust composition makes many artificial flavorings ideal for baked goods exposed to intense heat. That is why cookies and biscuits, in particular, benefit from the use of artificial flavorings that have good heat stability.

While many good artificial flavorings are on the market, no single flavoring works equally well in all products, and some bakery products are particularly sensitive to the quality of flavoring used.

EVALUATING NEW FLAVORINGS

Resist the temptation to judge the quality of flavorings by price alone or by smelling them straight from the bottle. Instead, evaluate flavorings in the actual products in which they will be used. For quick screenings, however, it is acceptable to use simple products. For example, evaluate vanilla flavorings in sweetened milk or whipped cream. Be aware, however, that flavor perception is complex, so don't expect a single flavoring to work equally well in all products. Vanilla that is wonderful in pastry cream may be weak and dull in sponge cake.

FINDING INSPIRATION

Flavorings often transform pastry from ordinary to distinctly different, even memorable. For new ideas on flavors, consider studying the foods of foreign cultures, including the Middle East, South America, Southeast Asia, and the Mediterranean. You'll find, for example, that a blend of orange, coffee, honey, and spices is a classic flavoring for chocolate in Sicily.

Read about food trends and popular flavors throughout history. There you will learn of flavorings—such as rosewater—that were popular with Europeans before the Spanish brought vanilla from the Americas.

Bring spices from the kitchen into the bakeshop. A small amount of black pepper, for example, provides a subtle yet important finish to pumpkin pie spice. This idea is borrowed from a nineteenth-century American cookbook.

In your travels, do not stray too far away from the familiar. Customers want variety, but they are more comfortable with variations on what they know, and they will always appreciate a well-made classic more than an ill-conceived new creation.

Many formulas call for flavorings to be added "to taste." This is necessary because different brands of the same flavoring often vary in strength. The first time a formula is used, determine the correct amount of flavoring to use. For example, to flavor a buttercream with vanilla extract, weigh out an amount of vanilla extract that is more than you will need. Next, add vanilla extract to the buttercream to taste. Weigh the amount of extract remaining, and subtract this amount from the original amount weighed out. The difference is the amount of extract that was added to the buttercream. Be sure to record this amount on your formula so you can refer to it time and again.

STORAGE AND HANDLING

Fresh herbs last from a few days to two weeks, as long as they are stored properly and of good quality when received. To keep from wilting and yellowing, bunch the herbs into a bouquet and place in a cup of water, stem side down. Cover leaves loosely with plastic wrap. Or, wrap leaves in damp paper towels and place in plastic bags in refrigerator.

Dried spices and other flavorings don't spoil so much as lose or change flavor and color. Certain ground spices also cake and clump. While spices retain some degree of flavor for years, they slowly degrade. Moisture, light, heat, and oxygen in air accelerate this degradation. This means that spices are best kept covered in a cool, dark spot. Whole spices last longer than ground spices because the flavors are protected by the spice's natural cell structure.

HELPFUL HINTS

The high heat from cooking and baking presents special challenges with flavorings prized for their volatile top notes. While it is difficult to eliminate flavor loss completely during cooking and baking, there are several ways to reduce it to manageable levels. First, consider supplementing natural flavorings with an artificial one specially designed for baking. With artificial vanilla flavorings, select one that contains ethyl vanillin, which is especially heat stable. Also consider encapsulated flavorings, for the same reason.

Avoid using flavorings that contain alcohol, such as extracts and liqueurs. Alcohol evaporates easily, and it can strip valuable top notes along with it. Instead, where flavor loss is a problem, try flavorings that contain nonalcohol solvents, such as glycerin and water.

Add flavorings directly to fat. For example, cream vanilla extract into butter instead of adding it to liquids. Since many flavors dissolve in fat, they are less likely to evaporate when captured by the fat.

Add flavorings as late in the cooking process as possible. For example, add vanilla extract to pastry cream after it is removed from the heat. Extract added too early evaporates, but if added too late, the alcohol will not evaporate and may detract from the flavor of the cream.

When handling spices and other flavorings, practice good inventory control. Ideally, purchase only enough for three to six months' use, and follow the FIFO rule—first in, first out. Do not open new containers until ready to use, because the containers are usually vacuum-sealed to exclude oxygen.

The American Spice Trade Association makes these additional recommendations for keeping ground spices as long as six months to one year.

- Close containers quickly and tightly after each use.
- Measure with dry utensils.
- Store at or below 68°F (20°C); if possible, refrigerate.
- Keep away from wet or humid locations, such as washdown areas and dishwashers.

QUESTIONS FOR REVIEW

1. Provide examples of where each of the following plant parts is used for flavoring food: leaf, seed, fruit, flower bud, root, and bark.

2. What is a flavor extract?

3. How is vanilla extract made?

4. How is peppermint extract made?

5. What are the advantages of vanilla extract and of vanilla bean?

6. What is meant by the fold of an extract?

7. When mixing batters and doughs, why is it best to cream an extract into the fat rather than add it with liquids?

8. Describe a product application where a concentrated liqueur flavor might be more desirable than using the liqueur itself.

9. In what type of product are flavor oils most likely used?

10. What is meant by a flavor compound?

11. List the advantages and disadvantages of imitation vanilla flavoring.

12. Of the following products, which might benefit the most from the use of artificial vanilla flavoring, which from pure vanilla extract or vanilla bean, and why: vanilla cookies, vanilla ice cream, buttercream?

13. Explain what flavor burn is and how to prevent it.

14. What should you do if a formula calls for a flavoring to be added to taste?

15. Describe two ways of storing fresh herbs.

16. List six points to consider for maintaining the flavor of dry spices.

EXERCISES AND EXPERIMENTS

1. Spice Smells

Fill wide-mouth small dark bottles with a layer of ground spices, some with one spice per bottle, others with a blend of spices. Top with a cotton ball, to hide the spice from view, and label each bottle on the bottom with its contents. Cover each bottle and shake gently, to stir up volatile molecules. Uncap and sniff, and see if you can identify the spice from smell alone. Repeat until you are able to identify all spices and all spice combinations.

2. How Different Brands and Types of Vanilla Affect the Quality of Vanilla Custard Sauce

OBJECTIVES

To demonstrate how different brands and types of vanilla affect the:
- Appearance of vanilla custard sauce
- Flavor strength and quality of vanilla custard sauce
- Overall acceptability of vanilla custard sauce

PRODUCTS PREPARED

Vanilla custard sauce made with:
- Pure vanilla extract (Madagascar)
- Imitation vanilla flavoring
- Imitation vanilla flavoring, double the amount
- Vanilla bean (Madagascar)
- Other, if desired (Tahitian vanilla bean, double the amount of pure vanilla extract, double the amount of vanilla bean, additional brands of pure extract, additional brands of imitation flavorings, etc.)

MATERIALS AND EQUIPMENT

- Vanilla custard sauce, enough to make 2 cups (½ liter) of each variation
- Stainless steel saucepans, 1½ quart or equivalent
- Heat-resistant spatulas
- Ice water bath

PROCEDURE

- Prepare vanilla custard sauce using the formula that follows or using any basic vanilla custard sauce formula. Prepare one batch of sauce for each variation.
- Cool samples in ice water bath, all to same temperature (about 40°F/5°C).
- Record any potential sources of error that might make it difficult to draw the proper conclusions from the experiment.
- Use cost information to determine the cost per batch for the vanilla used in each product. If you do not have costing information available, use the following values:
  - Pure vanilla extract, one-fold: $1.00/ounce
  - Pure vanilla extract, two-fold: $1.75/ounce
  - Imitation vanilla extract: $0.25/ounce
  - Vanilla bean (Madagascar): $1.00/each
  - Vanilla bean (Tahitian): $3.00/each
- Evaluate the sensory characteristics of completely cooled products and record evaluations in the Results Table, which follows. Be sure to compare each in turn to the control product, evaluating each of the attributes listed in the Results Table. For your evaluation of flavor strength and quality, consider the following:
  - Immediate vanilla impact
  - Lingering vanilla middle notes
  - Sweetness
  - Alcohol taste

Vanilla Custard Sauce

INGREDIENT	POUNDS	OUNCES	GRAMS	BAKER'S PERCENTAGE
Milk, whole		8	240	50
Heavy cream		8	240	50
Sugar, granulated		4	115	25
Egg yolks		4	115	25
Vanilla extract or flavoring		0.2	5	1
Total	1	8.2	715	151

Method of Preparation

1. Place milk, heavy cream, and sugar into 2-quart stainless steel saucepan and bring just to a boil.

2. Using a wire whisk, gently stir egg yolks; temper scalded milk mixture into yolks by slowly adding approximately ½ cup (125 milliliters) of it into yolks.

3. Add yolk/milk mixture back into scalded milk.

4. Cook mixture over low heat until it coats back of spoon (nappe), stirring constantly with a heat-resistant spatula.

5. Immediately remove from heat and transfer to a stainless steel bowl.

6. Place bowl in ice water bath.

7. Add vanilla extract/flavoring and continue to cool, stirring occasionally. *Note:* 1½ teaspoons (8 milliliters) can be used in place of 0.2 ounces (5 grams), if necessary.

Method of Preparation for Custard Sauces Made with Different Amounts of Vanilla Extract/Flavoring or Made with Vanilla Bean:

1. Follow the Method of Preparation for the control product (vanilla extract) above except for the following.

2. For double the amount of extract/flavoring, add 0.2 ounces (10 grams) or 1 tablespoon (15 milliliters).

For Vanilla Bean:

1. In step 1, add ½ vanilla bean, split and scraped, to milk/cream mixture.

2. In step 5, pass sauce through chinois after removing from heat, to remove vanilla bean.

3. In step 7, omit vanilla extract.

 **SOURCES OF ERROR**

RESULTS TABLE ■ SENSORY EVALUATION OF VANILLA CUSTARD SAUCES MADE WITH DIFFERENT TYPES AND AMOUNTS OF VANILLA FLAVORING

TYPE AND AMOUNT OF VANILLA	APPEARANCE	FLAVOR STRENGTH AND QUALITY	OVERALL ACCEPTABILITY	COMMENTS
Pure vanilla extract (control product)				
Imitation vanilla flavoring				
Imitation vanilla flavoring, double the amount				
Vanilla bean				

CONCLUSIONS

1. What were the main differences between the sauces made with pure vanilla extract (control product) and real vanilla bean? Were these differences small, moderate, or large?

_____

_____

2. What were the main differences between the sauces made with pure vanilla extract and imitation vanilla flavoring? Were these differences small, moderate, or large?

_____

_____

3. What were the main differences between the sauces made with imitation vanilla flavoring and imitation flavoring at twice the level? Were these differences small, moderate, or large?

_____

_____

4. Which was closer in flavor to the sauce made with real vanilla extract (control product): the sauce made with imitation vanilla flavoring or with twice the level of imitation flavoring? Explain.

_____

_____

5. Which sauce did you feel was most acceptable overall, and why?

_____

_____

6. Did you have any sources of error that might significantly affect the results of your experiment? If so, what could you do differently next time to minimize error?

_____

_____

7. How different are the sauces in cost? That is, are they different by pennies per batch, or dollars? In your opinion, does this price difference justify use of imitation flavoring in vanilla custard sauce? If not, why not?

_____

_____

CHAPTER 15

FRUIT AND FRUIT PRODUCTS

CHAPTER **OBJECTIVES**

1. Discuss different forms of fruit that can be purchased for the bakeshop.

2. Using apples and blueberries as examples, discuss factors to consider when selecting fruit varieties.

3. Discuss the ripening process.

4. Describe how to best store and handle fruits.

INTRODUCTION

Fruit is nature's sweet. It is the centerpiece of many traditional desserts, such as fruit tarts and pies, poached pears, and apple strudel, and it complements many plated desserts. Fruit is an important source of flavor, color, and texture in the bakeshop.

Fruit and fruit products today are different from those found in bakeshops as little as thirty years ago. Today, there is widespread use of frozen fruit purees, and flavors once considered exotic, such as mango and kiwi, are almost as common as strawberry and apple. New fruit varieties are continually being bred, such as the boysenberry and the Marion blackberry, and new ones imported and popularized, such as the sweet Meyer lemon and the nashi or Asian pear.

This chapter is not meant to be all-inclusive and it will not discuss each and every fruit. Instead, it focuses on a few common fruits and fruit forms, with the understanding that the principles of proper selection, storage, and use of fruit in general will provide the foundation for adapting to a changing industry.

HOW FRUIT IS PURCHASED

Fruits can be purchased fresh, frozen, canned, or dried. They can be whole, sliced, or pureed, packed in water or sugar, sold as jam or as a prepared pie or bakery filling.

More fresh fruit is available year-round, as early- and late-ripening cultivars of fruits are developed, and as more fruit from the Southern Hemisphere is exported to

HOW ARE NEW FRUIT VARIETIES DEVELOPED?

New and improved varieties of fruits are constantly entering the marketplace. New fruits often have improvements over older ones in flavor, texture, appearance, and size, providing a benefit to the consumer. Other times, the improvements are in disease resistance, yield per acre, and other benefits to the farmer.

How are new varieties developed, and who does the work? One technique that has been used for years is plant breeding. The first step in breeding plants is to select two plants with different desirable traits. For example, one strawberry might have great flavor and a firm texture but require large amounts of water to grow. A second plant might require little water, but it may have poorer flavor and texture. By transferring the pollen from one plant to another, the plant breeder hopes to generate seeds for plants with features that are the best of both. The only way to find out if this has happened is to plant seeds from the cross-pollination and determine if any grow into plants with the right combination of flavor, texture,

and water requirements. It is a time-consuming, expensive, hit-or-miss process, but most fruits are bred in this manner.

To get an idea of the size of such an undertaking, consider the following. Researchers at the University of California Strawberry Breeding Program grow around 10,000 seedlings in a nursery by crossbreeding parent plants. Each plant is evaluated for vigor, fruit quality, and yield, and about 200–300 are chosen and allowed to propagate and be planted in outdoor fields. Each outdoor-grown plant is further evaluated before one or more is selected for widespread planting.

The State of California relies on these traditional plant-breeding techniques, not on genetic engineering, to develop new strawberry cultivars. Why would the state spend so much time and money breeding a better strawberry? Over 80 percent of the strawberries consumed in North America are grown in California, making strawberries a multibillion-dollar business for the state.

North America during the winter. Ideally, fruit used in the bakeshop is fresh and fully ripe, but this is not always possible. For example, fresh blueberries purchased in the middle of winter might have poor color or flavor, or be prohibitively expensive. While some bakers and pastry chefs, for practical or philosophical reasons, use fruit only when it is in season locally, others like to use all types year-round, in season or not. Most common fruits, such as apples and strawberries, are available fresh year-round, but certain specialty fruits, such as pomegranate and lychee, are available only certain months of the year.

Purchasing fresh fruit in season is no guarantee of quality. Fruit is highly perishable, and poorly stored fruit will lose its value relatively quickly. Fruit is a natural agricultural product, and its quality varies throughout the season and from one growing region to the next. It also varies from one year to the next, partly because climatic conditions change from year to year. Depending on the amount of sun and rainfall and the length of the growing season, fruit can be weak-tasting and poor in color, or it can be sweet, vibrant, and bursting with flavor. Finally, different varieties of the same fruit can vary widely in quality.

Processed fruit—frozen and canned—provides certain benefits over fresh. Besides being available year-round, processed fruit is less perishable than fresh, and its quality is generally more consistent. When fruit is out of season, processed fruit often has better quality than fresh and it can be less expensive. Out-of-season fruit must be shipped long distances, often from South and Central America, Australia, and New Zealand. The cost of shipping is high, and its toll on quality even greater.

Even when fresh fruit is in season, reasonably priced, and high in quality, processed fruit products have a place in many bakeshops. Frozen puree, for example, need only be thawed and canned apples opened before use, with little manpower and no waste.

GRADING OF FRUIT

Fruits are natural products that vary greatly in quality. Both Canada and the United States have national programs for grading the quality of fruit grown and sold in their countries. The program run by the U.S. Department of Agriculture (USDA) is voluntary. Fruit in the United States that is not graded is not necessarily lower in quality; it could simply mean that the manufacturer chose not to take part in the USDA grading program.

Each fruit has a different set of standards to meet the grade, but the standards for all fruits are based on several common characteristics, including size, shape, color, and the amount of damage and decay allowed.

Frozen Fruit

Frozen fruit comes whole, sliced, diced, and pureed. *Straight-pack* frozen fruit is sold with the fruit placed directly into a pail or box, then frozen solid. Because freezing takes place slowly, straight-pack fruit often loses its piece integrity. Where this is not important, straight-pack fruit quality can be quite acceptable. A disadvantage of straight-pack fruit is that the whole pail or box must be thawed before use.

Individually quick frozen (IQF) fruit consists of whole fruit or fruit pieces that are quickly frozen and then packed into pails, boxes, or bags. As long as IQF fruit is not thawed and refrozen, the fruit pieces remain separate. IQF fruit is more expensive than straight-pack fruit, but it has one large advantage: With IQF fruit, as much or as little fruit can be used without thawing a whole container.

The faster freezing of IQF fruit means that smaller ice crystals form, and this often means less damage to fruit integrity than with straight-pack fruit. However, do not expect the same quality from IQF fruit as you would from peak-quality fresh fruit. Even when frozen quickly, fruit shrivels and exudes liquid. Certain fruits, such as cranberries and apple slices, freeze well, while others, like strawberries and raspberries, become unacceptably soft and mushy. IQF fruit often loses flavor, as well, after extended freezing. For the best color and flavor in frozen fruits, consider using sugar- or syrup-packed fruit.

Sugar- or *syrup-packed* frozen fruit has a certain amount of granulated sugar or glucose corn syrup added before freezing. Sugar-packed frozen fruit typically comes as a 4 + 1, 5 + 1, or 7 + 1 pack. The numbers refer to the ratio of fruit to sugar. For example, 4 + 1 strawberries consist of 4 parts strawberries to 1 part sugar, or 4/5 = 80 percent fruit and 1/5 = 20 percent sugar. It is very common for strawberries to be sold as a 4 + 1, just as it is common for cherries to be sold as a 5 + 1 pack (16.7 percent sugar) and apples to be sold as a 7 + 1 (12.5 percent sugar). The sugar is added to prevent browning of the fruit. Sugar also minimizes changes in flavor and texture of frozen fruits, so sugar-packed frozen fruit often has better quality than straight-pack or IQF fruit, often at a lower cost. When using sugar-packed

> **HELPFUL** HINT
>
> Before adding IQF fruit, such as blueberries, to muffin or coffee cake batter, coat the fruit with a light dusting of flour. This will make the juice from the thawing fruit less likely to mix with the batter and discolor it. Or, layer the fruit on top of the batter instead of mixing it in. During baking, as the fruit sinks, it will do so with a minimum amount of bleeding.

> **HELPFUL** HINT
>
> After thawing sugar- or syrup-packed fruit, thoroughly blend the sugar with the fruit before use, and account for the amount of sugar in your formula.
>
> Since 4 + 1 strawberries are 80 percent (0.80) strawberries and 20 percent (0.20) sugar, adjust your formula by dividing the weight of strawberries by 0.80 to determine the weight of 4 + 1 strawberries to use. Reduce the amount of sugar by the difference between the two. For example, for 1 pound (16 ounces) of strawberries, use 16/0.80 or 20 ounces of 4 + 1 strawberries and reduce the amount of sugar by 4 ounces (20 − 16). For one kilogram (1000 grams) of strawberries, use 1,000/0.80 or 1,250 kilograms of 4 + 1 strawberries and reduce the amount of sugar by 250 grams (1250 − 1000). Notice that the math is similar to that used when converting between shortening and butter or between granulated sugar and syrup.

fruit in place of fresh, be sure to adjust your formula for the amount of sugar added. As with straight-pack frozen fruit, the whole container of sugar- or syrup-packed fruit must be thawed before use, making it less convenient than IQF fruit.

FROZEN FRUIT PUREES

Frozen fruit purees are a convenient form of fruit, most commonly used in sauces, sorbets, Bavarian creams, mousses, and ice creams. Many pastry chefs consider frozen fruit purees a staple in the bakeshop, as important as prepared fondant, extracts, and liqueurs.

Fruit purees are made by straining and pureeing cleaned fruit, then heating to pasteurize and to deactivate enzymes. Some purees have sugar added, and pectin or other thickeners may be added to control consistency. Even single-strength purees are concentrated sources of fruit flavor, but some brands have water removed so that 1 measure of puree equals 2 or more measures of fresh fruit.

Purees come in a wide variety of flavors, with or without seeds. Some fruit purees, such as raspberry and cherry, can be of excellent quality. Others, such as kiwi, are more difficult for the manufacturer to heat-process without a loss in flavor and color. Use fresh puree as your guide before deciding if the quality of a frozen fruit puree is up to your standards.

HELPFUL HINT

Frozen fruit purees may look like ready-made sauces and coulis, but they are not. Before using one directly on a plated dessert, taste the puree. Chances are it is too sour and strong tasting, even if sugar is listed as an ingredient. Use the puree as a starting base, and add sweeteners, flavorings, and other ingredients to turn the puree into a sauce or coulis.

Canned Fruit, Fruit Fillings, and Jams

Expect canned fruit, fruit fillings, and jams to have less fresh flavor and often a softer texture than fresh fruit. Sometimes fresh fruit flavor, color, and texture are not the goal, however. Consider caramelized peach sauce, for example, slowly simmered with spices. Or consider a reduced orange glaze or strawberry jam, both with a fuller, deeper fruitiness than the fresh fruit. These are products where fresh fruit flavor, color, and texture may be a liability.

Canned fruits are purchased several ways, varying primarily in the amount of sugar and water added. *Solid pack* canned fruit has no water added, *heavy pack* has a small amount of water or juice, and *water pack* has water added. Besides these versions, canned fruit comes with added sugar or another sweetener. If one of these sweeteners is added, it is called a *syrup pack*. Depending on the amount of sweetener, the syrup is considered light, medium, heavy, or extra heavy. Do not confuse a heavy pack with a heavy syrup pack. One is heavy in fruit, the other heavy in sweetener.

HELPFUL HINT

Be clear on what is important in your final product before deciding which form of fruit will best suit your needs. For example, it may not be worth the time and expense to purchase fresh or even frozen fruit when the fruit is to be reduced and simmered at length.

Generally, the more sweetener added, the firmer the fruit and often the better the color and flavor. This is also true when fresh fruit is cooked in the bakeshop, as when preparing poached pears.

Canned fruit fillings are ready-to-use products, convenient for fruit pies, Danish, and other baked goods. They vary widely in quality, so try different brands before deciding which suits your needs and your budget. While not all canned fruit fillings contain additives, some might, to improve color, flavor, and consistency, and to minimize microbial growth. For example, calcium salts, like calcium chloride or calcium lactate, are sometimes added to firm up the fruit. Thickeners, like starches and pectin, are commonly added for thickness and to improve performance during baking. That is, so-called oven-stable fillings contain thickeners that reduce the tendency of fillings to thin out and run into pastry dough. This prevents the dough from becoming soggy and discolored.

POACHING FRUIT

To preserve the texture and often the flavor and color of cooked fruits, it is better to poach them in sugar syrup than in water. Some poaching syrups are very dilute; that is, some are as low as one part sugar to five or more parts water (or wine). Others are much more concentrated, having more than one part sugar to one part water. Before determining the amount of sugar to add to poaching liquid, consider the following.

When fruit is gently poached in sugar syrup, sugar and water freely diffuse, or move, in and out of the fruit. This diffusion continues until the amount of sugar and water in the syrup is the same as the amount in the fruit.

If the sugar syrup has more sugar than does the fruit, water diffuses out of the fruit to dilute the syrup. As this happens, fruit shrinks in size and often appears to have a vibrant, more appealing color (even as color diffuses out of the fruit). At the same time, sugar diffuses from the syrup into the fruit, sweetening the fruit and firming the pectin that holds it together. The more sugar in the syrup, the sweeter and firmer the fruit becomes but also the more it shrinks.

If the sugar syrup contains less sugar than the fruit, the opposite happens. Water diffuses into the fruit and sugar diffuses out. Often, enough water moves in so that the fruit gains weight and plumps appealingly. If the fruit is poached in water, however, large amounts of water move in. The force of the water disintegrates the fruit, reducing it to mush. While this makes water a poor cooking medium for whole or sliced fruit, it is an effective means of hastening the preparation of fruit purees and applesauce.

Each fruit is different, but often a good poaching liquid for sweetening and firming fruit contains two parts liquid to one part sugar. This allows some sweetening and firming of fruit without excessive shrinkage. To further assure firm poached fruit, poach gently without boiling, and add a small amount of lemon juice to the poaching liquid. Acid from the lemon juice firms the pectin that holds fruit cells together. Lemon juice also prevents browning and adds an appealing flavor.

Artificial color might be added to canned fruits that discolor easily, like cherries. Other common additives include mold inhibitors, like sodium benzoate, and inhibitors to browning, like citric acid, ascorbic acid (vitamin C), and sulfites. The mold inhibitors are not necessary to the canning process, because mold will not grow in properly processed canned foods. Instead, the mold inhibitor delays microbial growth in opened cans.

Some fruit products are packed into flexible pouches instead of cans. This usually indicates that the product has been aseptically processed. *Aseptic processing* is a means of heating, cooling, and packaging foods in a sterile environment. Like canned foods, unopened packages of aseptically processed foods can be stored at room temperature without the risk of microbial growth. Once opened, they must be refrigerated. For our purposes, there is little difference between canned foods and aseptically processed ones.

Dried Fruit

Fruit was originally dried to preserve it, but today dried fruits are used for their distinctive color, flavor, and texture. The most common dried fruit is raisins, but dried figs, dates, apricots, apples, and plums are also popular. In recent years, dried cherries, blueberries, strawberries, and cranberries have also become available for use.

Some dried fruit is sold as a paste. Fig paste, for use in products like fig bars, is the most popular. Dried plum paste is sold as a fat replacer. This will be discussed shortly.

FIGURE 15.1 Grapes can dry to become raisins
Courtesy of the U.S. Department of Agriculture

RAISINS

Any grape can be dried into raisins (Figure 15.1), but most raisins are dried from naturally sweet Thompson Seedless grapes, grown in the hot Central Valley of California. After they are harvested in late August, the grapes are laid out in rows in the sun for several weeks, to darken and dry before being cleaned and packed.

Raisins and raisin products—raisin paste, for example—contribute flavor, color, and sweetness to baked goods. They also extend shelf life of baked goods because they are hygroscopic and keep baked goods moist. Raisin products also contain small amounts of natural antimicrobial agents that help prevent mold growth.

Golden raisins are Thompson Seedless grapes that are tunnel-dried, rather than sun-dried, under carefully controlled conditions. Sulfur dioxide (or another source of sulfur, such as sulfites) is applied to the grapes, to bleach their natural pigments and to prevent darkening during drying. Golden raisins have a milder raisin flavor with a slight bitter aftertaste from the sulfur dioxide. Sulfur dioxide can be used to keep other light-colored dried fruits from darkening, including dried apricots, papayas, peaches, and pears. When products are treated with sulfur dioxide or another source of sulfur, they must have this information on the label.

Zante currant raisins are not related to the European red currant; Zante currants are raisins dried from Black Corinth grapes, a small dark purple grape sometimes marketed as the champagne grape. Zante currants are about one-quarter the size of regular raisins. Regular-sized raisins are also called select raisins. Figure 15.2 compares the size of currants with that of select raisins. While there are about 1,000 select raisins per pound (450 grams), currants can have up to 4,000 or more per pound (450 grams). Currants are popular in scones, but they can be used anywhere their smaller size is an advantage.

Baking raisins are Thompson Seedless raisins that are soft and moist because they have a higher moisture content than regular raisins. This makes them messy for out-of-hand eating, but it means that they are ready to add to baked goods and do not need to be conditioned first. Conditioning is discussed later in this chapter.

(a)   (b)

FIGURE 15.2 (a) Select raisins (b) Zante currants
Courtesy of the California Raisin Marketing Board

SWEETENED DRIED CRANBERRIES, CHERRIES, STRAWBERRIES, BLUEBERRIES

Most fruits do not have the high sugar content of the Thompson grape. If dried without added sugar, these fruits tend to be tough, dry, and sour. For softness and sweetness, cranberries, cherries, strawberries, and blueberries are first infused with sugar before they are dried in a tunnel drier under controlled conditions.

Sweetened dried fruits are expensive, so be selective about how they are used. For example,

WHAT'S THE DIFFERENCE BETWEEN PRUNES AND DRIED PLUMS?

There is no difference between prunes and dried plums; the terms are used interchangeably, but the preferred term today is dried plums. According to the California Dried Plum Board, however, not all plums dry well. The plum must dry in the sun without fermenting to be acceptable, and this is best done with plums that naturally contain high levels of sugar. Dried plums are not always sun-dried, however. As with raisins, plums can be dried in tunnel driers under carefully controlled conditions.

Tunnel-drying is beneficial when a milder-tasting, lighter-colored dried plum is desired.

The California plum for drying is a descendant of the La Petite d'Agen plum from southwest France. This is a deep purple-skinned oval plum with amber-colored flesh. Over 99 percent of the dried plums—or prunes—from California are of this one variety, and California supplies well over 70 percent of the world's supply of dried plums.

sweetened dried fruit works better than fresh or frozen fruit in applications where doughs are heavy or where products are low in moisture. They are good, for example, in cookies and scones. For one, the high moisture in fresh fruit is undesirable in these doughs, especially if cookies are crisp and dry. Besides, it is difficult to mix fresh fruit into heavy dough without tearing and breaking the fruit. Dried fruit, on the other hand, mixes into heavy doughs without tearing and breaking.

In most other applications, however, consider using other forms of fruit. Fresh, frozen, or canned blueberries have advantages over dried blueberries in muffins, for example. They provide a fresher, brighter fruit flavor that contrasts well with the bland taste of a muffin, and they cost less, too.

DRIED PLUM PASTE

Dried plum (prune) paste is sold as a fat replacer for baked goods. Because of its color and flavor, dried plum paste is best used in dark-colored products such as brownies and gingerbread.

Dried plum paste does not replace all the functions of fat, but it is effective at moistening and tenderizing baked goods. It contains several components, including fructose, glucose, pectin, and sorbitol, that provide these functions. Recall from Chapter 8 that sorbitol is a type of sweetener called a polyol, one that is very hygroscopic.

Dried plum paste can be purchased or it can be prepared by blending dried plums (prunes) with water in a food processor until smooth. Add about 12 ounces (750 grams) of hot water for every pound (kilogram) of dried plums. To use in baked goods, replace each pound (kilogram) of fat with one-half pound (500 grams) of dried plum paste. This is a starting point only; make adjustments as needed.

COMMON FRUITS

Many fruits are available to the baker and pastry chef—too many to discuss here. Whether peaches or pears, plums or cherries, the same general rules hold for selecting one variety over another. The following discussion focuses on selecting from among different varieties of apples and blueberries, but these same guidelines can be applied to all fruits.

DOES AN APPLE A DAY KEEP THE DOCTOR AWAY?

Modern science often rediscovers the truths of old wives' tales. Apples, for example, are a good source of dietary fiber and of polyphenolic compounds. Dietary fiber performs many functions in the body, including prevention of cancers and cardiovascular diseases.

Polyphenolic compounds—polyphenols—are a large class of compounds found in plant products, including fruits. Sometimes called flavonoids, polyphenols are powerful antioxidants that reportedly guard against cancer and cardiovascular diseases. Foods that contain polyphenols and other beneficial compounds are sometimes called functional foods, because they function beyond providing the common nutrients important for basic health.

Apples are not the only fruit beneficial to good health. Most fruits are good sources of dietary fiber, and many contain plant pigments that do more than provide color. Anthocyanins, for example, are the reds and purples in the plant world.

Anthocyanins are polyphenolic compounds, and like other polyphenolic compounds, they have antioxidant activity and many health benefits. Blackberries, blueberries, cherries, cranberries, pomegranates, raspberries, red grapes, and strawberries are all rich in anthocyanins that together contribute to good health.

Carotenoids are another class of plant pigments that are powerful antioxidants and contribute to good health. Carotenoids are yellow, orange, and orange-red pigments. Peaches, pears, melons, citrus, papayas, and mangoes are but a few fruits naturally high in carotenoids.

Health guidelines for North Americans include the recommendation to increase consumption of fruits and vegetables. In the United States, a program called 5 A Day for Better Health is sponsored by several health organizations to encourage Americans to eat five or more servings of fruits and vegetables a day.

Apples

There are many varieties of apples to choose from, and the apple industry continually comes out with new ones. In Canada, McIntosh is the number one apple. In the United States, Red Delicious, Golden Delicious, and Granny Smiths have been the three top varieties for the past decade or so. That is changing, as new tree varieties, such as Braeburn, Fuji, Gala, Jonagold, and Honeycrisp, planted in the 1990s, begin to bear larger harvests. Fuji is the most popular apple in Japan, while Jonagold is already well-known in Europe.

Each variety has its own characteristic color, flavor, and texture. Understand, however, that no one apple is ideal for all applications. For example, many consider Rome Beauty best for whole baked apples, Golden Delicious or Cortland for fresh fruit applications, and Granny Smiths for apple pies. Opinions vary, however, and that is why it is helpful to have some knowledge and personal experience with different apple varieties, so you can form your own opinions. The same is true for other fruits, as well.

When evaluating different varieties of any fruit, including apples, be aware that fruits are natural agricultural products that vary in quality over the course of the year and from year to year. Any conclusions reached about the relative quality of Granny Smith apples to McIntosh, for example, will be different when the evaluation is completed in the fall, when most apples are harvested, than if it is completed in the spring. Apples are harvested year-round, but each variety has its own peak harvest time. If it is not peak harvest time for a particular apple variety, the apple may have been stored in controlled atmosphere (CA) storage.

SELECTING AN APPLE FOR PIE OR STRUDEL

Much of selecting the appropriate apple for a pie or strudel is personal preference, or the preference of your customers. The important point to understand is that differences in apples do exist, and which apple you select will affect the quality of

WHAT IS CA STORAGE?

Controlled atmosphere (CA) storage is a method of storing fruits, like apples, so they remain fresh for a long time, as much as six months or more. CA stored apples are placed in large rooms that are kept at temperatures just above freezing, with the amount of moisture, oxygen, and other gases tightly controlled. CA apples may appear fresh, but noticeable changes can occur to both flavor and texture.

CA stored apples lose some of their sourness and aroma, but they often get sweeter. Their texture often becomes undesirably mealy, and they brown more quickly once sliced. If you find that the apples you receive are not up to par, change to a different variety, use frozen or canned, or offer an item only in season.

your pie. Here are some points to consider when selecting an apple variety for pie or strudel.

- *Aroma*—if the apple doesn't have the aroma of an apple, you'll end up with a sugar pie or a spice pie. Varieties that have a distinct, strong apple aroma include McIntosh, Empire, and Jonathan; apples with little aroma include Rome Beauty, Red Delicious, and Granny Smith. Some apples, including Golden Delicious, have a pear-like aroma.

- *Texture*—firm rather than soft apples are generally preferred in pies. Examples of firm apples include Cortland, Granny Smith, Northern Spy, and York Imperial. A soft apple is the McIntosh. Apples that are crisp fresh are not necessarily firm enough for baking. The crisp texture of Red Delicious apples, for example, make them good for fresh fruit applications but not necessarily so for baking.

- *Sourness*—generally, a sour apple is preferred in baking over one with little natural acidity. Acidity can be added, however, by adding lemon juice, but lemon juice adds a lemony taste, and may not be the flavor you are after. An apple that is high in acidity is the Granny Smith. Those that are low in acidity include Golden Delicious and Red Delicious.

- *Sweetness*—sweetness can easily be adjusted in an apple pie by adjusting the amount of sugar added. Apples that are low in sugar include the Granny Smith and York Imperial. Golden Delicious and Red Delicious are sweet apples.

Overall, the best apple for apple pie is one that has a strong apple aroma, firm texture, and is more sour than sweet. To achieve this, some bakers and pastry chefs combine apple varieties. For example, using Granny Smiths and McIntosh apples together in an apple pie provides the aroma of the McIntosh and the firm texture and sourness of the Granny Smith.

APPLES FOR WHOLE BAKING

Apples selected for baking whole or sautéing slices must hold their shape when heated. Rome Beauty apples are probably the best choice, because they hold their shape and do not explode or collapse when baked or sautéed. McIntosh apples, on the other hand, tend to break open and collapse when baked, literally bursting at the seams. As you might imagine, McIntosh apples are great for making applesauce.

APPLES FOR FRESH FRUIT APPLICATIONS

Apples selected for fresh applications should generally be more sweet than sour. Ideally, they will be firm and crisp, and more importantly, they should not brown quickly. Traditional choices for fresh presentations include Cortland and Golden Delicious.

MORE ON THE BROWNING OF FRESH FRUITS

Many fresh fruits—and vegetables—begin to brown within minutes of being cut. These same fruits and vegetables also brown when frozen and thawed. This fast browning happens at room temperature. Interestingly, heat can actually prevent it. Here's how.

The browning of fresh fruits and vegetables at room temperature is caused by an enzyme called phenolase, sometimes called polyphenoloxidase (PPO). Phenolase causes polyphenolic compounds in fruits and vegetables to combine, forming large molecules that absorb light across a broad spectrum of colors. This is what makes them appear brown.

All enzymes, including phenolase, are proteins that are inactivated by heat. The amount of heat needed to inactivate phenolase varies, but typically blanching (180°F/80°C or above) for sixty seconds or less is sufficient, as long as the piece size is small enough for the heat to penetrate throughout quickly.

Blanching is more typically used for vegetables than for fruits, which are too easily cooked by the heat. Instead, enzymatic browning in fresh fruits is usually delayed by lowering the pH by adding acid; excluding oxygen by soaking in liquid or coating with sugar or glaze; or by selecting a variety that browns slowly.

Fruits that brown through the action of phenolase include certain varieties of apples, bananas, cherries, peaches, and pears. Phenolase activity is not always undesirable. The brown color and distinct flavors of coffee, tea, and cocoa are partly due to enzymatic browning.

Newer varieties that work well include Cameo and Fuji. To further preserve whiteness, dip apples first in water enhanced with a small amount of lemon juice. The lemon juice slows the activity of enzymes that cause browning. Ascorbic acid (vitamin C) is sometimes used for this purpose, as well.

Blueberries

Blueberries come as two main types: wild and cultivated. Wild blueberries, also known as low-bush blueberries, grow on ground-hugging vines in the rocky soil of Maine and the Atlantic provinces of Canada. Cultivated blueberries, also called high-bush blueberries, grow on shrubs in several regions throughout the United States and Canada. Blueberries, depending on the species, sometimes go by other names, including bilberries, rabbiteyes, and huckleberries.

Cultivated blueberries, being relatively large, tend to provide a mouthful of juicy flavor when bitten into. They are typically preferred for fresh fruit presentations and for pies and tarts. Wild blueberries are generally more expensive per pound and less available than cultivated blueberries, yet they are often used in muffins and other baked goods. Their smaller size means that there are more wild blueberries per pound (or kilogram). Add a pound of wild blueberries to batter and there will be more points of color and flavor in your product, so less fruit can be used. The smaller size also means that there will be better uniformity of fruit throughout the batter. That is, it is less likely that there will be bites of muffin with no fruit while other bites are loaded with fruit.

Smaller fruit typically is less fragile than larger fruit, so a third advantage of using wild blueberries is that they can better withstand the abuses of mixing and heating. Finally, consumer perception is important. Wild blueberries, being less available and more expensive, are perceived as better and as having more intense flavor. Because they are perceived as being worth more, the higher cost of wild blueberries can be passed on to the consumer.

WHY MIGHT A GREEN RING FORM AROUND BLUEBERRIES IN BAKED GOODS?

Sometimes an unattractive green ring forms around blueberries in baked goods. In extreme cases, the green discoloration runs throughout the crumb. The discoloration forms when the anthocyanin pigments coloring the blueberries are exposed to a high pH—above 6 or so. This occurs because anthocyanin pigments are very pH-dependent, changing from red at a low pH to blue or purple at a medium pH, and to green at a high pH. In fact, anthocyanins are sometimes called nature's pH meter, because the pH of a substance can be predicted by how it alters the color of the pigment.

Discoloration can occur with any fruit or other ingredient that contains a high level of anthocyanins. Besides blueberries, cranberries, cherries, and walnuts are among the most common ingredients involved in this reaction.

The most likely causes of a high pH in baked goods are as follows:

- Too much baking soda or other alkali
- Too little cream of tartar or other acid
- A decrease in the amount of an acidic fruit or fruit juice, or its substitution with a less acidic fruit; for example, substituting half the cranberries in cranberry nut bread with apples
- A change from fast-acting to slow-acting baking powder
- Excessive bleeding of fruit into batter or dough

MORE ON THE RIPENING PROCESS

When fruits ripen, enzymes in the fruit break down large molecules to smaller ones. For example, starches break down to sugars, sweetening the fruit. Acids break down, so the fruit becomes less sour. Proteins and fats break down to molecules that have a pleasing, fruity aroma. Pectin, which holds fruits together, breaks down, making fruit softer and juicier.

FRUIT RIPENING

Ripening involves a series of changes that all fruits undergo as they age. Each type of fruit undergoes changes that are characteristic of that particular fruit. In general, however, fruits soften and become juicier, develop more color and flavor, and become sweeter and less sour as they ripen.

Some fruits can ripen after they are picked, or harvested. Table 15.1 is a partial list of fruits that are successfully ripened after harvest. While this list seems clear-cut, in fact, not all fruits ripen equally well. For example, bananas ripen better after harvest than probably any other fruit. They improve in all attributes, including color, flavor, sweetness, and texture. Cantaloupes and papayas, on the other hand, soften and develop color, but they will not sweeten or improve in flavor once they are harvested.

The ability of any fruit to ripen to its fullest depends on two factors. First, fruit must be fully mature. That is, it must have reached its full size before harvest, even though it might still be hard and green. Second, the fruit must have been stored properly before ripening. Many fruits, for example, will not ripen if first exposed to cold temperatures. Peaches, for example, do not ripen properly if they are stored below 46°F (8°C) for even a few hours prior to ripening. Some fruits will not ripen at all after they are harvested, even if stored properly. Table 15.2 is a partial list of fruits that cannot be successfully ripened after they are harvested. When purchasing these fruits, accept only those that are already fully ripe.

TABLE 15.1 ■ FRUITS THAT RIPEN AFTER HARVEST

Apples
Apricots
Bananas
Cactus (prickly) pear
Cantaloupe
Carambola (star fruit)
Cherimoya
Honeydew melons
Guava
Kiwifruit
Mangoes
Nectarines
Papayas
Passion fruit
Peaches
Pears
Persimmons
Plums

TABLE 15.2 ■ FRUITS THAT DO NOT RIPEN AFTER HARVEST

Berry fruits, including blackberries, blueberries, raspberries, strawberries
Citrus fruits
Cherries
Figs
Grapes
Pineapples
Watermelons

STORAGE AND HANDLING

Fresh Fruits

Fresh fruit can be expensive, so it is important that it be selected, stored, and handled properly. When a shipment of fruit arrives, for example, be sure to inspect it for quality and to always taste a sample before accepting the shipment. Remember that fruit is a natural agricultural product and quality can vary from one shipment to the next.

Fresh fruit that is consumed uncooked should be handled especially carefully, for sanitation reasons. Fresh fruit should always be washed before use, to remove dirt and microorganisms. Strawberries, in particular, grow close to the ground and pick up mold spores, while raspberries conceal insects in their caps. While fruit should be washed before use, it should *not* be washed before storage. Water left on the fruit encourages microbial growth, and washed fruit absorbs water into its cells. When this happens, the fruit swells and softens in an unappealing manner.

Melons, especially cantaloupe, must be washed before cutting. Melons grow on the ground, and cantaloupe, with its rough surface, tends to harbor microorganisms. When a knife passes through the melon, microorganisms on the melon's surface can be transferred to the fruit by the knife blade.

Several important tips for storing fresh fruit are listed below. While busy bakeshops with space constraints may not be able to follow all these tips, they should be followed whenever possible.

1. Store fresh fruits under high humidity, so they don't shrivel and dry. Often this means keeping them in their original packaging.
2. Do not store fresh fruit in closed plastic bags or plastic wrap for extended periods. Plastic cuts off oxygen, preventing plants, including fruits, from breathing, or respiring. If the fruit comes in plastic, however, it can be stored in this original packaging. Plastic packaging used for shipping and distributing fresh fruits and vegetables is not the same as plastic bags and plastic wrap used in the bakeshop.
3. Store ripe fruits at low temperatures, so they will respire more slowly and last longer. For most fruits, this means refrigerating them as close to 32°F (0°C) as possible. Avoid refrigerating unripened fruits, however. Recall that many fruits, such as peaches, will not ripen properly if exposed to cold temperatures.

DO PLANTS REALLY BREATHE?

Fresh, raw fruit is still living and breathing, or respiring, after it is harvested. As with human respiration, plant respiration involves taking in oxygen from the air, using it to continue life-sustaining processes, and giving off carbon dioxide. In the process, starches, sugars, and other molecules are broken down and used. As with humans, if respiration stops in plants, cells stop functioning and the plant dies.

While plants do respire, unlike humans, they also undergo photosynthesis. Photosynthesis is the opposite of respiration. That is, instead of taking in oxygen and giving off carbon dioxide, during photosynthesis plants take in carbon dioxide and give off oxygen. In the process, the plant forms sugar from carbon dioxide, using water from the soil and energy from sunlight. While mammals eat to take in sugar, plants undergo photosynthesis to create them.

DOES ONE BAD APPLE SPOIL THE WHOLE BUNCH?

Have you ever heard the expression that one bad apple spoils the whole bunch? It's true. Bruised and rotting fruit from Table 15.1, including apples, give off very large amounts of ethylene gas, which speeds up respiration in all fruits. If fruit is already ripe, exposure to ethylene gas causes them to rot.

While lower storage temperatures slow respiration, not all fruits, even when ripe, should be refrigerated. Cold temperatures cause chill injury to certain fruits, and this can damage their color, flavor, and texture. However, damage from chill injury is often not evident until after the fruit is returned to warmer temperatures. Chill injury is most likely to occur in fruits grown in tropical or semitropical regions, such as bananas, most citrus, mangoes, melons, papayas, and pineapples. Store these fruits at temperatures slightly above refrigeration, generally from 40°–60°F (4°–16°C).

Of course, it is not always possible to find a spot in the bakeshop that is warmer than the refrigerator yet colder than room temperature. If it is winter and there is a cool spot in the bakeshop, store tropical fruits there. If it is summer and it is extremely hot, refrigerate the fruit, but use it as quickly as possible.

4. Store fruits from Table 15.2 away from ripe fruits listed in Table 15.1, which naturally give off a gas called ethylene. Ethylene gas signals fruits to speed up respiration and to ripen. Since fruits from Table 15.2 cannot ripen any further, if these fruits are exposed to ethylene gas, they will begin to rot. That is why, for example, lemons should not be stored near ripe apples.

5. Before storing fruit, remove and discard any spoiled or rotten fruit.

6. To ripen fruit as fast as possible, store it at warm temperatures, and expose it to ethylene gas and oxygen. Closed paper bags and cardboard cartons allow oxygen in and out but trap ethylene. This means that paper bags and cardboard cartons are ideal for holding fruit for ripening. Place the paper bags or cardboard cartons in a warm spot and add a ripe apple or banana, for example, to give off ethylene.

Dried Fruits

Dried fruits are relatively safe from microbial damage, but it is still best to store dried fruits below 45°F (7°C). This prevents flavor changes and flavor loss, and it also prevents insect and rodent infestation. Since refrigeration space is often at a premium in the bakeshop, if dried fruits are held for one month or less, it is acceptable to store them in a cool spot in the bakeshop. Be sure they are well covered, to prevent moisture loss and infestation.

The glucose in dried fruit often crystallizes during extended refrigerator storage. This is sometimes called sugaring, and when it happens, the dried fruit becomes dry, hard, and gritty. Proper conditioning revives the flavor and texture of dried fruit that has sugared.

CONDITIONING RAISINS AND OTHER DRIED FRUITS

Conditioning is a process of soaking raisins and other dried fruits in water or another liquid before use. Conditioning plumps the fruit so it is not dry, hard, and flavorless in the final product. Conditioning also prevents dried fruit from absorbing moisture from batters and doughs. If too much moisture is pulled from batters and doughs, the product bakes up dry.

The raisin industry recommends that raisins not be soaked in hot or boiling water, because this easily overconditions them. Overconditioned dried fruits lose valuable flavor and sweetness to the soaking solution. They tend to tear during mixing and to stain batters and doughs.

Two methods are recommended for conditioning raisins and other dried fruits. Both require planning ahead by several hours. The first method involves spraying or submerging the dried fruit with slightly warm water (80°F; 27°C), draining immediately, and covering the fruit until surface water is absorbed. This takes about 4 hours. The second method involves adding about 1–2 ounces of 80°F (27°C) water per pound of dried fruit (or 80–120 grams per kilogram), covering, and soaking for about 4 hours, or until all water is absorbed. Stir or turn occasionally for even conditioning. Other liquids, such as rum or fruit juice, can be used in place of water.

Cut dried fruits, such as diced dates and sweetened dried cranberries, are probably best not conditioned. The cut surfaces readily pick up moisture, so there is little risk that they will stay hard in a batter or dough. The risk, instead, is that they will be easily overconditioned, resulting in fruits that bleed color and solids into the batter and that tear easily.

HELPFUL HINT

Even when properly conditioned, raisins and other dried fruits can tear during mixing. To minimize tearing, add dried fruits during the last minute or two of mixing, and set the mixer on low speed.

QUESTIONS FOR REVIEW

1. What are the advantages of using fresh fruit? What are the disadvantages?
2. What is meant by straight-pack fruit? What is meant by IQF fruit? What is a 4 + 1 pack?
3. What is the main advantage of IQF fruit over straight-pack, sugar-packed, or syrup-packed fruit?
4. Why use 4 + 1 frozen strawberries instead IQF strawberries in a fruit filling where flavor is most important?
5. How does the amount of sugar in poaching liquid affect the color, flavor, and texture of poached fruit?
6. What is the difference between a heavy pack and a heavy syrup pack in canned fruit?
7. Why might a canned fruit product, such as canned apple filling, contain calcium chloride?
8. Name some dried fruits that are most likely to contain sulfur dioxide (or another form of sulfur). Why is it added?
9. How are golden raisins similar to regular raisins? How are they different?
10. Why might sweetened dried blueberries be a better choice in cookie dough while fresh, frozen, or canned whole blueberries are better for muffins?
11. What is CA storage? How might it affect the quality of apples?
12. A shipment of underripe fresh fruit arrives that is not needed just yet. Which of the following should be done with the fruit, and why: Ripen the fruit and then refrigerate it until needed, or refrigerate first, then ripen?
13. Name four fruits that are best stored above 40°F (4°C); name four that are best stored below 40°F (4°C).
14. Where is ethylene gas found and how does it affect fruit?
15. Why should ripe bananas not be stored next to grapes?
16. A bin of ripe bananas contains one that is badly bruised. Why should the bruised banana be removed from the bin?
17. A carton of unripe pears that will be needed in just a few days arrives. How should the pears be stored so that they will ripen quickly?
18. What does it mean to condition raisins? Describe two methods recommended for conditioning raisins.
19. What might happen if raisins are underconditioned?
20. What might happen if raisins are overconditioned?
21. Why is it recommended that dried fruits be refrigerated for the long term?

QUESTIONS FOR DISCUSSION

1. List and explain five reasons why fresh fruit quality can vary.

2. Using the comparison of wild and cultivated blueberries as a guide, explain some advantages of Zante currants over raisins.

3. Why is it faster to prepare a cooked fruit coulis (sweetened fruit puree) by cooking the fruit in a small amount of water and withholding sugar until after the fruit disintegrates?

EXERCISES AND EXPERIMENTS

1. Strawberries and Sugar

A formula calls for 8 pounds (3.6 kilograms) of strawberries and 4 pounds (1.8 kilograms) of sugar. How much of a 4 + 1 pack and how much sugar should be used instead? Show your work.

_____

_____

_____

_____

_____

2. How Different Apple Varieties Compare in Quality When Consumed Fresh

OBJECTIVES

To demonstrate how apple variety and treatment of apples affects:
- The appearance, flavor, and texture of fresh apples
- The tendency of sliced fresh apples to brown
- The overall acceptability of different apple varieties in fresh-fruit applications

PRODUCTS PREPARED

Apple slices from:
- Granny Smith apples, untreated (control product)
- Red Delicious, untreated
- Golden Delicious, untreated
- McIntosh, untreated
- McIntosh, dipped in acidulated water for 30 seconds
- McIntosh, soaked in acidulated water for 15 minutes
- Other apple varieties, if desired (Braeburn, Cortland, Fuji, Gala, Honeycrisp, Jonagold, Macoun, Northern Spy, Rome, etc.)
- Other treatments, if desired (different amounts of lemon juice in water, different soak times, two crushed 200 mg vitamin C tablets dissolved in 14 fluid ounces [400 ml] water [0.1 percent ascorbic acid], commercial preps such as NatureSeal, etc.)

MATERIALS AND EQUIPMENT

- Apples, two or more for each variety and treatment
- Acidulated water: one tablespoon (15 milliliters) lemon juice into 16 fluid ounces (500 ml) water

PROCEDURE

- To evaluate the effects of treatments on the quality of fresh apple slices:
  - Pare and slice one McIntosh apple into six or eight slices of equal size. Discard any bruised or otherwise damaged slices.
  - Immediately place slices into acidulated water and soak for 15 minutes (longer, if time permits).
  - After 15 minutes, remove slices from acidulated water and lay in a row on parchment paper. Label row "15-minute soak."
  - Immediately slice another McIntosh apple and dip into acidulated water. Remove after 30 seconds and lay slices in a second row on parchment paper; label row as "dip."
  - Immediately slice a third McIntosh apple and lay slices in a third row on parchment paper. Label row "untreated."
  - Set aside at room temperature for 30 minutes.
  - After 30 minutes, evaluate apple slices and record results in Results Table 1, which follows. Be sure to compare each in turn to the control product and evaluate the following:
    - Amount of browning, from very little browning to extensive browning, on a scale of one to five.
    - Flavor (apple aroma, sweetness, sourness, etc.)
    - Texture (hard/soft, crispy, mealy, juicy/dry)
    - Overall acceptability, from highly unacceptable to highly acceptable, on a scale of one to five
    - Any additional comments, as necessary
  - Time permitting, repeat appearance evaluation after an additional 30 minutes and record results in Comments column of Results Table 1.
- To evaluate different apple varieties
  - Pare and slice two or more apples of each variety into six or eight slices of equal size. Discard any bruised or otherwise damaged slices.
  - Lay slices from one apple of each variety in a row onto parchment paper. Label each row with the name of the apple variety and record the time that samples were laid out.
  - In the meantime, evaluate remaining freshly-cut slices of each apple variety. Record evaluations in Results Table 1. Be sure to compare each apple in turn to the control product and consider the following:
    - Appearance (color, moistness/dryness, piece integrity and shape)
    - Flavor (apple aroma, sweetness, sourness, etc.)
    - Texture (hard/soft, crispy, mealy, juicy/dry)
    - Overall acceptability for fresh fruit consumption, from highly unacceptable to highly acceptable, on a scale of one to five
    - Add any additional comments, as necessary.
  - After 30 minutes, evaluate appearance of cut apple slices. Be sure to compare each apple in turn to the control product and focus on the extent of browning of each apple, from very little browning to extensive browning, on a scale of one to five.

■ Record any potential sources of error that might make it difficult to draw the proper conclusions from this experiment. In particular, be aware of variability that can occur from one apple of the same variety to another; also, note the seasonality of each apple variety and whether it is likely fresh-harvested or CA-stored.

SOURCES OF ERROR

RESULTS TABLE 1 ■ SENSORY CHARACTERISTICS OF McINTOSH APPLES TREATED TO PREVENT BROWNING

APPLE TREATMENT	AMOUNT OF BROWNING	FLAVOR	TEXTURE	OVERALL ACCEPTABILITY	COMMENTS
Untreated (control product)					
Dipped in acidulated water					
Soaked in acidulated water					

RESULTS TABLE 2 ■ SENSORY CHARACTERISTICS OF DIFFERENT VARIETIES OF FRESH APPLE SLICES

APPLE VARIETY	APPEARANCE WHEN FIRST CUT	FLAVOR	TEXTURE	AMOUNT OF BROWNING AFTER 30 MINUTES	OVERALL ACCEPTABILITY	COMMENTS
Granny Smith (control product)						
Red Delicious						
Golden Delicious						
McIntosh						

CONCLUSIONS

1. How well did the acidulated water dip and the extended soak work in delaying browning in McIntosh apple slices?

_____

_____

2. Did either treatment also change the flavor or texture of the McIntosh slices? If so, in what way?

_____

_____

3. Based on the results of this experiment, is it acceptable to soak McIntosh apple slices in acidulated water until they are needed for use, or is it better to dip, then set aside? Explain your answer.

_____

_____

4. What other fruits do you think would also benefit from either being dipped or soaked in acidulated water, to delay enzymatic browning?

_____

_____

5. Rank the different apple varieties from least sweet to sweetest.

_____

_____

6. Focusing on aroma only, which apple, to you, had the best apple aroma? Survey your class to determine, for each apple variety, the number of students that rated each as having the best apple aroma. How well did members of your class agree on this?

_____

_____

7. Which apple variety browned the fastest? Which browned the slowest?

_____

_____

8. Based on this experiment, which apple variety do you feel is most acceptable for fresh fruit presentations, and why?

_____

_____

9. Research the seasonality of each apple variety that you used in this experiment (www.bestapples.com; www.michiganapples.com; www.nyapplecountry.com). How might the results of this experiment be affected by the time of year (spring, summer, winter, fall) that this evaluation was completed?

_____

_____

10. Did you have any sources of error that might significantly affect the results of your experiment? If so, what could you do differently next time to minimize error?

_____

_____

3. How the Variety of Apple Affects the Overall Quality of Apple Crisp

OBJECTIVES

To demonstrate how apple variety affects:
- The appearance of apple crisp
- The firmness and juiciness of the apples in the crisp
- The overall flavor of the apple crisp
- The overall acceptability of the apple crisp

PRODUCTS PREPARED

Apple crisp made with:
- Granny smith apples (control product)
- Red Delicious
- Golden Delicious
- McIntosh
- Other apple varieties, if desired (Braeburn, Cortland, Gala, Jonagold, Northern Spy, Pippin, Rome, York Imperial, etc.)

MATERIALS AND EQUIPMENT

- Apples, 2 pounds (900 grams), approximately four large of each variety
- Streusel topping mix, enough to make a half sheet or hotel pan of apple crisp for each apple variety

PROCEDURE

- Preheat oven according to formula.
- Prepare apple crisp streusel topping using the formula that follows or using any basic streusel topping formula.
- Peel, core, and slice 2 pounds (900 grams) apples of each variety, slicing each apple into equal-sized pieces (fourteen slices for large apples).
- Add 1.25 ounces (40 grams) granulated sugar to apple slices and gently combine.
- Distribute sweetened apple slices into half sheet or hotel pan, spreading evenly.
- Top with an even layer of 10 ounces (275 grams) streusel topping.
- Use an oven thermometer placed in center of oven to read oven temperature; record results here _____.
- Place filled pans into preheated oven and set timer according to formula.
- Bake until control product (made with Granny Smith apples) is lightly brown and apples have softened slightly. Remove *all* apple crisps from oven after same length of time. If necessary, however, adjust bake times for oven variances. Record bake times in Comments column of Results Table 1.
- Transfer to cooling racks and cool slightly or to room temperature.
- Record any potential sources of error that might make it difficult to draw the proper conclusions from the experiment. In particular, be aware of how evenly apples were sliced; how evenly apples and streusel were spread in pan; and any problems with ovens.

- When apple crisps have cooled, evaluate their sensory characteristics and record evaluations in Results Table 1. Be sure to compare each in turn to the control product and consider the following:
  - Appearance overall (light/dark, wet/dry, firm/crumbly)
  - Crispness of topping
  - Texture of apples (crisp/soft, mealy, juicy)
  - Overall flavor (sweetness, sourness, apple aroma, brown sugar, butter, etc.)
  - Overall acceptability
  - Add any additional comments, as necessary.

Streusel Topping

INGREDIENT	POUND	OUNCE	GRAMS	BAKER'S PERCENTAGE
Flour, pastry		14	400	100
Sugar, light brown		11	300	77
Salt, ½ tsp. (2.5 milliliters)		0.1	3	0.8
Butter, unsalted		9	250	63
Total	2	2.1	953	240.8

Method of Preparation

1. Bring butter to room temperature.
2. Preheat oven to 400°F (200°C).
3. Combine flour, brown sugar, and salt on low speed of mixer using flat beater. If necessary, hold parchment paper over bowl opening during mixing, to prevent loss of streusel from bowl.
4. Cut butter into chunks and add to flour mixture. Stir on low speed for 2 minutes, or until well-blended and crumbly.
5. Set aside until ready to use.
6. Bake apple crisp for about 25–35 minutes.

 **SOURCES OF ERROR**

_____

_____

RESULTS TABLE 1 ■ SENSORY CHARACTERISTICS OF APPLE CRISP MADE WITH DIFFERENT APPLE VARIETIES.

APPLE VARIETY	APPEARANCE OVERALL	APPLE TEXTURE	OVERALL FLAVOR	OVERALL ACCEPTABILITY	COMMENTS
Granny Smith (control product)					
Red Delicious					
Golden Delicious					
McIntosh					

CONCLUSIONS

1. Rank the different apple varieties used in the apple crisps from least firm to most firm.

_____

_____

2. Rank the different apple varieties used in the apple crisps from least sweet to sweetest.

_____

_____

3. What were the main differences in appearance, flavor, and texture between the apple crisp made with Red Delicious apples and the apple crisp made with Granny Smith apples (the control product)?

_____

_____

4. What were the main differences in appearance, flavor, and texture between the apple crisp made with Golden Delicious apples and the apple crisp made with Granny Smith apples (the control product)?

_____

_____

5. What were the main differences in appearance, flavor, and texture between the apple crisp made with McIntosh apples and the apple crisp made with Granny Smith apples (the control product)?

_____

_____

6. Based on this experiment, which apple variety do you feel is most acceptable for use in an apple crisp, and why?

_____

_____

    a. In which other baked products would this apple variety also be good?

    _____

    _____

7. Why might your evaluations of the different apple varieties not apply from one year to the next, or even from one season or one shipment to the next?

_____

_____

8. What did you not like about the apples that were least acceptable for use in an apple crisp?

_____

_____

    a. How might the formula be adjusted (more or less sugar, lemon juice, spice, shorter bake time, etc.) to make the crisp more acceptable with these apples?

    _____

    _____

9. Did you have any sources of error that might significantly affect the results of your experiment? If so, what could you do differently next time to minimize error?

_____

_____

CHAPTER 16

NUTS AND SEEDS

CHAPTER **OBJECTIVES**

1. Describe the makeup of nuts and relate this to their nutrition.

2. Discuss factors that affect the cost of nuts.

3. List common nuts and describe their characteristics and uses.

4. Describe how to best store and handle nuts.

INTRODUCTION

Botanists differentiate nuts from seeds, legumes, and kernels. To a botanist, a nut is a dry, one-seeded fruit that does not split open at a seam when mature. While botanists classify chestnuts, hazelnuts, and sometimes walnuts as true nuts, other "nuts" are not. Almonds, coconuts, and macadamias are the seeds within the fruit's pit, or stone. Peanuts are seeds of a legume, and pine nuts are seeds of a pinecone. In most bakeshops, and for our purposes, all are considered nuts. Seeds are typically smaller than nuts and are not contained in hard shells. Examples of seeds are sesame, poppy, sunflower, and pumpkin.

Actually, all nuts are, or contain, the seed of a plant. Seeds consist of three main parts: an embryo that sprouts into a seedling, an endosperm that provides adequate food for the young seedling, and a seed coat that protects the seed. When planted, seeds grow into new plants.

Most nuts grow on trees. Tree nuts include almonds, cashews, hazelnuts, macadamias, pine nuts, pecans, pistachios, and walnuts. Not included in this category are peanuts, which grow underground on peanut plants.

Nuts are added to baked goods primarily for flavor, texture, and visual appeal. They can usually be used interchangeably in formulas without making adjustments to the formula. Taste, of course, will change, since nuts differ markedly in flavor. But, for the most part, nuts function similarly in baking. Chestnuts are the exception. Chestnuts are very different from other nuts and generally cannot be used in place of them.

COMPOSITION OF NUTS, KERNELS, AND SEEDS

Nuts are a good source of protein, fiber, vitamins, and minerals. While nuts are high in fat, the fatty acids in nuts (except coconut) are mostly unsaturated. From a health standpoint, unsaturated fatty acids are considered desirable. Nuts also contain

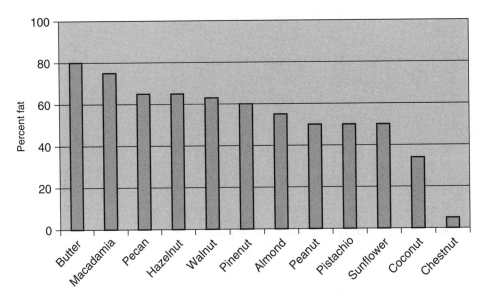

FIGURE 16.1 The amount of fat in nuts compared to butter

a significant amount of polyphenolic compounds, beneficial to good health. In fact, nuts are a part of a traditional Mediterranean diet, considered a model diet for good health.

Nuts vary in composition, but most contain more fat or oil than anything else. Figure 16.1 compares the fat content of nuts to butter. Notice that nuts vary widely in their fat content, but most range from 50–65 percent oil. Chestnuts and coconuts fall below this range, and macadamia nuts, at 75 percent oil, approach the amount of fat in butter. Because of their high oil content, most nuts should be used sparingly in low-fat baked goods.

THE UNIQUE HEALTH BENEFITS OF WALNUTS

While all nuts contribute to a healthful diet when consumed in moderation, walnuts are particularly rich in alpha linolenic acid (ALA). ALA is an omega-3 fatty acid that may reduce the risk of coronary heart disease.

Omega-3 fatty acids are low in the North American diet, especially in locations where oily fish, like salmon, are not a regularly consumed. Besides walnuts and fatty fish, the only other common food that is high in ALA is flaxseeds.

WHAT IS ANAPHYLACTIC SHOCK?

Anaphylactic shock is a severe and sometimes fatal allergic reaction that some individuals have to certain proteins, including those in tree nuts and peanuts. The body reacts to the presence of these proteins by releasing massive doses of chemicals, which causes shock, the swelling of air passages, and sometimes death. Often, only very small amounts of these foods are needed to trigger anaphylactic shock in hypersensitive individuals. The best way to prevent anaphylactic shock is to avoid those foods known to cause the reaction. Because death can occur within minutes, hypersensitive individuals often carry medication (an adrenaline kit) to take if they accidentally consume the wrong foods.

Customers should be specifically told when nuts are present in a product, because some people have severe allergic reactions to nuts. One easy and attractive way to remind customers of the presence of nuts in a product is to garnish the top with the type of nut it contains.

COST

Nuts are an expensive ingredient. They can range in price from several dollars to ten or more dollars per pound. Many factors contribute to the price of nuts. The main factors are as follows.

- *Type of nut*—certain nuts, like pine nuts and macadamia nuts, are significantly more expensive than peanuts or almonds, mainly because of difficulties in handling.
- *Added processing or difficulty in processing*—walnuts, for example, are fragile and difficult to remove from their shells intact. This makes walnut halves more expensive than broken pieces.
- *Crop year*—nuts are a natural agricultural product. If Georgia, which is a major producer of pecans, has heavy rains one year, this could wipe out its entire pecan crop, leading to an increase in price.
- *Packaging*—walnuts, for example, can be purchased in vacuum-packed cans (to prevent oxidative rancidity). Expect this type of packaging to add to the cost of the nuts.
- *Amount purchased at one time*—as with any ingredient, purchasing in bulk can lower costs.

COMMON NUTS, KERNELS, AND SEEDS

Almonds

The two main types of almonds are bitter and sweet. Bitter almonds are used for flavoring. Almond extract and amaretto liqueur, for example, can be made from the oil of bitter almonds.

Sweet almonds are used in baking. California is the largest producer of sweet almonds in the world. Sweet almonds are the number-one nut in America, at least in the bakeshop, and they have a long tradition of use throughout Europe. Almonds appear in many traditional formulas in the pastry shop, including meringues, marzipan, biscotti, macaroons, and pastry doughs.

Sweet almonds are mild-flavored, so they are best when toasted before use to develop flavor. Almonds come either natural—with the brown skin still intact—or blanched. The brown skin of natural almonds provides a contrast in color that is desirable for visual appeal. For example, the brown skin of natural almonds highlights the presence of the nuts in almond biscotti. The skin also provides a slight astringency that contributes to overall flavor. Recall from Chapter 4 that astringency is a taste characteristic that results in a drying sensation in the mouth from the presence of tannins.

Blanched almonds have the brown skin removed. They have a sweeter, milder flavor than natural almonds and are more common than natural nuts in the bakeshop. With their polished white appearance, blanched almonds have a more refined,

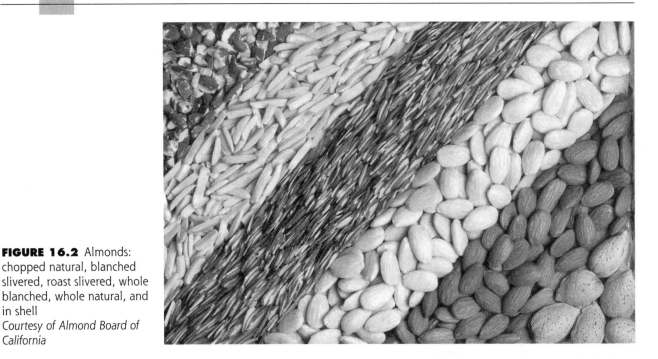

FIGURE 16.2 Almonds: chopped natural, blanched slivered, roast slivered, whole blanched, whole natural, and in shell
Courtesy of Almond Board of California

premium-quality image. To blanch almonds, pour boiling water over the nuts, let them sit for several minutes, then slide off the skins.

Almonds can be purchased in many forms, including whole, sliced, slivered, chopped, or ground into a butter, flour, or paste (Figure 16.2). Because of this variety in form, and because of its mild, pleasant flavor, almonds have a reputation as a highly versatile nut.

Almond paste consists of blanched almonds finely ground to a paste with sugar. Almond paste often contains binding and flavoring agents. Marzipan is almond paste and sugar mixed into pliable dough. Think of marzipan as edible modeling clay. Marzipan is traditionally colored and shaped into small fruits and whimsical animals. It can be rolled and used for covering cakes.

Cashews

Kidney-shaped cashew nuts are native to South and Central America. They have a sweet, mild flavor and an ivory white appearance. While the bulk of cashews are eaten directly as a snack, cashews are used in brittle and other confectionery, as well as in

HOW TO MAKE NUT BUTTERS AND NUT FLOURS

Nut butters do not contain butter; rather, they are pastes made by finely grinding nuts. Any nut can be used, but peanut, almond, and hazelnut are probably the most common nut butters.

To make nut butter, grind roasted nuts in a food processor until smooth. If necessary, add a small amount of oil to help achieve a smooth consistency. Salt, honey, or syrup can be added for flavor.

Nut flours are also made in the food processor. To make nut flour, nuts and granulated sugar are combined in the bowl of the food processor and pulsed repeatedly. The pulsing and the presence of sugar help keep the nuts from forming an oily paste. Nut flours are used in pastry doughs and cake batters.

cookies and other baked goods. Because of its bland flavor and pale color, cashews are sometimes soaked in water and blended into a smooth cream, which is used to replace dairy cream in frozen desserts and cheese in cheesecakes.

Cashews can be expensive because they are difficult to remove from their shells. Part of the difficulty is the presence of a skin irritant in the shell that is similar to the irritant in poison ivy and poison oak. To remove the shell without contaminating the cashew meat with this irritant, the nuts are steamed, roasted, or cooked in oil. This opens the shell so the nutmeat can more easily be removed, which is often done manually by skilled workers. These nuts are generally labeled raw, because while the shells were exposed to high heat, the nuts themselves were not roasted. The largest producers of cashews today are Brazil, India, and Vietnam, three countries with the tropical climate required for their growth.

Chestnuts

Chestnuts are very high in moisture and in carbohydrates, and very low—less than 5 percent—in oil. Chestnuts are cooked before use, giving them a characteristic soft, mealy texture. They are not interchangeable with other nuts.

Chestnuts are available fresh only in the fall and early winter months. During the rest of the year, they can be purchased already cooked, either frozen or canned, whole or pureed. Once opened, canned chestnuts should be refrigerated or frozen, to prevent mold growth. Chestnuts are also available dried and ground to a flour, or candied (*marrons glacés*).

Coconuts

Several products are derived from coconut meat, including coconut milk and desiccated, sweetened, or toasted coconut. Desiccated, sweetened, and toasted coconut products are cut to various sizes, from large shreds to fine flakes. Macaroon coconut is desiccated, sweetened, or toasted coconut that consists of fairly fine flakes.

Desiccated coconut is made by drying coconut from about 50 percent water down to less than 5 percent. Desiccated coconut, also called dried coconut, is a concentrated source of coconut oil and coconut flavor.

Sweetened coconut is made by cooking coconut with sugar before drying. Often, sweetened coconut contains additives to keep it soft and flexible (glycerin, for example) and to keep it white (sulfiting agent). Sweetened coconut is the form of coconut most familiar to North American consumers. It can be toasted to a golden brown color and sold as *toasted coconut*. Toasted coconut is used primarily as a garnish on cakes and doughnuts.

Coconut water is the clear liquid in the center of a mature coconut, sometimes consumed as a refreshing beverage. Coconut water is often mistaken for coconut milk.

WHAT'S THE DIFFERENCE BETWEEN COCONUT CREAM AND CREAM OF COCONUT?

Although coconut cream and cream of coconut sound like the same product, they are not. Coconut cream is the oil-rich layer that rises to the top of coconut milk. Like coconut milk, coconut cream is unsweetened. Cream of coconut is a thick, sweet liquid made from coconut milk and sugar. Cream of coconut is used primarily in mixed drinks, such as piña coladas. The two are not interchangeable.

Coconut milk is made by combining grated coconut meat with hot water and squeezing the liquid through a filter. Coconut milk is unsweetened and can be purchased canned or frozen. If a can of coconut milk is opened and the top layer, which is rich in coconut oil, is skimmed off, the skimmed-off layer is called *coconut cream*.

Hazelnuts

Hazelnuts are also called filberts. They are grown primarily in the Mediterranean region, but in the United States, small amounts are grown in Oregon. Hazelnuts have only recently become popular in North America. In Europe, they have been popular for many years, especially when paired with chocolate in desserts and confections. The combination of hazelnuts and chocolate ground smooth is called *gianduja*.

Hazelnuts can be purchased whole, diced, or sliced. As with almonds, they come with or without their skins, and toasting greatly enhances the distinctive flavor of hazelnuts, as it does with almonds. In fact, of all the nuts, hazelnuts probably benefit the most from toasting.

Macadamia Nuts

Macadamia nuts are native to Australia, but today they are more widely grown in Hawaii. Macadamia nuts are highest in oil of all the common nuts, which gives them a rich, creamy flavor and texture. Because the shell of the macadamia nut is hard to crack, shelled macadamia nuts are expensive and should be used only in baked goods with an upscale image and a price to match.

Pecans

Pecans are native to North America and in the United States, they are grown in the South and Southwest. As with walnuts, fancy pecan halves are expensive compared with the cost of pieces. Use the halves where appearance is important. Specialty items such as pecan pie, southern pralines, and butter pecan ice cream are three traditional uses of pecans.

Peanuts

Peanuts, being a legume, are higher in protein than tree nuts. They are native to South America and, while very popular in North America, are rarely used in Europe. The two most common varieties of peanuts are the Virginia peanut and the smaller Spanish peanut.

Peanuts are plentiful and inexpensive. Raw, untoasted peanuts have a beany flavor, so peanuts are typically toasted before use. Peanuts come whole, halved, diced, and ground into peanut butter. As with most nuts, peanuts pair nicely with chocolate.

Pine Nuts

Pine nuts are also called pignoli or piñon nuts. They are the seeds on the cone of a piñon tree, a type of low-growing pine. Fresh pine nuts have a mild, sweet flavor that is characteristic of certain Mediterranean, Middle Eastern, and Mexican specialties. Because they are difficult to remove from the pine cone, pine nuts are expensive and should be used with care.

Pistachios

Pistachio nuts have a unique green color that adds a different look to baked goods. While they are native to the Middle East, in recent years a large amount of pistachio nuts have been cultivated in California. Although pistachio nuts have traditionally been a snack nut, expect to see greater use of pistachios in the bakeshop, as the availability of shelled pistachio nuts increases.

Pistachio nuts are best used untoasted or lightly toasted, to preserve their bright green color and distinctive flavor. Pistachios are a traditional garnish on cannoli. They are also used in ice creams, biscotti, and baklava.

Walnuts

The English walnut is by far the most popular variety of walnut used in the bakeshop. A second variety, the black walnut, has a very strong flavor and a hard shell that is difficult to crack cleanly. Black walnuts are native to North America and can be purchased as a specialty item, but they are high-priced and have a strong flavor that is not appreciated by all.

Shelled English walnuts—walnuts sold out of their shell—come as fancy halves and in various-size pieces. They come in a variety of colors, from extra light to amber. The outside color of the walnut is an indication of how much sunlight the walnut received. The more sunlight, the darker the color, and the stronger the flavor. The characteristic flavor of a walnut is somewhat astringent. Its flavor is more pronounced than almonds, and for this reason it is not typically toasted before use.

About two-thirds of the world's supply of walnuts comes from California. Walnuts are very common in North American baked goods, such as brownies, quick breads, muffins, cookies, and coffee cakes. They are also used in pastries throughout Europe and throughout the Middle East, where they originated.

TOASTING NUTS

Nuts are toasted to develop flavor by allowing chemical reactions, including Maillard browning—the reaction of sugars and proteins—to occur. Toasting also improves the flavor of slightly stale nuts. Besides improving flavor, toasting also darkens the color and crisps the texture of nuts.

HOW TO TOAST NUTS

To toast, spread nuts in a single layer on a sheet pan. Place in an oven at 325°–350°F (160°–175°C) for 5–10 minutes or longer. Watch carefully; properly toasted nuts have a uniform, light brown color and sweet nutty taste. Different nut varieties require different toasting times, because of differences in size and oil content.

Do not try to toast nuts at too high an oven temperature or by cooking them on top of the stove. Stovetop heat, especially, is hard to control, and it is too easy to burn the outside of the nut while the inside stays raw and flavorless.

Once nuts are toasted, allow them to cool before use. Store leftover toasted nuts in an airtight container and refrigerate. Toasted nuts oxidize quickly, so they should be used within a few days.

STORAGE AND HANDLING

Nuts undergo oxidative rancidity when they are not handled properly. It is the oil in nuts that oxidizes, developing stale or rancid off flavors as it breaks down. Aged nuts are also more bitter and less sweet than fresh nuts. Recall from Chapter 10 that oxygen, heat, light, and metal catalysts all contribute to oxidative rancidity in fats. If these can be controlled, oxidative rancidity can be minimized. While the following suggestions are not always practical or necessary, they are worth considering.

- Keep nuts whole until ready to use. Chopped nuts have more surface area exposed to air and therefore oxidize faster.

- Do not toast nuts until ready to use; toasting initiates the oxidation of the nut oils.

- Store nuts at low temperatures, especially if toasted, since heat accelerates rancidity; refrigerate at 35°–40°F (2°–4°C), or freeze.

- Keep nuts away from sunlight; sunlight, like heat, is a form of energy that speeds up oxidative rancidity.

- Purchase nuts in vacuum packaging, to exclude oxygen.

- Purchase nuts with added antioxidants, like BHA, BHT, or vitamin E. Antioxidants interfere with the process of oxidative rancidity, greatly slowing it down. If antioxidants have been added to nuts, they will be listed on the label.

- One last consideration when dealing with nuts: always cover them when not in use. This keeps out odors from strong-smelling foods, such as onions, as well as insects and rodents. It will also keep away moisture, which makes nuts soggy, moldy, and likely to oxidize.

Some nuts are more easily oxidized than others are. How fast a nut oxidizes has more to do with the type of oil it contains than how much oil is in it. For example, walnuts oxidize faster than hazelnuts even though hazelnuts contain the same or slightly more oil than walnuts. This is because walnuts are highest in ALA, an omega-3 polyunsaturated fatty acid. Like all polyunsaturated fatty acids, ALA oxidizes at an extremely fast rate.

HELPFUL HINT

The following is a list of common nuts and the average amount of polyunsaturated fatty acids present in one ounce (30 grams) of each. Because the rate of oxidative rancidity is mostly related to the amount of polyunsaturated fatty acids, this chart is helpful in understanding which nuts will likely undergo rancidity rapidly. This, in turn, can help you decide on quantities to purchase at one time, or how to best store certain nuts.

Walnuts	13 grams
Pine nuts	9 grams
Pecans	6 grams
Peanuts	4 grams
Pistachios	4 grams
Almonds	3 grams
Hazelnuts	2 grams
Cashews	2 grams
Macadamias	1 gram

HOW MUCH LONGER WILL NUTS LAST WHEN REFRIGERATED?

Food scientists have a rule of thumb that they use to predict how much longer food will stay fresh when it is stored at low temperatures. The rule of thumb, which works reasonably well with nuts, is for every 15°F (10°C) decrease in temperature, product will last about twice as long.

Twice as long is huge. Let's assume, for example, that a bakeshop keeps their walnuts handy, near the ovens where it is quite warm (90°F/35°C). Let's also assume that the walnuts start tasting stale and rancid after about one month. If the walnuts are moved instead to a cooler spot, where the temperature is at 75°F/25°C, the nuts should now last about two months. And, if an even cooler spot is found (60°F/15°C), the walnuts should stay fresh about four months, which is twice as long again. Imagine how much more effective refrigeration and freezing is at extending shelf life of nuts.

Of course, the reverse is true as well, so that for every 15°F (10°C) increase in temperature, product will last about half as long.

QUESTIONS FOR REVIEW

1. What is anaphylactic shock?

2. What is an easy yet attractive way to remind customers of the presence of nuts in a baked product?

3. Which common nut is highest in oil? Which is lowest? What is the approximate oil content of each?

4. List and explain five factors that contribute to the cost of nuts.

5. What is the difference between natural and blanched almonds? Why might one be used over the other?

6. What is astringency? What part of the nut is most apt to be astringent?

7. What is the difference between almond paste and marzipan?

8. What is coconut milk?

9. What is the difference between coconut cream and cream of coconut?

10. What is gianduja?

11. What is ALA and its benefits? Which nut is it found in at high levels?

12. How does sunlight exposure affect the qualities of walnuts?

13. What is the main reason that walnuts oxidize at a much faster rate than most other nuts?

14. Name a nut that is relatively expensive; name one that is relatively inexpensive.

15. In what two ways does toasting nuts improve their flavor?

16. Name a nut that benefits greatly from toasting; name one that is probably best untoasted or only lightly toasted.

QUESTIONS FOR DISCUSSION

1. Why might it be better to purchase peanuts raw and toast them as needed, instead of purchasing them already toasted?

2. Assume that pine nuts you have just purchased are expected to remain fresh for only two months when stored at room temperature (70°F; 25°C). Use the rule-of-thumb relationship between temperature of storage and shelf life to calculate how long these pine nuts should remain fresh if refrigerated (40°F; 5°C).

EXERCISES AND EXPERIMENTS

1. How to Decrease Oxidative Rancidity in Nuts

Explain the reason that each of the following techniques works to decrease oxidative rancidity in nuts (for the purposes of this exercise, focus on decreasing oxidative rancidity only, even though some of the following might not be practical or desirable in all bakeshops). The first is completed for you.

1. Chop nuts immediately before use, rather than ahead of time.

Reason: Chopping exposes more surface area to air (oxygen), which initiates oxidative rancidity.

2. Store nuts under refrigeration until ready to use.

Reason:

_____

_____

3. Practice FIFO (first in, first out).

Reason:

_____

_____

4. Purchase and hold nuts in vacuum packaging.

Reason:

_____

_____

5. Store nuts in opaque, rather than clear, containers.

Reason:

_____

_____

6. Use hazelnuts or almonds rather than walnuts or pine nuts.

Reason:

_____

_____

7. If toasting nuts, toast just before use.

Reason:

_____

_____

2. How the Type of Nut Affects the Overall Quality of Cookies

 **OBJECTIVE**

To demonstrate how the type of nut affects the appearance, flavor, texture, and overall acceptability of cookies.

PRODUCTS PREPARED

Cookies made with:
- No added nut (control product)
- Walnuts, untoasted, chopped
- Pistachio nuts, untoasted, chopped
- Almonds, natural, untoasted, chopped
- Almonds, blanched, untoasted, chopped
- Almonds, blanched, toasted, chopped
- Other, if desired (hazelnuts, pine nuts, macadamia nuts, peanuts, etc.)

MATERIALS AND EQUIPMENT

- Drop cookie dough, enough to make 24 or more cookies of each variation
- Half or full sheet pans
- Parchment paper or silicone pads
- Small portion scoop, #30 (1 fluid ounce/30 milliliters), or equivalent

PROCEDURE

- Preheat oven according to formula.
- Prepare cookie dough using the drop sugar cookie dough formula, which follows, or using any plain drop cookie formula. Prepare one batch of dough for each variation.
- Line sheet pans with parchment paper or silicone pads; label with type of nut to be added to dough.
- Scoop dough onto sheet pans using #30 scoop (or equivalent). Space dough evenly, placing six on half sheet pan or twelve on full sheet pan.
- Use an oven thermometer placed in center of oven to read oven temperature; record results here _____.
- Place sheet pans in preheated oven and set timer according to formula.
- Bake cookies until control product (with no added nuts) is light brown, about 10–12 minutes. Remove *all* cookies from oven after same length of time. If necessary, however, adjust bake times for oven variances. Record bake times in Comments column of the Results Table, which follows.
- Remove cookies from oven and let stand 1 minute.
- Transfer to wire racks to cool to room temperature.
- Record any potential sources of error that might make it difficult to draw the proper conclusions from your experiment. In particular, be aware of differences in mixing and any problems with the oven.
- Evaluate the sensory characteristics of completely cooled products and record evaluations in the Results Table. Be sure to compare each in turn to the control product and consider the following:
  - Appearance (visibility of nuts/contrast in color with cookie)
  - Texture (crunchiness of nut, overall moistness and tenderness of cookie)
  - Overall Flavor (nut aroma, sweetness, saltiness, astringency, etc.)
  - Overall acceptability, from highly unacceptable to highly acceptable, on a scale of one to five
  - Add any additional comments, as necessary.

Drop Sugar Cookie Dough

INGREDIENT	POUNDS	OUNCES	GRAMS	BAKER'S PERCENTAGE
Shortening, all purpose		13	410	82
Sugar, regular granulated		18	565	113
Salt		0.25	8	1.6
Baking soda		0.25	8	1.6
Eggs		6	185	37
Flour		16	500	100
Total	3	5.5	1676	335.2

Method of Preparation

1. Preheat oven to 375°F (190°C).
2. Allow all ingredients to come to room temperature.
3. Weigh ingredients on digital or baker's scale. *Note:* If desired, use 2 teaspoons (10 milliliters) for 8 grams baking soda; use 1½ teaspoons (7½ milliliters) for 8 grams salt.
4. Blend flour, salt, and baking soda thoroughly by sifting together three times onto parchment paper.
5. Combine shortening and sugar in mixing bowl and mix on low for 1 minute; stop and scrape bowl, as needed.
6. Cream shortening/sugar mixture on medium for 3 minutes; stop and scrape bowl.
7. Add eggs slowly while mixing on low for 30 seconds; stop and scrape bowl.
8. Add flour to shortening/sugar/egg mixture and mix on low for 1 minute; stop and scrape bowl.
9. Stir in nuts.
10. Cover dough with plastic wrap and set aside until ready to use.

SOURCES OF ERROR

_____

_____

RESULTS TABLE ■ SENSORY CHARACTERISTICS OF COOKIES MADE WITH DIFFERENT NUTS

TYPE OF NUT	APPEARANCE	TEXTURE	OVERALL FLAVOR	OVERALL ACCEPTABILITY	COMMENTS
None					
Walnuts, untoasted					
Pistachio nuts, untoasted					
Almonds, natural, untoasted					
Almonds, blanched, untoasted					
Almonds, blanched, toasted					

CONCLUSIONS

1. What were the main differences overall in appearance, flavor, and texture among the cookies made without nuts and those made with nuts?

_____

_____

2. What were the main differences in appearance, flavor, and texture between the cookies made with natural almonds and those made with blanched (both untoasted)?

_____

_____

3. Which did you prefer—cookies made with natural or with blanched almonds? Why?

_____

_____

4. What were the main differences in appearance, flavor, and texture between the cookies made with untoasted almonds and those made with toasted almonds (both blanched)?

_____

_____

5. Which did you prefer—cookies made with untoasted or with toasted almonds? Why?

_____

_____

6. Based on this experiment, if a formula calls for one type of nut and you substitute another, how likely is it that your product will turn out acceptable? Explain.

_____

_____

7. Can you omit toasting nuts when they are used in a baked product, such as cookies—in other words, does the baking process substitute for toasting the nuts?

_____

_____

CHAPTER 17

COCOA AND CHOCOLATE PRODUCTS

CHAPTER **OBJECTIVES**

1. Describe the steps for processing cocoa beans and how these steps affect the quality of cocoa and chocolate products.

2. Define various cocoa and chocolate products and describe their makeup, characteristics, and uses.

3. Describe the nature of cocoa butter and the science behind tempering and handling chocolate products.

4. List the functions of cocoa and chocolate products and relate these functions to their makeup.

5. Describe how to best store cocoa and chocolate products.

INTRODUCTION

Chocolate is one of the most popular food flavors in the Western world, second only to vanilla. Unlike vanilla, however, which is essentially a flavoring, chocolate has been used over the centuries as food, medicine, aphrodisiac, and money. It was part of ancient religious rituals in Mayan culture, and became a ritual in daily life for seventeenth- and eighteenth-century Europeans who could afford their daily hot chocolate.

The cacao tree, the source of cocoa and chocolate, is a finicky plant that grows in relatively few regions of the world. Climatic conditions—rainfall in particular—affect the size of the annual harvest, as do the spread of fungus infections. Fungus infections have been a problem particularly in Brazil and other parts of South America in recent years. Political instability is also a threat to the size of the harvest in places like Côte d'Ivoire (Ivory Coast) in western Africa, the largest cocoa bean supplier in the world.

Yet, today more than ever, bakers and pastry chefs have a wide selection of cocoa and chocolate products from which to choose. Such a selection can seem bewildering, especially since cocoas and chocolates vary substantially in cost and quality. The first step in selecting cocoa and chocolate products for the bakeshop is to understand the makeup and functionality of each. Next, develop an educated palate by tasting and evaluating a wide range of products. Finally, include other important criteria—price, for example—in the selection process.

MAKEUP OF COCOA BEANS

Cacao—or cocoa—beans are the seeds or kernels from the fruit pods of the cacao tree. They are similar in many ways to other nuts and seeds, like almonds and sunflower seeds. Just as almonds and sunflower seeds are encased in a protective shell,

THE GROWING AND HANDLING OF COCOA BEANS

Cacao trees (*Theobroma cacao*) grow near the equator on small cocoa plantations or in tropical rain forests. Most commercial cacao trees grow in Africa, but other major growing regions include South and Central America and the islands of Indonesia and Malaysia in Southeast Asia. A limited number of trees are cultivated in other locales, such as Hawaii.

Cocoa pods grow off the limbs and trunks of cacao trees. Because the trees are fragile, the pods must be harvested by hand. Skilled workers cut down the pods with machetes, selecting only fully ripe ones for best flavor. Each pod holds about twenty to forty cocoa beans surrounded by a thin layer of white fruit pulp. The beans are removed from the pods—white fruit pulp intact—and are piled, covered, and allowed to ferment. Fermentation is the first step in the conversion of raw bean to flavorful chocolate, requiring two days to one week, depending on the type of bean. Fermentation

involves a complex series of reactions that occur as microorganisms ferment sugars in the pulp, and as enzymes break down various components in the bean. Fermentation darkens the bean's color and changes its flavor. It increases the bean's acidity, decreases its astringency and bitterness, and generates flavor precursors that are important to flavor development later during roasting and conching.

Once fruit pulp warms and liquefies, it drains from the beans. The beans are then dried, or cured, often directly in the sun, but sometimes over an open fire or with hot air. During drying, beans lose nearly half their weight and some acidity to evaporation. If dried improperly or incompletely, they pick up off flavors, including smoky or moldy flavors. Once dried, the beans are packed in burlap bags and shipped around the world to processing plants where they are cleaned, roasted, removed from their shells, and further processed.

In this cross-section of a whole cocoa pod, you can see the cocoa beans surrounded by the fruit.
Courtesy of the U.S. Department of Agriculture

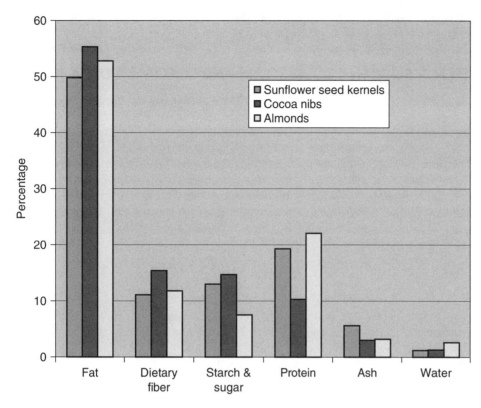

FIGURE 17.1 A comparison of the makeup of cocoa nibs to sunflower seeds and almonds
Adapted from data from the USDA Nutrient Database for Standard Reference, Release 19 (2006)

so, too, are cocoa nibs. Cocoa nibs—the edible part of the cocoa bean—are what are processed into cocoa and chocolate.

Like most nuts and seeds, cocoa nibs contain valuable nutrients. Figure 17.1 compares the makeup of roasted cocoa nibs to roasted almonds and sunflower seeds. Although there are some differences (most notably, almonds are highest in protein), there are many similarities. All are very high in fat and low in water, and all are a good source of dietary fiber and minerals (ash).

As with other sources of tropical fats, such as coconuts and palm kernels, cocoa nibs contain fat that is naturally saturated and is solid at room temperature. Although saturated, cocoa butter does not appear to raise blood cholesterol levels the way most saturated fats do. Besides containing fat high in saturated fatty acids, cocoa butter contains small amounts of lecithin and other natural emulsifiers.

Everything in cocoa beans that is solid but is not cocoa butter is collectively referred to as cocoa solids nonfat. *Cocoa solids nonfat* includes large amounts of proteins and carbohydrates. The carbohydrates in cocoa beans consist of starch, dietary fiber (cellulose and pentosan gums), and dextrins. *Dextrins* are starch fragments that are produced when starches are broken down by high heat, as when cocoa beans are roasted. Like starch, dextrins absorb water, but to a lesser degree.

WHEN TOO MUCH COCOA SOLIDS NONFAT IS A PROBLEM

Commercially sold chocolate syrup, used for flavoring milk and other beverages, has the best chocolate flavor when it contains a high amount of cocoa solids nonfat. The problem is, when there is a high amount of cocoa solids nonfat, there is a high amount of starch and gums that thicken the syrup. Over time, the syrup sets up and will not dispense properly from its package. To solve this problem, the enzyme amylase is sometimes added to chocolate syrup, to break down the starch so the syrup won't thicken.

WHAT'S THE DIFFERENCE BETWEEN COCOA SOLIDS AND COCOA SOLIDS NONFAT?

Because many chocolate products contain sugar and other ingredients, they are often labeled with a declaration of a minimum amount of cocoa solids, sometimes simply called percent cocoa or cacao. The European Union requires this by law of all its member countries. Cocoa solids, in this case, are not the same as cocoa solids nonfat. Instead, it represents the combined total of all cocoa ingredients, including ground cocoa nib and added cocoa powder and cocoa butter. In other words, it represents the combined total of cocoa solids nonfat and cocoa butter. The label declarations do not state how much of the cocoa solids are nonfat and how much are from added cocoa butter. All else being equal, a higher level of cocoa solids nonfat provides a stronger chocolate flavor. A higher level of cocoa butter means the product will be thinner when melted, which is important when chocolate is used as a coating.

Cocoa solids nonfat also includes small amounts of acids, color and flavor, vitamins and minerals, and polyphenolic compounds. Besides providing health benefits, polyphenolic compounds contribute to the color and flavor of cocoa beans. Finally, cocoa solids nonfat contains caffeine and theobromine, a mild caffeine-like stimulant. Theobromine, like caffeine, has a bitter taste, characteristic of chocolate.

While there are many types of cocoa beans, most fall into three main categories: forastero, criollo, and trinitario. The majority (90 percent or more) of cocoa beans are forasteros, considered basic or bulk beans. Forasteros are the workhorses of the cocoa industry. They originated in South American rain forests but today are grown throughout the cocoa-growing world, especially in western Africa. They are relatively easy to grow because they withstand changes in climate and are resistant to fungus and disease. The beans are dark and have a full chocolate flavor, with plenty of middle and base notes. While they provide a chocolate earthiness, forasteros lack the subtle top notes of criollo beans.

Light-colored criollo beans are considered "fine and flavor" beans. The industry term "fine and flavor" refers to the complex fruity aromatic top notes of these beans. Criollos are also typically low in bitterness and astringency. Criollo beans are expensive because the trees are susceptible to disease and are therefore difficult to grow. Criollo beans were the beans prized by the ancient Mayans. Today, less than 2 percent of the world supply of cocoa beans is criollo, and the size of the crop is shrinking as criollo trees are replaced with hardier varieties. Central and South America, the Caribbean, and Indonesia are known for their criollo and other fine and flavor beans.

WHY DO WE CRAVE CHOCOLATE?

Scientists have conducted numerous studies in recent years to determine if there is a chemical basis for the cravings many people report having for chocolate. Most studies have focused on determining if specific chemicals in chocolate have calming or euphoric effects, or act as mild antidepressants. In fact, chocolate does contain a mix of substances—theobromine, magnesium, tyrosine, phenylethylamine, anandamide, and N-acylethanolamine—that affect brain chemistry. However, many other everyday foods contain these same substances, often at higher levels. Yet, it is possible that chocolate contains a special combination of substances that provides an effect unique to chocolate. Or, it might simply be that the pleasurable sensory characteristics of chocolate—its taste, smell, and mouthfeel—are what we crave.

VARIETAL AND SINGLE-ORIGIN CHOCOLATES

Varietal chocolates, like varietal wines, are made from one type of bean. Single-origin chocolates—also called grand crus, in the tradition of wines—are made from beans grown entirely in a specific region or plantation. Many specialty chocolate manufacturers sell varietal and single-origin chocolates, at premium prices. Tasting single-origin chocolates is a way to broaden your knowledge of chocolate, although some of them are an acquired taste.

Look for chocolates made from the following varietal and single-origin flavor beans: Chuao, Maracaibo, and Porcelana criollos from Venezuela; Arriba, a criollo from Trinidad; Nacional, from Ecuador, a fine and flavor bean related to the forastero; Carenero Superior and Rio Caribe, two trinitario beans from Venezuela, and many more.

Trinitario beans are believed to be a cross between the forastero and the criollo, and they have characteristics of each. Like criollos, trinitarios are considered fine and flavor beans, although their flavor is less fruity and more earthy. Like forasteros, trinitario trees are hardy. They were first hybridized on the island of Trinidad in the 1700s, when forastero trees were imported to replace criollos destroyed by a major blight. Less than 5 percent of the world crop of cocoa beans is trinitario.

Most cocoa and chocolate products are produced from a blend of beans, with forasteros providing the base notes and the finish, and small amounts of flavor beans providing aromatic, often fruity, top notes.

COMMON COCOA AND CHOCOLATE PRODUCTS

Cocoa beans are grown in the tropics, but they are processed into cocoa and chocolate products where they are consumed—throughout Europe, North America, and other regions of the world. Cocoa and chocolate products can be categorized as cocoa products, chocolate products, and confectionery coatings. *Cocoa products* are unsweetened. They include cocoa nibs, chocolate (cocoa) liquor, cocoa powder, and cocoa butter. *Chocolate products* are sweetened. They are highly processed and more refined than cocoa products, and while they vary in price, expect to pay a premium for them. Chocolate products include bittersweet dark chocolate, sweet chocolate, milk chocolate, white chocolate, and couvertures. *Confectionery coatings* are low-cost products made from cocoa, vegetable fats other than cocoa butter, and sugar. Both chocolate products and confectionery coatings can be purchased as blocks—often 10 or 11 pounds (4.5 or 5 kilograms)—or drops, also called coins or chips. Because they are small in size, drops are convenient to melt and use.

Cocoa and chocolate products must meet minimum standards set by law. These standards clarify differences among products, but they do not eliminate the large variation in makeup and quality that exists between brands. Standards vary from one country to the next. The definition of milk chocolate, in particular, changes from North America, to Switzerland, to the United Kingdom.

In the descriptions that follow, U.S. and Canadian regulations are provided throughout, while Tables 17.1 through 17.3 and Table 17.5 summarize and compare product regulations for the United States, Canada, and the European Union (EU). The EU includes France, Belgium, Great Britain, Germany, and eleven other countries. Switzerland, an important chocolate producer, is not an EU member; it sets its own regulations.

A SHORT HISTORY OF CHOCOLATE—PART I

For thousands of years, chocolate was used by the Mayans in Central America as a drink in religious ceremonies, earning its reputation as food of the gods. It was also ground with maize and other seeds and grains, seasoned, and consumed as food. In its most refined form, chocolate beverages were poured from one vessel to another at great heights, creating quantities of foam. One reason beans were roasted was to intensify this foam.

When Christopher Columbus first met Mayan traders in 1502, he sensed that cocoa beans were held in esteem, but he did not fully comprehend their significance. Hernando Cortés, the Spanish conquistador, invaded Mexico in 1519. By then, the Spanish were aware of the importance of cocoa beans to the New World, at least in its role as money. More than a means of monetary exchange, however, *cacahuatl* was symbolic to the Aztecs of blood and the human heart. It was their most valued beverage, savored almost exclusively by nobility, warriors, and elite merchants. Spanish accounts report Montezuma, emperor of the Aztecs, sipping from fifty golden goblets of chocolate at a banquet feast.

As consumed by the Aztecs—cold, colored with red annatto, and flavored with dry chili—chocolate was rejected by the Spanish invaders. Eventually, however, chocolate made its way to the Spanish court (some say by Cortés himself). The Spanish heated chocolate, sweetened it with cane sugar, and flavored it with vanilla and cinnamon. Part medicine, part invigorating beverage, chocolate spread through western Europe, even as the Spanish kept its process a secret for years. As the 1600s progressed, hot chocolate became a trendy, healthful drink throughout Europe, enjoyed by those who could afford it.

The chocolate industry has changed over the years. At one time, the industry consisted of skilled craftsmen running small operations. Today, large manufacturers transform the bulk of the world's cocoa beans into cocoa and chocolate products. These manufacturers have the ability to produce consistent product at a moderate cost. One way they maintain consistency is by blending beans from around the world. Another way is through large-scale computer-controlled manufacturing processes.

At the same time that most of the chocolate industry has consolidated into a few large-scale mass producers, artisan chocolate manufacturers have begun producing small quantities of specialty products. Artisan chocolate manufacturers tend to use more traditional methods of processing beans, and they are likely to create specialty chocolates made from varietal or single-origin beans.

The first step in converting cocoa beans—single-origin or otherwise—into cocoa and chocolate products is to clean and roast the bean.

TABLE 17.1 ■ U.S., CANADIAN, AND EU STANDARDS FOR COCOA POWDER

REGULATING BODY	NAME	COCOA BUTTER	OTHER REGULATIONS
United States and Canada	Cocoa	10% (min)	In United States, 22% maximum
United States	High-fat cocoa	22% (min)	
European Union	Cocoa	20% (min)	Calculated on a dry weight basis
United States and Canada	Fat-free cocoa	0.5% (max)	
United States and Canada	Low-fat cocoa	10% (max)	
European Union	Fat- reduced cocoa	8–20%	Calculated on a dry weight basis

Data from U.S. 21CFR163 2002; Canada CRC, c.870, B.04 Dec 31. 2001; EU Directive 73/241/EEC

THE ROLE OF TECHNOLOGY IN CHOCOLATE MANUFACTURING

Chocolate has a rich and romantic history, and it is fun to learn about the role of kings, queens, and conquistadors in the story of chocolate. Yet, a closer look at chocolate's history reveals the importance of technology. Without technology, chocolate would never have risen in quality and popularity in quite the same way. The steam engine, a product of the Industrial Revolution, made chocolate affordable and appealing to the common man, for example. The invention of the cocoa press in 1828 reduced prices and increased appeal even more. Later in the 1800s, Rodolphe Lindt, a Swiss manufacturer, developed a means of refining the flavor and mouthfeel of chocolate through conching. Around the same time, another Swiss, Daniel Peter, created the first milk chocolate by incorporating Henri Nestlé's newly invented condensed milk into chocolate.

Advances in technology continue today, increasing the quality and maintaining the cost of cocoa and chocolate products. Look for references to these and other technology improvements throughout this chapter.

THE IMPORTANCE OF ROASTING

The roasting process is an important step in the transformation of bean to cocoa and chocolate. Roasting takes several minutes to an hour or more, at temperatures that range from about 200°–400°F (95°–200°C). Roasting conditions depend on the size and variety of bean, and on the end result desired. For example, criollo flavor beans are typically roasted for a shorter time or at lower temperatures than forasteros, so that valuable top notes are not lost to evaporation.

Roasting loosens the shell for easy removal, and it reduces the amount of moisture and destroys microorganisms and other undesirable pests, so that the bean is suitable for consumption. Roasting also darkens the color and changes the flavor of cocoa beans. The flavor changes as heat evaporates acids and other volatile flavor molecules. Heat also initiates many complex chemical reactions, including Maillard reactions, which involve the breakdown of sugars and other carbohydrates in the presence of proteins. As roasting progresses, Maillard reactions produce deep, earthy middle and base notes and darkly colored compounds.

While the traditional means of roasting is to dry-roast whole beans, newer roasting methods involve pretreating beans with steam or infrared heat. Pretreatment allows shells to be removed before roasting. Once shells are removed, nibs are broken into particles of uniform size. Alternatively, the nibs are reduced to a paste, which is roasted as a thin film. Either method provides the manufacturer with better control over the roasting process, so that beans are more evenly roasted.

As with coffee, people have personal preferences for the degree of roast that they prefer in their chocolate.

Cocoa Products

COCOA NIBS

Small bits of roasted cocoa nib can be purchased as a specialty ingredient. Just as cocoa beans can be thought of as nuts, cocoa nibs—also called cacao nibs—can be thought of as chopped nuts. Nibs contain everything that is found in the cocoa bean, including a large amount of cocoa butter and an almost equal amount of cocoa solids nonfat. Because they are unsweetened, cocoa nibs have a strong bitter chocolate taste. Like coffee beans, cocoa nibs provide instant impact in baked goods and confections, but they should be used sparingly.

CHOCOLATE LIQUOR AND UNSWEETENED CHOCOLATE

Chocolate liquor is produced by finely grinding chocolate nibs through a series of rollers. The word *liquor* refers to the liquid state of chocolate when it is warm; it does not indicate the presence of alcohol. If chocolate nibs are thought of as chopped nuts, chocolate liquor can be thought of as nut butter—nuts ground to a smooth paste. Unlike almond butter or peanut butter, however, chocolate liquor—also called cocoa liquor—hardens into solid blocks when cooled, because cocoa butter is solid at room temperature. When sold as solid blocks, chocolate liquor is called unsweetened chocolate, cocoa mass (*cacaomasse*), bitter chocolate, or baking chocolate.

Like nibs, unsweetened chocolate is high in cocoa butter. By law, unsweetened chocolate must contain a minimum of 50 percent cocoa butter (and, in the United States, a maximum of 60 percent). Because it is high in valuable cocoa butter, unsweetened chocolate is an expensive ingredient. It is often worth the price, however, because cocoa butter contributes to the full flavor of unsweetened chocolate. Unsweetened chocolate is the ingredient of choice for the richest chocolate flavor in baked goods.

Besides containing cocoa butter and very small amounts of moisture, unsweetened chocolate contains cocoa solids nonfat. Since it is made from pure nib, this is generally all that is in unsweetened chocolate (by law, however, it can contain small amounts of added milk fat, ground nuts, flavorings, and alkali). Recall that cocoa solids nonfat includes acid. The acid in unsweetened chocolate is available to react with baking soda in baked goods, producing small amounts of carbon dioxide gas for leavening.

NATURAL COCOA POWDER

When chocolate liquor is squeezed and pressed under high pressure, heat builds and melts cocoa butter, some of which drains from the chocolate. The remaining presscake is finely ground and sold as natural cocoa powder. The color of natural cocoa ranges from light yellowish brown—tan—to dark yellowish brown, depending on the source of bean and amount of roasting. Because valuable cocoa butter is removed and sold separately, cocoa powder is less expensive than unsweetened chocolate.

As with chocolate liquor, natural cocoa powder is acidic, having a pH typically between 5 and 6. The acids in natural cocoa react with baking soda to produce a small amount of carbon dioxide gas for leavening.

Cocoa powder does not contain added sugar. There are sweetened cocoas on the market, convenient for preparing hot cocoa and other beverages. These sweetened

A SHORT HISTORY OF CHOCOLATE—PART II

At the start of the 1700s, hot chocolate was too expensive for the common man. Joseph Fry, an English physician who counseled his patients on the medicinal qualities of chocolate, was the first to mechanize and mass-produce the grinding of cocoa beans. Before then, chocolate was manually ground as it had been for thousands of years, between a stone rolling pin and a stone surface (mano and metate). Mass production reduced the price of chocolate and improved its fineness, which increased its appeal.

Still, an unattractive slick of melted cocoa butter formed on the surface of hot chocolate. When C. J. Van Houten from the Netherlands developed a process in 1828 for pressing excess cocoa butter from chocolate, cocoa powder was produced and the problem was solved.

For a few years after cocoa powder was invented, nobody knew what to do with the left-over cocoa butter. Finally, in the mid-1800s, Fry and Sons combined cocoa butter and sugar with chocolate, creating the first popular chocolate candy bar. Because there was now a market for cocoa butter, the price of cocoa dropped, making hot cocoa available to the masses.

cocoas, which are also called hot cocoa mixes, are not used in baking.

One way to classify cocoa powder is by the amount of cocoa butter it contains. Regular medium fat cocoa powder, often simply called *cocoa*, is commonly used for baking in North America. Cocoa has a minimum of 10 percent cocoa butter by law, and it generally ranges around 10–12 percent. In fact, manufacturers often designate regular cocoa as 10/12 cocoa (see Figure 17.2).

Low-fat cocoa in North America has less than 10 percent cocoa butter, but some cocoas—labeled *fat-free*—contain 0.5 percent cocoa butter or less. Removing this much cocoa butter requires a special process (supercritical gas extraction, for one), so fat-free cocoas are expensive and not commonly used in the bakeshop.

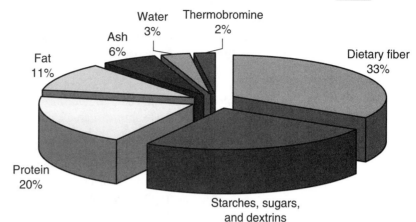

FIGURE 17.2 Makeup of 10/12 cocoa powder
Adapted from data from the USDA Nutrient Database for Standard Reference, Release 19 (2006)

A fourth category of cocoa powder sold in the United States is *high fat* or *breakfast cocoa*, which has a minimum of 22 percent cocoa butter. Manufacturers often designate it as 22/24 cocoa, because of its typical fat content. Either 10/12 or 22/24 cocoa can be used in baking, and while they can be substituted one for the other, higher-fat cocoas may provide a richer flavor.

Cocoa powder from the European Union is similar to American 22/24 cocoa in makeup. It is also often designated as 20/22 cocoa because of the amount of cocoa butter it typically contains. Table 17.1 summarizes government regulations in the United States, Canada, and the European Union for cocoa. Notice that cocoa considered fat-reduced in the European Union is not necessarily the same as North American low-fat cocoa.

SUBSTITUTING COCOA POWDER FOR UNSWEETENED CHOCOLATE

Cocoa cannot be substituted directly for unsweetened chocolate in baked goods because it is higher in nonfat solids and lower in fat. Less cocoa is needed compared with the amount of unsweetened chocolate, and fat—usually shortening—must be added along with the cocoa.

To calculate the amount of 20/22 (or 22/24) cocoa powder to use in place of unsweetened chocolate, multiply the amount of chocolate by 5/8, or 0.63. To calculate the amount of shortening to add, multiply the amount of chocolate by 3/8, or 0.37. This gives the following conversions for unsweetened chocolate:

1 pound unsweetened chocolate = 10 ounces 20/22 cocoa powder + 6 ounces shortening

1 kilogram unsweetened chocolate = 630 grams 20/22 cocoa powder + 370 grams shortening

Since shortening has twice the shortening power of cocoa butter, bakers and pastry chefs often reduce the amount of shortening by one-half (from 6 ounces to 3 ounces per pound of chocolate; from 370 grams to 185 grams per kilogram of chocolate).

For 10/12 cocoa, the substitution is 9 ounces cocoa and 7 ounces shortening (or 3.5 ounces, if reduced by half) for each pound of unsweetened chocolate, or 560 grams cocoa and 440 grams shortening (or 220 grams, if reduced by half) for each kilogram. The multiplying factors are 9/16, or 0.56, and 7/16, or 0.44.

To use cocoa powder, sift it with dry ingredients, cream it with shortening and sugar, or dissolve it in hot liquid. Some chefs find that dissolving cocoa in hot liquid before use releases flavor.

While the results are not identical when cocoa is used in place of chocolate, the product will be lower in cost, easier to make, and perfectly acceptable.

DUTCHED COCOA POWDER

Dutch process—dutched—cocoa is more common than natural cocoa in bakeshops. As with natural cocoas, dutched cocoas are typically sold as 10/12, 20/22, or 22/24 cocoas. Low-fat and fat-free versions are also available.

While natural cocoa has not been chemically treated, dutched cocoa has been treated with a mild alkali to neutralize the natural acidity of cocoa and to increase pH to 7 or above. An example of an alkali is sodium bicarbonate—baking soda—but this is not commonly used for dutching cocoa. Instead, potassium carbonate is often used. If cocoa has been dutched, its ingredient label will read: cocoa processed with alkali. The cocoa may be called alkalized, dutched, or European-style. In contrast, natural cocoa is sometimes called nonalkalized or regular cocoa.

The dutching process darkens the color of cocoa, making it look richer and often redder than natural cocoa. Dutched cocoas vary in color from light reddish brown to dark brown or dark reddish brown. The final color depends on the amount of dutching the cocoa has undergone. Because the alkaline treatment is applied to nibs before they are ground and pressed, unsweetened chocolate is also available dutched.

Besides affecting color, dutching changes the flavor of cocoa. Dutched cocoa has a smoother, mellower flavor than natural cocoa. It is less sharply astringent and acidic, is more full-bodied, and dissolves more easily in water.

Dutched and natural cocoas can be substituted for each other, despite differences between them. Deciding which to use is mostly based on personal preference. North American consumers tend to use natural cocoa in baked goods, while European consumers tend to use dutched cocoa. However, professional pastry chefs on both sides of the Atlantic typically prefer dutched cocoas for all applications because of its richer color and smoother flavor. Because natural cocoas are slightly acidic while dutched cocoas are alkaline, some chefs adjust the amount of baking soda and acid in formulas accordingly.

A SHORT HISTORY OF CHOCOLATE—PART III

Natural cocoa powder does not disperse easily in water. In 1828, the same year that he developed a method for producing cocoa powder, C. J. Van Houten discovered that by treating cocoa with alkali, cocoa powder dispersed easily. Because Van Houten was Dutch, the cocoa was called dutched cocoa. Dutched cocoa spread in popularity throughout Europe because it dispersed easily, but also because the alkali treatment gave the cocoa a darker, richer color and a mellower flavor.

WHAT IS CAROB POWDER?

Carob powder, or flour, is sometimes used in place of cocoa powder in confections, baked goods, and beverages. Although it looks like cocoa powder, carob powder is not a cacao product. It is made from locust bean (carob) pods that are roasted, then ground. Recall from Chapter 9 that another food ingredient, locust bean (carob) gum, is extracted from the bean contained in this same pod.

Carob powder is considered by some to be a healthful alternative to cocoa powder because it is low in fat and does not contain caffeine-like stimulants. However, some carob products, such as carob chips, can be high in fat. Carob has also been used as a low-cost cocoa substitute when prices of cacao products were high.

WHY IS COLOR AND FLAVOR REMOVED FROM COCOA BUTTER?

When purchased for the bakeshop, cocoa butter is highly-refined, that is, it is pale in color and mild in flavor. Why would pastry chefs want this bland product, instead of a richly-colored and flavorful cocoa butter, straight from chocolate liquor?

As described earlier, cocoa butter is often added to sweetened chocolate products, to alter their consistency. Because pastry chefs often pay premium prices for carefully selected and processed chocolate, they typically do not want anything—even another cocoa product—altering the flavor and appearance of their premium chocolate.

The second main use for cocoa butter is as a protective water-resistant coating on pastry. Once again, neutral flavor is desirable in this application, as well.

COCOA BUTTER

Cocoa butter, the fat naturally present in cocoa beans, is sold as pale yellow bars or flakes. When it is pressed from chocolate liquor during the production of cocoa powder, it has a deep tan color and a distinctively chocolate flavor. It is filtered to remove cocoa particles and partly or wholly deodorized to remove most, if not all, of its chocolate flavor.

Cocoa butter is an expensive fat, valued in the confectionery and cosmetics industries for its unique and pleasant melting characteristics.

Bakers and pastry chefs use cocoa butter for thinning melted chocolate and couvertures to the proper consistency for coating and dipping. While this is its main use, cocoa butter is also brushed onto pastry shells to provide some protection from getting soaked from moist fillings. Because it is highly saturated, cocoa butter resists oxidative rancidity, but it will eventually develop a rancid, off flavor.

Chocolate Products

BITTERSWEET DARK CHOCOLATE

Bittersweet dark chocolate is not the same as bitter, unsweetened chocolate. Like all chocolate products, bittersweet dark chocolate—also called bittersweet, dark, or semi-sweet chocolate, chocolate fondant, or simply chocolate—contains sugar in addition to chocolate liquor. Chocolate chips are one example of bittersweet chocolate commonly found in the bakeshop.

Besides containing a mix of chocolate liquor and sugar, bittersweet dark chocolate may contain small amounts of dairy, natural and artificial flavorings, emulsifiers, nuts, and cocoa butter. In a traditional chocolate factory, this mixture is ground or refined in a melangeur, then ground finer through a series of rollers. The grinding not only reduces particle size so that the chocolate is not gritty, it also releases fat from the particles, so that the chocolate flows better when melted. After chocolate is ground it is conched, to improve mouthfeel and flavor. The result is a smooth, homogenized mix of fine chocolate, milk, and sugar particles evenly suspended in cocoa butter.

After chocolate is conched, it is tempered, molded, and cooled. *Tempering* is a process of carefully cooling and holding chocolate products at the proper temperature to ensure that cocoa butter crystallizes properly. Tempering is the final step in assuring that chocolate has the proper mouthfeel and appearance. Since bakers and pastry chefs must temper chocolate products before use, tempering is discussed in more detail in a later section.

WHAT GIVES COCOA BUTTER ITS UNIQUE MELTING CHARACTERISTICS?

Cocoa butter is extremely hard and brittle at room temperature because it is high in saturated fatty acids. Yet, compared with other saturated fats, such as all-purpose shortening and lard, cocoa butter has a very sharp melting curve and a low final melting point, giving it a unique and pleasant melt-away mouthfeel. Figure 17.3 compares the melting curves of cocoa butter with all-purpose shortening. Notice that cocoa butter starts with a very high (85 percent) solid fat content at room temperature (68°F; 20°C), but that by 95°F (35°C), it has melted completely.

What makes cocoa butter so unique? Recall from Chapter 10 that most food fats contain a broad mix of fatty acids. Each fatty acid has its own distinct melting point, so most food fats melt slowly over a wide temperature range. Cocoa butter, in contrast, consists of relatively few types of fatty acids, which all melt just below body temperature. It is this uniquely homogeneous mix of fatty acids that gives cocoa butter its fast-melting pleasant mouthfeel.

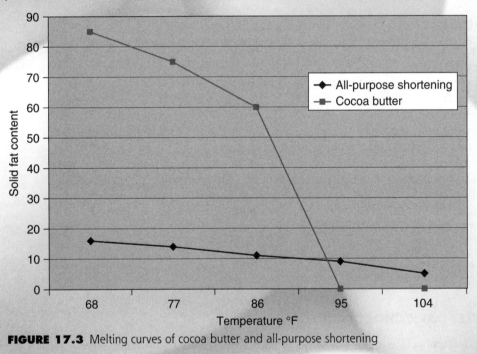

FIGURE 17.3 Melting curves of cocoa butter and all-purpose shortening

Bittersweet dark chocolate (often in the form of couverture, discussed shortly) is used in creams, mousses, ganache fillings and glazes, coatings, icings, sauces, and chocolate chip cookies (as chocolate chips). It is these products—not baked goods—that benefit most from the refined flavor and smooth mouthfeel of fine chocolate. While different brands of bittersweet dark chocolate can be used interchangeably, results vary because brands vary in color, flavor, and amount of sugar and cocoa solids.

Unlike unsweetened chocolate and cocoa powder, bittersweet dark chocolate is rarely used in batters and doughs. The use of bittersweet dark chocolate adds an unnecessary expense to baked goods because of the cost of added conching and refining. The contributions of conching and refining are clear only when chocolate is eaten as is, or in products such as creams, mousses, ganaches, and so on. Once highly refined and conched chocolate is added to batters and doughs, their mild flavor can be masked by other ingredients.

WHAT IS CONCHING?

Conching is a process in which ingredients are mixed, kneaded, and gently heated for several hours or days, depending on the type of equipment and on the desired end results. During conching, sugar and cocoa particles are ground smooth and coated with a film of cocoa butter. In a process that is the reverse of seizing, water evaporates from gentle heat, so the chocolate becomes smoother and shinier. Heat also drives off acids and other volatile ingredients, further refining flavor. Finally, heat continues the development of flavor from chemical reactions begun in the roaster. It is as if conching reduces the coarseness of both flavor and texture, and the chocolate changes from a dull, lumpy paste to a smooth, mellow-tasting liquid, ready for molding and cooling.

Rodolphe Lindt, a Swiss chocolate manufacturer, designed the first conch in 1879, creating the smoothest of eating chocolates, so smooth he called it fondant chocolate. The conch received its name from its shape, which followed the curve of a conch shell. The original conch had heavy rollers that plowed back and forth through waves of chocolate. Similar horizontal conches are still in use today in traditional chocolate factories. These conches often require seventy-two or more hours to complete the process and are said to produce the finest flavored chocolates.

Today, there are newer designs for conches that more efficiently complete the flavor and particle-size refinement processes. For example, rotary vertical conches are equipped with blades that vigorously scrape chocolate against ribbed walls and keep it in constant motion, while strong air currents blow through.

There is no one best process for conching, and manufacturers control the time, temperature, and speed of conching to achieve the results that they desire. This is one step among many by which manufacturers distinguish their brand of chocolate from others.

In North America, bittersweet chocolate must contain a minimum of 35 percent cocoa solids (in the United States, the 35 percent minimum must be of chocolate liquor), meaning that it can contain up to 65 percent sugar. Table 17.2 compares the U.S. standard for bittersweet chocolate with that for other chocolates. Table 17.3 compares Canadian standards for chocolates.

TABLE 17.2 ■ U.S. STANDARDS FOR CHOCOLATE

CHOCOLATE	CHOCOLATE LIQUOR (MINIMUM)	DAIRY SOLIDS	OTHER STANDARDS
Bittersweet	35%	12% (max)	
Milk	10%	12% (min)	
White	0%	14% (min)	20% (min.) cocoa butter; 3.5% (min.) milkfat; 5% (max.) whey; 55% (max.) sugar

From U.S. 21CFR163 2002

TABLE 17.3 ■ CANADIAN STANDARDS FOR CHOCOLATE

CHOCOLATE	TOTAL COCOA SOLIDS* (MINIMUM)	DAIRY SOLIDS	COCOA BUTTER (MINIMUM)	COCOA SOLIDS NONFAT (MINIMUM)	OTHER STANDARDS
Bittersweet	35%	5% (max.)	18%	14%	
Milk	25%	12% (min.)	15%	2.5%	5% (max.)
White	0%	14% (min.)	20%	—	Whey

*From chocolate liquor, cocoa powder, and cocoa butter

From Canada CRC, c.870, B.04 Dec 31, 2001

WHAT IF CHOCOLATE BROWNIES WERE MADE WITH BITTERSWEET CHOCOLATE?

Chocolate brownies are typically made with unsweetened chocolate (or with cocoa). If bittersweet dark chocolate was used instead, without adjusting the formula, the brownies would turn out differently. They would be lighter in color, have a milder chocolate flavor, and be sweeter. They would also be moister and more tender. In fact, depending on the brand used, they could look and taste more like blond brownies than chocolate brownies, because bittersweet dark chocolate is lower in cocoa solids than unsweetened chocolate is. In place of cocoa solids, bittersweet dark chocolate contains sugar—sometimes up to 65 percent sugar.

Because of the added processing that bittersweet chocolate undergoes, these brownies would likely be more expensive, too. In a pinch, however, 2 pounds (or 1,000 grams) of bittersweet chocolate can be used in place of 1 pound (or 500 grams) unsweetened chocolate (this assumes that the bittersweet chocolate is 50 percent chocolate liquor). Because bittersweet chocolate contains sugar, the amount of sugar in the formula should be reduced by 1 pound (or 500 grams).

Many bittersweet chocolates exceed these minimum standards, some containing 50 percent cocoa solids or more. Often, manufacturers use the term *bittersweet* when a chocolate contains more than 50 percent cocoa solids and semisweet when it contains between 35 percent and 50 percent, but there is no law that says they must. While price does not necessarily reflect quality, cocoa solids are more expensive than sugar, so the more cocoa solids in chocolate, often the higher the cost.

In the European Union, the equivalent to bittersweet dark chocolate is more often simply called chocolate. While European chocolate couverture does not meet minimum standards for bittersweet chocolate in North America, European dark couverture chocolate exceeds them. Dark couverture chocolate will be discussed shortly in more detail.

MILK CHOCOLATE

Milk chocolate is a sweetened chocolate product that is typically low in cocoa solids but contains a minimum of 12 percent milk solids (see Tables 17.2 and 17.3). As with bittersweet dark chocolate, milk chocolate often contains natural or artificial vanilla flavoring, emulsifiers, and cocoa butter. The rest is sugar. Milk chocolate undergoes refining, conching, tempering, and molding processes similar to those of bittersweet dark chocolate.

Most milk chocolates are sweet and mellow in flavor. While they lack chocolate bitterness, many do have interesting flavors from dairy solids. American milk chocolate, for example, often has a sour or ripened milk flavor, while Swiss chocolate has a mildly cooked milk flavor. British milk chocolate often is strongly caramelized from the addition of milk crumb. *Milk crumb* is a dry, crumbly powder made by heating condensed milk with sugar, with or without the addition of chocolate liquor. The caramelized flavors come from Maillard reactions that occur when milk and sugar are heated together.

Milk chocolate cannot generally be used in formulas designed for bittersweet chocolate because it is too low in cocoa solids and too mild in flavor to really work well. Its primary use (often in the form of couverture) in the bakeshop is for dipping and coating, and for chocolate garnishes and decorations.

WHITE CHOCOLATE

White chocolate is made from sugar, cocoa butter, milk solids, and natural or artificial vanilla flavoring; emulsifiers are optional. In other words, white chocolate is essentially milk chocolate without the cocoa solids nonfat. For many years, there was no permanent

WHAT IF CHOCOLATE MOUSSE WAS MADE WITH MILK CHOCOLATE?

Chocolate mousse is typically made with bittersweet dark chocolate. If milk chocolate was used instead, the mousse would likely come out quite different. It would be lighter in color; in fact, it might look more like butterscotch mousse than chocolate mousse, because milk chocolates are low in cocoa solids nonfat.

The low amount of cocoa solids also means that milk chocolate mousse would likely be softer and less firm than one made with bittersweet dark chocolate. In fact, some milk chocolate mousses fail to set up.

Finally, milk chocolate mousse would be sweeter than one made with bittersweet dark chocolate, maybe too sweet and too weak in flavor. The flavor often is more buttery, creamy, caramel, or vanilla than chocolate. These flavors come through aerated products more strongly than does chocolate.

Does this mean that milk chocolate should never be used in chocolate mousse? No, but it is often difficult to predict how well any particular milk chocolate will work without first trying it. To increase your chances of success, select a milk chocolate with a strong flavor and one that is relatively high in cocoa solids and low in sugar; use a combination of milk and bittersweet chocolates; or use a formula designed specifically for milk chocolate.

legal definition for white chocolate in the United States; this changed in 2002 when the FDA created a standard of identity for white chocolate. This standard is defined in Table 17.2 and is the same as that for white chocolate in the European Union.

The flavor of white chocolate is predominantly vanilla. White chocolate has essentially no chocolate flavor because the cocoa butter is typically deodorized before use. Because white chocolate is totally lacking in cocoa solids nonfat, it cannot be substituted directly for bittersweet or milk chocolate in most formulas. When it is, expect a softer set, even though white chocolate sets up faster than other chocolates. White chocolate is used in creams, mousses, ganache fillings and glazes, coatings, cheesecake, icings, various confectionery, and cookies (as white chocolate chunks).

COUVERTURE CHOCOLATES

Couverture is French for *coating*. Couverture chocolate is chocolate with a minimum of 31 percent cocoa butter (in the case of milk chocolate couverture, the minimum 31 percent includes milk fat). Think of couvertures as higher-quality chocolate products, with higher levels of cocoa butter adding to their cost.

Many bakeshops stock both milk chocolate and dark chocolate couvertures. Couvertures are used primarily for chocolate garnishes and decorations, or for dipping and coating cakes, cookies, and pralines. Couvertures can also be used interchangeably with regular chocolate products in creams, mousses, ganache, and icings. Couvertures are not typically added to batters and doughs for the same reason that chocolate is not.

Couverture has several advantages over chocolate. The added cocoa butter coats the sugar and cocoa particles, allowing them to flow past each other more easily. With particles flowing easily past each other, couvertures are thin, so they coat products easily. In contrast, when semisweet chocolate chips are melted, for example, the melted chocolate is thick. The sugar and cocoa particles tend to interact, thickening the chocolate. This thickness is necessary for the manufacturer to properly deposit chocolate into drops, but it means that melted chips designed for chocolate chip cookies are too thick to use for coating and dipping (unless cocoa butter or another fat is added).

The added cocoa butter in couverture also provides an attractive glossy finish—as long as the couverture is properly tempered. Because cocoa butter is extremely solid at room temperature, high-quality couvertures exhibit a characteristic snap that is absent from products with lower amounts of cocoa butter. Higher amounts of cocoa butter

WHAT IS GANACHE?

Ganache is a simple mixture of heavy cream and melted chocolate. To make ganache, bring fresh cream just to a boil, pour it over chopped chocolate, and stir until the chocolate melts completely. Ganache has many uses, including as a glaze or icing for cakes, as a filling for pralines, or, when whipped, as chocolate mousse.

The proportion of chocolate to cream in ganache can vary, with higher amounts of chocolate providing a firm consistency, and higher amounts of heavy cream producing a softer one. For further variety, other liquids—such as milk, juice, or coffee—can be substituted for heavy cream, and butter or egg yolks can be added for richness. Since chocolate products vary in the amount of chocolate liquor each contains, ganache consistency also varies with the type and brand of chocolate.

Scientifically, ganache is an emulsion of milk fat droplets and cocoa butter crystals suspended in liquid, stabilized by natural emulsifiers and proteins in milk and in chocolate. Too much bittersweet chocolate sometimes causes the emulsion to break and fats to separate from the liquid. When this happens, whisk ganache slowly into a small amount of heavy cream, to reemulsify.

THE USE OF EMULSIFIERS IN CHOCOLATES AND COUVERTURES

Just as emulsifiers interact and coat fat and flour particles in baked goods, so, too, do they coat and interact with particles in chocolates and couvertures. In particular, emulsifiers coat and interact with sugar particles. Through these interactions, emulsifiers allow particles in liquefied chocolates and couvertures to easily slide past one another. This thins the consistency of the chocolate, so that it flows smoothly and evenly.

Small amounts of the emulsifier lecithin are naturally present in chocolate liquor, and additional amounts are commonly added to chocolate products. Lecithin is approved for use in chocolates and couvertures in North America, as well as in Europe. Because it is less expensive and about ten times more efficient than cocoa butter at thinning chocolate, lecithin is often used for lowering the cost of chocolates. Lecithin is also added to expensive couvertures as a final adjustment of consistency. Since only a very small amount (usually 0.1–0.3 percent) of lecithin is needed, the chocolate flavor of the couverture is not diluted, as it can be when high amounts of cocoa butter are used instead.

also mean a smoother, more melt-away mouthfeel. Notice that these advantages are important when couvertures are used for coating and dipping or for creating chocolate garnishes and decorations; they are lost when couvertures are used in baked goods. Table 17.4 summarizes the important functions of cocoa butter in couvertures and other chocolate products.

European law defines couvertures; Canadian and U.S. laws do not. This does not mean that North American chocolate products never meet the standards of couverture; it simply means that they are not labeled as such. If it is important to know the amount of cocoa butter present in a chocolate product, ask the manufacturer. Table 17.5 summarizes European Union regulations for couverture chocolates.

TABLE 17.4 ■ FUNCTIONS OF COCOA BUTTER IN CHOCOLATE PRODUCTS

Thins viscosity of melted chocolate
Provides sheen
Provides firmness with snap
Provides a smooth, melt-away mouthfeel

Confectionery Coatings

Confectionery coatings go by many names, including compound coatings, summer coatings, or simply, coatings. Sometimes confectionery coatings are called chocolate coatings, but this is not legally correct. In North America, the word *chocolate* is reserved

TABLE 17.5 ■ EUROPEAN UNION REGULATIONS FOR COUVERTURE CHOCOLATES

COUVERTURE PRODUCT	MINIMUM COCOA BUTTER	OTHER REGULATIONS
Couverture chocolate	31%	> 2.5% cocoa solids nonfat
Dark couverture chocolate	31%	> 16% cocoa solids nonfat
Couverture milk chocolate	31% (includes milk fat)	> 2.5% cocoa solids nonfat; > 14% milk solids, and < 55% sucrose

Member countries of the European Union are allowed by law to add up to 5 percent tropical oils, such as palm oil or shea oil, into their chocolate products. However, these products cannot be legally sold as chocolate in North America.

for products that contain cocoa butter as the only fat (small amounts of milk fat are allowed). Confectionery coatings contain vegetable fats, such as partially hydrogenated soybean, palm kernel, or coconut oil, making them less expensive than chocolate products. The oils are specially processed—*fractionated*—so that they have melting properties similar to cocoa butter. While some are quite good in quality, coating fat is still imitation cocoa butter, just as margarine is imitation butter, so they are not identical.

Besides being low in cost, some confectionery coatings are easier to work with than couvertures because they do not require tempering. The fats in these particular confectionery coatings do not bloom, so the coatings stay glossy. Certain confectionery coatings have a higher melting point than cocoa butter. While too high a melting point gives the coating an unappealing waxiness, high-melting coatings resist melting in warm weather.

Confectionery coatings often sacrifice flavor and mouthfeel for low cost and ease of use. As with any ingredient, product quality varies from one brand to the next. If one is unsatisfactory, try another.

Confectionery coatings are available as dark, milk, and white versions. Coatings are also available in a rainbow of colors.

HANDLING CHOCOLATE PRODUCTS

Unsweetened chocolate and chocolate products are usually melted before use. They must be melted carefully, because they contain a mix of proteins and carbohydrates that are easily overheated. When chocolate overheats, it becomes thick, lumpy, and dull. If this occurs, throw out the chocolate and begin again. It is especially easy to overheat milk and white chocolates, because they contain dairy ingredients that burn and scorch easily.

Chocolate can be melted in a microwave or in a double boiler. In either case, never leave melting chocolate unattended, and be sure to stir often so hot spots do not develop and overheat the chocolate.

Keep water and steam away from melted chocolate. Be sure, for example, to dry off the surfaces of strawberries and other fresh fruits that are dipped in chocolate. Water causes chocolate to seize up and thicken, as hygroscopic sugar particles absorb water and become sticky. Sticky particles cannot flow easily past each other, greatly increasing viscosity or thickness. Once thickened in this manner, chocolate products are no longer useful for dipping and coating.

Cocoa butter, like all fats, is *polymorphic*, which means that it forms crystals with different shapes and forms. Each crystal form also has different properties. In the case of cocoa butter, there are six known crystal forms. The three most common for cocoa

HELPFUL HINT

Although no longer useful for dipping and coating, seized chocolate has its uses. By intentionally adding a small amount of water to chocolate, for example, chocolate is easily piped. Unintentionally seized chocolate can be used in ganaches, fillings, and other products that combine chocolate with liquid ingredients.

butter—listed in order of increasing melting point, density, and stability—are alpha (α), beta prime (β'), and beta (β). The beta form, sometimes called form V, is the most desirable of the three because it provides chocolate with snap, gloss, and a smooth mouthfeel. Beta crystals also have the highest melting point of the three, making them the most stable and the least likely to melt and bloom during storage. Beta crystals have these features because the triglycerides are more tightly packed than they are in other crystal formations.

When melted chocolate is allowed to cool without proper tempering, unstable alpha crystals form. Alpha crystals result in chocolate that is soft, dull, and does not snap when broken. Because alpha crystals do not pack as tightly as beta crystals, untempered chocolate placed in molds will be difficult to remove, since the chocolate does not contract.

While untempered chocolate will look somewhat acceptable when first hardened, the unstable alpha crystals transform to more stable beta crystals during storage. Yet, the beta crystals formed uncontrolled during storage are large and coarse. Eventually these crystals migrate to the chocolate's surface, where they appear as *fat bloom*, which are unattractive but harmless gray-white streaks or spots. With this change, chocolate becomes gritty, sometimes crumbly, in texture. Because texture affects flavor perception, bloomed chocolate does not have the right flavor, either.

Tempering Chocolate

To ensure that large numbers of small, stable beta crystals form, chocolate products are tempered. Tempering involves gently heating chocolate (115°–120°F; 46°–49°C) to dissolve undesirable low-melting crystals; cooling and agitating it at a temperature (78°–80°F; 26°–27°C) that encourages the formation of beta seed crystals; then warming it slightly (86°–90°F; 30°–32°C), before cooling gently to room temperature to set. As the chocolate cools, the presence of beta crystals from tempering encourages formation of more beta crystals. Because beta crystals take time to form properly, chocolate must be cooled and allowed to set slowly. In other words, tempered chocolate should not be placed in the cooler or freezer to speed the process.

The temperature ranges provided above are broad guidelines. Milk fat, emulsifiers, and other ingredients affect the crystallizing behavior of cocoa butter, which is why milk chocolates must be tempered at lower temperatures than bittersweet dark chocolates. Each brand of chocolate also has its own ideal tempering pattern, and it is best to ask the manufacturer for specific tempering guidelines.

There are several procedures for tempering chocolates. One way is to place chopped chocolate in a bowl set over hot water, and to melt, cool, and rewarm the chocolate in bulk. Another method is to add shaved bits of tempered chocolate to melted chocolate, to seed and cool it simultaneously. No matter the method used, the goal is the same—to form a large number of small, stable beta crystals for the most appealing appearance, texture, and flavor release.

FUNCTIONS OF COCOA AND CHOCOLATE PRODUCTS

Provide Color

Cocoa and chocolate products have colors that range from light tan to dark mahogany, even black. They vary in color for many reasons; the eight main ones are listed in Table 17.6. Of these reasons, the cocoa grower controls the first three while the

TABLE 17.6 ■ MAJOR CAUSES OF COLOR AND FLAVOR VARIATION IN CHOCOLATE AND COCOA PRODUCTS

Bean variety and country of origin
Bean maturity and ripeness
Handling of beans—fermentation, drying, and storage
Roasting conditions
Conching conditions
Amount of fat
Amount of dutching and final pH of cocoa or chocolate
Amount of baking soda and final pH of finished product (in baked goods)

manufacturer controls the next four. The last, the amount of baking soda and final pH of a baked good, is under the control of the baker or pastry chef.

Provide Flavor

Flavor is a primary reason for using cocoa and chocolate products in the bakeshop. There are regional preferences for chocolate flavors and styles of chocolate. For example, many French, Belgians, and Germans prefer dark chocolate, but most of the world prefers milk chocolate by a wide margin. A recent trend on both sides of the Atlantic, however, is the consumption of so-called extreme dark chocolates. Extreme dark chocolates are very dark and bitter because they are high in cocoa solids.

Cocoa and chocolate products vary in flavor for the same reasons that they vary in color (Table 17.6), but the two do not necessarily coincide. That is, a dark-colored chocolate does not necessarily have the strongest chocolate flavor. Recall that flavor-rich criollo beans are light in color, and that dutching darkens color while it mellows flavor.

The perception of chocolate flavor changes with context. That is, milk chocolate that seems well balanced on its own might taste weak when paired with other flavors. On the other hand, a bittersweet that seems strong and bitter when tasted alone could provide the right balance of flavor to a finished product. When selecting chocolate or couverture to use in products, be sure to taste a sample of the finished product before preparing large quantities.

WHY YOU CAN'T ALWAYS JUDGE COCOA BY ITS COLOR

Fat content is one of the eight major factors affecting color of cocoas and chocolates. The more cocoa butter in cocoa, for example, the darker and richer it appears. This makes 22/24 cocoa a good choice for dusting truffles and plated desserts.

You might think that 22/24 cocoa would also provide a darker, richer color in baked goods, such as cakes and cookies. Yet, the rich look of high-fat cocoa is an illusion. The more fat in cocoa, the fewer coloring agents it actually contains (the coloring agents are in the nonfat portion of cocoa). The rich look of high-fat cocoa is from the perception of light as it reflects off fat-coated cocoa particles. Once mixed into batters and doughs, cocoa powder takes on a different look. The color no longer depends on the amount of fat in the cocoa powder; it depends on the amount of coloring agents present in the cocoa solids nonfat. If there is any difference in appearance between a cake baked with a 22/24 cocoa and one baked with a 10/12 cocoa, it is the lower-fat cocoa that will provide a darker color (of course, other differences between the cocoas could affect color).

WHAT PUTS THE DEVIL IN DEVIL'S FOOD CAKE?

Recipes abound for devil's food cake, an American classic. Devil's food cake is mild tasting, yet it has a rich, dark, reddish brown color. It is typically made with cocoa, not chocolate, and the cocoa of choice is natural cocoa.

What makes devil's food cake dark and rich looking? Baking soda. Small amounts of baking soda react with acids in natural cocoa. This provides some carbon dioxide for leavening, but the baking soda also increases the pH of the batter.

This slightly higher pH darkens the cocoa and provides it with a smoother cocoa flavor. It is as if the cocoa were dutched right in the batter.

Care must be taken that excessive amounts of baking soda are not added to devil's food cake. Too much baking soda is detrimental to flavor, adding a chemically, off taste. Too much baking soda also overtenderizes cell walls. When this happens, the cell walls break, forming a coarse crumb and a cake that flattens unattractively.

Here are a few additional points to consider when working with chocolate flavor.

- Cocoa and chocolate products with a higher amount of cocoa butter typically provide a richer, fuller chocolate flavor because cocoa butter (when undeodorized) itself has flavor. That is why unsweetened chocolate—not cocoa powder—is preferred for the richest, most decadent chocolate desserts.

- Vanilla flavor is so commonly used in chocolate products in North America that sometimes the way to increase "chocolate" flavor in a product is to add a small amount of vanilla.

- Natural cocoas tend to have pronounced sharp, fruity, acidic flavors. Dutched cocoas have smoother, fuller flavors.

- Adding baking soda to baked goods is almost like dutching cocoa or chocolate right in the baked good.

Absorb Liquids

Cocoa solids nonfat is an extremely effective drying agent. In fact, cocoa powder absorbs more liquid than an equal weight of flour. It is proteins and carbohydrates—starches, dextrins, and gums—in cocoa solids nonfat that absorb liquids (water and oil) from cake batters, icings, fillings, mousses, and ganache. When extra cocoa is added to cake batter, for example, less flour is needed for the right batter consistency.

Provide Structure

Cocoa solids nonfat provides structure. The starches, in particular, provide structure when they gelatinize. Just as cake with extra cocoa requires less flour for the right batter consistency, it also requires less flour for structure. Likewise, chocolate mousse made with bittersweet chocolate has more structure and substance than one made from milk chocolate—which has much less cocoa solids nonfat—or from white chocolate, which has none.

Cocoa and chocolate products—even unsweetened chocolate, which is over 50 percent fat—are not considered tenderizers. Their structure builders are so powerful that they more than compensate for the mild tenderizing effect of cocoa butter. Cocoa butter is considered to have about half the shortening or tenderizing power of all-purpose shortening, partly because it is so solid at room temperature. In fact, cocoa butter itself provides firmness and structure through the formation of solid fat crystals.

WHAT IS ORAC?

ORAC stands for Oxygen Radical Absorbance Capacity. It is a sophisticated test that measures the antioxidant activity of food products in the laboratory. While it seems reasonable to assume that products with high antioxidant activity in the lab will also have high antioxidant activity in the human body, it is not necessarily the case. Clinical studies are needed to relate ORAC units to actual health benefits in humans. The high level of ORAC units in chocolate products, however, is impressive.

According to the USDA and American Chemical Society, the ORAC units for 100 grams of various food products are as follows:

13,120	Dark chocolate
6,740	Milk chocolate
5,770	Prunes
2,400	Blueberries
1,540	Strawberries
1,220	Raspberries
450	Onions
400	Corn

Provide a Pleasing Mouthfeel

High-fat cocoa and chocolate products, especially those that are highly refined and conched, have a pleasing mouthfeel that contributes to the overall sensory effects of coatings, creams, mousses, ganache fillings and glazes, and icings. The pleasing mouthfeel is primarily from the unique melting characteristics of cocoa butter and from the lack of grittiness in these products.

It might seem that if some smoothness is good, more must be better. Yet, if chocolate is ground too finely, it feels waxy. There are regional preferences for the mouthfeel of chocolate, just as there are preferences for flavor, with Europeans tending to prefer smoother chocolates than North Americans.

Add Nutritional Value

While cocoa powder contains cocoa butter (10–12 percent) and small amounts of moisture (about 3 percent), it consists mostly of cocoa solids nonfat (about 85 percent). It is especially rich in dietary fiber and other carbohydrates (Figure 17.2), as well as protein. Cocoa is also an important source of vitamins, minerals, and polyphenolic compounds. The level of polyphenols and the antioxidant activity of cocoa and chocolate products rivals that of many fruits and vegetables.

STORAGE

Chocolate products are a favorite food of rodents. For this reason, all chocolate should be well-wrapped and stored in covered containers.

Milk and white chocolates have the shortest shelf life of all cocoa and chocolate products because their milk solids undergo Maillard browning—the browning of sugars and proteins—even at room temperature. Stored properly, milk and white chocolates have a shelf life of six months to one year. Eventually, Maillard browning causes colors to darken and off flavors to develop. While cocoa butter is relatively stable to oxidative rancidity, milk fat is not. The milk fat in milk and white chocolates also contributes to off-flavor development in these products as it undergoes oxidative rancidity.

Other cocoa and chocolate products, including cocoa butter, have a shelf life that is longer than one year, but that is true only if they are stored properly. Ideally, cocoa and chocolate products should be stored well wrapped and at a cool, consistent 55°–65°F (13°–18°C), otherwise fat bloom forms on chocolate surfaces. Do not discard chocolate that has bloomed. Its baking qualities remain unaffected, and fat bloom disappears when chocolate is tempered before use, as long as it is not severe.

Sugar bloom occurs when chocolate picks up moisture. Sugar crystals melt in the moisture, only to recrystallize on the surface as larger crystals. The gritty white crystals affect both texture and appearance. Sugar bloom remains even after chocolate is tempered. To prevent sugar bloom, store chocolate where the humidity is below 50 percent; use gloves when handling chocolate, to avoid transfer of moisture from hands; and do not warm cold chocolate unless it is very tightly wrapped. This is critical with chocolate that has been refrigerated. As refrigerated chocolate warms to room temperature, water droplets easily condense onto its surface, solubilizing sugar crystals and forming sugar bloom.

Cocoa powder is hygroscopic. If it picks up excess moisture, it clumps, develops off flavors, and could be a source of food for microorganisms. Store cocoa in a tightly covered container and away from hot, steamy areas.

All chocolate products, but especially white chocolate, should be well wrapped and kept away from strong odors. Cocoa butter, like all fats, readily picks up odors.

QUESTIONS FOR REVIEW

1. How does the amount and type of fat in cocoa beans compare to that in almonds?
2. What is meant by cocoa nib?
3. A product is labeled 72 percent cocoa. What does this mean? How does this value differ from the amount of cocoa solids nonfat in a product?
4. What is the name of the caffeine-like stimulant found in cocoa nibs?
5. What changes occur in cocoa beans as they are roasted?
6. What is chocolate liquor called when it is sold as solid blocks?
7. What is the main difference in makeup between unsweetened chocolate and natural cocoa?
8. Which is more expensive to use, unsweetened chocolate or cocoa powder? Why?
9. Which should be used—unsweetened chocolate or cocoa—for the richest, most chocolate flavor in baked goods? Which should be used in low-fat products?
10. How is dutched cocoa made? How does it differ from natural cocoa in color, flavor, and acidity?
11. Why does cocoa butter provide a more pleasant mouthfeel than all-purpose shortening?
12. What is another name for semisweet chocolate?
13. How does bitter (unsweetened) chocolate compare with bittersweet chocolate in minimum percentage of cocoa solids?
14. What is meant by conching? Why is it important that chocolate products used for coating and dipping be conched? Why is it not important for unsweetened chocolate used in baked goods to be conched?
15. How does the amount of cocoa butter in chocolate products affect their properties?
16. You add a small amount of vanilla extract to chocolate and start to stir it in, but the chocolate thickens. Why? What has happened to the sugars and proteins in the mixture?
17. What does it mean when we say that cocoa butter is polymorphic?
18. What are the main differences between alpha, beta prime, and beta crystals?
19. Describe the process of tempering chocolate.
20. Why is the goal of tempering to form the largest number of beta crystals?
21. Which components in cocoa and chocolate make them drying or absorbing agents? Which make them structure builders?
22. How does cocoa butter compare to all-purpose shortening in its ability to shorten and tenderize?

23. What is meant by ORAC? How does chocolate compare to other food products in ORAC units?

24. What changes occur in white chocolate when it is stored for too long?

25. How should cocoa powder be stored? What changes happen to cocoa powder when it is stored improperly?

26. What is fat bloom? How can it be prevented?

27. What is sugar bloom? How can it be prevented?

QUESTIONS FOR DISCUSSION

1. From what you know of the minimum amount of cocoa butter that is in chocolate liquor and the minimum amount of chocolate liquor required in bittersweet dark chocolate in the United States, calculate the minimum amount of cocoa butter that can legally be in bittersweet dark chocolate (show your work). How does this compare to the minimum amount of cocoa butter that must be in European dark couverture chocolate?

2. A formula for chocolate cookies calls for unsweetened chocolate. If bittersweet dark chocolate is used instead, how might the cookies come out differently, and why?

3. A formula for ganache calls for bittersweet dark chocolate. If milk chocolate is used instead, how might the ganache come out differently, and why?

4. According to European law, what is the difference between milk chocolate and milk chocolate couverture? Which will be more expensive? Which is more likely to be used in the bakeshop for coating, dipping, and garnishing cakes, cookies, and confections?

5. For a stronger chocolate flavor in fudge cake, you add more cocoa to the basic formula. The result is a tough, dry, dense cake. Why?

6. To make a premium chocolate cake, you switch from unsweetened chocolate to an equal amount of expensive, superpremium dark couverture. The result is a pale, collapsed mess that is too sweet and has little chocolate flavor. Why?

7. You are out of unsweetened chocolate for brownies and are substituting bittersweet dark chocolate (or couverture) instead. How much bittersweet chocolate should be used for each pound (or kilogram) of unsweetened chocolate, and how should the amount of sugar be adjusted in the formula?

8. Why might chocolate cake contain baking soda? List three reasons.

9. Two fudge cakes are prepared in an identical manner using all the same ingredients in equal amounts, but different cocoas are used. List four reasons that could explain why one of the cakes looks darker than the other. Be specific. Why might a darker cocoa produce a lighter cake?

EXERCISES AND EXPERIMENTS

1. Replacing Chocolate with Cocoa and Shortening

Using the formula provided earlier in this chapter, how much cocoa and how much shortening should be used to replace 2 pounds (or 2 kilograms) of chocolate in a cake formula? Show your work.

2. Evaluating Chocolate

The best way to learn about chocolate flavor is to evaluate a range of chocolates. The chocolates should be at room temperature and, if possible, temper and mold each chocolate so that they are of the same size and shape for tasting. Use the following form to record your evaluations of the appearance, flavor, and mouthfeel of different brands of chocolate products. Use a separate form for each product. Compare white chocolates to each other, then repeat with milk chocolates, and finally bittersweet dark chocolates. Include one or two confectionery coatings in your tastings, and be sure to include products that range in price. Use only those terms you feel comfortable with. After some experience, add any other terms that you feel are important.

EVALUATION FORM FOR CHOCOLATE PRODUCTS

APPEARANCE	LOW				HIGH	OTHER COMMENTS
Gloss	1	2	3	4	5	
Color (darkness)	1	2	3	4	5	
Color (redness)	1	2	3	4	5	
TEXTURE						
Snap (firmness & brittleness)	1	2	3	4	5	
FLAVOR (SMELL)						
Vanilla	1	2	3	4	5	
Chocolate	1	2	3	4	5	
Fresh dairy	1	2	3	4	5	
Caramelized dairy	1	2	3	4	5	
	1	2	3	4	5	
	1	2	3	4	5	
FLAVOR (TASTE)						
Sweetness	1	2	3	4	5	
Sourness	1	2	3	4	5	
	1	2	3	4	5	
Mouthfeel						
Smoothness (gritty to smooth)	1	2	3	4	5	
Melt-away (slow to fast)	1	2	3	4	5	
AFTERTASTE						
Bitterness	1	2	3	4	5	
Creaminess (mouthfeel)	1	2	3	4	5	
	1	2	3	4	5	

Summarize your major findings from your chocolate tastings:

White chocolates:

_____

_____

Milk chocolates:

_____

_____

Bittersweet dark chocolates:

_____

_____

3. How the Brand and Type of Chocolate Affects the Overall Quality of Ganache

OBJECTIVES

To demonstrate how the brand and type of chocolate affects:
- Ganache appearance, flavor, and consistency
- Overall acceptability of ganache

PRODUCTS PREPARED

Ganache made with:
- Bittersweet dark chocolate or couverture (control product)
- Bittersweet dark chocolate or couverture, different brand
- Dark coating
- Milk chocolate or couverture
- White chocolate or couverture
- Other, if desired (milk coating, white coating, etc.)

PROCEDURE

- Line half sheet pan with parchment paper and label with type of chocolate to be used in ganache.
- Prepare ganache using the formula that follows or using any basic hard ganache formula. Prepare one batch of ganache for each variation.
- Pour hot ganache onto parchment-lined sheet pan and spread into an even, thin layer using a rubber spatula.
- Refrigerate to cool.
- Record any potential sources of error that might make it difficult to draw proper conclusions from the experiment. In particular, be aware of differences in time it took to boil the cream and in temperature of products when they are evaluated.
- Use *Brand Name* column in Results Table 1, which follows, to record any identifying information for each chocolate product used.

- Evaluate the sensory characteristics of completely cooled products and record evaluations in Results Table 1. Be sure to compare each in turn to the control product and consider the following:
  - Appearance (color, sheen, and consistency, or thickness)
  - Flavor (sweetness, bitterness, vanilla, caramel, cooked dairy aroma, etc.)
  - Mouthfeel (thick/thin, heavy, waxy, oily, etc.)
  - Overall acceptability
  - Any additional comments, as necessary.

Ganache

INGREDIENT	POUND	OUNCE	GRAMS	BAKER'S PERCENTAGE
Cream, heavy		7	200	50
Chocolate, finely chopped		14	400	100
Total	1	5	600	150

Method of Preparation

1. Place cream in heavy saucepan and bring just to a boil while stirring.
2. Remove from heat.
3. Stir in chopped chocolate and set aside for a few minutes to allow the heat from the cream to melt the chocolate.
4. Stir until smooth and chocolate is completely melted.

 **SOURCES OF ERROR**

_____

_____

RESULTS TABLE 1 ■ SENSORY CHARACTERISTICS OF GANACHE MADE WITH DIFFERENT BRANDS AND TYPES OF CHOCOLATE

TYPE OF CHOCOLATE	BRAND NAME	APPEARANCE	FLAVOR	MOUTHFEEL	OVERALL ACCEPTABILITY	COMMENTS
Bittersweet dark chocolate/couverture (control product)						
Bittersweet dark chocolate/couverture (different brand)						
Dark coating						
Milk chocolate						
White chocolate						

CONCLUSIONS

1. Rank the ganache samples from thickest consistency to thinnest. Were these differences predictable based on your knowledge of the makeup (approximate cocoa solids nonfat) of each chocolate product?

_____

_____

    a. How might you adjust the ganache formula for the thinnest ganache to make it thicker, while still using the same chocolate?

    _____

    _____

2. What were the main differences in appearance, flavor, and texture among the ganache samples made with the dark coating and with the different brands of bittersweet dark chocolate? Which of these three did you prefer, and why?

_____

_____

3. What were the main differences in appearance, flavor, and texture between the ganache made with milk chocolate and the one made with bittersweet dark chocolate (the control product)?

_____

_____

4. What were the main differences in appearance, flavor, and texture between the ganache made with white chocolate and the one made with bittersweet dark chocolate (the control product)?

_____

_____

5. Which ganache samples do you feel would be acceptable as a cake glaze, and why?

_____

_____

6. Did you have any sources of error that might significantly affect the results of your experiment? If so, what could you do differently next time to minimize error?

_____

_____

BIBLIOGRAPHY

This is a list of general references. Web addresses are accurate at the time of publication, but readers should consult a search engine, if necessary.

Agriculture and Agri-Food Canada. www.agr.gc.ca/index_e.php.

American Egg Board. "Egg Safety." www.aeb.org/Foodservice/eggsafety.htm.

Atwell, W. A. "An Overview of Wheat Development, Cultivation, and Production." www.namamillers.org/pdf/atwell.pdf.

Beckett, S. T. (ed.). *Industrial Chocolate Manufacture and Use, 2nd ed.* London, New York: Blackie Academic & Professional, 1998.

Beckett, Stephen T. *The Science of Chocolate.* Cambridge, UK: Royal Society of Chemistry, 2000.

Beranbaum, Rose, Levy. "Rose's Sugar Bible." www.thecakebible.com.

Berlitz, H. D., and W. Grosch. *Food Chemistry, 2nd ed.* Berlin, New York: Springer, 1999.

Calorie Control Council. "Questions and Answers about Polyols." www.caloriecontrol.org/redcalqa.html.

Calvel, Raymond, Ronald L. Wirtz (translator), and James J. MacGuire (ed.). *The Taste of Bread.* Gaithersburg, MD: Aspen Publishers, 2001.

Canada Department of Justice. Food and Drug Regulations (C.R.C., c. 870). http://laws.justice.gc.ca/en/ShowTdm/cr/C.R.C.-c.870.

Canadian Food Inspection Agency. "Food." www.inspection.gc.ca/english/fssa/fssae.shtml.

Chocolate Manufacturers Association. "Chocolate and Health." www.candyusa.org/Media/downloads/NCA_Chocolate_and_Health.pdf.

Chocolate Manufacturers Association. "The History of Chocolate." www.candyusa.org/chocolate/history.asp.

Coe, Sophie D., and Michael D. Coe. *The True History of Chocolate.* New York: Thames and Hudson, 1996.

Davidson, Alan. *The Oxford Companion to Food.* Oxford, England: Oxford University Press, 1999.

DGF Stoess. "Gelatine Production." www.gelita.com/dgf-deutsch/broschuere/pdf/gelatine_production.pdf.

European Union. EUR-Lex: "The Access to European Union Law." http://eur-lex.europa.eu/en/index.htm.

Fagrell, Eve. "Technical Bulletin: Raisin Usage in Baked Goods." Volume 14 (4). Kansas City, MO: American Institute of Baking, April 1992.

Fennema, Owen (ed.). *Food Chemistry, 3rd ed.* New York: Marcel Dekker, Inc., 1996.

Gisslen, Wayne. *Professional Baking, 5th ed.* Hoboken: John Wiley and Sons, 2007.

Hickenbottom, X. "Technical Bulletin: Use of Molasses in Bakery Products." Volume 18 (6). Kansas City, MO: American Institute of Baking, June 1996.

Hoseney, R. Carl. *Principles of Cereal Science and Technology, 2nd ed.* St. Paul, MN: American Association of Cereal Chemists, 1994.

Jackson, E. B. (ed.). *Sugar Confectionery Manufacture.* New York: Van Nostrand Reinhold, 1990.

Matz, Samuel A. *Ingredients for Bakers.* McAllen, TX: Pan-Tech International, 1987.

McGee, Harold. *On Food and Cooking: The Science and Lore of the Kitchen.* 2nd ed. New York: Scribner, 2004.

National Starch Food Innovation. "Modified Food Starches: Why, What, Where and How." http://www.foodinnovation.com/pdfs/modified.pdf.

National Starch Food Innovation. "Food Starch Technology." www.foodinnovation.com/pdfs/foodstarch.pdf.

Olive Oil Source. "Definitions: The Trouble with Definitions." www.oliveoilsource.com/definitions.htm.

Olive Oil Source. "Mill and Press Facts: How Olives Are Turned into Oil." www.oliveoilsource.com/mill_and_press_facts.htm.

Pyler, E. J. *Baking Science and Technology, Volumes I and II, 3rd ed.* Merriam, KS.: Sosland Pub. Co., 1988.

Pyler, E. J. "The Baking Process." In *Encyclopedia of Food Science and Technology, Volume 1,* Y. H. Hui (ed.). New York: John Wiley and Sons, 1992.

Reineccius, Gary (ed.). *Source Book of Flavors,* 2nd ed. Berlin, New York: Springer, 1998.

Sidhu, Punam Khaira. "The Delectable Story of Gur." www.tribuneindia.com/2002/20020316/windows/main2.htm.

University of California Postharvest Technology Research and Information Center. "Produce Facts." www.coolforce.com/facts/.

U.S. Department of Agriculture. "How to Buy Dairy Products." www.ams.usda.gov/howtobuy/dairy.htm.

U.S. Department of Agriculture. "How to Buy Eggs." www.ams.usda.gov/howtobuy/eggs.htm.

U.S. Department of Agriculture. "How to Buy Fresh Fruits." www.ams.usda.gov/howtobuy/fruit.htm.

U.S. Department of Agriculture. "The National Organic Program." www.ams.usda.gov/nop/.

U.S. Department of Agriculture. "USDA Food Composition Data." www.nal.usda.gov/fnic/foodcomp/Data/.

U.S. Food and Drug Administration Center for Food Safety and Nutrition. www.cfsan.fda.gov.

"Wheat into Flour: A Story of Milling." *Gastronomica: The Journal of Food and Culture,* 6(1): 84–92, 2006. www.ucpress.edu.

Witwer, Rhonda, "Understanding Glycemic Impact," *Food Technology,* 59(11): 22–29, 2005. www.ift.org.

INDEX